1992

LIBRARY OF THE HISTORY OF IDEAS

VOLUME VI

Essays on Political Philosophy

LIBRARY OF THE HISTORY OF IDEAS

ISSN 1050–1053

Series Editor: JOHN W. YOLTON

ESSAYS ON
POLITICAL PHILOSOPHY

Edited by

PATRICK RILEY

UNIVERSITY OF ROCHESTER PRESS

This collection first published 1992

University of Rochester Press
200 Administration Building, University of Rochester
Rochester, New York 14627, USA
and at PO Box 9, Woodbridge, Suffolk IP12 3DF, UK

ISBN 1 878822 08 X

Library of Congress Cataloging-in-Publication Data
Essays on political philosophy / edited by Patrick Riley.
        p.   cm. – (Library of the history of ideas,
ISSN 1050–1053 ; v. 6)
    Includes bibliographical references.
    ISBN 1–878822–08–X (alk. paper)
    1. Political science – History.   I. Riley, Patrick, 1941– .
II. Series.
JA81.E72   1992
320'.01 – dc20   92–4402

British Library Cataloguing-in-Publication Data
Essays on Political Philosophy. –
(Library of the History of Ideas Series,
ISSN 1050–1053 ; v. 6)
    I. Riley, Patrick   II. Series
    320.01
    ISBN 1–878822–08–X

This publication is printed on acid-free paper

Printed in the United States of America

TABLE OF CONTENTS

ACKNOWLEDGEMENTS

The articles in this volume first appeared in the Journal of the History of Ideas as indicated below, by volume, year and pages, in order.

Avineri, Shlomo, "The Problem of War in Hegel's Thought," 22 (1961) 463–74

Baron, Hans, "New Light on the Political Writers of the Florentine Renaissance," 8 (1947) 241–8

Beck, Lewis W., "Kant and the Right of Revolution," 32 (1971) 411–22

Berlin, Isaiah,"Reply to Orsini [on Feuerbach, Hegel and Marx]," 30 (1969) 91–5

Cassirer, Ernst, "Giovanni Pico della Mirandola: A Study in the History of Renaissance Ideas," 3 (1942) 319–38 (second chapter)

Crocker, Lester Gilbert, "The Problem of Truth and Falsehood in the Age of Enlightenment," 14 (1953) 575–603

Dewey, John, "James Marsh and American Philosophy," 2 (1941) 131–50

Gilbert, Felix, "The Composition and Structure of Machiavelli's *Discorsi*," 14 (1953) 136–56

Grene, Marjorie, "Hume: Sceptic and Tory?" 4 (1943) 333–48

Hadas, Moses, "From Nationalism to Cosmopolitanism in the Greco-Roman World," 4 (1943) 105–11

Kelley, Donald R., "*Foundations of Modern Political Thought*," 40 (1979) 663–73

Kelly, George A., "Liberalism and Aristocracy in the French Restoration," 26 (1965) 509–30

Krieger, Leonard, "History and Law in the Seventeenth Century: Pufendorf," 21 (1960) 198–210

Lovejoy, Arthur O., "The Meaning of Romanticism for the Historian of Ideas," 2 (1941) 257–78

Lukes, Steven, "The Meanings of Individualism," 32 (1971) 45–66

Macpherson, C. B., "The Economic Penetration of Political Theory: Some Hypotheses," 39 (1978) 101–18

Randall, Jr., John Herman, "Plato's Treatment of the Theme of the Good Life and his Criticism of the Spartan Ideal," 28 (1967) 307–24

Schrecker, Paul, "Leibniz's Principles of International Justice," 7 (1946) 484–98

Seliger, Martin, "Locke's Natural Law and the Foundation of Politics," 24 (1963) 337–54

Shklar, Judith N., "Jean d'Alembert and the Rehabilitation of History," 42 (1981) 643–64

Starobinski, Jean, "Eloquence and Liberty," 38 (1977) 195–210

Strauss, Leo, "Political Philosophy and History," 10 (1949) 30–50

Tillich, Paul, "Nietzsche and the Bourgeois Spirit," 6 (1945) 307–9

I

INTRODUCTION

By Patrick Riley

When an editor ventures to publish a collection of essays on political philosophy, he might be thought to have in mind a firm idea of what *counts* as political philosophy; but a little reflection will show that the distinguishing marks of "real" political philosophy are infinitely disputable. Indeed it should at once he said that unless one is prepared to decree that political philosophy obviously means such-and-such, it is by no means clear what it is. And that is because it is by no means clear what philosophy is, or what politics is; therefore the philosophy of politics combines uncertainties. To be sure, one can say, with Aristotle, that politics is the art of ruling and being ruled in turn by peers and equals;[1] that philosophy is the love of wisdom;[2] that political philosophy is therefore the love of wisdom concerning the art of ruling. And as a nominal definition this is beyond reproach. But anyone who is not a confirmed Aristotelian (or perhaps Thomist) will begin to have doubts that philosophical problems can be resolved by the confident issuing of *ex cathedra obiter dicta*.

In beginning to sort out what philosophy might be, and what politics might be, the notions of minimalism and maximalism are of great help. For it is clear that political thinkers from the pre-Socratics to the present have conceived either philosophy, or politics, or both, in "larger" and in "smaller" ways. At maximum, philosophy is the systematic knowledge of everything; it is, to quote Hegel, "the absolute science of the truth."[3] It is no longer mere philo-sophia, mere love of wisdom; it is the whole of wisdom concretely attained. (No one has gone beyond Hegel in this matter, because there is no beyond; no larger view of the claims of philosophy can be conceived.) At the opposite extreme, a perfect "minimalist" is a radical skeptic such as T. D. Weldon, who urges that philosophy's modest purpose is to "tidy up verbal confusions" in our ordinary

---

[1] Aristotle, *Politics*, ed. and trans. Ernest Barker (Oxford: Clarendon Press, 1952), 1278b35 ff.

[2] Aristotle, *Metaphysics*, ed. W. D. Ross (Oxford: Clarendon Press, 1928), 993b (inter alia).

[3] Hegel, *Encyclopedia of the Philosophical sciences*, cited in George Armstrong Kelly, *Hegel's Retreat from Eleusis* (Princeton: Princeton University Press, 1978), Ch. 1, p. 20.

language,[4] so that meaningless (or dangerous) claims can no longer be made. This sort of minimalist philosophizing can cast a narrow but powerful beam: for example in J. L. Austin's sorting out of the small but important difference between "unwillingly" and "involuntarily" in his justly famous essay, "A Plea for Excuses."[5]

And in between the maximalism of Hegel, which claims complete or "absolute" knowledge of the whole, and the minimalism of Weldon, which claims precious little knowledge of anything (even if Weldon finally emerges as a closet utilitarian who thinks that J. S. Mill is "perfectly right"),[6] there are middle positions such as Kant's — which deny real knowledge of what we most want to know (God, freedom, and immortality)[7] but nonetheless affirm that ideas such as freedom must be used by us as necessary practical hypotheses:[8] that we must take ourselves to be free if we are to conceive ourselves as responsible for acting rightly, that it is "practically" sufficient that no Hobbist can prove the truth of freedom-excluding determinism.[9] Other ways of treating philosophy are obviously possible: some view it as the search for certainty, others as the pitiless exposing of all grounds for certainty. Still, one can stretch philosophy along a *continuum*, with Weldon's modesty at one end and Hegel's spacious confidence at the other; philosophy can be very grand, or self-effacingly slight.

And the same is true of politics: some have seen it as the very center of human existence, as something supremely important. In Edmund Burke's sonorous and eloquent language,

Society is, indeed, a contract. Subordinate contracts for objects of mere occasional interest may be dissolved at pleasure; but the state ought not to be considered as nothing better than a partnership agreement in a trade of pepper and coffee, calico or tobacco, or some other such low concern, to be taken up for a little temporary interest, and to be dissolved by the fancy of the parties. It is to be looked on with other reverence; because it is not a partnership in things subservient only to the gross animal existence of a temporary and perishable nature. It is a partnership in all science, a partnership in all art, a partnership in

---

[4] T. D. Weldon, *The Vocabulary of Politics* (Harmondsworth, Middlesex: Penguin Books, 1953), Ch. 2, "The Logic of the Classical Theories."

[5] J. L. Austin, "A Plea for Excuses," in *Philosophical Papers* (Oxford: Clarendon Press, 1961), pp. 123 ff., particularly pp. 139 ff.

[6] Weldon, *Vocabulary of Politics*, op. cit., Ch. 5, p. 176.

[7] Kant, *Critique of Pure Reason*, trans. Kemp Smith (London: Macmillan, 1963 [orig. ed. 1929]), A568/B596 ff.

[8] Kant, *Fundamental Principles of the Metaphysic of Morals*, trans. T. K. Abbott (London: Longmans, 1909 [orig. ed. 1873]), pt. III, pp. 66–67.

[9] Kant, *Critique of Practical Reason*, trans. T. K. Abbott (London: Longmans, 1909 [orig. ed. 1873]), pp. 191 ff. Hobbesian freedom, for Kant, is only "the freedom of a turnspit" which suffers no external impediment to motion.

every virtue and in all perfection. As the ends of such a partnership cannot be obtained in many generations, it becomes a partnership not only between those who are living, but between those who are living, those who are dead, and those who are to be born. Each contract of each particular state is but a clause in the great primeval contract of eternal society, linking the lower with the higher natures, connecting the visible and invisible world, according to a fixed compact sanctioned by the inviolable oath which holds all physical and all moral natures each in their appointed place.[10]

This is certainly a maximalist view: though what one might call the "maximal maximum" is assuredly to be found in the final book of Plato's final work, Book XII of the *Laws* — in which Plato urges that the final truth about politics is

that no man, and no woman, be ever suffered to live without an officer set over them, and no soul of man to learn the trick of doing one single thing of its own sole motion, in play or in earnest, but, in peace as in war, ever to live with the commander in sight, to follow his leading, and take its motions from him to the least detail – to halt or advance, to drill, to bathe, to dine, to keep wakeful hours of nights as sentry or dispatch carrier, all at his bidding, in the stricken field itself neither to pursue not to retire without the captain's signal, in a word, to teach one's soul the habit of never so much as thinking to do one single act apart from one's fellows, of making life, to the very uttermost, an unbroken consort, society, and community of all with all. A wiser and better rule than this man neither had discovered, nor ever will.[11]

If there is a maximalist notion of what politics is, there are minimalist ones as well. John Locke (for example) argues that the political-legal order does little more than enforce the already-existing natural rights (such as those of property) which all men have in virtue of divine gift and their own labor;[12] hence Locke, revealingly, calls government a mere "judge," and resolutely reserves the term *sovereignty* for God alone.[13] (Indeed Locke's vocabulary in the *Second Treatise* is a cornucopia of judicial images and metaphors.) And in the next century Jeremy Bentham sticks to the minimalist view that since all law is moderately painful — because general laws never perfectly fit particular cases — the political-legal order should arrest only those pains (such as being murdered) which are more painful than the painfulness of government

---

[10] Burke, *Reflections on the Revolution in France*, in *Burke's Politics*, ed. R. Hoffman and P. Levack (New York: Knopf, 1959), p. 318.

[11] Plato, *Laws*, trans. A. E. Taylor, in Plato, *Collected Dialogues*, ed. E. Hamilton and H. Cairns (New York: Bollingen Foundation, 1961), Book XII, 942a–d.

[12] Locke, *Two Treatises*, in *The Works of John Locke*, (London: Rivington et. al., 1824), secs. 95, 128 (inter alia).

[13] Ibid., sec. 6, where Locke describes men as "all the servants of one sovereign master."

itself.[14] (Aristotle, who made a similar complaint about law's excessive generality, nonetheless avoided minimalist politics by offering "equity" as a particular *corrective* to that generality;[15] hence he could view the city, expansively, as "a rule of life such as will make the members of a polis good and just" [*Politics* III, 1280b]).[16]

Other political minimalists have different grounds for their modesty: Augustine, for instance, holds that the city of man is so inconsiderable compared with the City of God that human injustice is inevitable — even the benevolent judge will sometimes torment the innocent out of ignorance — and that a Christian's wish must be that of passing from this vale of tears to a realm of true felicity and justice ("though we acquit the judge of all malice we must admit that human life is miserable").[17] And a modern Augustine-admirer such as Michael Oakeshott says that politics should "never be taken for more than it is," and that what it is is only a set of minimal legal conditions to be "subscribed to" by *cives* in their pursuit of "self-chosen satisfactions" — that it is not a "joint enterprise" run by "teleocractic managers" who impose a common good on "anti-individuals."[18]

And just as, in philosophy, one can identify middle positions between Hegelian perfect knowledge and the mere Weldonian tidying up of verbal confusions, so too in politics the middle is fully inhabited — once again by someone like Kant, who holds that the political-legal order ("public legal justice") is indeed important, since it "realizes," through law, some of what ought to happen (peace, non-murder)[19] — but that, at the same time, public legal justice is inferior to the purely moral "good will" that is the only unqualifiedly good thing on earth, the only thing that might generate a Kingdom of Ends.[20]

Politics, then, as well as philosophy, can be large and important, or small and trivial. One can think, with Aristotle, that citizenship is su-

---

[14] Jeremy Bentham, *Principles of Morals and Legislation*, ed. L. LaFleur (New York: Hafner, 1948), Ch. XIV.

[15] Aristotle, *Ethics* 1137b, cited in *Politics*, ed. Barker, op. cit., p. 368.

[16] Aristotle, *Politics*, ed. Barker, op. cit., III, 1280b.

[17] Augustine, *De Civitate Dei*, Bk. XIX, 10.

[18] Michael Oakeshott, *On Human Conduct* (Oxford: Clarendon Press, 1975) ch. 3. For his minimalizing of politics, see "The Claims of Politics," *Scrutiny Vol. VIII, No. 2, September 1939, pp. 146–151.*

[19] Kant, *Rechtslehre*, in *Metaphysik der Sitten*, in *Immanuel Kants Werke*, ed. Ernst Cassirer (Berlin: Bruno Cassirer Verlag, 1922), Vol. 7, "Einleitung in die Rechtslehre," pp. 30 ff.

[20] Kant, *Fundamental Principles*, trans, Abbott, op. cit., pp. 9 ff., particularly pp. 45 ff. For the centrality of 'good will" in generating a Kingdom of Ends, see the editor's *Kant's Political Philosophy* (Totowa, N. J.: Rowman and Littlefield, 1983), Chs. 2 and 3.

premely important, that a man without a polis is "either a beast or a God";[21] or one can think, with Nietzsche, that "every great age of culture is an age of political decline," that culture alone really matters to a serious adult such as Goethe or Mozart or Raphael — who will not squander his limited psychic energy on a democracy which is merely a secularized, "under-handed" form of creativity-destroying Christian egalitarianism.[22]

II

Nothing could better illustrate the infinite gradation of possible meanings of both "philosophy" and "politics" than the present collection of political philosophy essays from the *Journal of the History of Ideas*; for every imaginable view of philosophy and politics (not to mention of "history" and of the "history of ideas") appears in this collection — which is held together by nothing more than the sheer excellence of the individual pieces. At one extreme one finds Leo Strauss' view ("Political Philosophy and History," 1949) that the Greeks (above all) saw "the political things" with incomparable freshness, that they revealed an unproblematical political truth unsullied by "historicist" and "relativist" doubts (of the sort that tormented Max Weber);[23] at the opposite extreme one finds C. B. MacPherson's worries about how much to deviate from the Marxian view that philosophy is the "epiphenomenal," superstructural echo or determined reflection of deep-lying material causes ("The Economic Penetration of Political Thought," 1978).[24] At one pole one finds Felix Gilbert's line-by-line exegesis of a single Machiavellian text, relating each fragment of the *Discorsi* to the surviving books of Livy, and showing that the first 18 chapters of the *Discourses* probably constitute the treatise on "republicanism" which Machiavelli refers to in *The Prince* ("Composition and Structure of Machiavelli's Discourses," 1953);[25] at the other one finds

21 Aristotle, *Politics*, trans. Barker, op. cit., I, ii, 9, 1253a.

22 Nietzsche, *The Twilight of the Idols*, in *The Portable Nietzsche*, trans. W. Kaufmann (New York: Viking, 1954), pp. 508–509. Nietzsche illustrates his dictum that culture needs political decline (but not *fall*) in his brilliant set-piece on Venice near the end of *Beyond Good and Evil*.

23 Leo Strauss, "Political Philosophy and History," *Journal of the History of Ideas*, Vol. X, No. 1, 1949, pp. 30 ff. For a fuller statement of Strauss' hostility to "historicism," see his *Natural Right and History*.

24 C. B. MacPherson, "The Economic Penetration of Political Thought," *Journal of the History of Ideas*, Vol. XXXIX, No. 1, 1978, pp. 101 ff. For MacPherson's best-known application of his demi-Marxian method, see *The Political Theory of Possessive Individualism*.

25 Felix Gilbert, "Composition and Structure of Machiavelli's Discourses," *Journal of the History of Ideas*, Vol. XIV, No. 1, 1953, pp. 136–156.

sweeping historical panoramas which manage to "capture" several centuries of French or German thought while treating comparatively few lines of actual text (as in Judith Shklar's "D'Alembert and the Rehabilitation of History" [1981] or A. O. Lovejoy's "The Meaning of Romanticism" [1941].[26] And in a different vein altogether one finds something like Cassirer's "Pico della Mirandola" (1941), which combines textual exegesis with an effort to make the great Italian humanist into a kind of honorary Kantian *avant la lettre* — not surprisingly, given Cassirer's tendency to see modern thought as leading up to, and then falling away from Königsberg.[27]

The mere mentioning of the names Lovejoy and Cassirer recalls the early, brilliant days of the *Journal of the History of Ideas*; and if the pieces representing those great scholars in the present collection are only partly "about" political philosophy, they are important as late-in-life contributions by the men who (earlier) gave us two of the works which define the "history of ideas" as a field — Cassirer's *Philosophy of the Enlightenment* and Lovejoy's *The Great Chain of Being*.[28] To be sure, Lovejoy's "The Meaning of Romanticism" ventures into very dangerous water — the effort to find the roots of fascism and Nazism in certain "Romantic" ideas of the period 1770–1820; and when Lovejoy urges that something like Kant's notion of "organicism" in the *Critique of Judgment* underwent a sinister transformation as it passed from the realm of biology into the sphere of the (so-called) "organic state," he perhaps does not show clearly enough how precisely Kant himself repudiated political "organicism" (together with the notion of political "mechanism") in section 90 of the *Third Critique* and in section 55 of

[26] A. O. Lovejoy, "The Meaning of Romanticism for the Historian of Ideas," *Journal of the History of Ideas*, Vol. II, No. 3, 1941, pp. 257–278. It is admittedly difficult to find a Lovejoy-essay which is centrally "about" political philosophy. But the "romanticism" essay is the most nearly suitable; a later *Journal* article on the "communism" of St. Ambrose is mainly translated Patristic text-fragments, linked up by Lovejoy commentaries.

[27] Ernst Cassirer, "Pico della Mirandola," in *Journal of the History of Ideas*, Vol. III, No. 2 (Part I) and Vol. III, No. 3 (Parts II and III). Only part II of this 1942 triptych is presented here: part I consists of very general reflections on Pico, and part III deals with Pico's attack on astrology. It is primarily part II which illuminates Pico's moral and political thought. For Cassirer's earlier (1926) treatment of Pico, see his *Individual and the Cosmos in Renaissance Philosophy*, trans. Mario Domandi (Oxford: Basil Blackwell, 1963), pp. 83 ff. For Cassirer's tendency to (subtly) Kantianize important pre-Kantian thinkers, see (inter alia) *The Question of Jean-Jacques Rousseau* or *Rousseau, Kant and Goethe*. Cassirer was, of course, the greatest Kant-editor of the twentieth century.

[28] Ernst Cassirer, *The Philosophy of the Enlightenment*, trans. F. Koelln and J. Pettegrove (Princeton: Princeton University Press, 1951); A. O. Lovejoy, *The Great Chain of Being* (Cambridge, Mass.: Harvard University Press, 1936).

the *Rechtslehre*.[29] (Those in search of a more reliable reading of Kant — which treats the Königsberg master *an und für sich*, not in the light of later "transformations" of his thought — can always repair to Lewis White Beck's magisterial "Kant and the Right of Revolution" [1971], which captures so beautifully the "space" between Kant's ethics and his politics.)[30] But Lovejoy shows clearly and fairly what Nazi apologists "did" to Nietzsche — and at a moment (1941) when fairness to Nietzsche was not exactly universal.

And if — in his "Pico della Mirandola" — Ernst Cassirer makes the Renaissance humanist "anticipate" Kant, he does so in a way which molds the great sweep of time from the Renaissance to the Enlightenment into a single intelligible, coherent movement:

> In Pico's oration [on the dignity of man], man is called his own almost arbitrary molder . . . it is as though from this position we could for the first time grasp completely certain sides of Michelangelo's nature . . . It contains nothing less than a kind of theodicy of art. For art . . . [now] expresses within its own sphere what characterizes and distinguishes mankind as a whole. Beauty becomes, to express it in Kantian terms, the 'symbol of morality': for in the capacity of man to produce from himself a world of forms, there is expressed his innate freedom.[31]

When Cassirer goes on to draw into this sweeping view figures as different as Ficino, Nicholas of Cusa, Giordano Bruno and Leibniz, one sees a large-scale capacity for depicting vast stretches of intellectual time in a manner virtually unparalleled since Cassirer and Lovejoy vanished from the scene.

If there are living historians of ideas who have something like this same range and sweep, they are surely Isaiah Berlin, Judith Shklar, and Jean Starobinski. To be sure, Sir Isaiah is represented here by nothing more than his "reply to Orsini" on Feuerbach, Hegel and Marx — his only substantial published piece in the *Journal of the History of Ideas*;[32] but surely it is worth reviving even a small contribution by the most learned and subtle of all Marx-biographers.[33] In any case nothing can

---

[29] Kant, *Critique of Judgment*, trans. J C. Meredith (Oxford: Clarendon Press, 1952), pp. 137 ff.; Kant, *Rechtslehre*, op. cit., pars. 55.

[30] Lewis White Beck, "Kant and the Right of Revolution," *Journal of the History of Ideas*, Vol. XXXII, No. 3, 1971, pp. 411–423. Beck is the *doyen* of American Kant-scholars, and his commentary on the *Second Critique* is invaluable.

[31] Cassirer, "Pico della Mirandola," op. cit., Vol. III, No. 3, p. 333.

[32] Isaiah Berlin, "Reply to Orsini" [on Feuerbach, Hegel and Marx], *Journal of the History of Ideas*, Vol. XXX, No. 1, 1969, pp. 91–95.

[33] Isaiah Berlin, *Karl Marx*, 4th edn. (London: Oxford University Press, 1978).

repay the debt which all students of philosophy owe to Sir Isaiah for his ringing assertion that "rationality rests on the belief that one can think and act for reasons that one can understand, and not merely as the product of occult factors which breed 'ideologies', and cannot in any case be altered by their victims. So long as rational curiosity exists . . . political theory will not wholly perish from the earth."[34] That eloquent passage, half-Platonic, half-Kantian, is meant to be an antidote to Freud's view — at the end of *Civilization and its Discontents* — that philosophy is merely the "effort to prop up illusions with arguments,"[36] that something like the pursuit of equality is not a reason-provided moral "ideal," but a passionate desire for equal subordination to quasi-paternal authority (*Group Psychology and the Analysis of the Ego*).[36] Sir Isaiah reminds us that there is good reason to worry about transforming good reasons into *ex post facto* "rationalizations" which have no efficacious bearing on conduct — though Freud was certainly not first to suspect that reason is the slave of the passions, since Pascal had insisted in the *Pensées* that *le coeur a des raisons que la raison ne connaît point*,[37] and was echoed in Nietzsche's assertion that philosophy is "desires of the heart, filtered and made abstract," which are then defended with "reasons sought after the fact" (*Beyond Good and Evil*).[38] And if we are denied Sir Isaiah's doubts and worries about Freudian and Nietzschean "rationalization" (and Marxian "ideology") in this present collection, in compensation we have Paul Tillich's brief but effective "Nietzsche and the Bourgeois Spirit" (1945)[39] — which says little about Nietzsche's suspicion that every great philosophy "so far" has been rationalized heart-desires, "personal and involuntary memoirs," but which brings out Nietzche's radical hatred of "bourgeoisdom" (at the time that some still viewed him as a crypto-fascist).[40]

Fortunately Judith Shklar, the most eminent living American student

---

[34] Isaiah Berlin, "Does Political Theory Still Exist?," in *Philosophy Politics and Society*, 2nd Series, ed. P. Laslett and W. G. Runciman (Oxford: Basil Blackwell, 1967), p. 33.

[35] Freud, *Civilization and its Discontents*, in *Civilization, War and Death*, ed. J. Rickman (London: Hogarth Press, 1953), p. 80.

[36] Freud, *Group Psychology and the Analysis of the Ego*, trans. J. Strachey (New York: Bantam 1960), Ch. IX ("The Herd Instinct").

[37] Pascal, *Pensées*, in *Oeuvres de Blaise Pascal*, ed. Léon Brunschvicg (Paris: Librairie Hachette, 1914), Vol. II, p. 380.

[38] Nietzsche, *Beyond Good and Evil*, trans. W. Kaufmann (New York: Vintage, 1966), pp. 12–13.

[39] Paul Tillich, "Nietzsche and the Bourgeois Spirit," *Journal of the History of Ideas*, Vol. VI, No. 3, pp. 307–309.

[40] e.g. Bertrand Russell in *A History of Western Philosophy*, New York, 1944.

of Rousseau and Hegel,[41] is represented here by one of the most brilliant essays she ever wrote — "D'Alembert and the Rehabilitation of History" (1981). It is hard to think of any other essay on this (comparatively) small scale which captures so many of the Enlightenment's reservations about history as an enterprise: Descartes' subordination of "mere" historical data to reason and the "method of doubt"; Locke's fear that history preserves (and thereby glorifies) cruelty; Voltaire's worry that historical evidence is far from reliable; D'Alembert's own conviction that geometry affords a certainty which is more satisfying than history's mere probability. Fontenelle, in his *éloges* of great scientists in the Académie des Sciences, Shklar urges, initiated a new kind of history that D'Alembert (and the Encyclopedists) could admire and practice: not the political history of "butchers" and conquerors, but the spiritual history of citizens of the Republic of Letters. The new history was to be nothing less than *oraisons funèbres* of the sort that Bossuet lavished on Condé or Queen Marie-Thérèse[42] — but now devoted to mathematicians and physicists and chemists.

The notion of a new epic had already occurred to Locke. Political society may be dominated by 'butchers,' but 'the commonwealth of learning is not . . . without its master builders.' They were Boyle, Sydenham, Huygenius, and, of course, 'the incomparable Mr. Newton.' Without the ancestral piety of the Romans there was no need to write their kind of monumental history, but to praise these truly great men, scientists all, might be as edifying as the record of battles was degrading. That was also to be one of the aims of the *Encyclopédie*. The victory of the moderns over the ancients did not mean the end of memory, but rather its redirection.[43]

And when Shklar goes on to add invaluable comments on Montesquieu, Condorcet, Diderot and Rousseau, one feels that the whole of early modern intellectual history has been pulled together and illuminated by a true "master builder." If any single piece in the present colleciton fully realizes the notion of what the "history of ideas" is supposed to be able to accomplish, it is surely Shklar's "D'Alembert."

[41] See Judith N. Shklar, *Men and Citizens: A Study of Rousseau's Social Theory* (Cambridge: Cambridge University Press, 1969); Shklar, *Freedom and Independence: A Study of the Political Ideas of Hegel's Phenomenology of Mind* (Cambridge: Cambridge University Press, 1976). The Rousseau book, *en particulier*, is a masterpiece.

[42] For Bossuet's political use of the "funeral oration," see the editor's edition of Bossuet, *Politics Drawn from the Very Words of Holy Scripture* (Cambridge: Cambridge University Press, 1991), Introduction, pp. xxv ff.

[43] Judith N. Shklar, "D'Alembert and the Rehabilitation of History," *Journal of the History of Ideas*, Vol. XLII, No. 4, 1981, p. 645.

(But Starobinski's "Eloquence and Liberty" is not far behind: its historical range is astonishing, stretching from Tacitus to Rousseau; and Starobinski shows effectively that once the "forum eloquence" of ancient republicanism was dried up by modern absolute monarchy, that eloquence migrated from the forum to the printing house — to Rousseau's *written* eloquence aimed at a newly-literate public.[44] And what he then says about Rousseau is supremely illuminating — not surprisingly, coming from the author of *Transparence et l'obstacle*. Like Shklar, Starobinski sees and depicts large, sweeping, general changes; like her, he has an eye for the bit of text which will support his *généralités* with relevant particulars.)

The remaining figure in this collection who vies with Berlin, Shklar and Starobinski as heir to the mantle of Cassirer and Lovejoy is, surely, the late George Armstrong Kelly – whose studies of Kant, Fichte and Hegel should now be re-published. (Has anyone else ever managed to make Hegel's *Philosophy of Right* wholly intelligible and largely persuasive, as Kelly did in *Hegel's Retreat from Eleusis*?)[45] Kelly's "Liberalism and Aristocracy in the French Restoration" (1965) shows how exquisitely Benjamin Constant and Mme. de Staël poised themselves between the revolutionary and the reactionary — and shows it in language fully worthy of those two eloquent writers.

Madame de Staël is Protestant in background, and so is Constant. This is incalculably important, not simply because it places her genetically in the tradition of modern revolution and "cosmopolitanizes" her rôle — attaching her to the Reformation in Germany, and above all, to the Glorious Revolution of 1688 — but because it symbolizes her whole psychological position in the liberal movement. She is intelligent, wealthy, independent, and free — with the candle of the Lord in her soul, when she cares to light it, and money in the bank. Furthermore, her God (and Benjamin's) can become at Whim an immanent conscience *à la Rousseau*, a rationalist teleological deity, or a Kantian metaphor that makes liberty immortal; none of the dark, secularized Calvinism of Guizot in her politics, none of the Catholic subordination or dogmatism, either. Instead, a sense that Protestantism, free of consistency and free of priestcraft, taken up or put down at will like a book of poetry, might be a good state religion for France; a sense that Protestantism is ancient and Catholicism modern.[46]

---

[44] Jean Starobinski, "Eloquence and Liberty," *Journal of the History of Ideas*, Vol. XXXVIII, No. 2, 1977, pp. 195–210.

[45] Kelly, *Hegel's Retreat from Eleusis*, op. cit., partic. Ch. 5 ("The Neutral State").

[46] George A. Kelly, "Liberalism and Aristocracy in the French Restoration," *Journal of the History of Ideas*, Vol. XXVI, No. 4, 1965, p. 514.

George Kelly left an important monument to his own love of French civilization in *Mortal Politics in Eighteenth Century France* — that remarkable study of death in French thought from Bossuet and Fénelon to Robespierre and the Terror;[47] the revival of his *Journal* essay extends this French excursion well into the nineteenth century. Few modern interpreters managed to cast equal light on both sides of the Rhine in the way that George Kelly did; his premature death, at 55, deprived the learned world of one of the best contributors to the *Journal of the History of Ideas*.

(It is lamentable — to say it in passing — that two eminent historians of ideas of a stature comparable to Cassirer's or Lovejoy's, namely Michael Oakeshott and Hannah Arendt, never published a word in the *Journal*. Oakeshott's brief but wonderful observations on Augustine, Montaigne, Montesquieu and Hegel in *On Human Conduct* [1975] make it clear that he could have contributed a remarkable essay on any of those figures — or even more on Thomas Hobbes,[48] whose greatest interpreter Oakeshott was. And Arendt's intriguing treatments of Duns Scotus, Kant and Nietzsche in *The Life of the Mind* make one regret that she never "floated" any of these set-pieces as articles in the *Journal*.)[49]

III

It is by now a received view in *Ideengeschichte* that prevailing "climates" of opinion may affect (if not effect) particular intellectual efforts; and this turns out to be true of some of the essays in the present collection. The *Journal of the History of Ideas* began publishing in the first full year of World War II; many European *émigrés* were among the earliest contributors; and it would be astonishing if the War had not left its mark on some of the articles in the *Journal*. Even Lovejoy's "Romanticism" owes (part of) its inspiration to the tracing of "monstrous" German political phenomena to supposed intellectual antecedents; even Cassirer's "Pico della Mirandola" discovers a proto-Kantian humanism in Renaissance Florence (at the very time that Cassirer was writing *The Myth of the State* and finding "ruthless" intimations of fascism in Hegel's *Philosophy of Right*).[50] And the War left an even clearer mark

---

[47] George A. Kelly, *Mortal Politics in Eighteenth Century France*, in *Historical Reflections* (Waterloo, Canada, 1986), Vol. 13, No. 1.

[48] See above all Michael Oakeshott, *Hobbes on Civil Association* (Oxford: Basil Blackwell, 1975), particularly the "Introduction" (1946) to *Leviathan*.

[49] Hannah Arendt, *The Life of the Mind: Willing* (New York: Harcourt, Brace Jovanovich, 1978).

[50] Ernst Cassirer, *The Myth of the State* (New Haven: Yale University Press, 1946), p. 267. Cassirer is horrified by Hegel's enthusiasm for "the truth which lies in power."

on other contributions published between 1940 and 1946: Moses Hadas'
search for "cosmopolital' political ideas in Greek antiquity (for
example) is not concerned with the sheer "pastness" of Greek civilization, but tries to show that the polis-envy of the Greeks was increasingly
countered by the notion of a universal *cosmopolis* (in late Stoicism, for
instance). And if the Greeks could move from the politan to the cosmopolitan, Hadas urges, might not we (moderns) move from exaggerated
nationalism to cosmopolitan internationalism?[51] In Hadas' "From
Nationalism to Cosmopolitanism in the Graeco-Roman World," the
sheer historicity of Greek theory and practice is subordinated to the
practical advantages to be got from seeing "parallels" between antiquity and modernity, between ancient and modern cosmopolitanism —
though Hadas was too good a classicist to extort "extra" meanings from
Homer or Pinder or Plato.

A comparable elevating of practical "lessons" and "parallels" above
historicity and sheer "pastness" appears still more strikingly in Paul
Schrecker's "Leibniz' Principles of International Justice" (1946), which
urges that

... the international law [Leibniz] strove for aimed at actualizing the community of mankind without impairing the liberty of the many individual nations to cultivate their particular civilizations ... he was also convinced that
every action complying with the laws of reason and justice would contribute,
be it but to an infinitesimal degree, to approaching this aim.
    The history of civilization is, of course, no continuous progress, and spo-
radic relapses into barbarism may always be expected to recur ... An alliance
of militarism and anti-intellectualism, this is what Leibniz considered the
deadly enemy of civilization.[52]

This formulation, while not false, certainly makes Leibniz into a
"good German," an anti-Nazi *avant la lettre*; since, however, as
Schrecker correctly says, Leibniz believed in demi-Platonic "eternal
moral verities," perhaps he is made not so much "contemporary" as
timeless. The only reasonable complaint one can raise about
Schrecker's study — which throws so much intelligent light on Leibniz'
magisterial *Codex Iuris Gentium* (1693)[53] — is that the Christian (more
specifically Pauline) element of Leibnizian ethics is downplayed in
order to make more room for a "reason" that all "mankind" can embrace. To be sure, Schrecker notes *en passant* that Leibniz defined

[51] Moses Hadas, "From Nationalism to Cosmopolitanism in the Greco-Roman
World," *Journal of the History of Ideas*, Vol. III, No. 1, 1942, pp. 105–111.
    [52] Paul Schrecker, "Leibniz' Principles of International Justice," *Journal of the
History of Ideas*, Vol. VII, No. 4, 1946, p. 497.
    [53] Ibid, p. 493.

justice as "the charity of the wise";[54] but that definition — which fuses
I *Corinthians* xiii ("the greatest of these is charity") with the Platonic
view that justice requires the rule of the wise[55] — is over-subordinated
to Leibniz' (perfectly genuine) devotion to Platonic reason and Roman
jurisprudence. Leibniz' insistence that "charity must prevail over every
other consideration in the world"[56] is never quoted; rather Schrecker
stresses Leibniz' (Platonic) conviction that there must be a *justice* which
is as universal and necessary as *truth*. Practical concerns with Leibniz'
"message" to us (in 1946) lead Schrecker to subordinate the possibly
"sectarian" — even Christian charity — to the "reason" that all rational beings can see. The post-war perspective does not falsify what
Schrecker says; but it clearly bends it in a certain direction. Paul is made
to cede too much to Plato; *Corinthians* yield too much to Athenians.

Almost certainly it was practical, and even immediately political,
concerns which led John Dewey to publish "James Marsh and American Philosophy" in 1941 — though the text itself was prepared as early
as 1929.[57] Of course Dewey really was concerned to point out Marsh'
debt to Kant and (particularly) Coleridge; and the occasion afforded
Dewey an opportunity to enlarge on Kant and Coleridge themselves, as
well as to praise Marsh as the intellectual ancestor of Emerson's "transcendentalism." But surely what suggested a 1941 publication was the
presence of Dewey's own larger reflections on American political
thought in this 1929 lecture-manuscript — reflections which viewed
American political thinking as a native product which had (fortunately)
broken with characteristic European obsessions:

In my judgment, this subordination of the state to the community is the great
contribution of American life to the world's history, and it is clearly expressed
in the utterances of Dr. Marsh. But recent events have tended to obscure it.
Forces have been at work to assimilate the original idea of the state and its
organization to older European notions and traditions . . . The constitution of
the state is treated not as a means and instrument to the well-being of the
community of free self-governing individuals, but as something having value
and sanctity in and of itself. We have, unconsciously in large measure but yet
pervadingly, come to doubt the validity of our original American idea.
  . . . the essence of our earlier pioneer individualism was not non-social,

[54] Ibid, p. 488.

[55] Plato, *Republic*, above all Book IV, 443d ff.

[56] Leibniz, letter to Mme. de Brinon, in *Die Werke von Leibniz*, ed. Onno Klopp
(Hannover: Klindworth Verlag, 1864–84), Vol. VII, p. 296. Cited and treated in the
editor's *The Political Writings of Leibniz* (Cambridge: Cambridge University
Press, 1972), pp. 3–4.

[57] John Dewey, "James Marsh and American Philosophy," *Journal of the
History of Ideas*, Vol. II, No. 1, 1941, pp. 131–150.

much less anti-social; it involved no indifference to the claims of society. Its working ideal was neighborliness and mutual service. It did not deny the claims of government and law, but it held them in subordination to the needs of a changing and developing society of individuals.[58]

This paragraph reveals Dewey's characteristic eloquence, his attachment to the New England ideals of Emerson and Thoreau which he saw evaporating. But Dewey's candor obliges him to admit that Marsh's speculative thought was as conventional and German-indebted as his social thought was freer and higher: "the period [of Dr. Marsh] was not favorable to far-reaching thought . . . he depended upon other, notably Coleridge and the German idealists."[59] For Dewey, then, Marsh's (admirable) political views did not flow irresistibly out of a larger, general philosophical perspective (in the manner of Plato, Aristotle, Kant, or Hegel); Marsh's self-limiting Americanism made him as speculatively unoriginal as it made him politically sound and solid. Europe for theory, America for practice — such seems to have been Dewey's view in 1929, and unchanged in 1941.

If the essays of Dewey, Schrecker, Hadas and others bear the mark of the War — the effort to see "relevant" parallels — some other pieces published in the *Journal* during the same period are remarkably timeless. Marjorie Grene's "Hume: Skeptic and Tory?" (1943), for example, with its subtle reflections on the relation between Hume's political writings and his history of England,[60] could have been written at any time after about 1920; the piece "ages" beautifully. And a later essay such as Steven Lukes' "The Meanings of Individualism" (1972) is again no period-piece; its painstaking dissection of the countless meanings of "individualism" in British and French thought shows no pressure-marks from the time in which it was written.[61] As for Leonard Krieger's "Pufendorf" (1960), it is "datable" only in the sense that Krieger was so early in taking seriously the figure whom Leibniz (a little unjustly) called "a bad philosopher and a worse lawyer"; only in very recent times has Pufendorf recovered some of the high reputation he enjoyed in the eyes of Locke and Rousseau — as evidenced by the inclusion of Pufendorf's *De Officio Hominis* in Quentin Skinner's new series of political theory texts for the Cambridge University Press.[62]

[58] Ibid, p. 146.

[59] Ibid, p. 149.

[60] Marjorie Grene, "Hume: Skeptic and Tory?," *Journal of the History of Ideas*, Vol. IV, No. 3, 1943, pp. 333–348.

[61] Steven Lukes, "The Meanings of Individualism," *Journal of the History of Ideas*, Vol. XXXII, No. 1, 1972, pp. 45–66.

[62] Leonard Krieger, "Pufendorf," in *Journal of the History of Ideas*, Vol. XXI,

(Krieger managed to show Pufendorf's importance at a time when he was being carefully treated only by Germans — for example in Hans Denzer's *Moralphilosophie und Naturecht bei Samuel Pufendorf.*)[63] And Shlomo Avineri's "The Problem of War in Hegel's Thought" is datable (to 1961) only in the sense that some time had to elapse, after 1945, before anyone could venture to put a more favorable gloss on Hegel's assertion that war preserves the "ethical health of nations" against the "foulness" that eternal peace would cause.[64] The meaning of those words could be more calmly considered in 1961 than in 1941 – and even more calmly now, in 1991. As is usual with him, Avineri redeems those parts of Hegel which seem most worrisome, or even offensive. (But then whoever thought that some of Hegel's political opinings should be ranked with his incomparable revelation of the unfolding or "becoming" of Western *Geist* in the *Phenomenology of Mind*?)[65]

To be sure, World War II was not the only immediately "practical" consideration which led historians of political thought to sacrifice sheer "pastness" to contemporary concerns: C. B. MacPherson's "The Economic Penetration of Political Thought" (1978) shows a (perfectly warranted) concern with social relations which are "exploitative," which rest merely on "power" and "control";[66] and he traces much of this misfortune to the rise of "market" relations in early modernity. It is one thing, however, to find a "capitalist" in Adam Smith, and quite another to press this phenomenon back into the Florentine Renaissance: Machiavelli, we are told, assumed that "economic relations set the dominant requirements of the political system."[67] But this is, to say the least of it, extravagant — surely Romulus did not pursue the historical "greatness" which Machiavelli praises in *Discorsi* I, ix (even justifying Romulus' murder of Remus)[68] by manipulating "economic relations."

No. 2, 1960, pp. 198ff. See also Leonard Krieger, *The German Idea of Freedom* (Boston: Beacon Press, 1957), pp. 50–59.

[63] Hans Denzer (ed.) *Moralphilosophie und Naturrecht bei Samuel Pufendorf* (Munich: Beck, 1972), passim. For Leibniz' critique of Pufendorf, see "Opinion on the Principles of Pufendorf," in *The Political Writings of Leibniz*, op. cit., pp. 64 ff 63.

[64] Hegel, *Philosophy of Right*, trans. T. M. Knox (Oxford: Clarendon Press, 1942), sec. 324, "additions," p. 210.

[65] For an intelligent privileging of the *Phenomenology* over the *Philosophy of Right*, see Shklar, *Freedom and Independence*, op. cit., passim.

[66] C. B. MacPherson, "The Economic Penetration of Political Thought," *Journal of the History of Ideas*, Vol. XXXIX, No. 1, 1978, pp. 101 ff.

[67] Ibid, p. 105.

[68] Machiavelli, *Discourses on Livy*, Book I, ch. 9. The following chapter (I, 10) then argues that Romulus' fratricidal boldness was justified by the advent — a milennium later — of a golden age of Antonine civic virtue.

And even Hobbes — who is said to have "deduced his whole system of political obligation from a model of bourgeois man"[69] — is turned into a kind of Andrew Carnegic in advance: leaving aside the fact that no one (not even Hobbes) can "deduce" a notion of obligation *from* "a model of bourgeois man," Hobbes' notions of appetite, aversion and covenant go back at least to Epicurus (as Oakeshott conclusively demonstrated).[70] (One remembers, of course, that Rousseau complained in *L'État de Guerre* that Hobbes had mistaken "a *bourgeois* of London or Paris" for the "natural man";[71] but it is merely erroneous to think that the word *bourgeois* had the same meaning for Rousseau in 1750 that it had for Marx in 1850). Rather than trace the "roots" of "market relations" to the banks of the Arno, MacPherson would (arguably) have done better to rely on Marx' greatest "left-Kantian" attack on exploitation in "Towards a Critique of Hegel's Philosophy of Right" (1843): "Criticism . . . ends with the doctrine that man is the highest being for man, with the categorical imperative to overthrow all social systems in which man is humiliated, abandoned, enslaved or despised."[72] Indeed, more generally, the best line of attack against exploitation surely lies in seeing a Kantian Kingdom of Ends (in which no one is used merely as a "means") partially realized in "democratic socialism" — in the "revionist" manner of Karl Vorländer or Lucien Goldmann.[73] But it is not helpful to "find" 19th century industrial dilemmas in Medici Florence (or even Malmesbury); the horrors arrive in their own good time, and one can just wait for them. MacPherson's (admirable) practical concerns deflected his historical judgment; but one should not let his historical mistakes lead to the automatic conclusion that his practical concerns were unfounded. For they were never that.

IV

The essays in the present collection, then, illustrate beautifully the infinitely various meanings which intellectual historians have attached to both "philosophy" and "politics"; they represent some of the best work in the history of political thought in the last half-century. But if an

[69] MacPherson, "Economic Penetration," op. cit., p. 105.

[70] Michael Oakeshott, "Introduction" to *Leviathan*, in *Hobbes on Civil Association*, op. cit., pp. 6 ff.

[71] Rousseau, *L'État de Guerre*, in *Rousseau: Political Writings*, ed. C. Vaughan (Cambridge: Cambridge University Press, 1915), Vol. I. p. 281 ff.

[72] Marx, "Towards a Critique of Hegel's *Philosophy of Right*," in *Karl Marx: Selected Writings*, ed. D. McLellan (Oxford: Oxford University Press, 1977), pp. 63 ff.

[73] Lucien Goldmann, *Immanuel Kant*, trans. R. Black (London: NLB, 1971). Goldmann is the most imaginative of the left-Kantians — though he owes a debt to Vorländer (and to Eduard Bernstein).

editor who aims at a "representative cross-section" of what has been thought must have what Oscar Wilde called "the impartiality of an auctioneer,"[74] that does not mean that that editor had no convictions of his own — convictions about the shape which the "history of ideas" must or might assume. And an editor may, finally, state those convictions in the form of a credo — which will, in a small space, unavoidably be dogmatic, since a large volume would be required to transform faith into reason.

Even if it is extravagant to think of all the members of the Great Tradition, from Plato to Rawls, as coexisting and conversing in a time-less *nunc stans*, it might still be that there are perennial, though not timeless, questions in philosophy that stretch over time. Since Plato's *Euthyphro*, for example, the question of whether there are any "eternal verities" that not even divine will can alter had recurred in every age of philosophy: in the seventeenth century, for instance, Descartes insisted that God would be neither creator nor omnipotent if A were necessarily equal to A, or if the good were necessarily good; but he was criticized by the neo-Platonists Leibniz and Malebranche, who argued that creation ought not to mean arbitrary willfulness, with Leibniz adding that *stat pro ratione voluntas* is "the motto of a tyrant."[75] And a century later Kant resurrected the same problems near the end of the *Critique of Pure Reason*, siding, more or less, with Leibniz.[76]

This is an example of a perennial speculative debate, and one that can and indeed must be carried on by abstracting a single thread — here the tension between always-having-been and coming-into-being — from the concrete wholeness of Platonism, Cartesianism, or Kantianism. To be sure, Descartes, as a Christian, worried about creation in a way that Plato did not: the *Timaeus* is less agitated than the *Response to the Six Objections* because salvation is not at stake.[77] But in looking at a perennial question one (designedly) minimizes the historical particularities of Platonism and Cartesianism precisely in order to stretch a sufficiently abstract notion over time and space. One loses something, to be sure (though others will retrieve it); but one gains a clear view of the fact that there are permanent and recurring questions in philosophy, even if recurrence is never simple recapitulation. To bring this out one

[74] *Oxford Dictionary of Quotations* (Oxford: Clarendon Press, 1974), p. 118.

[75] Cf. Leibniz, "Discourse on Metaphysics," prop. 2, in *Leibniz: Philosophical Papers and Letters*, ed. L. Loemker (Chicago: University of Chicago Press, 1956), Vol. I, p. 466.

[76] Kant, *Critique of Pure Reason*, op. cit., A819/B847.

[77] The authenticity of Descartes' Christianity has, of course, been doubted — most notably by Pascal in the *Pensées*.

heightens what is general and perennial; one subordinates what is particular and time-bound.

So too in political thought. Since Plato's *Crito* it has been a permanent question whether the legitimacy of government and the responsibilities of citizens depend on some free human action, for example the voluntary acceptance of benefits such as security and education, when one could have departed. To say that this question, very broadly conceived, appears in *Crito* and then twenty centuries later in Locke's *Second Treatise*, and then again in Michael Walzer's *Obligations*, is quite true.[78] To be sure, it does not appear in exactly the same form: Locke had a highly developed notion of the moral significance of "voluntary agreement," while Plato had not.[79] Furthermore, *Crito* is arguably anomalous in Plato's whole political corpus, since he usually stresses the rule of the wise rather than agreement. Locke, by contrast, must appeal to voluntary agreement, since for him all men are equal and there is no "natural" authority. And these differences cannot be explained without some historical reference to Christianity's "equality of all souls before God," and its idea that, in St. Augustine's phrase, "consent" must be "voluntary."[80] The notion of leaving history utterly out of account is absurd; but one can at least hope to find what Michael Oakeshott calls "the universal predicament" in the "local and transitory mischief."[81]

Philosophy is not timeless, but within time there is sufficient continuity and recurrence to speak of perennial questions, and the social contract (for example) is one of those question. Its central concern is to ask why political legitimacy and political obligation should be viewed as the voluntary creation of equal moral agents. That question, or at least the bare beginning of it, has been with us since *Crito*; but the most striking set of answers was provided by the "great age" of social contract theory, which flourished between the publication of Hobbes's *Leviathan* (1651) and Kant's *Metaphysical Elements of Justice* (1797).[82]

[78] Michael Walzer, *Obligations* (Cambridge, Mass.: Harvard University Press, 1970), particularly the "Introduction" and Chapter 1.

[79] For the absence of a strong theory of volition in Plato, see *Protagoras* 352b–c. Locke's theory of "voluntary agreement" in the *Second Treatise* needs to be fleshed out with his fuller treatment of volition in *Essay* II, 21 — particularly the sections beginning with #49.

[80] Augustine, *De Spiritu et Littera*, sec. 54; cited in Neal Gilbert, "The Concept of the Will in early Latin Philosophy," *Journal of the History of Philosophy* 1 (October 1963), p. 33.

[81] Oakeshott, "Introduction" to *Leviathan*, in *Hobbes on Civil Association*, op. cit., p. 7.

[82] See the editor's *Will and Political Legitimacy* (Cambridge, Mass.: Harvard University Press, 1982), Chapter 1.

Of course, there is something in Quentin Skinner's insistence that it is hard to claim to have achieved "historical understanding" of a "period" if we continue "to focus our main attention on those who discussed the problems of political life at a level of abstraction and intelligence unmatched by any of their contemporaries."[83] (Donald Kelley brings this out extremely well in his perceptive review of Skinner's *Foundations of Modern Political Thought*, which appeared in the *Journal* in 1979.)[84] But even Skinner himself is forced to draw a distinction between "classic texts" and mere "ideologies," finally allowing that the main reason for "focusing" on the study of ideologies is that "this would enable us to return to the classic texts themselves with a clearer prospect of understanding them." Perhaps jewels do shine more brightly in a setting of paste, as some theologians have imagined that the blessedness of the elect is heightened by the misery of the damned; but Skinner himself never mistakes the gems for the settings. His own intelligence, so formidably displayed in the *Foundations of Modern Political Thought*, leads, him, correctly, to "abstract" from an ideological "background" those feats of "abstraction and intelligence" that may indeed be qualitatively "unrepresentative" of a period but that do represent something higher: the possibility of remaining true enough over time to warrant being read. For surely the final reason to read Plato, Aristotle, Augustine, Hobbes, Locke, Rousseau, Kant, and Hegel is that they may conceivably be right, may possibly illuminate "the universal predicament."

That last phrase, of course, is Michael Oakeshott's; and if he officially published nothing in the *Journal of the History of Ideas*, one can nonetheless end this Introduction with the Oakeshott-passage which contains that celebrated phrase — for Oakeshott once intended to publish his "Introduction" to Hobbes' *Leviathan* (1946) as a free-standing monograph in the *Journal*, and refrained from doing so only because he did not want to shorten that essay to journal-length. (This he revealed to the editor on the occasion of their last meeting — in May 1990, a few months before Oakeshott's death.) Posthumously, then, one can place Oakeshott in the congenial company of Cassirer, Lovejoy, Berlin and Shklar — and at the same time gain one of the most brilliant of all readings of the "place" of political philosophy within the history of ideas.

---

[83] Quentin Skinner, *The Foundations of Modern Political Though* (Cambridge: Cambridge University Press, 1978), Vol. 1, "Introduction."

[84] Donald Kelley, review of Skinner's *Foundations of Modern Political Thought*, *Journal of the History of Ideas*, Vol. XL, No. 4, 1979, pp. 663 ff.

To establish the connections, in principle and in detail, directly or mediately, between politics and eternity is a project that has never been without its followers. Indeed, the pursuit of this project is only a special arrangement of the whole intellectual life of our civilization; it is the whole of intellectual history organized and exhibited from a particular angle of vision. Probably there has been no theory of the nature of the world, of the activity of man, of the destiny of mankind, no theology or cosmology, perhaps even no metaphysics, that has not sought a reflection of itself in the mirror of political philosophy; certainly there has been no fully considered politics that has not looked for its reflection in eternity. This history of political philosophy is, then, the context of the masterpiece. And to interpret it in the context of this history secures it against the deadening requirement of conformity to a merely abstract idea of political philosophy.

This kind of reflection about politics is not, then, to be denied a place in our intellectual history. And it is characteristic of political philosophers that they take a somber view of the human situation: they deal in darkness. Human life in their writings appears, generally, not as a feast or even as a journey, but as a predicament; and the link between politics and eternity is the contribution the political order is conceived as making to the deliverance of mankind. Even those whose thought is most remote from violent contrasts of dark and light (Aristotle, for example) do not altogether avoid this disposition of mind. And some political philosophers may even be suspected of spreading darkness in order to make their light more acceptable. Man, so the varied formula runs, is the dupe of error, the slave of sin, of passion, of fear, of care, the enemy of himself or of others or of both —

O miseras hominum mentes, O pectora caeca

— and the political order appears as the whole or a part of the scheme of his salvation. The precise manner in which the predicament is conceived, the qualities of mind and imagination and the kinds of activity man can bring to the achievement of his own salvation, the exact nature and power of political arrangements and institutions, the urgency, the method and the comprehensiveness of the deliverance — these are the singularities of each political philosophy. In them are reflected the intellectual achievements of the epoch or society, and the great and slowly mediated changes in intellectual habit and horizon that have overtaken our civilization. Every masterpiece of political philosophy springs from a new vision of the predicament; each is the glimpse of a deliverance or the suggestion of a remedy . . . for the masterpiece, at least, is always the revelation of the universal predicament in the local and transitory mischief.[85]

---

[85] Oakeshott, "Introduction" to *Leviathan*, op. cit., pp. 5–7.

PART ONE

ANCIENT POLITICAL PHILOSOPHY

II

PLATO'S TREATMENT OF THE THEME OF THE GOOD LIFE AND HIS CRITICISM OF THE SPARTAN IDEAL

By John Herman Randall, Jr.

Plato is not only an artist, as all will recognize; he is also an artist-philosopher, an artist who not only saw life, but loved wisdom, loved wisdom as only an artist can, and loved the kind of wisdom only an artist can see. Plato, in a word, is not merely an artist, but the philosopher of the artistic attitude, starting from the artist's experience, and developing the philosophic implications of the artist's outlook on life, employing the artist's method and technique to do so.

If we take Plato the artist-philosopher seriously, we shall find in the dialogues, not merely a dramatic picture of life, but a dramatic development of the implications of the artistic attitude and experience, a dramatic presentation of the artist's philosophy—almost the only one in our Western tradition.[1]

Plato could go as far as he did in developing the implications of the artist's outlook on life, because what we have been calling the "artistic attitude" was very conspicuous in Greek civilization. The greatest achievement of Greek life was an artistic achievement, and not only in architecture, sculpture and poetry, but also in religion, politics, ethics, and science. The ultimate intellectual interest of the Greeks, νοῦς, "Reason" in the sense of *Vernunft*, not *Verstand*, as leading to θεωρία, intellectual vision, was to see the world and human life as the artist sees them, to enjoy them as the artist enjoys them, and to remold them in imagination as the artist remolds them.

[1] With Plato may be joined Schelling, in his *Identitätsphilosophie*, and John Dewey. There are, of course, plenty of philosophies of the aesthetic attitude and experience, which is quite a different thing. It should be pointed out that Plato rarely uses the term τέχνη, "art," generically, as Aristotle so frequently does. The various "arts" usually mean for Plato the different "sciences," as Aristotle was to call them. On the other hand, Plato uses the term ἐπιστήμη, "science," or "true knowledge," generically: all "science" is for him, and for the Platonic tradition, ultimately *one*. Again, Plato *never* employs τέχνη or "art" to mean what moderns distinguish as the *beaux arts*, the "fine arts." For Greeks, this distinction simply did not exist. Consequently, there is in Plato *no* "theory of Art" in the sense of a theory of the Fine Arts. What has been taken by moderns to be Plato's "theory of Art" is actually his theory of poetry. Incidentally, that theory of poetry is *not* to be found in the *Republic*, Book X, in the discussion of μίμησις, "imitation." This discussion is *not* about poetry in general, but about what happens to poetry in the efficiently organized state, where it becomes mere "imitation"—in modern terms, where it is limited to "socialist realism." See Paul O. Kristeller, "The Modern System of the Arts," in *Renaissance Thought* II (1965), 163–227.

Plato was fortunate in being able to take over this attitude, elaborate it, and bring it to its highest expression. The whole relation of Plato to his environment is not that of the prophet opposing what he encounters, and proclaiming the one thing needful; it is not that of the scientist observing and describing what he sees and finds, picking it apart and manipulating it. It is that of the artist discerning its possibilities, and perfecting them in imagination. Plato was able to create an immortal vision of Greece—not of the Greece that actually was, but of what the artist could make out of it.

Hence it is a mistake to look for originality in the themes Plato selects to discuss and elaborate, or in the general notions and attitudes with which he starts his discussions, in the artistic materials he takes over from his culture and works with intellectually. It is easy to discover certain positions, certain assumptions underlying the discussions of the dialogues, and shared by all the characters:

1. Knowledge is essentially functional in character; it is directed toward knowing the uses, the possibilities, the ends of things.

2. The aim of politics is to organize and adjust different classes, by the "scientifically" trained expert, in the light of the best knowledge, and in the interest of bringing out the particular excellence of each class.

3. The Good Life is an achievement, an artistic masterpiece, to be attained by human intelligence and skill.

Now it is natural for most readers to assume that these ideas are distinctively "Platonic" conceptions, that this is "Platonic" doctrine, that these are the ideas Plato is trying to "teach," because we learn about them from his pages. In reality, these are the commonly accepted notions of the Greek, and especially of the Athenian, intellectual class. They differ widely from the notions on the same themes met with among the Hebrews, or the Romans, or the Christians, or modern Americans; but they are encountered again and again in Greek thought—in the Greek thought of the documents that have come down to us from the classic age.

Plato's originality—the distinctively "Platonic" note, "Platonic doctrine," if we will—consists not in these ideas themselves, but in what Plato *did* with this familiar material, in what he made out of it, in how he developed and elaborated its implications. These conceptions, in a word, are not Plato's philosophical *conclusions,* but rather the *starting-point* of Plato's philosophizing.

For example, we often imagine that Plato invented the idea that philosophers should be kings, that experts should rule the city, that education is the way out of our social problems. This is really like thinking that Abraham Lincoln "invented" democracy, or that Dante "invented" Christianity. We imagine that Plato was concerned to work out the details of what a "perfect city" would be like, or even that he was the first to sketch out a Utopia. And so we are apt to be shocked, when we are told, by Athenaeus and others, that the scheme of the perfect city in the *Republic,* down to almost the last detail, was merely taken over bodily by Plato from the familiar *Republic* of Protagoras, whose social philosophy Plato presents so sympathetically in the *Protagoras* dialogue.

Though we cannot check on these reports—Protagoras's Utopia is lost—they are quite credible. For it is clear the scheme of the perfect city, and the details of its organization, are quite irrelevant to Plato's political philosophy. It is clear that Plato's fundamental interest lies, not in the details of the Utopia of Protagoras, or of any other—least of all in one of his own devising—but in where men get when they try to elaborate a social ideal. It lies, formally speaking, in the nature and function of political discussion, in the nature and function of social idealism and social reform, in what a social ideal is, its values and its limitations. Naturally he had to take one particular social ideal for his illustration, to work with; and naturally he chose an ideal familiar to his audience: Protagoras's Utopia—or, if you prefer, the ideal of the Spartan state—as his philosophical material. But Plato might have chosen any other social ideal, and made the same points, developed the same political philosophy. He might, if he could, have taken the ideal of the Roman Empire, or of the Christian Church, or of Russian Communism, or of American Liberal Capitalism, or of the Welfare State—and carried out the same philosophical intent.

Now we may not be particularly attracted or seduced by Plato's own illustration—by the idealized Spartan state, clarified and elaborated, purified and perfected through discussion—though at least one modern state, Prussia, took this ideal as expounded by Socrates very seriously, in the XIXth century, and tried to model its *Beamtenschaftstaat* upon it—which, incidentally, is why Karl Popper during World War II came out with such venom and animus against Plato. And we must at least respect the power and the appeal of its closest analogue in our world today, the ideal of the totalitarian state— besides being in an excellent position to appreciate what Plato points out as the more unpleasant features involved in that ideal—in the ideal of the "perfectly just city." But we have ideals of our own, and we find Plato's dramatic comment on political ideals, his "philosophy of politics," as pertinent to our social ideals as to his Greek illustration.

Plato's philosophy of politics, pulled out of its dramatic setting, and stated crassly, would run something like this: political discussion has many values. The highest is to provoke vision, to discern imaginatively what would be really best, to have an ideal, to formulate it clearly, to see all it really involves. But—to *have* an ideal is not to *be* an ideal, it is to *use* it. Man cannot live without ideals, but equally man cannot live by ideals alone. That is not the Good Life, but fanaticism or lunacy. To take the *Republic* "literally," as a suggested practical program of political reform, is to make Plato a fanatic, and yourself an imperceptive reader.

We say, Follow the pole star. But does that mean, get a ballistic rocket and embark for the stratosphere? Do not *fly* to it, chart your course *by* it. To employ Plato's own figure: the sun is the only source of all light, of the possibility of any discrimination of objects. But does that mean, Look only at the sun? That would be crazy. "Platonists" do it, and go stark, raving mad.

Life must be lived by the proper use of natural human materials. Order it as wisely as you can, so that you may gain a vision of heaven, and in the light of that vision, go out and order it better. The ultimate end is vision: Plato is after all a Greek, not an American; he is devoted to θεωρία, not to endless "progress."

There is the constant temptation to live *in* the vision, rather than *by* vision: to want to go to Heaven, like the Christians, or to bring Heaven here to America, like the moderns, instead of living well a human life, *with* vision. There is the temptation to demand perfection, and to condemn all existence because it falls short of what it might be, as it naturally must, instead of using the vision of perfection to discriminate between what is better and what is worse in our relatively, and inevitably, imperfect world. This is just the difference between Plato and "Platonism," between Plato's "realism" and what it is the fashion to call today "perfectionism." This, it may be, is the truth that lies behind Plato's ironical warning that the effect of poets is often bad: because men are apt to be too stupid to realize that they *are* poets, and to take them literally, instead of seriously.

Something like this is what the artist-philosopher made out of the particular political discussion, the elaboration of the particular ideal of the Good Life furnished by Greek culture. And what he made out of Greek attitudes and "sensibility" is obviously a universal philosophy, applicable to any of man's ideals. Because he was an artist-philosopher, he was able to find the particular ideal of Greek culture very congenial: that the Good Life is not a theory to be expounded, nor a law to be proclaimed and followed, but an art to be practiced, a technique for the better ordering of human life, an artistic achievement.

What was this conception of the Good Life that had emerged in fourth-century Athens, and that was accepted, elaborated, and clarified by Plato? It was: 1. The Good Life is not righteousness, obedience to commands and law, either Divine or natural. Its converse is not "sin," taken as disobedience, transgression, breaking the law. This is the conception expressed in a central strain in Hebrew thought: that morality is a matter of taboos, of commandments, and obedience to the Law. This we call the ethics of Legalism.

2. The Good Life is not purity, holiness, it is not the ascetic flight from anything, involving so much repression of man's natural impulses that it is inevitably supernatural, and can come only through the miracle of grace and redemption. This is the conception expressed in a central strain of Christian thought; this we call the ethics of Asceticism.

3. The Good Life is not Pleasure, the mere enjoyment of the goods proffered by existence. Pleasure, the Greeks thought, is not something bad; it will be a natural part, an accompaniment, of the Good Life. But to aim at pleasure alone means missing so many possibilities of human living; and "pleasure" affords no means of discrimination: for anything can give one pleasure, especially if it is familiar and accustomed. This is the conception we call the ethics of Hedonism.

4. The Good Life is not "being natural," following impulse, "expressing oneself." This often seems to be our modern superstition. We used to say, "Be good, sweet maid, and let who will be clever." But more recently we have taken to saying, "Be yourself, kid, and let who will be careful." Did Sophocles write the *Oedipus* by just "being natural"? Did Ictinus and Pheidias build and adorn the Parthenon to "express" themselves? Some poems and plays are written for that purpose. In our modern world even some buildings seem to have been erected from that motive. But this hardly happened in Greece. Such a view was impossible in Plato's world. This is the conception we call Romanticism.

No, for the Greeks the Good Life is a conscious human achievement: it is an art, guided by vision and skill, a masterpiece to be created. Socrates is constantly appealing to the experience of the craftsman, the shoemaker, the weaver, the carpenter, the wagon-driver, the navigator. How can we find a τέχνη, a skilled craft for achieving a good man, like their skills? 'Αρετή in Plato means "skill," "craftsmanship," and its converse, ἁμαρτία, means "missing the mark," failing to achieve, clumsiness. Man is neither naturally full of original sin, nor is he naturally good. The good man is not developed by putting the child in a flower-pot, watering him, and just watching him grow in goodness.[2] The good man is a work of human art, not of nature.

---

[2] This is a figure used by Graham Wallas to characterize "permissive" education.

'Αρετή, "Excellence" (probably the most useful translation of this central Greek term into our vernacular), is "the health of the soul," say Plato and the Greeks. But does this mean that it is something spontaneous, natural, and effortless? Not to a Greek. For him health, bodily excellence, was a matter of constant exercise and intelligent concern.

"The Good Life" is what man can be made into, his possibilities, his "Idea," as Plato would put it—what our present-day existentialists call "man's essential being." To see man as suggesting it to the artist's imagination is to see man as he really is. There follows naturally the importance of *knowledge* of "the Good": it is the knowledge of man's possibilities. A good man is like a good horse, a good axe, a good ship: to know what is a good specimen of any of these things, you must know what that kind of thing is good for. To know what is a good axe, you must know what an axe is good for. To know what is a good horse, you must know what a horse is good for. To know what is a good man, you must equally know what a man is good for. This is the kind of "knowledge of the Good" Socrates and Plato are looking for.

Now to know what a man is good for is not an easy question to answer. For a man is obviously "good for" so many different and incompatible kinds of thing. To make the question a little easier, we can follow the Socrates of the *Republic* and turn to "man writ large," to society, to the city. We can ask, what is a good industrial system? To answer that question, we have to ask in turn, what is an industrial system good for? We have to explore the possibilities of our technology, to find its "Idea," the ends it might bring about. What could our machine and electronic technology give us? Clearly it could give us many things, some of which we should find "fitting," and should like to secure, like "freedom from want"; and some not so fitting, like H-bombs and ICBM's. This unfortunate but inevitable fact that an industrial and technological system is "good for" so many different and incompatible things, raises the fundamental problem of selecting and harmonizing, and it demands clearly the search for a principle of adjustment and adaptation. Just so it stands with the question, what is a man good for? That question raises the same problem of selecting and harmonizing; and it likewise demands the search for a principle of adjusting and adapting to each other the many different things a man is good for.

And since the highest object of knowledge is, what a man is good for, man's possibilities, what a man can become, we cannot help "loving" this highest object of knowledge and aspiring to it. For it is the "Ideas," or as we should say, the "ideals" arrived at by a realistic analysis of human nature—of what a man is good for. Hence "knowledge *is* ἀρετή," Excellence. For to "know" what we might become is to want to become it—it is to "love the Good." [3]

This is the theme of the "earlier," the Socratic or dramatic dialogues. The several ἀρεταί discussed in the *Charmides*, the *Lysis*, the *Laches*, the *Euthyphro*, and the *Protagoras* are different human "excellences"; they are all particular kinds of skill, appropriate to the occasions to which they are suited. To find the fitting excellence in any particular case implies an intelligent direction and ordering: it is a matter of "measuring," of correct proportion, of adjustment and adaptation to the occasion. It is thus a matter of what Aristotle was to call finding "the mean."

The Greek ἀρεταί, excellences, that appear in Plato: σοφία or wisdom, ἀνδρεία or courage, σωφροσύνη or self-control, and δικαιοσύνη or justice, are all human arts and techniques for dealing appropriately and fittingly with different situations. Thus Courage, in the *Laches* and the *Protagoras,* is knowing what is worth doing, when it is worth while to take the risk, and when it is not, and having the power of character to do it. This last, θυμός, is "spiritedness," "honor," what we call colloquially "will-power," strength of character: it is the nonrational factor in conduct, one of the noble steeds in the chariot figure of the *Phaedrus* myth. The whole of each excellence is thus knowledge adapting impulse to appropriate ends.

Knowledge thus enters into every "excellence" or ἀρετή, without being identical with it. This knowledge is fourfold:

1. Of what the possibility is, of its end.
2. Of its worth, the sense or feeling of it from within, in that sense of "knowing" in which to "know" self-control is to practice it.
3. Of skill in attaining it.
4. Of the occasions on which it is appropriate.

To "know" a good axe, we must know what an axe can do, the worth of doing it, how to do it, and when to do it. It is the same with these ἀρεταί or human excellences. But knowledge is only one factor in the Good Life; there must be impulses and enjoyments also. Knowledge is so important because we need both the vision of perfection, the imaginative insight into the possibilities, and also "intelligence," the skill, the ability to harmonize the impulses and get the right admixture, fitting to every occasion.

The fundamental problem of the Good Life, of ethics, thus becomes, to adjust all these excellences, through a principle of organization in the soul, which Plato calls δικαιοσύνη, "Justice," in the light

[3] This is the "existential" conception of knowledge that runs through the Socratic and dramatic dialogues.

of the totality of human excellences, which he calls "the Idea of the Good." The moral or point of the myth of Er at the end of the *Republic* is that the fruit of human experience is to have learned how to "mix" and harmonize them properly. The "mixed life" taken as the ideal in the *Philebus* seems to be an explicit statement of what is dramatically implied in the "earlier" or Socratic dialogues. There it is said, the Good Life is an intelligent and artistic blending of many materials, an affair like "weaving," "mixing," harmonizing, and adjusting, involving νοῦς both as insight, vision, and also as intelligence, ordering the ingredients in the right measure and proportion.

This whole conception demands all the materials available, all the natural and social goods. A good leaf must grow on a good tree, in a good soil, in a good climate. If you have not got the necessary elements—if you have no money, or live in a bad city—the good life will be impossible for you, you cannot be a good man. This may well be regrettable, but it remains a fact. Of course, if God has laid the injunction on man, to follow the law of righteousness—Be ye perfect, even as your Father in Heaven is perfect—it is then manifestly unfair to demand what is not possible for every man, however adverse his circumstances. The Good Life must then be pared down to an irreducible minimum—to righteousness or purity of heart. The great moral faiths of the East—Buddhism, Judaism, Christianity—express an ethic of despair, of renunciation. Such an ideal is natural enough in societies where the opportunities were very meager, in the poverty-stricken and class-ridden Oriental lands. They offer the promise that even the penniless beggar, the lame, the halt, and the blind, even they can attain the highest. It is clear why Nietzsche, saturated in this very different Greek ethic, called them forms of "slave morality."

But—if the Good Life is to be rather the best life conceivable in imagination, the kind of life men might lead in paradise, the creation of a perfect masterpiece out of natural human materials—how can you hope to make a good pair of shoes, if your leather is poor and you have no thread? How can you hope to make a good man, if the essential materials are lacking? This Greek conception is an ethic of achievement, for a situation in which the materials are all available. It is an ethic of prosperity, of abundance. In practice, given the actual paucity of materials available in classical Greece, it is the ethic of a privileged class, of an élite.

But, the modern objects, this is not democratic. Of course it is not. No art can be in that sense "democratic." It refuses to sacrifice its vision of the Good Life, just because the great mass of men has to put up with something second-best. There must be, Plato holds, no compromise with mediocrity. Plato shows he has no illusions about the actual privileged class in Athens: he portrays them as a pretty sad lot. But he is no democrat. He has no cheer for the oppressed. If that is what you are looking for, go follow Antisthenes, the "proletarian" philosopher. Be a Cynic! But at the same time, Plato offers no "opiate of the people," no "pie in the sky." Plato could sympathize with democratic moral ideals: they have never been more powerfully set forth than in the *Gorgias* and the *Phaedo*. Generations have read these dialogues, and exclaimed, "How Christian!" But Plato refused to give up his vision of the life that is really best.

No, the task of ethics and politics is alike: they face the same problem. It is not to find a type of goodness available to any man at any time, but to discern the possibilities of human life at its richest, fullest, and best, and to adjust these possibilities to each other, and to their natural basis and conditions.

We may here say a word on Plato's Philosophy of Education:

For such a conception of the Good Life as an artistic achievement, education is naturally of primary importance; just as for the legalistic morality, the important thing is moral training and the discipline of habits, and for the ascetic morality, the emotional shock of conversion. For Plato, the end of education will be to provoke a desire and love for the great things of life, to give a sense of what is worth while, a sense of relative values. Plato himself states it as "a discernment of all that is best in existence, and how they are related to each other."

Since for Plato the ultimate goal is θεωρία, vision, the means will be to remove the soul for a time from practice, so that it may get a disinterested outlook, and see what is, beyond all opinion and all debate. Plato thought that the only real science the Greeks had so far developed, except for the medical science of the school of Hippocrates, from which Aristotle was to set out, geometry, which takes the mind out of the welter of conflicting opinion, into a realm of fixed and certain knowledge, and confronts it with the compelling inevitability of what is, is the best preparation for seeing oneself and one's fellows with detached objectivity—for seeing impartially what you and they are, and what you and they might become.

For you can teach even an ignorant slave-boy the truths of geometry, for they are not debatable, while the wisest of men cannot teach their own sons moral excellence, ἀρετή. Only when we have escaped the relativities of opinion in that realm in which there can be no differences of opinion, in which what is true can be taught— the realm of τὰ μαθηματικά, the "teachable things," mathematics, can we hope to escape from mere opinion in that realm where there is no school and no teacher, where we must teach ourselves before we can expect to be taught, and where in the end it seems we have to fall back on the grace of God. Only when we have learned what is, in that world we never made, where our private preferences do not count, where we are not asked, "What do you think? What is your reaction?" but only, "How much have you found out?" can we hope to discern what is best, and to discriminate what we love. Plato is convinced, the best way of gaining imaginative insight into the problems and opinions of men, which is the goal of the philosophic life, and without which the intelligent direction of human life and of the cities of men is quite impossible, is the disinterested study of what is not man's to alter.

And this is Plato's "philosophy of education": the art of the Statesman must be founded on scientific knowledge; and the best way of preparing ourselves to find out what we must learn in order to guide human affairs wisely, is to study what the scientists have already discovered about the world, and to learn scientific method from them. Only thus can we escape the unending and inconclusive "discussions" of the Sophists and the professors of education.

Putting Plato's "philosophy of education" into modern terms, he definitely rejects: (1) a humanistic education in the classics, the traditional Greek education in the poets, and also our own traditional education since the Renaissance—though few modern men can still remember it. This was the philosophy of education of Protagoras, who was a classical humanist. In the dialogue that bears his name, Plato makes fun of Protagoras's literary humanism. (2) Plato rejects also any education in the "social studies"; that is all "mere opinion." There is no evidence that "good citizenship," which is what ἀρετή means in this context, can possibly be taught. (3) Plato comes out strongly for an education in the sciences. They can be taught, above all, the "teachable things," τὰ μαθηματικά, geometry. This conviction forms a large part of the attraction the Pythagoreans had for Plato.

It is significant that Plato does not stand for teaching the "social sciences": he was convinced there is no such thing. And though he talked much about a "science of the Good," according to the commentators it turned out to be nothing but mathematics. It seems clear that were Plato teaching today in a modern university, he would be teaching in the Faculty of Pure Science, and not in the "non-being" of the college of education.

All this philosophy of the Good Life is to be found in the *Republic*. It is brought out, partly in the words the characters are made to speak, partly in the author's dramatic commentary on those words. And we can neglect the latter only at the peril of wholly misconstruing Plato's "philosophy."

The *Republic* has as its central theme δικαιοσύνη, or "Justice"—
the principle of organization, of coordinating the separate "excellences" in men and in cities—the fundamental problem of Plato's
conception of the Good Life as a harmonizing of possibilities. This
principle of organization is clearly dependent on knowledge: it must
be an ordering by wisdom and intelligence. And so the treatment of
the theme of knowledge is inextricably interwoven with the treatment of the theme of the organization of the Good Life—of Justice.

How far can you carry the ideal of organization, of Justice; if,
because it is so obvious and essential a good, you take it as the
supreme and only good: if you let the mind play with it, as men do
in discussion, and push it as far as you possibly can? What would
an "absolutely just man," that is, a "perfectly adjusted man"; or
what would an "absolutely just state," that is, a "state organized
with perfect efficiency," be like?

It is clear, you can carry the ideal out to the bitter end, in imagination; and Plato shows the end is bitter! So Plato has Socrates,
maliciously and ironically, elaborate, shall we say, Protagoras's
scheme for a perfectly organized state—a "perfectly planned society,"
we moderns put it—till in the end we have a picture of αὐτὸ τὸ δικαίον,
of "Justice Itself," Pure Justice—the Perfect City, from which every
other consideration has dropped away, which exists for the sake of
Efficient Organization, and Efficient Organization alone.

But Plato warns us, we must know what we are about, just what
we have been doing. We have arrived at a vision of "Justice," of
what he calls the "Idea" of Justice. It is surely a marvelous guide
and inspiration—in imagination. But could we ever hope to make
the city of Athens—or the city of New York—like that? This question, Socrates is made to point out, is completely irrelevant to what
we have been doing. When pressed by his eager young hearers,
anxious to proceed forthwith, he replies, "Yes, we could—if we only
turned Philosophers into Kings—or perhaps Kings into Philosophers,
and then established a perfect system of education; if we drove all
the citizens over ten years of age out of the city, as hopelessly mis-
educated; and then proceeded to transform the human nature of the
children under ten left. Yes, we could then establish the Perfectly
Organized City on earth—if we only did a few more little things
like that."

Would we *want* to bring the Perfect City down from the sky—
which is clearly for Plato its only possible abode—and set it up
among the human cities of men? In order to achieve Perfectly Efficient Organization, would we really want to sacrifice everything else—
and Plato makes it abundantly clear, it would in the end involve just
that, in all its horror—the sacrifice of any individual happiness, of

any genuine moral education, of all poetry, art, wisdom, and philosophy—all would have to go by the board. Or, in individual terms, would you want to be, in Plato's unforgettable picture, a "Perfectly Just"—that is, a "Perfectly Adjusted man," and be at the same time perfectly miserable?

The answer, for any one in his senses, and certainly for any perceptive and imaginative reader of the *Republic*, is clear. "Justice," Organization, Efficiency, is only one element in the Good Life, or in the Good Society. Would you want any one excellence, at the expense of giving up all the rest? Would you want to be courageous, and nothing else? Or to be self-controlled, and nothing else? That way lies only madness.

No, Plato tells us, above "Justice," Organization, is the "Idea of the Good," a harmony of all values, not merely of Efficiency, Organization, "Justice." The more we contemplate the vision of the Perfectly Organized City, of the Perfectly Planned Society, the more we realize, without losing sight in the slightest of the very real importance of efficient organization, the need of adjusting the values of organization to all the other values, in the light of the totality of values—of the Idea of the Good.

Plato tells the myth of Er in order to point the moral of his long discussion of organization or "Justice." The souls gather at the river of Lethe to choose the lots that will determine what their next reincarnation will bring them: Plato is once more drawing on Orphic and Pythagorean mythology. The choice is made on the basis of what they have learned through their earthly experience in this life. The first soul to select makes a stupid choice: he chooses to be a tyrant, since he does not see he is fated to devour his own children, and suffer other horrors. Plato continues:

When he inspected his lot at leisure, he beat his breast, and bewailed his choice, not abiding by the forewarning of the prophet. For he did not blame himself for his woes, but fortune and the Gods and anything except himself. He was one of those who had come down from heaven, a man who had lived in a *well-organized society* [ἐν τεταγμένῃ πολιτείᾳ; emphasis mine] in his former existence, participating in excellence by habit and not by philosophy (ἔθει ἄνευ φιλοσοφίας ἀρετῆς μετειληφότα): and one may perhaps say that a majority of those who were thus caught were of the company that had come from heaven, inasmuch as they were unexercised by suffering. But the most of those who came up from the earth, since they had themselves suffered and seen the suffering of others, did not make their choice precipitately. For which reason there was also an interchange of good and evil for most of the souls, as well as because of the chances of the lot.[4]

Along came the soul of Odysseus, who had spent his life in any-

[4] Republic 619 C, D; tr. Paul Shorey.

thing but a well-organized and just city, but had knocked about the world more than most men.

And it fell out that the soul of Odysseus drew the last lot of all and came to make its choice, and, from memory of its former toils having flung away ambition, went about for a long time in quest of the life of an ordinary citizen who minded his own business (βίος ἀνδρὸς ἰδιώτου ἀπράγμονος), and with difficulty found it lying in some corner disregarded by the others, and upon seeing it said that it would have done the same had it drawn the first lot, and chose it gladly.[5]

Could Plato be saying more clearly that the moral of his whole discussion was to defend the Athenian ideal which he states explicitly in the *Laws*, to be good "not by external compulsion but by inner disposition"? The life lived in a "well-organized and just city without philosophy" brings no education in moral excellence.

Yet men have actually been so blind, as to read the *Republic*, and to imagine that Plato is urging a practical political program—they have been so insensitive as to think, Socrates is taking the stump for the Perfect City Party in Athens! They have thought that Plato was himself eager to catch a king, and to bulldoze him into becoming a philosopher. It is really incredible that over the ages readers of the *Republic*, with its layer upon layer of dramatic irony, have assumed that poor Plato himself wanted, or that any sane man in his sense could want, to *live* under such institutions as Socrates is made to elaborate—institutions so fascinating to talk about, but so intolerable to have to endure.

No, Plato is not offering a new constitution for Athens—or for Syracuse—or for any human, earthly city. He is trying, dramatically, to make us "see" where men get when, intoxicated with discussion, they talk about a perfect constitution. Plato is offering, not any political program, but a picture—the "idea" of Justice. "Idea" is a sight word, and means "something seen"—the picture of Perfect Organization, taken as an "end-in-itself." Plato is offering an imaginative vision, with all the imagination's ruthless disregard of any other value than that on which it is for the moment focused.

What is the value of talking about Perfect Organization, of contemplating it in discourse and in imagination, as Socrates and his companions are made to do in the *Republic?* What is the value of elaborating and clarifying an ideal of a perfect social order? It makes you see more clearly, surely, the very real value of efficient social organization—and it makes you realize also the importance of other things we want to possess. This, Plato shows us, is the value of clarifying any "ideal." We at once find it inextricably involved in other ideals; and we are led on to the problems of harmonizing and ad-

[5] Republic 620 C, D.

justing them all. This unification of values is the essence of what Plato calls "dialectic."

Plato is conventionally taken as the "first Utopian." In reality, while he is certainly a moving inspiration to social idealism, he is offering a vaccination against the Utopian spirit. The *Republic* is really a dramatic commentary on the nature and function of ideals—displaying what they can be, and do, and what they cannot. It s a dramatic exploration of the conditions of any realistic social idealism.

I have been saying, in the *Republic* Plato is conventionally taken as offering the first Utopia; while in reality, he is offering a vaccination against Utopianism. I should like not to be misunderstood—though I am pretty sure I will be by some. This is a cardinal illustration of the Greek maxim, "Know Thyself!" And it is almost impossible for a modern to understand that maxim. Our own maxim sounds very much like it, but the tune is quite different: "See things as they are!" To us, this means, Realize there is nothing to them. But it did not mean that to the Greek, and certainly not to Plato. To him it meant, "See things as they are, and realize all there *might be* to them," all you can make of them, if you see both what they are and what they are not.

The *Republic* is a dramatic commentary on the Utopian spirit, on social idealism. No one can read it, without being convinced that social idealism is about the most important thing in the world. It has made that impression for centuries, and such an impression is obviously intended by the author, by Plato. It is the greatest source of social idealism in the record of Western civilization—outside, at least, the Prophets and the Gospels. It inspires intense practical zeal. Yet it holds that zeal up and contemplates it with ironic detachment—with νοῦς. Are these two attitudes incompatible? If we find them so, then I am afraid we can never really understand Plato. We can never understand the Cave Myth, with its combination of detached vision and practical action. We can never understand Socrates' contention, at the close of the *Symposium,* that comedy and tragedy are ultimately the same.

But—no reader of the *Symposium* is ever tempted to minimize the idealizing power of love, because he is there made to see the actual human love of Alcibiades for Socrates. And no man need feel that Plato is counseling him not to vote, say, a Marxian ticket, because he is urging him to see Socialists and Communists as they are. In fact, if one wanted to put the central point of the *Republic* in a very different but perhaps more contemporary language, one might say, it is just what Karl Marx had in mind when he urged that Socialism should strive to be not "Utopian" but "scientific"—an advice many Marxians might still do well to heed.

One further illustration may clarify the point being insisted upon. Some years ago, in 1931, Bertrand Russell rewrote the *Republic*, in Part III of his volume called *The Scientific Outlook*, entitled "The Scientific Society." What Plato called the "Perfectly Just City," Russell brought up to date by dubbing "the Scientific Society," the society consciously planned so that every institution will be scientifically organized, and administered by scientific experts, in accordance with the best scientific techniques. Now Russell is the last man in the world to minimize the importance of science, or to try to persuade us not to be as "scientific" as we can. So he asks, what would a society be like, in which "scientific efficiency" were allowed free sway, and everything else subordinated to it? Russell's answer turns out to be identical, down to the last detail, with the scheme put into Socrates' mouth in the *Republic*.

There is one major difference: modern scientific organization would obviously demand a world-state. Hence there are in Russell's scientific society only two classes: there are no Platonic Guardian soldiers. There would, however, be no liberty, and no equality. There would be rule by an oligarchy of experts, who know what is best to do. Individuals would be ruthlessly sacrificed; Christian ethics is clearly "unscientific." There would be a scientific control of reproduction, and the community of women: the family would have to disappear. Every particular loyalty: of man and woman, of parents and children, even of friendship, would have to be sacrificed to an undeviating loyalty to the State, fostered by pills and propaganda. There would be an education of the working-class to be "docile, industrious, punctual, and thoughtless, 'cooperative,' and contented," by means of drugs and psychology; and of the governing-class of experts, in "intelligence, self-command, and command over others." Yet no one would be allowed to question the value of science; all fundamentally novel ideas would be discouraged. There would be a bureaucracy of experts leading to scientific stagnation.

Thus every institution would be perfectly "scientific," and every man perfectly miserable. At least, he would be, if he were not psychoanalyzed and fed pills to make him like it. There would be no poetry, no art, no love, no idealism, and no real science.

Now Russell is not a dramatic artist, like Plato, and so he has to state his point expressly, where Plato makes his reader "see":

The scientific society which has been sketched . . . , is, of course, not to be taken altogether as serious prophecy. It is an attempt to depict the world which would result if scientific technique were to rule unchecked. The reader will have observed that features that everyone would consider desirable are almost inextricably mingled with features that are repulsive. The reason of this is that we have been imagining a *society developed in ac-*

cordance with certain ingredients of human nature [emphasis mine] to the exclusion of all others. As ingredients they are good; as the sole driving force they are likely to be disastrous. The impulse towards scientific construction is admirable when it does not thwart any of the major impulses that give value to human life, but when it is allowed to forbid all outlet to anything but itself it becomes a form of cruel tyranny. There is, I think, a real danger lest the world should become subject to a tyranny of this sort, and it is on this account that I have not shrunk from depicting the darker features of the world that scientific manipulation unchecked might wish to create.[6]

This is the universal philosophy of Politics, of the nature and function, of the importance and limitations, of political theorizing, embodied by Plato in the *Republic*. It is clearly as applicable to the ideal of Communism, or to whatever we are willing to call our own social ideal, as to the Greek ideal Plato makes Socrates ironically expound.

But it is impossible not to believe that Plato had a very particular application in mind. To the audience for which the *Republic* was first written, the "Perfect City" of Socrates' ironical criticism could have had but one meaning: it was the Spartan ideal. Spartan institutions form the groundwork of the Perfect City: they are perfected and elaborated by Socrates into a Super-Sparta. We must remember that Sparta had defeated the Athenians in the long Peloponnesian War; and many Athenians were naturally fascinated by its harmonious and efficient military organization—it might well be the salvation of Athens to copy Sparta's successful military machine. In modern terms, many Athenians were tempted to collaborate. The *Republic* may even have taken form under the Spartan occupation of Athens: we do not know, of course, its exact date. But the situation is analogous to a Frenchman defending the ideal of French civilization against Prussian military bureaucracy under the German occupation of France during World War II.

We can well imagine Plato saying to the collaborators, All right! Let us take the Spartan ideal, and let us take it at its best, as Athenians would work it! of course, nothing so unenlightened and stupid as Sparta actually is could ever happen here. Let us take the Spartan ideal as a genuine ideal, and proceed to develop its implications, and see where we get. Of course, there would be no individual happiness, no moral responsibility; it could be made to work only by propaganda and "royal lies." There would be no art, and no poetry; scholars and scientists would all be "coördinated" with the Régime. Wisdom would be chained to a military machine. There would be a full eugenic pro-

[6] Bertrand Russell, *The Scientific Outlook* (New York, 1931), 260.

gram of mating, to prevent racial defilement and to improve Athenian blood. We should be left with business men, soldiers and bureaucrats, and Party members. Is that what you collaborators really want? Of course, we Athenians could stand a lot more sense of order and discipline and disinterested devotion to our city than we have got. But—do you really want to go Spartan? Or Nazi? the modern will add.

To the audience for whom the *Republic* was originally written, it must have been a sustained piece of dramatic irony, a magnificent defense of the Athenian ideal against the Spartan, Plato saw the genuine values of Spartan efficiency and military organization—especially for a War State, such as the Perfect City definitely is. But he was hardly rooting for Sparta—not even for a Super-Sparta.

There, organization takes precedence even over the Life of θεωρία, of imaginative insight. The philosopher is there forced back into the Cave, and is lucky if he can ever escape again. There, philosophers are good rulers because they hate the whole business, and are doing it only from a sense of duty, of "justice." There are much better philosophers in imperfect states, in actual human cities. There will be better art, better poetry, better life, better men—better everything but Efficient Organization.

This view of the *Republic* as an ironical defense of the Athenian ideal is confirmed by the *Laws*. There, the entire aim of the institutions of the new colony being planned should be not war, but peace and friendly feeling, the securing of permanent friendliness. The true Statesman will not prepare for war in time of peace, but even during war he will be ceaselessly preparing for peace. Military success is no valid test of the goodness or badness of institutions: it is largely accidental, and depends on power, not on worth.

This utter rejection of warfare is in marked contrast to—it is in fact the most striking difference from—the Perfect City of the *Republic*, where organization, efficiency, "Justice," is bent to the sole aim of military power, and the Efficient Organization or "justice" of the City is to be tested by whether its institutions will be effective in war, a project Plato proposes to undertake in the *Critias*. The Perfect City of the *Republic,* we have seen, is a War-State—it is the Spartan ideal.

Why this glaring contrast? The answer is simple. Sparta had fallen at Leuctra in 371 B.C., and finally had been completely overcome by the Thebans under Epaminondas at Mantinaea, in 362 B.C. The great War-State was an utter failure. Plato could now afford to say, "I told you so." His whole ironic defense of the Athenian ideal against the Spartan militarism in the *Republic* was now justified before the entire world. It was a damning indictment of Spartan institutions and the Spartan ideal, which had been attracting some Athenians. They aimed at power and military efficiency alone, and they failed to get even that. Power without wisdom, says Plato now, is ignorance of the greatest of human interests. No, institutions must develop men of Self-Control, men of character—not mere soldiers. One wonders whether the *Critias* was left incomplete because Sparta fell before it was finished.

War is a disease, to be avoided at all costs. It is caused, says Plato, by commercial greed; and Plato goes on to describe something close to what we have known during the past century as "economic imperialism." Such "imperialism" is fatal. Hence everything which leads to it must be shunned. So the three elderly planners propose a program of embargoes on commerce, neutrality laws, and the like.

The *Laws* merely confirms what the *Republic* dramatically develops—the inadequacy and incompleteness of the Spartan ideal of efficient organization for the sake of military power alone.

Columbia University.

III

NOTES AND DOCUMENTS

FROM NATIONALISM TO COSMOPOLITANISM IN THE GRECO-ROMAN WORLD[1]

By Moses Hadas

We need no ancient oracle to inform us that exaggerated nationalism is a Bad Thing and that the concept of the world as a single community might be a Good Thing. The experience of another civilization in moving from nationalism to cosmopolitanism may be interesting and instructive even if, in the nature of things, it cannot provide a blue-print for us to follow. No other stretch of history offers so convenient a parallel to our own problems as does the Greek; the springs of Greek conduct were very like our own, the span of their history is manageable, with beginning, middle, and end, and they were highly sophisticated and articulate in matters of political doctrine.

Vigorous nationalism appears as early as Homer. "One omen is best," says Hector (*Iliad* 12. 243), "to fight for one's native land." The word βάρβαρος ("stuttering, unintelligible, alien") is applied in the *Iliad*, in a compound form, to the Carians (2. 867). It is not applied to the Trojans and their allies for these, unlike the Carians, were known to the poet only from the saga. Their language, customs, dress, weapons, religion are thought of as being like the Greek; in early vase paintings Trojan warriors are represented as Ionian hoplites. After the Persian War nationalist feeling retrojected the term βάρβαρος in its pejorative sense to the Trojans; the drama represented them as different and inferior, and Trojan characters were dressed in barbarian costume.

Among themselves, of course, the Greek city-states were extremely particularistic, war rather than peace being the normal relationship between them. Callinus in Ionia, Tyrtaeus in Sparta, Solon in Athens all teach local patriotism. Pindar is concerned for Boeotian reputation. The Athenian dramatists, historians, and orators who wrote during the period of Athenian-Spartan hostilities all reflect Athenian partisanship in greater or less degree. But as opposed to the barbarians all Greeks regarded themselves as a single people. Similarly the enormous differences among various barbarian peoples were overlooked; their divergence from the Greeks was the paramount characteristic which imposed a unity upon them. The dichotomy between Hellene and barbarian is sharp and decisive from the very begin-

---

[1] The works which have been most helpful in the preparation of the first part of this paper are: Julius Jüthner, *Hellenen und Barbaren, Aus der Geschichte des Nationalbewusstseins* (Leipzig, 1923); Johannes Mewaldt, *Das Weltbürgertum in der Antike, Die Antike* 2 (1926), 177 ff.; Julius Kaerst, *Die antike Idee der Oekumene* (Berlin, 1903).

ning of Greek literature at the close of the Greek Dark Ages. From Hesiod onwards every classical Greek author reflects, with greater or less clarity, the conviction that the Hellenes are the elect and the barbarians their inferiors. The Greeks occupy the center of the world, and their usages are the norm by which lesser peoples are judged. Solemn proclamations excluded barbarians, along with criminals, from the celebration of the mysteries and from the national games. Sacred objects and sites, including the domestic hearth, were rendered unclean by contact with a barbarian.

The barbarian is strange and repulsive, uneducated, superstitious, awkward, stupid, unsocial, lawless; he is slavish and cowardly, unrestrained in passion, petulant, cruel, violent, faithless, greedy and gluttonous. In a word, the barbarian is a brutish creature; he stands in the same relation to a Hellene as an animal does to a man. The designation βάρβαροι was applied even to Egyptians, Babylonians, Assyrians, and Phoenicians, to whom Greek civilization owed so much. The designation is manifestly unfair, but it is not hard to see how it maintained currency. It originated in ignorance due to remoteness, and when the Greeks came to travel they were actually superior and the older civilizations retrograde. Eighth-century colonization in the West and in Southern Russia could only corroborate the traditional contempt. In the seventh century Scythian hordes overran Asia Minor and settled in Cappadocia. Unsavory Phoenician merchants and adventurers are traditional in the *Odyssey* and Herodotus. Lydians, Phrygians, and Syrians settled in Greece as metics and formed the larger part of the slave population, especially after the feeling against selling Greeks into slavery grew. These foreigners were not the best representativs of their people to begin with, and they were further corrupted by slavery. After the Persian invasion hatred increased and became traditional.

The tradition was first questioned, but only by implication, in the work of a medical man. In his *On Airs, Waters, Places* Hippocrates attributes human differences to geographic and climatic conditions; he implies, but does not state, the fundamental equality of diverse races. The implication was made explicit in the rising sophistic enlightenment. In the papyrus fragments of Antiphon's *On Truth*[2] the plain statement is made that "all men are created alike by nature in all respects, both barbarians and Greeks." The proof is that all men breathe through their mouths and nostrils; they are therefore alike in φύσις, and only different in νόμος, which is in the last analysis merely a matter of convention, dictated by the more powerful and calculated to serve their interests. Every δίκαιον is also ἄδικον: *summum ius summa iniuria.* The injustice of νόμος was particularly apparent during the period of the Peloponnesian war, when many small individual πόλεις were forced to change their νόμος overnight.

[2] *Oxyrhynchus Papyri XI*, no. 1364; most conveniently consulted in Diels-Kranz, *Die Fragmente der Vorsokratiker*[5] 87 (II, 346 ff., Berlin, 1935).

But Antiphon's statement of the equality of man remained merely a characteristic example of sophistic intellectual revolt, with no discernible influence upon thought generally. Atossa's dream in the *Persae* shows Aeschylus' well-bred contempt for the Persians. Sophocles' *Ajax* illustrates (in the Teucer passages) the contemporary attitude to half-breeds. Euripides favors the disinherited in many noble lines, but the general Athenian attitude seems to be reflected in such plays as the *Iphigenia in Tauris* and the *Helen*. "Dialect" jokes at the expense of foreigners are common to all comedy, but the bad Greek of the Scythian policeman in Aristophanes' *Thesmophoriazusae*, of the god Triballos in his *Birds,* and of Pseudartabas in the *Acharnians* seems a little malicious. But it is shocking to discover that Plato is equivocal on the subject of human equality and that Aristotle frankly upholds Greek superiority.

Plato readily acknowledges the influence of geography and climate in the formation of a people's character and makes a place for the influence of education.[3] Like Thucydides Plato deduces the character of the ancestors of the Greeks from that of contemporary barbarians. Plato goes beyond Hippocrates, then, in acknowledging the fundamental equality of humanity; but his theory does not prevent him from making the commonplace differentiation between Greeks and barbarians. Plato's nationalism appears most clearly in his discussions of the state. The ideal state is thought of as a Greek πόλις, with its traditional attitude towards barbarians. Strife among Greek cities is really civil war and should be avoided or carried on humanely; real war is against barbarians and should be carried on energetically. A story told of both Socrates and Plato is true probably of neither but characteristic nevertheless: the Greek is reported to have rendered thanks that he was born a man, not an animal, a man and not a woman, a Greek and not a barbarian.

If Plato's attitude is surprising, Aristotle's is shocking. At the beginning of the *Politics* he insists that slaves are such by nature, and that barbarians are naturally slaves. It is remarkable that Aristotle should embrace and justify the Greek prejudice, with no shred of logical proof. He is led into certain inconsistencies, as when he praises the constitution of Carthage: can a good state be comprised wholly of men who are slaves by nature?

Alexander's vision was broader than his teacher's; though his own ambition may have been merely to supplant the kings of Persia and become an oriental monarch, his victories did greatly accelerate the Hellenization of the Near East. "Greek" cities with characteristic theaters, libraries, games, dress, thought spread rapidly. These were the things which were supposed to set Greeks apart from other men, and now "Greeks" were to be found all over the world. Concomitantly alien cultural elements came to be appreciated. Babylonian astrology, Persian magic, Egyptian and Jewish

[3] The material is collected in F. Weber, *Platons Stellung zu den Barbaren* (Munich, 1904); cf. Jüthner, 22–28.

thought were studied; translations of Zoroaster, Mago, the Bible, were made; curiosity about foreign peoples was aroused and histories of them written, such as Berosus' work on Babylonia, Manetho's on Egypt, and Demetrius', Eupolemus', and Artapanus' on the Jews. The world was changed, the πόλις and Greece itself were transcended in a larger concept and the traditional distinction between Greek and barbarian obliterated.

The changes in the world were first recognized philosophically, it seems, by Theophrastus, Aristotle's successor as head of the Lyceum. A fragment of his[4] declares that all people are related, either because of an ultimate common ancestry, or because of their common sustenance, habits, and character. Here the implication of Hippocrates and the enlightenment of Antiphon are given scientific expression. The world had attained new dimensions, in fact as well as in theory.

And now we are prepared for the classic utterance of the Cynic Diogenes who, when he was asked of what city he came, answered, "I am a κοσμοπολίτης, a citizen of the world" (Diogenes Laertius 6. 72). But we must be careful to note that in Diogenes the statement does not bear the philosophic implications it acquired in later Stoicism, nor was Diogenes' cosmopolitanism the well-travelled man's interest in alien cultures, like that of Herodotus. It was rather a rebellious reaction against every kind of coercion imposed by the community upon the individual. The meaning is negative rather than positive; Diogenes is really saying, "I am not a citizen of any of your Greek cities."[5] The virtue which it is the function of the philosopher to teach is equally attainable by people of all classes regardless of sex or education. The morally good are all friends of one another, regardless of conventional barriers. Diogenes' cosmopolitanism, then, was the proud assertion of a ragged exile's consciousness of his own worth in the face of a bourgeois society which scorned him. But Crates of Thebes, the well-born disciple of Diogenes who renounced wealth and position and took up his master's scrip and staff and ragged cloak, gave a positive, philanthropic turn to the meaning of the word. "I am a citizen of the lands of Obscurity and Poverty, impregnable to Fortune, a fellow-citizen of Diogenes," he said (Diogenes Laertius 6. 93), but in his case it was evident that he had become naturalized in the larger community out of choice, and he preached its advantages over the smaller community out of love.

But it was the individual's happiness and not the well-being of the community, large or small, that the Cynics were interested in. It was the Stoics who thought primarily in terms of the community, insisting that nothing could be injurious to the individual if it was good for the community of which the individual was a part. The crucial point is the proper understanding of "community." Relationships of blood or race or country are

---

[4] Recovered by J. Bernays out of Porphyry; see his *Theophrastos' Schrift über Frömmigkeit* (Berlin, 1866), 97.

[5] See D. R. Dudley, *A History of Cynicism* (London, 1937), 34 f.

meaningless, political and social stratifications are rejected. All good men, whatever their social or geographic position may be, are equally citizens of the larger πόλις which embraces the entire cosmos: they are in fact κοσμοπολῖται, citizens of the world. The cosmos is a single organism which embraces the stars and the earth, men, animals and plants—all things which share in the animate being of the cosmos. The cosmos is the outer form of the divine animate spirit, and therefore God. Man is a favored part of the cosmos for he may possess an intelligent view of it and is therefore in a special sense a κοσμοπολίτης. Men and God are alike members of the same πόλις, which all must regard as their true fatherland. *Universus hic mundus una civitas communis deorum atque hominum existimanda est* (Cicero, *De Legibus* 23).

Zeno had sat under Crates, but unlike the Cynic's cosmopolitanism Zeno's involved expansion and assimilation rather than contraction and limitation. "Zeno's earliest work," writes Mr. Tarn,[6] "his Republic, exhibited a resplendent hope which has never quite left men since; he dreamt of a world which should no longer be separate states, but one great City under one divine law, where all were citizens and members one of another, bound together, not by human laws, but by their own willing consent, or (as he phrased it) by Love." With Zeno and his followers the doctrine of human equality and brotherhood was no mere specimen of enlightened wit, to be admired and ignored. The world was now become receptive to the notion. At a banquet at Opis Alexander had prayed for a union of hearts (ὁμόνοια) and a joint commonwealth of Macedonians and Persians (Arrian, *Anabasis* 7. 11. 9). Geographers had given up studying the world according to national boundaries but had developed the concept of the οἰκουμένη, the habitable world considered as a single unit. Nor were the Stoics the impractical perfectionists their austere doctrine would make them. Their theory recognized no degrees in virtue and assumed the equality of men; but they did in fact realize that men differ in ability, character, and circumstances; as Chrysippus put it, nothing could prevent some seats in the theater being better than others. Furthermore, the world being composed of ordinary men, ruled by people who were not philosophers and had no knowledge of the universal law, their world state was impossible of realization. But the Stoics were willing to compromise their perfectionism and to do what they could to bring their ideal nearer. They advised rulers, they wrote books on how states should be governed, they were ready to campaign actively against bad governments. Sphaerus of Borysthenes, for example, a disciple of Zeno, seems to have been a driving force behind Agis' and Cleomenes' social revolution in third century Sparta; and a century later Blossius of Cumae seems to have been responsible for much of the liberal program of the Gracchi. Notions of a just concord between states as well

[6] W. W. Tarn, *Hellenistic Civilisation* (London, 1930), 73.

as between citizens in a single state began to take shape. The germs of international law go back to third century Stoicism.

The Middle Stoa in particular was willing to relax the older ideals and accommodate itself to reality. Instead of ignoring existing states and dreaming of the ideal cosmic state teachers like Panaetius strove to introduce Stoic ideals into existing states. The first step was to place such states under the direction of a philosophical and moral élite. When Panaetius came into contact with Roman traditions and Roman power in the person of Scipio Aemilianus in the Scipionic Circle Stoicism came into position to influence a world power which was temperamentally sympathetic to it.[7] The Romans had their optimates: they needed only to become optimates in the Stoic sense; Roman world dominion needed only to take on the character of a Stoic commonwealth. Rome had succeeded magnificently in Latinizing Italy and moulding it into a unified nation, but its imperial domination, during the half century of the Punic Wars, had degenerated into organized plunder by an exploiting capitalist group which had no regard for the human or material degradation of subject peoples. The "mixed" constitution comprising all elements in the state urged in the sixth book of Polybius and in Cicero's *De Republica* is an echo of the Stoic doctrine of Posidonius current in the Scipionic circle; its goal is *civium beate et honeste vivendi societas*. The various elements in the state must not be separated by their private interests but must unite in the service of the greater commonwealth, under prudent oversight, for the freedom of individuals and for friendly relations between all individuals. The common nationality of the human race becomes the guiding rule for Roman statesmen and the basis for the cultural mission of the Roman world empire. Out of the *communis humani generis societas* (*De Officiis* 3.28) the Middle Stoa also evolved an ideal of law which should be valid for all subjects of the empire; the law of the πόλις makes way for the law of world society. Even the exercise of rule is to be based not on power but on law. The ideal of the unity of the human race gave rise to the new ethical principle of *humanitas*.

But besides the ideals of the mixed constitution and of the οἰκουμένη Stoicism was responsible for another development in Rome which is of perhaps greater significance in human history, and that is the ideal of the principate. The monarchic idea in Rome grew out of the prolonged military commands, but Greek influence was important in shaping it. In Julius Caesar himself and with the later emperors beginning with the Severi the monarchy was of the oriental Hellenistic type, based on the personal power and the divine character of the ruler. But the principate of Augustus preserved the character of a Roman magistracy and all the traditional Republican forms. Augustus' preeminence rested on the authority bestowed by his personal merits, and was not a private possession which he could transmit to his heirs.

[7] See J. Kaerst, *Scipio Aemilianus, Die Stoa, und der Prinzipat, Neue Jahrbücher für Wissenschaft und Jugendbildung* 5 (1929), 653 ff.

In the *Monumentum Ancyranum* he himself says he excelled in *auctoritas*, not *potentia*. Early Roman history exhibits numerous outstanding men, but no single genius surrounded with a nimbus of divine origin and super-human character until Scipio Africanus,[8] who was, significantly, the first to be impregnated with Greek ideas. Polybius thinks the mystery surround-ing Scipio was engineered for political reasons, but Scipio probably believed in his extraordinary gifts, in keeping with Stoic doctrine.

The idea of a single ruler endowed with special *auctoritas* who should be a *moderator* and *rector* of a commonwealth which should embrace the entire οἰκουμένη was the concept derived from Stoicism through the Scipionic circle and its followers which Augustus consciously adopted as the guiding princi-ple of his rule and which procured a large measure of peace and happiness for mankind for a period of two centuries.[9] Stoicism had led the struggle on behalf of *moriens libertas*, a struggle embodied in the Younger Cato, who is the martyr of republican freedom. Augustus' system was set up in conscious opposition to Caesar's, upon the pattern suggested by the Stoics.

Whenever succeeding emperors tended to regard their position as a per-sonal right rather than a ministry the Stoic opposition became vocal. That is why emperors like Domitian persecuted the "philosophers." Nerva and Trajan show their compliance with Stoic teaching by their rejection of com-pletely hereditary rule if by nothing else. Marcus Aurelius, who conceived his royal station as a duty something like a martyrdom is the truest repre-sentative of Roman Stoicism. And because he was incomparably the most influential man in his world his full recognition of the οἰκουμένη is profoundly significant. "All fits together for me which is well-fitted for thee, O thou Universe," he cries (*To Himself* 4. 23), "from thee are all things, to thee come all things; the poet saith 'Dear City of Athens,' but wilt thou not say 'Dear City of God'?" St. Augustine had ready to his hand not only the great phrase but also the outlines of the City of God, elaborated by genera-tions of socially-minded teachers that had gone before. The god who was a member of the city and its animate force altered his character; the out-lines of the city were blurred and its parishes developed separate modes of life. But from time to time, as especially in the sixteenth century, thought-ful men looked back upon it wistfully and were inspired to undertake a partial rehabilitation. Rehabilitation is sorely needed now, and inspiration if not light and leading may be drawn from the long struggle which men of old waged to bring cosmopolitanism out of nationalism.

Columbia University.

[8] See R. M. Haywood, *Studies on Scipio Africanus* (Baltimore, 1933).

[9] On the basis of a careful analysis of Cicero's *De Republica* R. Reitzenstein has demonstrated that the idea of the principate is a contribution of Stoicism through Panaetius and the Scipionic Circle: *Nachrichten der Göttingener Gesellschaft der Wissensch.*, 1917. Cf. A. M. Young, *The Stoic Creed on the Origin of Kingship*, *Classical Weekly* 28(1934), 116 ff.

PART TWO

POLITICAL THOUGHT
OF THE RENAISSANCE

IV

BOOK REVIEW

NEW LIGHT ON THE POLITICAL WRITERS OF THE FLORENTINE RENAISSANCE

By Hans Baron

ROBERTO RIDOLFI, *Opuscoli di Storia Letteraria e di Erudizione. Savonarola—Machiavelli—Guicciardini—Giannotti.* Firenze: "Bibliopolis," Libreria Editrice, 1942. Pp. VII, 217.

Contributions to the history of the Italian Renaissance published in Italy after 1939 are gradually finding their way across the Atlantic. Among these publications, the work of Roberto Ridolfi—published in "Bibliopolis" in Florence, a cover-name for the publishing house of Olschki under national-socialist suppression—deserves particular attention. Under its unassuming title we are given a selection of studies which often contain startling discoveries or refutations of accepted views on the lives and literary activities of four of the leading figures of the Florentine Renaissance. No student interested in the literary or political history of Florence in the Renaissance can afford to overlook the new facts uncovered in this work.

The method by which the author reaches his results owes much to the principle, as he puts it in his first study, that problems open to a strictly philological approach should be investigated along the road of "philological investigations" as far as possible, before any "arguments of a historical character" are called in to take the place of manuscript evidence and textual criticism (pp. 7, 18). While this seems to be self-evident as a rule of method, the harvest brought in by Ridolfi bears proof that students of political thought in the Florentine Renaissance often gave themselves up to inferences derived from more distant historical factors, before philology plain and simple had completed her sober task.

The following high lights from Ridolfi's studies will give an idea of the value and variety of the results achieved. To begin with Savonarola, the introductory chapter is devoted to a problem that has always intrigued students—the question of the authorship of the *Vita* of Savonarola traditionally ascribed to Fra Pacifico Burlamacchi, one of the most intimate and venerable followers of the reformer. The first to undermine the authority of this work, in which Savonarola is depicted, more than in any other source, as a prophet and miracle-worker, was Ranke in 1877. There are references in the text, Ranke pointed out, to events posterior to Burlamacchi's death in 1519. Though in a modified form, and partly with other arguments, the thesis of the late origin of the *Vita* was subsequently accepted by Villari, in the second edition of his *Savonarola*. More recently, however, J. Schnitzer and his school have included in their re-interpretation of Savonarola's figure an attempt to re-establish Burlamacchi's authorship by arguing that the doubts previously raised hold good only with regard to the Latin text, while the version handed down in Volgare was older and could be traced back to Burlamacchi. Ridolfi, by having philology answer the question as to which of the two versions was the model and which the translation, succeeds in solving the vexed problem with almost "mathematical" precision, as he boasts with good reason (pp. 5, 6). The cornerstone from now on is, that the Volgare-version was not the original text, but was translated from the *Vita Latina*—a statement of fact sufficient to overthrow all speculations of the last few decades, and vindicate in substance Ranke's theory of the late origin of the work of the Pseudo-Burlamacchi (now excellently characterized by Ridolfi as a piece of propaganda and apology by Savonarolian loyalists at the time of the last Florentine Republic).

An even greater shock to accepted views results from the second study. Ever since the early sixteenth century the so-called *Bible of Savonarola* in the Biblioteca Nazionale of Florence—an incunabula with handwritten marginalia and some homilies on stitched-in pages—has been looked upon with awe as an autographic relic of Savonarola. It has frequently served as a mine of information for the analysis of Savonarola's methods of biblical exegesis. Now Ridolfi adduces convincing chronological and paleographic arguments which show this "Savonarolian" legacy to have been the property and work, not of Savonarola himself, but of another Dominican friar in his circle (Fra Domenico Buonvicini da Pescia). Thus a long tradition both popular and scholarly has been exposed as a legend, and everything we have accepted about Savonarola's exegetical method must henceforth be re-examined.

As to Machiavelli, Ridolfi establishes a fact which, humble as it seems to be in itself, throws fresh light on the relationship of the author of the *Istorie Fiorentine* to the Medici. Investigations into the money value of the *fiorini di suggello,* the coin in which Machiavelli was paid by the Medici during his work on the *Istorie,* reveal that the actual amount of his salary was merely a fraction of what the nominal value suggests. He could not possibly have lived on this sum. Consequently, his position in those years was less akin to that of a hired official historiographer than has been usually assumed (cf. esp. p. 173). Elsewhere in the volume (p. 71 ff.) Machiavelli's comedy *Clizia,* which is generally ascribed to the carnival of the year 1526, is shown to owe its birth to the carnival week of 1525.

Regarding Guicciardini, Ridolfi's careful consultation of the manuscripts preserved in the archives of the Guicciardini family provides, for the first time, a clear idea of the sequence in which the books composing the *Storia d'Italia* were worked out. The first draft, we now see, did not take up the story in the fateful year 1494, when the Italian state-system of the Renaissance broke down under the onrush of the French invasion, but started out with the situation created by the battle of Pavia in 1525.   In other words, it provided only an account of contemporary events.   It was during the progress of his work that Guicciardini added, as a background, the celebrated picture of the Balance-of-Power in Quattrocento Italy and the history of the decaying Italian state-system from 1494 onward.   A by-product of these Guicciardini-studies is the discovery of the manuscript of a *Storia di Firenze,* a historical study in which Guicciardini, during the leisure provided by his absence from Florence at the time of the last Florentine Republic (1527–1529), returned to the theme of his earliest historiographical endeavor, the *Storia Fiorentina* of 1509 (cf. p. 190 f.).   Prior to Ridolfi's first communications about his find, in 1931, the very existence of his work had been unknown.   The subsequent essay on the *Fortune della "Storia d'Italia" guicciardiana prima della stampa* gives an account of the contemporaries who obtained access to the *Storia d'Italia* prior to its long-delayed posthumous publication in 1561.   Thus we are placed in a position to assess the debt to Guicciardini of the historical writers of Florence in the mid-Cinquecento.   From the result it is clear that the collection of relevant material recently included in V. Luciani's *Guicciardini and His European Reputation* (New York, 1936) is not entirely complete or beyond reproach.   (Cf. Ridolfi's findings, p. 213 f., in order to refute Luciani's mistaken conjectures on Benedetto Varchi's relationship to Guicciardini, p. 54.)

While the studies on Machiavelli and Guicciardini contained in the volume are revised reprints of articles first published in Italian periodicals during the last years preceding the War, the monograph on Donato Giannotti which fills the better half of the 217 pages of the work gives an entirely fresh synthesis of Giannotti's life, by integrating the author's numerous earlier specialized contributions on Giannotti.   Space does not permit a survey of the wealth of new information thrown on virtually every phase of Giannotti's career in this biography, largely thanks to the recovery of a substantial part of Giannotti's correspondence (previously published by the author in collaboration with C. Roth).   It must suffice to say that his monograph on Giannotti is the first and only account of his life drawn from a satisfactory range of primary sources.   As to Giannotti's literary works and their chronology, we owe to Ridolfi's review of the manuscript material essential improvements in the list published by Polidori in his introduction to Giannotti's works in 1850.   A novel addition (from a manuscript of the Biblioteca Nazionale in Florence) is the *Epitome Historiae Ecclesiasticae,* a major fruit (formerly believed lost) of Giannotti's studies in his later years when his historical interests in Papal Rome had turned in a new direction (pp. 140, 152).   Whether the supplementary *Cronologia e bibliografia delle opere di Giannotti,* announced by the author (p. 140), has been published by this time, I am unable to say.

So much about the content and the chief results of this indispensable work. Its strength, to recapitulate our observations, lies in the acumen with which the author discovers infirmities in the foundations of accepted views and employs every possible mans of philological critique to make a breach at these very points. "If discoveries from archival documents," he says himself, "have their fascination, an even greater one . . . lies for me in getting to the truth . . . across an erroneous interpretation or argument of another scholar, or in discovering the truth behind one of those amazing series of misunderstandings that have become inveterate by continuation through generations of students" (p. VI). The obstinacy with which the author sticks to this treasure-hunt has, however, its defects. There is in his studies a certain tendency to neglect—sometimes, to minimize or distort —such facts as do not lie in the focus of his particular interests, but none the less are indispensable for the precision of his results. A straw in the wind is an occasional lack of correlation of the conclusions reached with the results established by earlier students—a source of uneasiness to the reader, who is rarely in a position to detect omissions of this type. Take for instance the manner (p. 89 f.) in which Ridolfi's readers are informed about a mistaken hypothesis, put forth about fifty years ago, as to the authorship of one of our most important biographical sources for the history of the last Florentine Republic, the *Vita* of the gonfalonier Niccolò Capponi. This work, which has been handed down under the name of Bernardo Segni, was attributed to Gianotti in a study published by G. Sanesi in 1896. From Ridolfi's discussion it must appear as if Sanesi's contention went abroad unopposed until it was refuted in the present book. The truth is that it would be difficult to name any student who has upheld that daring theory. M. Lupo Gentile's *Studi sulla storiografia fiorentina alla corte di Cosimo I*, the fundamental work on the later phases of Florentine historiography, demolished the conjecture not long after it had emerged (in 1905). E. Fueter, in his *Geschichte der neueren Historiographie* (first published in 1911), expressly rejected it, calling the *Vita di Capponi* a work of Segni's, without any question-mark. This being the state of the preceding studies, the author must be said to fight a veritable battle against windmills when he declares, without any reference to Lupo Gentile's or Fueter's treatment of the subject, that "all the arguments accumulated by Sanesi . . . do not convince him" (p. 89). At a later point we shall be confronted with another, even more puzzling case of oversight of essential results already assured by a student intimately known to the author (i.e., by C. Roth, see below). Where earlier students happened to put their emphasis outside the particular avenues followed in Ridolfi's studies, the reader must be prepared to be confronted with characterizations that do not always strike a fair balance of the precursors' merits, as is especially true of the harsh and derogatory verdicts passed upon E. Zanoni's studies of Giannotti (pp. 57, 107) and P. O. Kristeller's pioneering essay on the statesman-humanist Giovanni Corsi

(p. 204). These may be minor blemishes, but they point to an underlying more vital flaw—the danger that the author in his own research may fall a victim to serious errors of perspective at points where the range of the relevant facts calls for a broader field of observation than a horizon that is often limited to textual analysis and manuscript investigations.

A glimpse at some of the author's suggestions for the chronology of Giannotti's literary works will reveal these pitfalls of his method. To start out with the pages devoted to the treatment of the *Libro della Repubblica de' Viniziani*, one of Giannotti's two major literary achievements, the author certainly succeeds in establishing some entirely new and fundamental facts. During the years 1525–1527, he proves, Giannotti visited Venice not once (as has been thought) but twice, and on the first of these trips had ten months (December 1525 to October 1526)—against seven or eight, formerly conjectured—for the preparation of his study of Venice. The trouble, however, begins when Ridolfi proceeds to proclaim that, given these corrections of fact for Giannotti's life, his stay at Venice was prolonged enough to suggest that the *Repubblica de' Viniziani* in all of its essential aspects was worked out during that Venetian sojourn (pp. 70 f., 99). Had the author taken into consideration that Giannotti's work, as known in the first printed edition of 1540, includes a fresh interpretation from the original sources for both the history and the constitution of Venice, he certainly would have wondered whether political and historical studies of this compass could be prepared in a number of months, whether ten or eight. A work like Giannotti's must have demanded a large amount of re-consideration and continued research subsequent to the foundations laid in 1526 in (at most) ten months. Moreover, this assumption tallies with Giannotti's later statements on the progress of his work. For if the *Repubblica de' Viniziani* was completed in 1526 in "a redaction almost entirely similar to the final one," how could it be that Giannotti stated as late as 1533 that "the diligent care used up to this time has been extreme, and that he would also employ it in the future"—a "diligent care" that continued until 1538 when he at last decided that his work was ready for publication. (Cf. the statements in Giannotti's letters, quoted by Ridolfi, pp. 99, 101 f., 107.) As to the evidence of the manuscripts, this, too, does not contradict the assumption of a gradual growth of Giannotti's work from 1526 to 1538, as Ridolfi knows and recognizes himself. (Cf. his last passages on p. 99.) There is, accordingly, no other apparent cause for his clinging to the year 1526 but the above-noted narrowness of ken—in this case, an inadequate attention to intrinsic evidence, once a suggestive discovery of external facts, like the one of Giannotti's prolonged Venetian sojourn, has arrested the author's interest.

A similar lack of comprehension of the time-element in the growth of ideas impairs Ridolfi's presentation of Giannotti's studies on the Florentine

constitution. While for the treatise *Della Repubblica Fiorentina* the manuscript tradition is merely listed with little enlightenment as to the successive
phases of the work (p. 102), we find a discussion of the circumstances of
origin for the *Discorso sopra il fermare del governo di Firenze,* a memoir
(written for the gonfalonier Niccolò Capponi) in which Giannotti first expressed some of the basic ideas of the *Della Repubblica Fiorentina.* According to Ridolfi's hypothesis, the *Discorso* was written as early as June
1527, almost on the re-institution of the Republic, at a time when Giannotti
had not yet been appointed secretary of the *Ten of War,* the office once held
by Machiavelli. The arguments put forward in favor of this suggestion are
1) that Niccolò Capponi concerned himself with plans for constitutional
reform particularly at the beginning of his office, during the months of June
and July, 1527, and therefore may have been interested in having Giannotti's advice at that very time; 2) that it would seem "impossible" to
assume (as Ridolfi thinks) that Giannotti dared to air a criticism of the
institution of the *Ten,* as strong as the one contained in the *Discorso,* at the
time when he was already serving as their secretary (p. 83 f.). Of these
arguments it may be said that they are nothing but mere guesses—leaps in
the dark, as it were, which are in striking contrast to the sureness of touch
found in the author's observations on manuscript and textual matters.
Quite independent of conjectures of this kind, the starting-point should be
an awareness of the fact that, if the author's thesis were correct, we should
have to regard Giannotti's program of constitutional reform, not as the
offspring of the practical experience garnered by a statesman (or, active
official) of the last Florentine Republic, but rather as a pre-conceived constitutional theory presented to the newly elected gonfalonier on the revival
of the Republic. As to the latter possibility, the touchstone lies in the observation that the *Discorso* clearly presupposes prolonged experience with
the workings of republican life, built on the institution of the *Consiglio
grande.* How, one must ask, could Giannotti have gathered this experience,
if a considerable number of months had not already passed after the restoration of the Republic and of the citizen-council about the middle of May?
Giannotti's critique of the prerogatives of the *Ten* is indeed developed in
terms of what already had happened "many times" ("le più volte") or
only "rarely" ("rare volte") with regard to the selection of the *Ten* by the
Consiglio grande, to the dealings of the *Ten* with the gonfalonier, etc. (Cf.
Giannotti's *Opere politiche e letterarie,* ed. Polidori, I (1850), 7 f.) When
it is added that the *Ten* did not take office in the new Republic until June
10th (cf. C. Roth, *Last Florentine Republic* (London, 1925), 50, 77), we
shall have to conclude that it is difficult from the outset to think of June
and July, 1527, as possible dates for Giannotti's critique.

Having established this clue, we shall find it easy to identify, in the text
of the *Discorso,* a number of events that clearly belong to a period con-

siderably later than June, 1527. For instance, we read: "Sometimes the *Ten* convoke the newly organized *Pratica* (i.e., board of counselors)," but rarely do they follow their advice. (ed. Polidori, 7.) There can be no doubt that in this mention of a newly organized *Pratica* we have to see a reference to the election by the *Consiglio grande* of twenty *Arroti* on August 18/19, 1528, delegates chosen to serve as counselors of the *Ten*. (Cf. Roth, *loc. cit.*, 116, for this date.) This term implies that the *Discorso* was written later than August 1528. Another paragraph, in mentioning the "*capitani* of the newly organized Militia" (ed. Polidori, p. 15), takes us beyond even the first half of November. For the law of the "newly organized" *Milizia e ordinanza del popolo fiorentino* was passed as late as November 6, 1528. The outcome is that Giannotti's *Discorso* must have been worked out some time between the end of November, 1528, and the middle of April, 1529, when Niccolò Capponi, for whom the *Discorso* was composed, lost his office of gonfalonier.

That Ridolfi should have failed to make any of these observations is all the more astonishing because C. Roth, in his *Last Florentine Republic*, had already pointed to the fact that the *Discorso* includes a reference to the reorganization of the *Milizia* in November 1528, and also mentions an event in foreign politics happening in June (Roth, *loc. cit.*, 109, n. 44). Did Ridolfi suspect these passages to be later insertions in a text otherwise written in 1527? If so, examination of the context removes any suspicion of this kind. For if it should be surmised that the text of the *Discorso* was revised on its preparation for presentation to Pope Clement VII, after the fall of the Republic—the only assumption commanding some plausibility—the refutation of this hypothesis lies in the fact that the paragraph on the *Ten*, in which most of the passages revealing a post-1527 experience are found, was written before the discontinuance of the republican offices, i.e., prior to August 1530. Giannotti's critique of the *Ten*—one of the offices characteristic of the Republic—indeed starts out with the phrase "in the *present* government . . ." (p. 7, top), includes the statement that "sometimes the *Ten* convoke (*chiamano*) the newly organized (*novamente ordinata*) *Pratica*," and winds up with a reference to the "government of the *present* administration" and to the "authority which [the *Ten*] *have at present*" (p. 8, bottom). Furthermore, there is the following conclusive argument: If the portions of the *Discorso* written later than 1527—and the whole paragraph on the *Ten* presupposes post-1527 experience, as we know—were really insertions in a draft of 1527, the entire criticism of the *Ten* would have to be excluded from the original version—which is tantamount to a rebuttal of any hypothesis of insertions. For the critique of the institution of the *Ten* is evidently an inseparable part of the program of constitutional reform as set forth in the *Discorso;* the paragraph containing this critique could not have been entirely missing in any early version. Consequently, if Giannotti's familiarity with the year 1528 in the *Discorso* cannot be accounted for in terms of subsequent alterations of the text, then any attribution of the work to the year 1527 is out of the question.   Even so puzzling an incident as the one to which Ridolfi seems to attribute significance (p. 83), namely that the date-mark "1527" appears in the title of the manuscripts— *Discorso sopra il fermare il governo di Firenze l'anno 1527*—has no force to undo the validity of these conclusions, for whatever causes that date may have erroneously slipped into the title-line.

   To sum up: it will be clear by now that, when a final study of Giannotti's works is once made—it is to be hoped, by Ridolfi himself, in his promised *Cronologia e bibliografia*—there will be need for a wider field of observation than the one employed in the present studies.   When all is said, it is from a more even balance between "philological investigations" and "historical arguments" that the ultimate answers must issue for critical problems of this type.   While the author's investigations have broken much virgin soil in these collected papers, especially as far as the philological aspects are concerned, there still remains room for revisions from historical vantage-points.

   Institute for Advanced Study and

      Johns Hopkins University.

V

GIOVANNI PICO DELLA MIRANDOLA

A Study in the History of Renaissance Ideas*

(Part II)

By Ernst Cassirer

SECOND CHAPTER

The Idea of the Microcosm and the "Dignity of Man"

It was no accident that Pico intended to preface the defense of his nine hundred theses with that great oration to which he gave the title: *"De hominis dignitate."* This was to be no mere rhetorical exhibition, to introduce the learned disputation and furnish a splendid if external proemium. The theme expresses rather the quintessence of all Pico's underlying ideas; it indicates the point in which all his manifold endeavors converge. If we place ourselves at this intellectual focus, then Pico's thought begins to appear as a self-contained whole. And at the same time, from this vantage-point his real and genuinely distinctive achievement becomes clear.

To be sure, even the general problem Pico's oration raises hardly falls completely outside the framework of tradition. An historical criticism of the sources, like that of Konrad Burdach, could point everywhere in Pico's oration to particular strains derived from the hermetic literature.[35] On the other hand, however, Pico himself indicated clearly and exactly the point at which he was departing from traditional and conventional views. The image of man as a "microcosm" is very ancient. It did not first arise in philosophical thought; it already belonged to mythical thinking, and is to be found, in the widest variations, in the myths of all times and all cultures.[36] But Pico is not satisfied with the interpretation

---

* Part I appeared in the previous number of *The Journal of the History of Ideas*, III (April, 1942), 123-144. Footnotes in Part II are numbered continuously with those in Part I. [See note 27 in the Introduction to this volume.]

[35] Cf. Burdach, *Vom Mittelalter zur Reformation*, III, 1 (Berlin, 1917), 293 ff., 314 ff.

[36] Cf. my article "Die Begriffsform im mythischen Denken," *Studien der Bibl. Warburg*, I (Leipzig, 1922), 38 ff.

of this image given in the philosophic schools. *"Tritum in scholis verbum est,"* he says, *"esse hominem minorem mundum, in quo mixtum ex elementis corpus et coelestis spiritus et plantarum anima vegetalis et brutorum sensus et ratio et angelica mens et Dei similitudo conspicitur."*[37] Should we take this doctrine literally, it would not so much illuminate the distinctive nature and worth of man as destroy them both. For man would then have nothing proper to his own nature which he would owe to himself. He would be nothing but a product and as it were a *"mixtum compositum"* of the world.

But Pico is not willing to take man as such an aggregate of all the cosmic elements. For him the chief thing is not to prove man's substantial *similarity* with the world; it is rather, precisely within this similarity, and without prejudicing it at all, to point out a *difference*—a difference that confers on man his exceptional and in a sense privileged position, not only as against the natural world but also as against the spiritual world. This is man's privileged position: unlike any other creature, he owes his moral character to himself. He is what he *makes* of himself—and he derives from himself the pattern he shall follow. The lines in which Pico has set forth this fundamental view of his are well-known and famous. But we must repeat them here, since they lead us to the very heart of his philosophy, and form the basis of any interpretation. "Neither a fixed abode, nor a form in thine own likeness, nor any gift peculiar to thyself alone, have we given thee," says the Creator to Adam, "in order that what abode, what likeness, what gifts thou shalt choose, may be thine to have and to possess. . . . Thou, restrained by no narrow bounds, according to thy own free will, in whose power I have placed thee, shalt define thy nature for thyself. . . . Nor have we made thee either heavenly or earthly, mortal or immortal, to the end that thou, being, as it were, thy own free maker and moulder, shouldst fashion thyself in what form may like thee best."[38]

This idea, that man is his own maker and moulder, adds a new element to the basic religious notion of "likeness to God." For it is no longer God who in his creation once and for all impressed upon man his own seal, and created him after his own image. The

---

[37] *Opera,* 8: *praefatio.*

[38] *De hominis dignitate, Opera,* 314 f.; tr. J. A. Symonds, *Renaissance in Italy,* II, 35.

likeness and resemblance to God is not a gift bestowed on man to
begin with, but an achievement for him to work out: it is *to be
brought about* by man himself. Just this ability to bring it about,
rooted in his own nature, is the highest gift he owes to the Divine
grace. Now we begin to see how little either the pure idea of creation, or the idea of emanation, is in accord with the main central
notion of Pico's thought, and how unsuited both ideas are to express that notion adequately. For in creation as in emanation
man appears always as a something either produced by the free
act of a Being outside and above himself, or arisen as a link in a
necessary process of development. Here on the contrary both
kinds of dependence are to be excluded; man does not bring with
him as his portion his real and deepest being, he owes that being
to his own acts.

Here once more is displayed the characteristic opposition
between the direction foreshadowed for modern philosophy by
Cusanus, and that foreshadowed by Pico. Cusanus sets out from
an analysis of the mathematical form of knowledge, in which he
sees the model for every type of certainty: *"nihil certi habemus in
nostra scientia, nisi nostra Mathematica."* And from this fact he
straightway derives the idea of a universal mathematical structure
and determination of reality, of a reality whose spiritual core and
origin is revealed in its being the subject of universal natural laws,
laws of number and magnitude. Pico is seeking after another
content of knowledge and another way of knowing. He employs
his *"abdita intelligentia"*; he plunges into Nature and into the
peculiar darkness of the soul. But in this darkness there suddenly
bursts upon him a new light, outshining all others: the light of
human freedom, standing higher than any necessity of nature and
elevated above it. This is the great theme which, especially in his
work against astrology, he treats again and again.[39] If we see in
Pico's oration, as is generally done, primarily a significant document for the history of civilization, we are easily led to the notion
that it is treating an ancient problem of metaphysics, that of the
freedom of the will, and supporting that freedom with familiar
arguments. Hence the value of the oration seems to rest not on
its content but on its form. But even this form cannot be regarded
as something merely external: it is the expression of a definite

[39] Further details in *Individuum und Kosmos,* 124 ff.

attitude and a definite personality.   Throughout the entire oration
we can trace the lofty rapture and the youthful fire with which Pico
sets about and carries through his task.   Only an age inspired by
and thoroughly permeated with a new ideal of man could strike off
such lines.   In this sense Jacob Burckhardt called the oration "*De
hominis dignitate*" one of the noblest legacies of the Renaissance.[40]

But we can hardly stop with such a notion and such a judgment.
The deeper meaning and value of Pico's oration are not revealed
until we place it in the context of his work as a whole and compare
it with that work in detail.   To our surprise we then become aware
that the whole of that work and its internal structure is determined
by the same underlying idea that Pico has made central in his oration.   Pico's metaphysics, his psychology and theology, his ethics
and natural philosophy—these all now appear as a continuous and
consistent unfolding of the underlying theme here announced.   To
perceive this clearly, we indeed need a patient and thorough analysis, an analysis that shall follow the theme of Pico's oration in all
its particular variations.

Let us first ask what the connection is between the principles of
"*docta ignorantia*" and of "*coincidentia oppositorum*," which
govern the structure of Pico's entire speculative philosophy, and
his ethics and his idea of human freedom.   Both principles, which
had dominated theological thought for centuries, suddenly take a
new turn in the fifteenth century.   Their general significance is
maintained; but they now receive a content of new problems and
new interests.   What had formerly been a negative principle of
theology now becomes a positive principle of natural philosophy,
cosmology, and epistemology.   Nicholas Cusanus proceeds from
his conception and interpretation of the idea of "*docta ignorantia*"
to an acute criticism of the Aristotelian logic and the Aristotelian
physics.   Aristotle's logic is unexcelled in the precise working out
of contradictions, in setting up the categories by which the classes
of being are distinguished.   But it is unable to overcome this opposition between the various classes of being; it does not press on
to their real point of unification.   Hence it remains caught in the
empirical and the finite; it is unable to rise to a truly speculative
interpretation of the universe.   The physical universe of Aristotle
is dominated by the opposition between "the straight" and "the

[40] Burckhardt, *Kultur der Renaissance*, II, 73.

curved''; motion in straight lines and motion in circles are for him essentially and radically distinct. But the transition to the infinitely large and the infinitely small shows that this is a matter not of an absolute but of a relative distinction. The circle with an infinite radius coincides with the straight line; the infinitely small arc is indistinguishable from its chord. In the same manner the spatial distinction of ''up'' and ''down'' becomes relative for Cusanus. There is no absolute up or down, no ''lower'' or ''higher'' sphere. No place in the universe differs in its nature from any other—and each can with equal right claim to be the center of the world.

All such cosmological consequences are alien to Pico's thought. The framework of scholastic physics he did not attempt to disrupt. But he consummated another revolution no less significant and distinctive, through which the whole picture of nature and the world worked out in the Renaissance first finds its inner completion. The principle Cusanus had applied to nature Pico applies to the specifically human world, to the world of history. The underlying idea is here in a sense carried over from the field of space to that of time. As in space no point has an absolute precedence or privileged value over any other, as each, with the same right, or lack of right, can be regarded as the center of the world, so are the moments of time equivalent to each other. What is the nature of man, and in what his specific dignity consists, can be judged only when we dissolve the fixed temporal distinctions, the now, the before and after—when we comprehend past, present, and future in a single vision. And in such a kind of ''seeing together'' there is first revealed the full meaning of human freedom. This freedom means for Pico, as we have seen, that man is not inclosed from the beginning within the limits of a determinate being. It is this fact that raises him above even those beings that stand higher than himself in the hierarchical order. Upon the angels and the heavenly intelligences their nature and their perfection have been bestowed from the beginning of creation: man possesses his perfection only as he achieves it for himself independently and on the basis of a free decision.

And this challenge stands not only for single individuals, it stands also for historical epochs. From each epoch to the next there is handed down a definite intellectual heritage; an uninterrupted chain of tradition binds the present to the past. It would be presumptuous and disastrous, according to Pico, to seek to break this *"aurea catena"* which binds together all times and all intellectual and moral life. But on the other hand each moment of history can and must be taken and interpreted as a new beginning and a fresh start. For without this meaning the basic principle of human freedom would be infringed. Just as to man, in distinction from all other natural and all other spiritual beings, God did not give the gift he bestowed all ready-made, but expected and demanded of him that he should achieve it for himself independently —so neither can history simply give to man goods all ready-made for him. | These goods must be faithfully guarded, and they must be handed on and on in uninterrupted succession. But each historical moment has at once the right and the duty to appropriate them in independence—to understand them in its own way and to increase them in its own way. Pico declares explicitly that no other form of knowing truth is granted man. Indeed, he almost anticipates the saying of Lessing, that not the possession of truth, but the search after it, is the vocation and the lot of man.

In this basic conception there is manifest the deep effect of the Platonic theme of *Eros,* that forms the distinctive idea underlying the world-view of the Florentine circle. He who serves Eros and regards him as the genuinely vitalizing force of philosophy, will not hold in possession, but will endeavor to earn for himself; he will not so much know as inquire. *"Amare Deum dum sumus in corpore plus possumus quam vel eloqui vel cognoscere. Amando plus nobis proficimus, minus laboramus, illi magis obsequimur. Malumus tamen semper quaerendo per cognitionem nunquam invenire quod quaerimus, quam amando possidere id quod non amando frustra etiam inveniretur."*[41] This form of love, that consists in seeking, not in possessing, according to Pico gives man that worth in which he needs yield to no other being: for nothing can be higher than the spiritual power that is expressed in the freedom of the will. This alone is to form man's goal and his "holy ambition," his *"sacra ambitio"*; but if he allows it to rule him in the right manner, nothing is for him unattainable: *"erimus illis,"* says Pico of the heavenly intelligences in the oration *"De hominis dignitate," "cum voluerimus, nihilo inferiores."*[42]

[41] *De ente et uno, Cap.* V, *Opera,* 250.
[42] *De hominis dignitate, Opera,* 316.

From this fundamental starting-point there follow at once a series of consequences of the greatest significance for the place of Pico's thought in intellectual history, and for the mission it filled in the whole philosophy of the Renaissance. On this basis we immediately understand the battles which Pico, for whom peace came first and whose highest aim was the *"pax philosophica,"* had to fight on all sides. We understand the conflict with the ecclesiastical system in which he was forced to engage from the very beginning of his teaching, from the announcement of his nine hundred theses. Pico is not only filled with a deep inner piety; to him any resistance to ecclesiastical authority, any spirit of rebellion, is quite alien. No man admired more sincerely the tradition of the Fathers and tried to hold to it more faithfully than he.[43] But here too it is not a fixed body of basic dogma he wants to preserve and defend under all circumstances; what he is seeking and what attracts him is the free dialectic movement of thought. He claims the right of free inquiry for himself as for any other thinker. This is the standpoint to which he adhered in his Apology for the nine hundred theses and upon which he based his defense. The teachings of the Fathers of the Church are to be accepted with due respect: *"non tamen sunt eorum dicta ita firmae authoritatis et immobilitatis, ut eis contradicere non liceat et circa ea dubitare."*[44] Thus even in this field, even in religious dogma, there is no real infallibility or "immobility." Faith too, like knowledge, has its history, and only in the totality of this history can its inner truth emerge.

The same sense of independence here revealed distinguishes also Pico's attitude toward Humanism. He stands quite in the center and inner circle of the great Humanistic movement; and in his admiration for the ancients, in particular for Plato and Aristotle, he is surpassed by none of the other Renaissance thinkers. But here too he rejects any dogmatic crystallization of the humanistic ideals and claims. To the dogma of classical antiquity he is as unwilling to submit as to any other. In this respect his famous letter to Ermolao Barbaro is really a declaration of war against the narrow "sectarian spirit" of Humanism. Pico here insists that no single epoch, no matter how admirable and deserving of

[43] Cf. on this point the comprehensive citations in Dulles' work, *Princeps Concordiae: Pico della Mirandola and the Scholastic Tradition* (Cambridge, Mass., 1941).

[44] *Apologia, Opera,* 143.

respect, can claim to represent the whole of mankind. This whole is to be found only in the totality of its intellectual history. He who forgets this fact, and fails to grant to each epoch its own substantial rights, he who makes mere splendor of style and speech the only criterion—he is judging not as a philosopher but as a philologist. Such a placing of words above content is contrary to truth. *"Est elegans res (fatemur hoc) facundia plena illecebrae et voluptatis, sed in philosopho nec decora nec grata."* And it is in terms of philosophy, i.e., in terms of the search for truth in its universal sense, not in terms of philology, that Pico is seeking to define essential and genuine *"humanitas."* Philosophy, not the science of speech or grammar, is for him the heart of science. *"Vivere sine lingua possumus forte, non commode, sed sine corde nullo modo possumus. Non est humanus qui sit insolens politioris literaturae. Non est homo, qui sit expers philosophiae."*[45]

But even the most immediate and concrete task which Pico was to accomplish in the history of thought bears this stamp of his personality and attitude. If we follow out the controversy between the *Platonic* and the *Aristotelian philosophies,* as it was conducted during the first half of the fifteenth century, we are struck by the fact that the real problem had not as yet been grasped, that the actual systematic and methodological differences between the two thinkers had not as yet been seen, let alone worked out with precision. The conflict takes the form of a mere polemic between two rival schools, and it is carried on in a most bitterly personal manner; it does not even shrink from personal innuendos and vilification. Bessarion entitled his work *"Adversus Calumniatorem Platonis";* and it bears this title not without justification, in view of the way in which the polemic was being conducted by the opponents of Plato. The *Comparatio Platonis et Aristotelis* of Georgius Trapezuntius had heaped upon Plato the most foolish reproaches, against both his person and his ideas.[46]

Another spirit and tone prevail in the School of Florence. Here for the first time there begins the genuine philological and intellec-

[45] Letter to Ermolao Barbaro, *Opera,* 357. On Pico's relation to Humanism and his polemic against the "grammarians," cf. the material in Anagnine, 19 ff., and in Garin, 61 ff.

[46] On the controversy between Platonists and Aristotelians, cf. G. De Ruggiero, *Storia della Filosofia,* III, *Rinascimento, Riforma e Controriforma* (Bari, 1930), I, 115 ff.

tual inquiry into the problem of Plato and Aristotle. Ficino is a mild and conciliatory spirit, anxious to extend the bounds of religious and philosophical truth as far as possible. He accepts amongst his "saints" and sages not only Christ and Plato, but also Moses, Hermes Trismegistos, Orpheus, and Pythagoras.[47] But in his judgments even he is not free from all partisan spirit. Plato stands for him as the real and indeed the only guide in all questions that concern spiritual being. To the Aristotelian doctrine he grants only a conditional and limited value, for the problems of natural philosophy. *"In Aristotile vero . . . humanum tantum, sed in Platone divinum pariter et humanum."*[48]

Pico is far from making any such distinction; from the very beginning he is concerned to apply the same rule to both. In his letter to Ermolao Barbaro, in which he speaks of his Platonic studies, he explains that he, the former scholastic and Peripatetic, is coming into the Platonic camp not as a deserter but as an explorer.[49] Pico desired to fight neither for nor against Plato; he wanted to be a free inquirer. And he remained true to this attitude even while he was working as second to Ficino in the Florentine Academy. His great work on the comparison of the Platonic and the Aristotelian philosophies, on which he labored with especial zeal, and whose completion was prevented by his early death, would certainly, had he finished it, have possessed a different character and served a different end than the commentaries of Ficino. We can imagine that Pico would have portrayed Plato and Aristotle in the way in which Goethe saw them: as two men who both in a sense shared in the possession of a common humanity, as the differing spokesmen for splendid but not easily reconcilable traits.[50]

All this is by no means mere "toleration," as it can seem at first glance—and as it seemed to Pico's contemporaries, when they called him *"Princeps Concordiae."* It is something different and more profound, which follows as the immediate consequence of Pico's idea of freedom. For this idea not only makes possible, it demands a new form of "individualism." It holds not only for

[47] Ficino, *Epistolae, Opera* (Basel), 866, 871; cf. *De christiana religione, cap.* xxii.

[48] Cf. Ficino, *Epistolae*, XII; cf. G. Saitta, *La Filosofia di Marsilio Ficino* (Messina, 1923); vid. also Garin, *op. cit.*, 78 ff.

[49] *Opera*, 368.

[50] Cf. Goethe, *Gesch. der Farbenlehre*, Weimar ed., II, 3, p. 142.

mankind as a whole, it holds also for each single individual, that
to him there can be assigned no fixed and determined position in
the realm of the spirit: he must seek his position independently.
This search is not only his right, it is his duty: in his pursuit of it
he must not be hindered. Pico rejects any inquisition, in the domain of knowledge as in that of faith. For him there are no heretics of the intellect. The intellect can be moved to accept a determinate proposition only when it produces the conviction of that proposition in itself; and this conviction must be founded on determinate grounds. Even in religious matters a proposition of faith
cannot be simply transferred externally; it must be appropriated
internally. Any compulsion in the things of faith is for Pico not
only to be rejected on moral and religious grounds: it is also ineffective and futile. For it is not in man's power to accept or reject a proposition of faith on external command. *"Non est in
libera potestate hominis credere articulum fidei esse verum, quando
sibi placet, et credere eum non esse verum, quando sibi placet."*[51]
Individual inquiry, ever-renewed examination, is therefore indispensable for the subsistence of every truth, philosophical as well
as religious; only from and through such inquiry can this subsistence be won and preserved. Pico's whole view is pervaded with
respect for this individual inquiry. If I am not mistaken, Pico
was the first thinker to see in the history of philosophy not only a
collection of opinions, not only a persisting set of problems and
solutions, but also an expression of individual intellectual personalities. In the contemplation of this rich and intricate world of
thought he loved to find absorption. He not only brings to each
particular philosophical "family" sympathy and understanding;
he also distinguishes within each family the characteristics of each
individual thinker and his distinctive manner of thinking. *". . .
in unaquaque familia est aliquid insigne, quod non sit ei commune
cum caeteris. . . . Est in Joanne Scoto vegetum quiddam atque
discussum. In Thoma solidum et aequabile. . . . Est apud Arabes
in Averroe firmum et inconcussum. . . . In Alpharabio grave et
meditatum, in Avicenna divinum atque Platonicum. Est apud
Graecos in universum quidem nitida, in primis et casta philosophia.
Apud Simplicium locuples et copiosa. . . . Apud Alexandrum con-
stans et docta. Apud Theophrastum graviter elaborata . . . et*

[51] *Apologia, De libertate credendi disp., Opera,* 224.

si ad Platonicos te converteris . . . in Porphyrio rerum copia et multiiuga religione delectaberis. In Jamblico secretiorem philosophiam et barbarorum mysteria veneraberis. In Plotino privum quicquam non est quod admireris, qui se undique praebet admirandum. . . .'[52] In his endeavor to comprehend the whole of philosophy, Pico never abandons a critical attitude and standards of his own. But with him the work of the dialectician should be preceded by the work of the "synopsist": he insists on surveying the intellectual achievement of the past in its totality and in the fulness of its individual differences, before undertaking to judge it. Each individual who, in the name of the philosophical Eros, has ever sought and inquired with genuine and devoted love for truth, he finds worthy of respect; for in each case the inquirer is an intellectual microcosm, a *"parvus mundus,"* mirroring the entire world of ideas.

If from this point we reconsider Pico's oration, we find that what is really important and essential in it lies less in what it immediately contains than in what it suppresses and rejects in silence. That man came forth from the hand of the Creator a free being, and that it is just in this freedom that his likeness to God consists, is the universally accepted doctrine of the theologians. But to this doctrine there is at once added, that man has lost this privilege forever through the Fall. What held for man in his "original state" the Fall transformed into its opposite. Henceforth man is driven forever from the paradise of innocence and freedom; and by his own powers he cannot find the way back again. Not any achievement of his will, but only a supernatural work of grace, can raise him up once more. When we consider with what vehemence Pelagianism had been fought in the medieval church since the days of Augustine, and how unconditionally it had been rejected as heresy, we must be astonished at the frankness and boldness with which Pico reaffirms the basic Pelagian thesis. For him man's sinfulness does not stand as an indelible stain upon his nature; for in it he sees nothing but the correlate and counterpart to something other and higher. Man must be capable of sin, that he may become capable of good. For this is just Pico's underlying idea, that in good as in evil man is never a completed being, that he neither rests ever securely in good, nor is ever a hopeless prey to sin. The way to both lies ever open before him—and the decision is placed within

[52] *De hominis dignitate, Opera,* 325.

his own power. An absolute termination of this process is inconceivable; for it would be equivalent to a denial of the specific nature of man. It lies in man's nature to find himself forever confronting the *problem* of good and evil, and to have to solve it independently and with his own powers. Hence however high he may rise, man must always expect a Fall: but at the same time no Fall, however deep, excludes the possibility of his rising and standing erect once more.

On this ground Pico defends in his theses even the teaching of Origen, that there can be no eternal punishment: he finds it unjust and disproportionate that to a fault of which a man had been guilty during his life, and hence in a finite extent of time, should correspond an infinite reparation.[53] An eternity of punishment would imply a form of finality which according to Pico's basic conception would contradict the real meaning of human existence. The freedom of man consists in the uninterrupted creativity he exercises upon himself, which can at no point come to a complete cessation. Such a cessation is in a certain sense the lot of every other nature except man. The heavenly intelligences are blessed in contemplating divinity—and this beatitude is a possession accorded them forever: for them it can never be troubled or diminished. Mere natural creatures, plants and animals, lead their lives within a narrowly limited circle and within a uniform and ever-repeated rhythm of existence. Their instinct impels them to follow certain paths, and within the channels of this instinct they move with unconscious security. But to man this security is denied. He must be forever seeking and choosing his own path: and this choice carries with it for him a perpetual danger. But this uncertainty, this perpetual peril of human existence—not in the physical, but in the moral and religious sense—at the same time constitutes for Pico man's real greatness. Without it he would not be what his destiny demands he should be.

Man's failure is hence for Pico not merely guilt; it is rather the expression of that same indestructible power that makes it possible for him to attain good. Only a being capable of, and as it were at the mercy of sin, can achieve that highest worth that lies in the independent overcoming of sensuality, in the free elevation to the

---

[53] Cf. *Apologia, De salute Origenis disputatio, Opera,* 207 ff. Cf. *"De poena peccati mortalis disp.,"* 150 ff.; *Conclus. in theologia* 20 (p. 94): *"Peccato mortali finiti temporis non debetur poena infinita secundum temporis, sed finita tantum."*

"Intelligible." "*Nascenti homini omnifaria semina et omnigenae vitae germina indidit pater. Quae quisque excoluerit, illa adolescent et fructus suos ferent in illo. Si vegetalia, planta fiet. Si sensualia, obbrutescet. Si rationalia, coeleste evadet animal. Si intellectualia, angelus erit et Dei filius. Et si nulla creaturarum sorte contentus, in unitatis centrum suae se receperit, unus cum Deo spiritus factus, in solitaria patris caligine qui est super omnia constitutus, omnibus antestabit.*"[54]

But this implies still another consequence, which likewise belongs among the most remarkable and surprising features of Pico's oration. What he here sets up as the distinctive privilege of man is the almost unlimited *power of self-transformation* at his disposal. Man is that being to whom no particular form has been prescribed and assigned. He possesses the power of entering into any form whatever. What is novel in this idea lies not in its content, but rather in the *value* Pico places on this content. For it is an extraordinarily bold step of Pico's to reverse at this point the conventional metaphysical and theological estimate. The latter proceeds from the basic notion that the highest and indeed in the end the only value belongs to what is immutable and eternal. This notion pervades Plato's theory of knowledge and Aristotle's metaphysics and cosmology. With them is joined the medieval religious world-view, which sets the goal of all human activity in eternity, and which sees in the multiplicity, in the mutability, in the inconstancy of human action but a sign of its vanity. So long as man fails to master this inner unrest of his, and in so far as he fails to end and conquer it, he cannot find the way to God. "*Inquietum est cor nostrum, donec requiescat in te.*"

But with Pico this inner unrest of man, impelling him on from one goal to another, and forcing him to pass from one form to another, no longer appears as a mere stigma upon human nature, as a mere blot and weakness. Pico admires this multiplicity and multiformity, and he sees in it a mark of human greatness. That man is confined to temporality, that even in his highest achievements he cannot overstep time, this now no longer appears merely a proof of his Fall, through which he has been alienated from his original divine nature. The fact that he is temporally conditioned and temporally mutable is the basis of the distinctive power of man. For the power of human freedom can be verified only in man's

[54] *De hominis dignitate, Opera,* 315.

moulding his own life, and for this moulding it must be possible for
him to pass through and in a sense make trial of the most varied
spheres of existence. The scholastic thesis: *"Essentiae rerum
sunt immutabiles"* may hold for all other beings; but with Pico it
does not hold for man. Man is a true chameleon, a being in a sense
iridescent with every color. But from this circumstance Pico does
not draw the same conclusion which Platonism or the medieval
ascetic world-view had drawn. He dares to affirm just what they
had denied. *"Quis hunc nostrum chamaeleonta non admiretur ?
aut omnino quis aliud quicquam admiretur magis?"*[55]

How was such a transformation possible? On what philosophical principle is it grounded? It is founded frankly upon that
distinction on which rests the entire structure of Pico's thought:
on the distinction between "Nature" and "Freedom." In the realm
of freedom the same standards do not hold as in the realm of
nature: the "Intelligible" and the "Sensible" must be measured
with different criteria. For natural things, for merely physical
things, it does indeed mean a limitation and a privation of being
that they are conceived in perpetual flux, that not for a moment do
they preserve their self-identity. This is expressed in their possessing no constant nature, in their being suspended in fluctuating
experience. But does the same conclusion follow for the world of
thought? Physical things do not change themselves, they are
changed. It is the operation of an external cause that produces
their change, and to this operation they are subject with complete
passivity. They do not themselves posit a definite change and
evoke it out of themselves; the change is rather forced upon them
by something else. But this manner of compulsion is transcended
in human action and production. Here there is an independent
setting of a goal: man *chooses* the form he will bring forth, at which
he will arrive in the very process itself. Thus man is not merely
subject to a passive becoming; he rather determines his own goal
and realizes it in free activity. It is this activity toward which
Pico's admiration is directed, and his oration is but the philosophical hymn in which he gives expression to this admiration. The
mind of man can be satisfied with no moderation, indeed, with no
possession of any sort that has fixed limits. His ambition, which
Pico calls "holy," consists in striving on and on. *"Invadat
animum sacra quaedam ambitio, ut mediocribus non contenti*

[55] *De hominis dignitate, Opera,* 315.

anhelemus ad summa adque illa (quando possumus si volumus) consequenda totis viribus enitamur."[56] Man can arrive at the highest only if he does not restrain this power of self-moulding he feels in himself, but allows it free scope in every direction; and this mutability, taken as the power of self-formation, constitutes not man's weakness but his greatness.

With this conclusion new light is thrown not only on Pico's philosophy, but also on the underlying intellectual attitude of the entire Florentine circle. It is as though from this position we could for the first time grasp completely certain sides of Michelangelo's nature. In Pico's oration man is called his own almost arbitrary moulder: *"sui ipsius quasi arbitrarius honorariusque plastes et fictor."* He is the "sculptor" who must bring forth and in a sense chisel out his own form from the material with which nature has endowed him. We can understand how such a view must have affected the aesthetics and the theory of art of the Renaissance. It contains nothing less than a kind of theodicy of art. For art, especially plastic art, is now no longer derived from pleasure in the imitation of the varied multiplicity of sensible things. It has found a different and a purely "spiritual" goal. It expresses within its own sphere what characterizes and distinguishes mankind as a whole. Beauty becomes, to express it in Kantian terms, the "symbol of morality": for in the capacity of man to produce from himself a world of forms, there is expressed his innate freedom. The artist in a sense possesses this freedom raised to a higher power; from it and because of it he can bring forth a new "Nature." This trait adds a new strain to the "cult of beauty" of the Renaissance. Pico too was suffused with this cult of beauty. He shared it with all the men of the Florentine circle—with Ficino, with Girolamo Benivieni, on whose *Canzone dell' amor celeste e divino* he wrote a philosophical commentary.[57] But in all this he is by no means merely "artistic"; his attitude is rather thoroughly universal; art is for him not a particular realm of human activity, but the expression and revelation of the primary "creative" nature of man.

It is obvious that at the same time the temporal character and the "historical nature" of man receives a new meaning and value. In its proofs for the immortality of the soul, Renaissance philosophy singles out an argument that is pushed more and more to the center

---

[56] *De hominis dignitate, Opera,* 316.

[57] Vid. *Opera,* 733 ff.

of attention, and that we find in various versions, in Nicholas of
Cusa as well as in Ficino. The guarantee for the continued existence of the soul lies in the fact that it is not subject to time; for
instead of being "in" time, time is rather in it. It is the mind itself that, by virtue of a native power resident in it, produces from
itself not only the ideas of number and magnitude, but also that of
time: how then could the mind be subject to that which it generates
from its own nature? "*Anima rationalis non est tempori subdita,
sed ad tempus se habet anterioriter, sicut visus ad oculum. . . . Ita
anima rationalis . . . non . . . ipsa subest tempori, sed potius
e converso.*"[58]

In this derivation of time from the thinking subject another interest, that of speculative idealism, comes to the fore. The thinking subject must be raised *above* time, must be in a sense withdrawn
from it, so that it can be revealed in its fundamental "transcendental" character, as the condition for all temporality. Pico
comes close to this conception; we can indeed say that it is this
notion that is in a sense at the basis of his entire criticism of astrology.[59] But he does not remain in this position. He does not simply
wish to elevate the mind above time, he wishes rather to locate it in
the midst of time: he sees the mind in its actual "history." But he
can see it thus without being forced to abandon or limit his spiritualism in any way. For to him history is no mere fate, and time
is not merely the external frame within which this fate is worked
out. History is no mere "occurrence" which seizes man from
without and carries him along with it, like the wheel of Ixion. It is
the sum-total of the intellectual forms which man produces from
himself. In his own history therefore man is not simply subject
to the temporality and transitoriness of things; in it he rather
reveals his own nature—a nature indeed mutable, but in this very
mutability free, because it is the self-changing, the eternal "Pro-
teus."[60] This Protean nature is elevated above the transitoriness
of natural existence, because it manifests no mere being acted upon,
but an activity, the sum-total indeed of human action.

And here we approach also the solution of one of the most difficult
problems the philosophy of Pico presents. In the historical and

[58] Cusanus, *De ludo globi, Lib.* II, 232; cf. Ficino, *Theologia Platonica*, VIII,
16 (further details in *Individuum und Kosmos*, 43 ff., 74 f.).

[59] Cf. the exposition of Garin, *op. cit.*, 177 f.

[60] Cf. *De hominis dignitate, Opera*, 315.

systematic interpretation of Pico's thought, the position it takes with regard to Averroism constitutes the real stumbling-block. That Pico in his first student years at Padua was under the influence of Averroism is easy to understand; for the School of Padua had long been the citadel of Averroistic teaching. But could he adhere to this teaching and defend it after he had become a "Platonist," and after he had come into the closest contact with the Florentine Academy? The goal of this Academy, set by its founder Marsilio Ficino, was the philosophic proof of the fundamental truths of Christianity. Among these for Ficino himself the doctrine of the continued existence of the individual soul, of personal immortality, held the first place. His whole *Platonic Theology* was directed toward this single goal. But it was just this doctrine that was most bitterly contested by Averroism. In a long series of writings, which reached their logical conclusion in Pomponazzi's treatise *De immortalitate animae,* this underlying theme is treated again and again. And the result is always the same: it is shown not only that reason is unable to furnish a proof for the continued existence of the individual soul, but that such a thesis is in direct contradiction to reason. For the "Intellect" to which alone belongs eternity is One for all mankind; it knows no differentiation or individuation. Accordingly, Ficino rightly saw in the Averroists the most dangerous enemies of his own basic position; against them he unceasingly directed his attacks.

Was it thus not treason to the cause of Ficino and to the Platonic Academy for Pico, though to be sure he did not accept the doctrine of the unity of the intellect, nevertheless to continue to display his admiration for Averroism, and in a sense to come to terms with it? This can indeed be explained only by making completely clear to ourselves wherein the connection between Pico's philosophy and Averroism consisted. The Averroists have been characterized as the "freethinkers of the Middle Ages." They treat the doctrines of the positive religions as myths; what they are seeking is a doctrine of God that shall remain within the bounds of mere reason. In this underlying aim of rationalism, Pico could and must feel himself related to them: for he too constantly defended the *"libertas credendi,"* and for the sake of this defense he too fell under the ban of the Church. But the relationship extends no further: for if Pico granted the *rationalistic* assumptions of Averroism, he rejected all the more sharply the *naturalistic* conclusions it had drawn from them. Averroism was in all its main forms bound up in the closest way with that astrological determinism and fatalism, in combatting which Pico saw one of the chief tasks of his philosophy. For the doctrine of human freedom there was in Averroism no place.

The transcendence of God has also taken on for Pico a new meaning. The basic presupposition of Neoplatonic doctrine, the absolute transcendence of primary Being, Pico never contested. He adhered strictly to the fundamental ideas of "negative theology." No predicate that we find in finite things can be applied to God, and every attribute by which we characterize them we must deny to him. God's essence lies beyond any comparison: "*finiti et infiniti nulla proportio.*" But there is none the less *one* form of understanding that escapes this criticism. If we can ascribe to the Divine Being no property or characteristic that belongs to things, there still remains a basic intellectual phenomenon by virtue of which we are not only related to Him but actually one with Him. For human *freedom* is of such a kind that any increase in its meaning or value is impossible, that it is elevated above any comparison. Thus when Pico ascribes to man an independent and innate creative power, he has in this one fundamental respect made man equal to Divinity. There is now a genuinely positive predicate that is bound to change the character of negative theology fundamentally. The entire world of ideas of Neoplatonism falls therewith into flux: for even "immanence" and "transcendence" are revealed as opposites which in accordance with the principle of the "*coincidentia oppositorum*" must be overcome and transcended. Where man appears not as a mere creature of nature, but as truly spiritual, i.e., as a creative being, he has risen above this opposition. In the *extent* of his creation he remains infinitely removed from God; but in the fact, in the *quality* of his creation he feels himself at the same time most intimately related to God.

What this idea of the "*coincidentia oppositorum*" means for the whole philosophy of the Renaissance, and what achievement remained for it to consummate—this we can best make clear, if at this point we compare the development reached in the *theory of knowledge* with that reached in *cosmology* and *physics*. The medieval Aristotelian physics rests on the basic idea, that the corporeal world is divided into two spheres. These two spheres are continuous with each other; and motions within the one continue in an uninterrupted causal chain into the other. But they remain none the less substantially divided from each other: the matter of which the celestial world consists is not the same as that of the "sublunar" world. The late Middle Ages had already dared to doubt this doctrine of the strict opposition between earthly and heavenly substance—and in the fourteenth century, as the studies of Duhem have shown, it was seriously shaken. But it could be truly overcome only when the idea of the *relativity* of place and motion had broken the way, and when this idea had found its speculative foundation in the system of Nicholas of Cusa.[61] Here the dualism between "above" and "below," between the "higher" and the "lower" world, ceases, because every position in space is made equal to every other. On this foundation Giordano Bruno was able to develop his doctrine of the infinity of worlds, which taken together form a genuine and true unity, and of which each on the other hand is self-contained. Instead of a single central point, or instead of two opposite poles, there are now an infinite number of completely independent centers. There are motions about an infinite number of centers; but they all in their totality make a whole: the unified life of the cosmos.

Pico's doctrine effects the same revolution for the intellectual and historical world. This world too appears now as a unified whole, filled with the most diverse forms of life. It too appears now—in accordance with the familiar analogy—as an infinite sphere whose center is everywhere and whose periphery is nowhere. For the periphery of the intellectual and historical world cannot be bounded and fixed; it is being perpetually extended by the work of men. But on the other hand we can be sure that this extension is no mere dissolution: even if the end is never reached, and even if the boundary is pushed ever further, we are at every point "within" truth. The real outcome of the movement here introduced was first presented in the thought of Leibniz. For it first placed by the side of the cosmological picture of Bruno the corresponding metaphysical picture: it saw reality as a whole of independent entities, each of which expresses the entire universe and represents it from its own particular "viewpoint." The sources of this "monadological" conception lie in the Renaissance. Leibniz was able to erect his system of "pre-established harmony" because he brought to-

[61] Further details in my work *Individuum und Kosmos*, 183 ff.

gether what in the Renaissance still remained separate; because
he sought to derive the new cosmology and the new intellectual and
historical world-view from a common underlying principle, and to
found them upon that principle.

VI

THE COMPOSITION AND STRUCTURE OF
MACHIAVELLI'S *DISCORSI*

By Felix Gilbert

A review of L. J. Walker's translation and edition of Machiavelli's *Discorsi*[1] is a puzzling and disturbing task; it is extremely difficult to arrive at a definite and unequivocal evaluation of the work. The first reaction which this edition evokes is that of gratitude; it is truly astonishing that there has been no scholarly edition of the *Discorsi*, explaining and commenting upon the many historical and classical allusions of the text, until the appearance of these two volumes. Mr. Walker's work goes far to explain the reasons for this delay; it shows the almost Herculean task involved in providing an edition which fulfills scholarly demands. The entire 390 pages of Mr. Walker's second volume are devoted to explanatory notes, to chronological tables, to discussion of the sources of the *Discorsi*, and to indices. Although a number of objections against details of the scholarly apparatus can be raised, there can be no doubt that now, for the first time, we have a scholarly commentary on the text of the *Discorsi;* all further discussion of Machiavelli's work will be based on Mr. Walker's edition.

Unfortunately, Mr. Walker has not limited himself to a purely editorial task; he would have given more if he had given less. As frequently happens, in pursuing his editorial function Mr. Walker arrived at a special and definite interpretation of the *Discorsi* and of the issues connected with them. He has presented his views in a long introduction; they penetrate into the scholarly apparatus and even invade the text, parts of which bear not only the titles given by Machiavelli but also headlines derived from Mr. Walker's views of the *Discorsi*. This is regrettable, because Mr. Walker's conception of the *Discorsi* is open to grave doubts. Since Mr. Walker's edition will and should be frequently used, his views may gain greater authority than they deserve. I shall not enter upon a comprehensive critical discussion of Mr. Walker's interpretation of the *Discorsi*, because previous reviews have proceeded along this line.[2] I shall take up one single issue, on which Mr. Walker has expressed very definite opinions, namely the question of " the composition and structure of the *Discorsi* "; in investigating this problem, the merits and the limits of Mr. Walker's edition will emerge clearly.[3] Thus the following study may serve as an example of the equivocal importance of Mr. Walker's edition; it will illustrate that Mr. Walker's work is of the greatest assistance to the study of the *Discorsi*, while his theories about the *Discorsi* should not be accepted without thorough reëxamination.

[1] *The Discourses of Niccolò Machiavelli.* Translated from the Italian with an introduction and notes by Leslie J. Walker, 2 vols. (New Haven, 1950).

[2] An important review is the one by J. H. Whitfield, *Italian Studies*, IV (1951), 100–106.

[3] The problem of the composition of the *Discorsi* formed the topic of a graduate seminar which I gave at Bryn Mawr College before the appearance of Walker's edition; but these investigations could never, or at least not so quickly, have led to definite results without Walker's edition.

I

Those who try to envisage the Machiavelli who emerges from the scholarly researches of recent years may sometimes wonder what our virtuous and law-abiding republican has to do with that conjurer of hellish powers, from whom former centuries learnt that

Might first made kings, and laws were then most sure
When, like the Draco's, they were writ in blood.[4]

Certainly, Machiavelli's teachings are so rich that in them each succeeding century can find answers for the political issues which are its main concern, and the myth of Machiavelli can grow and vary without losing contact with the personality which inspired it. It is probably fair to say, however, that in the case of Machiavelli the change in evaluation which critical historical scholarship has brought about has meant a particularly radical break with the picture which previous centuries had created. This development is reflected in the fact that, while to former centuries Machiavelli had been chiefly the author of the *Prince*, students of our century have given their chief attention to the *Discorsi* as containing the essence of Machiavelli's political teachings.[5] Nevertheless, the traditional emphasis on the *Prince* has exerted influence on recent scholarship still to the extent that, despite the assumption of the decisive significance of the *Discorsi*, they have not been considered in isolation, but have been studied chiefly in their relation to the *Prince*.

This at least seems to me a possible explanation for the strange lack of interest among students to investigate the formal questions connected with the *Discorsi*. We have no detailed structural analysis of the *Discorsi;* we have even no attempt to clarify a number of preliminary questions which can be solved on the basis of a careful reading of the text of the *Discorsi*, and which may help to define the problems involved in an examination of the structure of the *Discorsi*.[6] Such preliminary questions concern the time of the composition of the *Discorsi* and the problem of the formal unity of the work; scholars have been rather vague concerning these issues, though a mere analysis of the text certainly permits quite precise conclusions.

The standard works on Machiavelli refer to the time of the composition of the *Discorsi* by the very general statement that the *Discorsi* were written

[4] From the prologue of Christopher Marlowe's *Jew of Malta;* Machiavelli is the speaker of this prologue.

[5] For instance, see the statements of J. H. Whitfield, *Machiavelli* (Oxford, 1947), 106: " The *Discorsi*, whose composition extends over the years 1513 to 1519, represent the capital book of Machiavelli."

[6] So Whitfield, *op. cit.*, 106. An exception, apart from Walker's introduction to his edition of the *Discorsi*, is the article by Friedrich Mehmel, " Machiavelli und die Antike," *Antike und Abendland*, III (Hamburg, 1948), 152–186. However, the discussion of *The Prince* in this article lacks knowledge of the recent English literature, which leads beyond the point which the author presents; and though the author indicates the importance of Machiavelli's relation to Livy for disentangling the structure of the *Discorsi*, he makes no real attempt to carry through this approach.

between 1513 and 1519.[7] The year 1513 is set as the date of the beginning of the *Discorsi*, because Machiavelli composed the *Prince* in 1513,[8] and he states in the *Prince* that he has discussed republics in another place;[9] it has always been understood that this sentence is an allusion to the *Discorsi*. The year 1519 is taken as the end term for the completion of the *Discorsi*, because in the *Discorsi* Cosimo Rucellai, to whom the work was dedicated, and the Emperor Maximilian are mentioned as being alive, and both died in 1519.[10]

The *Discorsi* contain a great number of chronological references;[11] and on the basis of these references it is possible to give greater precision and meaning to the inference that the composition of the *Discorsi* extended over six years. Of course, many of the chronological references are so vague that for the purposes of exact dating they are of no value.[12] But two statements point to a definite date. In Book II, ch. 10, Machiavelli writes that "if treasures guaranteed victory . . . , a few days ago the combined forces of the Pope and the Florentines would have had no difficulty in overcoming Francesco Maria, the nephew of Julius the Second, in the war of Urbino."[13] This refers to a definite event, the conquest of Urbino in 1517. Another reference to a definite time can be found in book III, ch. 27. "Fifteen years ago Pistoria was divided, as it is still, into the Panciatichi and the Can-

---

[7] See note 5.   [8] See Machiavelli's famous letter to Vettori, 10 December 1513.

[9] The *Prince*, beginning of ch. 2: " Io lascerò indrieto el ragionare delle repubbliche, perchè altra volta ne ragionai a lungo." I use Niccolò Machiavelli, *Tutte le Opere Storiche e Letterarie,* a cura di Guido Mazzoni e Mario Casella (Florence, 1929), where this passage will be found on p. 5. English passages in the text are given according to Walker's translation.

[10] *Discorsi* II, ch. 11: " Come interverrebbe . . . a quel principe, che, confidatosi di Massimiliano imperatore, facesse qualche impresa " (*Opere*, 154).

[11] See " Table XIV, Discourses indicating dates," in Walker, II, 309–10.

[12] For instance, the expression " ne' nostri tempi " includes any development which took place in Machiavelli's life-time; an event which Machiavelli characterizes as having happened " pochi anni sono " occurred in 1495, and expressions like " prossimi tempi " and " freschissimo esemplo," which he uses interchangeably, refer to occurrences in quite different years, 1512, 1515, 1517; see Walker, II, 309–10.

[13] " E, pochi giorni sono, il Papa ed i Fiorentini insieme non arebbono avuta difficultà in vincere Francesco Maria, nipote di papa Julio II, nella guerra di Urbino," (*Opere*, 152). Walker, I, 43, suggests that this remark refers to the recovery of Urbino by Leo X on Sept. 17, 1517. Since the point of Machiavelli's statement is that a power which has money will be defeated by a power which has good soldiers, it would seem to me that he must have thought of an event which showed the strength of the financially weak Francesco Maria, *i.e.*, his reëntry into Urbino, and this campaign of Francesco Maria is mentioned also at another place, *Discorsi* II, ch. 24. But for the purposes of the argument of this article, it makes no difference whether the event which Machiavelli has in mind is the conquest of Urbino by Francesco Maria in February, or its recovery by Leo X in September. In our context, the important point is that the passage must have been written in 1517.

cellieri, but in those days they were armed, whereas today they have given this up."[14] Since Machiavelli refers here to the civil strife which had taken place in Pistoia in the winter of 1501–02, and about which he had reported in his "relation on the events in Pistoia," this sentence must have been written late in 1516 or in 1517. Other chronological indications also point to a special significance of the year 1517 for the composition of the *Discorsi*. A number of events which took place after 1513 are mentioned, allusions to events which happened as late as 1515, 1516 and 1517 are scattered over all parts of the work,[15] but there is no reference to any event which took place after 1517.[16] Thus a consideration of the chronological references leads to the conclusion, that of the six years during which the *Discorsi* are supposed to have been written, the year 1517 was particularly important.

If we ask what the significance of this year for the composition of the *Discorsi* might be, a possible answer would be that at this time Machiavelli gave the *Discorsi* the version which we possess today. For an examination of the text of the *Discorsi* suggests that their present structure developed very gradually. Undoubtedly the *Discorsi* were intended to appear as a consciously and systematically organized whole. Statements about the principles of organization can be found not only in prefaces and introductory chapters.[17] The place of single chapters is explained by references to the overall organization.[18] There are frequent references from one chapter to other chapters which include not only references from later chapters to earlier ones, but also—what is a more significant indication of a conscious composition—references from earlier chapters to later ones.[19]

On the other hand, the clearly-stated principles of organization do not seem really to have permeated the text of the work. There are chapters which deal with problems which have nothing or very little to do with the topic of the book within which they are placed.[20] Sometimes the same prob-

---

[14] "Sopra che non si può dare il migliore esemplo che la città di Pistoia. Era divisa quella città, come è ancora, quindici anni sono, in Panciatichi e Cancellieri; ma allora era in sull'armi, ed oggi le ha posato" (*Opere*, 238).

[15] See in particular the various references to the campaigns of Selim I in 1516 and 1517, and the chronological references, listed by Walker, II, 309.

[16] In general, see Walker, I, 42–44, and II, 133. There can be no doubt that the passage in *Discorsi* II, ch. 24, that Ottavio Fregoso was able to hold Genoa without protection of a fortress against 10,000 men, does not refer to events of the year 1521, but to Fregoso's ability to remain in power when Francis I invaded Italy in 1515.

[17] *Discorsi* I, ch. 1; II, preface; III, ch. 1.

[18] For instance, *Discorsi* I, ch. 15: "E benchè questa parte più tosto, per avventura, si richiederebbe essere posta intra le cose estrinseche; nondimeno . . . mi è parso da connetterlo in questo luogo . . ." (*Opere*, 83).

[19] *Discorsi* I, ch. 35 to I, ch. 40; II, ch. 20 to III, ch. 6; II, ch. 26 to III, ch. 6; II, ch. 29 to III, ch. 1.

[20] The organization seems particularly loose in book III, formally devoted to the question "how much the action of particular men contributed to the greatness of Rome and produced in that city so many beneficial results"; aside from ch. 6, On

lems are treated in quite different parts of the work, so that the impression of a certain repetitiveness is created.[21]   Scholars have debated whether the issues that Machiavelli proclaims form the principles of organization of his work were really the problems in which he was interested, or whether the collecting and grouping of the material was actually determined by different concerns.[22]   The possibility of doubts on this point supports the view that the formal structure was not clear in Machiavelli's mind when he began his work.   The present organization seems to be more an afterthought, a framework which was imposed from the outside to give his work a unified and presentable pattern.

This examination of the most manifest chronological and structural data of the *Discorsi* cannot be regarded as having provided definite proof that in the year 1517 Machiavelli transformed the material which he had previously collected into that work which has come down to us.   But this preliminary analysis has certainly revealed some rather rough seams in the structure of the *Discorsi*, and suggests that an investigation of the composition of the *Discorsi* might have significant results for an understanding of the work.

Conspiracies, chapters like 26 (How women have brought about the downfall of states), 27 (How unity may be restored to a Divided City, and how mistaken are those who hold that to retain possession of cities one must needs keep them divided), 29 (That the faults of Peoples are due to Princes), 35 (What dangers are run by one who takes the Lead in advising some Course of Action; and how much greater are the Dangers incurred when the Course of Action is Unusual), have nothing to do with the main theme.   Though the topic of the first book (internal affairs) is very comprehensive, chapters like 41 (A sudden transition from Humility to Pride or from Kindness to Cruelty without Appropriate Steps in between is both imprudent and futile), 43 (Those who fight for Glory's sake make Good and Faithful soldiers), 56 (Before Great Misfortunes befall a City or a Province they are preceded by Portents or foretold by Men), 59 (What Confederations or other Kinds of League can be trusted most; those made with a Republic or those made with a Prince), hardly belong to this theme.   The second book (external affairs) comprises everything that has to do with war.

[21] The outstanding example is the treatment of military affairs, which are the chief topic in book II, but which are also discussed in various chapters of books I and III, so that, for instance, the theme of mercenaries appears at different places. The " Subject Index " in Walker, II, 345–390, gives some insight into the treatment of the same topics at various places.

[22] Whitfield, *op. cit.*, 108, says that " out of Taine's discovery of an opposition between the *Prince* and the *Discorsi* arose a feeling in others of an indifference in Machiavelli to the matter he was analysing, an indifference which was interpreted as cynicism "; Walker, I, 135, assumes the existence of a difference between the logical sequence of Machiavelli's ideas and the historical order adopted by him in the *Discorsi*.

II

What means do we have to gain further insight into the process of the genesis of the *Discorsi* and to advance the analysis of the composition of the *Discorsi* beyond the stage which we have reached? The original manuscript of the *Discorsi* no longer exists.[23] Thus we have only one lead for establishing the method of the composition of the *Discorsi:* the *Discorsi* are commentaries on the first decade of Livy's *History of Rome;* through clarifying the relation of the chapters of the *Discorsi* to Livy we might be able to reconstruct Machiavelli's procedure. Such a confrontation will be of a very technical character, but as the reader will see, the results will permit some fundamental observations on the position of the *Discorsi* in Machiavelli's work and on the development of his ideas and the influences which formed them.

The idea of using the relation to Livy as the key for an understanding of the composition of the *Discorsi* is not a new one, but an analysis along these lines has never been fully carried through.[24] The reason is that such an investigation encounters an obstacle which seems to make clear-cut results impossible. Though almost half the chapters of the *Discorsi* comment

[23] On the various manuscripts in which the *Discorsi* are handed down to us, see Machiavelli, *Opere,* 54; the only material written by Machiavelli himself is a draft for the introduction. Two early manuscripts of single chapters are in existence— both in Florence: the one in the *Biblioteca Nazionale,* Msc. Palat. 1104 (not 1020 as erroneously stated in *Opere*), the other in the *Archivio di Stato,* R. Acquisto Rinuccini, X di Balia, Responsive N. 119; but I have made sure that they are copies of a text of the entire manuscript and do not permit insight into the genesis of the *Discorsi.*

[24] The exception is Walker, who uses this approach for a discussion of the genesis of the *Discorsi* in the introduction to his edition. The difference between Walker's approach and mine is that Walker lists the various Livy passages which are mentioned in a chapter of the *Discorsi* side by side, without making any distinction about their importance (see the "Analytical Table of Contents," Walker, I, 165– 198), while I try to differentiate between them and to establish the "Main Reference," around which the chapter is grouped. The results of my analysis are shown in the table. The processes by which I arrive at this result are explained in footnotes 25–31. Note 25 lists those chapters of the *Discorsi* which mention only one Livy passage, and generally these statements are analogous to those by Walker. The following footnotes 26–31 show how I arrived at the establishment of a "main reference" in those chapters, which mention two or more Livy passages, and naturally this analysis has no model in Walker. It should be easy for the reader to reconstruct my procedure and to reëxamine its results on the basis of my table and footnotes 25–31. I want to add that, as I explain later on—quite in agreement with Walker, 61—the first 18 chapters of the first book of the *Discorsi* are of a somewhat exceptional nature, and a reëxamination will best begin with chapter 19 of the first book. Necessarily account is taken only of passages in Livy's first decade. Moreover, since Machiavelli frequently comments on entire stories from Livy, the references are frequently not to single Livy chapters, but to a series of chapters.

on only one chapter or story from Livy,[25] there are a large number of chapters which quote several Livy passages, and which therefore seem to prevent the establishment of a definite scheme of relationship.

Chapters in Machiavelli's *Discorsi*	Livy references in Book I of the *Discorsi*	Livy references in Book II of the *Discorsi*	Livy references in Book III of the *Discorsi*
1	general	general	general
2	no	general	I, 56–59
3	II, 27– 33	general	II, 4, 5
4	same	V, 33–34	I, 42, 46, 48
5	IX, 26	same, no	I, 49–58
6	no	general	no
7	II, 34–35	V, 30	same (as chapter 5)
8	VI, 15	V, 33, 34	II, 41; VI, 11, 14–20
9	I, 7, 14	VII, 29–31	same, no
10	no	same	VII, 12
11	I, 19–21	same	IV, 48
12	V, 22	same, no	IX, 1
13	same	VIII, 4	II, 39·
14	X, 40	same	II, 64
15	X, 38–39	same	IV, 31
16	II, 1–5	VIII, 7–11	no
17	same	same, no	no
18	same, no	II, 20, general	IV ¯7–39
19	I, 4–31	VII, 38	_, 58–60
20	same	VII, 38–41	· V, 27
21	same	IX, 20	same, no
22	I, 24–30	VIII, 11	VII, 4–10, 33; VIII, 7–10
23	same	VIII, 13, 21	V, 23
24	same	same, no	VIII, 26
25	II, 1–2	II, 44, 45	III, 26, 27, 29
26	same, no	same	IV, 9–10
27	same, no	same, no	same
28	II, 2 and 7	V, 35–36	IV, 13–15
29	same	V, 37–38, 48–55	V, 28
30	same, no	same	VI, 6
31	V, 8–11	VIII, 24	VI, 7
32	II, 9	VIII, 22–23, 25–26	VI, 21
33	II, 18	IX, 35–36	VI, 28–30, 41
34	same		VII, 5
35	III, 32–54		VII, 6
36	II, 46		VII, 10
37	II, 41		VII, 11
38	III, 6		VII, 32
39	III, 9		VII, 34

[25] Namely the following 63 chapters contain only one Livy reference:

Discorsi I, ch. 3, 5, 12, 14, 16, 19, 22, 25, 32, 33, 35, 36, 38, 40, 47, 50, 51, 53, 55, 56, 58, 60

Discorsi II, ch. 4, 7, 9, 13, 16, 19, 20, 21, 22, 25, 28, 31, 33

Discorsi III, ch. 2, 3, 4, 5, 10, 11, 13, 18, 19, 20, 25, 28, 29, 30, 31, 32, 34, 35, 38, 39, 40, 41, 42, 43, 44, 45, 46, 47

Chapters in Machiavelli's *Discorsi*	Livy references in Book I of the *Discorsi*	Livy references in Book II of the *Discorsi*	Livy references in Book III of the *Discorsi*
40	III, 31–39		IX, 2, 3
41	same		IX, 4
42	same		IX, 8, 9
43	same and III, 41–42		X, 10
44	same and III, 44–53		X, 16
45	same and III, 54–59		X, 28–29
46	III, 65		IX, 33, 34
47	IV, 6		IX, 38
48	IV, 7		X, 3, 4
49	IV, 8		VIII, 18; IX, 46
50	IV, 26		
51	IV, 59, 60		
52	same		
53	V, 24, 25		
54	same		
55	V, 25		
56	V, 32		
57	VI, 4		
58	VI, 14–20		
59	same, no		
60	VII, 32		

EXPLANATIONS:

" no " are chapters without Livy reference.

" general " are chapters of a quite general character; they cannot be considered as comments on the Livy passages they mention.

" same " are chapters which comment on the same Livy passage as the previous chapter.

" same, no " are chapters which continue the line of thought of the previous chapter without referring to Livy.

But this difficulty is actually less serious than it appears. For a careful consideration of the *Discorsi* chapters with several Livy references shows that it is generally possible to establish one particular Livy passage as the main reference among several.

In a number of chapters containing allusions to several Livy passages, the decisive importance of one particular quotation is evident.[26] Then there are Livy stories on which Machiavelli comments in a consecutive series of

[26] Namely in the following 18 chapters:

Discorsi I, ch. 7, 8, 11, 15, 31, 46, 57

Discorsi II, ch. 8, 18, 32

Discorsi III, ch. 12, 14, 15, 23, 24, 26, 37, 48

Example: *Discorsi* III, ch. 26, where the riot in Ardea is the main reference, and not the outrage to Lucretia or Virginia.

chapters;[27] in considering the same story from different angles, additional material from Livy is sometimes adduced but the subordination of this additional material to the Livy passage which started the whole discussion remains obvious. A few chapters summarize an entire development of Roman history; in such cases the Livy passage which describes the beginning of that development is the main reference.[28] In one case all uncertainty about the relative importance of various Livy references in the same chapter is solved by statements in a later chapter.[29] Altogether only in the case of very few, namely of three [30] chapters, doubts remain as to their main reference.[31]

A first survey of the relationship between the individual chapters of the *Discorsi* and Livy reveals one striking fact: in extremely few cases only has the same Livy story served as main reference in different *Discorsi* chapters, *i.e.*, duplications are extremely rare,[32] so rare that their paucity cannot be

[27] These 24 chapters are:
Discorsi I, ch. 4, 13, 17, 20, 21, 23, 24, 29, 34, 41, 42, 43, 44, 45, 52, 54
Discorsi II, ch. 10, 11, 14, 15, 26, 30
Discorsi III, ch. 7, 27
Example: *Discorsi* I, ch. 23 and 24 are tied to the fight between the Horatii and Curiatii described in ch. 22.

[28] These 4 chapters are *Discorsi* I, ch. 37, 39, 48, 49
Example: *Discorsi* I, ch. 37, deals with " the scandals to which the Agrarian Laws gave rise in Rome "; the main reference is the Livy passage which describes the origin of the Agrarian Laws.

[29] The main reference in *Discorsi* III, ch. 36, follows from ch. 37.

[30] I mean *Discorsi* III, ch. 8, 22, 49, which comment on two or more Livy passages from different books of Livy, and with regard to which I cannot find one reference to be more crucial than the other. I also have not been able to decide on a " main reference " in the following five cases: *Discorsi* I, ch. 9, 28; II, ch. 23, 29; III, ch. 33, but in these cases the situation is somewhat different. The two Livy passages, to which these chapters refer, are taken from the same Livy book and are to be found in chapters which follow rather closely upon each other; moreover they deal with related subjects so that it would have been rather repetitive to form independent chapters.

[31] In order to complete this analysis, I shall now mention those 24 chapters which have not been discussed in the previous footnotes 25–30: A few chapters (*Discorsi* I, ch. 1; II, ch. 1, 2, 3, 6; III, ch. 1) are so general that, though Livy is mentioned, they were not conceived as comments on Livy. A certain number of chapters contain no Livy references at all; *i.e.*, six of these chapters (namely *Discorsi* I, ch. 2, 6, 10; III, 6, 16, 17) are quite independent, others (namely *Discorsi* I, ch. 18, 26, 27, 30, 59; II, ch. 5, 12, 17, 24, 27; III, ch. 9, 21) continue a trend of thought, which was discussed in the previous chapter, though they have no connection with the Livy reference, which started the discussion of the previous chapter.

[32] There are four cases in which the same Livy reference is used in different books of the *Discorsi*: Livy II, 4–5, in *Discorsi* I, ch. 16 and III, ch. 3; Livy II, 14–20, in *Discorsi* I, ch. 58 and III, ch. 8; Livy VII, 32, in *Discorsi* I, ch. 60 and III, ch. 38; and Livy VIII, 7–10, in *Discorsi* II, ch. 16 and III, ch. 22. There are seven cases

accidental. This fact proves that we are on the right track in pursuing an investigation along this line. Evidently Machiavelli intended each chapter, or sequence of chapters, of the *Discorsi* to be a commentary on a different chapter or story from Livy, and it seems a worthwhile attempt to find out whether, from a closer and detailed analysis of this relation, a scheme will evolve which will permit the reconstruction of the process which Machiavelli followed in composing the *Discorsi*.

No pattern with regard to Machiavelli's use of Livy can be discerned in the first eighteen chapters of the first book of the *Discorsi*, but from the nineteenth chapter on a sequence can clearly be observed. Till the end of the book, or at least till chapter 56,[33] Machiavelli comments on successive chapters of Livy's first five books. There are only two exceptions: chapters 25 to 37 are tied to passages from Livy's second book, but chapters 31 and 35 are commentaries on passages from later books of Livy. One of these chapters, however, is evidently a later insert.[34] Thus these chapters are a striking example of exceptions confirming the rule; they reinforce the view that the section was conceived as a commentary on successive Livy chapters.

Another sequence of a similar character can be found in the second part

---

in which the same Livy passage forms the basis of discussion in two different chapters of the same book of the *Discorsi: Discorsi* I, ch. 8 and 58, 9 and 19, 16 and 25; *Discorsi* II, ch. 4 and 8, 16 and 22; *Discorsi* III, ch. 2 and 5, 22 and 34 discuss the same Livy passages. It should be remarked, however, that the number of duplications would become still smaller if the first 18 chapters of the first book of the *Discorsi*, which, as we mentioned above, were somewhat exceptional, were not counted. Moreover, *Discorsi* III, ch. 22, which appears twice on this list, is one of those chapters which have no definite " main reference." As will be shown later on (see p. 147, note 38), all the duplications appear in chapters which do not form part of the fundamental pattern of the *Discorsi*. It is of no great help to bring the frequency of duplications into a statistical form: there are 11 duplications in the 142 chapters of the *Discorsi*, but if the exceptional 18 chapters of the first book of the *Discorsi* and the fact that frequently a series of successive chapters is concerned with the same Livy passage, are taken into account, the relation 84 to 7 might be more correct.

[33] Formally, the sequence continues till the end of the first book of the *Discorsi*, since chapter 56 comments upon passages from Livy V, and chapters 57–60 on passages from Livy VI and VII; but a coverage of Livy VI in but two chapters is so much less complete than the coverage of the previous Livy books in the preceding chapters of the *Discorsi* that it must be assumed that the sequence ends with chapter 56; see also below, p. 147f.

[34] There can be no doubt with regard to *Discorsi* I, ch. 35; in the previous chapter, Machiavelli had praised the wisdom of establishing the institution of dictatorship and explained that extraordinary powers given to one man, if legally clearly defined, are no danger to freedom. When he later comes to the Decemviri, he must have realized that their story seems contradictory to this previously expounded thesis, and so he inserts chapter 35 to remove this contradiction. Probably a case could also be made for chapter 31 being a later insert, because of the somewhat conscious attempt, in the first paragraph, to justify the place of this chapter by tying it up with the previous ones. But this is speculation.

of the third book of the *Discorsi*. From chapter 30 on, Machiavelli comments on successive chapters from books 6, 7, 9, and 10 of Livy.[35] Two aspects of Machiavelli's procedure in this part of the *Discorsi* deserve attention. The one is the fact that in this section he is commenting on books of Livy's with which Machiavelli had not been concerned in the series of successive comments of the first book. The other is the conclusion which must be drawn, if the two series of successive comments in the first and third book of the *Discorsi* are taken together; then it emerges that in their successive coverage of Livy's first decade these two sections contain no discussion of Livy's eighth book and only very few comments on his fifth book. It is striking that comments on chapters from these two books form the bulk of the Livy material on which the second book of Machiavelli's *Discorsi* is based.

Thus we find an underlying pattern in those sections of the *Discorsi* we have analyzed. These sections originated as a series of successive commentaries on Livy's first decade; when this material was transformed into a literary work, the series was broken in the middle, and the second part arranged into two books: The comments on Livy's fifth and eighth book, which chiefly deal with military and foreign affairs, were lifted out and assembled in a special, second book, while the remainder of the material forms the third book.

Let us now look at those parts of the *Discorsi* which do not fit this pattern: there are first single chapters like the last chapters of all three books and the first three chapters of the second book, which stand outside the series of successive comments; then there are two large sections, namely the first halves of the first and third book of the *Discorsi*, which likewise do not permit the establishment of a pattern, but intermingle references to different books of Livy's first decade. It is obvious why the Livy references which are used in the last chapters of all three books and in the first chapters of the second book break up the pattern of successive comments. These chapters have a concluding or introductory character and Machiavelli picked out Livy passages which were suited for such purposes.

The fact that neither the first eighteen chapters of the first book nor more than half of the third book fit the pattern of successive comments raises a much more serious problem. Do we really have the right to consider successive comments on Livy's first decade as the basis of Machiavelli's *Discorsi*, if a large part of the work is outside such a scheme? But if we examine closely one of these unrelated parts—namely, chapters 1 to 29 of the third book of the *Discorsi*—it emerges that this part has unique and irregular features through which it stands out from the rest of the book and which point to a composition of this part at a rather late stage.

First of all, there are external signs for the special character of these chapters. In this part duplications [36] and chapters with doubtful main

---

[35] As the table above shows, chapters 46, 47, 48 should precede chapter 43, to make a perfect successive order.

[36] Five of the duplications are concerned with the first 29 chapters of the third book of the *Discorsi*.

references [37] are particularly frequent; as a matter of fact almost all [38] such irregularities can be found in chapters or sections which do not belong to the original order of successive comments on Livy. Then this section is especially closely knitted together; Machiavelli states frequently in the closing sentences of one chapter the topic with which he will deal in the next. Such a device which clearly indicates a planned and conscious composition, is used here almost regularly, much more often than in any other part of the *Discorsi*.[39] But also the contents of these chapters suggest that this section stands somewhat separate from the rest of the third book of the *Discorsi* and forms a unit in itself. The connection of these first 29 chapters with the leitmotif of the third book of the *Discorsi*, namely " the example of Rome's great men," is closer than in the rest of the book.[40] The organization in the first part of the book seems to be more systematic; in the rest of the book, the chapters have more the character of a commentary and take up topics of very different scope and importance.

Machiavelli's procedure in composing the *Discorsi* has now become clear. The composition developed in two stages. The first stage was that of giving a series of successive comments on Livy's first decade. Thus, in contrast to what has been frequently assumed, Machiavelli's original intent was not the presentation of a systematic treatise on politics. This feature emerged only in the second stage of his work, in which he rearranged his material: By dividing the material into three different groups, by adding some new material, and by providing introductions and conclusions, three books were created which were to discuss different aspects of the same general political problem, so that the whole work would appear to form an interconnected and unified whole.

These observations are not meant to convey that when Machiavelli rearranged his material and brought it into the form which we possess, he proceeded mechanically, just placing completed chapters into a new order

---

[37] The three chapters with doubtful main references are *Discorsi* III, ch. 8, 22, 49; *i.e.*, the first two belong to the first 29 chapters of the book, the last one is the concluding chapter of the book.

[38] See above notes 30–32. The two exceptions are the duplications in *Discorsi* II; they are not very significant duplications. In the first case (ch. 4 and 8), the chapters are close to each other and it could be questioned whether this is really a duplication or a continuation of the discussion of the same section; in the second case (ch. 16 and 22), the first time Machiavelli comments on a whole story, contained in several Livy chapters, while the second time he comments only on the last chapter of that story. I listed these two cases as duplications, however, so that the reader should not feel that I gloss over difficulties.

[39] This device is used 13 times in these 28 chapters (in ch. 1, 2, 3, 4, 5, 8, 9, 16, 19, 20, 21, 22, 26); it is used only once in the rest of *Discorsi* III (ch. 37), and only 17 times in *Discorsi* I and II (I, ch. 2, 4, 6, 7, 16, 22, 25, 28, 47, 58; II, ch. 1, 4, 11, 16, 19, 20, 31); seven of these 17 instances belong to introductory or concluding sections, which, as we showed, do not belong to the general pattern of successive comments on Livy.

[40] The rest has a number of chapters which have little or nothing to do with great men; for instance, ch. 29, 32, 33, 35, 36, 40, 41, 43, 44, 48.

and writing introductions and conclusions. It seems much more likely that he reworked the whole manuscript, adding suitable material from other parts of Livy. He might have elaborated single ideas into complete new chapters, so that now some Livy passages are dealt with in a series of chapters, discussing the same story from different angles. He might have condensed comments on different passages, which were related in contents, into one greater and more comprehensive chapter.[41] A precise and detailed reconstruction of the manner in which Machiavelli proceeded, seems hardly possible, however, on the basis of the material we have. But although there is no intention of being too categorical about the details of the process out of which the present version of the *Discorsi* developed, the main fact which our analysis has brought out and which has important implications for the understanding of Machiavelli's doctrine, is that the basis of the *Discorsi* was a commentary on successive chapters and books of Livy's first decade.

III

Before we discuss the wider implications of the results of our analysis, it might be appropriate to give some attention to the one part of the *Discorsi* which we have not so far examined at any length: the first eighteen chapters of the first book of the *Discorsi*.

This section of the *Discorsi* needs to be treated separately and in some detail, because its investigation opens up a somewhat different problem; the analysis of the first 18 chapters of the *Discorsi* has its bearing upon the question regarding the time when the *Discorsi* were composed. It has been mentioned that the manner in which these chapters are tied to Livy does not reveal any clear order or pattern. The references to Livy are taken from the most different books and are used without any regard to chronological sequence or to their place in Livy. In addition, the relation between the Livy reference and the contents of the chapter is frequently very loose, so that the connection with Livy seems to derive from a wish to adjust the chapters to the general pattern of the book rather than from inner necessity. Moreover, this section contains a number of chapters without any reference to Livy, and it is remarkable that here Machiavelli's " Romanism " is somewhat subdued and that, apart from Rome, Sparta and Venice serve as patterns of republican life. Above all, this part stands out because of its systematic approach; it contains detailed discussions about the various types of republics, the reproduction of Polybios' theory of the constitutional cycle, the thesis of the increase of political vitality through civil strife and of the usefulness of religion for the maintenance of political order, and finally the pessimistic reflection on the small chance of reintroducing a free government in a corrupt society. Briefly, Machiavelli presents here his basic ideas about the nature of republican institutions.

[41] This is suggested by Bernardo di Giunta in his letter of dedication, which precedes the *Giunta edition of the Discorsi* (Florence, 1531); there he says he had heard that Machiavelli intended " di ridurre i lor capi a minor numero."

It would seem entirely natural that Machiavelli wanted to place considerations of a general character at the beginning of his work, and this
purpose would satisfactorily explain the peculiar features of the section.
But the question may be raised whether the discussion of the fundamental
problems of a republic in these chapters has still other roots. It was mentioned that, in this part, the " Romanism " of the *Discorsi* is not pronounced
and the connection with Livy is not very close. Machiavelli uses a large
number of other historians here, and examples are taken from other peoples
and times quite as much as from the Roman period. Machiavelli himself
seems to have felt that the discussions of this part are rather outside the
stated scope of his work, because he makes a strangely apologetic remark
about his slowness in arriving at the discussion of Livy's tale of Rome's
beginnings.[42]

In all these respects Machiavelli's approach in these first chapters of the
Discorsi is very similar to that in the *Prince*. There are even passages
which have a quite close interconnection. The ideas of the nineteenth chapter of the *Prince* and of the tenth chapter of the first book of the *Discorsi*—
both concerned with the Roman emperors—seem like two parts of a rather
comprehensive reflection on the same subject.[43] The great state founders,
Moses, Lycurgus, Solon, who have been characterized as the real heroes of
the *Prince*,[44] make their appearance in these chapters.[45] Most of all, the
statements about different kinds of principalities given in the *Prince*, and
about different kinds of republics given in the *Discorsi*, complement each
other, so that taken together they provide a classification of all forms of
government.

We have said that in the *Prince*, Machiavelli mentions having written a
treatise on republics,[46] and that this sentence has always been regarded as
referring to the *Discorsi*. But are the *Discorsi* correctly described as a work
on republics? The name which Machiavelli's contemporaries gave to the
work, was *Discorsi su Tito Livio*.[47] Certainly, since Machiavelli presents
his ideas in the form of comments on the history of the Roman republic, the
issues of republican life and of the successful functioning of a republican
constitution are in the foreground of his interest. It should not be overlooked, however, that frequently his reflections are relevant to both mon-

[42] Beginning of ch. 9: " Ei parrà forse ad alcuno, che io sia troppo trascorso
dentro nella istoria romana, non avendo fatto alcuna menzione ancora degli ordina-
tori di quella repubblica . . ." (*Opere*, 72).

[43] See Walker, II, 28–29.

[44] Meinecke in his introduction to Machiavelli, *Der Fuerst, Klassiker der Politik*,
VIII (Berlin, 1923), 27.

[45] *Discorsi* I, ch. 9 (*Opere*, 73).

[46] See above note 9.

[47] See the foreword of the Giunta edition, or Filippo de' Nerli, *Commentari de'
Fatti Civili occorsi dentro la Città di Firenze* (edition of 1728), 138, or Jacopo
Nardi, *Historie della Città di Firenze* (Lyon, 1582), 177 (in the seventh book).

archical and republican institutions, that many chapters deal with political problems of the most general character which have no special relation to republican government, and that a large part of the work is devoted to discussions of warfare.[48] It seems legitimate to ask whether, without a systematic treatment of the problems of republican government in the first eighteen chapters of the *Discorsi*, there would be much justification for entitling the *Discorsi* a book on republics. Because the treatment in these chapters is rather different from the rest of the book, and because the approach is rather similar to that of the *Prince*, it seems possible to suggest that Machiavelli had been working on a treatise on republics when he was composing the *Prince*, and that he used this manuscript when he gave the *Discorsi* their final version and realized the necessity of providing them with a fuller introduction.

It is hardly in accordance with the rules of sound scholarship to suggest the existence of a treatise of which no mention is made and no manuscript is preserved, if such a thesis is not forced upon us by otherwise inexplicable contradictions in our source material. There are weighty reasons, however, for doubting that the above mentioned statement in the *Prince*, which has always been assumed to refer to the existing version of the *Discorsi*, can have had this meaning, and there is a need for finding a different explanation of that sentence. It is the question of the date of the *Discorsi* which makes a new interpretation of the allusion to the work on republics in the *Prince* necessary.

We have distinguished two different stages in the composition of the *Discorsi*. The later, the second stage, which was a rearrangement of previously gathered material, resulted in the version which we have today, and the analysis which we have previously made of the chronological references in the *Discorsi* permits the conclusion that this work of rearrangement and revision took place in the year 1517.

But when did the first stage of Machiavelli's work on the *Discorsi* take place? This first stage was the writing of a serial commentary on Livy's first decade. We have inferred the existence of such a first stage from an analysis of the relation of the *Discorsi* to *Livy's History of Rome, i.e.*, from internal evidence. Now it must be emphasized that we have statements by contemporaries on the origin of the *Discorsi*, and this external evidence fully confirms the results of our analysis. In general, the accounts of Machiavelli's contemporaries emphasize the novelty of Machiavelli's attempt to transform the teachings of history into definite rules; [49] one of them, Nerli,

---

[48] Of course, this has been frequently observed, for instance in Walker, I, 56, without drawing any conclusion from this observation.

[49] Nardi, *op. cit.*, 177 v: " . . . Opera certo di nuovo argumento e non più tentata (che io sappi) da alcuna persona," or the foreword of the Giunta edition: Machiavelli " è stato il primo che dell'utilissimo campo historico ci ha insegniato mietere e riporre copiosissimo frutto, e che le attioni pubbliche e civili ha ridotte si fattamente a regola, che ogni ben tardo ingegnio può facilmente comprendere, come, e in quanti modi si fondino, e ordinino le Città, in che maniera prudentemente si governino, e a quelle s'acquisti, et mantengasi larghissimo imperio."

even gives a somewhat more detailed report about the origin of the work. He narrates that a number of literati, among them Machiavelli, came together in the Rucellai gardens: " There they trained themselves, through the reading of classical works, and the lessons of history, and on the basis of these conversations, and upon the demand of his friends, Machiavelli composed his famous book the *Discorsi on Livy.*" [50] Since others also mention the meetings of the Rucellai gardens in connection with the *Discorsi*,[51] and since Nerli himself participated in these meetings, the authenticity of this report cannot be doubted.

An important aspect of Nerli's statement is that it gives us the possibility of establishing the time when Machiavelli was concerned with the first stage of the work, the serial commentary on Livy. For Machiavelli's participation in the meetings of the Rucellai gardens cannot have taken place before 1515; this conclusion must be drawn from our knowledge of Machiavelli's life as well as from the information we possess about the Rucellai circle.

After the Medici had returned, Machiavelli was in disgrace and spent most of his time in his villa outside Florence, in a self-imposed exile, cut off from friends and from Florentine society. Only gradually did his appearances in Florence become more frequent and extended, and his letters mention the names of new friends acquired through the meetings in the Rucellai Gardens not before 1519.[52] When Machiavelli attended the meetings in the Rucellai Gardens, their guiding spirit was Cosimo Rucellai, to whom Machiavelli expressed his attachment and obligation in the *Discorsi* as well as in the *Art of War.* Cosimo was born in 1495 and can have entered upon the rôle of host and intellectual leader of the Rucellai Gardens meeting only after the death of his grandfather Bernardo, *i.e.*, after 1514.[53] Moreover, the many references to the flowering of the Rucellai Gardens as a center of intellectual activity under Cosimo Rucellai all point to the years 1515 to 1517. It is evident, therefore, that in the *Prince*, which Machiavelli wrote in 1513, he cannot have referred to a work which owed its origin to readings

[50] Nerli, *op. cit.*, 138: " . . . avendo convenuto assai tempo nell'orto de' Rucellai una certa scuola di giovani letterati, e d'elevato ingegno mentrechè visse Cosimo Rucellai, che morì molto giovane, ed era in grande aspettazione di letterato, infra quali praticava continuamente Niccolò Machiavelli (e io ero di Niccolò, e di tutti loro amicissimo, e molto spesso con loro conversavo), si esercitavano costoro assai, mediante le lettere, nelle lezioni dell'istorie, e sopra di esse, ed a loro instanza compose il Machiavello quel suo libro de' discorsi sopra Tito Livio, e anco il libro di que'trattati, e ragionamenti sopra la milizia."

[51] Nardi, *op. cit.*, 177 v.

[52] I believe this conclusion can be drawn from a reading of the letters written by Machiavelli during these years. See Machiavelli, *Lettere Familiari*, ed. Alvisi.

[53] For these dates see Walker, II, 3; and in general, my article " Bernardo Rucellai and the Orti Oricellari," *Journal of the Warburg and Courtauld Institutes*, XII (1949), especially 114–118, and the literature quoted there, particularly the great Machiavelli biographies by Villari and Tommasini.

and lectures in the Rucellai Gardens held after 1515.[54] Thus some explanation like the one we have provided is needed for the passage in the *Prince* alluding to a work on republics.

But it should be obvious that our explanation of the special character of these first 18 chapters may appear probable but cannot be regarded as more than a hypothesis. Because this part of our study is speculative, it must be emphatically stated that this theory about an early treatise on republics by Machiavelli is independent of the other results of our study which have a quite definite character, showing that in the framework of discussions held in the Rucellai Gardens after 1515 Machiavelli wrote a series of comments on Livy's *Roman History*, and that soon afterwards, in 1517, he transformed these notes into the book of the *Discorsi sopra la prima deca di Tito Livio* which we possess today.

Perhaps a glance at the political development during these years of Machiavelli's occupation with the *Discorsi* may help to explain why he was interested in giving, in his final product, a special slant towards the problems of republican politics. Whoever discusses Machiavelli's creative processes will go back to Machiavelli's own description in the famous letter to Vettori [55] when Machiavelli was composing the *Prince*. He writes that during the day he is sunk in vulgarity and involved in trifles, but in the evening, he puts on regal and courtly garments and enters into the ancient courts of ancient men, where, being lovingly received, he speaks with them and asks the reasons for their actions and receives courteous answers. In this letter, Machiavelli makes it clear that he was studying the ancients in order to clarify his thoughts about the problems of government, and that the advancement of Giuliano Medici to Captain General of the church—with all the speculation aroused by it—gave him the idea of summing up the results

[54] It must also be mentioned that in the *Discorsi*, the *Prince* is mentioned as a completed treatise; see *Discorsi* II, ch. 1; III, ch. 19 and 42. In explanation of this fact, Luigi Russo, *Machiavelli* (Bari, 1949), 39, assumes that Machiavelli left the *Discorsi* aside to work on *The Prince*, after he had finished the first book of the *Discorsi*; but because also the first book of the *Discorsi* contains references to events which occurred after 1514 (when *The Prince* was completed), such an easy explanation of this difficulty is not possible. Chabod, in his article " Sulla Composizione de ' Il Principe ' di Niccolò Machiavelli," *Archivum Romanicum*, XI (1927), 348, uses the argument that in the summer of 1514 Machiavelli must have had finished the *Prince*, because he writes in a letter to Vettori that, having fallen in love again, he has "lasciato dunque i pensieri delle cose grandi e gravi; non mi diletta più leggere le cose antiche, nè ragionare delle moderne." If this letter is considered as a serious argument for establishing the date of the composition of the *Prince*, it must also be taken as an argument against continuous composition of the *Discorsi* in the period between 1513 and 1519. These passages show that previous writers have been well aware of the difficulty of harmonizing the common opinion that the *Discorsi* were composed in the period from 1513 to 1519 with the facts, even if they did not initiate a thorough reëxamination of the whole problem.

[55] Letter to Francesco Vettori, December 10, 1513; I use the translation of A. H. Gilbert in Machiavelli, *The Prince and other works*, University Classics (Chicago, 1941).

of his studies in a small book, useful to a new " prince." Thus in *The Prince* Machiavelli makes use of more comprehensive studies for a clearly delimited, particular purpose.[56] Three years later, Giuliano Medici was dead, and Lorenzo Medici had become duke of Urbino; the Medici family had no obvious candidate for the rulership over Florence. The Medici themselves played with the idea—or at least pretended to—of restoring freedom to Florence. The Florentines were deeply excited about this prospect; the following years saw a great number of writings, one of them by Machiavelli, discussing the way in which a republican constitution could be reintroduced, and the form which the republic should take. The question of the advantages of republican institutions had again become a practical concern in Florence.[57] Though the *Discorsi* are more general and theoretical than the *Prince*, Machiavelli must have been aware that if, in giving his comments on Livy a more literary and systematic form, he placed special emphasis on the problems of republican government, he was again transforming his theoretical knowledge into practical usefulness. He was too good a student of the ancients not to know about the power of καιρός.

IV

It remains to investigate the implications of the result of our study for the understanding of Machiavelli's political science and intellectual evolution. They are rather far-reaching, and lead into the center of the questions with which students of Machiavelli have been concerned. The following, therefore, will be only a sketch indicating briefly to what extent these questions may appear in a new and different light.

The crucial issue on which our investigation has bearing is that of Machiavelli's " new method," the question of what he conceived to be the " new way as yet untrodden by anyone else," on which he had decided to enter.[58] The results of our investigation bring this problem into new and sharp relief. For while in the past *The Prince* and the *Discorsi* have been considered as having been composed at the same time and therefore as using the same methodological approach, our analysis eliminates the possibility of a simultaneous conception of *The Prince* and the *Discorsi*. Even though not more than two or three years separate the composition of the two works, Machiavelli could not have placed such emphasis on the novel character of the method applied in the *Discorsi* if he had already used the same approach in *The Prince;* he must have believed that with the *Discorsi* he had

[56] The treatise on the republics, which, as we have suggested, formed the basis of the first 18 books of the *Discorsi*, might have belonged to the layer of general studies on the problems of government.

[57] Most historical treatments of this period of Florentine history discuss this situation; the best treatment seems to me Antonio Anzilotti, *La crisi costituzionale della Repubblica Fiorentina* (Florence, 1912).

[58] Proemio of the first book of the *Discorsi:* " Ho deliberato entrare per una via, la quale, non essendo suta ancora da alcuno trita, se la mi arrecherà fastidio e difficultà, mi potrebbe ancora arrecare premio " (*Opere*, 56).

undertaken something which he had not done before.

In order to avoid misunderstandings, it must be said immediately that the extent to which the methods of the *Discorsi* differ from those applied by Machiavelli in his previous works and especially in *The Prince* is limited. From the time he began to write on politics, Machiavelli's thoughts moved around the same fundamental questions; the necessity of transforming politics into a science, the significance of history for political practice, the importance of the ancients.[59] Changes in method are limited, therefore, to variations in the combination of these elements and to changes in the relative weight given to each of them. Within this framework, however, there seems to be some justification for Machiavelli's claim of having entered with the *Discorsi* a " path as yet untrodden by anyone else," for taken by themselves the methods of *The Prince* and of the *Discorsi* are somewhat divergent.

This difference emerges chiefly in Machiavelli's attitude to history. The historical material which Machiavelli uses in *The Prince* comes chiefly from modern times and the contemporary scene; in the *Discorsi*, the bulk of the illustrations is taken from ancient history, and Machiavelli sometimes even makes an apologetic remark when he refers to contemporary events in proof of a thesis.[60] Even though the greater emphasis placed in the *Discorsi* on ancient history comes to a large extent from the purpose of this work, the lower evaluation of contemporary history remains significant. For it is accompanied by a change in the attitude to the importance of history for the construction of a political system. In *The Prince*, though Machiavelli's realism leads to new results, history is used in the same way as it had been used in the previous political literature; history serves as example, it illustrates a general statement. In the *Discorsi*, history provides the material from which a general conclusion is drawn; the theoretical statement arises from an analysis of the empirical facts of history. While the " political laws " of *The Prince* are deductions, the *Discorsi* represent an attempt at carrying through an inductive method.[61] Machiavelli's contemporaries

[59] See, for instance the passage, quoted by H. Butterfield, *The Statecraft of Machiavelli* (London, 1940), 36, from Machiavelli's early memorandum on the " Method of dealing with the rebels of the Val di Chiana," and the other quotations on this and the next page 37.

[60] For instance, *Discorsi* I, ch. 17: " E benchè questo esemplo di Roma sia da preporre a qualunque altro esemplo, nondimeno voglio a questo proposito addurre innanzi popoli conosciuti ne' nostri tempi " (*Opere*, 86).

[61] An interesting discussion of Machiavelli's " inductive method " will be found in Butterfield, *op. cit.*, particularly in the section on " The rise of the inductive method "; Butterfield's views are disputed by Walker, I, 92–3. Certainly, Butterfield is right in cautioning against identification of Machiavelli's inductive method with induction in the modern sense of the term; we would hardly consider the facts reported by an ancient historian as empirical data. But if we abstract this difference in Machiavelli's and our own view of what empirical data are, we can say that he tries to arrive from the observation of facts to general rules; this approach seems to me more thoroughly used in the *Discorsi* than in *The Prince*.

agree fully with his own view that, with the *Discorsi*, he had entered a
" path untrodden by anyone else; " their accounts all stress the novelty of
his undertaking, in particular they characterize his new method as an attempt to " gain from history definite rules which everyone could easily comprehend; " [62] these attempts seemed to them the sensational feature of the
Discorsi. We would now hardly regard the abstract and even meaningless
norms to which the richness of empirical observations and realistic insights
is condensed as the most significant aspect of the *Discorsi*. Yet it frequently
happens that contemporaries misjudge the true significance of an intellectual
achievement. Instead of realizing that its impact derives from a fundamental incompatibility with the traditional system of thought, they concentrate their attention on those somewhat more superficial results which are
slight additions to the prevailing intellectual system and which build on it
without bursting the framework. Thus Machiavelli's contemporary readers,
like Machiavelli himself, saw in the *Discorsi* chiefly an attempt to achieve
for the field of politics what humanist scholars were trying to do in other
areas of learning, *i.e.*, an attempt to rediscover the laws the ancients had
known and followed in the various fields of human activity.

In the introduction of the *Discorsi*, Machiavelli remarks that " the civil
law is nothing but a collection of decisions, made by jurists of old, which the
jurists of today have tabulated in orderly fashion for our instruction; nor,
again, is medicine anything but a record of experiments performed by doctors of old, upon which the doctors of our day base their prescriptions."
Following these examples Machiavelli wanted to deduce from the experiences of ancient history the laws of political behaviour. Our analysis that
before the *Discorsi* took their present form they were strictly a series of
comments on Livy, gives still greater emphasis to the point that, in the *Discorsi*, Machiavelli followed a method which he believed to be the recognized
scholarly procedure of his time. The *Discorsi* were conceived in the form of
a traditional literary genre and in line with what Machiavelli considered to
be the modern scholarly tendency of elaborating general rules from ancient
authors.[63] In other words, with the *Discorsi* Machiavelli adjusted his new
political concepts to the method and normative approach of humanism, the
dominating intellectual trend of his time.

In pointing out this aspect of the *Discorsi*, we touch upon the other significant issue on which our study has bearing; it sheds new light on Machiavelli's intellectual evolution and on his relation to the intellectual trends of
his time, in particular humanism. Unquestionably Machiavelli's later works,
the *Art of War* and the *Florentine History*, have a strongly humanist
flavour. There is an obvious difference between the *Prince*, which was
written in direct opposition to the usual contemporary treatments of this

[62] See above note 49.

[63] Perhaps Machiavelli's relation to sixteenth-century commentaries on classical
authors would deserve closer study and clearer definition.

subject,[64] and the later two works which fit the prevailing humanist pattern. The *Art of War* is mainly a modernization of an ancient author in the classicizing form of a dialogue. In the *Florentine History* Machiavelli uses a method, namely the reduction of historical events to typical situations, which is pointedly humanistic. Our investigation would suggest that these two works were only further stages in a development toward adoption of humanist concepts which had begun with the *Discorsi*. This view would also be supported by observations on changes in Machiavelli's style which, it has been said, from the *Discorsi* on begins increasingly to show rhetorical and Latinizing features.[65] The methodical differences between *The Prince* and the *Discorsi* can be considered, therefore, as a first sign of Machiavelli's inclination to accept orthodox humanism and the contrast between the political realism of *The Prince* and the political idealism of the *Discorsi* would appear to be the result of an intellectual development rather than an expression of a tension in Machiavelli's mind.

It is easy to explain biographically Machiavelli's increasing interest in the humanist approach. When Machiavelli composed the *Discorsi*, he had become a member of that humanistically inclined group which assembled in the Rucellai gardens; he was in closer touch with the prominent intellectuals of his time than he had ever been before.[66] But there is also an inner logic in this development: for there are few if any who, after having once stared unblinkingly into the face of what man is, have been able to hold to that vision and have not escaped into dreaming of what he ought to be.[67]

Bryn Mawr College.

[64] See my article, " The Humanist Concept of the Prince and ' The Prince ' of Machiavelli," *The Journal of Modern History*, XI (1939), 449–483.

[65] See Leonardo Olschki, *Geschichte der neusprachlichen wissenschaftlichen Literatur Italiens*, II (Leipzig, 1922), 313–4; also F. Chabod's article on Machiavelli in the *Enciclopedia Italiana*.

[66] See note 65 and particularly Toffanin, *Machiavelli e il Tacitismo* (Padua, 1921).

[67] This, of course, is a paraphrase of the famous sentence in the 15th chapter of the *Prince*.

VII

FOUNDATIONS OF MODERN POLITICAL THOUGHT

REVIEWED BY DONALD R. KELLEY

Quentin Skinner, *The Foundations of Modern Political Thought,* Cambridge University Press (Cambridge, 1978), 2 vols., xxiv + 306 pp. and vi + 406 pp.

The history of modern political thought, like the history of philosophy, has tended to remain in, or revert to, a historically naive and abstract condition. The main reason for this, the general indifference of the practitioners of "normal" political science and professional philosophy to the concrete history of their disciplines, is understandable enough. Certainly uncovering the complex process of discovery, debate, and formulation of ideas in social and political context is more difficult and perhaps less immediately useful than prescribing a simple and up-to-date set of standards and, in the consequent artificial perspective, to construct a plausible tradition based on the linking of familiar "major" figures by predetermined argument. Just as in the history of philosophy the temptation has been to jump directly—metaphysically—from Thomas Aquinas to Descartes, from one familiar "-ism" to another, so in political thought the tendency has been to seize upon certain heroic conceptualizers and to distribute them along a narrative argument that is often anachronistic as well as overreasoned. It may be that every discipline falls victim to its own version of that "Whig fallacy" lamented years ago by Herbert Butterfield,[1] but even for elementary purposes of self-perception and professional utility, such perfunctory text-book constructions have little value or pedagogical durability. This is the first and most conspicuous reason why it is useful to have the extraordinarily sensitive and informed survey of the foundations of modern political thought by Quentin Skinner, newly appointed Professor of Political Science at Cambridge University.

Another reason is that, besides a conceptually and historically mature interpretation, the book offers an unusually, almost unprecedentedly, broad synthesis, encompassing what scholarly convention has normally segregated, despite chronological overlap, as medieval and Renaissance phases. The consequences of segregation have been unfortunate and sometimes ludicrous, revealing though they may be about minor academic chauvinisms. One obvious impediment to a clear perspective on early modern history has been the ingrained tendency to define or to hypostasize a "Renaissance" on the basis of some highly selective conception of bourgeois culture and consciousness. The intellectual imperialism of "Humanism" is an historical reality, but it is hardly adequate to take humanist views of their significance

---

[1] Herbert Butterfield, *The Whig Interpretation of History* (London, 1931).

(and that of their adversaries) as a valid characterization of Renaissance thought in general, and especially not of political thought. Another distorting tendency has been the lack of appreciation of "medieval" patterns of thought in, or perhaps the institutional inability of medievalists to attend to, the fifteenth and sixteenth centuries, to go no further. Medievalists have laboriously investigated, and are still investigating, scholastic philosophy and the intricacies of civil and canon law without, at least until recently, seriously exploring the post-conciliar period. Yet the sixteenth century was not only an extraordinary age of resurgent scholasticism and restored civil law but in a sense the culminating period of canonist (and concomitantly of anti-canonist) thought: for what was the "Lutheran scandal" if not a debate on canon law? On the whole Skinner's book is remarkably successful in overcoming such obstructions.

On a more conventional level Skinner presents a coherent and comprehensive view of the major contours of political thinking from about 1300 to the late sixteenth century. He attends to the major themes and dilemmas of the human—political and social—condition: problems of liberty and authority, of obedience and resistance, of "absolutism" and "constitutionalism," of oppression and revolution, and most generally of the emergence of the "State" and modern "political" consciousness. In the course of this survey we are given sometimes fresh, always thoroughly grounded interpretations of such familiar figures as Machiavelli and More, Luther and Calvin, Montaigne and Bodin; but careful attention is always given to historical context and to many of the lesser known, though not necessarily less seminal, grapplers with political questions. Historians of all sorts can learn much from this synthesis; political scientists and philosophers can learn more (if only they will).

Skinner's point of departure is the emergence of modern ideas of "liberty" (in the sense of political independence as well as republican self-government) attending the rise of the Italian city states. Following Nicolai Rubinstein, he presents an illuminating discussion of Marsilio of Padua in the light of this urban development, historically more relevant and closer to Marsilio's experience than the government of the imperial client for whom he wrote his *Defender of Peace*.[2] Still more significant, it seems to me, is the prominence Skinner gives to the role of civil law. In this case following the classic work of Cecil Woolf, Skinner attributes "a revolutionary political claim" to Bartolus' defense of the *de facto* sovereignty of the city republic (in his famous formula, *civitas sibi princeps*).[3] What he does not stress is the still more radical defense of the *de jure* independence of national monarchies on the basis of arguments largely of canonist devising. Although Bartolus' position and the complex of private rights in civil law elaborated by him and his colleagues, were essential for ideas of self-government,

[2] Marsilius of Padua, *The Defender of Peace*, trans. Alan Gewirth (New York, 1956), and Nicolai Rubinstein, "Marsilius of Padua and Italian Political Thought of his Time," in *Europe in the Later Middle Ages*, ed. J. R. Hale, J. R. L. Highfield, and B. Smalley (London, 1965).

[3] C. N. S. Woolf, *Bartolus of Sassoferrato* (Cambridge, 1913).

political independence was more intensively cultivated by his "ultramontane" rivals serving the French and other monarchies. Both were important for the theme of liberty which Skinner pursues throughout both of his volumes.

Perhaps the most valuable aspect of this analysis is the care with which Skinner discriminates between various strands of libertarian thought, especially between scholastic argumentation, exemplified by Ptolemy of Lucca, as well as by Marsilio and Bartolus, and the rhetorical tradition, whose connections with the medieval *ars dictaminis* he demonstrates with a wealth of illustration. Related to the latter tradition were two genres of seminal importance for later political thinking, a new type of city chronicle and increasingly popular handbooks of counsel, which are arguably ancestors of Machiavelli's *Florentine Histories* (1520-25) and *The Prince* (1513). Not surprisingly this bifocal perspective brings Skinner into confrontation with recent interpretations of "civic humanism," and his reaction is to find the view of Hans Baron "misleading" for its proprietary claims (on behalf of Bruni) over both republican enthusiasm and critical historical consciousness. In contrast to Baron, too, he doubts both that the association of wealth and virtue was a discovery of *quattrocento* humanists and that the distrust of private wealth was a specifically Franciscan or even Christian theme. In arguing for the specifically Stoic roots of the distrust of private wealth Skinner introduces one of his consciously revisionist views and returns to it in several contexts, especially in connection with the "state of nature." But if Skinner dissents from Baron's view of humanism (partly because he is less interested in specific social contexts), he does not find P. O. Kristeller's contrasting interpretation entirely satisfactory either.[4] If Skinner's perspective prevents him from contemplating the creation of ideas out of one, however urgent, political crisis, it also discourages him from interpreting humanism in a purely academic fashion, devoid of social content or political implications; as he tries to bridge Renaissance and Medievalist bias, so he tries to avoid the extremes of ideology and value-free history of ideas.

Such an effort seems altogether praiseworthy: surely the latter-day scholasticism generated by the Renaissance, and now the Humanism, Debate has gone on long enough—too long, many may think, since the conceptual level of the discussion seldom matches the learning marshalled by the disputants. Yet there is an important methodological issue here, and Skinner himself raises it briefly (I, 102), namely, the debate between what historians of science like to call the "externalist" and "internalist" interpretations of the history of thought.[5] Neither extreme is humanly plausible: neither the notion that ideas sprout directly out of a mindless social process, nor the notion that they are carried along in an historical equivalent of an eternal mind. For some purposes of analysis the investigation of social and political conditions has priority; for other purposes a more formal history of thought may be appropriate. Only when a metahistorical effort of synthesis (and more

---

[4] The seminal statements include Hans Baron, *The Crisis of the Early Italian Renaissance* (Princeton, 1966), and P. O. Kristeller, *Studies in Renaissance Thought and Letters* (Rome, 1956), esp. 553-83.

[5] See Thomas S. Kuhn, *The Essential Tension* (Chicago, 1977), 118-22.

particularly *explanatory* synthesis) is undertaken does the paradox become disturbing; and it does seem to me that the dilemma ought to be discussed with more methodological awareness than has usually been apparent. The gentle charges of being "misleading" aside (and there are more such to come in this book), Skinner's moderate position, between history and theory as well as between internalism and externalism, does seem appropriate for his own attempt at synthesis. Yet the argument on the whole places this book in the "internalist" school (illustrated by one of the few lapses into what used to be called "reasoned history," which has Bartolus and Baldus in the late fourteenth century being "quickly followed by the French jurists under Philip the Fair," instead of the reverse, in developing the famous doctrine of *rex in regno suo est imperator*[6]), and its value for disciplines outside of history is enhanced accordingly.

In his first half-dozen chapters Skinner presents an incomparably broad, well informed, and skillfully argued groundplan of the "foundations" to be examined in succeeding sections. In particular he sets the scene for a comprehensive appraisal of Machiavelli and the later career of republicanism. Machiavelli is appropriately set in an intellectual continuum of humanist concerns with political virtue, princely counsel, and republican values; yet the "highly subversive" tendency of his views on leadership and policy is by no means underestimated. Nor does Skinner lose sight of the continuing significance of scholasticism, especially as reflected in the ideals of Savonarola (following the interpretation of Donald Weinstein).[7] The Italian part of this survey concludes appropriately with a notion of "the end of republican liberty"—which, however, did not signify the end of the ideas thereof and debates thereover.

Despite fresh insights, novel connections and revisionist views, the rubrics of this book are often conventional, and the first volume concludes with a discussion of "the Northern Renaissance." Again, the importance of the law is admirably drawn out, following (if not going quite so far as) Walter Ullmann, one of Skinner's teachers for whom the legal tradition is indeed sovereign.[8] In this connection it might be suggested that the conceptual value of "legal humanism" is somewhat exaggerated, but the fault lies less with Skinner than with some of his authorities (including this reviewer). In general the political views of jurists like Zasius and even Alciato owe more to their medieval (professional) forebears than to their humanist (amateur) colleagues.[9] The point is marginal, however, since Skinner is concerned above all with the recognizable humanist themes, largely Italianate in character and associated with various practical problems of counsel, the qualities of leadership, the princely virtues, and the role of education. Once again the

[6] In general see Gaines Post, *Studies in Medieval Legal Thought* (Princeton, 1964), 453-82.

[7] Donald Weinstein, *Savonarola and Florence* (Princeton, 1970).

[8] Recently, Walter Ullmann, *Medieval Foundations of Renaissance Humanism* (London, 1977).

[9] See my "Civil Science in the Renaissance: Jurisprudence Italian Style," *Historical Journal*, forthcoming.

social content of humanist attitudes is emphasized, and indeed one of the characteristics of the advice-books of English, French, and Spanish authors was attention to morality and injustice. It might be added, though Skinner does not quite say, that the work of Erasmus and More seems to have involved a shift away from strictly political thought; but of course it is impolitic, if not impossible, to leave *Utopia* out of a history of political thought in this period, even if it does have to be justified as a "humanist critique of humanism."

In moving from "The Renaissance" (volume I) to "The Reformation" (volume II) Skinner also takes leave of "humanism" for the most part and comes to grips with more recognizably modern political themes: Absolutism, Constitutionalism, and Revolution. Skinner is sympathetic towards, though not uncritical of, the views of J. N. Figgis, who likewise made a valiant effort to establish a bridge between medieval and modern times.[10] Besides generally endorsing the thesis (seconded by Harold Laski and, more recently, by Francis Oakley) about the Conciliarist origins of modern constitutional thought,[11] Skinner is inclined to associate Luther as well as Machiavelli in the apparently inexorable drift toward the modern absolute State. Yet— central paradox of modern political thought!—this drift in no way stood in the way of the opposite tendency toward revolution; and indeed the main thrust of Skinner's interpretation of Lutheranism is to insist on its inherent radicalism. As in the first volume, Skinner prepares the ground for his analysis (following Heiko Obermann and others)[12] with a discussion of medieval antecedents of the many-sided—theological, ecclesiastical, ecclesiological, political, and social—Lutheran movement. Particularly valuable is his assessment of the followers of Gerson, Zabarella, and D'Ailly, especially Jacques Almain and Jean Mair, who carried on the critique of papal absolutism. In general Skinner is careful to emphasize "forerunners" and heretical continuities linking the Reformation with medieval traditions.

Like Machiavelli, however, Luther was more than an inheritor. In his analysis of the "subversive stand of Lutheranism," Skinner rightly rejects the literal minded view that Luther never departed from the Pauline convention of passive resistance. Like Calvin, and even less surreptitiously, Luther accommodated himself to political reality, if only by handing over the responsibility for judgment to the lawyers. Anabaptism may have raised "the spectres of communism and revolution," but Lutheran resistance theory had in the long run a more upsetting impact on political thought and action, first in the civil war in Germany and then in the Calvinist struggles in France and the Netherlands. Equally "revolutionary" was the impact of Lutheranism on the relationship between church and state; and Skinner traces the development from the notion of the church as a simple "congregation of the faithful" through the social and political changes of the reforma-

---

[10] J. N. Figgis, *Political Thought from Gerson to Grotius* (Cambridge, 1907).

[11] See especially Francis Oakley, "On the Road from Constance to 1688," *Journal of British Studies*, I (1962), 1-32.

[12] See especially *The Reformation in Medieval Perspective*, ed. Steven Ozment (Chicago, 1971).

tion to the culmination in the enforcement of religious uniformity—the obverse, in a sense, of the concurrent idea of political resistance. In this connection the ideological contours of the English Reformation are treated with special thoroughness.

The importance of Roman law for absolutism is a commonplace, but its role in the elaboration of constitutional and especially resistance theory is less appreciated, and it is another virtue of this book that these connections are not overlooked. In particular (and presumable following the terminology of Ullmann[13]) Skinner refers to the "populist way of interpreting the *Lex Regia*," which is the ancient Roman law by which the prince receives the *imperium* from the people. What Skinner calls "the Bartolist theory of popular sovereignty" was employed by Andrea Alciato (among others who might be mentioned) but most instructively, he thinks, in the work of Mario Salomonio, who rejects on this basis the counterbalancing Roman formula of absolutism (*princeps legibus solutus*). As for resistance the Romanist argument stems from the private-law (and some would argue natural-law) principle that it is always permitted to repel force with force (*via vi repellere licet*). What might be added to this argument is the consideration that private law in general constituted a haven for individual liberties and right, and specifically that it was at least technically immune from political or legislative interference. The prohibition of legislators to alter private law, the provisions of civil as well as customary law, often went without saying; and while investigating such tacit limitations poses problems for orthodox historical investigation, the principle represented a powerful check on sovereignty and deserves further exploration.

Equally valuable in Skinner's presentation is the unusually sympathetic attention given to scholastic thought in the sixteenth century. This includes not only the "mainstream of radical scholastic political thought" traceable back to Gerson and ultimately to Ockham, but also the *via antiqua,* especially the revived Thomism elaborated on by Spanish apologists.[14] Many of the energies of these late-late scholastics were devoted to countering the errors of humanists like Erasmus and naturalists like Machiavelli; but they also made positive contributions, especially in employing the device of the "state of nature," ancestor of social contract arguments. Acknowledging the significance of scholastics for constitutional arguments, Skinner prefers to emphasize their services to absolutist theory, in contradiction to the populist opinions of the *via moderna* and especially of the Bartolists. Above all, they added to the "foundations of modern political thought" by establishing a vocabulary and pattern of argument for the classic natural-law theorists of the next century.

In the last part of his work Skinner comes to the final cornerstone of modern political thought and the dénouement of controversies carried on

[13] Walter Ullmann, *Principles of Government and Politics in the Middle Ages* (London, 1961).

[14] A recent treatment of importance not cited here is *La Seconda Scolastica,* ed. Paolo Grossi (Milan, 1973).

over three centuries, namely, "the theory of revolution." Once again his analysis moves admirably not only horizontally through a long perspective but also vertically from immediate reactions to historical predicaments to higher levels of political legitimation and theory. The point of departure is "Lutheran radicalism," which Skinner finds initially more receptive than Calvinism to the idea of active resistance; and the analysis concentrates on the two main ingredients of this idea.[15] One is the constitutional thesis, championed by Philip of Hesse as early as 1529 and elaborated especially by Martin Bucer; the other is the private law notion, "to repel force with force," first urged by John of Saxony. Lutheran theologians and jurists developed these ideas, which reemerged again in the late 1540's and were expressed most famously in the Magdeburg Confession of 1550. As Skinner points out, Calvinists came late to this line of argument; but when they arrived, they carried it much further, partly because of the failure of toleration and the still greater urgency of their predicament in the wars of religion, first in France and then in the Netherlands.[16] They also added the final ingredient, which was the argument, expanded mightily from Calvin's initial suggestion, that the prior duty to God might justify resistance. Joined with the potentially subversive motion of "inferior magistrates" and the fundamentalist notion of the "covenant," these arguments established the basis for the modern theory of popular revolution, a theory, Skinner adds, "destined to enter the mainstream of modern constitutionalist thought."

Skinner's analysis is sound and penetrating, and it seems to me that he is right in refusing to accept the theory of passive resistance as an adequate characterization of Luther's or Calvin's view. Certainly their contemporaries would have agreed. The idea of resistance was an extension, not a betrayal of their position in the context of civil war. One comment that might be made about the genesis of this idea, however, concerns the importance of both the feudal and civic notions of "liberty," which converged with the "Christian liberty" preached by Luther. It was above all this fusion that had a politicizing and radicalizing effect. In the Empire this occurred relatively early, and so did the confrontation of parties. In France the explosive combination did not take effect until the constitutional crisis following the death of Henry II in 1559; and it is this circumstance, rather than any inherent conceptual recklessness or caution, that makes Lutheranism even more "advanced" in developing resistance ideas. The availability of the necessary arguments has been generously demonstrated by Skinner; the essential condition of a full-fledged theory of revolution was a political predicament that led powerful men and groups to sponsor, indeed to commission, such theorizing. From this point of view what Luther and Calvin had to offer was largely their blessing, and perhaps *ex post facto* benediction.

---

[15] See the important collection by H. Scheible (ed.), *Das Widerstandsrecht als Problem der deutschen Protestanten* (Gütersloh, 1969).

[16] See R. M. Kingdon, "Was the Protestant Reformation a Revolution? The Case of Geneva," in *Transition and Revolution,* ed. Kingdon (Minneapolis, 1974), 53-107.

In terms of the evolution of ideas, in any case, Calvinist radicals of the 1550's, especially the exiled Ponet, Goodman, and Knox, took the next step toward the "defense of popular revolution." The program of the Marian exiles was for the most part abortive, however; and it was rather the French, soon followed by the Dutch, Huguenots of the next decade who represent the "mainstream" referred to by Skinner. From the early 1560's there is a clearly traceable trajectory, several points of which he notes, between the "Declaration" made by the Prince of Condé at the outset of the civil wars and the propaganda generated in its wake, and the major revolutionary works of the 1570's, in which "a direct attack on the Valois monarchy" was launched, including at least suggestions of tyrannicide.[17] And again the political context was crucial, in this case the panic caused by the massacres of St. Bartholomew and the "conspiracy theory" developed by the Huguenots. Yet Skinner is surely right in opposing the view put forward by Michael Walzer (whether or not it is "Weberian")[18] that the revolutionary ideology of that incandescent age was essentially Calvinist; he reminds us that scholasticism had its own radical heritage and needed only political provocation to be employed. He goes further and argues that the main revolutionary argument of the Huguenots, the contract thesis, was actually scholastic in provenance.

This revolutionary train of thought did not obstruct, rather it helped to provoke rival trends of absolutist and constitutionalist thought, which Skinner in a sense factors out and analyzes separately. But it may be better to regard these views as different aspects of the same face (just as the revolutionary view is the obverse) of the coin. On the one hand, the classic expression of the "constitutionalist" thesis, Seyssel's *Grand Monarchy of France* (1515), was designed to celebrate and to enhance as well as to put "bridles" on royal authority; on the other hand, royal legists, setting out to flatter the crown and inflate its image, assumed (when they did not acknowledge) those same "bridles."[19] During the religious wars troubled observers ransacked all these traditions, often exaggerating or distorting them further. As well as the theory of popular revolution, Skinner finds a growth or regrowth of both the absolutist and constitutionalist lines. What began as differing points of view, however, turned increasingly into different schools of thought, and muted disagreement broke out into ideological wars after St. Bartholomew. On the one side was Jean Bodin, who came to champion absolutism in its most stark form; on the other, the "monarchomachs"—especially Beza, Hotman, and Mornay, who sought relief from "tyranny" in a variety of constitutionalist and revolutionary arguments.[20] In Skinner's panoramic view, which encompasses disillusioned passivists like

[17] The subject of my *The Beginning of Ideology: Consciousness and Society in the French Reformation.*

[18] Michael Walzer, *The Revolution of the Saints* (London, 1965).

[19] Seyssel, *La Monarchie de France,* ed. J. Poujol (Paris, 1961), translation by J. H. Hexter, ed. D. R. Kelley (forthcoming).

[20] See especially Hotman, *Francogallia,* ed. R. E. Giesey and translated by J. H. M. Salmon (Cambridge, 1972); Beza, *Du Droit des Magistrats,* ed. R. M. Kingdon (Geneva, 1971); and Julian H. Franklin (ed.), *Constitutionalism and Resistance in the Sixteenth Century* (New York, 1969); also *Jean Bodin, Verhand-*

Montaigne and still-illusioned tolerationists, the story is neither so simple nor so dramatic; and he rightly points out both the constitutionalist survivals in Bodin and the opportunistic character of the Huguenots' apparent traditionalism. He points out, too, the notorious turnabout of the 1580's, when Catholics and Protestants in effect exchanged ideologies. But from the point of view of political thought the dialectical pattern is clear and represents the most visible part of the "foundations" in the book's title.

With an account of the formation of modern theories of absolute monarchy and of revolution Skinner brings his book to a close, and closes it with a paradox not fully examined. The culmination of the Bodinian idea came in the later sixteenth century with the addition of the Pauline notion of divine right, in the work of various Gallican writers and especially William Barclay, whom Locke regarded as one of the greatest "assertors" of the principle. By contrast the idea of revolution received its fulfillment, according to Skinner, when it was totally *divorced* from religious considerations, in the work of certain of those whom Barclay called "monarchomachs," especially George Buchanan. In contrast to the view of some writers, such as Julian Franklin and the present reviewer, Skinner, applying the test of secularism, seems to make Buchanan, not the earlier French monarchomachs, "by far the most radical of all Calvinist revolutionaries." Does not the same test make Bodin "more radical" than his divine right successors? But perhaps there is no quarrel here: the judgment is made not on the grounds of historical context, after all, but of logic and strictly political thought according to an "internalist" standard.

This brings up another and more general unexamined question about the attempt to write the history of political thought and do justice to absolutist apologetics and "revolutionary" experimentation. One way to pose the problem is to inquire about the difference between arguments based on law, or designed for legal purposes, and more general attempts at legitimation or philosophical persuasion. Although historically these may all be regarded as part of an intellectual continuum, there are certain dangers in treating them as if they are on the same level.[21] Appealing to constitutional principle (as did, for example, Philip of Hesse) is quite a different matter than rejecting sovereignty (as did some of the French monarchomachs, for exampe, and the Seventeen Provinces); both are different from constructing a theory of political organization, even on the basis of positive law (as Bodin did for the most part) but especially on the basis of natural and divine law (which was the inclination of the *Vindiciae contra tyrannos,* for example). More generally, arguing a case of a client (as Hotman and other Huguenots did for the Prince of Condé) is something apart from taking a stand on principle. Or, from the standpoint of political thinking,

---

lungen der internationalen Bodin Tagung in München, ed. Horst Denzer (Munich, 1973), especially the article by Salmon.

[21] Aspects of this largely neglected problem are touched on by J. G. A. Pocock, *Politics, Language and Time* (New York, 1973) and much more extensively in a genre apparently, and unfortunately, unknown to historians of ideas, i.e., the hermeneutics of law. See, e.g., Emilio Betti, *Teoria generale della interpretazione* (Milan, 1955).

is it? It is to Skinner's credit, in any case, that he grapples with an unusually
—for synthetic works an unprecedentedly—wide range of political con-
ceptualizing, from the most transient *livres de circonstance* to the most
systematic treatises, from the most flagrant propaganda to the most utopian
flights.

In the sixteenth century, although the most extreme political concepts
were formulated, the methods of arguing continued to be extraordinarily
eclectic. Roman, canon, and feudal law, theological and Biblical texts,
formal political and moral philosophy, legislative precedent and curial
"style," historical examples and literary sources, all were part of the apparatus of political thought, and all were utilized, without much discrimination, by philosophers seeking the broadest base of theory and practice as
well as by lawyers arguing *in utramque partem*. Roman lawyers did not
hesitate to borrow from their canonist rivals; the sharpest critics of civil
law, like François Hotman, did not hesitate to appeal to Romanist sources
when it suited them or their clients; and philosophers like Bodin did not
hesitate to cite historical anecdotes as if they had the authority of a text
from Ulpian or scriptures. It was in the context of this pandemonium of
inherited wisdom and unprecedented ideological ferment—of traditional
values and expedience—that the foundations of modern political thought
were laid.

What Skinner has achieved in some 600 pages is a conspectus of the
emergence of the modern *homo politicus* from the fourteenth-century
"political Renaissance" (illuminated by the work of Alois Dempf, Georges
de la Garde, Francesco Ercole, and others)[22] down to the crucible of
Europe's first world war in the late sixteenth century (discussed by Figgis,
Allen, Mesnard, Weill, Caprariis, Salmon, A. J. Carlyle, and others[23]).
Perhaps the most conspicuous product of this transformation was the appearance of the modern State; and although it was left to the northern nations
to create the new leviathan, it was the Italians, and especially the predecessors of Machiavelli, who created the concepts and terminology for understanding it. Beginning at least with Bruno Latini, and continuing especially
in the work of Italian and French humanists, "political science" became a
special branch of knowledge identified with a particular method and point
of view. The second major theme of Skinner's book is the emergence of
this discipline, a discipline (it may be noted) which was indebted not only

[22] Dempf, *Sacrum Imperium* (Darmstadt, 1954), esp. part III, "Die Politische
Renaissance"; Lagarde, *La Naissance de l'esprit laïque au declin du moyen-âge*
(Louvain, 1956-70); Ercole, *Da Bartolo all'Althusio* (Florence, 1932).

[23] Figgis (see n. 10); J. W. Allen, *Political Thought in the Sixteenth Century*
(London, 1927); Pierre Mesnard, *L'Essor de la philosophie politique au XVIe
siècle* (Paris, 1969); Georges Weill, *Les Théories sur le pouvoir royal en France
pendant les guerres de religion* (Paris, 1894); Vittorio de Caprariis, *Propaganda
e pensiero politico in Francia durante le guerre di religione* (Naples, 1959); and
J. H. M. Salmon, *The French Religious Wars in English Political Thought* (Oxford,
1959); and A. J. Carlyle, *A History of Medieval Theory in the West*, VI (London,
1950).

to the revival of Aristotelian philosophy and Machiavelli's "new route" but also to the "civil science" of professional jurists. In general the political consciousness attendant on this development Skinner sees advancing first in Italy, then in France, and finally in England; and he follows this epic story, a special episode of a broader "translation of studies," down to the threshhold of the heroic age of political speculation.

Some readers may be disappointed that this book stops at the ground level, as it were, and does not go on to the larger edifice of political theory, especially in the seventeenth century, a field in which the author has few peers; but Skinner's decision to stop short of the Hobbes-and-Locke complex seems to me sensible. He has laid out the essential themes admirably, uncovering most if not all of "the foundations" of his field; and in any case explicating the work of the familiar textbook figures is another job or work— ideally one that henceforth will be carried out in the light of Skinner's survey. In the seventeenth century natural law overwhelmed positive law; pure reason replaced erudition and legal tradition as the means of persuasion and justification. But if the words changed, the music in a sense remained the same; and the familiar themes of Hobbesian absolutism, Lockean constitutionalism, and (*pace* Pocock[24]) Harringtonian republicanism are traced to their earlier and more obscure formulations in terms especially of scholastic, conciliarist, civic humanist, and Protestant thought. What Etienne Gilson did for (or to) Descartes, which was to show his unacknowledged debts to medieval philosophy,[25] Skinner has done more broadly for the political philosophers of Descartes' age, at least implicitly. His book in large part supplants the classic works of his predecessors—not perhaps that of Gierke (who would essay that?)[26] but certainly the pioneering efforts of J. N. Figgis (to which Skinner's view owes a substantial debt), of J. W. Allen (penetrating in its cranky way but historically unsatisfactory), of A. J. Carlyle (learned and ground-breaking but narrowly and legalistically focussed), and to some extent of Pierre Mesnard (though his work is still essential for analyses of some major figures and for older bibliography). Skinner's book is the new standard and will in time attain its own place as a classic.

University of Rochester.

---

[24] Pocock (ed.), *The Political Works of James Harrington* (Cambridge, 1977).

[25] Gilson, *Etudes sur le rôle de la pensée médiévale dans la formation du système cartésien* (Paris, 1951).

[26] That section of Gierke's *Genossenschaftsrecht* translated by Ernest Barker as *Natural Law and the Theory of Society 1500 to 1800* (Cambridge, 1934).

PART THREE

THE SEVENTEENTH CENTURY

VIII

HISTORY AND LAW IN THE SEVENTEENTH CENTURY: PUFENDORF *

By Leonard Krieger

There seems to be a connection between the social growth of a profession and its intellectual ambitions. Before its practitioners achieve autonomy, its field is ancillary to other kinds of knowledge. After the profession is absolutely secure, intellectual autonomy aspires to intellectual sovereignty. Certainly for many historians today the independence of their calling has as its intellectual counterpart an historical attitude toward life in general which mobilizes principles only recently well established. The relationship between historical experience and extra-historical presupposition has become a crucial problem in determining the principles of knowledge and of conduct. It may be worthwhile to refresh ourselves with the recollection of the original function of history at a time when its devotees were separating it out from other kinds of knowledge and in the person of an early professional caught in the process of parturition.

The time is the XVIIth century. For historiography this age was an interlude, its framework inherited and its efforts within that framework a store for the future. The great political history of the Renaissance statesmen, Machiavelli and Guicciardini, lay in the past; the great cultural history of the Enlightenment men of letters—Voltaire, Gibbon, Herder—was still to come. Certainly, as the historiographical manuals attest,[1] there was progress during the XVIIth century, but it was progress not so much in the products as in the materials of historical writing—the collections of sources, the criticism of documents, and the auxiliary sciences. The failure of the historical works that were raised upon this improved foundation to achieve new insights or interpretations of the historical process can be attributed to the continued prevalence of extra-historical occupations among the historians and of extra-historical preoccupations in their writings. The historians were politicians or officials, classicists, clergymen, and jurists. Where their vocational attachment was not to the state or the church it was to universities in which they occupied chairs of theology, law, or of combined humanistic and historical studies—History and Poetry, History and Rhetoric, History and Philology, and the like. They were concerned, correspondingly, with clarifying ecclesiastical or legal tradition, with revising the traditional academic chronicles of universal history, and with refining the humanist tradition of history as exemplary past politics in its application to classical, national, or territorial materials.

---

* In slightly different form, this paper was delivered at a session of the American Historical Association on December 28, 1958.

[1] E.g., Eduard Fueter, *Geschichte der neueren Historiographie* (3rd ed., Munich, 1936), 307–310.

The primary importance of the XVIIth century for historiography, then, has less to do with the study of history itself than with developments in the reigning non-historical conceptions which favored the growth within them of an historical dimension. These developments went beyond the much-remarked external connection between the critical empiricism of the new science and the progress in historical techniques, for they affected the very substance of the authoritative political and philosophical values. The most pertinent of these developments, for our purposes, were those which heightened the centrality of law.[2]

In politics, the dominant tendencies in both external and domestic relations favored the exposition of law in historical forms. Public attention was increasingly diverted from static ideals of the Christian community of rulers on the international stage and of the Christian hierarchy of authorities at home to the aggressive claims of independent territorial states against one another and of their sovereigns against their privileged subjects. Since this shift was an expansion rather than a rejection of the accepted standards of political conduct it called forth the enunciation of uniform legal principles in forms that would harmonize the old order with the new facts. Hence when princes or councils desired the justification of their foreign policies to the rulers, officials, and scholars of other powers in the new unstable system of states it was to the jurists that they turned for the historical validation of their acts. When governments or parties desired to justify their rôles in recent internal convulsions, commissioned scholars or advocates wrote national or contemporary history to show the constitutional and moral lawfulness of their actions. And when the wonted framework of universal history which had integrated politics into the religious scheme of the four empires was undermined during the XVIIth century by the growing secularism of political interests, it was to jurisprudence that the benefits of theological retrenchment accrued. The extension of its influence over the field of the political present entailed its predominant responsibility for reordering the political past, for the purpose both of explaining present politics and of setting examples for recommended policies. Thus the

---

[2] It should be emphasized here that the relations of law and history made up but one strand in the historiographical development of the XVIIth century. The relations of religion and history, which provided the framework simultaneously for the growth of pragmatic church history and for the improvement in the critical techniques of historical research, constitute the other main line in the emergence of history as an autonomous discipline. Despite the parallels that can be established for the growth of historical dimensions in legal and in religious doctrines, the problem of religion and history in the XVIIth century had its own process and will be considered towards the end of this paper only at the point where Pufendorf had contact with it.

limited consciousness of the historical requirements of jurisprudence, which had emerged during the XVIth century in the ' French mode ' of commentary upon Roman Law, grew by the end of the century into the more general coincidence of law and history in politics. If we take only the most prominent figures in the annals of political history and political theory between the late XVIth and the end of the XVIIth century this coincidence of law and history is striking indeed. The best-known political historians were probably de Thou, Bacon, Clarendon, and Pufendorf—all were jurists. Of the political philosophers, Bodin wrote on the philosophy of history, while both Grotius and Pufendorf were practicing historians. Hobbes, Spinoza, and Locke wrote no history,[3] but none of them was a lawyer either, whether by education or profession. Leibniz, the only one of the great metaphysicians of the century who applied himself to history, was trained in law at the University of Jena, and the juristic stamp was patent in his historical writing.

The juristic met the philosophical dimension of law in the secularized doctrines of natural law, which came to dominate XVIIth-century thought in the fields of ethics and politics. The impact of natural law upon history worked in two opposite directions at once. It established rules of behavior that were universally applicable to all times and places, and it assigned to human reason and human will, operating in *particular* times and places, the function of recognizing and of applying them. The problem posed for general history by these two facets of natural law during the XVIIIth century provided Friedrich Meinecke with the starting-point of his study on historicism.[4] But it was a problem that characterized the XVIIth-century

[3] That is, they wrote no independent historical works. This is not to deny Hobbes' and Spinoza's interest in history. Hobbes translated Thucydides' *Peloponnesian War* into English in 1629, and his *Behemoth: or an Epitome of the Civil War in England from 1640–1660*, published in 1679, can be considered a species of contemporary history, while his *Historical Narration concerning Heresie and the punishment thereof*, of 1680, falls overtly into the genre of religious history. But the Thucydides' translation was a humanist exercise undertaken before Hobbes turned either to philosophy or politics; the *Behemoth* is a moralistic dialogue; and the history of heresies was a brief pamphlet in defense of the *Leviathan*. It is generally agreed that for Hobbes historical knowledge occupied a distinctly derivative and merely rhetorical place. See Leo Strauss, *Political Philosophy of Hobbes: its Basis and Genesis* (Oxford, 1936), 80–107, and Raymond Polin, *Politique et philosophie chez Thomas Hobbes* (Paris, 1953), 81–86. As for Spinoza, his introduction of historical criticism of the Bible in the *Theologico-Political Treatise* of 1670 had little that was specifically historical about it. He admitted that his "method of interpreting scripture does not differ widely from the method of interpreting nature—in fact, it is almost the same," since it consists in "inferring the intentions of its authors as a legitimate conclusion from its fundamental principles" just as the definitions of natural phenomena are deduced from fixed axioms. See Ernst Cassirer, *The Philosophy of the Enlightenment* (Boston, 1955), 184–186.

[4] F. Meinecke, *Die Entstehung des Historismus* (2 vols., Munich, 1936).

proponents of natural law as well. Since, in the earlier century, the framework of absolutes was more inclusive and the sphere of history less inclusive, the issue was not yet the combination of general ethical and concrete historical factors into a system. Rather it was the dawning relationship of history to a system maintained as valid without it. It is true that for the XVIIth century as for the XVIIIth the relation of rational to empirical truth was the primary problem of knowledge, but empirical facts were themselves so much less homogeneous for the XVIIth century than they were to be for the XVIIIth century that the distinction between the empirical and the historical was a far more pressing problem for the earlier period than for the later. So we find that in the natural-law jurists of the XVIIth century the problem of history took two forms: it involved first the integration of empirical facts, in the form of legal precedent and custom, into the framework of rational principles; but it also involved the rôle of historical facts, in the form of separate works of political narration, *vis-a-vis* this empirico-rational legal system as a whole.

So much for the age. Now what about the man? Samuel Pufendorf was unique for the balance of law and history which characterized his professional life and influence. He was a jurist and an historian not by virtue of having simultaneous interests but by successive and exclusive profession. Between 1661 and 1677 Pufendorf was a professor of law, at Heidelberg until 1670 and thereafter at the Swedish University of Lund. His professional commitment to law during this period worked as a powerful personal drive within him; it bulked large in his decision to move from his native Germany to Sweden, for his irregular position as law teacher in Heidelberg's philosophical faculty rankled as much as the prospect of the post as top-ranking professor in Lund's law faculty gratified.[5] His subsequent dedication to history was hardly less complete. When Charles XI of Sweden appointed him to the joint post of court historian and secretary of state, Pufendorf abandoned both university and law, never to return. His function as secretary of state, moreover, was honorary rather than active;[6] the only extant evidence of activity in this capacity, a report in 1680 on the Franco-Swedish alliance, was largely historical in approach,[7] and what there is of his correspondence, silent as it is on any political or administrative business and full as it is of

[5] Erik Wolf, *Grosse Rechtsdenker der deutschen Geistesgeschichte* (3rd ed., Tübingen, 1951), 325.

[6] Heinrich von Treitschke, " Samuel Pufendorf," in *Historische und Politische Aufsätze* (Leipzig, 1897), IV, 268–269.

[7] This is apparent from its title: *Dissertatio de Occasionibus Foederum inter Sueciam et Galliam*—title given in Paul Meyer, *Samuel Pufendorf: Ein Beitrag zur Geschichte seines Lebens* (Grimma, 1894), which contains the most complete listing extant of Pufendorf's works.

his historical concerns, reveals how unreservedly he held his duty to be that of state historian.[8] Nor did Pufendorf's move to Berlin in 1688 change the professional tenor of his life. He went as court historian and privy counsellor to Brandenburg's Great Elector, and his final years were absorbed in writing the history of the two Electors under whom he served.

The pattern of Pufendorf's publications confirms this clear-cut division of his career, for his writings as well as his functions were concentrated first on law and then on history.[9] During his historical phase he wrote on law only in the special context of religion,[10] a con-

[8] For Pufendorf's repeated acknowledgments that his historical labors left him no time for any other pursuits, see letters of Pufendorf to Thomasius, March 24, 1688 and Jan. 7, 1693, in Emil Gigas, ed., *Briefe Samuel Pufendorfs an Christian Thomasius* (Munich, 1897), 19, 71–72; also Pufendorf to Paul von Fuchs, Jan. 19, 1688, and to Ernst von Hessen-Rheinfels, July 8 or 18, 1690, in Konrad Varentrapp, ed., " Briefe von Pufendorf," *Historische Zeitschrift*, LXX (1894), 26–27, 196.

[9] His main works on law were all published by 1677: *Elementorum Juris Prudentiae Universalis Libri Duo* (The Hague, 1660), recent English translation by W. A. Oldfather (Oxford, 1931); *De Obligatione erga Patriam* (Heidelberg, 1663); *De Statu Imperii Germanici ad Laelium Fratrem Dominium Trezolani Liber Unus* (Geneva, 1667), published under pseudonym Severinus de Monzambano Veronensis at The Hague, recent edition and German translation under title *Über die Verfassung des deutschen Reiches* (Berlin, 1922) by H. Bresslau; *Dissertatio de Republica Irregulari* (Lund, 1668); *De Jure Naturae et Gentium Libri Octo* (Lund, 1672; expanded ed., Frankfurt, 1684), recent English translation by C. H. Oldfather and W. A. Oldfather (Oxford, 1934); *De Officio Hominis et Civis Mixta Legem Naturalem Libri Duo* (Lund, 1673), an epitome of the *De Jure Naturae*, English translation by Frank G. Moore (New York, 1927); and assorted brief articles in *Dissertationes Academicae Selectiores* (Upsala, 1677).

Pufendorf's historical works were, with one exception, post-1677: *Einleitung zur Historie der vornehmsten Reiche und Staaten in Europa* (Frankfurt, 1682). Extended sections on the Papacy—the exception, published in 1674—and on Sweden were published separately. *Commentariorum de Rebus Suecicis Libri XXVI ab Expeditione Gustavi Adolphi Regis in Germaniam ad Abdicationem Usque Christinae* (Utrecht, 1686); *De Rebus a Carolo Gustavo Sueciae Rege Gestis Commentariorum Libri Septem* (Nurnberg, 1696); *De Rebus Gestis Friderici Wilhelmi Magni Electoris Brandenburgici Commentariorum Libri XIX* (Berlin, 1695); *De Rebus Gestis Friderici III Electoris Brandenburgici, post Primi Borussiae Regis Libri III Complectentes Annos 1688-1690. Fragmentum Posthumum ex Autographo Auctoris Editum* (Berlin, 1784). The only legal writing which Pufendorf undertook during his historical period was a series of rebuttals to criticisms of his *De Jure Naturae* (most, but not all, of these rebuttals were published in *Eris Scandica qua Adversus Libros de Jure Naturali et Gentium Objecta Diluuntur* (Frankfurt, 1686) and a revision of his *De Statu Imperii Germanici* (the basis of the new edition published by J. P. Gundling for the Berlin Academy in 1706).

[10] His *De Habitu Religionis Christianae ad Rem Publicam* (Bremen, 1687) and his *Jus Feciale Divinum sive de Consensu et Dissensu Protestantium, Exercitatio Posthumus* (Lübeck, 1695).

text, which, as we shall see further on, made this activity consistent with his concern for history. Pufendorf admitted frankly, in his correspondence during the 80's, that his professional responsibilities as historian precluded any further work by him on the system of natural law, despite his acknowledgment of the need for it.[11] In terms of influence, moreover, Pufendorf alone, among his contemporaries, wrote works that were widely used as text-books for both juristic and historical students. Both his study *On the Law of Nature and Nations* of 1672 and his general history of Europe of 1682 were so applied. They were republished frequently down to the middle of the XVIIIth century, and appeared in Latin, German, French, English, and Russian editions.[12]

But, as this reception indicates, Pufendorf was unique in his combination of law and history rather than in the quality of his work on either. Indeed, one is attracted to the paradox that his uniqueness consisted primarily in his being more representative than anyone else of the professional and intellectual attributes of his age. Neither the cautious courage of his legal doctrines, permitted by the limited autonomy of his position as professor of law, nor the political conformity of his history, dictated by governmental surveillance of his position as professional but official historian, was extraordinary. His application of the revolutionary geometrical method to jurisprudence; his eschewal of the revolutionary implications of natural-law doctrines for positive law and politics; his channelling of documentary sources into the humanist tradition of pragmatic political history; his retention of an orthodox religious faith—in his case Lutheranism—alongside his devotion to natural law and humanist history: these tendencies—and the problems implicit in them—were all characteristic of the times.

[11] Pufendorf to Thomasius, Mar. 24, 1688, in Gigas, ed., *Briefe Pufendorfs*, 19.

[12] The prevalence of piracy in copyrights during the XVIIth and early XVIIIth centuries makes it difficult to establish the precise number of editions which these works went through. I have counted 9 Latin editions of the *De Jure Naturae* by 1759, 7 French editions by 1771, 5 English editions by 1749, and single editions in German, Russian, and Italian; 16 Latin editions of the *De Officio* (a compendium of the *De Jure Naturae* designed specifically for student use) by 1769, 7 French editions by 1756 and single French editions in 1822 and 1830, 4 English editions by 1716, and a German edition in 1691; 5 German editions of the *Einleitung zu der Historie der vornehmsten Reiche* . . . *in Europa* by 1746, 10 English editions by 1764, 5 French editions by 1759, 3 Latin editions by 1704, and a Russian edition of 1718. For recent acknowledgment of the influence exercised during the XVIIth and XVIIIth centuries by Pufendorf's treatises on natural law, see Robert Derathé, *Jean-Jacques Rousseau et la science politique de son temps* (Paris, 1950), 78–84. For the use of Pufendorf's general history in German universities, see Emil Clemens Scherer, *Geschichte und Kirchengeschichte an den deutschen Universitäten* (Freiburg, 1927), *passim*, esp. 179.

They held even for Leibniz, creating an intellectual connection with Pufendorf over and above his substantive philosophical differences with and his explicit hostility toward the latter.[13] What distinguished Pufendorf was his articulation of the implicit relations among ideas which were generally shared.

What then, were Pufendorf's solutions for the problems of law and history?

His solution to the problem of working an empirical content into his natural-law doctrine offers few difficulties, for the merger of natural-law principles with traditional positive law and institutions was the most prominent feature of his system. Consequently, the procedure which he adopted toward this end is patent throughout his legal and political writing. Essentially, this procedure consisted in the adoption of a both-and attitude which was a testimony less of logical rigor than of the urge to account for as much of existence as possible. This attitude determined each of the three basic steps of his formal thought. First, the fundamental principles of morality included both rational principles, or ' axioms,' whose truth " flows from reason itself, . . . merely from the bare intuition of the mind," and experimental principles or ' observations,' based upon " the comparison and perception of individual details uniformly corresponding with one another." [14] This juxtaposition of empirical and rational approaches induced Pufendorf to insist upon man's temporal context—that is, to exclude the ideal of a perfect, or pre-lapsarian state of nature entirely from consideration [15]—and still to endow him with a constant character within that context. In the analysis of this character Pufendorf's syncretistic method led him to replace the psychological abstractions of social appetite and self-seeking passions, which Grotius and Hobbes had raised as polar opposites, with the more flexible notions of ' sociability (*socialitas*) ' and ' weakness (*imbecillitas*),' which he conceived as complementary permanent attributes of human ' nature,' knowable from both the observation of the human experience

---

[13] The common influence stemmed from the Cartesian mathematician at Jena, Erhard Weigel, who taught both men. For Leibniz' strictures upon Pufendorf and for the misinterpretations upon which they were in part based, see Gaston Grua, *Jurisprudence universelle et théodicée selon Leibniz* (Paris, 1953), 23, 418, 421–423.

[14] Pufendorf, *Elementorum* (transl. W. A. Oldfather), II, 209. This dual approach characterized his later natural-law work as well. " Now the dictates of sound reason are true principles that are in accordance with the properly observed and examined nature of things, and are deduced by logical sequence from prime and true principles." *De Jure Naturae* (transl. C. H. and W. A. Oldfather), II, 203.

[15] *Ibid.,* II, 154–155; Samuelis Pufendorfii, *Eris Scandica, qua Adversus Libros de Jure Naturali et Gentium Objecta Diluuntur* (Frankfurt, 1759), 19, 32–33.

and the dictates of moral reason, and interacting in proportions that varied with time, place, and circumstance.[16]

Secondly, in treating the substantive principles of natural law, Pufendorf's inclination was ever to subdivide his principles into propositions of equal validity, one categorical, the other comprehensive and adapted to experience. This natural law was founded both upon the rule of reason and upon the positive command of a superior.[17] It prescribed both duties that were absolute and duties that were conditional.[18] It legitimated both rights that were perfect—that is, valid and enforceable—and rights that were imperfect—that is, valid but unenforceable.[19] Thirdly, the application of natural to civil law was oriented toward the imposition of absolute criteria not so much for discriminating among positive laws and institutions as for recognizing, relating, and rationalizing them. Thus he acknowledged a broad field of discretion in the execution of natural law itself, since many of its precepts were ' indefinite,' and beyond this he admitted an even broader field of ' permission.' Here, natural law applied only very indirectly, through the derivative and formal criteria of equity and " the particular advantage of individual states." [20] In public law Pufendorf admitted the legitimacy of both absolute and limited sovereignty; [21] in private law he admitted the bulk of Roman law, with an admixture of German.[22]

But what does all this have to do with history? Actually we find no recognizable historical description or narration in Pufendorf's works on natural law. We cannot go beyond the observation that Pufendorf's appreciations of the alternative within the context of men's action in political society opens his system to a place for history. The kind of history which was possible whithin his natural-law system appeared not in his theoretical works but in his treatise on the

[16] Pufendorf, *De Jure Naturae*, II, 205–219; Hans Welzel, *Die Socialitas als oberstes Prinzip der Naturrechtslehre Samuel Pufendorfs* (Heidelberg, 1930), 8–17; Wolf, *Grosse Rechtsdenker*, 319–320, 343–346.

[17] Pufendorf, *De Jure Naturae*, II, 217–221.

[18] Pufendorf, *Elementorum*, II, 159.

[19] Pufendorf, *De Jure Naturae*, II, 118–119; *Elementorum*, II, 289.

[20] Pufendorf, *De Officio* (F. G. Moore Eng. tr.), II, 125–126; *De Jure Naturae*, II, 32–33, 1132–1137.   [21] *Ibid.*, II, 1063–1079.

[22] R. Stintzing and Ernst Landsberg, *Geschichte der deutschen Rechtswissenschaft* (Munich, 1898), III, 15–16. But Pufendorf was no Romanist. He claimed that he had refused an appointment in Roman Law at Heidelberg, and he grounded both his appreciation of it and his deviations from it on the conformity of large parts but not all of the Roman Law with the natural law. Pufendorf to Thomasius, Oct. 16, 1688, in Varentrapp, ed., " Briefe," *Historische Zeitschrift*, LXX, 36–37; Dec. 1, 1688 and Apr. 9, 1692, in Gigas, ed., *Briefe Pufendorfs*, 32, 67; Pufendorf, *Eris Scandica*, 125.

German constitution,[23] the only publication of his juristic period which contained narrative history. His historical sketch of German constitutional development was in the context of his emphasis upon the real rather than the formal relationships of the German Empire, but in the final analysis it was not autonomous history, for it served primarily to be measured against Pufendorf's natural-law principle of sovereignty and to be used as evidence for the label of 'monstrous' which he affixed to the constitution.

What, then, was the relationship of Pufendorf's system to the independent historical works which he wrote as a professional historian? Certainly there was some continuity between the two. In terms of vocation, it can be pointed out that Pufendorf's general history of Europe, which received final form and publication while he was court historian in Stockholm, was apparently based upon lectures which he had given as professor of natural law at the University of Lund.[24]

The connection between the law and the history can be made in terms of ideas as well. In both his general and his archival histories, Pufendorf's concentration on political and contemporary history, his pragmatic dictum that the value of history is, besides pleasure, its usefulness for policy-makers by showing examples of good and bad actions, and his frank espousal of 'the real interest' of states as the canon of such actions,[25] all manifest the mould of lawful politics into which his history was poured. This notion of 'the real interest' of states, in the more familiar designation of *raison d'état*, has been particularly stressed as the point of union between the natural-law system and the history,[26] for Pufendorf had used this idea in his theoretical writing to cover the flexible union of the duty prescribed upon the ruler to govern for the good of the people and his permitted right to interpret this duty variously in varying empirical conditions.

But we can carry the implications of Pufendorf's natural-law system even further, for it is an aid toward understanding the assump-

---

[23] Severinus de Monzambano, *De Statu Imperii Germanici ad Laelium Fratrem, Dominum Trezolani, Liber Unus* (Geneva [actually The Hague], 1667). It was written in 1664.

[24] Pufendorf, *Einleitung*, preface; H. Treitschke, "Pufendorf," in *Aufsätze*, IV, 274.

[25] Pufendorf to Thomasius, Nov. 26, 1692, in Gigas, ed., *Briefe Pufendorfs*, 69; Pufendorf, *Einleitung*, preface.

[26] Thus Ernst Salzer, *Der Übertritt des Grossen Kurfürsten von der schwedischen auf die polnische Seite während des ersten nordischen Krieges* in *Pufendorfs 'Carl Gustav' und 'Friedrich Wilhelm'* (Heidelberg, 1904), 13–19; F. Meinecke, *Die Idee der Staatsräson in der neueren Geschichte* (Munich, 1924), 279–303; Wolf, *Grosse Rechtsdenker*, 357–358.

tions of Pufendorf's historical methodology. Pufendorf contended
that the historian must be at the same time impersonal and partial.
On the one hand, he must be no ' advocate,' but he must " report
things as they happened, without favor or aversion "; he must reveal
" not his own judgment " but " the uncorrupted truth from authentic
sources for posterity." [27]   On the other hand, however, Pufendorf insisted just as categorically that the historian " expresses with his pen
the sentiments of the lord he serves "; " as public interpreter of the
acts and motives of the prince or commonwealth whose history he
writes he cannot avoid expressing their views." [28] Pufendorf himself
never tried to reconcile these two assumptions of his history, but his
political notion of the reason of state seems both objective enough
and particular enough to cover them. Thus the outstanding characteristics of his archival histories of Sweden and of Brandenburg seem
explicable by his use of ' reason of state ' as his historical criterion:
on its objective side, the focus on the contemporary history of foreign
policy, the concentration on the discussions and negotiations leading
to decisions rather than on causes or events, the treatment of individuals as spokesmen of policies rather than as personalities, and the long
verbatim excerpts from the documents; on the subjective side, the approach in each history from the position of the state for which he
wrote, the deliberate restriction to sources from the archives of that
state, the manufacture of discussions to fill in particular gaps of
validly established policies, the occasional suppression of material
still deemed confidential, and the abstention from general interpretations.[29] Politics, in short, was for Pufendorf the meeting-ground of
law and history, for his politics had its base in his natural-law system and it projected the framework for his historical work. Through
politics the ' moral science ' of law was sufficiently loosened for history to have a place in the nature of human things.

This kind of interpretation has, in varying forms, been applied to
Pufendorf by his commentators, from Droysen to Wolf. It is clear
and it is valid. It is also inadequate. It leaves unaccounted some-

[27] Pufendorf to J. F. von Seilern, Mar. 5, 1690, in Varentrapp, ed., " Briefe,"
Historische Zeitschrift, LXX, 43–44; Pufendorf, *De Rebus Gestis Friderici Wilhelmi Magni*, preface and 445; Salzer, *Der Übertritt des grossen Kurfürsten*, 5, 8.

[28] Pufendorf to Paul von Fuchs, Jan. 19, 1688 and Pufendorf to J. F. von Seilern,
Mar. 5, 1690, in Varentrapp, ed., " Briefe," *Historische Zeitschrift*, LXX, 27–28,
43–44.

[29] For analyses of Pufendorf's archival histories, see Salzer, *Der Übertritt des
grossen Kurfürsten*, Johann Gustav Droysen, " Zur Kritik Pufendorfs," in *Abhandlungen zur neueren Geschichte* (Leipzig, 1876), and Hans Roedding, *Pufendorf als
Historiker und Politiker in den ' Commentarii de Rebus Gestis Friderici Tertii '*
(Halle, 1912).

thing that was absolutely essential for Pufendorf. Meinecke caught a glimpse of this something in a negative way when he complained of the gap between Pufendorf's announcement of 'reason of state' as an historical principle and the absence of any general principle in his actual history-writing.[30] Meinecke attributed this gap to a flaw which ran all through Pufendorf and the XVIIth century—the want of a conceptual capacity to integrate the rational and the empirical. But what was a flaw and a want for Meinecke was something quite positive for Pufendorf. Pufendorf did not attempt such an integration for the simple reason that for him the truth of law and the truth of historical existence belonged to two different orders of knowledge, each equipped with its own validity, its own authority, it own methods, its own empiricism. From the very beginning of his writing on natural law Pufendorf distinguished between the *necessary* truth of the *relations* among particulars, which was perceived by reason as a natural law, and the *contingent* truth of the particular facts themselves, which depends on probability and faith.[31] In his only reference to 'the historian' in the works on natural law, Pufendorf explicitly assigned historical knowledge to the order of contingent existence.[32] But this division of knowledge did not ever mean, for Pufendorf, the deprecation of the 'contingent' in favor of the 'necessary.' On the contrary, if the truth of moral laws was 'necessary' in a logical sense, it was also 'hypothetical' in a metaphysical sense—that is, its reality was conditional upon the existence of its particular subject, and the proof of this existence lay outside the realm of moral or legal science.[33] The two kinds of existence in which he was particularly interested were revealed religion and history. They could not, of course, be known in the same way, but they shared the quality of positive rather than rational knowledge and they both lay outside the natural-law system, since from the facts which they supplied no propositions could be deduced. It is hardly fortuitous, then, that after his juristic period Pufendorf wrote not only on history but on religion as well, nor is it surprising that the only kind of knowledge which he permitted Scripture to furnish for 'speculative discipline' was historical knowledge.[34] In the correspondence of his historical period Pufendorf himself explicitly connected his religious and historical interests by proposing canons for the writing of ecclesiastical history along impersonal and pragmatic lines avowedly analogous to those of 'civil

---

[30] Particularly in reference to Pufendorf's general history. Meinecke, *Die Idee der Staatsräson*, 288.

[31] Pufendorf, *Elementorum*, II, preface.

[32] Pufendorf, *De Jure Naturae*, II, 37.

[33] *Ibid.*, II, 23; *Eris Scandica*, 24–25, 256, 273.   [34] *Ibid.*, 276.

history.'[35]   Here the two main lines of XVIIth-century historiography, the political and the religious, converged in Pufendorf, and their relationship in him reflected the larger connection for the century as a whole—the meeting in history of kinds of facts that were irreducible to science.

In the light of this interpretation Pufendorf's whole enterprise takes on a pattern quite different from the one which would make his history simply a further step in the specification of his moral and legal system. He was not a man who sought to move the facts of existence on the fulcrum of his natural-law principles. He was rather a man who accepted the positive institutions of his time, placed their existence outside his system of reason, and sought to rationalize the ideas about them and the relationships between them. He has been adjudged representative of the bourgeoisie by virtue of the rationality of his principles and the practical common-sense of his application of them,[36] but is must be remembered that he was a XVIIth-century burgher too in his recognition of where real authority lay, his acceptance of this authority, and the orientation of his criticism simply to the removal of its obfuscations. The two stages of his intellectual career should be seen as a process of development in which he first sought to weave the reasonable network of law into the institutional world he observed around him, and then moved outside this network to deal directly with the facts of religion and political sovereignty upon whose existence his legal system hinged. The difference between these two stages has little to do with the banal distinction between rationalism and empiricism. The natural-law system of his first phase was, as we have seen, itself both rational and empirical, while the common element of the religious and historical works of his second phase was their concern with facts that were not observable. The difference in his approaches to law and history was epitomized in his distinction between the *relations* among moral actions already committed, which were subject to the universal principles of legal science, and the *process* of bringing such actions into existence, which was a work of moral freedom, flexible in its operation upon different times and circumstances but unknowable by merely applying general law.[37] The distinction here was not between a greater or lesser empiricism but between an order of reality that was

---

[35] Pufendorf to Thomasius, Dec. 30, 1688 and Nov. 6, 1692, in Gigas, ed., *Briefe Pufendorfs*, 35–36, 69.   [36] Wolf, *Grosse Rechtsdenker*, 330–331.

[37] " And so long as we deliberate, we are properly called free, while the effects that will follow our actions are properly called, with respect to that liberty, contingent; but when we have determined upon some action, the relation between our acts and all the effects depending thereon, is necessary and quite natural, and therefore capable of demonstration." Pufendorf, *De Jure Naturae*, II, 26.

susceptible to general reason and an order of reality that was susceptible to particular judgment.

It was not incapacity or neglect on Pufendorf's part to have supplied his history with a pragmatic purpose drawn from his legal system and then to have refrained from drawing the generalities which would have led from his historical facts to it. The restraint was deliberate. " If the moral is to be drawn from history," he declared, " the reader must supply what the historian does not venture to write." [38] Between history and moral law, in other words, there was an inevitable gap. His firm conviction that he was serving the cause of historical truth while frankly representing the side of his prince was not simply an anomaly explicable by the flexible principle of *raison d'état*. Pufendorf did not feel the tension within this conviction, because he assumed a strict independence between the realm of historical facts and the realm of political reality to which they led.

Two principal conclusions emerge from this early case-study in the growth of a modern historical sense. First, the feeling for historicity did not always grow within the sheltering confines of theological, metaphysical, or moral systems until the dissolution of these systems in the late XVIIIth and the XIXth centuries gave it independence. Even in the most systematic stages of this process there were men like Pufendorf who viewed history as an autonomous realm with an irreducible content that not only moderated but set ultimate limits to the applicability of systems. Secondly, this pattern of knowledge was not merely unstable, transitional, or schizoid. It derived its strength and its persistence from the circumstance that the realms of absolute principle and of historical fact, while not reducible to each other, were related to each other. This relationship consisted of more than the obvious positive connection between principles that were open to historical specification and an experience that required principled guidance for history in the making. At least as potent was the negative connection whereby the spheres of life that were rationally grounded afforded a secure spring-board for the adventure into those spheres of life which, like history, were not. For such men as Pufendorf, the distinctiveness of reason's field has served both to permit the recognition of different kinds of reality and to instill the confidence that the past and the transcendent can be organized around the firm certainty of the here and now in the co-operative quest for knowledge.

Yale University.

[38] Pufendorf, *Einleitung*, II, preface, quoted in E. Salzer, *Der Übertritt des grossen Kuerfürsten*, 8, note 25. This division of function between the historian and everyman was so essential to Pufendorf that he repeated his statement of it both in his *Commentariorum de Rebus Suecicis*, preface, and in his *De Rebus Gestis Friderici Wilhelmi Magni*, 445.

IX

LEIBNIZ'S PRINCIPLES OF INTERNATIONAL JUSTICE*

By Paul Schrecker

All commentators and interpreters of Leibniz agree that universality was one of the main features of his thought. To use a figure introduced by Leibniz himself, we might say that he was a living mirror of the universe—a *mirror* because he reflected more or less clearly and distinctly the whole realm of nature and civilization, and a *living* mirror because he not only passively reflected but actively shaped and concentrated the enormous variety of rays emanating from his world. Just as the monads diversely unify the infinite variety of the universe, so Leibniz's function in the history of human thought was to conciliate forces that seemed most opposed, not only of scientific and philosophic thought, but of religion, politics, and history as well.

This universality was not merely an accident of his personality; it was not the result of insatiable curiosity or the manifestation of his multifarious gifts, but rather an essential postulate of his program and the innermost core of his method not only of conceiving but of organizing the world. The world, indeed, has been divided for the practical purposes of limited creatures into separate provinces: body and soul, science and religion, theory and action, justice and politics. In reality, according to Leibniz, the universe is the creation of one indivisible and universal spirit, called God in the realm of religion, Reason in the realm of knowledge, and Justice in the realm of action.

Descartes had founded the unity of science on the unity of the human intellect in dealing with the variety of objects to which it applies itself. He had guaranteed the truth and reality of science by the veracity of God, who, he declared, could not wish to deceive us in what we perceive most clearly and distinctly. In two directions Leibniz advanced far beyond his predecessor. First, he generalized, science is not the only system whose unity is required by the unity of our intellect, which demands unity of our entire human civilization. If conflicts arise between various religions, between science and religion, between justice and particular

* Read at the meeting in celebration of the tercentenary of Leibniz held by the Conference on Methods in Philosophy and the Sciences at the New School for Social Research, New York City, May 5, 1946.

interests, or between theory and practice, these conflicts are of the same order as the inconsistencies and contradictions which, without prejudice to its ideal unity, science contains at every stage of its history. The progress of science consists in gradually eliminating inconsistencies within the system, and contradictions between any system and experience. The same is true of the totality of civilization. Conflicts springing up between its several divisions are imperfections brought about by human limitation. But they are by no means phenomena before which we have to capitulate. All human effort, therefore, must be devoted to overcoming these conflicts which are symptoms of disturbances that can be cured.

It is true that the unity of civilization is thus never actually reached. But neither is the unity of science, which is nevertheless the aim that inspires all research. This is Leibniz's first extension of the Cartesian postulate of the unity of science. Despite the diversity of aims pursued in its various fields, civilization is a potential unity, and every effort ought to be devoted to actualizing this potentiality.

There is still another direction of no minor importance in which Leibniz universalized the Cartesian conception. According to Descartes, all truths, even those of reason, have their source in God's unfathomable will. This mediatization of truth is absolutely inconceivable to Leibniz. Truths of reason, that is, those the contrary of which implies self-contradiction, are, as he says, more inviolable than the Styx, and God Himself cannot but respect them in His creation. We do not, therefore, need any additional guarantee for these truths, their very necessity warranting their reality. This principle would, however, be insufficient and ineffectual in the field of action were it not inseparably accompanied by another which completes it and renders it practicable. What reason is to knowledge, justice is to action. And the principles of justice are as independent of the Divine Will as necessary truths are of the Divine Intellect. Now, since in the divine unity two definite perfections, wisdom and justice, can never be at variance, injustice can never be reasonable, nor can disobedience to reason ever be just. No incongruity is thus possible between true theory and just action. Truth and justice are the two correlative universal ideas which should dominate the entire field of human conduct.

These two sovereign and seemingly very simple ideas are the key to the often cryptic achievements of Leibniz. Just as a small number of axioms virtually contain the whole of geometry, so the ideas of reason and justice virtually contain all manifestations of genuine civilization.

Whereas, however, the idea of reason as conceived by Leibniz seems incontrovertible, the idea of justice, alas, appears much less solidly founded and still less universally recognized. For while we have a fairly good idea, imperfect as it may be, of what is to be understood by the concept of truth, while the reach of this idea has been considerably enlarged during the course of history, while it may rely upon a certain number of indubitable principles—justice, on the contrary, seems a word devoid of any precise meaning, or at least subject to such wide variations in space and time that it appears ridiculous to proclaim it the sovereign principle of human actions. History, moreover, does not seem to lead to the progress of justice as it undoubtedly has led to the progress of knowledge. Where, indeed, is the stable starting-point which would correspond in the field of action to the first and indubitable principles which guarantee the progress of our knowledge? Is there one single principle of justice as generally and universally accepted as the principle which expresses the contrary of justice, namely, that might destroys right?

In opposition to these sceptical and cynical objections, Leibniz affirmed the certainty and actuality of an idea of justice, the content of which may vary constantly, and which, moreover, may be ceaselessly violated by positive law as well as by the actual conduct and condition of man, but which nevertheless remains the only idea capable of directing human action towards the general good. No civilized society aiming at the improvement of its civilization would indeed be possible, were it to renounce the idea of justice. This certainty, according to Leibniz, rests on first principles of life in society, which are as incontrovertible and valid as the axioms of logic.

What are these principles of justice called upon to unify human society, analogous to the principles of reason which unify our knowledge? Leibniz first proclaims a universal principle, namely, that everything must be directed towards the general good. This supreme norm is articulated by three more particular principles which Leibniz borrowed from the Roman lawyers and which correspond to the traditional three degrees of justice. The first, expressing strict law, is: *Neminem laedere*—to harm no one; the second, expressing equity, is: *Suum cuique tribuere*—to grant to each what is his; finally, the highest degree, called piety by Leibniz, is the expression not of particular but of universal justice, or as we should rather call it, of morality, and runs: *Honeste vivere*—to live honestly.[1]

What is common to these principles is that they are purely formal and not substantive, just as truths of reason grasp only the order of things, not their substance. They do not suggest, therefore, any concrete decisions to be taken in individual cases. Here, too, the analogy with formal science is complete, since material laws of nature, constants, for instance, are not deducible from logical and mathematical principles. And if the common aim of these principles of justice is to direct human actions toward the general good, they fail to teach us what the general good is. Leibniz tried to elaborate on these principles by defining justice as the conduct of the *vir bonus*. This, however, by no means renders easier unequivocal decisions, since every civilization produces a different ideal type of *vir bonus*.

A closer analysis of the principles of justice, however, shows that their function is not at all to determine human actions directly and immediately, but to serve as regulative principles for the legislation and government of civilized communities. Here again there is a striking analogy to the truths of reason. These truths, indeed, neither serve nor suffice to determine facts, but only to create a method leading towards comprehending facts in one single and consistent system of knowledge. The principle of contradiction, for instance, prescribes the admission of a proposition into the scientific system or its exclusion therefrom, but not its discovery. The same is true of the social system. If, and in so far as, its legislation and government do not comply with the principles of justice, they must be rejected. For then this society is not a lawful community, but only a *de facto* association, not distinguishable from the well-organized gangster-band bound merely by egoistic interests and fear.

Truths of reason, Leibniz stated, are those the contrary of which implies self-contradiction. Should it not be possible be formulate a similar definition for the principles of justice? The analogy seems to be unquestionable. Can a system of law or a govern-

---

[1] *Codicis Juris Gentium Praefatio* (*Werke,* ed. Onno Klopp, VI, 457 sq.); *Mittheilungen aus Leibnizens ungedruckten Schriften,* ed. Mollat, 5, 8, etc.

ment be conceived, constituted by principles diametrically opposed to those Leibniz considered the axioms of justice? Can we imagine a genuine civilization reposing on the principle that everyone ought to harm everyone else or to refuse every man what is his? Such a civilization would necessarily involve a moral obligation to dishonesty. It would consider it honest to be dishonest, virtuous to be without virtue, and pious to be impious. A more obvious contradiction can hardly be imagined.

True, the determination of an unjust injury or the criterion of property is variable, just as is the criterion of honesty and piety. This variability, however, by no means destroys the value of the principles, the less so since the same applies to the truths of reason. Two and two are four, whatever may be the nature and reality of the objects counted. Two unicorns and two unicorns are four unicorns, even though none may ever have existed, and it is certainly not the business of arithmetic to decide upon this issue. Just as the power of the truths of reason appears most conspicuously where they have been neglected, from the very absurdity of the result, so also is the power of the sovereign idea of justice evinced in the very cases in which it is most flagrantly violated. Never, indeed, in the course of history has might destroyed right without veiling its misdeed behind a mask of sham reason and sham justice. Often a pseudo-principle of justice has been evoked in order to cloak the worst kinds of violence in the guise of justice.

Leibniz frequently defined justice as *caritas sapientis,* the charity or benevolence of the wise. It is, indeed, inconceivable that injustice could conform to universal reason wherein the wise participates, since "by obeying reason one carries out the orders of Supreme Reason." [2] The harmony between reason and justice is thereby proven complete, and justice is nothing else but "what complies with wisdom and goodness joined together." [3] These two inseparable ideas thus define the general aim of civilization as well as the duty of anyone wishing to participate in it. By fulfilling this duty, that is, by following reason and justice, man actually is made to God's likeness. "Indeed," wrote Leibniz, "His goodness and justice as well as His wisdom are different from ours only because they are infinitely more perfect." [4]

[2] *Philosophische Schriften,* ed. Gerhardt, VI, 27.
[3] Ed. Mollat, 48.
[4] Ed. Gerhardt, VI, 51.

How can these principles apply to the organization of social life? Again the analogy to the truths of reason may provide a clue. Just as every true proposition must be capable of figuring in one and the same consistent system of knowledge, so also there can be no irreconcilable conflict between individuals and communities, nations, churches, or classes, in so far as they are inspired by the universal ideas of reason and justice. The use of brute force, constraint, and persecution exercised for the purpose of fighting adverse doctrines and convictions is, therefore, always an infallible symptom of a defection from reason and justice.

These are the principles which Leibniz, even in his adolescence, indefatigably attempted to apply to the conflicts which had provoked the Thirty Years' War. Wherever he turned, he observed moral and material devastation, the aftermath of the conflict, which the Peace of Westphalia had not succeeded in eliminating. The main ideological struggle was that between the Roman Catholic and Protestant Churches, together with the dissension of the Protestant Churches themselves, Lutheran and Calvinist, the latter evincing at times more violent bitterness than the hatred both entertained for the common enemy. From his twentieth year to his death, Leibniz devoted himself to reconciling the churches. The history of these attempts at reunion and union has often been written, though much important material still remains unpublished.

The principles, however, which inspired his activity in this direction have hardly ever been clarified. Since each denomination and each of the many Christian sects conceived itself as the genuine depository of the true Christian religion, and since reason and justice exclude the possibility of there being more than one, the problem arose as to whether the apparent divergencies dividing the several doctrines really existed, and if so, whether they were fundamental and barred the union of all believers in one single and oecumenic community. Now, what instrument would be of more avail for the purpose of resolving this problem than reason which participates in Supreme Reason? and what norm would be more competent to rule relations among the Churches than the idea of justice, derived from divine goodness? Rational analysis thus became in fact the method to which Leibniz subjected the principal divergencies of the Christian denominations. And he reached the conclusion that the doctrinal antagonisms were only quarrels about words, and that wherever genuine dogmatic differences existed, they were not fundamental and did not present any real obstacle to reconciliation. Just as the Roman Catholic Church, without prejudice to its unity, embraced doctrines as divergent as those of Saint Augustine and Aquinas, oecumenic Christian unity would not necessarily demand complete uniformity of doctrines.

Here again the idea of monads may be applied. Each of the Churches represents the same divine institution, though each represents it from a different viewpoint. Schisms are, therefore, contrary to reason. And the effect they have had—religious wars and the bloody persecutions of heretics and non-conformists—are also contrary to justice, divine as well as human. "I believe," wrote Leibniz to Father Des Bosses,[5] "that persecutions of doctrines which do not instigate crime are the worst of all things, and that one should not only abstain from such persecutions, but strive to make them execrated by those over whom we have some authority. It is permissible to refuse honors and advantages to which they are not entitled to those who abet doctrines we deem harmful. But I do not think it permissible to confiscate their property, and still less to use rigor against them, by means of proscriptions, chains, the galleys, and evils still worse. Is this not, indeed, a species of violence which one could not escape but by a crime, to wit, by forswearing what one believes to be true? The greater a man's value the more he will suffer under this tyranny."

The reconciliation of the Christian Churches demanded by reason and justice thus seemed to Leibniz an indispensable condition for the pacification of Europe. Unfortunately for us, the antagonism between ideologies which engenders cataclysms merely suffers changes of form. If religious wars, since the American and the French Revolutions, have become obsolete, wars under some other ideological pretext have not been suppressed by the decay of religious passions. However, everything Leibniz denounced as unreasonable and unjust in those religious struggles holds still more strongly for the ideological divergencies which have replaced them. The new credos, be they economic, philosophic, national, or what not do not even share the incomparably higher dignity of religious ideals or the legitimate claim to universality naturally inherent in them. Whatever the ideological motives for

<hr>

[5] Ed. Gerhardt, II, 337 (Original text in Latin).

the recourse to brute force, the universal ideas of reason and justice reject them *a priori* as incompatible with genuine civilization.

Such are the reasons which moved Leibniz to execrate war between civilized nations. "War," he wrote,[6] "is the state where one avows the intention of fighting by force for the purpose of obtaining something. If we could believe that God always grants victory to the just cause, war would be an appeal to divine judgment or a kind of decision by lot. God, however, for other and stronger reasons, allows the unjust cause the greater weight. This is why an appeal to divine judgment amounts to tempting God, just as if one wanted to test whether there is a God or whether He is just, starting from the erroneous conviction that God cannot allow evil." More than a hundred years later, Fichte used the same argument, stating that "war would be a safe and perfectly legitimate means of securing lawfulness in international relations if one could only find a means of always assuring victory to the defendant of the just cause."[7] To prevent the victory of a nation which seeks to violate justice in international relations or at least to render such a victory more difficult and less probable—is this not one of the main objectives of the United Nations Organization?

What did Leibniz think of the possibility of such an international organization? He shared the opinion of Hobbes that in the state of nature man is a wolf to his fellow-man. What has ended the war of all against all and given birth to civil society organized in the State is civilization, that is, the reign of law, which, following the elementary principles already pointed out, forbids the commission of harm against anyone, guarantees everyone the possession of what is his, and aims at the common good. Thus the state is called upon to be the framework of any civilization, provided it is based on the idea of justice. "The aim of political science with respect to the doctrine concerning the forms of government," wrote Leibniz,[8] "ought to be to promote the flourishing of the authority of reason. . . . Arbitrary power is the form of government directly opposed to the authority of reason." It would, indeed, be absurd and blasphemous to exempt a despot from the laws of justice and reason, to which, according to Leibniz,

[6] *Opuscules,* ed. Couturat, 507 (Latin).

[7] *Grundlage des Naturrechts* (1797), II, 260 (German).

[8] Ed. Gerhardt, III, 277 (French).

God Himself is subject as the Creator and Supreme Governor of the world.

Leibniz was perfectly conscious of the dangers involved in autocracy, and he stated that frequently the insomnia of a prince and his resultant bad temper have provoked decisions bringing death to thousands of human beings.[9] However, just as Leibniz was opposed to any form of despotism, so was he also opposed to granting arbitrary freedom to the citizens. "True liberty," he wrote,[10] "is one of the greatest jewels of human nature, but comes after reason. Liberty, indeed, should be nothing else but the capacity of following reason." Since one and the same reason is called to direct the legislation and the government of a State as well as the conduct of every citizen, no legitimate conflict can arise between just law and reasonable liberty.

Still more than between men in the state of nature is war the natural relation between States, so much so that, as Leibniz wrote, peace between the Powers is only like the intermission in a fight between gladiators when they get a breathing spell.[11] This means that in the state of nature peace between the nations is not a rule of law, but only a *de facto* state without guarantee of duration and without sanction against infractions. However, Leibniz declared,[12] "just as, when the state is established by men who have not before been bound by obligations, each one binds himself by a common tie, so also several sovereign powers may accept a common tie as if they were as many free persons, be it by law, or by a declaration of their will, or by custom." What Leibniz proposed here was in the nature of a covenant or social contract between nations, and the idea which inspired him was the analogy between isolated states and isolated individuals. Just as the relations between the citizens of one and the same state are not ruled by arbitrary force, but by positive law, so also the relations of the states among themselves may be governed by a system of positive law, subject, like the positive law of the state, to the principles of reason and justice. By this means Leibniz attempted to overcome the conflict, still acute today, between the idea of national sovereignty and the idea of international law. Since national

[9] *Cod. Jur. Gent. Praefatio.*

[10] Ed. Gerhardt, III, 278 (French).

[11] *Cod. Jur. Gent. Praefatio.*

[12] *Opera*, ed. Dutens, IV, 270 sq. (Latin).

sovereignty is a legitimate claim only in so far as it respects the ideas of reason and justice, and since these same ideas ought to control international law, no justifiable antagonism between the two systems seemed possible.

The execution of any general plan for the pacification of the world may proceed along two different paths, analytically or synthetically, as it were. One may first elaborate on what, at a given point of time, international relations actually imply as reciprocal obligations, either in the form of treaties or of usage. One may, on the other hand, strive to establish a universal organization of civilized states ruled by a constitutional charter which would determine the lawful working of this society of nations. Leibniz devoted himself mainly to the former task, a task for the historian and jurist. But, as will soon appear, he by no means neglected the problem of political synthesis. The assiduous work he devoted in the first direction produced his *Codex Juris Gentium Diplomaticus* of 1693, followed, in 1700, by a supplement, the *Mantissa*. They contain a compilation of the most important international treaties, pacts, and other documents beginning with the 11th century which evince the existence of certain rules of international law established and accepted *via facti*.

But, disregarding the historical interest presented by such a collection, does it prove anything with regard to international law? Most of these pacts were not abrogated by agreement of the contracting parties, but died a violent death. Far from testifying to the value of international law, this graveyard of broken engagements seems an impressive monument to the powerlessness of law in international relations. Whereas agreements between private persons are guaranteed execution by positive law, pacts between sovereign states seem to be valid only so long as the stronger stipulator so desires it. This, of course, is a fact it would be absurd to deny. However, as Grotius had already pointed out, a right without coercive power is not thereby rendered ineffective. The absence of power capable of enforcing respect for international obligations does not destroy international law any more than an unpunished crime destroys penal law.

Logically, the voluntary conclusion of treaties between sovereign states doubtless implies recognition of at least that international law which imposes strict compliance and qualifies the breach of stipulated engagements as unlawful and unjust acts. The prin-

ciple qualifying such infractions as unjust derives directly from
the first principles of justice proposed by Leibniz. What could
be more obviously contrary to the *suum cuique tribuere* than not
to grant to a state possession of what has been voluntarily
recognized by a pact as legally belonging to it? Or what could be
more strikingly contrary to the *neminem laedere* than to inflict
upon a state an evil to abstain from which the contracting partner
has expressly engaged himself?

The first commandment of international law and the basis of
all others is therefore, according to Leibniz, the faithful observance of treaties. In the preface to the *Codex* he violently attacked
those Powers which, as he says, play with treaties as children with
nuts. He does not admit that alleged obligations of honor may
justify or even excuse violations of the given word. "All obligations of law," he wrote,[13] "are also obligations of honor, above all
those which derive from the pledged word: it is dishonest to violate
them even if one may sometimes have excuses which would be
valid if taken in the strict sense, but which are suitable for lawyers
rather than princes. Honest people, the world at large, posterity,
and our own conscience are not always satisfied with what may
be valid in the courts." And in another passage Leibniz expressly
and sarcastically opposed the widespread abuse of allowing considerations of prestige to prevail over considerations of justice.[14]

Pufendorf was therefore wrong, according to Leibniz, in denying that nations could create international law by their agreements, and in basing his denial on the absence of any superior
power capable of enforcing the obligations deriving from these
pacts.[15] Those, indeed, wrote Leibniz,[16] "who base all obligations
on constraint and consequently take power for the standard of
law," fall back on "the concept implied by that tyrannical definition of Plato's Thrasymachus, who said that justice is nothing but
what pleases the most powerful."

The historical development of international relations embodied
in pacts and alliances thus necessarily implies the recognition of
international law founded on the idea of justice. Any violation
of this law consequently appears as a heinous offense against jus-

[13] Ed. Klopp, V, 253 (French).
[14] Ed. Gerhardt, VII, 509.
[15] Ed. Dutens, IV/3, 275.
[16] Ed. Gerhardt, VI, 35.

tice. These considerations lead to the proscription of war as a means of international policy. They demand that the most energetic and tenacious efforts of the peace-loving nations be directed towards creating an efficient organization for the observation of treaties. This observation should not merely comply with their always ambiguous texts, but with the spirit of reason and justice, which is the unique source of their strength. Loyalty thus becomes the capital virtue of statesmen. "To preach love of peace," wrote Leibniz,[17] "when one makes others feel all the effects of war, to refuse the allegation of rights, to refuse to consider modifications, to dictate equivalences and strict conditions; not to tolerate precautions taken by others in making alliances or levying troops, openly to mock the given word, to pretend such reasons as one is wont to invent for putting off simple and stupid persons when desiring to ridicule them, to add chicanery to violence and insult to spoils—these are traits a thousand times worse even than ruin."

While abhorring war and considering it not merely impious, but even inept,[18] Leibniz did not neglect the necessity of taking precautionary measures against a neighbor whose policy might not be inspired by the ideas constituting civilization. He by no means adopted the absolute pacifism of non-resistance to evil, but, on the contrary, insisted on the duty of being strong and contributing all sacrifices necessary to one's efficient defense against unjust aggression. Nor would he have agreed to a policy of appeasement and expediency. "By concessions and disgraceful submissions," he wrote,[19] "minds will become more and more intimidated and depressed; they will eventually lose their sensitivity, become callous to maltreatment and accustomed to patience. It will seem as if this had to be so owing to a decree of fate. Finally, all will travel the road to serfdom."

Leibniz even concerned himself with the technical and organizational details of mobilization and armament necessary to the safeguarding of liberty and law against warlike nations, and he violently attacked the use of inhuman arms, specifically bombs, that "result of human ingenuity for inventing new evils," which within "a small cone carry the force of an earthquake and in a few hours destroy the work of centuries." [20]

[17] Ed. Klopp, V, 254 (French).   [18] *Ibid.*, II, 221.

[19] *Ibid.*, V, 255 (French).

[20] *In Bombos Epigramma*, ed. Klopp, V, 636.

As already pointed out, Leibniz, while particularly concerned with the analytical methods of developing international law, did not neglect the pacification of the world by synthetic means, that is, by the creation of an international organization of civilized nations. Thus, when asked his advice on the *"Projet pour rendre la Paix perpétuelle en Europe"* of the Abbé Castel de St. Pierre, he agreed in principle to its proposals. "It is very certain," he wrote,[21] "that if men wanted to, they could free themselves from those three great scourges: war, pestilence, and famine. As to the two latter, any sovereign could do it. But against war an agreement of the sovereigns would be necessary, which it is difficult to obtain."

Sectarianism under whatever name, so much execrated by Leibniz, he rightly expected to oppose itself to the realization of this aim; sectarianism, which, as he wrote,[22] "consists in insisting that others rule their conduct by our maxims, while we should be satisfied with seeing that all approach the principal aim." This principal aim is not the welfare of one nation, one class, or one race gained at the expense of all others, it is not the hegemony of any one people believing themselves called upon to rule the world, it is the welfare of mankind. "Provided something of consequence is achieved," he wrote to a French friend,[23] "it is indifferent to me whether it originates in Germany or in France, for I desire the welfare of mankind; I am neither a philhellene nor a philoroman, but a philanthropist." And in a letter to Count Golofkin, chancelor to Czar Peter the Great, he declared: "I do not discriminate against any one nation or party, and I would prefer to see the sciences rendered flourishing in Russa, to seeing them poorly cultivated in Germany. The countries where they prosper best will be the most dear to me, since the whole human race will always profit therefrom, and the real treasures of the human race will thereby be increased. The real treasures of mankind are the arts and the sciences. They distinguish man from beast and cultivated peoples from barbarians."[24]

These are but a few quotations illustrating how Leibniz applied his fundamental ideas to what we may call the rationalization of international relations. They will suffice, I hope, to prove that

[21] Ed. Gerhardt, III, 637 (French).

[22] Ed. Dutens, I, 470 (French).

[23] Ed. Gerhardt, VII, 456 (French).

[24] *Oeuvres,* ed. Foucher de Careil, VII, 503 (French).

Leibniz's ideas were by no means the more or less utopian dreams and illusions of a doctrinaire spirit alien to the realities of the world. Leibniz's thought was, on the contrary, thoroughly realistic. But the reality he envisaged was not confined within the horizon of those narrow-minded politicians whose reach does not stretch far beyond what their eyes can see and their hands can grasp.

Leibniz's hope of promoting the establishment of international law designed to rule the relations of nations, analogous to the law that rules the relations of the citizens of one and the same civilized state—this hope rested on the universality of his ideas of reason and justice. The international law he strove for aimed at actualizing the community of mankind without impairing the liberty of the many individual nations to cultivate their particular civilizations. Leibniz knew very well that this task could not be carried out in one generation, or in one century. But he was also convinced that every action complying with the laws of reason and justice would contribute, be it but to an infinitesimal degree, to approaching the aim. In one of his letters to the Landgraf Ernst of Hesse-Rheinfels he presented this paraphrase of an old Latin adage: *Labora diligenter, semper aliquid haeret*— Work diligently, something of it will always remain.

The history of civilization is, of course, no continuous progress, and sporadic relapses into barbarism may always be expected to occur. The spiritual forces of mankind are, indeed, limited and rather quickly exhausted. However, in order to crush civilization it would be necessary, said Leibniz,[25] "for all functions and the entire authority to be in the hands of military men who would have to be barbarians, enemies of science, and who would have to set out to destroy intellectuals as the disturbers of public peace." An alliance of militarism and anti-intellectualism, this is what Leibniz considered the deadly enemy of civilization.

Our own epoch presents in this respect a state of mind very similar to that which, near the end of his life, moved Leibniz to this pathetic complaint: "It is the misfortune of mankind to be finally disgusted with reason itself and weary of light. Chimeras begin to return and to please because they have something mysterious."[26] How many chimerical mysticisms, irrationalisms,

[25] Ed. Gerhardt, VII, 162 (French).
[26] *Ibid.*, VII, 417 (French).

and charlatanisms disguised as science have we seen reborn, which we believed definitively conjured away by the progress of civilization? However, all such set-backs were incapable of affecting Leibniz's optimism, so often mocked at and so rarely understood. What, indeed, could be more optimistic than his conception of a world in which only very few things are apparently conformable to reason and to justice, but which tends naturally to carry out those supreme ideas in all the walks of civilization? His optimism was never seriously shaken, despite all the blows his conciliatory and pacificatory attempts suffered time and again in all the fields of his activity. His perseverance found the most simple and also the most pathetic expression in the passage of a letter he wrote an old friend after a renewed, seemingly final, defeat of his project for the union of the churches: *"Ipsa se res aliquando conficiet"*—Some day the thing will by itself break into reality.[27]

New School for Social Research.

[27] *Epistolae ad diversos,* ed. Kortholt, I. 124.

X

LOCKE'S NATURAL LAW AND
THE FOUNDATION OF POLITICS

By M. Seliger

The belief that politics can and must be guided by injunctions of reason has been persistently maintained by natural law theorists, during decisive phases of the development of political thought. It is proposed to show that the inner consistency of Locke's natural law doctrine lies in its vindication of a specific conception of the political process, and of popular participation in it, held to be in accord with reason and with the different abilities of men to ascertain and apply generally valid dictates of reason. A re-interpretation of Locke's conception of natural law from this point of view seems to be in order.

It is almost generally agreed that in Locke's conception of natural law theorems of utility coexist with traditional norms of perfection and virtue.[1] Disagreement exists as regards the contention that Locke surreptitiously followed Hobbes, intimating by way of contradictions in his writings that he regarded as ineffective the traditional hierarchy of ends to which traditional natural law teaching, pagan and Christian, stands committed.[2] What appears to be contradictory in Locke's statements on natural law, however, does not necessarily bear upon the question of whether utilitarian theorems and traditional norms are compatible with each other, or whether the former are easier to apprehend than the latter. In the first place, political theories do not necessarily differ in their conception of human nature, and of the requirements of political organization, because they differ in the nature

---

[1] See L. Stephen, *English Thought in the Eighteenth Century*, 2 vols. (3rd ed., London, 1902), II, 135–41; S. P. Lamprecht, *The Moral and Political Philosophy of John Locke* (New York, 1918), 9, 30, 39, 81f.; C. E. Vaughan, *Studies in the History of Political Philosophy before and after Rousseau*, 2 vols. (new ed., Manchester, 1939), I, 140, 170, 181; W. Kendall, "John Locke and the Doctrine of Majority-Rule," *Illinois Studies in the Social Sciences*, XXVI, 2 (1941), 68f.; W. Simon, "John Locke and Political Theory," *American Political Science Review*. XLV (1951), 386–8f.; J. W. Gough, *John Locke's Political Philosophy* (repr. Oxford, 1956), 19f., 22, 114; R. I. Aaron, *John Locke* (2nd ed., Oxford, 1955), 256f.; R. Polin, *La Politique Morale de John Locke* (Paris, 1960), 53f., 81f., 92, 113f., 119–20, 126; H. Moulds, "John Locke's Four Freedoms in a New Light," *Ethics*, LXXI, 2 (1961), 122–3; R. Singh, "John Locke and the Theory of Natural Law," *Political Studies* (June 1961), 114. Cf. H. R. F. Bourne, *The Life of John Locke*, 2 vols. (London, 1867), II, 64.

[2] This has been maintained with unrivalled brillance by Leo Strauss, *Natural Right and History* (2nd impr., Chicago, 1957). Even if one cannot go the whole way with Prof. Strauss, it is his indisputable merit to have put the utilitarian elements in Locke's conception into the sharpest possible relief and in this way to have raised problems of interpretation of which one might otherwise have remained unaware. The present writer readily admits his indebtedness in this respect. Special thanks are due to Mr. Maurice Cranston and Mr. Peter Laslett for their encouragement and helpful criticism.

of their ethical premises. Hobbes denied what Plato had affirmed, and traditional natural law theorists had continued to maintain, namely that absolute norms of virtue ought to have precedence over rationalized needs of convenient self-preservation. Yet, both Plato and Hobbes were agreed in so far that they were sceptical of human nature. According to Plato, ordinary men cannot become really virtuous; while for Hobbes, virtue by itself appears to have little, if any, relevance for men. The two philosophers were sufficiently united by their scepticism to advocate the imposition of standards of political behavior by authoritarian rule. In this respect Plato, Machiavelli, and Hobbes were as much at one as they were different from Aristotle and Locke. Yet, in their conception of ethics, Plato and Aristotle had as much in common as had Machiavelli and Hobbes.[3]

Evidently, the significance of ethical premises for political theories must be judged in the light of the forms of political organization and the nature of the political rights and obligations which are advocated. For the correspondence between moral contents and the forms of political action, though far from being immaterial,[4] shows itself to be highly equivocal in systems of thought. The complexity of this relationship is further enhanced, since conflicting moral and political maxims have often been derived from identical theological and metaphysical premises, just as similar moral and political maxims have been based upon divergent theological and metaphysical premises.[5]

Secondly, in theories concerned with the political realization of ethical principles, the mutual exclusiveness of motives and rules of conduct associated with different ethical premises has seldom been fully maintained. This might even be said of Hobbes. As J. S. Mill's humane utilitarianism shows, the reliance upon the eventually assured harmony of individual interests is not divorced from the imperative of human perfectibility and dignity in its own right. In traditional natural law theories, considerations of convenience and individual happiness were subjected to absolute norms of perfection. In their purity, however, such norms were to serve only for passing judgment. For purposes of civic action they are necessarily diluted by conventional right.[6] Indeed, Plato did not stipulate that the best state could come about, or even function, with a total disregard for conventional motives and rules of conduct. The greater part of the city, from whom a measure of consent is also to be obtained, cannot

[3] See also below text to notes 47–50.

[4] Cf. N. Rotenstreich, "Rule by Majority or by Principles," *Social Research*, XXII, 4 (1954), 411–27.

[5] As regards Locke, see for instance J. W. Yolton, *John Locke and the Way of Ideas* (Oxford, 1956), vi, 13 and *passim*, and introduction to his edition of Locke's *An Essay Concerning Human Understanding*, 2 vols. (Everyman's Library, 1961), I, ix–x.　　　　　　　　　　　　　　　　　　[6] Strauss, *op. cit.*, 146, 152–3, 165.

shake off its utilitarian standards. In fact it must live by them in order to enable the guardians to fulfill their function. The Platonic division of labor depends as much upon the effectiveness of the lower rated as of the higher rated motives and norms of behavior.

Thirdly, although post-Lockean utilitarianism and idealism dispensed more and more with the notion of natural law, they preserved with varying emphases a belief that political life cannot be ordered without reference to rational standards. As Green said, so far as the institutions of civil life operate as "giving reality to these capacities of will and reason and enabling them to be really exercised . . . they may be said to correspond to the 'law of nature' . . . according to the only sense in which that phrase can be intelligibly used." [7] In utilitarian theories men's desires and interests, while thought to be by themselves the criterion of eventual harmony, nevertheless necessitate the mediation of reason for the attainment of the greatest possible happiness of all. In other words, dictates of reason are reverted to in order to restrict human arbitrariness irrespective of whether human motives and ends are predicated on men's personal desires and interests or are subjected to an objective teleological order. In both instances dictates of reason have an identical function. Justice is effected through a rational reconciliation of interests. The contents of what such dictates enjoin often differs according to the motivational and teleological nature of the underlying ethics. But there is also some fundamental correspondence in what variously based dictates of reason are held to enjoin. Both utilitarian and idealist political theories acknowledge—though on different grounds—the necessity of political organization; nor do they differ in all that men must and must not do in order to maintain it.

Indeed, Locke's reliance upon reason is not questioned when it is maintained that he intended to insinuate that natural law in the traditional sense cannot be known by, and hence does not exist for, mortals.[8] If no more were conceded than that, it could be agreed that

[7] T. H. Green, *Lectures on the Principles of Political Obligation* (new impr., London, 1959), sec. 7.

[8] Straus, *op. cit.*, 203–4, 209, 212, 217, 219–22, 226–8; and "Locke's Doctrine of Natural Law," *American Political Science Review*, LII, (1958), 490, 492, 493, 496, 500, where Strauss argues that this was Locke's esoteric intention, against von Leyden, who explains contradictions as a change of mind on the part of Locke (W. von Leyden, *John Locke, Essays on the Law of Nature* [Oxford, 1954], 52, 132, 198). R. H. Cox, *Locke on War and Peace* (Oxford, 1960), 35f., 52f., 75f., 85f., 111, 117, has elaborated upon Strauss' thesis and revealed the inexactness of Locke's references to biblical and other accepted authorities. These are regarded as premeditated and intended to indicate Locke's acceptance of a thoroughly naturalistic political construct of self-preservation. A. P. Brogan, "John Locke and Utilitarianism," *Ethics*, LXIX, 2 (1959), allows neither for contradictions between traditional and utilitarian ethics, nor for the coexistence of both in Locke's *Essay* and his political writings (83–4, 86, 90–1). He regards these as consistently following the explanation

the question of the knowability and applicability of dictates of reason is, to some extent, detachable from the controversy as to Locke's attitude towards traditional natural law. At any rate in this way the consensus as to the central function of dictates of reason in Locke's system is maintained. Yet, in fairness it must be said that, indirectly at least, it is also admitted that, in what they enjoin, dictates of reason in Locke's doctrine and in traditional natural law correspond to some extent with each other.[9]

Lastly, whatever view one takes of the extent to which the strands of Locke's philosophical work are consistent with each other,[10] one has to bear in mind that the mature Locke refrained from a full exposition and logical examination of the concept of natural law in his philosophical *Essay*.[11] In the latter, natural law is scarcely mentioned. The opposite is true, however, of his political *Treatises*. In the *Second Treatise*, in which Locke's political doctrine is fully developed, he stated that it is "besides my present purpose, to enter here into the particulars of the law of nature"; [12] yet he referred to it time and time again in order to demonstrate what men may and are able to do to make political life conformable with injunctions of reason. Accordingly, one may conclude that Locke thought that his natural law concept did not need further epistemological elaboration to serve as a major premise of his political theory.[13] There is thus a particular reason why the distinctive feature of Locke's natural law teaching lies less in a concern with the question of the compatibility of theorems of utility and traditional norms than in the purpose of justifying a competitive diffusion of political authority.

of voluntary action in both egoistic and hedonistic terms; that is, as in Hobbes and the utilitarians of the XVIIIth century (82f.). Brogan admits only that this cannot be said of the earlier *Essays on the Law of Nature* and the later *Reasonableness of Christianity* (87–90).

[9] See below, text to notes 29–30 and 46.

[10] Polin, *op. cit.*, esp. 97, 115 and Singh, *loc. cit.*, argue in favor of the unity underlying all Locke's works. So does Strauss for a different interpretative purpose. See text to note 29. M. Cranston, *John Locke, A Biography* (London, 1957), 208, stresses the non-philosophical character of the *Treatises*. P. Laslett, *Locke's Two Treatises of Government* (Cambridge, 1960), 80, is also of the view that the *Treatises* are no extension of Locke's general philosophy into the field of politics, but agrees that this may be overstating the case (89).

[11] See von Leyden, *op. cit.*, 59–60, 73f., 75–7, 80, and "John Locke and Natural Law," *Philosophy*, XXI (1956), 27, 34 for a criticism of Locke's natural law concept and the latter's undiminished faith in natural law as providing an absolute basis for moral and political obligation. Similarly, J. W. Yolton, "Locke and the Law of Nature," *Philosophical Review*, LXVII (1958), 487–8; and Kendall, *op. cit.*, 76f., 81.

[12] Sec. 12. All quotations are from the *Second Treatise*, unless otherwise stated. The text is that of Laslett's edition but quotations are rendered in modernized English. All italics are mine. [13] Cf. von Leyden, *op. cit.*, 80f.

On Locke's terms, the only manner in which ordinary men can bring their political judgment to bear directly on the management of political society is by way of revolt.[14] Since revolt is justified by natural law, the appeal to heaven—which involves an appeal to arms —is not merely a matter of will but of right. "He that appeals to heaven must be sure he has a right on his side," since he is accountable—like, we may add, the monarch by divine right in conducting government—to "a tribunal that cannot be deceived." [15] The question is, how sure can ordinary men be that they have a right on their side? Locke's statements provide not only a positive but also a rather negative answer to this question.

According to one aspect of Locke's statements, it ought not to be difficult for ordinary men to know when they have a right and hence reason on their side. Locke said that natural law was plain—even plainer than positive law—to rational creatures.[16] He postulated, and assumed as given, the possession of reason as a condition for being under the obligation of natural law or any other proper law.[17] Man is born free and rational and "age that brings one, brings with it the other too." [18] However, while men have equal natural rights, they are not equally endowed by nature. Men, as "creatures of the same species and rank promiscuously born to all the same advantages of nature, and the use of the same faculties, *should* also be equal one amongst another." [19] Equality is a moral postulate. Natural equality is "the foundation of that *obligation* to mutual love" upon which are built "the *duties* they owe one another," and from whence are derived "the great maxims of justice and charity." [20] This the law of nature, which is reason, "teaches all mankind who will but consult it." [21]

---

[14] What is said on revolution in the present article will be demonstrated in detail in another chapter of my forthcoming study on *The Liberal Politics of John Locke*.

[15] Sec. 176.   [16] Secs. 12 and 124. Similarly Secs. 6 and 11.

[17] Secs. 57, 58, 60, 63, 98.

[18] Sec. 61 and Secs. 87, 95 and 170. Cox, *op. cit.*, 80, note 7, quotes ". . . we are born free as we are born rational, not that we have actually the exercise of either." To omit what immediately follows, namely "age that brings one, brings with it the other too," is hardly a convincing way to demonstrate that Locke never explicitly says, but leads one only to believe that he says, that natural law can be known by reason. See below note 22.

[19] Sec. 4. Cf. Laslett, *op. cit.*, 287, on the reading of "should" "as imperative in feeling" and the additional evidence adduced for Locke's recognition of the inequality of capacities. However, Laslett does not suggest how to reconcile this cogent comment with his assertion (*ibid.*, 96) that the *Second Treatise* contains nothing to support a theory of differential rationality. Similarly Polin, who admits that Locke addressed an elite which by its rationality merits alone the name of man (*op. cit.*, 91), denies that Locke distinguished among classes according to rationality and income (273).

[20] Sec. 5.   [21] Sec. 6.

Evidently, not all mankind does consult what reason enjoins, nor can men do so equally well. Though born to use the same faculties, men do not invariably nor equally make use of reason, and hence of their physical endowments.

The unequal use of both mental and physical capacities is persistently reckoned with, even in Locke's idyllic picture of the state of nature in the second chapter, which deals extensively with the right to punish offenders so "that all men may be restrained from invading other's rights," as well as with the right to secure reparations.[22] Consequently, Locke directed the absolute imperative inherent in natural equality against that subordination which "may authorise us to destroy one another, as if we were made for one another's uses, as the inferior ranks of creatures are for ours." [23] Far from giving cause to misinterpret his statements on natural equality, Locke referred back to them in explaining that "I cannot be supposed to understand all sorts of equality." Hence it is consistent with natural equality—i.e., with equally binding mutual obligations and duties—that "age or virtue may give men a just precedence; excellency of parts and merits may place others above the common level; birth may subject some, and alliance and benefits others, to pay observance to those whom nature, gratitude or other respects have made it due." [24] There are, then, no more contradictions and ambiguity in Locke's views of natural equality than in any egalitarian argument which is not absolute, i.e. not chimerical. Nature having provided the same advantages to all, has provided at the same time for the differential use of these advantages. Hence also the justifiable precedence of "the industrious and rational" as regards the acquisition of property.[25]

[22] Secs. 7 and 8–12. Cox, *op. cit.*, 77, 79, maintains that in order to convey that men in truly natural conditions cannot know natural law, Locke used the device of a "progressive and systematic alteration" of what he says in this respect and of a parallel reversal of the statements on natural law, the divide being in the middle of the *Treatise*. As to Locke's by no means infrequent references to the negative aspects of the state of nature well before the divide, these are set aside as ambiguous and not of "the essential quality" (note 5 to p. 77 and note 1 to p. 78). Apparently we must say this also of other far from ambiguous statements, as when Locke affirmed the understanding by grown-ups of the rule of reason, "whether, it be the law of nature, or the municipal laws . . . they are to govern themselves by." This statement, in spite of the reversal, occurs well beyond the divide, i. e. in sec. 170. Cox's attempt to resolve the complexity of Locke's statements results in dissolving the logical ground on which Locke could account for the emergence of political society. Compare, for instance, what Cox says on pp. 88–9, 209, and 94 with his interpretation (93,102). A similarly gratuitous quandary follows from Macpherson's interpretation. See note 25.

[23] Sec. 6. *First Treatises*, Secs. 35–8.   [24] Sec. 54. See also Polin, *op. cit.*, 254.

[25] Sec. 54. See also Strauss, *op. cit.*, 233. C. B. Macpherson, "The Social Bearing of Locke's Political Theory," *Western Political Quarterly*, VII, 1 (1954), 15, 18, regards Locke's views on equality as conflicting and ambiguous. Setting aside his

Thus, not everybody is, or can be, "a studier of that law." [26] To know natural law properly is the concern of those who by nature and occupation are more rational than others. But this does not mean that no one else can have a notion of that law; nor that the less rational or irrational must blindly follow the student of natural law. Ordinary people are not unable to distinguish between true and false interpreters of that law. "So plain was it writ in the hearts of all mankind," that its precepts are reflected in deep-set convictions. It is likewise affirmed by the voice of the Scriptures—which "is the voice of reason confirmed by inspiration." [27] To interpret statements like these as pointing to conditions which are non-existent [28] is not only at variance with the language of the text. It also seems to be questionable in respect of the explanation that the non-philosophical presentation of Locke's political doctrine in the *Treatise* accounts for its considerable concessions to scriptural principles. These concessions are made because the greater part of men cannot know but must believe, and hence are best left to be instructed by the precepts of the gospel.[29] But to make such concessions amounts to acknowledging that this form of political education suits the political principles which the *Treatise,* by itself an attempt at political persuasion, sets forth. It follows that, for civic purposes, dictates of reason based on natural laws of self-preservation are not counter-acted by scriptural principles. For it is not maintained that the instruction of the people in scriptural precepts interferes with the ability of the majority to be a better guarantor of individual self-preservation than monarchic and oligarchic rulers; nor with the exercise of the special right of more reasonable men to lead the way towards self-preservation and happiness.[30]

One might, therefore, conclude that Locke had no intention of breaking rigorously with the conception of an immutable law of nature which is fully in accord with reason and partly in accord with

---

earlier hesitation (see "Locke on Capitalist Appropriation," *ibid.,* IV, 4 [1951], 551), Macpherson in his later article (pp. 11, 12, 16, and note 35), maintains unreservedly that Locke regarded rationality as not inherent in man, but socially acquired as the result of different economic positions. Rationality is, therefore, identical with accumulation, and of significance only in relation to it. Locke is thus made to fit the popular Marxist view of a bourgeois philosopher. Macpherson's instructive analysis of Locke's views on property and labor might have been put to better use, had he compared it with Marx's doctrine of the self-alienation of man.

[26] Secs. 6, 12, 124.

[27] Secs. 11, 31 respectively. See also *First Treatise,* Sec. 86. Brogan, *loc. cit.,* 87, does not consider these passages when he maintains that only after having published the *Essay* and the *Treatises* did Locke extol faith as consistent with reason and as suitable for popular use.

[28] Strauss, *op. cit.,* 225.   [29] *Ibid.,* 221.   [30] *Ibid.,* 232–4.

scriptural teachings, despite deviations from the latter.[31] According to such an interpretation it is, therefore, conceded that something of a *tour de force* is implied in the way Locke connected the belief in reason with the belief in Christianity. For the Scriptures, like convictions and common-sense, only confirm the voice of reason; they cannot contradict it but are tested by it. Since the obligations of the law of nature bind even God Almighty,[32] Locke's law of nature would reflect the rational order of the world even if there were no revelation.[33] Yet, Locke made it plain that the ascent from sense data through discursive reasoning, or by direct inference or intuition through the "light of nature," are preferable ways of gaining knowledge of standards of action, but not the only way.[34] To the extent that natural law is not studied, or reason fails men, what natural law implies may still be known through other media, or acknowledged when expounded rationally by the student of natural law.

Clearly, even on the evidence of Locke's positive statement alone, it is going too far to maintain that he regarded the people as the proponent of "the legitimacy and the infallibility of reason itself." Nor can it be said without qualifications that on Locke's showing everybody is authorized to set himself up as an interpreter of natural law, with the consequence that the existence of the state becomes impossible.[35] In any case, Locke's skeptical statements raise the ques-

[31] The deviation is admitted by Yolton, "Locke and the Law of Nature," *loc. cit.*, 484f., and Polin, *op. cit.*, 102f., 117, whereas for Strauss this deviation in the *Treatise* (*op. cit.*, 221), must be evaluated in the light of his conclusion that, according to Locke, a natural law in the proper sense must be known to be given by God and conform in all its parts to the New Testament (214–19, 233).   [32] Sec. 195.

[33] For Strauss, *op. cit.*, 214, this serves only as a provisional definition of Locke's natural law. According to Polin, *op. cit.*, 57, 123, this is the modification in the *Treatise* of the relation between reason and natural law whereby reference to God is not however precluded. Cf. Gough, *op. cit.*, 11–12. In fact in the *Essay* (I, ii, 6), too, Locke said in one instance that the existence of God and obedience to him is "so congruous to the light of reason" that a great part of mankind "give testimony to the law of nature"; while in the other instance (I, iii, 13) natural law is "a law knowable by the light of reason, i.e. without the help of positive revelation."

[34] On intuition as Locke's ideal of knowledge identified by him with reason as well as with the act of knowing, see Aaron, *op. cit.*, 222f. On Locke's prevarications and confusion of issues in this respect, see von Leyden, *Essays*, 59; and "John Locke and Natural Law," *loc. cit.*, 23f., 28. Similarly already Lamprecht, *op. cit.*, 85f.; and also Yolton, *loc. cit.*, 482. On alternative or conjunctive ways of knowing and on the relation between reason and revelation, see Aaron, *op. cit.*, 253, 264–6, 296f., 305; Yolton, "Locke and the Law of Nature," 481–3, 486, 489, 491; Polin, *op. cit.*, 3f., 25, 40f., 55f., 68f., 91f., 117, 121; Simon, *op cit.*, 389f.; Gough, *op. cit.*, 11f., 17; and Laslett, *op. cit.*, 87–8, 92f.

[35] Polin, *op. cit.*, 235, and Vaughan, *op. cit*, 168–170 respectively. Vaughan disregarded the fact that the revolutionary judgment is a collective one and that what he said in favor of the prevalence of the wise few (178) is Locke's own view.

tion whether natural law amounts after all to no more than an arbitrary rationalization of contrivances, the only justification of which lies in that they are consented to. Locke cast serious doubt, if not on the knowability of immutable natural laws, then on their applicability, in pointing to the variety of opinions, the partiality of men and the contrariety of interests, and drawing the conclusion that laws grounded on consent must serve as the standard of right and wrong.[36] It does not follow, however, that Locke intended to grant men unlimited competence to change natural law by agreement.[37] For if men are completely divided by the contrariety of interests and opinions and by partiality, consent to anything is out of the question. This much was already recognized by Hobbes. He distinguished between passions which make for strife and passions which incline to peace, from whence the possibility that "reason suggests convenient articles of peace, upon which men may be drawn to agreement.[38] In exchange for the benefits of political society Hobbesian men agree on articles of peace by which they renounce once and for all the right to dissent collectively from established authority. According to Locke the capacity to reach informed agreement goes further, so that ordinary men can be trusted to retain the right to dissent collectively from established authority—and in accord with natural law at that. Locke therefore thought that recurrent consent—in the form of recurrent dissent from authority—was possible and feasible, men's divisions of interest and opinions notwithstanding. Even if he thought that men are more likely to agree to changes of natural law than to heed it, it does not follow that he regarded the heeding as impossible, and much less that he conceded men the right, as distinct from the capacity, to change natural law by consent.

Thus there is little reason to doubt that, for Locke, the validity of natural law is in principle independent of consent, for not only in his theory of labor and property,[39] but in his *Essays on the Law of*

[36] Secs. 13, 123, 125, 124, respectively. These sections clearly contradict Lamprecht, *op. cit.*, note to p. 135; Vaughan, *op. cit.*, 171; and Gough, *op. cit.*, 34, who refers to R. Niebuhr, ¡*The Children of Light and the Children of Darkness* (1945), 25, as regards the view that Locke thought public and private interests easily reconcilable with each other.

[37] Cf. Kendall, *op. cit.*, 82, 85. This is implied also by Strauss and Cox in so far as Locke is held to have thought it easier for men to be guided by considerations of their temporal happiness than by those of virtue in its own right. According to Macpherson, "On Capitalist Appropriation," *loc. cit.*, 552, 568, the subjection of natural law to consent applies only to property relations. Already Stephen, *op. cit.*, 133–4, had maintained that the compact outshines natural law.

[38] *Leviathan*, ch. 13.

[39] Cf. Ch. H. Monson, "Locke and His Interpreters," *Political Studies*, VI (1958), 126–7.

Nature Locke had rejected the hypothesis that universal consent could be proof of the existence of natural law.[40] Accordingly, in the *Treatise* he omitted any reference to this hypothesis. Instead he emphasized that although by "the law of nature; common to them all . . . mankind are one community," men must "separate from this great and natural community and by positive agreements combine into smaller and divided associations," because of "the corruption and viciousness of degenerate men." [41] It follows that if natural law were fully observed by all men, they would live in one world-community and thus be united by universal consent. This is not to say that all that is universally agreed is, for that reason, in accord with natural law.[42] Conversely, and by the same token, the existence of positive agreements proves no more than the impossibility of universal consent, and not that natural law does not exist or is dependent on consent. Although it is the basis for the realization in society of natural law, consent does not necessarily testify to the observance of natural law. Indeed, since degenerate men seem to be in the majority,[43] it would have been self-defeating to maintain that the greater the number of people who consent to something, the greater is the observance of natural law; exception being made for the hypothetical case when all mankind, and not just the majority, are inclined to live peacefully in one world-community. On principle, consent remains subject to natural law; it is the rightful instrumentality for applying natural law. Men incorporate into political society to establish a legislature for making laws by consent. But the legislature has only as much competence as the law of nature gave men for their preservation and that of mankind.[44]

However, "the first fundamental natural law . . . the preservation of the society and (as far as will consist with the public good) of every person in it," [45] states so vast a generality that an almost unlimited number of derivations can be made from such a law. One might, therefore, object that Locke had saved the superiority of natural law over consent at the price of conceiving the former in such a way as to leave it with little definite meaning as regards the manner of its realization. Evidently, this objection applies to any natural law doctrine, if for no other reason than that the derivation of particular rules in any natural doctrine is a matter of human understanding. For this reason, although in all natural law doctrines

---

[40] Cf. von Leyden, *op. cit.*, 42.   [41] Sec. 128.

[42] As Locke said in the *Essay*, I, iii, 6: "several moral rules may receive from mankind a very general approbation, without either knowing or admitting the true ground of morality."

[43] Sec. 123 as quoted below in text to note 57.   [44] Sec. 135.

[45] Sec. 134. See also, Secs. 16, 123, 128, 129, 149, 159, 168, 220.

an elite is entrusted with leadership, they are acutely aware of the discrepancy between the observed management of civic affairs and the injunctions of natural law. In point of fact, Locke was largely preoccupied with justifying effective ways and means of reducing this discrepancy. He set about this not by detracting from the moral claims of traditional natural law. Locke's first fundamental natural law of self-preservation was meant not to do away with, but by its generality to accommodate, the traditional limitations by which a proper civil society is distinguished from a happy-go-lucky gang of robbers.[46] While in this decisive respect a correspondence of the content and intent of laws of self-preservation and traditional injunctions is thus maintained, the distinctive feature of Locke's natural law teaching emerges in the justification of guarantees against the necessarily defective implementation of generally valid rules. In conformity with his view of ordinary men as capable of having a notion of such rules, Locke advocated the social diffusion and institutional diversification of the authority to invoke natural law effectively.

A traditional natural law theorist like Thomas Aquinas was well aware that deviations from natural law are attendant upon the rule of men by men. He emphasized that such deviations from reason result in unjust or tyrannical laws. But on the strength of Pauline teachings, such laws are still seen to bear the imprint of the eternal rule. They retain the quality of law because their objective, to assure full obedience, is as such wholesome and necessary.[47] Consequently, notwithstanding his distinction between moral and legal obligations,[48] and despite his eloquent condemnation of tyranny, Aquinas allowed for the limitation and deposition of rulers only where legal provisions or customs to this effect are established. He unequivocally rejected tyrannicide and active extra-legal resistance on the part of an aggregate of private citizens.[49] This conclusion was accepted by Hobbes, who identified right and law in public matters, although one might well query how consistent he was in doing so. Locke was at one with Aquinas in rejecting the identification of right and law, but unlike

[46] Secs. 176, 177, 228. Strauss, *op. cit.*, 227, 229, agrees that Locke was forced to make this distinction because he was aware that to live in a gang of robbers may be more conducive to temporal happiness than to live in a proper political society. This means that what is said to be a requirement of consistent speech and action is, in fact, not happiness but true, i.e. virtuous, happiness. Cf. *Essay*, II, xxi, 50–2, 56–7; and Polin, *op. cit.*, 21–4, 49f., on the distinction between happiness and true happiness in Locke. This distinction is the more easily admitted if, like Aaron, *op. cit.*, 257, one identifies Locke's hedonism with the Christian hedonism of the kind in Gassendi, and not as deriving from Hobbes' materialist brand. See also Lamprecht, *op. cit.*, 90 and von Leyden, *op. cit.*, 71f.

[47] *Summa Theologica*, qu. 93, art. 3; qu. 92, art. 4; qu. 95, art. 2.   [48] *Ibid.*, qu. 100.

[49] *De Regimine Principum*, ch. VI. There are, however, many affinities between Locke and Aquinas which bear a close analysis.

both his predecessors, he maintained the right of private citizens to engage in concerted resistance. In this instance, at least, Locke was more consistent than both Aquinas and Hobbes, and especially more than the latter, from whom he took the emphasis upon the principle of self-preservation. For Hobbes, the first law of nature is nothing but a command of prudence turned into the right of individuals to do all they can for the preservation of their life. But for Hobbes, prudence does not require more than to secure to the individual the right of evading military service, imprisonment and giving testimony against blood-relations,[50] all of which are rather futile bulwarks against the political insecurity of individuals.[51] Locke went further and invoked prudence against putting a practically irrevocable trust into any government. But his insistence on the right of the subjects to implement their judgment of the government's performance by concerted resistance does not rest on the principle of self-preservation alone. It is intimately allied with, because justified by, the moral imperative of natural equality. That is why self-preservation is not merely the physical condition for the attainment of virtue but part of the hierarchy of ends. After all, for Locke, the iniquity of tyranny, similar to that inflicted by thieves and robbers, does not necessarily and exclusively consist in a threat to life and possessions; it is no less a threat to an honorable and virtuous life.

In the context of a doctrine of "natural political virtue," [52] in which rights reflect individual wants and needs, yet correspond to duties of dignity and virtue, the diffusion of the authority to consent to particularizations of natural law might well be designed to provide for the best possible application of natural law. By placing political authority in more than one hand, the fallibility of the prince is evidently offset by his obligation to collaborate with an elective and an hereditary body of legislators. The fallibility of the two collective bodies is checked in exceptional cases by prerogative and, that of legislators and princes alike, by the right of revolt. The diffusion of political authority in this way obviously indicates that the authority to apply natural law and judge the appositeness of its application, is made a matter of competition between governmental agencies and between them and the people. Indeed, in dealing with the relationship between the legislative and the members of society, Locke stated that "the law of nature stands as an eternal rule to *all men, legislators as well as others*" so that "no human sanction can be good or

---

[50] *Leviathan*, ch. xxi.   [51] Cf. Strauss, *op. cit.*, 233.

[52] In these aptly chosen terms Laslett, *op. cit.*, 108, defines the intention of Locke's natural law. It is the merit of Kendall, *op. cit.*, 68, 76, 79f., 105f., 113, although he has overstated the case, to have exposed the misapprehension that Locke stressed rights instead of duties. However, even Vaughan, *op. cit.*, 138, was aware that natural law, "this accommodating oracle" (140) also enjoins duties.

valid" in opposition "to the law of nature, i.e. the will of God." [53]
This obligation stands, whether the legislative is "placed in one or
more." So does the right of revolt.

If Locke had not wished to provide for the best possible observance of natural law, it would have been uncalled for to extend the
authority to consent to human laws beyond what traditional natural
law theorists, as well as Hobbes, were prepared to accept, with the
explicit provision that no human sanction ought to contravene natural
law. To extend the authority to compete on a socially inclusive scale
in regard to the application of natural law does not run counter to
Locke's distinction between the different ways and grades of knowing
natural law. The people's authority does not extend further than to
check their betters. In all forms of proper political activity, the ini-
tiative lies with the more reasonable members of society.

The conclusions reached so far need further confirmation. In
principle, one might regard consent as subject to natural law and
competitive consent as most conducive to its proper realization. Yet
one may still think that, while men are capable of knowing that law,
in practice they have become increasingly incapable of heeding it.
Considering Locke's insistence on human frailty and baseness, one is
led to ask whether human sanctions, granted they were once good and
valid according to the eternal rule, will not increasingly deviate
from it, and by competitive consent at that. The wider sharing in
political power, i.e. the placing of several parts of it into different
hands, is on Locke's showing the product of historical experience and
development.[54] This development would seem to indicate a departure
from men's allegiance to natural law. For how can positive laws go
on reflecting the ceaseless obligations of natural law, and the latter
even become "drawn closer," if with the vanishing of the "golden age"
of "the infancy of commonwealths," governors have become worse
and subjects more vicious? [55] The moral deterioration of subjects
certainly necessitates more legislation, and that of the governors a
diffusion of power. The moral deterioration of both governors and
subjects is hardly propitious for an increase of the correspondence of
legislation with natural law. The conditions for any correspondence
would seem to become worse as history goes on.

We are thus again confronted with the extreme scepticism which
appears to be conveyed by the negative aspects of Locke's natural law
doctrine. Moreover, if it could be said that, according to Locke, moral
deterioration is an uninterrupted process it would be unnecessary to
resort to the device of cancelling out the positive views by the
negative views concerning men's susceptibility to be guided by natural
law. However, it can still be shown that, in accordance with the

---

[53] Sec. 135.   [54] Secs. 94, 107.   [55] Secs. 135, 111, 110, respectively.

textual evidence, these views supplement rather than contradict each other.

In the first place, the evolutionary argument of moral deterioration does not offset the fact that Locke's positive and negative statements on the knowability of natural law refer to men as men, that is, to human nature in general. Moreover, the evolutionary argument does not denote a unilinear process. Retrogression follows after men have progressed from the state of nature to the stage of early and minimal government. The "golden age" of early government is a stage of harmonious simplicity; and an advance beyond the inconveniences of the state of nature. For to be under natural law alone, i.e. in the state of nature, entails great inconveniences, fears and dangers,[56] "all being kings . . . and the greater part no strict observers of equity and justice." [57] It follows that, in the infancy of governments, men were not only better fitted to observe natural law than in more developed stages, but also were so before the golden age, that is, prior to the institution of government. Evidently, moral deterioration is not the consequence, but the cause, of the institution and intensification of government. Government provides the means to cope with moral deterioration. Governors, rather than government as such, also become the cause of deterioration, because the social and economic development achieved, due to good and wise princes, offers unworthy successors an increased temptation to abuse power for their private interests.[58] The misuse of governmental authority does not discredit its positive function but induces men to make provisions against its abuses.

Since the early age of government compares favorably with a previous non-political condition as well as with a posterior political one,

[56] Secs. 13, 37, 92, 101, 123, 124, 126, 127, etc.

[57] Sec. 123. The line of argument suggested here not only disproves the view of Vaughan, op. cit., 161–2, that the admission of retrogression ought to have led Locke to Paine's conclusions, but is also additional evidence for Lamprecht's argument, op. cit., 127, against Stephen, op. cit., II, 137, namely that the state of nature and "the golden age" are not identified by Locke. Strauss, op. cit., 216, asserts the identity of the two states. Yolton, op. cit., 492–3, distinguishes between a semi-romantic and an inclusive state of nature, the latter including all that falls short of Locke's prescriptive notion of political society. In this way, the "golden age" is again identified with the state of nature. Cox, op. cit., 94, 101, 172, defines early government merely as a less complete state of savagery than a truly natural condition. The most satisfactory interpretation has been suggested by Laslett, op. cit., 357–8, 360. He accepts Lamprecht's conclusion but adds that military leadership is a transitional and internally largely harmonious stage between the state of nature and political society. As to the much advertised concern of Locke with minimal government, it is well to remember that he thought it to be coeval with a bygone condition of harmony and simplicity, and with paternal-authoritarian rule at that.

[58] Secs. 42, 94, 107, 111, 162, 166.

development is not identified with deterioration. The existence of government is not only compatible with the observance of equity and justice, but this observance is greater when government exists than when it does not. A further increase of equity and justice is likewise not precluded. Although the observance of equity and justice has decreased in the development subsequent to the golden age of early government, governors and subjects are said to have become worse but not incorrigible. This holds equally true of men as they are by nature —that is, as they are depicted by Locke in his idyllic as well as in his de-idealized version of the state of nature—and of men as they develop under bad government on the one hand and under the strain of social and economic differentiation on the other. The institution and intensification of legislative activity, and consequently the enlargement of political competitiveness, remain the means to ensure—and possibly to increase—the observance of equity and justice. No contradiction is, therefore, involved in the assumption that a tolerable degree of equity and justice must, and can, be ensured when the ceaseless obligations of natural law "in many cases are drawn closer, and have by human laws known penalties annexed to them, to enforce their observation." [59] This is the less inconsistent, as Locke considered wisdom and virtue to be in all stages of development the properties of the few who, either as legislators or as leaders of resistance, are capable of evoking eventually, though not with certainty, a favorable response on the part of the many.

The foregoing interpretation is only one indication of a liberalism more level-headed or frank with regard to government activity than that of many of Locke's later disciples. Nor is it adversely affected by the fact that, on Locke's terms, rules of conduct which are sanctioned by human law, although they become thereby more effective, are not for that reason alone more in harmony with natural law. A great part of "the municipal laws of countries" reflects the "fancies and intricate contrivances of men, following their contrary and hidden interests put into words." [60] What is thus put into words is not right, since positive laws "are only so far right, as they are founded on the law of nature, by which they are to be regulated and interpreted." While it is again made plain that men have no authority to flout natural law by consented laws, it is also made clear that a correct adaptation of consented laws to natural law is not impossible. Locke was far from denying that men may conceive law "in its true notion." [61] As this possibility is the prerequisite of the obligation to honor laws, the denial of such a possibility would have amounted to preaching anarchy. This was obviously besides Locke's purpose. For, "where there is no law, there is no freedom." [62]

[59] Sec. 135.   [60] Sec. 12.   [61] Sec. 57.   [62] Secs. 94 and 57, respectively.

That Locke did not intend to discredit, by a sleight of hand, the belief in the applicability of natural law, is further confirmed by his alignment of the gist of his sceptical and optimistic statements in two consecutive sentences. In these, Locke maintained that consented law is "plain to all rational creatures" and that "men being biased by their interests as well as ignorant (of natural law) for want of study of it, are not apt to allow for it as a law binding to them in the application of it to their particular cases." [63] What is stated here is neither different from traditional natural law teaching nor self-contradictory. The argument is simply that in view of men as they are, natural law cannot be applied to particular cases without the intermediacy of government and positive law. Because this is due to the bias and ignorance of men, but not of all men, positive law may still reflect natural law through the prevalence of those who are neither ignorant nor biased. Thus Locke spoke first of what is plain "to all rational creatures" and not of what is plain to all men. But when he spoke of bias and ignorance he referred simply to "men" and not to "all rational creatures." If this appears to be an excessively hair-splitting exegesis, it is confirmed by the undeniable fact of Locke's acknowledgment of the differential capacities of men. What is more, in the very section which is adduced to prove that according to Locke natural law is of no avail, he made it clear that, because natural law is "unwritten, and nowhere to be found but in the minds of men, they who through passion or interest shall miscite and misapply it, cannot so easily be convinced of their mistake where there is no established judge." [64] Evidently, not all men are misled by passions and interests. Otherwise nobody would be left to try and convince anybody. And, what is not easy is clearly not impossible. This applies, according to Locke, where there is no established judge, and much more, where there is one. Clearly, there is, then, a foundation for the interpretation that men as men, and ordinary men at that, may know natural law, and that the correspondence between natural and positive law is possible and even increasable. In order to try to attribute to Locke the opposite intention, one must, indeed, leave out the part of Sec. 136 which we have just quoted,[65] and rely exclusively on the other part, which says that natural law "serves not as it ought to determine the rights, and fence the properties of those that live under it, *especially* where every one is judge, interpreter and executioner of it too, and that in his own case." However, the "especially" is a qualification which establishes the connection with the foregoing part of the section.

These statements only confirm further that Locke's distinction between the state of nature and political society is not meant to be com-

[63] Sec. 124.   [64] Sec. 136.
[65] Thus Cox, *op. cit.*, 80–1; and Strauss, *op. cit.*, 225–6.

plete.[66] Otherwise the validity of natural law, and the possibility of becoming convinced of mistakes made in citing and applying it, could not hold good in all conditions of human existence. In other words, because the hypothesis of a non-political state of nature illustrates what men are by nature and to what extent they are capable of knowing and applying natural law, Locke could not set political society completely apart from the state of nature. Indeed, Locke's political society minimizes, but does not eliminate, the necessity of every one being "judge, interpreter and executioner" of natural law. Arbitrary rule, which is even worse than the state of nature, causes revolt. This brings back the state of nature in the sense of a state of war, though it does not dissolve society.[67] Everybody becomes again judge and interpreter by himself, but executioner only in unison with the majority. By engaging with others in revolt, men act within political society— as in the state of nature—by appealing directly to the law of nature, the common superior having disqualified himself by the act of putting himself into a state of war with society. Revolt is as often directed against the infraction of positive laws as against objectionable positive laws. Not only is revolt unprovided for by positive laws, but, as likely as not, entails an infraction of positive laws. Locke recognized that inconveniences which are characteristic of the state of nature do not only follow upon the infraction of laws by rulers, or upon legislation which is arbitrary because it contravenes natural law. He knew also that such inconveniences may be attendant upon the revolutionary appeal by, or in the name of, the majority to natural law. For he admitted that revolt may be unjustified. If Locke's political society were meant to be entirely immune from the pitfalls of the state of nature,[68] it would be impossible to explain why Locke should have considered the causes of revolt and its justification as applicable to each form of government, and have made these considerations the pivotal and most belabored single issue of the whole *Treatise*.

It follows that in each human condition imagined by Locke a natural law of self-preservation and human dignity obligates and sanctions individual and collective rights and duties. To be applied most effectively and fairly, it requires the extension and institutional diversification of the authority to appeal to and act upon the eternal rule of reason.

[66] Cf. Vaughan, *op. cit.*, 136; Laslett, *op. cit.*, 99; and Polin, *op. cit.*, 185.

[67] Secs. 13, 137 and 243 respectively. See the cogent argument of Strauss, *op. cit.*, note 100 to p. 232, for the consistency of Locke's assumption of the continuation of political society in revolution.

[68] That Locke's political society was not meant to be perfect and utopian is pointed out by Polin, *op. cit.*, 150. The opposite view is held by Simon, *loc. cit.*, 398, and Yolton, *loc. cit.*, 492–5; but there is, after all, a great difference between Locke's attitude towards the existing order and, say, Plato's.

To sum up: considered as basic to Locke's theory of political action and obligation, and as fundamental to his belief in the necessary predominance of rational criteria in political life, his statements on natural law do not suggest an intention to deny its knowability and applicability. They suggest his awareness of the difficulties involved in making dictates of reason prevail. Since the injunctions of natural law, like any standards that cover a multiplicity of cases, are necessarily of a rather general nature, they may be said to be plain to all rational creatures, and eventually also to the majority. By the same token, the specification and application of such standards as regards particular cases is less plain and more controversial. In this respect there is no difference between traditional natural law teaching and Locke's version of it, nor between his *Treatise* and his *Essay*. There, too, Locke took it for granted that men on occasion know with certainty. And, although very little knowledge is certain, the probable knowledge, i.e. "the grounds and degrees of belief, opinion and assent" which men can achieve, is sufficient for their needs.[69]

Related to each other, Locke's statements on the knowability and applicability of natural law reflect a division of labor between the more and the less enlightened members of society. The student of natural law necessarily faces the difficulty of communicating his superior knowledge to those who are either ignorant or whose bias and interests distort their judgment. Those who know better consequently face the difficulty of inducing the many to respond to what by nature they are not incapable of knowing and responding to. The many are capable of this response, not primarily as a result of reasoning, but by dint of common-sense or deep-set convictions, which are in accord with tradition and Scriptural teachings, inasmuch as they confirm the voice of reason.

The important difference which sets Locke's version of natural law apart, not only from the traditional one but also from that of Hobbes, consists in the extension of the authority to invoke natural law, and especially in the granting to the common people of the right to veto by revolt their betters' particularizations of the eternal rule. The metapolitical foundations which Locke's natural law doctrine provides serve to justify a view of politics as a continuously competitive process of maintaining or re-establishing, by reference to rational criteria, a tolerable balance between powers which represent individual and collective rights and capacities.

The Hebrew University of Jerusalem.

[69] *Essay*, I, i, 2 and 4; and Aaron, *op. cit.*, 78–9.

PART FOUR

ENLIGHTENMENT
POLITICAL THOUGHT

XI

JEAN D'ALEMBERT AND THE REHABILITATION OF HISTORY

By Judith N. Shklar

One of the great problems of Enlightenment thought was to find an appropriate place for history among the sciences. This preoccupation has often been dismissed as a sign of a lack of "historical spirit" in most *philosophes*. The absence of "historism" did not, however, imply an indifference to or a willful ignorance of the past.[1] On the contrary, they were deeply interested in accurate information about other ages and in the possible uses of such knowledge. History was, however, both an epistemological and moral puzzle because there was no obvious location for it on the map of the sciences. It was difficult to justify history in the eighteenth century because genuine knowledge was supposed to be both certain and useful, and it was far from obvious that history was either one.

Jean d'Alembert (1717-83) has been long recognized as particularly important among those who tried to offer answers to the pressing questions raised by history, but his contribution to the theory of history has not been fully appreciated.[2] That is partly due to his general eclecticism. He was above all a mathematician, and only secondarily a man of letters. While he wrote some remarkable essays about historiography, he composed no concentrated treatise on the subject. And while he considered the history of any subject he treated, he did not write a single work of historical scholarship. Nevertheless, as part of his work as an encyclopedist and as a theorist of science he was forced to confront the history of ideas directly. In

---

[1] For the notion of Enlightenment historiography as merely preparing the way for genuine history: Friedrich Meinecke, *Historism*, trans. J. E. Anderson (New York, 1972). The philosophes were not concerned to explain the growth of such "individual" wholes as nations and classes within the development of world history, which was to become the mark of post-Napoleonic historiography, as particularly well described by Otto Hintze, "Troeltsch and the Problems of Historicism" in *The Historical Essays of Otto Hintze*, ed. Felix Gilbert (New York, 1975), 368-421. The defense of the Enlightenment's approach to history, on which I have relied, is to be found in Ernst Cassirer, *The Philosophy of the Enlightenment*, trans. F. C. A. Koelln and James Pettegrove (Boston, 1951), 197-233. Peter Gay, *The Enlightenment*, 2 vols. (New York, 1966 and 1969), and esp. Georges Gusdorf, *L'avènement des sciences humaines au siècle des lumières* (Paris, 1973).

[2] Cassirer, *op. cit.*, singled him out, but mostly as a step toward Kant's philosophy of history. The best treatment of d'Alembert as a historian of science is Georges Gusdorf, *De l'histoire des sciences à l'histoire de la pensée* (Paris, 1966), 47-92.

his capacity as the permanent secretary of the *Académie Française* he felt, moreover, obliged to memorialize the life and work of its recently deceased members. That unavoidably forced him to defend both the scientific and social status of biography and of the history of ideas generally. For not only did a significant part of his public doubt the value of these endeavors, d'Alembert himself at times showed little respect for history. Yet, he did ultimately restore history to a more secure and dignified position in the world of learning than any that it had occupied for over a century.

By the middle of the eighteenth century traditional history had suffered a century of massive abuse. D'Alembert's occasional contempt was quite normal and owed much to his admired predecessors, Descartes and Locke. When he spoke of history as idle entertainment suitable at most for teaching moral lessons to children, he was only repeating what he had learned from some of his forebears.[3] However much these two differed on other subjects, they were remarkably at one in their views on history. Most books on history were nonsense and, in any case, most book-learning was a waste of time. The only knowledge worth acquiring was self-generated. Of the two charges the latter was the more devastating, since even sensible history is largely second-hand information, but the first was damaging also. What could be more condescending than Descartes' remark that a little history is good for us because it saves us from a narrow parochialism? A little learning is quite enough, however, for even the most truthful historians are so given to exaggeration that they endanger one's realism and common sense.[4] Locke at least thought that an English gentleman who expected to enter public life should know the history of his own country. History is, after all, "the great mistress of prudence and civil knowledge." Nevertheless, he was unhappy about the moral impact of historical literature. It glorified cruelty. For what were all those celebrated conquerors but "the great butchers of mankind"?[5] Severe as these strictures may seem, they do not utterly condemn all history to oblivion. The possibility of a reliable and morally useful history remains open. Even Descartes implicitly accepted at least the historical element inherent in the very pursuit of science. He expected future scientists to build on his work. Science is a collaborative effort in which scientists depend on their predecessors even though they must critically re-examine the latter.

[3] "Collège," *Encyclopédie ou Dictionaire raisonné des sciences, des arts et des métiers* (Paris, 1751-65), III, 632-38; "Erudition," *ibid.,* V, 914-15.

[4] René Descartes, *Discours de la méthode* in *Oeuvres et Letters,* ed. André Bridoux (Paris, 1949), 95.

[5] John Locke, *Some Thoughts Concerning Reading and Study for Gentlemen* in *Works* (London, 1823), III, 296-97; *Some Thoughts Concerning Education,* IV, 182-84, 116.

It is indeed a pity that ancient philosophy had been so falsely represented to us, but if one now reports one's own work carefully, such
errors could be avoided in the future. That is why he, Descartes, had
after much inner doubt decided to publish his researches. Science, in
short, writes its own history and so forms a link between past, present, and future.[6] Descartes may not even have recognized this continuity or scientific heritage as a form of history. It was altogether
new, but it was to be one of the overt objectives of the *Encyclopédie*
as a work of history, according to d'Alembert. Characteristically, he
added that there was much curiosity and sheer vanity in that hope.[7]
The lure of fame was clearly not unknown to scientists, but it might
be a good thing. The notion of a new epic had already occurred to
Locke. Political society may be dominated by "butchers," but "the
commonwealth of learning is not . . . without its master builders."
They were Boyle, Sydenham, Huygenius, and, of course, "the incomparable Mr. Newton."[8] Without the ancestral piety of the Romans there was no reason to write their kind of monumental history,
but to praise these truly great men, scientists all, might be as edifying
as the record of battles was degrading. That also was to be one of the
aims of the *Encyclopédie*. The victory of the moderns over the ancients did not mean the end of memory, but rather its redirection. The
critique of traditional history did not preclude the creation of a new
kind of history, new in its subject matter, in its greater reliability and,
above all, new in its aims. Contemporary history thus became very
important. It would secure for future generations history worth
knowing.

The most serious obstacle to any possible history was raised by
the doctrine of systematic doubt. History is not direct experience. It
depends on information, on documents and artifacts that must, to
some minimal degree at least, inspire trust in the historian. It is derivative knowledge and it is neither clear nor certain. For Descartes
that was a decisive flaw. His program for the future of knowledge had
no room for political history. Custom must be rejected entirely and
everything be grounded solely on one's own opinions. These could
emerge only after one had washed all received opinions out of one's
mind. The world must be thought anew and one begins with knowledge of self to read the great book of the world.[9] History cannot
survive such a declaration of individual self-reliance. One can repeat

---

[6] *Discours de la méthode*, 134-44.

[7] *Discours préliminaire de l'Encyclopédie* in *Oeuvres Complètes de D'Alembert*
(Geneva, 1967), I, 36.

[8] *An Essay Concerning Human Understanding* in *Works*, I, 1.

[9] *Discours de la méthode*, 97-98, 101-04, 110-11; *Règles pour la direction de
l'esprit, ibid.*, 7-19 *et passim*.

scientific experiments, but history is a matter of trust. This part of Descartes' philosophy flourished, for it was reinforced by Locke at every turn. Who ever scoffed more effectively than Locke did at those who "read, and read and read on yet make no great advance in knowledge?" Because they depend upon the erudition of other men, they let their poor minds be "bound by citations and built upon authority."[10] Indeed, "the floating of other men's opinions in our brains makes us not one bit more knowing, though they happen to be true."[11] The trusting man is simply a fool. This was independence indeed. Knowledge was not worth having unless it began in direct experience. Then it could be stored in one's memory to form one's intellectual capital, honestly acquired and entirely one's own. That it must be merely probable knowledge did not trouble Locke as it would have disturbed Descartes. Probable knowledge was "sufficient to govern our concernments."[12] A Lockean might endure the relative uncertainty of historical knowledge at least, but he could not bear its submissiveness, its dependence on other minds. History had been expelled from the "commonwealth of learning" only to await further blows.

Descartes' and Locke's polemic was certainly directed at sacred history, but not exclusively or directly. That task was reserved for Bayle and biblical criticism generally. From the critical examination of traditional ecclesiastical history it moved on to what Bayle called "historical Pyrrhonism." His review of all that was unreliable and unbelievable led him to doubt everything except a few basic historical facts. The same impulse led more pious historians to reject everything save the revelations of the Holy Spirit.[13] It was also shared by Voltaire, d'Alembert's immediate predecessor as heir to Descartes' doubts and Locke's hopes for an alternative history. Although he claimed that he was not an "outré" skeptic, Voltaire was certainly haunted by Bayle's skepticism. He saw no particular reason to doubt that a city called Peking existed, but he would not wager his life on it.[14] Because he put so much passion and effort into the discrediting of miracles and every other sort of traditional religious and classical lore, he fell victim to an overwhelming state of suspicion. As an

---

[10] *On the Conduct of the Understanding* in *Works*, III, 24, 250-52.

[11] *Essay*, I, Bk. I, ch. IV, 2-3, 79.   [12] *Ibid.*, Bk. I, ch. I, 6, 4-5.

[13] For the historical doubts of believing Christians, see R. R. Palmer, *Christians and Unbelievers in Eighteenth Century France* (Princeton, 1947), 67-76, and generally Paul Hazard, *The European Mind*, trans. J. Lewis May (New Haven, 1953), 29-52, 106-14, 162-67, 185-97.

[14] "Le Pyrrhonisme de l'histoire," *Oeuvres Complètes de Voltaire* (Paris, 1877-85), XXVII, 235; "Histoire," *Dictionnaire Philosophique*, XIX, 346-70, and "Certain/Certitude," *ibid.*, XVIII, 117-21, which dealt mostly with historical uncertainty.

historian Voltaire often could not bring himself to believe anyone or anything. The mission of his age, as he saw it, was to destroy error.[15] Nevertheless, he did write history because he recognized that the means of recovery were at hand. Voltaire did much to establish rational procedures for historical research. Because he found it so very difficult to accept mere probability, he devised rational ways to mitigate it. One must authenticate documents, judge the reliability of witnesses, doubt all oral evidence committed to writing long after the event, and one must never accept accounts of events that are out of the common course of nature.[16] Methods for the protection of the historian against fraud were also safeguards against the despair of perfect doubt. Moreover, Voltaire had hoped to be the creator of a new kind of history, social and intellectual, which would be broad in scope, elevating and accurate. It would deal with the experiences of peoples rather than wars.[17] In practice his historical writings fall very far short of his proclamations. The arts receive far less space than the wars of the great patron-king in *Le siècle de Louis XIV*. There are only a few pages devoted to daily life and customs and a very great many to popular superstitions and to royal politics in *Essai sur les moeurs*. That is not really surprising, since Voltaire admired "the great" and especially kings. He could never believe that Tacitus was reliable because it seemed to him incredible that emperors should be so monstrous.[18] But d'Alembert was perfectly ready to believe the worst about rulers. He deeply admired Tacitus' message and translated him carefully even though he thought him too rhetorical.[19] Kings and courtiers were, in his eyes, a corrupting menace as patrons of the arts. He was therefore never tempted to write their history as his older friend had been.[20] In fact, throughout their gossipy correspondence history is never seriously discussed, and although d'Alembert often praised Voltaire's historical writings, he never explained their merits in any detail.[21] He did share Voltaire's severe skepticism and

[15] "Le Pyrrhonisme," 236-37.

[16] In a letter to a fellow historian Voltaire claimed that in writing *Le siècle de Louis XIV* he had consulted all the available personal memoirs as well as the reports of the intendants, "Voltaire à Jean Baptiste Dubos, 30 octobre, 1738," *Voltaire's Correspondence*, ed. Theodore Besterman (Geneva, 1954), VII, 424-28. More generally his program is set out in "Histoire," *loc. cit.*, and in *Encyclopédie*, VIII, 220-25; J. H. Brumfitt, *Voltaire Historian* (Oxford, 1958), 32-34, 84-86, 98-104, 136-47 *et passim*; H. T. Mason, *Pierre Bayle and Voltaire* (Oxford, 1963), 128-33 *et passim*.

[17] Brumfitt, *op. cit.*, 48-70; Paul Hazard, *op. cit.*

[18] "Le Pyrrhonisme," 356-61.

[19] "Réflexions sur l'histoire," *Oeuvres*, II, 6.

[20] The difference in their attitudes to "the great" put a strain on their relations generally and made d'Alembert quite cautious in his dealings with Voltaire. See John N. Pappas, *Voltaire and d'Alembert* (Bloomington, 1962), *passim*.

[21] E.g., "Discours préliminaire," 79-80.

the urgent need to overcome it, but he looked to other intellectual models for practical instruction.

Voltaire was not the only advocate of a renovated history. Leibniz, Fontenelle, and Condillac proposed the same program without suffering from debilitating doubts, and d'Alembert learned much from them, directly and indirectly. Fontenelle (1657-1757) especially had done as much as Voltaire to discredit the fables that passed for historical facts. He was, however, perfectly confident that reliable history could be, and indeed had already been, written, most notably by Leibniz. In extending the scientific spirit to historical studies Leibniz had, according to Fontenelle, provided so sound an account of the past that it provided the means for making predictions about the future.[22] History had, in short, already joined the other advanced sciences. Nor did Fontenelle entertain doubts about the usefulness of history. A mere recital of the facts was not enough, but historians who linked natural causes and effects explicitly could tell us much about human motivation. History was applied psychology. To achieve that it must learn to deal with ordinary people. For the scientific study of conflict, Fontenelle noted, a lawsuit between two bourgeois is just as important as a war between princes.[23] D'Alembert was to agree with most of these views, but he could never share Fontenelle's or Leibniz's serene optimism.[24] The notion of history as a predictive science plays no part in his thought.

Fontenelle's real importance was his contribution to the history and glorification of science. As permanent secretary of the *Académie des sciences* he not only contributed to the writing of its history but also wrote the *éloges* of those of its members who had died since 1699. These memorials were entirely his own invention. The history of other academies, notably Bishop Sprat's, existed and speeches in honor of academicians were not unknown. There had, however, never been anything quite like Fontenelle's regular series of reviews of the achievements of notable scientists. Other academies did not have them, his predecessors did not deliver them, and he was not obliged to write them as part of his official duties. The genre was entirely the invention of this gifted nephew of the great Corneille. The fact that the *Académie* had just become a more open society with

[22] "Eloge de Leibniz," *Oeuvres Complètes de Fontenelle* (Paris, 1818), I, 228-35.

[23] "Sur l'histoire," *Oeuvres,* II, 424-35. For Fontenelle's general approach to the social sciences see Leonard M. Marsak, *Bernard de Fontenelle: The Idea of Science in the Enlightenment* in *Transactions of the American Philosophical Society, N.S.,* **49,** Part 7 (1959), 40-59.

[24] D'Alembert in general had a low opinion of Leibniz, for the same reasons that made Voltaire ridicule him. See W. H. Barber, *Leibniz in France* (Oxford, 1955), 156-58, 176. Fontenelle was admired but also criticized for superficiality and pliancy, "Eloge de la Motte," *Oeuvres,* III, 137-41.

sessions open to the public probably inspired him, for it gave him the opportunity to promote the fortunes of science and to present scientists as heroes of the intellect.[25] He certainly knew that these were "lay funeral orations" designed to replace a solemn religious rite.[26] They were clearly intended to raise the intellectuals to a new and superior social level, one comparable to that of the highest clergy. In setting out and praising the characteristic virtues of scientists these *éloges* were also meant to encourage solidarity and cooperation within the republic of science. Finally, Fontenelle hoped that young scientists would be moved to emulation by the example of their distinguished elders and so ensure the progress of science and the triumph of the moderns over the ancients.

The style of these *éloges* mirrored the very qualities that Fontenelle expected scientists to cultivate: seriousness, simplicity, refinement, and an impersonal, selfless devotion to science. Sainte-Beuve quite justly admired them for their "grandeur of spirit spent on great matters." They were "exact, spiritual, and serious," as Fontenelle claimed his subjects had been.[27] Theirs were not, very obviously, the aristocratic or princely virtues. Cassini cared more for the progress of science than for personal glory, while Homburg's style was notably simple, methodical, and without superfluity. Viviani's Régis', and Lémery's *éloges* mentioned the simplicity of their manners.[28] These were the social virtues needed for unity among scientists, the end which the academies were meant to achieve and which became constantly more urgent as specialization advanced. With less optimism d'Alembert as usual came to share Fontenelle's program for ordering the social world of the intellectuals.

The social cooperation of scientists and the use of history as a way of promoting intellectual unity among the sciences became particularly important when the belief in the inherent oneness of science waned. Leibniz had still believed in the Cartesian notion of a single truth, a universal science, from which all others would be deduced. He thought, however, that until that unity was known, all existing kinds of knowledge should be organized in a convenient encyclopedic form. For d'Alembert the metaphysical unity of science remained a very faint hope, probably beyond human intellectual powers. He

---

[25] These remarks owe much to a private communication from Professor Roger Hahn; see also his *The Anatomy of a Scientific Institution: The Paris Academy of Sciences 1666-1803* (Berkeley, 1971), 35-57.

[26] Gusdorf, *De l'histoire des sciences,* 55. An unpublished paper by George A. Kelly, "The History of the New Hero: Eulogy and its Sources in Eighteenth-Century France," expands on this challenge to religion.

[27] *Causeries de Lundi* (Paris, n.d.), I, 392-94.

[28] *Préface de l'histoire de l'académie des sciences, depuis 1666 jusqu'en 1699* in *Oeuvres,* I,II: "Eloges," 176-77, 200-01, 65, 95, 193.

therefore turned to the encyclopedic scheme as the only practical way to preserve a semblance of order among the sciences.[29] The history of science—both as a way of unifying the diverse sciences and of celebrating the fame of the great genii of science—replaced the now untenable metaphysics of a universal science. History for d'Alembert had both a moral and an intellectual function in the republic of learned men. The history of science, accurate in form, with the pursuit of truth as its content was obviously worthwhile, even if it was limited in scope.

Voltairean skepticism and Fontenelle's confidence in history generally and in its uses for the enterprise of science particularly were not d'Alembert's only inheritance. It was complicated by a third author whom he admired far more, Montesquieu, "the legislator of nations" as he was to call him.[30] As that compliment implies, Montesquieu was not interested in the history of daily usages and customs for their own sake or as an alternative to the history of governments. They were to be studied as part of the rise and fall of states. His broad generalizations were remote from the specificity that Voltaire and Fontenelle demanded. Lastly, Montesquieu was not interested in praising great men, least of all intellectuals. L'Esprit des lois is highly impersonal and is addressed to lawmakers and to their critics. It was not compatible with Voltaire's or Fontenelle's purposes, yet d'Alembert was wholly convinced of its usefulness and philosophic importance. It was the great textbook of applied psychology and of "moral causes," and if it was neither predictive nor certain, it was an immensely instructive book. It did not deal with men who pursued truth; it was not exact. On the contrary, it was a tale about errors and it was often vague. Epistemologically it did not meet the standards for a respectable science. It did, however, fulfill one task of history admirably: to warn men against tyranny and superstition and, above all, it made sense out of the chaos of politics.[31] Nevertheless, it rendered the science of history more problematic for d'Alembert. History was supposed to meet two philosophical ends, certainty and utility, but the two were not identical.[32] The new Tacitus seemed to demand a reconsideration of the nature of historical knowledge because he widened the gap between them.

[29] Robert McRae, The Problem of the Unity of the Sciences: Bacon to Kant (Toronto, 1961), 69-88, 107-22.

[30] "Eloge de Montesquieu," Oeuvres, III, 499.

[31] Réflexions sur l'histoire in Oeuvres, II, 7; "Mémoires et réflexions sur Christine, reine de Suède," II, 120.

[32] Elémens de philosophie in Oeuvres, I, 127-28; "Apologie de l'étude," Oeuvres, IV, 9-10.

Montesquieu had never been troubled by the doubts that tormented Voltaire. He had chosen an intellectually far less hazardous course. He could escape unending self-interrogation because he did not devote himself to the systematic destruction of historical errors. He could concentrate on the creation of his kind of new history, sociological and philosophical, without incessant doubts. That did not earn him Voltaire's admiration.[33] It also disturbed d'Alembert who was only too familiar with Descartes', Locke's, and Bayle's misgivings, both philosophical and practical. His first reaction to L'Esprit des Lois was, therefore, predictably hostile. Montesquieu's book, he wrote to a friend, "resembles those physical dissertations . . . where the author explains phenomena so easily that he could just as well have explained completely different phenomena by the same principles."[34] He eventually absolved Montesquieu from that mistake, but he thought that all other authors who attempted to write about the rise and fall of empires were given to just such abuses. They were like "demonstrative chemists" whose causes can produce any set of effects whatever.[35] How can one know historical causes at all? The smallest incident which no contemporary would notice or bother to record might produce the most momentous consequences. That certainly is one of the difficulties of Cleopatra's nose. Given the defective materials with which historians work, how can effects be traced to their causes? It is all highly conjectural.[36]

Then there is the problem of distinguishing moral from physical causes. D'Alembert entirely agreed with Montesquieu that there were moral causes at work in history. Climate was far from accounting for everything. The only way, however, one can impute moral causes to events is by observing their physical manifestations, that is, human actions, which may have any number of psychological origins. How does one get to moral causes then? D'Alembert saw the difficulties of social history clearly enough, but could find no way of overcoming them.[37] His admiration for Montesquieu's work was, nevertheless, intense once he could accept its inevitable guesswork. Mainly he was impressed by the historical use of physical psychology, and by its moral and political implications. He was obviously convinced by the theory of climate and the related notions of national character. The article he wrote for the Encyclopédie on these topics is essentially a

[33] "Lois (Esprit de)," Dictionnaire Philosophique, XX, 1-15, "Commentaire sur quelques principales maximes de L'Esprit des Lois," XXX, 407-64, Brumfitt, op. cit., 116-21.

[34] Unpublished letter quoted in Thomas L. Hankins, Jean d'Alembert: Science and the Enlightenment (Oxford, 1970), 81.

[35] Réflexions sur l'histoire in Oeuvres, II, 7.

[36] "Eloge de Montesquieu," Oeuvres, III, 448-49.

[37] "Causes Finales," Encyclopédie, II, 789-90.

summary of and a tribute to Montesquieu. The theory of climate had a sound empirical basis, and one of d'Alembert's collaborators was to give a more detailed review of it than Montesquieu had.[38] There was plenty of medical evidence to back up the latter's observations. Even *Sauerkraut*, it seems, is healthful for some people in some places! The study of populations that Montesquieu presents is thus a contribution to physiology. It also helps one to separate long-term general from short-term particular causes in history. The immediate causes are clearly more "moral," political in character, and therefore more open to speculation than the climatic influences.[39] Given a man of impartiality, circumspection, and probity, however, even this part of history can be of immense value, "a series of experiments on mankind." We are in the realm of group psychology here, but it is not the scientific accuracy but the utility of this kind of history that continued to earn d'Alembert's praise. Scientifically, he observes, it is just as unreliable as medicine and just as necessary. It also holds out the same hope: we need both as our only chance for finding a cure for our afflicted condition.[40]

Montesquieu's glory is political and moral rather than scientific, for like a good physician he has to be content with hit-or-miss methods. The more facts a physician or a historian has, the better off he is, but facts without theory are simply pointless. The mere recital of data, history uninformed by philosophy, is the very least of "the human sciences" in d'Alembert's view.[41] His approach is not, to be sure, an invitation to forget the evidence but to remember the purpose of history: to know mankind, not to gather information for its own sake.[42]

Merely piling up accurate information, especially about antiquity or the past generally, d'Alembert regards as useless erudition. At times he thinks one should respect all forms of knowledge; at other times he is sure that we already know all that is worth knowing about antiquity.[43] Surely we should be more selective in what we choose to remember. Perhaps one should pick out the really useful facts every

---

[38] Montesquieu, in fact, shared many of d'Alembert's concerns about causality in history and psychology, e.g., "Essai sur les causes qui peuvent affecter les esprits et les caractères," *Oeuvres Complètes,* ed. A. Masson (Paris, 1955), III, 397-430. But this essay remained long unpublished.

[39] "Climat" and "Caractère," *Encyclopédie,* III, 533-36.

[40] "Elémens des sciences," *Encyclopédie,* V, 491-97. This is a truly splendid essay, a summing up of d'Alembert's entire philosophy. Why he changed his mind about Montesquieu is not clear, but it was not merely because of the latter's anti-clericalism.

[41] "Mémoires et réflexions sur Christine, reine de Suède," *Oeuvres,* II, 119.

[42] "Apologie de l'étude," *Oeuvres,* IV, 7-9.

[43] "Erudition," *loc. cit.;* Discours préliminaire," *Oeuvres,* I, 55-56, 61-62, 75.

hundred years and burn up the rest.[44] In the history of the exact sciences, this process takes place spontaneously. Errors are simply forgotten. That is why, as the sciences become more perfect, the history of science becomes shorter. Who records mere opinions and errors in mathematics? It does not have a history of sophisms.

Montesquieu's history was certainly speculative, but it was not random, for as Condillac had said of his own history, "the art of conjecture has its rules." [45] When d'Alembert raged against the practices of current historians, it was not their selectivity that he deplored but their aimless erudition. If the moral and political lessons of history were compensations for its lack of rigor, then intelligent selection, such as Montesquieu's sophisticated real order amid apparent confusion, must be the model.[46] The trouble with most readers of history was that they were not ready for that kind of history. They were people who were unwilling to think, even if they were not prepared to vegetate entirely. They tended to turn their backs on the good historians in favor of unedifying recitals of errors and wars that were simply not worth remembering.[47] At times d'Alembert was utterly exasperated. History was good only for children whose moral principles were not yet set. After thirty it was useless. To the young it should, moreover, be taught backward, from the present to the past, so that they might see its relevance to their own time.[48] For the rest, history was just idle curiosity.

Even though most of what the public received was of obscure origin or made up by authors, history could be reformed.[49] D'Alembert would not join those "sad Diogenes" who shunned history altogether because he recognized that philosophical history "instructs, consoles, and encourages us." [50] His answer to the "bitter critics of history," however, also suggested that "facts not verbiage" would effectively reform historical literature.[51] Rigorous history based on accurate chronology, geography, authentic documents, artifacts, monuments, and especially memoirs and letters would render it truthful. And still following Voltaire, an elevating content would dignify it. The *Encyclopédie* explicitly omitted saints' lives, genealogies of noble houses, and the lives of conquerors, all of which low subjects

[44] "Mémoires . . . sur Christine." *Oeuvres*, II, 119.
[45] "Histoire ancienne," *Oeuvres de Condillac* (Paris, 1798), IX, 20.
[46] "Eloge de Montesquieu," *Oeuvres*, III, 450-51.
[47] "Réflexions sur l'histoire," *Oeuvres*, II, 1; "Essai sur les élémens de philosophie," *Oeuvres*, I, 127; "Discours préliminaire," *Oeuvres*, I, 79-80.
[48] "Collège," *loc. cit.*
[49] "Réflexions sur l'histoire," *Oeuvres*, II, 1-3, "Apologie de l'Etude," IV, 5-8.
[50] "Réflexions sur l'histoire," *Oeuvres*, II, 5; "Discours préliminaire," I, 36-37.
[51] "Elémens des sciences," *loc. cit.; *"Essai sur les élémens," *loc. cit.*, I, 168-74, 346.

were of no use.[52] D'Alembert never tired of calling the roll of great names from Galileo to Boerhaave. These were the real heroes of the human spirit that history was to celebrate.[53] He agreed with all that Fontenelle had claimed for them. Their history could be both true and useful. The history of science is the history of a very few men of genius in each epoch. They are an inspiration to new scientific experiments and their history a direct service to science, to the pursuit of truth. Science is a self-correcting process, slow work, possible at all for only a very few men, and work that becomes ever more difficult as the sciences advance.[54] Most of the history of science is recent history, and as scientists leave accurate accounts of their labors it is easy to write true history. In all these ways the history of science is true and good.

Accurate and improving as the history of science is, it does not and cannot touch our public consciousness. In what ways does rigor console us, or even broaden our sympathies? Diderot drew the obvious conclusion. He did not care how good or bad the evidence was if history turned its readers into heroic defenders of freedom.[55] Rousseau began his inspired account of the origins of human inequality by simply putting the facts aside.[56] For d'Alembert such an easy solution was impossible; he was certain that truthfulness and utility would have to be combined. The easiest way to achieve that was to argue that enlightenment was bound to ensure general progress. The more men knew the better they would become. D'Alembert did in fact hope that this was the case, but he did not see it as a law of development or a certainty. It was only a possibility, and history was not the record of past gains and the vision of future glories. He was given to neither gloom nor hope about the future of mankind. Civilization was thin ice. He welcomed amateurs, he once noted sardonically, because they make it less likely that we shall relapse into barbarism, "our natural element."[57] Even without a complete relapse, civilization was a matter of ups and downs, an exchange of gains and losses. The image of the ocean waves that deposit something on the shore, but also take something out again, appealed to him. New knowledge

---

[52] The *Encyclopédie* explicitly refused to concern itself with these topics. "Préface au troisième volume de l'Encyclopédie," *Oeuvres*, IV, 389. D'Alembert used this occasion to insist that usefulness, not just certainty, must be a standard in selecting the subject matter for discussion (*ibid.,* 391).

[53] *Ibid.,* and esp. "Discours préliminaire," *Oeuvres*, I, 63-78.

[54] "Elémens des sciences," *loc. cit.;* "Essai sur les élémens," *loc. cit., Oeuvres*, I, 123.

[55] Gay, *op. cit.,* II, 385.

[56] "Discours sur les origines et les fondemens de l'inégalité, parmi les hommes," *Oeuvres complètes* (Paris, 1964), II, 132-33.

[57] "Discours préliminaire," *Oeuvres*, I, 81-82.

could often be destructive. The growth of the critical spirit, for example, so good for the sciences had stifled poetry.[58] Truth was certainly preferable to error, but its moral and social advantages remained to be proven.[59]

What was the moral place of rigorously factual history? The Voltairean program applied to the history of science and of learning generally had its own distinct moral advantages, different and apart from the political lessons of Montesquieu's conjectural history. The former stimulated intellectual growth while the latter educated political man. For d'Alembert there was another moral benefit. He did not want merely to promote the reputation and social standing of intellectuals, as Fontenelle and Voltaire had, but also to raise their standards of conduct. The pursuit of truth has immediate effects upon the character of scholars; it makes better persons of them. The impact of geometry upon the mathematician is direct. It molds his mind into a finer form. That much was implicit in Descartes' *Discourse on Method*, and d'Alembert greatly expands upon it. Mathematicians, unlike artists or men of letters, do not depend upon the public for approval. They are their own judges and so are peculiarly self-sufficient. They pursue the truth for its own sake and for the certainty it imparts, and they would be as happy with that on a desert island as in Paris. Of all men, they, and they alone, achieve a rational autonomy.[60] The rest of the republic of letters is not fortified against the temptations of patronage. Artists and authors work for an audience, which tends to degrade them to a servile dependence on their public, especially the rich and powerful. Scientists are not amusing and so do not attract the interest of idle patronage. The frivolous do not pursue mathematicians.[61] These happy circumstances are not, however, all; it is not just the absence of temptation that preserves the independence of mathematicians. Mathematics is inherently purifying. "La géométrie," he wrote in his eulogy of Jean Bernoulli, "est pour ainsi dire la mesure la plus précise de notre esprit, de son degré d'étendue, de sagacité, de profondeur, de justesse. Si elle ne peut nous donner

---

[58] *Ibid.,* 78-79; "Réflexions sur l'usage et sur l'abus de la philosophie dans les matières de goût," *Oeuvres,* IV, 396-97; "Essai sur les élémens," I, 121-23. See generally René Wellek, "The Price of Progress in Eighteenth Century Reflections on Literature," *Studies of Voltaire and the Eighteenth Century* (1976), **155**, 2265-84.

[59] It was an expression of this faith that led d'Alembert to argue that the people should be told the truth about religion. Voltaire considered it too dangerous, but d'Alembert thought that it could and should be done with tact and slowly. See Lester G. Crocker, "The Problem of Truth and Falsehood in the Age of the Enlightenment," *Journal of the History of Ideas,* **14** (1953), 575-603.

[60] "Apologie de l'étude," *Oeuvres,* IV, 10.

[61] "Essai sur la société des gens de lettres et les grands," *Oeuvres,* IV, 341, 348-50.

ces qualités, on conviendra du moins qu'elle les fortifie, et fournit les moyens les plus faciles de nous assurer nous-mêmes et de faire connaître aux autres jusqu' à quel point nous les possédons.'' [62] The great mathematicians deserve to be remembered because they embody the essence of what is good in the human spirit. If material utility were really what we prized, d'Alembert went on to say, we should honor manual laborers and soldiers. If we were really to do that and forget the great mathematicians, then we would put an end to civilization. Geometry may be of no obvious use, but mathematicians are far from frivolous in their profession. They are all that stands between us and barbarism which is so natural for us. What emerges here is that personal autonomy and civilization are ends in themselves to which the pursuit of truth contributes. That is how truth becomes morally useful.

D'Alembert did not think that the probity that marked the pure mathematician could be shared in its entirety by other intellectuals. That was because geometry is our only example of what perfectly certain knowledge is like. Geometry is our sole intimation of what perfected science might be. D'Alembert could not give up the idea of a single truth from which all others must follow. His empiricism was therefore always uneasy. It is because we are intellectually too feeble to perceive that one truth that we can only hope to approximate it by pursuing individual sciences in terms of the principles inherent in each. The more facts we can gather and organize, the more complete the sciences become. That does not, however, alter their inherent instability. If we could see the truth whole, it would be like geometric knowledge in its clarity and certainty, but such omniscience must elude us forever. [63] What we can and should do is to imitate and approximate the geometric model. The *Encyclopédie* was meant to do just that. By showing all the interconnections among the individual sciences it would give us a vision of the whole, even though it was a very imperfect one. To be sure, it was also to remind us of the purely conjectural state of most of our knowledge. Even the highest degree of probability is not a demonstration of truth. For historical knowledge that means that even its high level of uncertainty is not a difference in kind from the other empirical sciences. There is no special reason to worry about whether Caesar existed. It also meant that historical knowledge, however speculative, had its place in a whole

    [62] ''Eloge de Bernoulli,'' *Oeuvres*, III, 354.
    [63] ''Elémens des sciences,'' *loc cit.*; Ronald Grimsely, *Jean d'Alembert* (Oxford, 1963), 222-45; Hankins, *op. cit.*, 104-31; Keith M. Baker, *Condorcet* (Chicago, 1975), 99-109. D'Alembert also believed that there were stable standards of beauty and taste even if only very few people could ever grasp them; see Dennis F. Essar, ''The Language Theory, Epistemology and Aesthetics of Jean d'Alembert,'' *Studies on Voltaire and the Eighteenth Century* (Oxford, 1976), 106-12.

that we could never quite reconstruct. Finally, there was a political message in this acceptance of the merely probable. As long as no one knows, everyone has a right to enjoy the most "extreme liberty" of expressing his own opinions.[64] Geometry remains a moral and intellectual beacon in this wilderness because of its certainty. It disciplines scholars and sets the standards for all scientific work. Conjectural knowledge, however, also has its moral advantages. It teaches us our limitations and invites moderation.[65]

D'Alembert's commitment to certainty has often been misunderstood.[66] It is said that he was so infatuated with certainty that he could accept nothing between it and utter skepticism. In fact, d'Alembert saw himself as the guardian of conjectural knowledge not only in his encyclopedic labors but also in his defense of the less rigorous kinds of history. What really disturbed him was the tendency to treat probable knowledge as if it were certain. That did not mean that conjectural knowledge was of small value. Montesquieu's kind of history and medicine were necessary if they were appreciated properly and not misused. But uncertain knowledge should inspire caution, especially when applied to public policy.

D'Alembert was not alone in drawing a very sharp line between certainty and probability. Voltaire did so also. He took the Abbé de Prades severely to task for arguing that if all Paris claimed to have witnessed something, a miracle for example, then it was a certain truth. Only mathematicians are certain and truth is not a matter of majority votes.[67] Voltaire did, however, regret that probability was all one could achieve, and he would have liked to render all knowledge immediately more nearly certain. D'Alembert, on the other hand, was afraid of premature mathematization of probabilities and of the pseudo-certainty that it might engender. Undoubtedly, his low esteem for literary men in general did nothing to lessen his worry about their hasty desire to apply the newly discovered calculus of probability to daily life. He knew that our only hope for fairness in courts of law, as in daily life, depended on the probity and decency of the judges, not on mathematical calculations. Voltaire, however, could not settle for that, and he was immediately anxious to see that the new calculus of probability be applied to judicial evidence. In practice, these efforts to attach mathematical weights to evidence in judicial proceedings were no better than the old system of fractional

[64] "Essai sur les élémens," *Oeuvres*, I, 173-76; *L'abus de la critique en matière de religion*, I, 553.

[65] "Portrait de l'Auteur, fait par lui-même," *Oeuvre*, I, 9. "Essai sur les élémens, *loc. cit.*, 127-28.

[66] E.g., Arthur M. Wilson, *Diderot* (New York, 1972), 431.

[67] "Certain/Certitude," *loc. cit.*; Gay, *op. cit.*, II, 379; and Mason, *op. cit.*, *passim*. For Prades see "Certitude," *Encyclopédie*, II, 845-62.

proofs against which he and Beccaria had so rightly protested.[68] Doubt was for Voltaire a weapon against the Church, not a principle to live by. He railed against d'Alembert's lack of zeal even though the latter was, in his quiet way, a very determined *philosophe*.[69] Condorcet, in his eulogy of d'Alembert, continued to reprove his dead friend for his caution in attacking prejudice. D'Alembert was in fact singularly devoid of autocratic impulses. He did not like to dictate, which was quite in keeping with his acceptance of all the psychological and social implications of living in a permanent state of doubt. If everything is conjectural, one must respect common sense, be sure of one's facts, practice forebearance, and be perfectly tolerant. Condorcet did not particularly care for such a temper. D'Alembert, he noted, pushed rigor and fact-finding too far. He was too fond of geometry and its manner of thinking and therefore thought of the human spirit as too limited in its scope, especially in matters of morals and politics where there were few if any certain principles. It was not a very generous eulogy.[70]

Condorcet's strictures had their roots in d'Alembert's critique of the calculus of probabilities. D'Alembert had noted that the connection between mathematical and physical probability was assumed, not proven. From this he concluded that the mathematical calculation of probable truths did not render them more certain or make them a surer guide to practical conduct. In the art of practical conjecturing, mathematics is useless.[71] He even criticized Bernoulli for a futile effort to apply mathematics to human physiology.[72] It is now generally agreed that however poorly he presented his argument d'Alembert was quite right: there was no proof that the laws of mathematical probability accurately describe the physical world. The moral and social implications were for him especially worrying, for he knew where to expect trouble. The application of the calculus of probability to social policy was not limited to the judicial process. It was also suggested that it justified making inoculation against smallpox compulsory. The chances of dying from the disease could, after all, now be exactly proven to be so much higher than the likelihood of dying from the inoculation. The theory of infection being still unknown, this was not a proposal to prevent the spread of the disease but to save the ignorant and superstitious from themselves. D'Alembert strongly ap-

---

[68] "Essai sur les élémens," *loc. cit.*, 167-68; Baker, *op. cit.*, 231-35.

[69] Grimsely, *op. cit.*, 113, 293; John N. Pappas, *Voltaire and d'Alembert*, 33-41; *Essai, op. cit.*, 137-50.

[70] Condorcet, "Eloge de d'Alembert," *Oeuvres de d'Alembert*, I, i-xxviii.

[71] "Doutes et Questions sur le calcul des probabilités," *Oeuvres*, I, 451-66. "Essai sur les élémens," *ibid.*, I, 157-80; Hankins, *op. cit.*, 146-49; Baker, *op. cit.*, 171-80.

[72] "Eloge de Bernoulli," *Oeuvres*, III, 358.

proved of inoculation, but he was utterly opposed to the use of compulsion. When one's own life is at stake, everyone must be left free to make his own decision as he may see fit. He warned especially that orphans and abandoned children under public care should not be made the object of medical zeal.[73] Even Condorcet was moved by the plea to recognize that in this case an "exaggerated patriotism" would have infringed upon the rights of the individual.[74] It was not he, however, but d'Alembert who raised his voice against this proposal, one may assume because his own helpless childhood made him more sensitive. That may also have contributed to his dislike and fear of the social and political ambitions of the intellectuals, whose general outlook he shared in most respects and with whom he lived amicably enough.

Such views about the art, rather than the science, of conjecturing have considerable bearing on history such as Montesquieu's. Common sense was everything in this highly conjectural field, and mathematics could do nothing here. The philosophy which d'Alembert urged upon historians was really only a general critical spirit, with which Montesquieu was already amply endowed. Philosophy can teach careful methods of weighing evidence, but history also teaches philosophers how to make the most of insufficient factual materials. If history cannot compete with the sciences, given its low store of reliable facts and the unlikelihood of making new discoveries, it remains valuable as an incomparable school of wisdom. It shows us what men are by revealing to us what they once were.[75] It is the master of common sense, and it is of supreme importance that we develop that faculty because we must not overstep it. Hence the greatness of Montesquieu whose inspired guesses did not need the misapplied support of mathematics.

These precepts also guided d'Alembert's own practices as an historian. His task was, like Fontenelle's, to write notices of the life and work of former members of the *Académie Française* of which he was the permanent secretary. While he recognized Fontenelle's achievement as the real inventor of these panegyrics, he did not wish to imitate him entirely. He found Fontenelle's style mannered, too familiar, and too informal.[76] The real difference was, however, that d'Alembert had to eulogize many people who were completely undistinguished. The members of the *Académie des sciences* were all bona fide scientists, while the *Académie Française*, like most purely literary societies, was not so selective. The question of how truthful he

[73] "Réflexions sur l'inoculation," *Oeuvres,* I, 467-514.

[74] Condorcet, "Eloge de d'Alembert," *loc. cit.,* xx-xxi.

[75] "Eloge de Montesquieu," III, 448-49.

[76] "Réflexions sur les éloges," *Oeuvres,* II, 152; "Eloge de La Motte," *Oeuvres,* III, 171-74.

should be was therefore a far more pressing one for d'Alembert than it had been for Fontenelle. The obligations of an historian to posterity were for him a real burden. He could not simply sing the virtues of scientific man. In fact, he wrote the *éloge* of only one mathematician; all the others were more or less literary men. D'Alembert was determined not to prevaricate under any circumstances. If the work of a dead member was bad or his life disgraceful, just pass over it in silence, he advised.[77] Leave out the bad, but do not invent virtues. The Abbé de Saint-Pierre was remembered for his total lack of common sense and his poor style as much as for his good intentions.[78] Other *éloges* are tellingly brief. "I write your history and not your eulogy," he wrote of Jean Bernoulli.[79] The Abbé Dubos' only notable achievement was to have been refuted by Montesquieu.[80] Fléchier was only a second-rate orator.[81] Truthfulness, even when tempered by tact, was not d'Alembert's only achievement. He knew that he was using history as a replacement for a religious rite. He even claimed that Massillon would have preferred to write history instead of his celebrated *oraisons funèbres*.[82] The two were for d'Alembert competing ceremonies, defining two wholly incompatible views of man's destiny. History was meant for posterity, and it demanded accurate biographies in order to study mankind carefully and scientifically. On occasion d'Alembert, perhaps remembering Tacitus' biography of Agricola, parts of which he had translated, dwelled on the pettiness, especially that of the court, which threatened but did not overwhelm remarkable men such as Bossuet or Fénélon. These were, however, not models to be emulated by the young, such as Fontenelle's subjects had been. The biographies of intellectuals should be just as unflattering as those of kings if that was deserved.[83] D'Alembert was not only serving future historians, he was also reminding intellectuals to consider their future reputations. History had its disciplinary uses. Here accuracy and didactic purpose meet.

The history of science, the history of men of learning, and philosophical political history all have their diverse uses and aims. In the *Encyclopédie* all were to come together, the certain and elevating as well as the psychologically and politically conjectural, for d'Alembert here developed a new notion, history as the science of man, that could embrace them all. In the end he was able to bring a measure of coherence into the conflicting tendencies he had inherited. History as

---

[77] "Réflexions sur les éloges académiques," *Oeuvres*, II, 150-53.
[78] "Eloge de Saint-Pierre," *Oeuvres*, III, 255-58, 262, 274-75.
[79] "Eloge de Bernoulli," *loc. cit.*, 164, 338.
[80] "Eloge de Dubos," *ibid.*, 208.
[81] "Eloge de Fléchier," *ibid.*, 325.
[82] "Eloge de Massillon," *ibid.*, 223.
[83] "Eloge de Perrault," *ibid.*, 238.

the science of man illustrates the pattern by which men learn. Everything that can be called knowledge at all, whether certain or merely probable has its place here. That makes history more than a form of moral education. The notion of an encompassing history may well have come to d'Alembert from Condillac's belief that change begins in the human spirit and is then reflected in mores which in turn determine politics.[84] In d'Alembert's version the process of learning is a psychology of intellectual change which, with all its ups and downs, is an historical framework within which all knowledge and conduct find a place. As an encyclopedic umbrella, history is not merely good for us. History can make an integral contribution to knowledge in general. It can serve as a method of organization, a way to order our otherwise overwhelming stock of facts.

History is our collective remembering and that mental faculty is a far from passive one. Memory is passive, a mere attic, but without it all our other knowledge is useless to us. Remembering is active. The retrieving from memory what has been stored up is, like perception, an activity of the human mind without which there could be no human understanding. Memory is indeed the mother of all the muses, as the ancients had said, d'Alembert recalled.[85] It inspires work. Considerations such as these led him to assign to history, as active remembrance, a central place in the universe of knowledge. These new functions were not related to the moral and political uses of history, but they were scarcely less important. The sheer amount of history in the *Encyclopédie* is staggering. Most topics seem to have their history. D'Alembert and Haller introduced their discussions of individual sciences with a brief historical outline even if other authors did not do so. Some sciences did not have much of a history to recite, and most of d'Alembert's articles dealt with aspects of specific sciences that required merely definitions. However, whenever possible, he did mention the work, especially of antiquity, that preceded the present state of a science.[86] Even the history of previous encyclopedias and the debt the latest one owed to them received due attention.

Whether he discussed physics, literature, academies, or the expulsion of the Jesuits from France, d'Alembert had always found it necessary to begin with a history. How can one understand the

---

[84] "Histoire ancienne," *Oeuvres*, IX, 3-6, 20-22. Isabel F. Knight, *The Geometric Spirit* (New Haven, 1968), 224-25, 267-69.

[85] Locke, *Essay, ed. cit.*, Bk. II, Ch. X, *Works*, I, 137-43; "Discours préliminaire," *Oeuvres*, I, 51, 103-04.

[86] Nelly N. Schargo, *History in the Encyclopédie* (New York, 1947), 141-53 *et passim*. Lynn Thorndike, "L'Encyclopédie and the History of Science," *Isis* (1924), 6, 361-86. For the extremely technical and definitional character of d'Alembert's contribution see John Lough, *Essays on the Encyclopédie* (Oxford, 1968), 230-51. More generally, Jacques Proust, *L'Encyclopédie* (Paris, 1965), 106-41.

character of a religious order, or a system of patronage, or the structure of a learned society without first presenting its history? How else can one organize what one knows about it? How else is one to place it and explain its present status?[87] The need to write history, whether of the sciences or of social groups, was forced upon d'Alembert by the imperatives of systematization, of which the *Encyclopédie* was the ultimate and most expansive expression. It was history designed to retrieve all knowledge and to situate its individual forms. As such, it assumed the very style of its subject matter. D'Alembert strove to eliminate every trace of rhetorical embellishment from his narrative and to make it as plain, as unadorned, and as close to scientific exposition as possible.[88] Here his debt to Fontenelle's style became very evident, for their intentions coincided.

Encyclopedic organization required more history than prefaces to the main subjects. Active memory, remembering, was needed to grasp the totality of available knowledge. The Baconian universe of knowledge followed the three main faculties of the human mind: memory, reason, and imagination which engendered history, philosophy, and the arts respectively. The first, however, played a part in each of the others. It was the storehouse of each, and in the act of remembering it played a decisive part in every development.[89] It also had the very special task of organizing the unified whole. From a purely philosophical perspective all knowledge should be seen as a single interconnected whole, as a chain. The philosopher stands above the whole and gets a bird's-eye view of all the relationships that bind the sciences into a single unit. He can do that even without knowing that single truth that forever escapes us. The encyclopedic organization of knowledge follows this pattern through a system of exhaustive alphabetical listings which are linked by a complete system of cross-references. And each link and each branch of knowledge has its history, thus giving history an expansive character that d'Alembert had not originally foreseen. It could not be confined to one of the three categories into which he had tried to divide all knowledge.[90]

---

[87] "Essai sur les élémens," *Oeuvres*, I, 337-42: "Discours sur l'expulsion des jésuites," *ibid.*, II, 15-27: "Essai sur la société des gens des lettres," *ibid.*, IV, 337-39: "Description du Gouvernement de Genève, *ibid.*, IV, 411-15.

[88] Peter France, *Rhetoric and Truth in France, Descartes to Diderot* (Oxford, 1972), 96-112: Ralph S. Pomery, "Locke, d'Alembert and the Anti-rhetoric of the Enlightenment," *Studies of Voltaire and the Eighteenth Century*, 154 (1976), 1657-75.

[89] "Discours préliminaire," *Oeuvres*, I, 43-53.

[90] Hugh M. Davidson, "The Problem of Scientific Order Versus Alphabetic Order in the Encyclopédie," *American Society for Eighteenth Century Studies*, 2 (1972), 33-49; Hankins, *op. cit.*, 105-08.

When he defined history directly, d'Alembert had sliced it into three segments. First there was sacred history, then the history of man, civil and intellectual, and finally natural history. The last covered both the order of nature and the use man made of it. The history of the human intellect was, however, of a peculiar kind, since it embraced all knowledge whether it be imaginative, mnemonic, or rational. Art, history, and science properly so-called all fell within its realm. Indeed, they fell into both an historical and a parallel psychological sequence. The arts, most sensual, come first, then imaginative belles-lettres, and finally, philosophy and science, expressions of the critical spirit. This series does not show any sort of progress; indeed, there are real losses here as dry reason seems to destroy the inspiration of the fine arts. The work of history, it becomes clear, escapes definition as a separate or isolable topic because remembering is not just memory—it is active. Any reasoned dictionary, even a purely grammatical one, must be a philosophical history pursuing its subjects from their infancy to their maturity, and on to their old age and decline.[91] The tree of knowledge grows, whether as the accumulated work and virtue of great men of science or as the work of obscure mechanics; knowledge increases through the ages and acquires an even longer past. Remembering these achievements, the historian in his work provides the only way to bring the growth of knowledge to our present consciousness, to give us any view of the whole and all its parts.

D'Alembert's replacement for a discredited tradition of history has its peculiarities. In the history of science there is no enduring place for the history of fraud and error which become eliminated as non-knowledge. Such centennial discarding of useless facts that d'Alembert had suggested makes perfectly good sense here. His new history was not to be confused with mere traditonalism, as much of nineteenth-century "historism" was. Philosophical history was to be a master science.[92] As the organizer of human knowledge generally, it could not just preserve the whole past as equally precious. It had, moreover, to embrace an endless future, for the childhood of the sciences is long, or to be exact, eternal.[93] History cannot, given its purpose, keep such a mass of matter in perpetual consciousness. If one knows, as d'Alembert did, what the uses of history are, then one can choose information that is worth remembering and periodically eliminate the worthless from the scholarly memory. There are things

[91] "Discours préliminaire," *Oeuvres,* I, 40-42, 48. "Essai sur les élémens," *ibid.,* 123-26; "Dictionnaire," *Oeuvres,* IV, 494-95, 500-01.

[92] "Elémens des sciences," *loc. cit.*

[93] "Expérimental," *Encyclopédie,* VI, 299.

that might well be fit for forgetting if they do not help us to order our moral and intellectual conduct.

The intense concern for the usefulness of history may not, in practice, be helpful to the working historian, but it led d'Alembert to find a commanding place for history among all the other forms of knowledge. He provided an answer to the outstanding questions about historiography, an answer which allowed history to survive and grow in a scientific intellectual climate. He also suggested reasons why the history of ideas generally, and of science particularly, has a special function in the world of knowldege, where it was not only a member but a master.

Harvard University.

XII

ELOQUENCE AND LIBERTY*

By Jean Starobinski

This essay intends to study, in the works of eighteenth-century French writers, the occurrence of an idea borrowed from Tacitus' *Dialogue*[1] and from the last chapter of Pseudo-Longinus' treatise *On Sublimity*[2]: eloquence, in order to develop all its powers, needs freedom and even civic disorders; when freedom disappears, eloquence degenerates accordingly.

In Tacitus' *Dialogue,* this idea is expounded in the final speech of Maternus, but Maternus does not deplore the condition of his time which left eloquence reduced to a minor role. Thanks to the emperor's authority, public affairs are now peaceful, the flame of civil wars is extinguished. Maternus invites his friends not to regret an art which flourished with that "licence which fools call liberty." He himself has chosen to devote his talent to poetry: consequently, he expects not to be blamed if he spends most of his time writing a tragedy of *Cato.* It is significant that this subject brings Maternus' mind back to the days of the Republic, the very same past which he declares not to regret. Taken literally, Maternus' speech could be read as a lesson in the historical relativity of the arts: there is a time when great minds cannot help being involved in public quarrels; there is another time when, things being held firmly in the hands of an authoritarian government, gifted men would just waste their time pleading petty lawsuits; they can do better, if they devote themselves to more pleasant or to more useful tasks.[3] As we shall see, in the eighteenth century Maternus' thesis gave occasion to some generalizations: peace and prosperity are not the proper stimulus for artistic achievement: but are not peace and prosperity preferable? And, if in the present time eloquence and even poetry are weaker, should the citizens of Europe blame their century, which in so many other respects has made them happier and more secure? One could define this interpretation as an optimistic one: if the best minds are busy with matters of public welfare, they cannot be also orators,

---

*Read before the International Society of the History of Ideas, Fourth Conference on "Freedom of Thought and Expression in the History of Ideas" held at the Cini Foundation in Venice, Sept. 28–Oct. 2, 1975.

[1] Ch. XXXVI–XLI.   [2] Ch. XLIV.

[3] For the interpretion of the *Dialogue,* see Ronald Syme, *Tacitus* (Oxford, 1958), I, 100–11; Kurt von Fritz, "Aufbau und Absicht des Dialogus de Oratoribus," *Tacitus,* ed. V. Pöschl (Darmstadt, 1969).

poets, painters; they are engaged in practical negotiations which dispense with eloquence.

But another interpretation was possible, supposing that Maternus was either cautious or ironic when he mentioned the "licence which fools call liberty." Perhaps he did really intend to incriminate the loss of liberty: was it possible for him to speak more openly? To this interpretation, the authority of Longinus gave an additional weight. Every schoolboy could have read Longinus in Boileau's translation and apply to French conditions what the Greek author said about his own times:

> Je ne saurais assez m'étonner . . . d'où vient que dans notre siècle il se trouve assez d'orateurs qui savent manier un raisonnement, et qui ont même le style oratoire . . . mais qu'il s'en rencontre si peu qui puissent s'élever fort haut dans le sublime: tant la stérilité maintenant est grande parmi les esprits. N'est-ce point . . . ce qu'on dit ordinairement, que c'est le gouvernement populaire qui nourrit et forme les grands génies: puisque enfin jusqu'ici tout ce qu'il y a presque eu d'orateurs habiles ont fleuri et sont morts avec lui? En effet . . . il n'y a peut-être rien qui élève davantage l'âme des grands hommes que la liberté, ni qui excite et réveille plus puissamment en nous ce sentiment naturel qui nous porte à l'émulation, et cette noble ardeur de se voir élevé au-dessus des autres. Ajoutez que les prix qui se proposent dans les républiques aiguisent, pour ainsi dire, et achèvent de polir l'esprit des orateurs, leur faisant cultiver avec soin les talents qu'ils ont reçus de la nature. Tellement qu'on voir briller dans leurs discours la liberté de leur pays.
>
> Mais nous . . . qui avons appris dès nos premières années à souffrir le joug d'une domination légitime, qui avons été comme enveloppés par les coutumes et les façons de faire de la monarchie lorsque nous avions encore l'imagination tendre, et capable de toutes sortes d'impressions; en un mot, qui n'avons jamais goûté de cette vive et féconde source de l'éloquence, je veux dire de la liberté: ce qui arrive ordinairement de nous, c'est que nous nous rendons de grands et magnifiques flatteurs. . . . Ainsi la servitude, je dis la servitude la plus justement établie, est une espèce de prison où l'âme décroît et se rapetisse en quelque sorte.

No mention is made here of a shift of interest from eloquence to other arts or to practical activities. Servitude, even under a just ruler, prevents the full development of the soul's faculties. A deterioration occurs in the innermost part of man's nature. There seems to be no compensation, such as general peace and prosperity, which can be relied upon to make us accept without regret the new state of things. This leads to a pessimistic view of human history: except for two short periods in Athens and in Rome, eloquence did not flourish in antiquity; it must be concluded that despotism and tyranny were constantly stronger than liberty. The decline of Greece and the fall of Rome were both announced and accompanied by the decay of eloquence. It is not difficult to generalize the close relation just established between eloquence and freedom and to extend it to all arts and sciences. Only a free republic can foster their rise and progress.[4]

It is easily seen that these ideas, although at first applied in interpreting ancient history and civilization, were general enough to be retained and to become a sort of commonplace expression to test the present state of affairs and to pass judgment upon it. What interests us here, at least, is the manner in which a *topos* concerning the political and literary history of antiquity, already considered as trite by Pseudo-Longinus,[5] has been utilized as a model for the understanding of a contemporary situation. As soon as this happens, the main issue becomes this one: Is our situation under absolute monarchy similar to that of Rome under the emperors? Are we threatened by the same fate? Is the loss of liberty irretrievable? Or do we have a chance of developing other crafts and trades, to compensate for a lost state of licence, which altogether should not be regretted? The topos, in both its versions, optimistic or pessimistic, becomes interesting for us, insofar as it works as an analytical or interpretative tool, through which eighteenth-century writers tried to gain an understanding of their present situation, or to express their discontent. This set of questions, borrowed from classical writers, fitted exactly the needs of "intellectuals" who, perhaps for the first time in modern Europe, were concerned with the interaction of literature and socio-political conditions. For them, the history of taste could less and less be disassociated from the history of political institutions and of what Montesquieu calls "l'esprit général." Thus, they tended to treat contemporary literature as an index of their socio-political situation, and, conversely, to refer to the existing political regime in order to justify their literary options or to excuse their failures.

As long as no criticism is directed against the principle of monarchy, the lower quality of modern eloquence, as compared to that of the classics, can be explained harmlessly enough. For Guillaume Du Vair, at the end of the sixteenth century, one of the main causes of the absence of a genuine achievement in oratory among the French is the nobility's neglect of literary culture. But this neglect itself is not severely blamed, as it has a moral excuse: "Ils s'estoient persuadez qu'il valloit mieux bien faire que bien dire, et, contents du rang que leur donnoit leur naissance ou vaillance, ils ne

---

[4]"It is impossible for the arts and sciences to arise at first among any people, unless that people enjoy the blessing of a free government," Hume writes in 1742, *Essays, moral, political, and literary,* Part I, xiv; new ed. (Basle, 1793), 116.; also Condillac, *Cours d'Étude pour l'Instruction du Prince de Parme* (London, 1776), VI, 60–74 of *Introduction à l'étude de l'histoire ancienne,* Bk. III, Chap. IX.

[5]The word used is *to thruloumenon.*

cherchoient point d'autre honneur que celuy des armes à la guerre et du mesnage en la paix."[6] Another excuse for the lower quality of French eloquence is the monarchic rule, which is a good in itself: "Nostre estat François a dès sa naissance esté gouverné par les Roys, la puissance souveraine desquels ayant tiré à soy l'authorité du gouvernement nous a à la verité deslivré des miseres, calamitez et confusions qui sont ordinairement és estats populaires, mais aussi nous a privé de l'exercice que pouvoient avoir les braves esprits et des moyens de paroistre au maniement des affaires."[7] Such an explanation might have provided a good reason for dispensing with eloquence. Nevertheless, Du Vair, himself an orator, hopes that there will be a French eloquence, and gives advice on the means to foster and to acquire it. Except for the tone of Renaissance optimism concerning the future growth of arts and skills which have not yet been fully rediscovered, Du Vair's arguments (partially borrowed from Tacitus) were to be repeated again and again. They could be somewhat modified and, instead of mentioning the wisdom of the ruler, one could mention the complexity and greater perfection of the body of laws, which left little to be submitted to the arbitrary feelings of the judge, and therefore made useless the forensic orator's efforts to influence those feelings. In this manner the inferiority of modern eloquence could be ascribed to the actual superiority of civil government. Ideas of this sort were expounded by some of the major English authors of the eighteenth century, for instance by Hume[8] and Gibbon.[9] But they were also put forward in France, even by some of the authors who, on other occasions, had expressed opinions very critical of the French absolutistic pattern of government. There is an interesting page of Diderot, where he seems to extend to all the arts one of the main propositions of Maternus, the character in Tacitus' *Dialogue*. In a world where commerce and international trade have become the main activity, violence and war, both civil and external,

---

[6] Guillaume du Vair, *De l'Eloquence française*, ed. René Radouant (Paris, n.d.) 150. For a general view, see Hannah H. Gray, "Renaissance Humanism: the Pursuit of Eloquence," *JHI*, **24** (1963), 497–514.

[7] *Op. cit.*, 148.

[8] "Of Eloquence," in *Essays, moral, political, and literary*, Part I, xiii.

[9] *Essai sur l'Étude de la Littérature* (London, 1762), XII: "Les anciennes Républiques de la Grèce ignoraient les premiers principes d'un bon gouvernement. Le peuple s'assemblait en tumulte pour décider plutôt que pour délibérer. Leurs factions étaient furieuses et immortelles; leurs séditions fréquentes et terribles; leurs plus beaux jours remplis de méfiance, d'envie et de confusion: leurs citoyens étaient malheureux; mais leurs écrivains, l'imagination échauffée par ces affreux objets, les peignaient comme ils les sentaient. La tranquille administration des lois; ces arrêts salutaires, qui, sortis du cabinet d'un seul ou du conseil d'un petit nombre, vont répandre la félicité chez un peuple entier, n'excitent chez le poète que l'admiration, la plus froide de toutes les passions."

tend to disappear, or to be reduced to short and insignificant outbursts. In such a situation, the arts lack the very element of which they are made: passion, hope, hatred, heroism. They cannot but decline, whereas general well-being increases:

Si l'on me demande ce que deviendront la philosophie, les lettres et les beaux-arts sous le calme et la durée de ces sociétés mercantiles où la découverte d'une île, l'importation d'une nouvelle denrée, l'invention d'une machine, l'établissement d'un comptoir, l'invasion d'une branche de commerce, la construction d'un port, deviendront les transactions les plus importantes, je répondrai par une autre question, et je demanderai qu'est-ce qu'il y a dans ces objets qui puisse échauffer les âmes, les élever, y produire l'enthousiasme? Un grand négociant est-il un personnage bien propre à devenir le héros d'un poème épique? Je ne le crois pas. Heureusement que cette espèce de luxe n'est pas fort essentielle au bonheur des nations. . . . Quelle est la cause des progrès et de l'éclat des lettres et des beaux-arts chez les peuples tant anciens que modernes? La multitude d'actions héroïques et de grands hommes à célébrer. Tarissez la source des périls, et vous tarissez en même temps celle des vertus, des forfaits, des historiens, des orateurs et des poètes. Ce fut au milieu des orages continus de la Grèce, que cette contrée se peupla de peintres, de sculpteurs et de poètes. Ce fut dans les temps où cette bête féroce, qu'on appelait le peuple romain, ou se dévorait elle-même ou s'occupait à dévorer les nations, que les historiens écrivirent et que les poètes chantèrent. Ce fut au milieu des troubles civils en Angleterre, en France après les massacres de la Ligue et de la Fronde, que des auteurs immortels parurent. A mesure que les secousses violentes d'une nation s'apaisent et s'éloignent, les âmes se calment, les images des dangers s'effacent, et les lettres se taisent. Les grands génies se couvent dans les temps difficiles, ils éclosent dans les temps voisins des temps difficiles.[10]

Usually Diderot himself and most of his contemporaries establish a close link between liberty and the growth of the arts.[11] Instead, Diderot refers here to "storms" and to bestial cruelty, using the concepts which were familiar to those writers who were diffident of popular rule. If one has to pay such a high price for "great geniuses," who would not prefer security, accompanied by a relative cultural mediocrity? In any case, if the historical conditions for the birth of literary geniuses are those supposed by Diderot, there is no reason— at least no *moral* reason—to complain about the decline of eloquence and of the arts in general, once they have occurred. Political improvement may be accompanied by aesthetic decline. A weakening in the arts should not be taken as an ill omen for the destiny of a nation. No

---

[10]Diderot, "Pensées détachées ou Fragments politiques échappés du portefeuille d'un philosophe," *Oeuvres complètes* (Paris, 1971) X, 80–81.

[11]In his *Essai sur la vie de Sénèque le philosophe* (Paris, 1778), Diderot writes: "Ne cherchez la véritable éloquence que chez les républicains" (Ch. X, 39).

decrease in the amount of liberty enjoyed by a people can be diagnosed on that basis.

An additional argument, current among the "moderns," but widely accepted, contends that true eloquence is a natural gift, not unknown to primitive cultures and apt to manifest itself at all times and in every country.[12] In such a broad definition, which no longer limits eloquence to the knowledge of rhetoric and to its use at the bar, it is not likely ever to be lost. In different ages, eloquence manifests itself in different literary genres. Thus, the flourishing French pulpit eloquence ("éloquence de la chaire"), unknown to pagan antiquity, compensates for the lack of a truly great forensic eloquence ("éloquence du barreau"). Voltaire, in the article "Eloquence" written for Diderot's *Encyclopédie,* starts with the traditional mention of liberty as the condition of eloquence:

> L'éloquence sublime n'appartient, dit-on, qu'à la liberté; c'est qu'elle consiste à dire des vérités hardies, à étaler des raisons et des peintures fortes. Souvent un maître n'aime pas la vérité, craint les raisons, et aime mieux un compliment que de grands traits.

Voltaire cannot refrain from showing, once more, his admiration for England, where the rewards of forensic eloquence are the same as in the great republics of ancient times. But in France, eloquence has, so to speak, migrated in another field:

[12]For instance René Rapin, (1621–87) in his "Réflexions sur l'usage de l'éloquence," writes: "Aristote, Cicéron, Quintilien, et Longin, qui nous ont laissé des traités de rhétorique les plus accomplis de l'antiquité, remarquent que cette éloquence, telle qu'on l'a vue autrefois dans Athènes et dans Rome, avant que ces deux républiques eussent perdu leur liberté, ne peut régner que dans un peuple libre. . . . C'est l'avis de ces grands hommes, qui étaient à la vérité bien capables d'en juger; mais qui cependant se sont un peu laissés prévenir en faveur du gouvernement où ils avaient été nourris: je ne suis pas tout-à-fait de leur sentiment. Car l'éloquence peut régner partout, quand elle est véritable, et qu'elle a de quoi se faire écouter" *Oeuvres du P. Rapin* (La Haye, 1725), II, 2–3. Rapin, like many of his contemporaries attributes to Quintilian the *Dialogus de Oratoribus.* In his *Saggio sull'Eloquenza,* Saverio Bettinelli (1718–1808) defines eloquence as "un'arte di rivolgere i precetti della ragione all'imaginazione sì fortemente, che la volontà, e gli affetti ne sian percossi," and he adds: "Dell'eloquenza cosi definita ed intesa son capaci tutti gli uomini, tutte le nazioni, tutte le lingue, e tutte l'arti," *Opere* (Venice, 1782), VIII, 26–27. Turgot, in an essay written in 1748, while he was a student at the Sorbonne, insists on the same point: "Nous devons remarquer une chose sur l'éloquence, c'est que, quand nous parlons de ses progrès et de sa décadence, nous ne parlons que de l'éloquence étudiée, des discours d'apparat; car, chez tous les peuples et dans tous les temps, les passions et les affaires ont produit des hommes vraiment éloquents. Les histoires sont remplies d'une éloquence forte et persuasive dans le sein de la barbarie," *Oeuvres de Turgot,* ed. G. Schelle (Paris, 1913), I, 129.

Charles Perrault, in his *Parallèle des anciens et des modernes,* devotes one dialogue, out of five, to prove the superiority of modern eloquence, and particularly of religious eloquence: "Au lieu des séditions qu'il fallait émouvoir ou apaiser du temps

La grande éloquence n'a guere pu en France être connue au barreau, parce qu'elle ne conduit pas aux honneurs comme dans Athènes, dans Rome, et comme aujourd'hui dans Londres, et n'a point pour objet de grands intérêts publics: elle s'est réfugiée dans les oraisons funèbres, où elle tient un peu de la poésie.

Quoting a famous page of Massillon on the Last Judgment, Voltaire praises it as "un des plus beaux traits d'éloquence qu'on puisse lire chez les nations anciennes et modernes." Furthermore, there are admirable speeches in modern works of history, like that of Mézeray. Voltaire ends his article with a declaration of trust in his own century and in human genius: "Dans un siècle éclairé, le génie aidé des exemples en sait plus que n'en disent tous les maîtres."[13]

In all the examples we have quoted thus far, Tacitus' and Longinus' interpretation of the decline of eloquence as the result of the loss of liberty, although dutifully mentioned, was either applied in an anodyne way to the contemporary scene, or limited to the particular fate of Athens and Rome. But it could be utilized with the effect of justifying modern literary and political discontent. In other words, Tacitus' and Longinus' interpretations of their own historical situation offered a means of interpreting the present world in a similar way, and furthermore of predicting a downfall similar to that which brought Rome to its pitiful end. It was possible to construe it, for learned readers, as a fateful simile, as a warning. These writers, once decided to proclaim the wrongs of their nation, could prophesize the worst, as soon as they had established the "fact" of the absence or decline of eloquence: this "fact" once acknowleged, was the premise of a syllogism, where a regular law of historical development, from rude beginnings to decline, was taken for granted and thought to be

---

des républiques anciennes, nos prédicateurs n'ont-ils pas lieu d'employer les mêmes figures de rhétorique, ou à exciter les pécheurs à secouer le joug de leurs passions tyranniques, ou à calmer les troubles que ces mêmes passions élèvent continuellement dans le fond de leurs âmes. Jamais les matières n'ont été plus heureuses pour l'éloquence puisqu'elles ne sont pas de moindre importance que le salut et la vie éternelle," ed. H. R. Jauss and M. Imdahl (Munich, 1964), 243. The same idea is developed by Z. Pearce in *The Spectator,* No. 633 (Dec. 15, 1714): "The design of this paper shall be to show, that the moderns have greater advantages towards true and solid eloquence, than any which the celebrated speakers of antiquity enjoyed. . . . Our ideas are so infinitely enlarged by revelation, the eye of reason has so wide a prospect into eternity, the notions of a deity are so worthy and refined, and the accounts we have of a state of happiness or misery so clear and evident, that the contemplation of such objects will give our discourse a noble vigour, an invincible force, beyond the power of any human consideration."

[13]Voltaire's article "Eloquence" was included later, with minor modifications, in his *Dictionnaire Philosophique.* In the *Encyclopédie,* Voltaire's article was supplemented by an article by Marmontel, where the superiority of the "éloquence poétique" over the "éloquence oratoire" is demonstrated.

the same for successive civilizations. Let us go over a few examples, in order to show how constantly the topos "eloquence lost = liberty lost" was put forward by those who were critical of their times and institutions.

In his important *Lettre à l'Académie* (1716), Fénelon develops, among other projects, the idea of a Rhetoric ("Projet de Rhétorique") and reviews the past history of eloquence. After a description of Greek city life, where "tout dépendait du peuple, et le peuple dépendait de la parole," he adds:

La parole n'a aucun pouvoir semblable chez nous; les assemblées n'y sont que des cérémonies et des spectacles. Il ne nous reste guère de monuments d'une forte éloquence . . . Tout se décide en secret dans le cabinet des princes ou dans quelque négociation particulière: ainsi notre nation n'est point excitée à faire les mêmes efforts que les Grecs pour dominer par la parole.[14]

In a first version, Fénelon had mentioned Rome. And Roman history was for him the occasion of a dichotomy, which was later to be more fully developed by Rousseau. In Fénelon as in Rousseau, this dichotomic view of history even occurs twice over. It consists first in attributing more value to the rude beginnings of the republic, where eloquence was not yet discovered; in those times, doing was preferred to speaking, action was what mattered more than words:

Les Romains s'appliquèrent fort tard à l'éloquence et à la poésie. Quoiqu'ils vécussent en république, ils étaient moins touchés du talent de parler, que des armes, de l'agriculture, du commerce d'argent, de la justice au dedans et de la politique au dehors. . . .

As opposed to the virtues of ancient times, eloquence and poetry are symptomatic of moral decline.

But a second dichotomy, concerning later conditions, separates the age of servitude and the age of eloquence. In a similar way, what comes later makes us regret what was before. Nostalgia has always a golden past to lament over:

L'éloquence vint enfin dans la République et elle y éclata jusqu'à ce que les Empereurs la fissent tomber avec la liberté.[15]

No doubt, in the *Lettre à l'Académie,* it would be hard to find an explicit criticism of social conditions in contemporary France. But there is an undertone which links it unmistakably with the writings in which Fénelon expressed his misgivings about the royal administration.

[14] Fénelon, *Lettre à l'Académie,* ed. A. Cahen (Paris, 1902), 26.
[15] *Op. cit.,* 186.

Some compelling analogy might have existed in Fénelon's mind between imperial Rome and the French kingdom, where decisions are taken "en secret, dans les cabinets des princes."

At mid-century, the criticism sharpens; new "facts" were advanced which seemed to tie in with the loss or the absence of true eloquence, and to bear the same relationship to the lack of liberty: these "facts" are the changes observed in language, and interpreted as signs of corruption and degeneration. Remarks on this subject can be found in various authors, among which we shall give particular attention to only two: d'Alembert and Rousseau.

As a matter of fact, d'Alembert's writings on the exact sciences and their history express a very optimistic view of their progress from the "renaissance des lettres" on; further advances are taken for granted. But at the same time, d'Alembert does not do away with the idea of decline and decadence. He feels concern about the too close relationship between the intellectuals ("les gens de lettres") and the wealthy and noble classes ("les grands"). In their submission to rich patrons, the "gens de lettres" adopt their manners and their ways of speaking. The worst, in this moral alienation, is its effect on language. Literature is invaded by "ce langage entortillé, impropre et barbare."[16] D'Alembert is convinced that "notre langue se dénature et se dégrade."[17] And he goes as far as to insinuate the impending risk of an irreversible decline, similar to the decline of the Latin language, which was in some measure responsible for the decline of Roman morals and finally of Roman civilization. If the "gens de lettres" remain unable to defend themselves against "le ramage éphémère de nos sociétés,"[18] if they don't go back to "le vrai et le simple,"[19] France will suffer the fate of Rome: "Il y a bien de l'apparence que ce sont des circonstances pareilles qui ont corrompu sans retour la langue du siècle d'Auguste."[20] It is evident here that, to the eyes of d'Alembert, servitude and servility not only prevent the blooming of true eloquence (which he calls elsewhere "fille du génie et de la liberté"[21]), but affects language itself. Collective well-being and political health being based on the sound state of language, it is not just a pedantic bias to insist on purity and clarity of language: the future of the national community is at stake, and the considerations on language take a socio-political turn.

This is peculiarly evident when d'Alembert comes to suggest the

---

[16] D'Alembert, *Mélanges de littérature, d'histoire et de philosophie* (Paris, 1763), I, "Essai sur la société des gens de lettres et des grands," 384.

[17] *Op. cit.*, 385   [18] *Ibid.*

[19] *Op. cit.*, 386   [20] *Ibid.*

[21] *Op. cit.*, II, "Réflexions sur l'élocution oratoire et sur le style en général," 317.

remedies. What should be done by the "gens de lettres"? They ought to take the vow of "liberté, vérité, pauvreté"[22]; they must live in harmony, "vivre unis,"[23] which is the surest way to obtain respect. If they follow his advice, d'Alembert does not hesitate to promise power to the intellectuals. As a reward for their integrity, they can "donner la loi au reste de la nation sur les matières de goût et de philosophie."[24] Although this power remains apparently limited to matters of taste and philosophy, it is evident that through taste and philosophy the intellectuals could become the true rulers of the nation.

This essay of d'Alembert shows very clearly how the threat of decadence and ruin is put forward, in order to give an additional inducement, a sense of urgency, to the proposed solution, relying on the unity of action among the intellectuals. In a way, it is good rhetoric, and it makes the appeal "intellectuals, unite" sound more convincing. And what is here implicitly affirmed is that the freedom kept alive in their limited circle by the "gens de lettres" can still regenerate the liberty of the whole community, and lift it from the wretched state where it is now.

Rousseau, in many respects, is a disciple of Fénelon, and his interpretation of Roman history, as regards the growth and decline of eloquence, is the same. But Rousseau is more outspoken in his contempt for the present state of civilization and, at the same time, he tries to develop a more articulate and elaborate theory to account for the causes and mechanisms of changes occuring in history: he pays particular attention to the way in which the factors interact. Thus, he develops a more radical system, where philosophy of history, philosophy of language, and political theory are tied together far more tightly. The last chapter of the posthumous *Essai sur l'Origine des Langues* can be mentioned as an example of Rousseau's way of thinking: the present state of things in language, politics, and manners is analyzed as the final stage of a gradual deterioration. The first languages were synthetic, passionnate, warm, musical; their expressive power was maximal. The primal unity, once split, gave way to separate and specialized progress,[25] which heightened the practical usefulness of language, its referential precision; manners became polite and hypocritical; music cultivated the pleasures of the ear at the expense of those of the heart. In all these fields, a cooling of expressive power, a clouding of immediacy gradually occurred. The

---

[22]*Op. cit.,*I 399.

[23]*Op. cit.,* 410.   [24]*Ibid.*

[25]The splitting of a primitive synthetic language into the idioms of song, verse, and prose is an 18th-century commonplace, going back to Strabo.

last chapter of the *Essai sur l'Origine des Langues* is pervaded with the spirit of indictment. The state of affairs described is thought to be the worst in history: man has practically lost the ability to communicate what matters, i.e., his inner feelings. Human language and free eloquence have been replaced by the all too clear, but mute, signs of despotic violence:

Dans les anciens temps, où la persuasion tenait lieu de force publique, l'éloquence était nécessaire. A quoi servirait-elle aujourd'hui que la force publique supplée à la persuasion. L'on n'a besoin ni d'art ni de figure pour dire, *tel est mon bon plaisir.* Quels discours restent donc à faire au peuple assemblé? . . . . Les langues populaires nous sont devenues aussi parfaitement inutiles que l'éloquence. Les sociétés ont pris leur dernière forme; on n'y change plus rien qu'avec du canon ou des écus, et comme on n'a plus rien à dire au peuple sinon *donnez de l'argent,* on le dit avec des placards au coin des rues ou des soldats dans les maisons; il ne faut *assembler* personne pour cela: au contraire, il faut tenir les sujets épars; c'est la première maxime de la politique moderne.

Il y a des langues favorables à la liberté; ce sont les langues sonores, prosodiques, harmonieuses, dont on distingue le discours de fort loin. Les nôtres sont faites pour le bourdonnement des divans. Nos prédicateurs se tourmentent, de mettent en sueur dans les temples, sans qu'on sache rien de ce qu'ils ont dit. Après s'être épuisés à crier pendant une heure, ils sortent de la chaire à demi-morts. Assurément ce n'était pas la peine de prendre tant de fatigue.

Chez les anciens on se faisait entendre aisément au peuple sur la place publique; on y parlait tout un jour sans s'incommoder. . . . Toute langue avec laquelle on ne peut pas se faire entendre au peuple *assemblé* est une langue servile; il est impossible qu'un peuple demeure libre et qu'il parle cette langue-là.[26]

One question arises: Supposing we admit Rousseau's arguments, could political changes alone be sufficient to bring back some sort of better government? Apparently, as long as language remains in its degenerate state—and what power can undo at a blow what slow transformations have done?—the restoration of a more free and more legitimate community is not to be thought of. In the chapter of the *Contrat Social* devoted to the demonstration that sovereignty should not be represented, Rousseau lets us understand that where a people has a language unfit for public assemblies, it is doomed to serfdom, and can never have a democratic constitution.[27]

[26] Rousseau, *Essai sur l'origine des langues* (1781, posthumous), ed. Porset (Bordeaux, 1968), XX, 197–201. On the importance of sound, Rousseau leans on Duclos.
[27] *Contrat social* [1762], III, xv (*Oeuvres complètes,* [Paris, 1964], IV, 428–31). It is necessary to add that Rousseau can also be chosen as a good example in the tradi-

A few remarks should be added here.

First, let us say that the chapter of Rousseau we have just partly quoted is in itself a very eloquent piece of literature. The absence of a forum eloquence, of a public oratory, gives rise to a very elaborate and—as the success of Rousseau among his contemporaries tells us—to a very efficient *written* eloquence. Although we could recognize here the figures, the rhythms, the syntactic devices of rhetoric, Rousseau's work is different both in the fact that it is meant from the beginning for the press, and in that its pathos is a nostalgic one. It is eloquent, while complaining about the destruction of eloquence.

Another remark should start with the reminder that one aspect of the debate, in Tacitus' *Dialogue,* was the choice made by Maternus to write poetry instead of practicing legal oratory. It was traditional in education to divide the *Belles Lettres* into three great categories: poetry, oratory, and history. And it was traditional, too, in the colleges, to enlarge upon their comparative value and usefulness; one would show, for instance, that they had much in common; that oratory could be poetic, that poetry could be also eloquent, and so on. But rarely, in these academic exercises, were the inner motivations for the choice of, say, poetry against oratory, taken into full account.

Now it is obvious that Rousseau, although not formally a poet, is one of the main sources of French romantic poetry. And his way to poetry seems to be a direct consequence of what has just been put into focus. If true political eloquence has become impossible because of the lack of public liberties, there is another eloquence, the source of which is the inner freedom of the individual, the "voice of conscience." This new type of eloquence is not only based on the nostalgia of what has disappeared from public life; it tends to identify itself with poetry, and more specifically with poetry conceived as an expression of the self.[28] The written word of the poet receives life and warmth from liberty, as did the spoken word of the orator, but liberty has now to be understood as a subjective power, as the individual will

---

tion of hostility and diffidence against eloquence, which starts with Plato's *Gorgias* and includes Montaigne's essay LI ("De la vanité des paroles") in Book I of the *Essais,* and John Locke's attack on rhetoric in his *Philosophical Essay* (III, X, §34). As can be expected, Rousseau prefers always the spontaneous communicative power of inner feelings to any sort of learned skill. The first *Discourse* includes an attack on eloquence. *Emile's* Book IV brings important elements to this subject. We should remark here that the famous "Profession de foi du Vicaire Savoyard" is supposed to be a *spoken* lesson in religion, delivered to a single listener. The Vicaire Savoyard is a preacher. The "inner feelings" give rise to a specific eloquence, which conceals its rhetorical nature.

[28] M. H Abrams, *The Mirror and the Lamp* (Oxford, 1953).

rescued from the wreck of the general will.[29] The inner certitude of truth had always been one of the presuppositions of eloquence[30]: truth being now inseparable from conscience itself, to be eloquent and to express oneself are one and the same thing.

In such a withdrawal from outside to inside, from public life to the inner feelings, eloquence seems to be condemned to give up its direct impact on the crowd. Actually, the poets, the writers, and Rousseau himself knew that words carried by books work more slowly and more obscurely than words pronounced in public assemblies. But they didn't accept easily that their message should remain secret and reserved for the few. Although a belated one, their had to be also a widespread action and, above all, an action of the utmost *energy*. Written eloquence, for them, was still supposed to keep the power which public eloquence was endowed with: "se rendre maître des esprits par la parole."[31] The dream of playing the legislator's or the prophet's role was not lost.[32] It could be clearly demonstrated that the neoclassical imitation of Greek authors—for such a poet as André Chénier—was regarded as a means of infusing new warmth, new energies into the French Language. The revival of antiquity was supposed to rejuvenate modern poetry.[33] Some of the poets and theorists of that period took a new interest in the Pindaric ode because its enthusiastic character seemed appropriate to generate the feeling of a rebirth (or of a *regeneration*, to use a word then fashion-

[29] Previously, some treatises of rhetoric recommend forestalling the tiresome effects of a too well constructed discourse. It is preferable to give an impression of freedom and improvisation: the Jesuit Father B. Gisbert writes: "L'éloquence veut de la liberté. Elle aime un caractère aisé, dégagé, naturel, qui règne dans toutes les parties du discours. . . . Elle consiste, cette liberté, dans un style où l'art et l'étude ne se font point remarquer, où la nature est toujours la dominante: je dis une nature cultivée et polie; une nature à qui la réflexion, l'étude, le commerce du monde a ôté ce qu'elle a de grossièreté et de rudesse, depuis la corruption du péché. Parlez, exprimez-vous, dites les choses comme vous les auriez dites dans l'état d'innocence, et votre style sera aisé, libre, simple, naïf. C'est pour en venir à ce point qu'il faut employer toute la force et toute la finesse de l'art. L'art ne doit servir qu'à rétablir la nature dans sa première perfection: s'il ne va pas jusque là, il est défectueux: s'il va au-delà, il est vicieux." *L'éloquence chrétienne dans l'idée et dans la pratique* (Lyon, 1715), VI, 69.

[30] E.g., Milton, "True eloquence I find to be none, but the serious and hearty love of truth," "An Apology," in Milton's *Complete Prose Works*, ed. D. M. Wolfe *et al.*, (New Haven, 1962), III, 263.

[31] Claude Fleury, *Traité du choix et de la méthode des études,* nouvelle édition (Paris, 1753), 235.

[32] Paul Benichou, *Le sacre de l'écrivain: 1750–1830* (Paris, 1973).

[33] This idea finds its expression particularly in the poem "L'Invention" by André Chénier, *Oeuvres complètes* (Paris, 1946), 123–32.

able) of political freedom. Diderot's somewhat intellectual and programmatic essay in dithyrambic poetry is significantly called *Les Eleutheromanes*.[34] Chénier's only poem published during his lifetime is the Ode, *Le Serment du Jeu de Paume*, dedicated to the painter David. The opening statement announces the resurrection of poetry, and echoes Winckelmann and many others in adding that the arts cannot flourish, except in a free country.[35] Liberty helps poetry; then poetry propagates freedom; in a further development, Chénier again invokes personified Poetry:

> La liberté,
> Pour dissoudre en secret nos entraves pesantes,
> Arme ton fraternel secours.
> C'est de tes lèvres séduisantes
> Qu'invisible elle vole, et par d'heureux détours
> Trompe les noirs verrous, les fortes citadelles,
> Et les mobiles ponts qui défendent les tours,
> Et les nocturnes sentinelles.[36]

No doubt, in the circumstances of the Revolution, the age of Athens and Rome seemed to have returned. Madame de Staël said in 1800: "Les premières époques de la Révolution ont fourni à ses orateurs des sujets d'éloquence antique."[37] Many of the discourses delivered at the revolutionary assemblies (in so far as their precise wording has been kept) cannot be read today without a smile.[38] Their oratorical excess, however, can be explained: our study has shown how deeply, at the end of the eighteenth century, writers were convinced of the connection between liberty and eloquence. In seeking sublimity in patriotic eloquence, the revolutionary orators convinced themselves of the restoration of democratic liberty.[39] They thought that they

[34] Diderot, *Oeuvres complètes* (Paris, 1971), X, 15–26.

[35] Winckelmann, *Histoire de l'Art chez les anciens*, trans. Huber (Paris, an II, 1793), IV, 7, 323; also Hugh Blair's Lessons XXV and XXVI, in his *Lectures on Rhetoric and Belles Lettres* (London, 1790).

[36] *Op. cit.*, 168.

[37] *De la Littérature*, I, xvi, *Oeuvres complètes de Madame la baronne de Stael-Holstein* (Paris, 1836), I, 271.

[38] Successful orators, during the Revolution, were immediately attacked by members of the opposite parties as "déclamateurs," "flatteurs du peuple," "Démosthènes de la halle": such definition can be found in Chénier's polemical papers against the Jacobins. The power of intellectual and sentimental domination, which has been ardently sought for, is then denounced as dishonest manipulation. We deliberately abstained from taking into discussion the traditional debate about true and false eloquence. See note 27.

[39] See F.-A. Aulard's series of studies: *L'éloquence parlementaire pendant la Révolution française* (Paris, 1882–86). To many observers the use of the same rhetorical ways of speaking to defend the most contradictory causes brought about a

were bringing it about while speaking. Knowing that Napoleon was to follow, it is too easy for us to say that something of magic incantation and of wish fulfillment was present in this behavior.

If I am putting an end here to my investigation, it is because the Tacitean and Longinian *topos* seems to be almost forgotten after the Revolution.[40] Of course, the French "gens de lettres" did not cease to be attracted by political "engagement." Some of them, up to our times, acquired a rather intimate acquaintance with parliamentary eloquence, or with journalistic oratory. But theoretical considerations about the relationship between eloquence and freedom were no longer in the foreground. *Eloquence,* at least in French, is now a

---

sense of fatigue, monotony, and hypocrisy. In an article written in 1797, Benjamin Constant offers an analysis of the terrorist rhetoric: "Dans toutes les luttes violentes, les intérêts accourent sur les pas des opinions exaltées, comme les oiseaux de proie suivent les armées prêtes à combattre. La haine, la vengeance, la cupidité, l'ingratitude, parodièrent effrontement les plus nobles exemples, parce qu'on en avait recommandé maladroitement l'imitation. L'ami perfide, le débiteur infidèle, le délateur obscur, le juge prévaricateur, trouvèrent leur apologie écrite d'avance dans la langue convenue. Le patriotisme devint l'excuse banale préparée pour tous les délits. Les grands sacrifices, les actes de dévouement, les victoires remportées sur les penchants naturels par le républicanisme austère de l'antiquité, servirent de prétexte au déchaînement effréné des passions égoïstes. Parce que, jadis, des pères inexorables, mais justes, avaient condamné leurs fils coupables, leurs modernes copistes livrèrent aux bourreaux leurs ennemis innocents. . . . La foule, corrompue à la fois par le péril et par l'exemple, répétait en tremblant le symbole commandé, et s'épouvantait du bruit de sa propre voix. Chacun faisait nombre et s'effrayait du nombre qu'il contribuait à augmenter. Ainsi se répandit sur la France cet inexplicable vertige qu'on a nommé le règne de la terreur. Qui peut être surpris de ce que le peuple s'est détourné du but vers lequel on voulait le conduire par une semblable route" ("De la Terreur et de ses effets," *Oeuvres politiques de Benjamin Constant,* ed. Charles Louandre [Paris, 1874], 359). In the tenth of his *Zwölf Reden über die Beredsamkeit und deren Verfall in Deutschland* (1812; Leipzig, 1816), Adam Müller says: "Die französische Revolution schien ein ungeheures Feld für die Beredsamkeit eröffnet zu haben: jede der aufeinanderfolgenden Regierungen aber ist der andern gleich in ihren Deklamationen und Proklamationen. Der einzige Moniteur enthält so viel Ausrufungszeichen und Gedankenstriche, als die ganze übrige Literatur der Beredsamkeit zusammengenommen: die Gesetze selbst haranguirten die Nation . . ." ed. Arthur Salz (Munich, 1920), 225.

[40]To Tocqueville, at least, democratic oratory, as exemplified by American parliamentary eloquence, seems to be worth a reflection: "Je ne vois rien de plus admirable ni de plus puissant qu'un grand orateur discutant de grandes affaires dans le sein d'une assemblée démocratique. Comme il n'y a jamais de classe qui y ait ses représentants chargés de soutenir ses intérêts, c'est toujours à la nation tout entière, et au nom de la nation tout entière que l'on parle. Cela agrandit la pensée et relève le langage. . . . De là naît dans les discussions politiques d'un peuple démocratique, quelque petit qu'il soit, un caractère de généralité qui les rend souvent attachantes pour le genre humain. Tous les hommes s'y intéressent parce qu'il s'agit de l'homme, qui est partout le même" *De la démocratie en Amérique* (Paris, 1951), II, 96–97.

slightly disparaging word: it is no longer fashionable, although the rhetorical tricks are not at all abandoned. To account for the successful speeches of leaders and statesmen, one never says today that they are eloquent, but that they possess (or are possessed by) charismatic power. Usually, freedom is then out of the picture, although *liberty* and *liberation*—as could be statistically proven—belong to the group of the most frequently employed words in the political vocabulary.

University of Geneva.

XIII

HUME: SCEPTIC AND TORY?

By Marjorie Grene

Boswell's report of his last interview with Hume,[1] as well as Hume's statement in *My Own Life*,[2] indicate in the philosopher's own mind a sense of sympathy with the Stuart as against the Parliamentary cause in the history of the seventeenth century—a sympathy developed in the course of studying the period in order to compose the *History*. It has been suggested that this presumptive Tory leaning, dogmatic as it seems in Hume's own formulation, especially in *My Own Life*, needs somehow to be reconciled with the general sceptical position that appears in other parts of Hume's writings. One way of effecting such reconciliation is to show, as Mr. E. C. Mossner did in his recent article in this journal, that Hume's Tory leaning was not as strong as Hume in *My Own Life*, presumably for reasons of policy, said it was.[3] But an alternative solution to this apparent problem is, I think, equally possible. Hume's basic philosophic position may, it is true, be said to be consistent with his professed "Tory" sympathy if that sympathy be reduced to a "leaning" rather than a dogmatic assertion of partisan views, so that the moderate and hesitant philosopher takes his place beyond party lines as an objective spectator in some broadly liberal, non-partisan sense. But it may be insisted with equal force that Hume's philosophic position entails a Tory leaning in a somewhat more positive way: that is, that a man of Hume's position, in a study of seventeenth-century history, would naturally be led more and more by his own fundamental premises to a view very definitely on the Tory rather than the Whig, or at any rate the Roundhead, side of the dispute. There is good evidence, e.g., from the above-mentioned conversation with Boswell, or from Hume's late revisions of the *Dialogues*,[4] that Hume did not in his later years essen-

---

[1] *Dialogues Concerning Natural Religion*, ed. Norman Kemp Smith (Oxford, 1935), 97–100.

[2] *Essays, Moral, Political, and Literary*, ed. Green and Grose (London, 1889), I, 11.

[3] Mossner, Ernest Campbell: "Was Hume a Tory Historian? Facts and Reconsiderations," in this journal II, 2 (1941), 225–235, *passim*. Mr. Mossner's general interpretation of Hume as historian ["An Apology for David Hume, Historian," *PMLA*, LVI (1941), 657–690] seems to me entirely sound; what I am suggesting here is an alternative view of the narrower political question based on a different emphasis but not, I think, on a radical difference in interpretation.

[4] See Norman Kemp Smith's introduction to the dialogues (*op. cit.*).

tially alter his fundamental philosophic views. There is also good evidence, in *My Own Life* and the Boswell interview, that as he grew more intimately acquainted with the history of the Civil Wars, he did emphasize increasingly the Stuart side of the case; in fact, he felt himself to have vindicated the first James and Charles so completely that they would never be attacked again. From these two well-established facts one may fairly infer, as an hypothesis plausible enough for serious consideration, that Hume's Tory leaning developed not inconsistently with and perhaps even as a positive outcome of his general philosophic views.

Certainly Hume is not exclusively a Tory in the most extreme eighteenth-century or Jacobite sense, nor in what he considers the somewhat earlier sense of a defender of passive obedience. Certainly there is always in his statement of political theory and his accounts of political practice a peculiar duality of emphasis; a tension between the two poles of liberty and authority, neither of which can be entirely renounced. That does not necessarily indicate, however, that Hume's leaning to the Stuart side in his historical view is a mere appendage, expressive of a personal liking for James and Charles I, to a thoroughly Whig political philosophy. It is rather an indication that, in politics conspicuously, but actually in the whole of his philosophy, Hume's basic distinctions are almost always of degree. Although, as I shall try to show, Hume's philosophic views do indicate at least in history a definite Tory leaning that is not merely a personal weakness intruding on Whig principles, every such leaning is for Hume just a leaning, not a complete or radical decision; it corresponds in the sphere of moral and political judgment to the logical status a probable inference can have in the field of causal generalization. For that reason his Tory sympathies can always be toned down in the interest of substituting good-humored politeness for angry factionalism. For kindness was Hume's besetting virtue; in fact his ''scepticism'' as well as his politics is rather the offspring than the source of that fundamental trait. To be sure, such a basic temper does in good part eliminate dogmatism from the philosophy of its possessor; but it does not eliminate an emphasis one way rather than another on moral, political and scientific issues.

The notion that Hume's views in various subsidiary fields are consistent with and in fact demanded by his fundamental sceptical position in the *Treatise* needs further exposition in several directions: with regard to Books II and III of the *Treatise,* to the views presented in the various *Essays* on politics and aesthetics, to the arguments on natural religion in the *Dialogues* and *History of Natural Religion,* and even with regard to the application of the methods of the first book of the *Treatise* to itself. To treat the *History,* whose subject matter seems the most remote from general epistemological considerations, independently of the other, more obviously integrated portions of Hume's writings, is, in a way, to take the last of a chain of inferences before the intervening ones. But if a case can be made out for the connection here, perhaps the case for the integral connection of other, more obviously associated parts of Hume's thought will be strengthened.

The thesis here proposed, that Hume's scepticism underlies his Tory leaning, depends, first, on the interpretation of the crucial terms "sceptic" and "Tory" as they apply to Hume, and secondly, on tracing Hume's metaphysical scepticism through his general moral philosophy (which follows, as he presents it, from his fundamental position) to his particular political bias in the *History.*

In order to connect Hume's sceptical philosophy with his views as an historian it is first essential to establish just what "scepticism" means as applied to Hume. The problem indeed exists because of the conventional notion that a sceptic is one who is chary of "positive" opinions on any subject—and correlatively, one who is especially chary of reactionary opinions, which to the liberal critic, seem more opinionated than any others. But Hume's mitigated scepticism involves, as we all know, an affirmative as well as a negative position.[5] To put it very briefly, the cornerstone of Hume's scepticism is the reduction of all cognitive and moral judgment to perception: perception transformed and transfigured, no doubt, by the laws of association—but those laws themselves are just statements of the patterns in which perceptions, by their own inexplicable chemistry, do generally happen to group themselves. Such a reduction, minimizing the role of "reason" as a faculty of demonstration, making belief sensation and inference custom, is certainly "sceptical." But such a sceptical reduction does not forbid a reasonable though calm adherence to opinions on all sorts of subjects: reasonable because well grounded in a broad foundation of experience vividly retained. In fact, in its analysis of gen-

[5] See, for example, R. W. Church, *Hume's Theory of the Understanding* (Ithaca, 1935), *passim;* especially the treatment of the natural relations and their significance for Hume's system.

eral rules and their self-correcting nature, in its careful distinction between knowledge, proofs, probabilities of cause and chance, and unphilosophical probabilities, and in its enumeration of simple, workable rules for causal inference,[6] Hume's exposition provides in his view an ample basis for natural, moral and political philosophy.[7]

For what Hume means by the "Tory side" the obvious text to consult is his own, in the essays *Of Parties in General* and *Of the Parties of Great Britain.*[8]

In differentiating between Whig and Tory Hume points out three stages which bear on his attitude toward present and past. There is first the distinction between Roundhead and Cavalier, of which Hume says:

> The hopes of success being nearly equal on both sides, *interest* had no general influence in this contest: so that ROUNDHEAD and CAVALIER were merely parties of principle, neither of which disowned either monarchy or liberty; but the former party inclined most to the republican part of our government, the latter to the monarchical. In this respect, they may be considered as court and country party, inflamed into a civil war, by an unhappy concurrence of circumstances, and by the turbulent spirit of the age. The commonwealth's men, and the partisans of absolute power, lay concealed in both parties, and formed but an inconsiderable part of them.[9]

Secondly, there is the distinction between Whig and Tory prior to the Revolution. It is here that the "absurd principles" of passive obedience and indefeasible right make their appearance, though only briefly. But with the Revolution the true nature of the Tories appeared, as against their fantastic avowals of abso-lutism in the preceding period: "The Tories, as men, were enemies to oppression; and also, as Englishmen, they were enemies to arbitrary power."[10]   They are not entirely happy about the "set-

---

[6] *Treatise*, Book I, Part III, sec. XIII; sec. I and XI–XIII; sec. XV.

[7] The close connection of Hume's system of the passions and of morals with the causal logic of Book I is repeatedly emphasized in Books II and III. See for example Book II, Part I, sec. IV, V and XI. The account of the passions results from the same principles (i.e., of perceptions and their associations; see sec. IV) and is analogous in its content (sec. XI) to the analysis of the understanding in the first book.

[8] *Essays*, I, 127–144.

[9] *Ibid.*, 137. Hume here calls the decision between the two sides a very difficult and uncertain one. One senses here, as against the *History*, the difference in emphasis to which the passage in *My Own Life* doubtless refers: a shift, again, of degree not of kind, which a closer acquaintance with the major figures of the civil wars could easily occasion.

tlement in the Protestant line," partly out of affection, partly out of principle. But they showed by their conduct at the Revolution once for all that, though they love monarchy, they love liberty as well. Thus in Hume's terms, the two parties may be contrasted in their personal sympathies, and also in their principles—not radically, to be sure, but in the ordering and emphasis of their abstract allegiance:

A TORY, therefore, since the *Revolution*, may be defined, in a few words, to be *a lover of monarchy, though without abandoning liberty, and a partisan of the family of Stuart:* as a WHIG may be defined to be *a lover of liberty, though without renouncing monarchy, and a friend to the settlement in the Protestant line*.[11]

It is to be noted, moreover, that Hume here distinguishes Tories from Jacobites, in terms of his own century: a Tory does not necessarily advocate either the Roman Catholic cause, or the violent restoration of the Stuarts.[12] Hence, the issue of Stuarts or Hanoverians is—with significant application to Hume himself—rather complicated for partisans on the eighteenth-century scene.

In order to determine the relation between Hume's basic sceptical view and his Tory sympathies, it is necessary to keep in mind just what kind of moral judgments Hume the sceptic could allow Hume the historian to make. It is the essence of Hume's philosophy to derive all the types of human experience from their simplest elements. So, just as the more and the less vivid impressions arising from sensation are sufficient to account for all our cognitive judgments, the calmer and the more violent passions, distinguished in terms of degrees of intensity, are adequate to explain human emotion, together with patterns of association similar to those operative in the other field. This analysis of the passions Hume feels to be not only consistent with but closely analogous to and therefore confirmatory of his analysis of knowledge in the *Treatise*, Book I. And on the basis of this unified treatment of thought and emotion, it is possible to explain the nature and origin of moral judgments, still in terms of "perception" as the psychological material for all aspects of human life. The central question of ethical theory is put clearly and explicitly in terms of this principle: whether it is by impressions or by ideas (the two basic types of perception) that we distinguish between vice and virtue. The

---

[10] *Ibid.*, 138.

[11] *Ibid.*, 139.

[12] *Ibid.*, 141 (from editions A to P).

answer, of course, is that our judgments of right and wrong depend on a moral sense, occurring "when a character is considered in general, without reference to our particular interest"—a kind of consideration which in turn depends for its possibility upon the "calm determination" of the passions.   Such judgments, or better, feelings are divided into four groups: "For we reap a pleasure from the view of a character, which is naturally fitted to be useful to others, or to the person himself, or which is agreeable to others, or to the person himself."[13]   And in his account of the four types Hume places greatest emphasis on the "gentler affections" or "social virtues"; benevolence, generosity, etc., as opposed to the more energetic characters like courage and ambition which may be good or bad depending on circumstances.

Hume's analysis of the moral sense explains in general how the historian can pass moral judgment.   Moral judgments depend at their very core on the only kind of impartiality possible to any man, a wider range of imagination than the pressure of interest usually permits.   The partiality of an historian should be just such an impartial partiality, determined by a wide, disinterested view, in which sympathy in the literal sense dominates the imagination, instead of the narrower vision of the self-interested office-seeker or violently impassioned zealot.   Such impartiality, like the probabilism of the mitigated sceptic, of which it is the practical corollary, allows and even demands positive moral judgment: judgment not positive in the sense of "dogmatical" but nevertheless definite enough.

In contrast to the natural virtues, the virtue of justice rests remotely on considerations of interest as well as sympathy.[14]   The most general social conventions first of all, and the institution of government secondly, depend ultimately for their existence on the end of private advantage they originally served.   But by the operation of custom and general rules, political institutions have come to rely for their sanction on a consideration of public rather than private interest.   So when public interest is flagrantly violated the conventions themselves and the judgments based on them would

[13] *Treatise,* Book III, Part III, Sec. I (ed. Selby-Bigge, second edition, Oxford, 1896), 591.

[14] *Ibid.,* Book III, Part II, Sec. I and *passim.* Though the distinction between natural and conventional is toned down in the *Enquiry* the situation described there is fundamentally the same.

presumably collapse;[15] and here Hume denies emphatically the doctrine of passive obedience—though, as we shall see in the concrete context of the history, with a peculiar twist that restricts the practical importance of the right to revolution far more stringently than the doctrine, for instance, of Paine or Locke. But against such general considerations, one must—remembering the all-embracing rôle of perception or feeling in this sceptical system—place in the balance several other factors which influence allegiance and counteract the tendency to question government's authority when it acts against the public interest.

Where the public good does not evidently demand a change, it is certain that the concurrence of all those titles, *original contract, long possession, present possession, succession,* and *positive laws,* forms the strongest title to sovereignty, and is justly regarded as sacred and inviolable.[16]

So factors of custom have, as one might expect, a powerful influence on the judgment, or rather the sentiment, of allegiance; and where long inheritance or law is lacking, other elements, like present possession, exert some influence. Partly summing up and partly supplementing all these considerations in a given case, moreover, there is the general tenor of public opinion which forms an important weight on the delicate scale of political judgments.[17] In short, here as everywhere, and more than for the natural virtues, those feelings we call judgments result, when they are reliable, from the self-correcting nature of general rules which teach us by experience how to let various factors take their just weight to bring about a calm and reasoned rather than a hot and hasty choice. Against the abstract considerations of public interest and the right of subjects to maintain such interests against tyrannical rulers, these influential psychological factors must in most cases be weighed, and the decision made in terms of the resulting balance of many values and many feelings.

In the light of this theory of moral judgment, closely integrated as it is with his basic sceptical position, what particular political judgments would Hume be likely to draw (a) in studying the history of the preceding century and (b) in looking at the events of his own time and the more recent past?

[15] *Ibid.,* Book III, Part II, Sec. IX, 550–553.

[16] *Ibid.,* Book III, Part II, Sec. X, 562.

[17] This is partly implicit in Hume's treatment of the preceding five factors, partly in his statement (Book III, Part II, Sec. VIII, 546) of the peculiar authority of opinion in moral matters.

First, on the conflict between Cavaliers and Roundheads, what would the judgments of Hume the moralist be? The political virtues take the center of the stage in this historical controversy. Here there is at first sight on the side of the Roundheads as against the Cavaliers a principle of liberty essential to social and political institutions. Certainly, as we saw above, Hume denies the principle of passive obedience and insists on the right of subjects to resist extreme oppression. Against that abstract principle, however, there are at least two important factors in favor of the Stuarts.

The question was not one of absolute monarchy or liberty, but of the balance of the two; and as the history of the Commonwealth showed it was in fact the presumptive seekers after extreme liberty who actually brought the nation, as Hume seems to think is usually the case, to the extremest tyranny instead.[18] Liberty is all very well, and all very necessary in the abstract as a basis for political conventions; but as the essay on the British Government suggests,[19] too much liberty, as it may occur in republican governments, more frequently turns into an extreme of despotism (the despotism of a man of ill-breeding like Cromwell!) than does an excess, within a balanced government, of monarchical authority. The British con-stitution is blessed in having monarchy better mixed with liberty than the French, Hume thinks—but blessed too in having the balance of the mixture somewhat to the monarchical rather than the popular side. So, despite instances like the Star Chamber or the ship money, the question of public interest is not automatically decided in favor of the Commonwealth men as against the Cavaliers.

In fact, the *Treatise,* the *Political Essays,* and the *History* concur in sustaining, within the continual polarity of Hume's political view, an emphasis on the dangers of liberty rather than its converse. Hume is against passive obedience, proud of British free speech, etc.; but he is extremely conscious of the dangers of a fanatical zeal for liberty—of the fury of the mob when roused to an overkeen consciousness of its rights. A Nero or a Caligula deserves rebellion and perhaps even punishment on the part of his

[18] "The slavery into which the nation, from the too eager pursuit of liberty, has fallen." *History of England,* ed. Porter and Coates, 5 vols., following Hume's last corrections (Philadelphia, no year), IV, 545; cf. 549.

[19] *Whether the British Government Inclines More to Absolute Monarchy, or to a Republic. Essays,* I, 122–6.

subjects, but in the case of Charles I, a prince sometimes rash or weak but on the whole virtuous and well-intentioned, there is for Hume no question of justifying such extremes.[20]

There are two passages in the *History,* the second of which is paralleled in the *Treatise,* which bear most significantly on the question of Hume's emphasis here.   In his account of Charles's trial Hume relates how the Parliament introduced for their own purposes ''a principle noble in itself and which seems specious, but is belied by all history and experience, *that the people are the origin of all just power.*''[21]   Surely for Hume the philosopher, as for Hume the objective and impartial historian, a principle belied by all history and experience is no principle at all, but a superstitious illusion to be dispelled by judicious consideration of past and present.   But can Hume the liberal philosopher deny the very key-stone of liberalism, the central expression of those laws of nature which, indeed, in Hume's view, men and not gods have made for their own interest, but which are nevertheless basic to organized society?   No; the abstract principle of liberty stands for Hume, despite this striking denial of an empirical foundation: practically, because it would not be the part of a gentleman and a humanitarian to deny it; intellectually, because there is in Hume's system no apparatus for its denial—no superstate or supersovereign to sanction a source of power other than the human beings who compose society and whose interests necessitate the foundation of the state. And it is of course a principle jointly acknowledged, in Hume's view, by Whig and Tory in his own day.

But the principle is singularly attenuated in its practical application, not only indirectly in the above denial of its historical validation, but more pointedly in the treatment of men's basic right of revolution both in the *History* and in the *Treatise.*   In both these works Hume insists generally that while extreme tyranny provokes, and justifies, rebellion, there is no need to tell every one about it— when the case is extreme enough, the rebellion will come of itself; and in the meantime one had better hush up this provocative (though undeniable) principle.[22]   Why?   Because the end of gov-

[20] *History,* IV, 492.

[21] *Ibid.,* IV, 480.

[22] *Ibid.,* IV, 491: "Government is instituted in order to restrain the fury and injustice of the people, and being always founded on opinion, not on force, it is dangerous to weaken, by these speculations (i.e., on the right to revolution) the reverence which the multitude owe to authority, and to instruct them beforehand that the

ernment is (at least, according to the statement of the *History*) to restrain mob violence (a lesson easily learned from the Civil Wars); and mob violence would be only encouraged by a universal consciousness of universal rights. Such is in the main the tenor of Hume's argument, in general in the *Treatise* (Bk. III, Pt. II, sec. X) and in particular in the discussion relative to Charles I's execution in the *History* (Ch. LIX).

This is at first sight an amazing statement on the part of a signally mild and humane philosopher, whose trust in human benevolence is proverbial. Philosophically the situation here is similar to that in the first book of the *Treatise* with respect to causal inference and the general causal principle. Intellectually, there is no thoroughgoing, "rational" validation for a causal law; but it is demanded practically and practically sanctioned by custom and imagination. Here, conversely, there is no intellectual, rational justification for a *denial* of the libertarian principle and the right to revolution; but practical need demands its public denial or at any rate its concealment in most circumstances. As with knowledge Hume's intellectual doubt gives way to his practical naturalism, so here the intellectual liberalism which the latter in turn demands (because it offers no alternative view of the *raison d'être* of organized society) gives way for practical purposes to a much more qualified and conservative view of political education. In neither case does the one principle cancel the other; but where practice and experience, or in short perception, is the test of truth and of values, it does significantly balance and perhaps even outweigh the abstract generality to which, as pole to pole, it is at once related and opposed.

Compare Hume's view here with Locke's position in the *Second Treatise of Civil Government*. Both stress the libertarian basis for civil society, deny passive obedience, and thus suggest the view of political society as a commonwealth of free men. Both mention the unruliness of the passions as an important fact relative to the need for and end of political organization. But in Locke, the friend of Shaftesbury, and in Hume, the acknowledged partisan of

---

case can ever happen when they may be freed from their duty of allegiance. Or should it be found impossible to restrain the license of human disquisitions, it must be acknowledged that the doctrine of obedience ought alone to be *inculcated* and that the exceptions, which are rare, ought seldom or never to be mentioned in popular reasonings and discourses." Cf. *Treatise*, Book III, Part II, Sec. X, 555–6 and 563–4.

the Stuarts, the emphasis on these two concomitant elements is significantly at variance. For Locke it is the commonwealth of free men with their parliamentary rights and liberties that is continually, practically as well as abstractly, of importance; the *motif* of the passions enters as an explanatory factor relative to the account of the organization of society with its apparent limitation on men's native liberties. For Hume, liberty is basic, it is true; the end of the state is the maintenance of these liberties, but *through* the continual control and suppression of the violent passions, and especially the prevention of mob violence—a means so necessary and so important that it can on occasion be called the end of political institutions: "government is instituted in order to restrain the fury and injustice of the people."[23]

Let us look carefully, in the light of these general considerations, at Hume's treatment of Charles I's trial and execution. Hume's general consideration in the *History* of the right of subjects to depose, judge and execute their sovereign,[24] coming after his continual stress on the unjust conduct of the Parliamentarians and the nobility and virtue of the wronged king, may look ambiguous and inconclusive. But it is clearly consistent with the closely parallel passage in the *Treatise* and its ambiguity consists, not in a hesitation on Hume's part as to whether the deposition (perhaps even execution) of sovereigns is *ever* permissible—clearly it sometimes is; nor in a hesitation as to whether the treatment of Charles was just—clearly it was not. It arises rather from the duality inherent in Hume's political theory: a duality which, however, does not prevent a strong and consistent emphasis on one of the two elements involved. Liberty is necessary to government; but the zealous pursuit of liberty often leads—and in the case of the Civil Wars, did lead—to the extremest slavery, and hence to the negation of the public good on which alone society is ultimately based. The right of revolution is necessary to government; but its untoward exercise often leads—and in the case of the Civil Wars did lead—to the violation of honored and honorable persons, the arbitrary overthrow of ancient institutions, and the chaotic play of violence against violence, the avoidance of which is among the primary constituents of that basic "public good."

Consequently, in terms of the heavier emphasis on monarchy than on liberty (while retaining a belief in both), Hume's own

[23] See note 21 above (p. 341).

[24] *History,* IV, 491; see note 22 above (pp. 341-2).

position, with regard to the events of the seventeenth century, fits his own definition of Tory.

In addition to the primary factors of public interest which enter into such problems of allegiance as those facing partisans in the period of the Civil Wars, there are, as we noticed above, a group of other factors centering chiefly in phenomena of popular custom and of public opinion, which need likewise to be taken into account in a cool and reasoned evaluation of the various parties' claims. "Where the public good does not evidently demand a change," Hume says, the questions of original contract, long possession, present possession, succession, and positive laws all enter into account. Where these secondary factors concur, there is no difficulty in deciding the issue; vexed questions arise—as in any causal inference—only through a conflict in the influences impelling our judgment one way and another. With regard to Charles I, as we have seen, the public good was not so grossly violated as clearly to demand a change. On the other hand, the influence of "original contract" in this case is rather hard to see; but in his initial description of these elements in political judgment Hume isolates the first as a factor sometimes occurring in some states, and mentions long possession in particular as a sort of alternative to it.[25] The five are, after all, not abstract canons of right, but lines of psychological and associative influence, and it is only in a few cases (as for instance later in the constitutions of the North American states or revolutionary France) that the consciousness of a contractual relation plays an important part in the imagination of a people. Usually they have been governed so long that their judgments on political matters have come to feel as natural as their judgments on the natural virtues—and the question of a voluntary and contractual foundation of the state is not one that plays an important part in forming their opinions. It is for that reason perhaps that Hume with his eye always on the psychological basis for his moral theory hesitates to make universal and necessary the social contract theory of political origins.[26]

The other four factors, however, certainly do concur in this instance. Long possession, present possession, succession, and positive law are all on the Cavalier side, with no contrary pressure from the remaining principle. Long possession, in particular, combined with positive law, provides a strong source of authority

[25] *Treatise,* Book III, Part II, Sec. X, 554–5.
[26] *Ibid.,* Book III, Part II, Sec. VIII, 541–2.

for the supporters of the king.[27]   In fact that is the point made by Hume himself in the letter to Mrs. Macaulay quoted by Mr. Mossner in the above-mentioned article:

> For as I look upon all kinds of subdivision of power, from the monarchy of France to the freest democracy of some Swiss cantons, to be equally legal, if established by custom and authority; I cannot but think, that the mixed monarchy of England, such as it was left by Queen Elizabeth, was a lawful form of government, and carried obligations to obedience and allegiance; at least it must be acknowledged, that the princes and ministers who supported that form, tho' somewhat arbitrarily, could not incur much blame on that account; and that there is more reason to make an apology for their antagonists than for them.[28]

To be sure, in Hume's own day, the well-established possession of the crown by the House of Hanover is sufficient to preclude, in Hume's view, a need for violent restoration of the Stuarts.   But at the same time long possession and legality were, a century earlier, very definitely strong enough forces to put the burden of proof on the Parliamentarians—who in the violence and fanaticism of their behavior furnished no very persuasive argument on the other side.   Granted that history and true philosophy teach us according to Hume "to regard the controversies in politics as incapable of any decision in most cases, and as entirely subordinate to the interests of peace and liberty."[29]   Still the concurrence of all the subordinate principles, he goes on to say, "forms the strongest title to sovereignty, and is justly regarded as sacred and inviolable."[30]   They did concur in the case of Charles I; and his title and his person were therefore to be respected accordingly.   (Not to mention, of course, that the interest of peace and even, as it turned out, of liberty, too, might well have been better served by the Royalists than the Cromwellians.)   In short, however specious the abstract principles sponsored by the Roundheads, their concrete

[27] See for example in the *History* (IV, 454) on the king's hopes for a reasonable settlement: "A people without government and without liberty, a Parliament without authority, an army without a legal master; distractions everywhere, terrors, oppressions, convulsions; from this scene of confusion, which could not long continue, all men, he hoped, would be brought to reflect on that ancient government under which they and their ancestors had so long enjoyed happiness and tranquillity."

[28] Mossner, *op. cit.*, 234–5.   From *European Magazine and London Review,* (November, 1793), 33.

[29] See *Treatise,* Book III, Part II, Sec. X, 562.

[30] *Loc. cit.*

and psychological claims to allegiance certainly did not suffice to justify the impeachment, let alone the murder (for as such Hume saw it) of their lawful sovereign, and within a brief space the overthrow in all but the semblance of the parliamentary institutions in defense of which, ostensibly, they had condemned their king. Here, again, the sympathy with established authority in general and the Stuart family in particular prevails.

But the subordinate principles of long possession, etc., have a further importance: their introduction suggests a reason for Hume's reactionary view of political education and for his view that peace and the maintenance of order are at least as basic an end of government as liberty itself. For here once more is the omnipresent principle of custom with its influence on imagination and hence on the intensity and direction of human passions. Interest is the foundation of states; and the fair principles of liberty are the dictate of interest. But with long custom that basis is forgotten: custom makes subjection and allegiance feel as natural as any extra-political sentiment. And custom, that great guide of human life, cannot be lightly overturned—nor should it be, for its overthrow lets loose a chaos of violent passions unchecked by general rules. Calm reflection, combined with a distant view, can operate only in the gentle and sheltered atmosphere of an orderly society: and liberty itself, always present as the foundation of the state, is in the extremest danger when custom, in its dual form of inherited rule and civil law, breaks down and "the madness of the people" and "the furies of fanaticism"[31] are let loose.

Looked at another way, finally, the subordinate principles sum up to a statement of factors forming and influencing public opinion. And taking them in that sense, their weight is once more on the Royalist side. For, whatever abstract sanction the principle of liberty might have given the Roundheads (had that principle been genuinely involved as an issue, as by the time of the institution of the Commonwealth it certainly was not), against that abstract consideration there would stand the very concrete and effective factor of the present issuance of political habit into public sentiment. The Commonwealth was a real tyranny in the sense that no one or only a very few men wanted it, and only the stupor of exhaustion after long civil war made its initiation possible at all.[32]

[31] *History,* IV, 493.

[32] See the account of the stupor and astonishment of the people at the events leading up to the king's death (486); their reaction to it (488). Compare the ac-

One may conclude that Hume's moral judgment, that is, his disinterested judgment—such judgment as his sceptical position allows and in fact demands—would incline him to the Tory side in his view of the Civil Wars.

With regard to the contemporary scene, Hume's position is different. His Stuart sympathies (though short of Jacobitism) might remain; as would his preference for a good safe balance of monarchy first with liberty second. He would certainly not accept the notion of passive obedience; but, as he himself says, that goes only with a part of the Pre-Revolution Tory notion,[33] and even there, is more talk than genuine belief. So his view might still be found to fit fairly well his own definition of Tory with regard to his own time. But despite that sympathy he professedly disapproves of Jacobites:[34] for he would not sympathize with the Catholic cause as it grows more openly equated with that of the Stuart family, nor would he desire a violent renunciation of the *status quo* so long as the *status quo* is fairly comfortable for most of the people he cares about. He would not, like Hobbes, accept any *status quo*, even the Commonwealth: it was too uncomfortable for every one. But the Protestant succession is, first of all, Protestant (an advantage where Protestantism wears a less positively religious front than the Roman church—the reversal of the seventeenth-century situation); and secondly, fairly secure by Hume's time. So there is, despite the agreeable character of the Stuarts and even the legitimacy of their claim, no particular reason to upset the present settlement. If that is to be a Whig, or at least less of a Tory, then Hume is, if not a Whig, at least less of a Tory in contemporary politics than in his historical view. A sense of the delicacy and uncertainty of political decisions, a liking for calmness and good-nature, as it makes him outspoken against the fanaticism of the Roundheads, blunts the edge of his partiality in respect to his own times, when the side of greater religious bigotry seems to have shifted, when the peaceful present compels allegiance, and when the demands of politeness and a philosophical disposition prevent the adherence to what is now a revolutionary cause. It is this side of his peculiarly double-edged position that appears in the essay

---

count of the authority behind the Commonwealth (497) and the account of the Restoration, *passim*.

[33] *Essays*, I, 137–8.
[34] *Ibid.*, I, 143–4.

on the Protestant succession,[35] in the note on the Revolution in the *Treatise*,[36] and in the latter part of the paragraph from the letter to Mrs. Macaulay quoted above:

> I grant, that the cause of liberty, which you, Madame, with the Pyms and Hampdens, have adopted, is noble and generous; but most of the partizans of that cause, in the last century, disgraced it, by their violence, and also by their cant, hypocrisy, and bigotry, which, more than the principles of civil liberty, seem to have been the motive of all their actions. Had those principles always appeared in the amiable light which they receive from your person and writings, it would have been impossible to resist them; and however much inclined to indulgence toward the first James and Charles, I should have been the first to condemn those monarchs for not yielding to them.[37]

As against the legality of the English constitution prior to the Civil Wars, as against his disapproval of violence and cant, perceptible as the prime motives in the seventeenth-century Parliamentary party, as against an indulgence, in contrast, to the first James and Charles, Hume stresses the fair character of liberty (a principle admitted both by Whigs and Tories, according to his definitions, though with unequal emphasis), and professes to admire Whig principles when they are placed in "so amiable a light"; that, is, when they are transferred from affiliation with violence and fanaticism to the politer and more moderate surroundings of Hume's own world. The mildness and complacency of Hume's disposition involve, philosophically, a serious emphasis on the importance of the public peace and on the correlative sanctity of well-established custom. That emphasis issues, in practical terms, in a genuine sympathy with a conservative politics in general and in particular with the Stuart side of the historical dispute; and in an equally genuine approval of a convenient settlement approved at its outset by the moderates of both political parties and guaranteeing, by the manner of its allegiance to liberty, not the violent upheavals consequent on the libertarian avowals of "the Pyms and Hamdens," but an agreeably well-ordered existence in a decent, moderate and enlightened state.

The University of Chicago.

[35] *Ibid.*, I, 470–480.
[36] *Treatise,* Book III, Part II, Sec. X, 563–6.
[37] See note 28 above.

XIV

THE PROBLEM OF TRUTH AND FALSEHOOD IN THE AGE OF ENLIGHTENMENT

By Lester Gilbert Crocker

" Ye shall know the truth, and the truth shall make you free."

The new critical rationalism of the Age of Enlightenment conceived as its mission the task of freeing the world from a morass of falsehood. The errors and prejudices that the eighteenth century attacked, and its own explanation of things, have been intensively studied. But the controversy over the premise itself, that errors and prejudices should be destroyed, has been neglected. And yet on no question did the rationalists assemble greater concentration of interest.

The problem involved in that premise has been a constant focus of discussions and struggles. More than a clash of ideas, it is the expression of a conflict between social forces and their ideologies, a conflict whose roots lie deep in the history of human thought and social relationships. In the ancient and modern world, writers, great and small, have debated the values of truth and falsehood perennially. The debate seems to have acquired renewed vitality whenever a revolutionary movement threatened the continuance of an established society. In the eighteenth century, it assumed epidemic form.

There is no space here to analyze in detail the earlier history of the controversy.[1] The ancients had discussed the relation of truth to virtue and happiness; and also, whether the innate tendency of the human mind is to accept truth or falsehood. But even more important, they had launched the debate over the political expediency of using deceit as a weapon of government.[2] The Middle Ages, on the other hand, approached the discussion largely from a moral and theological bias. Its chief contribution was the debate over the permissibility of the " mensonge officieux "—a falsehood prompted by altruistic motives. The sixteenth century, a period of instability and revolt, explored more freely knotty matters such as the rôle of truth in government and society, and questioned accepted values. At a time when relations of the State to morality and to organized religion were most confused, the political implications of the problem again came to the fore. The three leading figures were Machiavelli, Mon-

---

[1] Among the Ancients the debate was waged between the schools of Zeno and Epicurus, in the writings of Plato, Plutarch, Cicero, Seneca and Lucretius. (Benjamin Farrington has touched upon the question in *Science and Politics in the Ancient World* [New York, 1940].) Among medieval writers, St. Augustine, St. Jerome, St. Chrysostomus, St. Thomas Aquinas, Synesius and others were involved.

[2] For Lucretius and the Epicureans, the struggle against superstition, lies and errors was the struggle to free men and their minds from the yoke of privilege and persecution. Plato urged the use of lies, Cicero the foisting of superstition upon the people, the better to manage them.

taigne and Charron.[3]   The Renaissance mind viewed society as a state of perpetual strife between rulers and ruled, as well as among princes themselves. Consequently, ruse and violence seemed better instruments of government than truth and reason. There was a definite current of belief in a double standard of truth, the one philosophical (or for philosophers), the other practical and religious. Truth must be considered as a social institution and therefore at times must be opposed by a diametrical doctrine. As Giordano Bruno said, " Quel che è vero è pernicioso alla civile conversazione, e contrario al fine delle leggi."

The seventeenth century combined preoccupation with Christian morality (le mensonge officieux) with humanistic interest in man's nature. Psychological analysis dominates the writings of the period.[4] Political discussion was suppressed in France. However, the bickerings of the Jesuits and the Jansenists gave rise to a bitter debate over Machiavelianism applied to religion.[5] Although the use of falsehood was a subject of dispute, there was rather general agreement that truth was a dangerous instrument, to be handled gingerly.

Not until the eighteenth century did the theme of truth and falsehood develop from a scattered discussion into a universal and pressing question, into actual public and private debate. Pressure for intellectual, economic and eventually for political and social liberation is

---

[3] Machiavelli seeks only a " good " (a chosen end) of the moment and denies any inherent prerogative to what men call " truth." Falsehoods, of all types, are essential to those who would dominate, especially since men accept falsehood as readily as truth and live by it as if there were no distinction. (Il Principe, XVIII; Istorie Fiorentine, VII, 30.) Typical is Charron's purposeful confusion of the values of good and evil: necessity is above law, and therefore he who does evil by necessity does no wrong. (De la sagesse, II, 1.) Both Charron and Montaigne (like Plato) reserve to rulers the privilege of lying. For Montaigne, however, lying, in social intercourse, is a betrayal of society: communal existence, dependent on mutual intelligence, relies upon the sanctity of the word. (Essais, II, 18; I, 9; III, 1.) Alone Etienne de la Boëtie refused to accept the debasement of humanity, and denounced the alliance between superstition and oppression. (De la servitude volontaire [Paris, 1924], 33.)

[4] Many nuances were contributed to the grosser discussion of the sixteenth century by men such as Descartes, Boileau, Bossuet, La Mothe Le Vayer, Massillon, La Fontaine, Molière, Pascal: and in other countries, by Bacon, Hobbes and Leibniz. Pascal reversed Montaigne's famous theory, and claimed that the very existence of society is based on mutual deceit. (Pensée 100, éd. Brunschwicg.)

[5] Jesuit casuists frequently sanctioned lies and deception as a means to a worthy end, the end itself being the criterion of right and wrong. More direct political applications of the question of truth and falsehood were made outside of France by Pufendorf and Grotius (on the conservative side), and by Hobbes and Spinoza. The latter declared that nature gives men the right to liberty (the goal of any legitimate government), and that truth is the inseparable handmaiden of liberty (Tractatus theologico-politicus [London, 1900], 5).

the essence of the history of eighteenth-century France. By an alliance possibly unique in human record, those who sought dignity and selfish freedom in commercial enterprise found themselves arrayed against the same foe as those who sought the dignity and freedom of the human mind. The debate over the values of truth and falsehood contains the very pith of this historic struggle. The liberals were impelled by the conviction that "mankind had been corrupted and betrayed by false doctrines. Their essential task was to destroy these false doctrines." [6] They believed that the rejection of truth meant the rejection of morality and justice in social organization; that deceit was a weapon of the strong to continue indefinitely their oppression of the weak. On the other side, those who fought to perpetuate the feudal organization of society inevitably opposed a philosophy which insisted on the exclusive utility of truth; inevitably, they justified deceit and prejudice on both political and moral grounds.

The essential questions were few in number. What is the relation between truth and happiness? Are all truths useful, and should they be told? Are all falsehoods harmful, and should they be destroyed? What, finally, is the origin of prejudice and error, and does that origin allow us to envisage the possibility of their destruction? All of these questions possess much more than an obvious abstract interest; each one is capable, according to the answer given, of condemning or justifying the web and fabric of the Old Régime.

Four general divisions can be distinguished among the large number of contributors. There was, in the early years of the century, a survival of the purely religious group, some of whom denounced all lies, while others defended the "mensonge officieux." Most of these were gradually absorbed, under the pressure of anti-religious propaganda, into the new party, the upholders of the *status quo*. Although few conservatives admitted their support of deceit and prejudice as political weapons, their replies to the stated questions leave no doubt as to what they were really defending. They maintained that truth was inimical to happiness and socially dangerous; that illusions and prejudices were vital to individual felicity and social well-being: that prejudices and errors were an unavoidable outgrowth of human nature, and therefore could never be destroyed. Theirs was a purposeful, and perhaps, realistic philosophy of defeatism. The most effective argument of the conservatives was that unbelief would weaken the foundations of morality and social order. In an age when men had as yet freed themselves only speculatively from medieval authoritarianism, even philosophers retreated on this question, fearing a practical application of their own rationalism. The third fac-

[6] Becker: *The Heavenly City of the Eighteenth Century Philosophers* (New Haven, 1932), 122.

tion—the shock-troops of the "philosophic" assault—categorically denied each of these contentions and advanced opposite conclusions. Of particular importance was their own view on the origin of error. For if falsehoods, as they and many Ancients held, were systematically imposed by an oppressive class, then we could hope for their eventual extermination. But was it not evident that this program involved, perhaps even contemplated, extermination of the oppressors? Between the two extremist groups a more moderate party was distributed. Among its adherents we find a greater variation. Most maintained that some truths, at least, were not useful, or possessed certain elements of danger, and advised a slow and cautious destruction of prejudice. Others were inclined to favor the retention of "useful" prejudices, and leaned more to the conservative side.

It is interesting to note the stand taken by the more famous thinkers of the age. Fontenelle was basically a conservative; Hume, Diderot, d'Holbach, Helvétius and Condorcet were "radicals"; d'Alembert belonged to the moderate group; Bayle and Rousseau were uncertain and contradictory; while Voltaire was so "moderate" that he may be said to have had one foot in the enemy camp. The question of truth and falsehood may well be considered one test of a given *philosophe's* liberalism. The division in the ranks also shows us the "enthusiasts" facing the cynics, or realists.

The moral approach gradually oriented itself to one important matter, already adumbrated by a few seventeenth-century writers, the relation between truth and happiness. The question of the "mensonge officieux" acquired renewed importance. Up to this point, theologians and moralists had been asking whether it was *right* to lie for a good purpose. When eighteenth-century thinkers took up the problem, they posed the question differently. They asked whether it was *useful* to tell a lie. The *philosophes* were not interested primarily in the "mensonge officieux" but in the lie used as a social weapon, in superstition and political deceit. However they were forced to consider the "mensonge officieux" because their opponents seized upon the moral issue and used it as a strategy of confusion. The defenders of the Old Régime tried to establish an inverse ratio between truth and human happiness; their object was to prove the usefulness of falsehood and deceit, including the "mensonge officieux" as well as superstition and prejudice. They pretended to see no fundamental distinction between falsehood used by the ruling classes for systematic propaganda and oppression, and "a white lie" told for a purely altruistic purpose. Death—and life—wrote Frederick the Great, are acceptable only because of error and illusion. Formey, De Boufflers, Jaucourt and many other writers upheld falsehood both on a personal and a social plane, as a bulwark of human happiness.[7]

To such arguments the *philosophes* responded in various ways, often typical of their shape of mind. A few favored an extreme line of reasoning, least calculated, perhaps, to advance their cause. This first group flatly contradicted the preceding viewpoints and proclaimed the invariable and exclusive utility of truth.[8] Voltaire, Diderot and d'Holbach belonged to a second group. They replied more cannily. By admitting all that the defenders of lies claimed in special circumstances, they shook off the question of the " mensonge officieux " and went on to their main business, the attack on social lies.[9] Many other writers did not touch upon the question of the " mensonge officieux " but maintained, from the social viewpoint, the exclusive utility of truth. This group included Helvétius and L. S. Mercier.[10] In rebuttal, enemies of the *philosophes,* such as De Boufflers, ridiculed the notion that truth is useful. " Vous me demandez si l'erreur est utile aux hommes; il fallait le demander de la vérité." [11] Fontenelle adopted a different approach. Reason, after

[7] Cf. Frederick the Great: *Dissertation sur l'innocence des erreurs de l'Esprit,* in *Oeuvres* (Berlin, 1848), VIII, 42; Formey, " *Examen de la question, Si toutes les vérités sont bonnes à dire,*" in *Nouveaux Mémoires de l'Académie de Berlin,* Année 1777 (Berlin, 1779), 343–5; De Boufflers concluded that the more we are deceived, and the more we help to delude each other with useful lies, the happier we all shall be (*Sur l'erreur,* in *Oeuvres* [Paris, 1813], II, 329–30). See also Jaucourt ("Mensonge " in the *Encyclopédie*).

[8] As Vauvenargues put it, " c'est être bien impertinent de vouloir faire croire qu'on n'a pas assez d'erreurs pour être heureux." (*Maximes,* CCCLXXXIII; CCLXXXI; CCCLXXII; DLXXIV.) Also Champfort (*Maximes,* CLII); Hume (*Dialogues on Natural Religion,* X).

[9] Voltaire, *Traité de métaphysique,* ch. IX; *Dictionnaire philosophique,* art. " Préjugé "; *Stances* (*Oeuvres,* VIII, 545); Diderot, *Diderot et l'abbé Barthélemy* (Paris, 1921), 261; d'Holbach, *Système Social* [Londres, 1773], I, 21; *Morale Universelle* (1776) [Paris, 1820], I, 232–3, 139–41, 220.

[10] See Helvétius: *De l'Homme,* IXe partie, ch. 5; Mercier: *Du théâtre* (Amsterdam, 1773), 223–4.

[11] *Oeuvres* (Paris, 1813), 327. It was Formey who undertook the most serious and systematic attack upon the " philosophic " position, in his spirited if loose-jointed essay, *Examen de la question: Si toutes les vérités sont bonnes à dire.* He divides truth into three classes: theory (mathematics, abstract science), fact, and feeling. Theoretical truths can never cause harm, although they are frequently useless. The question begins with factual truths, " au moment où les connaissances acquises, les vérités découvertes, peuvent influer sur l'état de la société, le troubler et le déranger." It is obvious that many hypothetical discoveries (such as the philosopher's stone) and many inventions (such as the flying machine) would bring more grief than happiness to mankind. Most important of all are truths relative to morals, politics and religion. If there were, in this field, any truths contrary to accepted doctrine, they would sap the foundations of society, destroying law and order in the home and in the nation. Perhaps such revolutions are of lesser consequence among the *élite,* but the latter should at least keep them from the eyes and

all, supplies us only with a small number of certain maxims, not enough to satisfy our mind's needs. Since most men cannot suspend judgment (" un état violent pour l'esprit humain "), prejudices fill the gaps, and save our minds from the intolerable state of a vacuum.[12] Fontenelle's opinion is summed up in his apocryphal statement, oft quoted in the eighteenth century: " Si je tenais toutes les vérités dans ma main fermée, je ne daignerais pas l'ouvrir."

Toussaint—and this is particularly interesting—was the only *philosophe* who rejected any solution based on the criterion of utility. He sweeps away all pretended justifications of the " mensonge officieux ": " Misérables prétextes, qu'un mot seul va pulvériser! Il n'est jamais permis de faire un mal pour qu'il en arrive un bien." Toussaint, however, although he recognized the central weakness in the reasoning of his fellow *philosophes,* the confusion between utility and morality, did not possess the philosophic resources to erect himself a universal principle of truthfulness. This task only one man, Immanuel Kant, was able to accomplish, later in the century. The first step for Kant is to distinguish prudence from duty. On the basis of prudence, it may seem useful to lie, but when we consider the possibility of unforeseen consequences, it acually turns out more prudent to act according to a universal maxim. But this is still only a maxim " based on an apprehensive concern with consequences," not a moral principle. The concept of the action must itself contain a law, regardless of results for the individual. The answer is readily obtained in this question: " Would I be content that my maxim should hold as a universal law," for others as well as for myself? " I immediately see that I could will the lie, but not a universal law to lie." Obviously, the basis of mutual confidence would be destroyed. Later, in answer to Benjamin Constant's defense of the *mensonge officieux,* Kant points out that a lie always harms another, " for it vitiates the source of law itself." The law of a duty is destroyed once we admit exceptions to the principle, which by definition must be universal. A principle is a moral imperative, limited by no expediency.[13]

The discussion of the usefulness of truth had the following question as its counterpart: are some prejudices, errors, superstitions socially useful, even necessary? The fundamental attack of the *philosophes* upon the existing social, religious and political system is involved in this question.

---

ears of the people. The author's ostensible solicitude about the effects of truth on men's happiness and welfare is obviously a thin mask for his true concern.

[12] *Dialogues des morts,* " Dialogue entre Straton et Raphael d'Urbin."

[13] Toussaint: *Les Moeurs* (Oxford, 1749), 231; Kant: *Foundations of the Metaphysics of Morals* (1785); " On a Supposed Right to Lie from Altruistic Motives," in *The Critique of Practical Reason and other writings* (Chicago, 1949), 63–4, 346–50.

The discussion was reopened, for the eighteenth century, by Bayle. In theory, Bayle supports the freedom to search for truth even in defiance of religion.[14] But Bayle, as Voltaire puts it, " se combat lui-même." Prejudices must be foisted upon the common people, he insists time and again, so that government and society can properly function.[15] Elsewhere he goes even further, asserting that the existence of human society depends on men keeping their thousand false prejudices. Errors, passions, prejudices are a necessary evil, and if philosophers succeeded in making all men think and act reasonably, " on peut être très assuré que le genre humain périrait bientôt."

The " encyclopedic group," of course, assailed uncompromisingly the citadel of prejudice. D'Holbach, Helvétius and Diderot declared time and again that because of the unavoidable link between all our ideas there are no useful errors. With them stood men like Maupertuis, Mercier, Morelly and Thomas Paine.[16] To the theory of the legitimacy of deceit in government, Mercier (loc. cit.) framed the typical answer of the philosophes: " . . . l'erreur n'est jamais utile, parce que le prestige se dissipe nécessairement et que l'indigence, la faiblesse et le désespoir saisissent l'homme détrompé: il retombe alors au-dessous du terme de l'avilissement humain."

Voltaire, at once a conservative and a rebel, was, as might be expected, a fence-sitter. His opinion changed according to the convenience of the moment. Under " Fraude " in the Dictionnaire philosophique, he supports the inevitable utility of truth, the inevitable harmfulness of falsehood. But in that article he is attacking " l'infâme." Also in a letter to the Duke de Saint-Mégrin, he condemns those who argue that because a prejudice is solidly established and universally respected, we must uphold it; the fatal results of such a doctrine are only too evident.[17] More often, however, did this realist side with the defenders of prejudice. Voltaire's arguments in their favor were typical. He is certain that prejudices—some, at least—may be beneficial to society. Voltaire distinguishes a class which are " universels, nécessaires, qui sont la vertu même "—faith in God, love of father and mother, hatred of stealing. What is a good

[14] " On ne doit jamais faire quartier à l'erreur, de quelque espèce qu'elle soit." (Pensées diverses, Pensée XCI.)

[15] Pensées diverses, Pensée XCI; Nouvelles lettres critiques sur l'histoire du calvinisme; Lettre XVII, par. 8 (Oeuvres diverses, II, 284): Réponse aux questions d'un provincial, ch. CIII, ibid., III, 708. Nouvelles lettres critiques, Lettre XVI, par. 6, II, 274.

[16] Maupertuis, Essai de cosmologie, Oeuvres (Dresde, 1752), Préface; Mercier, op. cit., 221–3; Morelly, Le Code de la Nature (Paris, 1941), 126, 95, 141–9; Thomas Paine, Age of Reason, Part I, ch. 12.

[17] Le 4 novembre, 1768. In Oeuvres, XLVI, 159.

prejudice, then? Quite simply, one "que le jugement ratifie quand on raisonne." [18]   To this strong argument other *philosophes* would have doubtless replied that under those circumstances it was not a prejudice! [19]   The remaining species of prejudices, according to Voltaire, are the natural variety (*e.g.*—the sun rises), and errors of gullibility (religion, of course).

Not many writers dared admit their belief in lies and prejudices as a valid instrument for preserving the *status quo* in society.   Frederick the Great, for instance, affirmed that our speculative errors and beliefs have little social importance, but his ardent defense of prejudice belies his own statement. [20]   Mirabeau—"l'ami des hommes," not the revolutionary—approves of truth, but only behind closed doors. [21]   Religion, whether true or false, must be respected for the sake of social order. On this point Voltaire belongs with the conservatives. [22]   De Boufflers, like Bayle, was more frank: "L'erreur est encore plus utile qu'elle n'est agréable; c'est elle qui soumet les peuples au joûg, en leur persuadant qu'ils sont plus faibles que leurs maîtres" (an interesting confirmation of La Boëtie's theme). [23]   On the other hand, many *philosophes* denied specifically the social importance of religion.   D'Alembert echoed Bayle's famous paradox, [24] and Hobbes, Boulainvilliers and Helvétius followed a similar line of argument. [25]

In the group of moderates were men who favored the eventual triumph of truth over prejudice, but who also feared the social consequences of hasty changes.   To this group, aside from d'Alembert and

[18] *Dictionnaire philosophique*, art. "Préjugé."   An identical opinion is expressed in a letter to Tronchin (18 avril, 1756, *Oeuvres*, XXXIX, 30): "Il est des préjugés utiles, il en est de bien dangereux."   Similarly in *Nanine* (II, ii, *Oeuvres*, V, 34).

[19] Compare, however, statements similar to Voltaire's.   Duclos, "Un préjugé, n'étant autre chose qu'un jugement porté ou admis sans examen, peut être une vérité ou une erreur." (*Considérations sur les moeurs*, in *Oeuvres* [1820], I, 167.) And Mme. de Lambert, "C'est mal parler que de traiter la religion de préjugé: le préjugé est une opinion qui peut servir à l'erreur comme à la vérité." (*Avis d'une mère à sa fille*, in *Oeuvres* [1764], 60–61.)   Also, Formey, "Considérations sur le fanatisme," in *Mémoires de l'Académie Royale de Sciences et Belles Lettres* (Berlin, 1798), 7–10; Shaftesbury, *Characteristicks* (London, 1723), III, 44–9.

[20] *Op. cit.*, 43–4.

[21] *L'ami des hommes* (Avignon, 1756), 178–80.

[22] *Oeuvres*, XXV, 100–2; XXXVII, 356; XLIII, 191.   See especially his cynical letter to d'Argental (20 avril 1769, *Oeuvres*, L, 454).

[23] *Op. cit.*, 43–4.   ("L'erreur établit la paix et l'union dans les sociétés et dans les familles, en cachant à l'un qu'il est méprisé, à l'autre qu'il est haï, à l'autre qu'il est trompé.")

[24] *Eléments de philosophie*, in *Oeuvres* (1805), XI, 214–16.

[25] *De l'Esprit*, IXe partie, 48–9 (ch. VII); Boulainvilliers: *Réfutation des erreurs de Spinoza* (Paris, 1731), 303.

Voltaire, belong Duclos, Champfort, Antoine Thomas, La Mettrie.[26] The case of Marmontel is particularly interesting, because he became involved in a significant confusion of values, to which we shall again have occasion to refer. Having intimated that all truth is useful, he goes on to say that the ruler will recognize truth by its utility. " Pour lui, le vrai, c'est le juste et l'utile: c'est dans la société, le cercle des besoins, la chaine des devoirs . . . . " The next step is a concession that public interest and truth do not always match. This finally leads to a conclusion quite opposed to Marmontel's starting point: the prince is not to be concerned at all with truth and falsehood; his but to judge of the good or harm that may result from either of these.[27]

Connected directly with the central questions and as frequently pondered, were two other matters: the origin of prejudice and error in the human mind, and the possibility of their destruction—two questions that are themselves inseparably linked.

The more outspoken of the liberal group pinned the blame for the ascendancy of error on the " oppressors " of mankind. Condillac and Volney accused the tyrants of inciting the priests.[28] Others were inclined to place on the priests themselves the burden of guilt.[29] Most of the liberal writers, however, lumped priests and princes together in a common category of oppressors. In a class apart are three English authors, Shaftesbury, Bolingbroke and Pope. They were the only apologists of falsehood who at the same time accused exploiting groups of fostering it.[30]

> Force first made Conquest, and then conquest, law;
> Till Superstition taught the tyrant awe,
> Then shared the Tyranny, then lent it aid,
> And Gods of Conqu'rors, Slaves of Subjects made.

By far the greater number of writers attributed errors and prejudice to the frailties inherent in human nature, or in the human mind. Nature wants men to be happy, declared Fontenelle, and not to think.[31] Error is easy to believe, held Bayle, easy to spread—and

---

[26] Duclos, *op. cit.*, 26; Champfort, in *Recueil des pièces couronnées par l'Académie de Marseille*, (Marseille, 1765); Thomas, *Discours de réception à l'Académie française*, in *Oeuvres* (Paris, 1822), vol. IV; La Mettrie, *Histoire naturelle de l'âme* (La Haye, 1745), 227–8, 97, 173–4; D'Alembert, *Discours préliminaire*.

[27] *Bélisaire*, in *Oeuvres*, VII, 74–5, 164–6.

[28] Condillac, *Histoire ancienne, Oeuvres*, X, 441–2; Volney, *Les Ruines*, ch. VIII.

[29] Hume, *Works* (Boston, 1854), III, 82ff.; *An Enquiry concerning the Human Understanding*, Sec. X, part 2.

[30] *Characteristicks*, III, 44–9; *Essay the Second on Human Knowledge, Works*, IV, 28–42; *Essay on Man*, Ep. III, v. 245–8:

[31] *Dialogues des morts*, " Callirhée et Pauline," " Parménisque et Théocrite de Chio." The inconsistency in Fontenelle's position of scepticism towards truth and resignation to falsehood lies in his own attacks on errors and traditions, in his own illuminating search for the origin of superstitions and fables.

almost impossible to uproot.[32] For Bayle, the question of truth and
falsehood was not essentially a social or a psychological problem. He
was tormented by the quest for truth and its frustration by universal,
unending error, involuntary and willful. Thus he slipped more and
more into an absolute Pyrrhonism, even as he struggled to find some
certainty. Against this cynical, or perhaps realistic, appraisal of
human nature, there were various protests. Jean Leclerc, Hume and
others called the love of truth, based on natural curiosity, an inherent
part of human nature.[33]

The conservatives of course followed Bayle in proclaiming the
futility of the crusade against errors and prejudice. Frederick the
Great took delight in pointing out the endless procession of philosophic and scientific theories and systems. The path to truth, he
declares, is a trackless labyrinth leading to abysses that our feeble
lights can never pierce. " Aussi, lui dis-je, l'erreur est notre partage
. . . . Pour extirper l'erreur de l'univers, il faudrait extirper tout le
genre humain." [34] In England, Swift satirized the adage that " Truth
will at last prevail " with one of his own coinage: " Falsehood flies,
and Truth comes limping after it." Because of the natural disposition
in many men to lie—and in the multitudes to believe—the lie is a
powerful political weapon. " It can conquer kingdoms without fighting, and sometimes with the loss of a battle."—Here, indeed—although Swift is morally opposed to it—is the fundamental philosophy
of totalitarian propaganda.[35]

A small group of *philosophes* held hopes for a more successful
outcome to their struggle against lies and prejudices. D'Alembert,
Diderot, d'Holbach, Morelly and Condorcet were certain of eventual

---

[32] *Nouvelles lettres critiques*, IXe lettre, 6e objection; *Critique générale de l'histoire du Calvinisme*, Lettre XXVIII; *Pensées diverses*, Pensées IV, XL. Many
18th-century writers held to these viewpoints. Voltaire, in his frequent fulminations
against the " prêtre fourbe," agreed with d'Holbach that popular prejudices are
sometimes imposed and entertained by oppressive groups. However he also adhered
to the school of Bayle.

> L'homme est né pour l'erreur; on voit la molle argile
> Sous la main du potier moins souple et moins docile
> Que l'âme n'est flexible aux préjugés divers
> Précepteurs ignorants de ce faible univers. (*Temple du goût*)

Zadig is almost an act of faith: man, with his limited view of things, cannot attain
the truth.

[33] Comment on Grotius: *The Truth of the Christian Religion* (London, 1761
[1729]), 322–4; *A Treatise of Human Nature*, Part 3, Sec. 10.

[34] *Op. cit.*, 36–45. Frederick's discussion is lengthy, and the arguments many.

[35] " On the art of Political Lying," in *Prose Works* (London, 1904), IX, 80–2.
In *Gulliver's Travels*, he put it even more explicitly: the servant of tyranny " never
tells a truth but with an intent that you should take it for a lie, nor a lie but with
a design that you should take it for a truth."

victory. To a certain extent, they were supported by Voltaire, Morellet, Malesherbes and Turgot. Volney, at the height of the Revolution, went so far as to proclaim that the final victory against falsehood had been won.[36]

The last word in the controversy was had by Antoine de Rivarol, a partisan of deliberate deceit and a diehard defender of the Old Régime. In one of his most serious works, Rivarol devotes fifty pages to a defence of superstition.[37] What men need most, he asserts, is stability, not truth; something to be sure of, something that will not change. Thus Rivarol seeks to suspend the law of change and evolution, which the eighteenth century had rediscovered. In addition to thé usual arguments, Rivarol emphasizes that only religion offers a recompense for good behavior, as well as a punishment for transgression. People need something to look forward to. Therefore society cannot exist without religion.[38] The great mistake of the *dévots,* in the century just ended, was to answer the cry of the *philosophes* for *proofs.* Both sides treated religion as a problem of truth and falsehood, instead of something to be respected, and not discussed. A religion, regardless of its abstract truth, " jouit d'une vérité politique." In a word, there is no relation between the abstractions of thought we call " truth " and the exigencies of life, which form a higher truth. And let the *philosophes* not call this hypocrisy, since it is for the good of all! Rivarol thus glibly assumes the most dubious point. Not only does deception of the people result in their happiness, but it is done for that very purpose. Truth shall be banished, and society will be forever happy with whatever lies necessity and convenience dictate. Will it be just? For Rivarol, justice is probably as vainly philosophic as truth. His conscience is easy: it is all for the general welfare.

At this point we must mention two cases which have particular interest in that they show how profoundly the controversy gripped men's souls. The abbé de Mably, in some of his writings, proclaimed the right of insurrection against tyranny, and foresaw the fall of the French régime. He blamed property for society's ills, and lay the blame for property on the wilful duping of the multitude by a few clever exploiters. A successful society must be based on truth, but unfortunately, class spirit has thwarted the search for it. Obviously, Mably was a liberal. But Mably never published these conclusions. On the contrary, he fought them bitterly. His communism was akin to Rousseau's *Contrat Social* and Diderot's amoralism—the imaginary voyages of a philosopher in his study, the offspring of an unchained,

---

[36] *Les Ruines,* 267.

[37] *De l'homme intellectuel et moral* (1801), in *Oeuvres choisies* (Paris, 1880), I, 1779.

[38] " Il y a donc un contrat éternel entre la politique et la religion."

irresponsible logic, that evaporated in the light of real situations. In real life Mably was a Christian moralist, ignorant of economic problems, " content to praise a natural order remotely staged in the past or future." [39] Consequently, in his published writings he defended the doctrine of deliberate fraud as the very basis of social order.[40]

One man, Jean-Jacques Rousseau, may be said to have been less involved in the general controversy than torn by it within himself. At one moment he leaned gingerly towards the side of truth.[41] In the *Contrat Social*, however, he took the other side; his " civil religion " is a matter of utility and not truth. Elsewhere he asserts that intellectual prejudices may be destroyed, but not those based on vices inherent to human nature—unless human nature itself is changed. Rousseau tells the *philosophes* that they have done everything wrong. " Vous voulez commencer par apprendre aux hommes la vérité pour les rendre sages, et tout au contraire, il faudrait d'abord les rendre sages pour aimer la vérité." [42]

On the purely moral side, Rousseau had his own conception of the " mensonge officieux," which he evolves in the fourth *Rêverie*. A white lie is justifiable only when it is to no one's profit or disadvantage. Such cases are rare and difficult to determine. Truth is the most precious of all things; it is the eye of reason, the eye of man. " C'est par elle que l'homme apprend à se conduire, à être ce qu'il doit être, à faire ce qu'il doit faire, à tendre à sa véritable fin." But any particular truth may be bad, or indifferent. We have no property over useless truths, no right to demand them, no right to divulge them. Therefore, if I tell a falsehood in such cases I am not lying. But are there such cases, are there truths, " si parfaitement stériles qu'elles soient, de tout point inutiles à tout? " And how shall I be the judge of their utility? There is constant opposition of interests among individuals, between individual and public welfare. Shall I withhold or declare the truth that helps one and hurts the other? Shall I think of justice, " la justice distributive," or of public good? What do I owe to myself? Rousseau adds one more precept—ever a favorite one when he felt his reason sinking into deep waters. In case of doubt,

[39] K. Martin, *French Liberal Thought in the Eighteenth Century* (London, 1929), 250.

[40] *De la législation* (1776), *Oeuvres*, IX, 387–8, 401–8, 426–31; *De la Superstition, Oeuvres*, XIII, 299–352. We are all subject to errors and prejudices, and are none the worse off for them. Men are essentially imbeciles, swayed by fear, hope, avarice and ambition. What can reason do against these? Mably ends up by supporting a ruthless philosophy of exploitation by the strong, cynically indifferent to justice and the common good. To it, he adds the same purposeful defeatism that Frederick the Great, and other reactionaries since, have spread.

[41] *Lettre à M. de Beaumont*, in *Oeuvres* (Paris, 1835), II, 775.

[42] Cf. *Correspondence générale de J-J. Rousseau*, éd. Th. Dufour, VII, 202–5.

in this and all difficult moral questions, we must follow the voice of our conscience.

Rousseau's torments center around the usefulness of truth. That word for him meant two things: justice and happiness for men. This usefulness he tries at times to identify with truth, in the fourth *Rêverie* and elsewhere, but he clearly holds it to be paramount. And in the *Profession de foi*, he turns their own argument against the *philosophes*. " Jamais, disent-ils, la vérité n'est nuisible aux hommes. Je le crois comme eux, et c'est à mon avis une grand preuve que ce qu'ils enseignent n'est pas la vérité." In his heart, Jean-Jacques wanted truth and utility to be two words for one thing. But before the " truth " of the *philosophes,* in the bitterness of disillusion, and in the chains of his own confused system, he did not succeed in making them always tally. At those difficult moments, the abstract, indefinable shadow men call Truth lost to a tangible, though still more ephemeral reality.

It is obvious that the thinking on both sides, about the origin and destruction of prejudice and error, was not often objective; it was determined to a large extent by the position each man had taken toward the central question of their social value. Exaggerated optimism or pessimism was the inevitable consequence. The conservatives sought to prove the futility of combating prejudices (as they had tried to demonstrate its danger) by attributing them to ineradicable qualities of human nature. The liberals, as they had upheld the value of truth, supported the possibility of finding it, and still more, the possibility of exterminating the man-made obstacles of prejudice and error. These obstacles are no more an invincible part of human nature than the selfish short-sightedness that uses them as a method of oppression and exploitation. Education and good government can conquer both. This was the faith of the Age of Enlightenment.[43]

POLEMICS

It was against this background of current opinion, individually expressed, that several heated discussions and debates arose—some private, others public. The first, and the briefest, was an exchange of letters between Voltaire and Mme. du Deffand. There were seven or eight letters in all, six of which we have. In their discussion, Mme. du Deffand was the defender of the *status quo*, while Voltaire appears as the rather timid, almost reluctant defender of the " philosophic " movement. It was the famous *salonnière* who began it, on December

[43] Mirabeau—the liberal, the black sheep of an aristocratic family—proclaimed that only truth can form a free and happy society. In place of Voltaire's motto, *Ecrasez l'infame!,* Mirabeau would substitute another watchword: *Eclairez les hommes!* (*Essai sur le despotisme* [1772], in *Oeuvres* [Paris, 1835], vol. I, 8.)

28, 1765, by an apparently unprovoked challenge: " Mais, M. de Voltaire, amant déclaré de la vérité, dites-moi de bonne foi, l'avez-vous trouvée?—Vous combattez et detruisez toutes les erreurs, mais que mettez-vous à leur place? " [44] Besides, she queried, why do you bother? The people pay no attention, the wise already know, and it is useless to try to enlighten the fools.

Voltaire's reply to these typically clever and pointed remarks is missing. Apparently he said something about the harm caused by popular errors. Mme. du Deffand's answer, dated January 14th, 1766, was all the more deft in that it echoed the real opinion of Voltaire himself. " Si vous ôtez à ces sortes de gens leurs préjugés, que leur restera-t-il? C'est leur ressource dans leur malheur (et c'est en quoi je voudrais leur ressembler) ; c'est leur bride et leur frein dans leur conduite, et c'est ce qui doit faire désirer qu'on ne les éclaire pas; et puis pourrait-on les éclairer? " [45] Truth, she concludes with customary pessimism, cannot be found, nor is it important to find it.

Next we have two replies from Voltaire,[46] an intermediary letter from Mme. du Deffand probably having been lost. In them Voltaire seeks chiefly to avoid discussion; he defends his position by claiming rather weakly that the search for truth keeps him busy and makes the troubles of this world seem very petty.[47] Upon receipt of these vacillating letters, Mme. du Deffand decided to press her advantage and seek a decision. She therefore inquired, on February 28th, whether, since Voltaire thinks it possible to know truth, he deems it of any importance.[48] This clear-cut interpellation did not evoke an equally precise answer. Voltaire continues to beg the question, to sit on his fence. The notions on which men differ are not necessary, he replied, since they are hidden from them. Men are every where in agreement on what is necessary to them. " Tout ce qui est un éternel sujet de dispute est d'une inutilité éternelle." [49] Knowledge beyond our reach is therefore useless, but the search for it, reiterates the Patriarch, is a most agreeable intellectual exercise.

This " pragmatic " argument is so obviously fallacious that Mme. du Deffand disdained to criticize it. Evidently, in the light of his previously examined opinions, Voltaire was ill-chosen to defend the march of ideas against one who argued the cause of obscurantism. To all practical purposes, he was in agreement with his adversary. It was out of party loyalty, loyalty to the group who, with him, attacked the " infâme," that he undertook a reluctant defense of truth against falsehood. His weakness lay in Mme. du Deffand's generalization of the question; for Voltaire was in favor of *some* prejudice.

---

[44] In Voltaire, *Oeuvres*, XLIV, 154.   [45] *Ibid.*, 182.

[46] Dated January 27, 1766, and February 19, 1766.   [47] *Ibid.*, 224.   [48] *Ibid.*, 231-2.

[49] *Ibid.* This idea, according to Voltaire, destroys the legitimacy of all superstition.

A somewhat lengthier epistolary debate was held by d'Alembert and his patron, Frederick the Great. D'Alembert had become wearied of the abstract, scholastic questions chosen as prize subjects by the Academy of Berlin, especially those dealing with the origin of things. Accordingly, in a letter to the Prussian monarch, dated December 18, 1769, he proposed one of his own: " S'il se peut faire que le peuple se passe de fable dans un système religieux." [50] To the suggestion he added his own comment. " Je pense, pour moi, qu'il faut toujours enseigner la vérité aux hommes, et qu'il n'y a jamais d'avantage réel à les tromper."

Frederick replied on January 8, 1770, and at some length, for the subject happened to be a favorite one. He suggests that the proposed topic amounts in essence to this other question: whether a man will believe his common sense rather than his imagination. His own answer was, of course, negative: " parce que le système merveilleux séduit, et que l'homme est plus raisonneur que raisonnable." [51] The experience of all ages proves that a successful religion must be a mixture of necessary morality based on absurd fable. After all, there is only an average of one thousand cultured people per ten million, and these are not in agreement. Common sense is therefore limited to a fraction of the nation, and imaginary systems are destined to sway forever the masses of men. The obvious conclusion (and this was the end-all of Frederick's reasoning) is that we should not waste time trying to enlighten humanity.

" L'imperfection, tant en morale qu'en physique, est le caractère de ce globe que nous habitons; c'est peine perdue d'entreprendre à l'éclairer, et souvent la commission est dangereuse pour ceux qui s'en chargent. Il faut se contenter d'être sage pour soi, si on peut l'être, et abandonner le vulgaire à l'erreur en tâchant de le détourner des crimes qui dérangent l'ordre de la société." [52]

Responding on the ninth of March, d'Alembert decided to broaden his question and rephrased it in this fashion: " Si en matière de religion, ou même en quelque matière que ce puisse être, il est utile de tromper le peuple." He concedes one of Frederick's points: that superstition is the food of the people. But he is not equally sure that such is their inevitable destiny. [53] It is most difficult, indeed, to uproot a long established prejudice, but if absurd and reasonable opinions were presented, even to the ignorant multitude, at the same time and for the first time, superstition would probably lose out. [54]

[50] D'Alembert, Oeuvres, XVII, 140–1.   [51] Ibid., 145.   [52] Ibid., 148.   [53] Ibid., 154.

[54] " Il me semble qu'il ne faut pas, comme Fontenelle, tenir la main fermée quand on est sûr d'avoir la vérité: il faut seulement ouvrir avec sagesse et avec précaution les doigts de la main l'un après l'autre, et petit à petit la main est ouverte tout à fait, et la vérité en sort tout entière. Les philosophes qui ouvrent la main trop

Frederick did not wait as long as his correspondent to give answer; his letter was dated April 3rd. By now thoroughly warmed to the subject, he declares that a proper rejoinder would require an *in-folio*. If we were at the first day of the world—in other words, speaking abstractly—it would not be wise to deceive the people, to introduce unknown superstitions and errors. However, we are not in such a position, and the world is full of prejudice. History shows two kinds of impostures. The first, based on superstition, fabricated by priests and prophets; as for these, " je vous les abandonne." Here Frederick appears even more anti-clerical than Voltaire. Second, the moulding of the people's minds, to their own advantage, by princes, and by means of prejudices. These are necessary impostures; auguries in Rome, for instance, halted popular seditions. Frederick, apparently, is speaking from his own practical experience, when he declares that all those who have to lead multitudes toward a common goal must deceive them. There is no harm in this, since some kind of super-stition is inevitable anyhow.

" Il serait beau sans doute de jouir du spectacle unique d'un peuple sans erreur, sans préjugé, sans superstition, sans fanatisme; mais il est dit dans les centuries de Nostradamus, qu'on ne le découvrira qu'après en avoir trouvé un sans vices, sans passions, sans crimes." [55]

Frederick, not unlike Rousseau, is at the opposite pole from those *philosophes* who considered vices and crimes the *result* of errors and prejudices. Again he mocks the utility of their efforts: a few cultured men will agree; the *bonzes* and *lamas* will shout; and an infinity of imbeciles will stop up the holes of their caves. Calas, Sirven, the burning of witches in Rome, these and many other things prove that even in the century of philosophy, there has been little genuine prog-ress. " Oh! mon cher Anaxagoras, l'homme est un animal incorrigible, plus sensible que raisonnable."

D'Alembert's answer to this long letter, delayed because of ill-health, was finally sent on April 30th. He adds little to his previous argument: that the birth and introduction of errors should be opposed by all possible means; that those already established should be at-tacked with finesse and patience, by the establishment of opposing truths.[56]

---

brusquement sont des fous; on leur coupe le poing et voilà tout ce qu'ils y gagnent; mais ceux qui la tiennent fermée absolument, ne font pas pour l'humanité ce qu'ils doivent."

[55] *Ibid.*, 160.

[56] The rationalist replies to the realist in these terms: " Il ne faut pas braquer le canon contre la maison, parce que ceux qui la défendent tireraient des fenêtres une grêle de coups de fusil; il faut petit à petit élever à côté une autre maison plus habitable et plus commode; insensiblement tout le monde viendra habiter celle-ci, et la maison pleine de léopards sera desertée! "

Again Frederick's reply followed closely, on the seventh of May. His letter provides the link between this debate and the more bitter one that followed, with the radical wing of the *philosophes*. He too had been ill. During his convalescence, the first book that fell into his hands was d'Holbach's *Essai sur les préjugés* (1770). This book aroused him from his inertia and impelled him to use all his energy to think through its mistakes. "J'ai éprouvé des mouvements répulsifs aux sentiments de l'auteur, qui prétend que la vérité étant faite pour l'homme, il faut en tout temps la lui dire." Especially he resents the author's insults to kings, generals and poets, "parce que j'ai l'honneur d'être assez mauvais poète (ou empoisonneur public), parce que j'ai eu l'honneur de me battre quelquefois en qualité de général (ou de bourreau mercenaire), parce que j'ai l'honneur d'être un roi (ou de [*sic*] tyran barbare)." The author is a "chien enragé" and deserves to be treated as one. Frederick, moreover, has decided to refute this monstrous book and is sending his dissertation for d'Alembert to judge.

D'Alembert informed his patron, on June 8th, that he had not been able to get a copy of the *Essai*, which was commanding a very high price. Besides, he is tired of books against what Voltaire calls "l'infâme." He is tempted to say of the title of *philosophe* what "Jacques Rosbif dit de celui de Monsieur dans la comédie du *François à Londres:* je ne veux point de ce titre-là, il y a trop de faquins qui le portent." [57] Instead of insulting priests, *philosophes* should make religion useful to man's happiness, and enlighten sovereigns.

The royal philosopher was still fuming when he answered d'Alembert on July 7th. Hardly had he sent along his refutation of the *Essai sur les préjugés*, when another "vicious" work fell into his hands. It was titled *Du Système de la nature*. Frederick did not suspect their common authorship. Although he felt less violently about this one, he decided that he would refute it, too, and send his remarks to d'Alembert. He admits that they are "malsonnantes, hérétiques, sentant l'hérésie et dignes d'encourir les foudres du Vatican. Cependant, ce qui m'a consolé, c'est que mon adversaire sera pour le moins doublement cuit et rôti, si je le suis une fois dans l'autre monde." [58] Again he emphasizes the uselessness of the "philosophic" effort. It is not in our nature to reach perfection. "Croyez, mon cher, qu'un homme qui aurait l'art de vous faire bien digérer serait plus utile au monde qu'un philosophe qui en bannirait tous les préjugés." [59]

After several extraneous exchanges, Frederick returned to the subject once more, in his letter of October 18, 1770. There he urges attacking superstitions with the weapon of ridicule and leading all minds to a spirit of universal tolerance: "qu'importe alors à quel culte le peuple est attaché?" [60] And d'Alembert replied (November 30),

[57] P. 172.   [58] P. 178.   [59] P. 178.   [60] P. 197-8.

echoing again the general tone of his correspondent's mood, urging this time that religion be reduced to its essential moral elements, for then superstition will easily be destroyed. In this last letter, he returns to one of his first themes. " Le peuple est sans doute un animal imbécile qui se laisse conduire dans les ténèbres, quand on ne lui présente pas quelque chose de mieux; mais offrez-lui la vérité: si cette vérité est simple . . . il me parait infaillible qu'il la saisira et qu'il n'en voudra plus d'autres." [61]

Thus ended the discussion, neither man having budged from his initial position. It was a controversy valuable for its relation to the thought of the century, and no less important for the light it throws on the minds of the disputants. D'Alembert appears timid and lost in rationalistic abstractions, but sincere in his idealism and humanitarianism. Frederick is always the cynic, the realist, bending reason to fact and to selfish interest; keen in his dislike of the Church— rather than of religion—a lion in defense of the social *status quo* against the menace of an idea; an idea whose potential implications he realized far better than its very proponents.[62]

From this epistolary debate, we are led to the larger one with which it is connected. In this more acrid controversy, d'Holbach, Frederick the Great and Diderot were the participants. D'Holbach tackles directly the question of truth and falsehood in most of his works. In condemning all errors and prejudices, involuntary or imposed, he is only carrying to its extreme logical—if not always practical—conclusion, the sense and core of the " philosophic " struggle against the Old Régime. The *Essai sur les préjugés* (1770), like the *Système de la nature* (1770), was an all-out attack on the " tyrants,"

---

[61] P. 215-6.

[62] It is interesting to note that Frederick had also written to Voltaire about his refutation of the *Essai sur les préjugés* (24 mai 1770, in Voltaire, *Oeuvres*, XLVII, 85-6). Voltaire replied (8 juin 1770, *ibid.*, 102) that he had tried to read the *Essai*, but " n'ayant vu qu'un verbiage sans esprit, j'avais jeté là le livre. Vous lui faites trop d'honneur de le critiquer; mais béni soyez-vous d'avoir marché sur des cailluox, et d'avoir taillé des diamants." To d'Alembert, however, Voltaire expressed not quite identical opinions. He wrote to him on June 11, asking whether Diderot, Damilaville or d'Helvétius might be the author of the *Essai*. " L'auteur . . . a de la force, mais il fait trop de prose." And about Frederick: " le roi a aussi les siens (i.e., préjugés) qu'il faut lui pardonner; on n'est pas roi pour rien." (*Ibid.*, 104). On July 27, he commented shrewdly about Frederick's attack on the *Système de la nature:* " vous voyez qu'il prend toujours le parti de son tripot, et qu'il est fâché que les philosophes ne soient pas royalistes." (*Ibid.*, 152-3.) D'Alembert, contrary to Voltaire, expressed the same opinions to him as to Frederick: " D'ailleurs, independamment de l'incertitude de la matière, je ne sais pas si on fait bien d'attaquer directement et ouvertement certains points auxquels il serait peut-être mieux de ne pas toucher." (4 aout 1770, *ibid.*, 162.) This, again, is characteristic of the two men.

political and religious, who " enslave and exploit " their fellow-men. They were assertions of the democratic principle that society exists for the happiness of the ruled, and not of the rulers, who usually exercise a selfish and usurped power. This power, according to d'Holbach, is based on violence and fraud. The fraud consists in keeping men in ignorance, in hiding and distorting truth, and in systematically imposing prejudices and errors. By attacking falsehood, then, d'Holbach is attacking one of the two pillars of tyranny.

In the *Essai sur les préjugés*, d'Holbach lays open this universal conspiracy to deprave the human reason, to extinguish the light.[63] " Public welfare " and " religion " are the two pretexts used by oppressors to veil the truth. But men should know that fear of truth is an infallible sign of imposture. D'Holbach had a fanatical hatred of priests. He asserts that their invariable maxim will always be to perpetuate the errors of the human race, to make it blind and submissive, fortified against reason. It follows that error is the source of all human evils, and truth the remedy, the only possible source of genuine happiness and virtue.[64] Falsehood can have only a specious and temporary usefulness or usefulness to a few selfish men.[65] To doubt whether it is good to disillusion men of their prejudices is to doubt whether they are better off happy than unhappy, rational than irrational, virtuous than vicious.[66]

D'Holbach rests much of his argument on utility. If morals, for instance, have made no progress among men, it is solely because they have been founded on the lies, errors and prejudices of a Church. It is equally false that truth would be dangerous to a sovereign. The strongest prince is the ruler of a free people, of one that knows its interests, rights and obligations. To govern men it is not necessary to use violence, trickery, the chimerical terrors and rewards of another life, nor is it required to reduce them to the condition of brutes. For the man without truth will never be more than a discouraged slave, beaten down by oppression, ready to receive all vices and prejudices that those he depends on wish to inculcate in him. These cannot be cooperative members and intrepid defenders of a great society.[67]

---

[63] *Essai sur les préjugés* (Paris, 1822), chap. I. D'Holbach also accuses both education and custom: " tout conspire en ce monde . . . à mettre l'homme en garde contre la vérité."

[64] *Ibid.*, ch. II.   [65] *Ibid.*, 81.

[66] " Non, la vérité ne peut jamais être funeste aux hommes; elle ne peut être à craindre que par ceux qui se croient faussement intéressés à les tromper . . . . Il n'est point d'erreur utile au genre humain." (P. 95.) This idea is often repeated by d'Holbach. Cf. *Système de la nature* (Londres, 1771), I, 373–4, 522–3; II, 388–90 (" to say that error is useful is to say that poison is useful "), 403, 422–3, nb. 92, 439–41.

[67] Cf. *Essai* . . . ch. III.

D'Holbach's conclusion is optimistic. It is an insult to humanity to say that error is pleasing to it. Man is in error because "tout conspire à le tromper." [68] But the human mind is perfectible. Sooner or later necessity will lead all men to the North Star of truth, and all errors will be discovered and destroyed. To fight against this is to fight against natural law. Some day truth will form "un vaste fleuve qui entraînera toutes les erreurs et les barrières impuissantes qui s'opposent à son cours." [69] Liberty and education will solve all our problems, for they will enable men to use their reason. Some day, perhaps not in all the world, but at least in part of the world, for part of the time, reason will triumph and men will be happy.[70]

D'Holbach's argument is an impassioned and sincere one. Its weaknesses, quite evidently, are its abstractness, its ignoring of realities, its assumption of all that has to be proved. Frederick the Great took advantage of these deficiencies in his refutation, the *Examen de l'Essai sur les préjugés*. Repeating opinions he had expressed elsewhere, Frederick points out that truth is not made for man, since manifestly he has not found it. "L'expérience me montre l'homme, en tous les siècles, dans l'esclavage perpétuel de l'erreur . . . et des préjugés qui règnent d'un bout du monde à l'autre." [71] The cause is clear: man's own nature, and his limitations. "Qu'en puis-je conclure autre chose, si ce n'est que l'homme est fait pour l'erreur?" Frederick's argument, in contrast with d'Holbach's rationalism, is exclusively empirical.

The one who became most excited about this dispute, with his usual impetuosity and enthusiasm, was Diderot. To him it was clearly a fight between the forces of progress and obscurantism. He probably lost no time in taking up the cudgels in defense of his side, and wrote his impassioned *Lettre sur l'Examen de l'Essai sur les préjugés*.[72] Diderot repeats many of d'Holbach's gratuitous abstractions. Errors pass, truth alone remains. Therefore man is made for truth: and truth is made for man, since he is constantly pursuing it, and embracing it whenever he finds it. And Diderot points for proof to the progress we have made from barbarism.

[68] P. 365–6.   [69] P. 397.

[70] D'Holbach's optimism is much more cautious in the *Système de la nature*. "Ne nous flattons point cependant que la raison puisse délivrer tout d'un coup la race humaine des erreurs dont tant de causes réunies s'efforcent de l'empoisonner . . . . Des êtres ignorants, malheureux et tremblants se feront toujours des Dieux . . . . Ne nous proposons donc que de montrer la raison à ceux qui peuvent l'entendre; de présenter la vérité à ceux qui peuvent soutenir son éclat . . . ." (II, 345–6.)   [71] *Oeuvres*, IX, 132.

[72] Not published until 1937, by Jean Thomas and Franco Venturi. The editors assign no date to the ms., nor does their volume have any page numbers.

The main cause of error, Diderot retorts to Frederick, is not man's weakness. " Si le monde est plein d'erreurs, c'est qu'il est plein de scélérats prédicateurs du mensonge." And Diderot repeats almost exactly an argument of Bayle's: that the triumph of error is an homage to truth, because the dupes of tyrants, in accepting their lies, do so only under the name of truth.[73] Society is based on virtue (not on force), and virtue on truth; therefore, concludes the mathematical philosopher, society is based on truth. Frederick's defense of " le mensonge officieux " he brands a deliberate attempt to confuse the issue. In all matters regarding society, " il n'y a aucun exemple que la vérité ait été nuisible ni pour le présent, ni pour l'avenir." And Diderot concludes with a violent denunciation of tyrants and a prediction of the universal triumph of truth.

The editors of the *Lettre*, it may be said in passing, have missed its true scope. They treat it exclusively as a violent outbreak against a tyrant. The deep significance of Diderot's discussion lies in its link to the underlying philosophic question. His attack was only secondarily on the manifestations of tyranny itself; primarily it was a denunciation of a moral and political philosophy of truth that justified and implemented any tyranny, that made man the chattel of his oppressors, debased his dignity and compromised his future.

D'Holbach was less perturbed than his friend over Frederick the Great's refutation of his essay. He replied in later works. In the *Système social* (1773), he again linked truth and happiness, and took pains to point out that the matter of the white lie concerns individuals—not society as a whole. He denied that there is any political danger latent in truth; it is error that produces factions and fanatics. D'Holbach's conclusion is again that man's self-interest will eventually assure the triumph of truth, despite tyranny and imposture. " L'esprit humain n'est point fait pour revenir sur ses pas; son essence est d'aller en se perfectionnant." [74]

In one shape or another, we find the question of truth and falsehood recurring from time to time in academic records. It was forced upon the ears of the Académie Française, despite that august body's sedulous avoidance of dangerous subjects. The Académie de Marseille chose as essay subject for the year 1750, " *Lequel des deux est le plus nuisible à la société, des vices du coeur ou des erreurs de l'esprit?* " The Société Economique de Berne, in 1762, considered this question: *Est-il des préjugés respectables qu'un bon citoyen doive se faire un scrupule de combattre publiquement?* Again we find the Académie de Marseille, in 1765, listening to a discourse by no less a personage

---

[73] Cf. *Nouvelles lettres critiques,* Lettre IX, 6e objection (*op. cit.,* II, 226).
[74] *Ibid.,* III, 157-8.

than its director, M. de Paul, on the task of enlightening mankind through discovery of truth and attack on prejudice. By 1785, academicians were even bolder. *Quelle est la meilleure manière de rappeler à raison les nations tant sauvages que policées qui se sont livrées à la superstition et aux erreurs de tout genre?* On this subject Le Roy de Flagis addressed the Académie de Dijon. He finds man's ignorance only one obstacle to his purpose, and not invincible, despite the fact that three-fourths of humanity are stupid. The greatest impediment is formed by some of the upper, more intelligent fraction. In that group, " il en est trop d'ingénieux, d'éclairés et d'intéressés à entretenir la superstition. Elle a jeté de trop profondes racines dans le corps politique pour qu'il ne soit pas bien plus difficile de la déraciner." Le Roy de Flagis sees only two solutions: revolution, or preferably, a voluntary example set by the upper stratum: the aristocracy should renounce their privileges, and the priests their superstitions.[75]

But of all the academic appearances of our question, the most noteworthy was its choice as a prize-topic by the Academy of Berlin in 1777. This episode, a typical example of the essay contests that played such a large rôle in the intellectual life of the eighteenth century, brought about the most extensive public debate over the problem of truth and falsehood.

D'Alembert, it has already been mentioned, was annoyed by the scholastic nature of the prize-essay subjects selected by the Royal Academy of Berlin—especially those dealing with the origin of things. The culmination came in 1777 with a long and unintelligible question on the " Recherche d'une force primitive et permanente, à la fois substance et cause." On September 22nd of that year, d'Alembert wrote to the King, again urging the choice of more useful matters, " faites pour contribuer à l'amélioration de la société." As a help, he proposed a possible topic, one he had already mentioned seven years earlier.[76] Reluctantly, the metaphysically minded academy accepted it, in essence, after Frederick himself had ordered a special prize conferred for it.[77] The matter was first propounded in the Academy's *Mémoires* for 1777.[78]

---

[75] Cf. Roger Tisserand, *L'Académie de Dijon, de 1740 a 1793* (Vesoul, 1936), 450–2.

[76] " S'il peut être utile de tromper le peuple." D'Alembert's next comment is interesting. " Nous n'avons jamais osé à l'Académie française proposer ce beau sujet, parce que les discours envoyés pour le prix doivent avoir, pour le malheur de la raison, deux docteurs de Sorbonne pour censeurs, et qu'il n'est pas possible avec de pareilles gens d'écrire rien de raisonnable." Apparently, the possibility of using this topic may have been discussed by the French Academy.

[77] Cf. Christian Bartholmess: *Histoire philosophique de l'Académie de Berlin* (Paris, 1850), I, 230–2.   [78] Berlin, 1779, 14.

L'Académie a fait imprimer dans le mois de Novembre 1777 un programme à part par lequel la Classe de philosophie spéculative propose la
Question suivante.

*Est-il utile au Peuple d'être trompé, soit qu'on l'induise dans de nouvelles
erreurs ou qu'on l'entretienne dans celles où il est?* Les Pièces sont admises
au concours jusqu'au 31 Décembre 1779, et le prix sera adjugé le 31 Mai
1780.

A similar announcement the following year added that the prize
would be " une Médaille d'or de cinquante Ducats," [79] and in 1779 an
identical notice was published. None of the papers submitted, unfortunately, is at present available, since they probably lie within the
archives of the Royal Academy. The *Mémoires* for 1780, however,
give us the essential results.[80] There were no less than forty-two
entries, in French, German and Latin. Of these, five were excluded
for arrival after the deadline, and four others because the authors did
not follow the rules for anonymity. Of the remaining thirty-three
twenty espoused the affirmative, thirteen argued for the negative.
These figures are significant: the total number as to the popularity of
the problem; the division of opinion, as to its status in contemporary
thought. It should be added that some of the contestants took sides
only with reservations and modifications. In contrast with the size
of the two groups is the number of papers selected as distinguished:
four among the affirmative theses, seven among the negative. To
indicate that they took no sides (and perhaps no interest) in this
imposed question, the Academy made a double award. For a negative paper, the prize was given to a " M Becker, Gouverneur de M. le
Baron de Dachemoeder, à Erfurt en Thuringe," for the affirmative, to
" F. de Castillon, professeur de mathématiques à l'Académie Royale
des Gentilshommes." The former's motto was " Homo sum, humani
nihil a me alienum puto," the latter chose Tasso's lines:

> Così all'egro fanciul porgiamo aspersi
> Di soave liquor gli orli del vaso,
> Succhi amari ingannato in tanto ei beve
> E dall'inganno sua orta receve.[81]

It might be assumed that no one of any importance felt impelled
to contribute to the contest. If true, such a conclusion would not
reduce the value of the testimony as to the widespread, indeed universal interest in the problem; but aside from the fact that it is not at
present possible to verify the identity of all the participants, we do

---

[79] *Ibid.*, 1778 (Berlin, 1780), 30.   [80] Berlin, 1782, 9–10.

[81] Some of the other *devises* are worth quoting, as revelatory of the attitudes and
approaches adopted. " Neque hic lupis mos, nec fuit leonibus unquam "; " Lucri
odor bonus ex re qualibet "; " Non refert qua via; sed quo tendam "; " Candide, sed
caute."

know that one renowned philosopher, at least, was stimulated to write his piece for the competition. That was Condorcet, and we know it simply because he decided, for an unstated reason, not to send in his essay.[82] In the present instance, that was a fortunate decision, for Condorcet's essay reveals to us the details of the program and is possibly a representative sample of the arguments used by the thirteen who spoke for the negative.

The program set forth by the Academy consists of eight questions. First a general query: " Des erreurs nouvelles sont-elles utiles au peuple? " Condorcet replies that a people should know " l'ensemble de toutes les vérités morales et politiques qui influent sur son bonheur," for it is clear that " le plus grand nombre voudra nécessairement ce qui est utile au plus grand nombre." [83]

The second question had also been aired by earlier writers. " Est-il utile au peuple d'appuyer des vérités par des erreurs, sous prétexte qu'il est plus aisé de lui faire adopter une erreur absurde que de lui faire entendre les preuves d'une vérité? " Error, rejoins Condorcet as others had before him, is a fragile base for truth, for if one perceives the falsehood of the supporting arguments, he will be tempted to reject the entire fabric.

The next question and Condorcet's reply are similar to the second. " Est-il du moins utile d'inspirer aux peuples certaines erreurs, uniquement dans la vue d'en tirer des motifs sensibles et à sa portée, de se conformer, dans sa conduite, aux règles de la morale? " Erroneous motives, Condorcet points out, indicate bad reasoning. If a man reasons badly on the motives, he will reason badly on the principles as well, and on their applications. The belief that true motives are insufficient is used by sophists who wish to degrade the human race in order to deceive them for their own profit.

The fourth question was more probing. " Si l'erreur est toujours nuisible en général, n'y a-t-il pas du moins quelques objets sur lesquels elle soit, pour ainsi dire, nécessaire, ou parce que la raison seule est insuffisante, ou parce que la vérité n'est pas à la portée de tous les hommes? L'erreur n'est-elle pas nécessaire pour certaines classes d'hommes? " The necessary truths, retorts Condorcet are not complicated, at least to grasp superficially. Like d'Holbach, he asserts that if the people are stupid, it is because " on a tout fait pour rendre

---

[82] *Dissertation philosophique et politique, ou Réflexions critiques sur cette question: S'il est utile aux hommes d'être trompés?* (1779, published 1790), in *Oeuvres,* éd. Arago-O'Connor (Paris, 1847), vol. V.

[83] P. 347–8. " L'avantage général du genre humain, d'une nation, d'un corps d'hommes, est de connaître la vérité sur les objets généraux de la société, quelle que soit cette vérité. Nous pouvons donc conclure généralement qu'il ne peut être utile aux hommes d'être trompés."

les hommes stupides et fous." [84] Crimes are due to bad laws, which are due to errors, and cannot therefore be corrected by other errors. Condorcet's viewpoint is typical of the relations which eighteenth-century rationalists perceived between morals and legislation. He does not answer the last part of the question; by " certain classes " he assumes women and children to be meant.

Next the Academy turned to remedial measures. " Si nous considérons les hommes livrés à des erreurs, peut-il être utile de les leur laisser, d'en détruire une partie pour laisser subsister le reste, ou de combattre une erreur par d'autres erreurs moins nuisibles? " Condorcet's reply is categorical. " Innocent errors " produce " extravagances monstrueuses et funestes . . . . Si l'erreur n'est jamais utile, il faut chercher à la détruire où elle se trouve." [85]

" Si les erreurs ne sont pas d'une utilité générale," the contestants were next asked, " ne peuvent-elles pas être, pour en peuple particulier, d'une utilité momentanée? " This Condorcet grants, for the exception proves the rule. Some errors may have contributed to the greatness of some nations: the belief in a miraculous statue may have acted like a strong liquor—but we cannot erect drunkenness into a principle of politics. Loss of the illusion would, moreover, be disastrous.

Here, then, is a reservation on Condorcet's part. And in response to question seven, he continues his retreat. " N'y a-t-il aucun inconvénient " asked the Academy, " à dire au peuple la vérité tout entière? De quels ménagements est-il utile et permis d'user en attaquant les erreurs populaires? " Condorcet allows that precautions must be taken with certain errors that influence the private or public conduct of men. Truth, once known, will be useful, but the passage from error to truth is sometimes dangerous. " Il ne suffit pas de faire le bien, il faut le bien faire." [86] It is like tearing down a house—we must do it in a way not dangerous. There are two essential problems. The first is to destroy religious prejudice without destroying morals. This can be accomplished by books, for the ruling class, by education and legislation, for the people. The second is to teach peoples their political rights without provoking disorders. By spreading the fundamental truths which are common to all forms of government, the erroneous opinions on which the power of oppressors is founded will be demolished.[87] Condorcet's discussion, abstract all along, is especially distant from realities at this point. He holds that even if men, having learned the truth about their rights and the violations of them, started civil disorders, it would not be the fault of such truth, but rather of

[84] P. 359.
[85] P. 365-6. Cf. Helvétius and Thomas Paine.
[86] P. 373.
[87] P. 375-9.

another error: that is, their assumption that they could demand their rights at any time and by any means.

The final question deals more directly with truth itself. " N'y a-t-il pas des vérités qui deviendraient nuisibles au peuple, parce qu'il ne les entendrait pas, et qu'elles instruiraient ceux qui veulent lui nuire des moyens de l'empêcher de s'éclairer? " This is true, admits Condorcet; if the majority were not ripe for receiving the truth, tyrants could stifle it. Like a general, philosophers must keep their plans hidden, await the proper moment, prepare the ground meanwhile. There are four cases when truth should not be recklessly dealt out: religious morals; the right of resistance to oppressive governments (except in democracies, where there is freedom of opinion); truths that will help enemies of humanity strengthen their power and retard progress; premature truths, for which the people are not ready, and which tyrants could crush.[88]

Condorcet concludes that, with the above exceptions, " la vérité est toujours utile au peuple, et que si le peuple a des erreurs, il est utile de les lui ôter . . . . C'est trahir la cause des hommes, que de soutenir des erreurs, puisque l'erreur ne peut être utile . . . . Concluons, enfin, que de toutes les erreurs nuisibles, l'opinion qu'il y a des erreurs utiles aux hommes est la plus dangereuse et renferme toutes les autres." [89]

The Academy of Berlin, apparently, repented in its opposition to this type of essay subject. In 1781, it proposed a similar topic, but narrower in scope. " Quelle est la meilleure manière de rappeler à la raison les nations, tant sauvages que policées, qui se sont livrées à l'erreur et aux superstitions de tout genre? " [90] The prize was to be awarded in 1783. This time, however, the question had a less fortunate fate. When the prize year came, the academy reproved the competitors for having misinterpreted the subject. Their mistake was a significant one. They had debated whether errors *are* harmful and should be extirpated, whereas the question, explained the Academy, assumed that some errors are harmful and should be destroyed, and sought the best methods of attaining this expressed purpose.[91] Consequently, an extension of two years was granted. The prize was finally awarded in 1786, but with no details or fanfare, to " M. Ancillon, pasteur de l'Eglise française de Berlin."

[88] P. 382.
[89] Cf. p. 381–9.
[90] *Mémoires* . . . , Année 1781 (Berlin, 1783), 11. Cf. Le Roy de Flagis, *supra*.
[91] *Ibid.*, Année 1783, 11.

CONCLUSION

Brought into strong relief by the controversy over truth and false-hood is the dominantly utilitarian direction of eighteenth-century thought. The utility of truth as a means to personal and social wel-fare, rather than abstract reasons of morality, justice, or right and wrong, was the sole factor in the judgment of each group. While some thought falsehood best served these aims, others proclaimed truth to be exclusively useful, and a third group held that a given truth or prejudice might, according to the circumstances, be either beneficial or harmful. The liberal group defended truth on the sole ground that it is always useful; they condemned deceit on the sole ground that it is always harmful. As d'Holbach and others admitted, they would favor falsehood if it could ever be socially useful—a proposition which they categorically denied.

Such an outlook was natural to the new middle-class cast of mind. It was inevitable at a time when thinking was forced into the channel of social problems and many thinkers scorned the spider-webs of meta-physics. To the humanism of the *philosophes,* it was particularly akin, since theirs was a philosophy of relativity, that judged all by the measure of man. This is especially true of the materialists, who, while championing social morality and justice, excluded the abstract notion of good or evil from a purely mechanistic universe.[92] Because of their peculiar fusion of utilitarian materialism and idealism, the eighteenth-century liberals did not see a danger underlying their stand. To pro-claim an idealistic faith that was the opposite of their adversaries', they adopted their adversaries' criterion of utility.

The matter of the " mensonge officieux " is a concrete instance of this confusion. Previously, this question had been a discussion of abstract values of right and wrong; now it was a matter of utility in regard to happiness. Previously it had been a point in dispute among Christian writers; now we find a combination of devout be-lievers, political conservatives and many *philosophes* united in its favor. The motives for this strange bedfellowing are significant on both sides. When faced with the menace of rational criticism, many believers who had condemned all lies on purely moral grounds found themselves in the new conservative or " devout " party, opposed to an all-out stand for truth. The *philosophes,* in turn, conceded the value of the " mensonge officieux," because a " mensonge officieux " was use-ful, and where they supported truth it was only because of its utility.

Of those who accepted or rejected the " mensonge officieux," only

[92] As Mirabeau admitted, " c'est précisément parce qu'on me convainc qu'il est de mon intéret d'être juste, que je regarderais la justice comme mon premier devoir . . . . La méchanceté est donc évidemment une erreur de calcul aussi bien qu'un sentiment pervers . . . le respect de la vertu n'est qu'une institution politique fondée sur l'utilité." *Oeuvres,* I, 110, 144–5.

Toussaint and Kant renounced the criterion of utility. They maintained that right is right and wrong is wrong. They declared that it is
never permissible to do wrong, to use deceit, in order to achieve a good
end, while the other liberals were saying that it is never *possible* for
a wrong, or a falsehood, to produce a good end—except in this case.
They evidently did not realize the full implications of their concession. Their acceptance of the " mensonge officieux " was no less than
an avowal that the end justifies the means. The artificial restriction
of the usefulness of lies to individuals and the distinction of " social
truths " was no effective dike against universal application of their
own admission, that truth is good only because it is always useful,
that falsehood is bad only because it is never useful. It would not be
difficult to maintain that, at bottom, they were arguing the cause of
their enemies. For if we identify truth and utility, we may either
assume, as they did, that all truth is useful, and insist on its exclusive
reign; or else we may decide what is useful, and truth being relative
to utility, declare false and iniquitous whatever impedes the chosen
end. That is what Rousseau and Robespierre did in declaring the
" philosophic " ideas false because of their danger.[93] From this viewpoint, we can see how Frederick the Great, arch-defender of deliberate
fraud, would have accepted as his own the argument that whatever is
true is useful, whatever useful true. Admittedly, most of those engaged in the controversy on the conservative side did not adopt this
bias; rather did they accept the distinction and claim utility more
important than truth. It was the liberals who insisted on the identity,
but in reality it made little difference, for they could not maintain
their stand. They had to accept the white lie as useful, and should
anything at all be proven eternally useful, as d'Holbach admitted,
they would have to believe it true, or else accept it anyhow.

Such was the latent danger of their position, and several of their
opponents profited from it. Yet, in all justice, we must realize that
these liberals had a special conception of usefulness. They were thinking of ultimate, not immediate utility. The latter kind seemed to
them specious, the former alone general and genuine. It was this
" ultimate usefulness " that they equated with truth. This conception
led them, not to a realistic view of the useful—the view of Machia-
vellians, that it is relative and can be determined by every man in his
given situation; it led them rather to a faith in ideals and absolutes:
the rights of man, truth, justice.

[93] Robespierre, attempting to impose the Cult of the Supreme Being, defended
the belief in God and the after-life in these terms: " Et comment ces idées ne
seraient-elles point des vérités? Je ne conçois pas du moins comment la nature
aurait pu suggérer à l'homme des fictions plus utiles que toutes les réalités." (" Discours du 18 floréal," an II, in *Oeuvres*, III, 621–6.) Cf. Mably (*Oeuvres*, IX, 408):
" Si la vérité est toujours utile, l'athéisme n'est donc pas la vérité, car il est toujours
plus funeste aux hommes que la guerre, la famine et la peste."

There is another important inference to be drawn from the discussion. Fundamentally, those who upheld the side of truth were believers in what we today call democracy: for their stand was founded on faith in the people, faith in their ultimate discernment of the good and the true, faith, also, in the power of education. It was Thomas Jefferson who most clearly perceived this relationship.[94]

And in the eighteenth-century controversy, it was the reactionary, the vindicator of deceit and prejudice who held that the people are stupid and dangerous. Oppressors naturally fear and scorn the oppressed. The triple link is constantly evident between defense of falsehood, defense of the oppressive organization of society, and vilification of the common people who were the victims. Rightly or wrongly, the defenders of falsehood view men as more animal than human.[95]

In the new revolutionary cataclysm of the present era the values of truth are again an important aspect of the philosophical side of a social and political struggle. Thanks to the discussion waged in the eighteenth century, we can see that any order that avows only the law of might, that submits belief in truth, morality and justice to an arbitrary criterion of utility, cannot tolerate a system that makes truth alone the test of ideas and moral justice the test of actions. We can understand, with deep historical perspective, why such an order, bending its genius to propaganda, makes a recognized weapon of falsehood, recalling the words of Montaigne: "Notre vérité de maintenant, ce n'est pas ce qui est, mais ce qui se persuade à autrui."

The dualism of man's animal heritage and human aspirations condemns him to an eternal struggle. He must join forces with one of two groups. There are those who consider society a continuation of the state of war that is the law of animals living according to nature's way. "Nature is pitiless, and that is why we too shall have to be cruel," said Adolf Hitler to Hermann Rauschning. And there are those who hope to supersede that rule with the human law of cooperation. It may happen that the attempt to cooperate, that the promises of rationalism will fail, as in the last generations. Then men will succumb to the despairing view of human nature of the totalitarian philosophies. This is man's eternal struggle, unless he fall again to brutishness, or rise to an angel's sphere.

Goucher College.

[94] Cf. Jefferson, *Democracy*, ed. S. K. Padover, 146–9, 137, 141, 144.

[95] The doctrine that "might is right" is always accompanied by a cheapened evaluation of human beings. Cf. Machiavelli, *Il Principe*, ch. XVIII; Hitler, *Mein Kampf* (New York, Stackpole, 1939), 661.

XV

KANT AND THE RIGHT OF REVOLUTION

By Lewis W. Beck*

Kant's enthusiasm for the French Revolution, the American Revolution, and the Irish efforts to throw off the English yoke is well known. It earned him the unenviable epithet of "the old Jacobin"; though he condemned the excesses of the Reign of Terror and the execution of the King and Queen, these events which turned many of his compatriots against the Revolution and all its works did not make Kant modify his adherence to the principles of the Revolution; and even it was believed that he was to go to Paris as advisor to Sieyès.[1]

When, therefore, in 1793 he sent his essay, *On the Saying: "That may be true in theory but it does not hold in practice*," to the *Berlinische Monatsschrift*, the editor wrote him with obvious relief: "To speak quite openly, it pleased me all the more since it refuted the rumor (which I had suspected from the start) that you had come out in favor of the ever increasingly repulsive French Revolution, in which the actual freedom of reason and morality and all wisdom in statecraft and legislation are being most shamefully trampled under foot...."[2] For this essay of Kant's denies the right of revolution, when the editor had reason to believe that Kant would defend it. But what was a relief to Biester, the editor, has been a paradox to others.

How could a man of Kant's probity sympathize with revolutionists and yet deny the right and justification of revolution? I say a man of Kant's probity; for it has been suggested that Kant's condemnation of revolution in his published works was deceptive, a sop to the censor. Of course we cannot disprove this accusation; but while it is not improbable that Kant was intimidated by the censor, I find it incredible, for Kant's actual response to the censor in 1792 was silence, not deception. In 1766, he had written Moses Mendelssohn, "Although I am absolutely convinced of many things that I shall never have the courage to say, I shall never say anything I do not believe."[3] I think that was as true in the 1790's as in the 1760's; and therefore, I must try to find some other way to explain the apparent inconsistency in Kant's attitudes.

We can understand Biester's delighted surprise in finding in Kant's essay a denial of the right of revolution. Not only had Kant's reputation as a Jacobin

*A slightly revised version of a paper presented at a symposium on "Kant on Revolution" held at Temple University, Dec. 5, 1969. I am grateful to my fellow-symposiasts, Professors Sidney Axinn, Charles Dyke, and John E. Atwell for criticisms; also to Professors Jeffrie G. Murphy and John B. Christopher for comments on an earlier draft.

[1] An account of this rumor will be found in G. P. Gooch, *Germany and the French Revolution* (London, 1920), 276–77.

[2] Biester to Kant, Oct. 5, 1793; *Kants Gesammelte Schriften*, Prussian Academy edition (hereafter cited as "Ak."), XI, 456; *Kant's Philosophical Correspondence*, trans. Arnulf Zweig (Chicago, 1966), 208–09.

[3] Kant to Mendelssohn, April 8, 1766; Ak. X, 69; Zweig, 54.

spread to Berlin, but also in his *Idea for a Universal History* published nine years earlier, even before the French Revolution, Kant had spoken the hope that "after many reformative revolutions, a universal cosmopolitical condition ... will come into being."[4] In fact, one might almost suppose that the conclusion of *Theory and Practice* came as a surprise to Kant himself; for in unpublished notes we find Kant writing that resistance to government may be justified provided some constitutional provision is made—as he believed it was made in England[5]—under which there can be a formal legal finding that the original contract has been broken by the monarch; and even without such a constitutional provision he held in certain cases that revolution is justified:

Force, which does not presuppose a judgment having the validity of law [*rechts-kräftig Urtheil*] is against the law; consequently [the people] cannot rebel except in the cases which cannot at all come forward in a civil union, e.g., the enforcement of a religion, compulsion to unnatural sins, assassination, etc., etc.[6]

—and the etceteration is Kant's own. Given what we know of Kant's theory of natural law and of the justification of positive law by reference to it—a theory as susceptible to a Lockean as to a Hobbesian development—it is easy to suppose that Kant could have asserted the right of resistance to a tyrannical government which denied autonomy to the legislation of the citizens. In fact, one of his disciples, August Wilhelm Rehberg, in the following issue of the *Berlinische Monatsschrift*, replied to Kant and drew precisely this conclusion from Kantian premises:

If a system of *a priori* demonstrated positive specifications of natural law is applied to the world of men, nothing less than a complete dissolution of present civil constitutions would follow. For according to such a system, only that constitution is valid which accords with the determination of the ideal of reason. In this case, no one of the existing constitutions could stand.... If these constitutions contradict ... the first requirements of a rational constitution, the human race is not only permitted, it is required, to destroy these constitutions which are opposed to the original moral law. The form of

[4]Ak. VIII, 28; *Kant on History*, ed. L. W. Beck (Indianapolis, 1963), 23. The words translated "reformative revolutions" (*Revolutionen der Umbildung*) do not suggest (as the English words may) that these revolutions were to be bloodless.

[5]Reflexionen 8043, 8044; Ak. XIX, 590, 591. But popular violence (*turbas*) is forbidden. In *Über den Gemeinspruch: Das mag in der Theorie richtig sein, taugt aber nicht für die Praxis* (Ak. VIII, 303) he approves of the silence of the "contractual arrangement" made in 1688 with respect to the right to overthrow a monarch who does not fulfil it.

[6]Reflexion 8051; Ak. XIX, 594–95. The passages cited by H. S. Reiss, "Kant and the Right of Rebellion," *J. H. I.*, XVII (1956), 190–91, as evidence that Kant justified seeking to overthrow government under the saying, "We ought to obey God rather than men" (*Religion innerhalb der Grenzen der blossen Vernunft*, Ak. VI, 99n; Greene and Hudson trans., 90n.) do not seem to me to go beyond the justification of passive disobedience, and not even to go that far when the politico-civil law does not command anything "in itself evil."

the constitution of the state is a matter of indifference, so long as complete equality is established; but to establish this, everything else must be sacrificed.–Thus the theory of revolution is a necessary consequence of the physiocratic system.[7]

Kant spurned Rehberg's essay (without specifically mentioning the putative deduction of the right of rebellion),[8] and his tentative justification of the Glorious Revolution of 1688 remained hidden in his notes. In his published works, there is only one halfhearted commendation for revolution (cited above) and one passage (later than the contribution to Biester's journal) which excuses, if it does not justify, revolution. It occurs in the *Rechtslehre*, where Kant speaks of a people's having "at least some excuse for forcibly [dethroning a monarch] by appealing to the right of necessity [which knows no law]."[9] But otherwise Kant's denial of the right of revolution is as firm and clear as his express sympathy for the French Revolution.

I shall proceed to examine this paradox as follows. I shall first state Kant's jurisprudential objections to the right to revolt; next I shall give a brief summary of those parts of his political theory which provide a context for his understanding of the events of 1789; then I shall discuss the nonjurisprudential ground of his sympathy with the Revolution. In conclusion, I shall draw some comparisons between his views and those of Hegel.

1. Kant's argument against the right of revolution is brief to the point of lucidity. By virtue of the ideal of the social contract, sovereignty is indivisible. A constitution cannot have within it a positive law permitting the abrogation of the constitution; there is a contradiction in the conception of a publicly constituted *Gegenmacht*.[10]

The constitution cannot contain any article that would allow for some authority in the state that could resist or restrain the chief magistrate in cases in which he violates the constitutional laws. For he who is supposed to restrain the authority of the state must have more power than, or at least as much power as, the person whom he is supposed to restrain . . . ; in other words, he must be able to command the resistance publicly. But then the latter would be the chief magistrate, not the former; and this supposition contradicts itself.[11]

To permit any opposition to this absolute power (an opposition that might limit that supreme authority) would be to contradict oneself, inasmuch as in that case the power (which may be opposed) would not be the lawful supreme authority that determines what is or is not to be publicly just.[12]

In this argument, we see Kant's formalism *in extremis*. There cannot be a

[7]*Über das Verhältnis der Theorie zur Praxis* (1793) in *Über Theorie und Praxis*, ed. Dieter Henrich (Suhrkamp, 1967), 128.

[8]Kant to Biester, April 10, 1794 (Ak. XI, 496–7; not in Zweig).

[9]*Rechtslehre* (Part I of *Metaphysik der Sitten*), Ak. VI, 321n; cf. 236; *Metaphysical Elements of Justice*, trans. John Ladd (Indianapolis, 1965), 87n; cf. 42.

[10]*Über den Gemeinspruch . . .*, Ak. VIII, 303.   [11]*Rechtslehre*, Ak. VI, 319; Ladd, 85.

[12]*Ibid.*, Ak. VI, 372; Ladd, 140–41.

law which permits lawlessness, nor an institution of power that provides for its own forcible dissolution.

It seems to me that no one should be unduly shocked by Kant's argument; and if one is not convinced, it is because one objects to the narrowness of Kant's base, not to the stringency of his proof erected upon it. The revolutionist does not appeal to the terms of the constitution for justification of his efforts to overturn the constitution; at most he appeals to the constitution for reform of administrative practices, or perhaps to the preamble of the constitution with its adumbration of natural, not positive, law as a basis for criticism of the positive law and the constitution which he rejects. In the *Rechtslehre*, which is concerned with the *a priori* foundation of civil society, Kant could have drawn no other conclusion. Revolution abrogates positive law; therefore positive law and its system condemn revolution. Revolution means a return to nature, which the contract establishing positive law renounces.[13]

Up to this point it may appear that Kant is making a point of boring obviousness, namely, that there can be no *legal* right of revolution. Revolution by its very nature is a denial that established legal and constitutional claims are indefeasible; and to tell a revolutionary that he should desist from his revolutionary activity because he is breaking a law would be met with derision.

In *Perpetual Peace*, however, there is another criticism of the putative right of revolution, a criticism which is more deeply rooted in Kant's moral philosophy than in his metaphysics of jurisprudence. The previous argument, as it were, is a legalistic consequence of the categorical imperative in the form which forbids us from acting on maxims which are self-contradictory when universalized. The new argument is derived from the form of the categorical imperative which requires us to treat human beings as end-setting ends-in-themselves, and it leads to what Kant calls the "transcendental formula of public law": "All actions relating to the right of other men are unjust if their maxim is not consistent with publicity." "The illegitimacy of rebellion," he infers, "is thus clear from the fact that its maxim, if openly acknowledged, would make its own purpose impossible. Therefore [the maxim to revolt on occasion] would have to be kept secret"[14] in order to be effective, and is therefore illegitimate. The maxim to put down revolution, however, passes this test and is likely to be most effective when given the widest publicity.

In place of revolution, Kant favors evolution. The evolution of the state to a more just form and administration, Kant believes, is inevitable only if there is public enlightenment and freedom of the press. The free press is the palladium of human rights.[15] It permits the reform of the state by apprising the rulers of the dissatisfactions of the subjects, and it is to the interests of the

[13]*Ibid.*, Ak. VI, 355; Ladd, 129.
[14]*Zum ewigen Frieden*, Ak. VIII, 381; in *Kant on History*, 129–30.
[15]*Über den Gemeinspruch...*, Ak. VIII, 304.

rulers themselves that these dissatisfactions be removed, since an irrational legislation—one decided for the people in a way in which the people would not decide for themselves[16]—makes for instability in the government and insecurity of the rulers. Reform can be effected only by the sovereign,[17] but it can be undertaken by him with wisdom only if he is made aware of the inequities and inadequacies of his administration.

Until this reform is effected, however, the people must obey. For to disobey is to return to the state of nature and to leave it to chance, or Providence, whether the new government yet to be established will be better or worse than the one which is overthrown. Reform means progress, the metamorphosis of the state; revolution means palingenesis[18] of the state, a new beginning of civil society from the state of nature without profit from the steps previously taken on the path away from the state of nature.

That a government may have been established by an act of lawless violence does not impugn its legal authority and validity, nor reduce its claim to allegiance. Kant is willing to believe that all governments began with power, not with contract. But to inquire into the historical origin of a government for the purpose of thereby impugning its authority is itself punishable.[19] This principle of the irrelevancy of historical origin to judicial validity is used to legitimize the government which is, in point of historical fact, established as a result of insurrection.[20] The new government cannot legitimately punish the fallen ruler, since he could, under the previous constitution, have done no (punishable) wrong.[21]

2. I turn now to Kant's theory of government, in which the doctrine of the separation of powers is the most basic principle.

The sovereign (*Beherrscher*) or lawgiver of a people (the head of the state) derives his rightful authority from the united people under the contract.[22] It is as though he held his legislative authority from the perfect lawgiver, God.[23] But his actual authority is in all probability based upon his power, with only a *post facto* justification of it by the ideal of the contract. The sovereign has rights with respect to the subject, but no coercive duties.[24] Hence the sovereign can do no wrong[25] in the sense that nothing he does is punishable: "There is no right of sedition, much less a right of revolution, and least of all a right to lay hands on or to take the life of the chief of state."[26]

The head of the government (*Regent*) is the agent of the sovereign. His commands are not laws but only ordinances and decrees.[27] He is obligated to the sovereign and subject to the laws given by the sovereign. His decrees must be obeyed by the subjects, and even if he proceeds contrary to the law, the

[16]*Rechtslehre*, Ak. VI, 327; Ladd, 95.

[17]*Ibid.*, Ak. VI, 321–2; Ladd, 88.   [18]*Ibid.*, Ak. VI, 339–40; Ladd, 111.

[19]*Ibid.*, Ak. VI, 319, 339–40, 372; Ladd, 84, 11, 140.

[20]*Ibid.*, Ak. VI, 323; Ladd, 89.   [21]*Ibid.*, Ak. VI, 317, 341; Ladd, 82, 113–14.

[22]*Ibid.*, Ak. VI, 315; Ladd, 80.   [23]*Ibid.*, Ak. VI, 319; Ladd, 84–85.

[24]*Ibid.*, Ak. VI, 319, cf. 241; Ladd, 85, cf. 47.   [25]*Ibid.*, Ak. VI, 317; Ladd, 82.

[26]*Ibid.*, Ak. VI, 320; Ladd, 86.

citizens must not actively resist him except by exercising their freedom to criticize and petition for reform.[28] But the head of the government may be deposed by the sovereign and the sovereign may modify his administration.[29]

Various abortive forms of government arise when the legislative, judicial, and executive functions of government are confused or lodged in the same moral or physical person. If the same person both makes and executes the laws—if, that is, the sovereign is himself the head of the government or the supreme judge—the system of checks and balances is not in effect, and the government is despotic.[30] A government may be monarchical in form while republican in spirit if the sovereignty resides in the united people, and the person of the sovereign represents the interests and rights of the people.

The ultimate agency of legitimate reform in the government lies in the person of the sovereign, as we have seen; but there are limits even on his right to change the constitution. The sovereign, for example, cannot validly arrange a transformation of one constitution to another (e.g., from an aristocracy to a democracy), for these are matters only for the collective will of the people to decide. "Even if the sovereign were to decide to transform himself into a democracy," Kant writes, "he would be doing the people an injustice, because the people themselves might abhor this kind of constitution and might find that one of the other two was more advantageous to them."[31]

When the chief of state allows himself to be represented in a body of deputies of the people, sovereignty *ipso facto* reverts to the collective people; the surrender of sovereignty by the person of the monarch has already occurred,[32] and it cannot be regained at the end of some specified time unless it is freely granted by the body of the people or their deputies. This event, according to Kant, took place on May 5, 1789 when "the sovereignty of the monarch disappeared completely ... and passed over to the people, to whose legislative will the property of every citizen now became subject." What was not justified was, first, the surrender of his sovereignty by Louis XVI to the Estates General; and, second, the execution of the former monarch—an act which "fills the soul, conscious of the ideas of human justice, with horror."[33]

But the success of the Revolution, in spite of the illegitimacy of its begin-

---

[27] *Ibid.*, Ak. VI, 317; Ladd, 82.

[28] *Ibid.*, Ak. VI, 319; Ladd, 85.   [29] *Ibid.*, Ak. VI, 317, 321–22; Ladd, 82, 88.

[30] *Ibid.*, Ak. VI, 317, 319; Ladd, 82, 85.   [31] *Ibid.*, Ak. VI, 340; Ladd, 112.

[32] *Ibid.*, Ak. VI, 341; Ladd, 113. The King had plenty of warning against convoking the Estates General, with such admonitions as "Un roi qui subit une Constitution se croit dégradé: un Roi qui propose une Constitution obtient la plus belle gloire qui soit parmi les hommes . . . ." and besides "It is illegal!" (See Jean Egret, *La Pré-révolution française* [Paris, 1962], 322, and George Lefebvre, *The Coming of the French Revolution* [New York, 1959], 27). But the notion that it was radically "unconstitutional" (like an act of revolution itself) seems to be original with Kant. More study of the polemical literature of the time, however, might reveal earlier sources for this singular idea.

[33] *Rechtslehre*, Ak. VI, 321n.; Ladd, 87n. There is, however, an inconsistency in Kant's comparing the execution of Louis XVI to an act of state suicide, since it follows

ning and the crimes which marked its effectuation, "binds the subjects to accept the new order of things as good citizens, and they cannot refuse to honor and obey the suzerain (*Obrigkeit*) who now possesses authority."[34]

Kant's fervid denial of the right of revolution, therefore, is historically focussed not against the Estates General and the successor government, but upon the efforts at counterrevolution and restoration of the Bourbons. Thus he specifically denounces the right claimed by other sovereigns to intervene in French affairs so as to undo the Revolution.[35]

Our exposition has perhaps let it appear that Kant's formalism—the notion that a legal right to rebel is self-contradictory and a moral right to rebel is unjustifiable—makes him oppose all revolutions yet to come, while precisely the same formalism permits him to accept all successful revolutions of the past, especially those of 1688, 1776, and 1789. His enthusiasm for these revolutions, especially that of 1789, is made compatible with his denial of the right of revolution, for "revolution" now means "Restoration." This, however, would seem to me to be time-serving dishonesty which one would not willingly attribute to Kant if a more ingenuous resolution of the original paradox is possible.

But even if one hesitates to apply to Kant the maxim that what matters is "whose ox is being gored," there is a sophistic legalism in his theory of a non-juridical transfer of sovereignty from Louis XVI to the Estates General. He seems to be exculpating the Estates from the charge of rebellion, saying rather that they discharged the duty that legally devolved upon them to "reform" the government. This outcome, to be sure, removes the paradox with which I began this paper: Kant disapproved of revolutions, but what was called the French Revolution was not really a revolution or, if it was a revolution, the only revolutionary was Louis XVI![36] Surely, however, this is explaining away one paradox by means of a greater one.

3. To remove the paradox requires us to consider things not from a moralistic or legalistic point of view, which is perhaps the one most natural to Kant, but from the standpoint of his teleological conception of history. For from this point of view alone can Kant justify comparing a state before and after a revolution and thus pronounce a moral judgment on a revolution unjustified *a priori* on grounds of positive law and on the natural law that authority must be obeyed.

In so doing, however, Kant cannot, without being unfaithful to his moral principles, appeal to a utilitarian justification for a revolution. And he does not do so;[37] whether a people is happier before or after a revolution is as

---

from his thesis that Louis was no longer sovereign. He suffered injustice, to be sure, and one can sympathize with Kant's abhorrence of this act without putting it into a special class "more heinous than murder itself," inexplicable except as "the pure Idea of extreme perversity" (Ak. 322n.; Ladd, 88n.).   [34]*Ibid.*, Ak. VI, 323; Ladd, 89.

[35]*Zum ewigen Frieden*, Ak. VIII, 346; *Kant On History*, 89.

[36]Cf. Dieter Henrich, "Einleitung," *Theorie und Praxis*, 32.

[37]*Rechtslehre*, Ak. VI, 318; Ladd, 83.

irrelevant from the standpoint of the judgment of the philosophy of history as it is from the standpoint of positive or moral law. Progress in history is not measured by the happiness of the people but by the formal criterion of the rule of law and the scope of juridical freedom.

The perfect civic constitution, Kant holds, is republican, for it alone derives from the idea of the original compact which is the norm, if not the historical genesis, of all government:

> The republican constitution is the only enduring political constitution in which the law is autonomous and is not annexed to any particular person. It is the ultimate end of all public law and the only condition under which each person receives his due peremptorily.... [Under any other form of government] it must be recognized that only a provisory internal justice and no absolutely juridical state of civil society can exist.[38]
> The republican constitution is with respect to the law the one which is the original basis of every form of civil constitution.[39]

Thus Kant can distinguish between revolutions towards the better and revolutions towards the worse, though *qua* revolution both are to be condemned. Since revolution produces an *interregnum* which is equivalent to the state of nature, revolutions probably have a tendency to end in a worse government than the government which could have been achieved by gradual reform. Political wisdom, therefore, stands on the side of reform to make the constitution better accord with the ideal of law; but "when nature herself produces revolutions," political wisdom will use them "as a call of nature for fundamental reforms to produce a lawful constitution founded upon principles of freedom, for only such a constitution is durable."[40]

When nature herself produces revolutions . . . ! The *Idea for a Universal History* is like a theodicy, asking "Is it reasonable to assume a purposiveness in all the parts of nature and to deny it to the whole?"[41] Kant answers: "The history of mankind can be seen, in the large, as the realization of Nature's secret plan to bring forth a perfectly constituted state...."[42] The unsocial sociability of mankind, the competition among tribes and states which leads to war, and revolutions—all of which are judged, juridically and moralistically, to be evil—are the means nature uses in realizing her "secret plan" for mankind.

That the French Revolution is to be understood at least by analogy to natural teleology is made clear in the *Critique of Judgment*. The organization of nature, Kant tells us, has nothing analogous to any causality known to us, but it throws light on "a complete transformation, recently undertaken, of a great people into a state" where

---

[38]*Ibid.*, Ak. VI, 341; Ladd, 112–13.
[39]*Zum ewigen Frieden*, Ak. VIII, 350; *Kant on History*, 94.
[40]*Ibid.*, Ak. VIII, 373n.; *Kant on History*, 120n.
[41]*Idee zu einer allgemeinen Geschichte in weltbürgerlicher Absicht*, Ak. VIII, 25; *Kant on History*, 20.   [42]*Ibid.*, Ak. VIII, 27; *Kant on History*, 21.

the word "organization" has frequently, and with much propriety, been used for the constitution of the legal authorities and even of the entire body politic. For in a whole of this kind certainly no member should be a mere means, but should also be an end, and, seeing that he contributes to the possibility of the entire body, should have his position and function in turn defined by the idea of the whole.[43]

But the French Revolution is not to be understood only by analogy to natural teleology; it has a distinctively moral dimension too. In the *Strife of the Faculties*, Kant draws a moral conclusion from the French Revolution. The passionate participation in the good, *viz.*, the disinterested enthusiasm with which the Revolution was greeted, could have no other cause, Kant thinks, than a moral predisposition in the human race to seek what is ideal and purely moral.[44] It gives hope and evidence of the moral progress of mankind. The participants in the Revolution, of course, were not morally disinterested; but the impartial spectators approved, and "such a phenomenon in human history"—Kant is not now speaking of the Revolution, but of the moral enthusiasm it engendered—"*is not to be forgotten*, for it revealed a tendency and faculty in human nature for improvement such as no politician, affecting wisdom, might have conjured out of the course of things hitherto existing, and one which nature and freedom alone, united in the human race in conformity with inner principles of right, could have promised."[45]

4. Kant does not have a categorial scheme adequate to take account of the juxtaposition of the illegality and immorality of a man who makes a revolution and what might be called his higher morality when, through revolutionary activity, he establishes a better stage of political culture as a basis for further moral development. He does not accept the doing of evil that good may result. He does not do so in part because his political ethics reduces to the maxim of my station and its duties except in so far as complaining and striving to reform a government are imprescriptible rights; and in part because his conception of natural law is static.[46] Not only is it static; it is in fact inconsistent, for it includes both the teleology of seeking to bring about the rule of law under a republican constitution (which may, in fact, require not merely efforts at reform but actual violence[47]) and a formalism of obedience

---

[43]*Kritik der Urteilskraft*, Ak. V, 375n; *Critique of Teleological Judgment*, trans. J. C. Meredith (Oxford, 1952), 23n.

[44]*Der Streit der Fakultäten*, Ak. VII, 85–86; *Kant on History*, 144–45.

[45]*Ibid.*, Ak. VII, 88; *Kant on History*, 147.

[46]Not natural law, of course, in the sense that the study of empirical nature gives rise to it; it is a law of reason. But it functions in the same way as natural law, as a norm and warrant for positive law. See Leonard Krieger, "Kant and the Crisis in Natural Law," *J. H. I.*, XXVI (1965), 191–210, esp. 201, 207.

[47]As certainly the first step from a state of natural savagery to civil society required the exercise of a natural right to violence: "... Everyone may use violent means to compel another to enter into a juridical state of society," *Rechtslehre*, Ak. VI, 312; Ladd, 76–77.

to the powers that be. The duty we have to contribute to the progress of mankind is a duty of imperfect obligation, is unenforceable, and leaves elbow-room for its realization. The latter, the duty we have to fulfill the requirements of the established law, is a duty of strict or perfect obligation, and is thus for Kant prior in its claims to the former.[48] As consequences of this priority of duties of perfect over duties of imperfect obligation are those famous cases which have served for generations as a *reductio ad absurdum* of Kantian ethics, e.g., the denial of the right to lie in order to save the life of an innocent man. A like consequence is here drawn in Kant's political philosophy. We are to work towards the end of the improvement of mankind by striving to secure a political stage on which the rights of man will be respected and war will be abolished. But in so doing, we are not to overthrow by violence even a tyrannical government which blatantly traduces these rights, for to do this would conflict with a duty of perfect obligation. We are not, therefore, justified in killing a tyrant in order to preserve the lives of thousands or millions of his subjects. The most I can morally do is to expose the abuses of his power and make proposals for his reform, to disobey him if he commands me to do something immoral and to suffer martyrdom if necessary.[49]

A conception of natural law which is evolutionary can profit from an understanding of the inconsistency into which Kant falls in condemning revolution while holding that the enthusiasm for the French Revolution sprang from a moral disposition in mankind. The moral aspirations of mankind are not satisfied by punctilious obedience to the powers that be; they demand that the powers that be should earn our respectful obedience, and they sometimes justify the disobedience to the positive law out of obedience to a "higher law." Both obligations are rational and natural, and it takes deep moral and historical insight to adjudicate their conflict, and this adjudication need not and does not always lead to the same decision. An evolutionary view of morality and of the law of nature draws a distinction between the morality of stable societies, which is necessary to maintain or to gradually improve the *status quo*, and the historical demands which abrogate static laws and institutions when they fall significantly below the level of moral aspiration; but no rules can be given for this adjudication which will decree an all-or-none answer in periods threatened by, or promised, radical changes.

The agents whose acts are directed against the stable moral order are, descriptively, criminals; but they may be, in Hegel's terms, men whose "words and deeds are the best of the age."[50] If they succeed, their words and ideas will be the ruling words and ideas of the new moral community they will pro-

---

[48]*Zum ewigen Frieden*, Ak. VII, 377; *Kant on History, 124.*

[49]*Kritik der praktischen Vernunft*, Ak. V, 155–56; trans. L. W. Beck (New York, 1956), 159f., on the effort of Henry VIII to suborn a witness against Ann Boleyn.

[50]*Die Vernunft in der Geschichte (Einleitung in die Philosophie der Weltgeschichte), Sämmtliche Werke*, ed. G. Lasson (Leipzig, 1930), VIII, 76. *Reason in History*, trans. R. S. Hartman (Indianapolis, 1953), 40.

duce—and if they fail, they will (rightly) be hanged as common criminals against the stable ethical order.

Such an evolutionary conception—an evolutionary conception which is meant to justify revolution, if that is what is required for progress—is found in Hegel's dialectic of private morals (*Moralität*), public ethics (*Sittlichkeit*), and the egotism of world-historical individuals whose crimes against the first two are converted, by the cunning of world-reason, into quantum-jumps in the moral progress of the community or state:

> The basis of duty is the civil life: the individuals have their assigned business and hence their assigned duties. Their morality consists in acting accordingly.... But each individual is also the child of a people at a definite stage of its development.... A moral whole [a specific moral community], as such, is limited. It must have above it a higher universality, which makes it disunited with itself. The transition from one spiritual pattern to the next is just this, that the former moral whole is abolished.... It is at this point that appear those momentous collisions between existing acknowledged duties, laws, and rights, and those possibilities which are adverse to this system, violate it, and even destroy its foundations and existence.... These possibilities now become historical fact; they involve a universal of an order different from that upon which the permanence of a people or a state depends. This universal is an essential phase in the development of the creating Idea, of truth striving and urging towards itself.[51]

Thus arises the conflict between the morally good man who fulfills the duty of his station and the man who breaks down that system—the "world-historical individual" who is impudently judged to be immoral by schoolmasters and valets, "those exquisite discerners of spirits."

> But the history of the world moves on a higher level than that proper to morality.... Those who, through moral steadfastness and noble sentiment, have resisted the necessary progress of the Spirit stand higher in moral value than those whose crimes have been turned by a higher order into means of carrying on the will behind this order.... They stand outside morality. The litany of the private virtues of modesty, humility, love, and charity must not be raised against them.[52]

This is a teleological suspension of the ethical, to adapt Kierkegaard's terminology to a new use.

Kant's enthusiasm for the French Revolution is based upon his teleological conception of history, which is a forerunner of Hegel's definition of history as "the progress of the consciousness of freedom." That the final purpose of the world is moral, not eudaemonistic, makes it possible for Kant to have a

---

[51] *Ibid.*, 73–75 (Hartman [slightly modified], 38–39). No inferences must be drawn, of course, from this passage concerning Hegel's own view of the right of revolution and, specifically, the French Revolution; much else entered into his judgment on these questions.

[52] *Ibid.*, 153, 154 (Hartman, 82; trans. slightly modified).

moral enthusiasm for the Revolution which his formalistic moral system does not justify. Had Kant's approval of the Revolution been eudaemonistic, the inconsistency would have been greater. But some inconsistency remains because Kantian ethics is not adequate to resolve the painful problems of conflicting duties.[53]

The University of Rochester.

[53]He even denies that conflicts of duties exist: *Metaphysik der Sitten, Einleitung,* Ak. VI, 224; Ladd, 25.

PART FIVE

NINETEENTH CENTURY
POLITICAL PHILOSOPHY

XVI

THE PROBLEM OF WAR IN HEGEL'S THOUGHT

By Shlomo Avineri

One often encounters the assumption that Hegel's political thought paved the way for the crystallization of a theory of state both nationalist and totalitarian. This view has been presented in a particularly forceful manner since the rise to power of the Nazis in Germany, when many efforts were made on the part of enemies of Nazism to find similarities between the philosophical premises of Hegel's thought and the institutional image of the nationalistic state in its extreme manifestations.[1]

This opinion needs re-examination, as is often the case with a hypothesis which has taken root, gained acceptance, and become fixed to such a degree that it seems to require no proof or confirmation. One can, without much difficulty, indicate the historical associations which contributed to the understanding of Hegel's philosophy in a nationalist spirit, just as one can show that this is not the only interpretation applicable to Hegel's thought. Rudolf Haym's *Hegel und seine Zeit* (Berlin, 1857) is a bitter invective against Hegel, accusing him of being blind to the national aspirations of German unity; and Haym's book is only one example.

We shall not undertake here an exhaustive attempt to examine afresh Hegel's connection with German nationalism. The aim of this paper is to trace the meaning of war in Hegel's thought and try to find out, whether this meaning can be assumed to have contributed towards a nationalistic-militaristic ideology culminating in Nazism and Fascism.

It would not be difficult to find passages in Hegel which seem to justify *prima facie* the opinion of those scholars who have found that the Hegelian concept of war resembles, in a way that leaves no room for doubt, the "new totalitarian-étatistic" or fascist ideas.[2] In one of his early works, called "The System of Ethics" (*System der Sittlichkeit*), written about 1801–1802, Hegel says: "Morality must display

---

[1] See e.g. H. Heller, *Hegel und der nationale Machtstaatsgedanke in Deutschland* (Leipzig & Berlin, 1921), 118; W. M. McGovern, *From Luther to Hitler* (N. Y., 1941); K. R. Popper, *The Open Society and Its Enemies* (Princeton, 1950), 259. This opinion, uncritically accepted, found its way into general text books of political philosophy, e.g. J. Bowle, *Politics and Opinion in the 19th Century* (London, 1951), 43. The opposite opinion is no less widespread; see F. Rosenzweig, *Hegel und der Staat*, 2 vols. (Munich & Berlin, 1920); H. Marcuse, *Reason and Revolution*, 2nd ed. (London, 1955); E. Weil, *Hegel et l'État* (Paris, 1950). Cf. also Georg Lukacs' "Der deutsche Faschismus und Hegel," in his *Schicksalswende* (Berlin, 1948), 37–67.

I wish to express my gratitude to Prof. J. L. Talmon for the help and advice I was privileged to receive from him while doing research on this subject under his supervision.

[2] D. A. Routh, "The Philosophy of International Relations," *Politica* (Sept. 1938), 223–35.

its vitality in something different from itself. . . . This something different is the enemy, and the dissociation from him, which takes shape in relation to one's fellow man as the opposite of survival . . . is the fear of fighting." [3] In another work dating from the same period, "On the Methods of Scientific Treatment of Natural Law" (*Über die wissenschaftlichen Behandlungen des Naturrechts*), these criteria are transferred from the inter-personal to the inter-state level: "War is the moral health of peoples in their struggle against petrifaction. . . . Just as the breeze saves the sea from foulness, which is the result of continued complacency, so does war for peoples." [4]

But the most extreme formulation is that which appears in the "Phenomenology of Mind" (*Phänomenologie des Geistes*), which was completed in 1806—precisely on the eve of the Battle of Jena—and whose outlook is strongly influenced by the charismatic experience of the Napoleonic personality and its historical operation: "In order not to let [the citizens] get rooted and settled in this isolation and thus break up the whole into fragments and let the common spirit evaporate, Government has from time to time to shake them to the very centre by War. By this means it confounds the order that has been established and arranged, and violates their right to independence, while the individuals (who, being absorbed therein, get adrift from the whole, striving after inviolable self-existence (*Fürsichsein*) and personal security) are made, by the task thus imposed upon them by Government, to feel the power of their lord and master, death. . . ." [5]

These formulations, in all their intensity, can be taken as the unmitigated consecration of the force of war, and it might appear from them that there is no distinction between Hegel and the formulations of Treitschke [6] or even those of the Fascists.[7] But those quotations should be studied within the context of Hegel's general theory of state, most maturely expressed in his *Philosophy of Right*.

Here we encounter Hegel accepting the challenge of one of the most difficult, and perhaps most thankless, theoretical tasks: namely, the painstaking effort to try and give a meaning, in a general philosophical context, to the phenomenon of war. He was not the only one

---

[3] *Hegels Schriften zur Politik und Rechtsphilosophie*, ed. G. Lasson (Leipzig, 1913), 470.

[4] *Ibid.*, 432.

[5] G. W. F. Hegel, *The Phenomenology of Mind*, trans. by J. B. Baillie, 2nd ed. (London, 1949), 474.

[6] H. v. Treitschke, *Politik*, ed. M. Cornicelius, 5th ed. (Leipzig, 1922), I, 24, 39, 60; II, 362, 371, 519.

[7] Cf. Mussolini's article "Fascismo" in the *Enciclopedia Italiana* (Rome, 1932), XIV, 847–850, for the strong emphasis on 'positive' values of war. See also W. Ebenstein, *Modern Political Thought* (New York, 1958), 330–337.

to do so in his generation; a contemporary of his, Adam Müller, tried to tackle the same problem in a series of lectures, delivered in 1808/9 and later published under the general title of *Elemente der Staatskunst*. But Müller reached quite different conclusions on the moral plane: he recognized the expansionist urge of the state and distinguished between "just" and "unjust" wars—a distinction which is completely alien to Hegel's thought, as will be shown later.[8]

Hegel, on the other hand, attempts to understand war in its human setting, "to recognize the rose in the cross of the present." [9] Hegel realizes that we customarily evaluate war as a deviation from the normal condition of peace; under the influence of various schools of Natural Law, war is conceived as a reversion, a regression to something prior to the rational socio-political order, a reversion to an elemental, barbaric state.[10]

This explanation seems to Hegel insufficient: the moral negation of war does not explain it away. War seems to be the product of some specific human ingredient, and seeing it as a mere accident, a product of sheer arbitrariness, only begs the question as to the motives of this outrageous eruption. Seeing fighting as a departure from the norm of peace means sliding into wishful thinking. This might be lauded from the point of view of personal subjective morality, but it cannot be an adequate philosophical explanation, when philosophy means comprehending *that which is*. Here, as with other social phenomena, Hegel holds that moral indignation cannot suffice.

He does explicitly condemn war: "Hence in war, war itself is characterized as something which ought to pass away . . . implying . . . that the possibility of peace be retained." [11] He does not rest on this but goes further in order to explain the inner necessity of the causes which bring about war as part of the cultural world shaped by man.

[8] A. Müller, *Elemente der Staatskunst*, ed. J. Baxa (Jena, 1922), I, 5, 7, 85ff. Meinecke, in his *Weltbürgertum und Nationalstaat*, 146, sees in Müller the forerunner of Ranke's thoughts on war, while Hegel's thought, which is free from the romantic obsession with the vitalistic and organic growth of the state, is of a completely different mold. This seems to be true in spite of Hegel's remark that literature, and mainly epic literature, is nourished by wars of conquest (*Werke*, ed. Glockner [Stuttgart, 1928], XIV, 354, recently quoted and discussed by W. Kaufmann, *From Shakespeare to Existentialism*, 122–124). It seems that here, once more, a mere statement of what seemed to Hegel to be a historical fact was construed as if it meant moral approval.

[9] *Hegel's Philosophy of Right*, trans. by T. M. Knox (Oxford, 1945), 12. On the specific Lutheran connotations of this expression, which occurs also in Goethe, cf. K. Löwith, *Von Hegel bis Nietzsche* (Zurich, 1941), 24.

[10] Montesquieu is perhaps the first among the moderns who sees in war a result of the social condition of man, and not a relapse into some traumatic pre-social state. *L'Esprit des Lois*, I, ch. ii–iii.

[11] *Philosophy of Right*, § 338; see also addition to § 339.

That our ideas about how this world *should have been* are different from historical reality, is in itself a proof of the human capacity for working out the ideal out of the actual.

First of all, Hegel goes on to explain that war cannot be justified by the utilitarian motive of the defense of life and property. This idea, which Hegel recognizes as one of the commonplace answers to the question of the moral justification of war, would lead to an absurd situation: for it is impossible to demand that men sacrifice, in the act of war, those very things towards the preservation of which it is waged.[12] Every attempt to justify war by reference to needs will necessarily culminate in a dubious code of ethics according to which A will have to pay with his life to preserve B's life or merely property. This amounts, in other words, to an absolute violation of Kant's categorical imperative, which is also the basis of Hegel's personal morality: "Be a person and respect others as persons." [13] Where war is defended from the point of view of Civil Society (i.e., the realm of needs), there necessarily emerges this violation of the basic imperative of morality, since man thus serves as a mere tool and means at the hands of his fellow man.[14]

However strange this may seem *prima facie,* Hegel's theory of war tries to avoid this difficulty and find an explanation, and justification, for war without infringing on the Kantian imperative. According to Hegel, there lies in war an ethical (*sittlich*) element inasmuch as it exposes the accidental, the arbitrary, and finite in life. It prevents the particular interest from becoming the master of the universe. By demanding everything from all, it places the concrete world of phenomena in its true transitory place, it serves as an ethical *memento mori:*

"The ethical moment in war is implied in this. . . . War is not to be regarded as an absolute evil and as a purely external accident, which itself therefore has some accidental cause, be it injustices, the passions of nations or the holders of power, &c., or in short, something or other which ought not to be. It is to what is by nature accidental that accidents happen, and the fate whereby they happen is thus a necessity. Here as elsewhere, the point of view from which things seem pure accidents vanishes if we look at them in the light of the

---

[12] *Ibid.,* § 324. Without directly drawing on this paragraph, this utilitarian-liberal argument was criticized on the more general level of political obligation by Hegel's English disciple, B. Bosanquet, *The Philosophical Theory of the State,* new edition (London, 1958), 76, n. 1.

[13] *Philosophy of Right,* § 36; Hegel's *Enzyklopädie,* § 49. Compare this with the Nazi maxim: "The individual as such has neither a right nor a duty to exist, as all the rights and duties derive exclusively from the community," stated by the Nazi jurist Otto Dietrich in his article in the *Völkischer Beobachter* (November 11, 1937). [14] *Philosophy of Right,* § 324.

concept and philosophy, because philosophy knows accident for a show and sees in it its essence, necessity. It is necessary that the finite —property and life—should be definitely established as accidental, because accidentality is the concept of the finite." [15]

Hegel himself sees the affinity of his train of thought with religion, and comments that one often hears sermons of this sort from the pulpit. But, he goes on to remark, every one hearing in church that all the goods of this world are ephemeral, still thinks that on the day of judgment *his* life and property will be spared. But when the day of wrath does come and shows up here, in this world, and not in some remote other-worldly existence, "if this insecurity now comes on the scene in the form of hussars with shining sabres and they actualize in real earnest what the preachers have said, then the moving and edifying discourses which foretold all these events turn into curses against the invader." [16]

According to these paragraphs, war is only the permanent writing on the wall, the embodiment of "unto dust thou shalt return." Thus it is not an outcome of a real will of any concrete human being, nor is it waged with an eye towards the aggrandizement of any particular person or group. It is, in a way, a rod of anger, to use the biblical expression, unrelated by itself to any goal, just as the wars of Nebuchadnezzar were unrelated to any ethical purpose, though in the eyes of the pious they always had, behind the scene, the hidden meaning of providential scorn.

This metaphysical explanation will not receive much approval nowadays and may certainly seem dated if not obscurantist. On the other hand, it would not be welcome by any ideology which might be termed militaristic, as it is completely devoid of the ethos of war itself. It is, however, related only to the *concept* of war, and does not yet refer to any *concrete, historical* war. Hegel distinguishes, on another level, between the concept of the state and the concrete state; the latter belongs ultimately to the realm of the accidental and the arbitrary, and so this distinction serves Hegel here also: "This [concept of war], however, is said to be only a philosophic idea, or, to use another common expression, a 'justification of Providence,' and it is maintained that actual wars require some other justification." [17] Obviously this implies that the philosophical significance of the *concept of war* cannot serve as a justification for *waging any concrete war*. In this regard there was a marked development in Hegel's thought after the *Phenomenology of Mind* had been written; there Hegel had not yet arrived at a clear distinction between the conceptualization of war and its concrete incidence.

[15] *Ibid.*   [16] *Ibid.*, addition to § 324.
[17] *Ibid.*, § 324. It is interesting to note that Popper, *op. cit.*, 262, 269, did not

What, then, is the essence of concrete wars for Hegel?

Hegel asserts that the essence of a state's existence as a unity, an individuality, lies in its relations with other states.[18] This personality of the state, this "fictitious man," to use Hobbes' language, must be distinguished from other personalities in order to find its identity: "The nation as a state is mind in its substantive rationality and immediate actuality and is therefore the absolute power on earth. It follows that every state is sovereign and autonomous against its neighbors." [19]

This *absolute* power of the state derives from the empirical fact that nations have no praetor to preside over them, as Spinoza once put it, for there is no judicial institution before which nations can litigate [20]; but it should be emphasized that this absolute power is *on earth,* and not to be viewed as eternal, *sub specie aeternitatis.* This is a factual, descriptive statement about the non-existence of an institutionalized supranational law. That we may want things to be different, Hegel would argue, belongs to the realm of hope, and not to the province of reality.

What makes Hegel's statements sound as if they meant that war could never be avoided (and hence they were viewed as obnoxious) is the fact that he criticizes even the *possibility* of ever achieving lasting peace. To understand the reason for his position, it is necessary to examine carefully the language Hegel uses to explain it: "But the state is an individual, and individuality essentially implies negation. Hence even if a number of states make themselves into a family, this group as an individual must engender an opposite and create an enemy." [21]

A proper understanding of this sentence is possible only in the light of Hegel's epistemology, whereas most of those who have relied upon it have not understood the connection. As the state is seen by Hegel as a person, an 'individual writ large,' we should turn to Hegel's notion of how a person identifies himself. Put into a nutshell, Hegel's answer is that the individual is a *person* by virtue of his being recognized by others and thus distinguishing himself from them [22]—and this holds true also for the state which has the attribute of a *person.* Its existence is possible only through the objectification of its desires as they come into contact with the world external to it. This contact is possible only by means of opposition and struggle——just as with the individual, who distinguishes himself from his fellow man, sets himself in opposition to him, and in doing so attains to

---

make the distinction, falling therefore into the pitfall of identifying Hegel with Treitschke and Moeller van den Bruck.   [18] *Philosophy of Right,* § 323.

[19] *Ibid.,* § 331. Hegel writes: *"Das Volk als Staat . . .";* since Knox translated this as "the nation-state," which only begs the question, I have had to render my own translation of this phrase.   [20] *Ibid.,* addition to § 324.

[21] *Ibid.* The Korean and Congolese experiences might perhaps be cited as illus-

self-identification. To make the point clearer, one may paradoxically say that if *states,* in the plural, cease to exist, there cannot, by definition, remain *a* state in the singular.

But this complication, in which Hegel became enmeshed because of the dialectical nature of his epistemology, is apt to lead to yet another surprising conclusion: if the state exists *because it is recognized as such by other states,*[23] it follows that the state is not independent, "sovereign," a monad enclosed within itself. It seems to be limited in its omnipotence, its sovereignty, as it needs *for its very existence* the co-existence of its fellow-states. This is the startling point from which Hegel derives dialectically the need for the existence of international law as of vital importance for the very existence of the states themselves. The negation of the possibility of a *comprehensive and perpetual* international order does not therefore, according to Hegel, constitute the denial of the existence of international law itself.[24]

The dialectical paradox is that Hegel's state is sovereign only in so far as the other states recognize it as such, and the essential need for the existence of a *comitas gentium* arises from just the apparently unlimited sovereignty of the state. To the uninitiated, this may sound a bit overstrained; to Hegel, this would only prove that the infinite must necessarily be limited and restricted by its own dialectical reason. And so Hegel comes to the treatment of International Law in that section of the *Philosophy of Right* entitled "Sovereignty *vis-à-vis* foreign States." Here clearly it is incorrect to assume that Hegel denied the existence of international law. He only denies the existence of an aprioristic international law, which would be based only on abstractions of things-as-they-ought-to-be. Hegel stresses, however, the difference between international and intranational positive law. As international law derives its authority not from its essence but rather from the particular wills of the parties involved, it is more like a contract than law.[25] But its very existence (and Hegel here employs a concept with the intense concrete significance of *Wirklichkeit*) is never denied by him.[26]

Hegel even goes further to prove that the norm of international behavior is inherent in what seems *prima facie* its very negation:

---

trations to Hegel's contention how the existence of an international organization might enmesh this very organization in what is to all practical purposes an act of war. Assertions that those experiences tend to strengthen the authority of the UN only corroborate Hegel's insight, as the same might be said of an individual state confronted by the challenge of war. [22] *Ibid.,* § 71. [23] *Ibid.,* § 323.

[24] Cf. the interesting study on this subject by Dr. Adam von Trott zu Solz, *Hegels Staatsphilosophie und das Internationale Recht,* Abhandlungen des Seminars für Völkerrecht und Diplomatie, Heft 6 (Göttingen, 1932), 87–91.

[25] For the difference, according to Hegel, between law and contract, see his *Enzyklopädie,* §§ 493–495. [26] *Philosophy of Right,* § 333.

Even in war—the state of affairs when rights disappear and force and chance hold sway—a bond wherein each counts to the rest as something absolute always remains. Hence in war, *war itself is characterized as something which ought to pass away*. It implies therefore the proviso of the *jus gentium* that the possibility of peace be retained (and so, for example, that envoys must be respected), and, in general, *that war be not waged against domestic institutions, against the peace of family and private life, or against persons in their private capacity*.[27]

Here the non-totalitarian aspect of Hegelian war is emphatically stressed, and this stands miles apart from the prevailing outlook of that period as characterized by the German Romantics, e.g. Adam Müller, who complains that war was still considered in Germany the exclusive business of the standing army; according to him, "the fire of war should penetrate all the families, all the laws and institutions of peacetime life."[28] It is in Müller's expressions that we encounter the roots of the ideology of total war. Hegel's distinction, on the other hand, between State and Civil Society enables him to safeguard an autonomous region, eminently personal and particular, which should be respected even in war—as war is waged between states, never between individuals. Hegel even comes to the conclusion that modern warfare characterized by the anonymity of battle made possible by the discovery of gunpowder expels personal enmity from the act of fighting itself.[29] This might seem a rather naïve appreciation of the horrible possibilties of modern warfare, and it might be that Hegel became himself a victim of that wishful thinking so much obnoxious to him. But this attests to the fact that Hegel *wanted* to see war humanized or minimized in spite of his conviction that it could not be abolished altogether. In any case, the individual must be safeguarded from the emotional horror of warfare.

This cannot be interpreted as the modern concept of a people's nationalist war, which needs the concentration of every human effort in the community. As a consequence Hegel stresses his point that the term of *patriotism* should not mean the irrational enthusiastic battle-cry, but rather the day-to-day identification with the laws, institutions, and values of the state in *peace time*.[30]

Moreover, according to Hegel war and victory in war can never suffice to indicate which party was right. A concrete war can never decide matters of justice; the victors are never necessarily the righteous, nor the vanquished the villains in the piece: *Might is not Right*. Hegel first took this position as to the ethically neutral outcome of

---

[27] *Ibid.*, § 338 (my italics). Cf. also the addition to this paragraph, as well as § 339. This is strikingly similar to clause 6 of Kant's "Preliminary Articles of Perpetual Peace" in his *Perpetual Peace*, trans. by M. Smith (London, 1903), 114.

[28] *Elemente der Staatskunst*, I, 9. 　　　[29] *Philosophy of Right*, addition to § 338.

[30] *Ibid.*, § 268.

war in his essay "On the Constitution of Germany" (*Die Verfassung Deutschlands*) in 1802, saying:

The various possibilities of conflict are so numerous that it is impossible to express them at the outset on the basis of human reason. The more they are explicitly stated and formulated, i.e., the more rights that are set down, the more readily will conflict spring up between these rights. . . . Each side bases its position on the right which it claims as its own and charges the other party with violating this or that right. . . . The public takes sides and each party argues that justice is his, and both sides are right: the difficulty is that these just rights themselves have caused the conflict. . . . Law is the utility of the state as asserted and confirmed in contracts and treatises. But since in these contracts the different interests of the state are stated in a general way, while as rights they are exceptionally many-sided, these interests, and with them the rights themselves, must come to conflict. It depends only on the combination of forces, i.e. on the judgment of politics, whether the interests and rights which are thus endangered will be defended by all available means and force, or not. In such a case it is obvious that this right is also reserved by the other party, as it has the interest opposite to it, as well as the right to this interest. And war, *or any other means*, is what will decide the matter: *not which of the two rights is the more just— for both sides have just rights—but which of the rights will yield to the other.* War must decide this, for just the reason that the two mutually contradictory rights are equally true and just.[31]

The same principles, but in less cumbersome and more mature philosophical garb, Hegel expressed twenty years later in his *Philosophy of Right:* "A state through its subjects has widespread connections and many-sided interests, and these may be readily and constantly injured: but it remains inherently indeterminable which of these injuries is to be regarded as a specific breach of treaty or an injury to the honor and autonomy of the state. The reason for this is that a state may regard its infinity and honor as at stake in each of its concerns, however minute, and it is all the more inclined to susceptibilties to injury the more its strong individuality is impelled as a result of long domestic peace to seek and create a sphere of activity abroad." [32]

This is a rare insight into the self-righteous attitude every state is apt to adopt towards a real or imagined infringement on what it considers its rights.[33] Thus every war creates the unfortunate situation wherein both sides may have a claim to a certain portion of justice, and as a result war cannot be "justified" from the point of view of *one* party alone. This assumption precluded any possibility of relating the Hegelian concept of war to the idea of a national war, since the national movement, even in its humanitarian phase, e.g. Mazzini, has had recourse to the concept of a 'just' war: otherwise it cannot

[31] *Hegels Schriften zur Politik und Rechtsphilosophie*, 99–101 (my italics).
[32] *Philosophy of Right*, § 334.　　　　　　　　　　　[33] *Ibid.*, § 335.

justify a national *levée en masse*, or a people's war against the 'national enemy,' not to mention wars waged on pretexts of rectifying historical injustices or preventive wars.

According to Hegel, no war can be inherently just, for a concrete war does not take place in a realm which is at all relevant to the concept of justice. Thus the circle has been closed: first the *concept* of war has been understood in the ethical sphere of general philosophical speculation, and then *concrete* war retreats to the realm of the accidental. The philosophical solution, in spite of its dialectical brilliance, may seem unsatisfactory, but if so, the failure derives from Hegel's unwillingness to consecrate the phenomenon of concrete war. The solution adopted by Treitschke, who saw a positive moral ingredient in national wars or wars of conquest, or Carl Schmitt's radical treatment of war as the essence of a human and political creature might be more consistent, though morally abhorrent. For Hegel concrete war is always a conflict between accidental-particular desires which contain nothing necessary,[34] and thus no philosophical justification can be given to that or any other war.[35]

From this Hegel draws some institutional conclusions: as war should not be part and parcel of the life of the community at large, it should be conducted by a standing professional army, and not through a *levée en masse*.[36] Universal conscription should be avoided, as the courage and skill needed in war are themselves individual characteristics and not collective mass-psychology virtues.[37] In harmony with this, the military power should be absolutely under civilian authority, and a military state like the late Roman praetorian Empire is cited by Hegel as the inversion of the normal order of things.[38]

This is unquestionably a radically different conclusion from the *prima facie* impression one gets from the passages quoted at the beginning of this essay, but the distinction, occurring over and again, between the concept and the concrete phenomenon is essential to the understanding of Hegel's position. Thus Hegel can exalt the concept of war, without identifying himself with any concrete war. This ambivalence might perhaps be compared (on a rather superficial level, of course) to the Christian attitude to sin. The *concept* of sin is the cornerstone of Christian theology, and is *sine qua non* to the concept of grace. Yet every *concrete* sin is a subject for negative moral evaluation.

Thus Hegel concludes the passages on war in a vein which correctly expresses his feeling of crucifixion in face of the fact that war is so much with us; yet in spite of his assertion not to turn to wishful thinking, he sees in Europe of the post-Napoleonic period the possibility of minimizing the incidence of war: "The European peoples

---

[34] *Ibid.*, § 334.   [35] *Ibid.*, § 337.   [36] *Ibid.*, §§ 325, 328.
[37] *Ibid.*, § 327.   [38] *Ibid.*, addition to § 271.

form a family in accordance with the universal principle underlying their legal codes, their customs, and their civilization. This principle has accordingly modified their international conduct in the state of affairs [i.e. war] otherwise dominated by the mutual inflicting of evil." [39]

This universalistic attitude towards the unifying concept of the modern world, of contemporary Europe, Hegel also uses in order to stress the fact that the politico-national boundaries dividing the European states are of secondary importance, since the cultural partnership is dominant. Political unity is secondary to cultural unity, as the realm of the state itself is philosophically subordinated to the realm of the absolute spirit. Thus Hegel puts it in his *Philosophy of History:* "States in the Modern World seek independence of one another, and this is their honor. This obstinate tendency toward an absolute position of autonomy they have in common with the Greek city-states. . . . But despite all the differences between the individual states . . . , there also obtains a unity among them, *and therefore we should view even political independence as a merely formal principle.* Today there is not the same absolute chasm between the states of Europe which prevailed between Greece and Persia. When one state is annexed to the territory of the other, it loses, to be sure, its formal independence: but its religion, its laws, the concrete in its life remain intact. The trend of the states is, therefore, towards uniformity. There prevails among them one aim, one tendency, which is the cause of wars, friendships, and the needs of dynasties. But there also prevails among them another uniformity, which parallels the idea of hegemony in Greece, except that now it is the hegemony of Spirit." [40]

Although Hegel does not accept, on what seems to him solid philosophical considerations, the vision of an aprioristic eternal peace scheme such as Kant's or that of the Holy Alliance, his empirical de-

[39] *Ibid.*, addition to § 339. Hegel uses a similar expression in his lectures on aesthetics when he remarks: "In contemporary Europe every nation is limited by another one, and cannot, therefore, embark on a course of war against another European nation" (*Werke*, ed. Glockner, XIV, 355).

[40] G. W. F. Hegel, *Vorlesungen über die Philosophie der Weltgeschichte*, ed. G. Lasson, (Leipzig, 1920), 761 (my italics). I have had to render my own translation, as this passage, like so many others, does not appear in Sibree's English translation, which was based on the very fragmentary early German edition of Hegel's lectures on the Philosophy of History. Only at the beginning of this century did Lasson compare this edition with Hegel's own notes and publish the fuller edition. It is a pity that the English-reading public has to rely on such an incomplete version. Cf. also Hegel's opposition to the claim for 'natural' frontiers, most vociferously claimed in Germany by Arndt. Hegel contends in his *Philosophy of Right*, § 247, that such a claim only causes endless dangers and provokes further wars, as there exists no objective criterion for the 'naturalness' of the frontiers. It is fascinating how deeply an early XIX-century philosopher could foresee the hollowness of this nationalistic catchword, so much still *en vogue* in our own century.

scription of contemporary Europe is much in the same vein. If there
might be raised objections to it, they are on the ground that he has
not rightly sensed the pulse of his time.

For it seems doubtful that Hegel's position about war could, or
should, be defended. It might seem hardly praiseworthy to explain
the immanence of war in human history by reference to its being a
continuous *memento mori;* still, it should be remembered that by this
notion Hegel did not try to defend any actual war, only to explain it
conceptually. Similarly, it may be questioned whether there really are
no 'just' wars in the sense that in *any* war both sides have an equal
portion of justice. Contemporary history certainly could supply us
with ample cases in which Hegel's notion would not stand when
tested by his own standards.

Yet, apart from the question whether Hegel has supplied us with
an *adequate* philosophical explanation of war, it must be maintained
that, on the other hand, he did not supply arguments from which the
nationalist case for war could be sustained. The last paragraphs
quoted amply suggest that Hegel did not speak the language of nationalism or expansionist militarism. His dream of a relatively tran-
quil Europe was shattered, like all the other dreams of the Restoration period, in 1830 and later, with greater force, in 1848. At that time
a new chord was struck, which enabled men to praise war as morally
justified under those circumstances which suited them ideologically.
Thus Mazzini, the *humanitarian* nationalist, encouraged his followers in his *Duties of Man,* written in 1844, to be concerned that the
blood spilt by them should be *ad magnam patriae gloriam;* Wilhelm
Jordan, member of the German Constituent Assembly in Frankfort,
justified the continued occupation of Polish areas by a unified national Germany with the following words: "Our right in Poland is
the right of conquest, the right of the stronger . . . , and I am proud
of it" [41]; and the Student Fraternities (*Burschenschaften*) which declared "we believe that war puts an end to conditions of degeneration
and that it is the first and irrepressible way to the final goal of national unity" [42]—all those various trends of thought do not speak the
language of Hegel, and the philosophical lineage of those attitudes
cannot be ascribed to him.

The Hebrew University, Jerusalem.

[41] Cited in T. Klein, *1848—Der Vorkampf deutscher Einheit und Freiheit*
(Munich, 1914), 294–295. On this problem in the history of modern, and especially
German, nationalism, cf. J. L. Talmon, *Political Messianism: The Romantic Phase*
(London, 1960), 479–486.

[42] H. Haupt, *Quellen und Darstellungen zur Geschichte der Burschendschaft
und der deutschen Einheitsbewegung* (Heidelberg, 1911), II, 37. For Hegel's attitude to the extreme nationalism of the Fraternities, see my "The Hegelian Position on the Emancipation of the Jews," *Zion, Quarterly for Research in Jewish
History* (Jerusalem, 1960), XXX, 134–136 (in Hebrew).

XVII

REPLY TO ORSINI
[on Feuerbach, Hegel and Marx]
By Isaiah Berlin

Professor Orsini brings two specific charges of unequal gravity against me. He accuses me (a) of describing a reference by Marx to the writings of Feuerbach in a way that is inaccurate to the point of being misleading and (b) of seriously misrepresenting Feuerbach's criticism of Hegel, and, as a direct consequence of this, making unjust charges against Croce.

On (a) I plead guilty. If Professor Orsini had confined his strictures to my bibliographical shortcomings I should, without more ado, have acknowledged their justice and, after due acknowledgment, taken steps to correct the relevant reference in the text of my book on Marx to which he refers. I am, however, far more concerned about Professor Orsini's more serious charges collected under (b). These seem to me baseless, and I see no reason for withdrawing the relevant statements either in the review or the book in which Professor Orsini discovered them.

(a) Firstly, Marx on Feuerbach. When Professor Orsini points out that Marx not only did not, but could not, review Feuerbach's Theses on Hegelian Philosophy, because no such work can be found in the twelve (surely not twenty?) volumes of Feuerbach's collected works, what he says cannot be controverted. The document of which I had been thinking (and to which I should have made a more precise reference) is not a review but a letter, written by Marx on March 13, 1843 to Arnold Ruge, in which he refers not, indeed, to Theses on Hegel, for that is not the title of Feuerbach's work in question, but to his *Vorläufige Thesen zur Reformation der Philosophie*, (in fact the philosophy of Hegel) which appeared, as Professor Orsini correctly states, with Marx's own article on the Prussian censorship in Ruge's *Anekdota zur neuesten deutschen Philosophie und Publizistik* (MEGA 1/2 pp. 305–306). In this essay Feuerbach expounds some of the anti-Idealist doctrines to which Marx alludes in his *Theses on Feuerbach* and elsewhere. Professor Orsini, it is clear, accepts Mehring's assertion in his *Karl Marx* (pp. 52–53 of the English translation) that it was indeed this work by Feuerbach, and not, as Engels asserts, the celebrated *Essence of Christianity*, that proved to be "a revelation for Marx," but I have never felt at all convinced by Mehring's argument. It has always seemed to me that Engels probably knew the facts; but that in any case, an even clearer formulation of the relevant thesis is to be found in Feuerbach's *Zur Kritik der Hegel'schen Philosophie* (written in 1839, two years before *Das Wesen des Christentums*)—an essay which Marx, who refers to Feuerbach's views even before 1839, can scarcely not have known. Marx was, after all, not notable for acknowledging intellectual debts. It was this work that, thirty years ago, I misnamed *Theses* on (instead of *Critique* of) the Hegelian philosophy, and supposed to have been the subject of Marx's "review," i.e., letter to Ruge. For this confusion of titles with references I apologize.

251

(b) Now as to the weightier charges. In the *Critique* Feuerbach advances the proposition, which he is to repeat in many guises later, that Hegel's efforts to deduce the real from the ideal, existence from essence, only succeed in establishing in the conclusion what had been assumed in the premisses: that Hegel can extract whatever he wishes—e.g. the historical process —out of the category of pure Being because he has already inserted all that he needs into it at the outset. Let me cite Feuerbach's words from the *Critique of Hegel* of 1839: "The Absolute Idea . . . posits itself in advance as the truth. What it posits as the Other, already posits in its very essence the truth of the Absolute Idea again. The proof is therefore purely formal," i.e., circular.[1] What these dark words come to (pace Professor Orsini's admiration for Feuerbach's "terse and vigorous" style) is that the "deduction" of the real world from the Idea only works because all the characteristics of the real world have been previously imported into the Idea, and that therefore all that is being proclaimed by Hegel is that things are as they are in the real world because they are as they are in the Idea, which, according to Feuerbach, is nothing but a mythological projection of, and requires to be translated back into, the real, empirical world of which it is a kind of transcendent copy. Indeed, this is the very process of "demythologising" of which Feuerbach was one of the original champions, a method which Marx later used to such devastating effect. In the *Holy Family* [2] Marx says "the speculative philosopher . . . smuggles the well known characteristics of the apple and the pear as they are in experience into the logical determinations which he affects to have discovered" and then pretends to "deduce" them as "differentiations" of an "organic whole" or (concrete) "universal," which he calls "the fruit." This is pure Feuerbach. In the previous year, towards the end of the Paris MSS., Marx gives this account of Feuerbach's dialectic: "Hegel begins from the alienation of substance . . . from the infinite, abstract universal . . . i.e. in ordinary language, from religion and theology. Then he supersedes the infinite and posits the real, the perceptible, the finite and particular (philosophy, supersession of religion and theology). Then he supersedes the positive and re-establishes the abstraction, the infinite (restoration of religion and theology)." This is the circle which Marx, in my view quite correctly, regards as the heart of Feuerbach's critique of Hegel. Feuerbach's central thesis is that "the abstract understanding can only give things names" not create entities; empirical characteristics are first transmogrified into mysterious metaphysical entities, and then used to account for their own original empirical selves, which they are held, in some sense, to have generated.

Professor Orsini complains that I have reduced Feuerbach to a nominalism that might "have come straight out of an Oxford Common Room of the present day." Indeed, and why not? When, for example, Feuerbach says "my brother is called Johann, Adolf, but in addition there are innumerable others called Johann, Adolf. Shall I then conclude from this that my Johann is not a reality, that only in Johannheit is the truth? For sense perception

---

[1] Quoted from Feuerbach's *Collected Works*, II, 20, by Sidney Hook in *From Hegel to Marx* (London, 1936), 226–27.

all words are names, *nomina propria* . . . only signs to be used to achieve the ends . . . in the shortest way." [3] What is there in this passage to which an "Oxford nominalist" could take exception? Whether the Absolute Idea is Hegel's equivalent of God, or a mythical projection of the real world (which to Feuerbach is the same), makes no difference to the central thesis of the positivist creed—that to find the origin of things in the Absolute Idea is to invent imaginary entities and realms of theology and transcendental metaphysics, which can and should, in the interests of truth, be "demystified" into their unmysterious empirical bases. Indeed this doctrine is Feuerbach's link with eighteenth-century materialism—a commonplace of all monographs on Feuerbach and histories of western ideas. On this view, to explain empirical phenomena by reference to an impalpable *Geist* or "Absolute" (or, in the case of history, the *Zeitgeist*), is to explain these phenomena in terms of an occult relationship to a mythical version of them, i.e., to pretend that a heavily disguised form of the original question is itself the answer to it. This is the tautology of which I spoke, and which Professor Orsini fails to find in Feuerbach. Yet this reduction of *a priori* metaphysics to empirical states of mind or feeling—in Feuerbach's case a reduction to propositions of psychology—is the weapon which made a deep impression not on Marx alone, despite all his strictures, but on others, from Wagner to Lenin. It is at once one of Feuerbach's primary claims to fame and the central thesis of naturalist positivism of all breeds. When Marx in a celebrated passage of *Das Kapital* says that the ideal is only the material world reflected by the human mind, he is echoing his own summary of Feuerbach's theses in the Paris MSS. cited above, a position he shares with Holbach and his fellow materialists of the eighteenth century, with Feuerbach, Bakunin, Comte, as well as the nominalists and positivists of our day, influenced by the development of modern logic and analysis, some of whom are undeniably members of the Oxford Common Rooms to which Professor Orsini has directed a rhetorical flourish. I cannot, therefore, see where I have gone astray. It seems to me that I merely reaffirmed what has always been considered Feuerbach's just historical due. And this brings me to Croce, and Professor Orsini's complaint that I criticize Croce for ignoring Feuerbach's central objection to Hegel's metaphysics, which, according to my opponent, Feuerbach never propounded.

That Feuerbach did propound it seems to me sufficiently established by the quotations I have given (even if we pay no attention to the general consensus of scholars). But when Professor Orsini assumes that my motive for so perversely denying Croce and Collingwood a place "among the intellectual innovators of our time" comes solely from my belief that they failed to meet the arguments of Feuerbach and Marx, this is not so. My sole and sufficient reason for making this historical judgment is that it asserts a historical fact. It seems to me that no reasonably objective historian of philos-

---

[2] MEGA abt. 1 Bd. 3 p. 231.

[3] Quoted by Sidney Hook, *ibid.* Hook's translations and account of the matter seem to me quite correct.

ophy could deny (even if he thought it a disaster, as Russell, for example, regarded the influence of Kant, or Broad that of Hegel) that it is the new logic, which began with Frege and Russell, and the new analytic movement closely connected with it, and not the neo-Idealist school, that constituted a turning point in the history of modern philosophy. This truism was, in any case, only an *obiter dictum* in a review concerned with Croce's opinions in the translated collection the title of which Professor Orsini, I expect rightly, considers inappropriate. I did not wish to do an injustice to a thinker with whose views I did not feel myself to be in particular sympathy. Consequently, it seems to me, that I almost lean over backwards in describing Croce as a civilized, original, illuminating, penetrating thinker, a man of humane, fastidious, and generous culture, the possessor of a richly imaginative mind, with a gift for original and fresh *aperçus*. Yet none of this, I fear, satisfies Professor Orsini. For my crime is not only to be myself blind to the true character and value of Croce, although this would have been bad enough, but to have caused similar blindness in others. According to Professor Orsini, it is I, and none other, who have spread a heresy (by means of a short review) which has seeped into the opinions of Professor Guido Calogero, Father Vincent Turner, and (*via*, I gather, Mr. Turner's essay) Professor Edgar Wind. These distinguished thinkers do not need me to defend them against Professor Orsini's thunderbolts. So eminent an Italian thinker and philosophical scholar as Professor Calogero may be assumed, I think, to have arrived at his opinion of Croce's thought independently of my brief remarks in the pages of *Mind* in 1952. Nor need Father Turner or Professor Wind be suspected of deriving their convictions of the fallacies of Hegel's Idealism, or of the criticisms of it by Feuerbach, from a few lines written by me, even if they do me the honor of agreeing with me on these points. But, of course, Professor Orsini is perfectly right in supposing that I regard Feuerbach's (and Marx's) criticisms of Hegel in this regard as possessing substance; and that I think that Croce's failure to meet them, his hostility to naturalistic explanations of historical, and, in particular, aesthetic and cultural developments—in short his "spiritualism" (despite his disavowals of belief in transcendent entities outside empirical experience), and, indeed, his inability to free himself from hypostatizing empirical concepts and categories—that I think that all this does vitiate his and every other Idealism. This is, I take it, the view common to myself and to my three eminent "victims," which Professor Orsini deplores. He may, on this, stand with Hegel and Croce and not with Feuerbach, Professor Calogero or the empiricists; but I cannot for the life of me see where I can be considered to have misrepresented Hegel, Croce, Collingwood, or anyone else.

These seem to me the only matters of serious importance raised by Professor Orsini. There remains the question of Croce's view of Feuerbach. I do not know whether Croce anywhere discussed Feuerbach's views at any length. Professor Orsini does not tell us. My assumption—not, it seems to me, wildly eccentric—was that Croce, who abhorred positivism and naturalism, could not have thought highly of Feuerbach who was, to say the least, plainly influenced by such views. But on this Professor Orsini, who has, after all, written an admiring monograph on Croce, speaks with authority, and I defer to his expert opinion. He tells us that Croce wrote sympathetically about Feuerbach's follower, Eugen Dühring. If Croce could admire Dühring, who but for Engels' famous onslaught, would have been utterly (and justly) forgotten, it is, I admit, difficult to be sure what he might not have thought; his polemic against Comte and his followers, on which I relied, is evidently not a dependable pointer. Perhaps Croce thought that consistency is a virtue of small minds. At any rate I am ready to retract my rash extrapolation if only to please Professor Orsini, whose view, on this, must, I assume, carry weight.

As to my characterization of Feuerbach's literary style, Professor Orsini is entitled to his preferences, and I to mine. Brought up as we evidently have been in somewhat different philosophical traditions, this is perhaps unavoidable. Fortunately Professor Orsini's own style, despite his admiration for them, does not seem to have been influenced by Hegel, Feuerbach or even Croce. For he writes so clearly and pungently that I have had no difficulty in understanding his assertions, and therefore in concluding that beyond my avowed bibliographical error, and my naive belief that Croce was a consistent anti-positivist, I have no need to apologize either to the reader, or to my three distinguished contemporaries who have, according to my critic, so blindly followed me into the anti-Idealist abyss—least of all to the learned, mordant, but (I cannot help thinking) over-zealous champion of Croce, Professor G. R. G. Orsini himself.

Oxford.

XVIII

LIBERALISM AND ARISTOCRACY IN THE FRENCH RESTORATION

By George A. Kelly

Critical of both the ancient and the revolutionary pasts, the Liberals of the Restoration are, nevertheless, prepared to find in them the germs and seedlings of liberty. Conserving gains, thrusting back reaction, they are dimly hopeful of a future that can extend the boons of progress and security, even if it cannot promise the millenium. As Stanley Mellon observes in his description of the political uses of history in the Restoration,[1] the Liberals have three main tasks: to preserve the civil acquisitions of 1789, to cleanse themselves of the guilt of violence, and to prepare for the possession of power. This they do with the pen and the printing press, and they compel the Ultras to accept these weapons of choice, since terror and *arbitraire* are passing out of style. There are Liberals and Liberals, going under the labels of "doctrinaires" and "indépendants." Several sharp distinctions divide the two groups, even though in total theory and tactics the groups do not differ widely. The "indépendants"—Constant, Lafayette, Manuel, Sebastiani, Foy, *et al.*—are children of opposition, not so much setting the rules of government as establishing boundaries which governments should not transgress. The "doctrinaires," on the other hand, are enduring an apprenticeship of opposition and preparing for their own day of dominance, which will come in the July Monarchy.[2]

One of the hallmarks of a Restoration Liberal is that he sees the progress of liberty sanctioned and insured by a certain social order, neither too egalitarian nor too tolerant of privilege, constructed according to Montesquieu's famous formula of "mixed government." It is fairly clear that for François Guizot and his *doctrinaire* tribe, fervently middle-class in spirit, the restored aristocracy becomes a kind of trophy of their splendid victory and a testimony to their reasonableness. The Chamber of Peers is a warrant of the fulfilled revolution and a reward for new "capacities"; but there is no doubt that 1789 and 1814 have installed the bourgeoisie in the driver's seat:

[1] S. Mellon, *The Political Uses of History: A Study of Historians in the French Restoration* (Stanford, 1958), esp. 1–57, 193–5.

[2] The Revolution of 1830 was, to be sure, a coalition effort of the bourgeoisie, Liberal in attitude, and some radicals and republicans emerged from underground. But the prize of power went to the Guizots, de Broglies, and Casimir-Périers. As for the independents, Constant remained in the opposition until his death in December. The *doctrinaires* and *indépendants*, aside from their organization in separate cliques and salons, are best distinguished by their respective interpretations of sovereignty and of the organization of the "liberal" state.

The people formerly conquered had become conquerors. In their turn they conquered France. By 1814 they controlled it beyond dispute. The Charter recognized their possession, proclaimed this fact to be law, and provided representative government as its guarantee. . . .[3]

By this historical procedure they manage to "nationalize" the Revolution, representing it as the culmination of a millenial social struggle engendered in the very origins of the French race.[4]

With Constant and other "indépendants," the notion of class movement and ascendancy is not so visceral. As generally hostile to the abuses of the *ancienne noblesse* as are the "doctrinaires" and indeed more libertarian in principle, they are not as concerned to legitimize a new social basis for government. Guizot and his party are no doubt erudite, but the erudition of the independent Liberals is more aristocratic, more abstract, more cosmopolitan. They are the grandchildren of Montesquieu and they share his appetites, if not some of his individual preferences.[5]

We need not go back as far as Montesquieu and his critics to see precisely what the Liberals had in mind. Both their hopes and fears were concentrated and exposed in the closing days of the Old Regime and in the ideologies of the Constituent Assembly. An honor roll of moderate constitutionalism adorns all their historical and political writings: Turgot, Malesherbes, Mounier, Malouet, Clermont-Tonnerre, Necker; above all, Jacques Necker, Anglophile, *créancier d'Etat*, patriot, and literal grandfather of Restoration Liberalism. Against these heroes stands a host of bloody names, but there is one, guilty of no blood in particular, yet seen as the inventor of twenty years of anarchy and tyranny: it is the oracular Sieyès, whose explosive pamphlet *Qu'est-ce que le Tiers Etat?* in 1788 had set a spark to the long fuse of turbulence.[6]

[3] François Guizot, *Du gouvernement de la France* (Paris, 1820), 3. Quoted by Mellon, 50.

[4] The history of the French race was charged with revolutionary significance in the XVIIIth century. Aristocratic writers like Boulainvilliers and Montesquieu tended to praise the Frankish conquest and legitimize the feudal order: Dubos, Voltaire, Mably, and others attacked the foundations of French nobility as a usurpation. The complicated question is well treated by Jacques Barzun, in *The French Race* (New York, 1932). As pointed out ahead, Sieyès resumed these arguments in 1788, equating the Tiers Etat with the Gallo-Roman elements of the French population. Guizot expanded this theory in his Sorbonne lectures of 1820, and it received added emphasis in the historical writings of Augustin Thierry.

[5] See *De l'Esprit des lois*, II, iii–iv; III, vii; V, vii–xi; VIII, ix, xvi; XI, vi–vii; XIX, i–iv; XXVIII–XXXIII, *passim*.

[6] The *Tiers Etat* was by far the most resonant of Sieyès's three revolutionary pamphlets of 1788. It sold 30,000 copies in three weeks, and, in the words of Malouet, "perverted the public." For background, see Glyndon G. Van Deusen, *Sieyès: His Life and His Nationalism* (New York, 1932), 33–34.

Sieyès and Necker are our two basic poles within the spectrum of constitutional government. Solutions lying outside this range are either arbitrary despotism or simple mass fury. But, in the opinion of the Liberals, the one man's system leads to freedom and security while the other's degenerates into chaos and fear.

Essentially the doctrine of Sieyès was a bowdlerized Rousseau, plus representative government. Two of his points deserve our particular attention. The first is that the institution of hereditary nobility is excess and worthless baggage for the French nation to carry; the Tiers, in fact, is the Nation:

It is not enough to have shown that the Privileged Class, far from being useful to the Nation, can only weaken and harm it; we must further prove that the noble order has no part in the social organization; that it may well be a burden for the Nation since it cannot be part of it.[7]

The only hope for the nobility in France, in the eyes of Sieyès, is "their rehabilitation in the order of the Tiers Etat." [8] All special corporations of citizens must be abolished so that "the common interest is assured of dominating the particular interests"; the duty of the Nation is to see that it does not "degenerate into aristocracy." [9] As a corollary to the thesis of Sieyès, all "mixed government" becomes literally impossible: the monarch is no more than a symbol of the people's power, and all conceivable aristocracies are abolished. This leads Sieyès to attack the much vaunted freedom of England. The English constitution, perhaps of some merit in 1688, is gothic and arbitrary by the standards of a hundred years later. It is the "product of chance and circumstances much more than of enlightenment." [10]

The second line of argument is more complicated and more interesting. Here the customarily abstract Sieyès turns to history—the history of Dubos and Voltaire—for his most crushing indictment of the nobility. By this thesis, the opposite of that of Boulainvilliers and Montesquieu, the "noble Germans" are usurpers who have held the French people in illicit bondage ever since late Roman times. The Gauls are the Tiers Etat:

Why should [the Tiers] not send back to the Franconian forests all those families who preserve the mad pretension of descent from the Conquerors and inheritance of their rights?

Thus purged, the Nation will, I think, take consolation in being left to believe that it is composed only of the descendants of the Gauls and the Romans. . . . Why not? Turn about is fair play; the Tiers will once again be Noble in becoming the Conquering Race in its turn! [11]

[7] Emmanuel Joseph Sièyes, Qu'est-ce que le Tiers Etat? (2nd edition, Paris, 1789), 8.   [8] Ibid., 14.   [9] Ibid., 118.
[10] Ibid., 68.   [11] Ibid., 12–13.

Curiously enough, the conservative *doctrinaires* led by Guizot will pick up and expand the radical historical arguments of Sieyès, altering the Tiers Etat to fit the bourgeoisie of their heart's desire; whereas the independent Liberals will at least waveringly credit their Montesquieu.

Jacques Necker, the man of a thousand virtues and pieties, loved with a fierce filial devotion by Madame de Staël, lauded by Constant, hailed by almost all the moderates, was above all an admirer of the English constitution and of the biases of that freedom-loving and commercial island. His system had consisted in making the customs, politics, and constitution of France as much like those of England as possible, while time remained. This meant, in sum, the antithesis of the Sieyesian doctrine: cultivation of a responsible aristocracy, primogeniture, a bicameral legislature, and mixed government *à la Montesquieu,* decentralization of administrative responsibility in the provinces and a constitutional monarch who would not be without power. The Anglomania of the Neckers leaves no doubt.[12] But the Neckers' fancy did not of itself create the total *idée fixe* of Restoration Liberalism. It was the violent elimination of all other constitutional solutions—except the English, which had never been tried— that gave the "beau système" of Montesquieu [13] an air of finality and perfection in the eyes of the *amis de la liberté.*

According to the Liberals, 1791 had taught that no king could survive without the support of hereditary aristocracy. In 1814 France had both a king and a nobility which, despite its countless duplicities and stupidities, had been redeemed by force. The extraordinary Liberal attempt will be to find a place for this institution within the system of liberty, treating it not merely as a necessary evil but as an additional barrier to arbitrary power. It is not without some inconvenience that the Liberals make the gesture; but the idea is, in the words of Dominique Bagge, to create a "libéralisme assez hérédi-

---

[12] To take a non-political instance: Madame Necker languished hopelessly in love with a wayward Edward Gibbon for a number of years before accepting Jacques; it was seriously proposed that Germaine should marry William Pitt the Younger; and, even unto the third generation, Albertine (later Duchesse de Broglie, daughter of the great blue-stocking and, conceivably, of Benjamin Constant) appears to have been intended at one moment for Lord Byron. For a full account of Neckerian Anglophilia, see Robert Escarpit, *L'Angleterre dans l'oeuvre de Madame de Staël* (Paris, 1954).

[13] Montesquieu, basing his judgment on the histories of Caesar and Tacitus, notes the early propensity of the Germanic tribes for mixed government. This, for him, is the source of the English system and serves as a link between the experiences of England and the continental peoples. His famous *mot:* "Ce beau système a été trouvé dans les bois." *De l'Esprit des lois,* XI, vi.

taire" [14] and, in the phrase of Constant himself, to leave some insulation between the sheer power of men and the scaffold.[15] In the remainder of this essay we shall examine three exhibits of this form of virtuosity.

Madame De Staël: Aristocracy Without Tears

Germaine de Staël, who is both proto-doctrinaire and proto-independent, inherits her father's predilection for England and "mixed government" and makes it her own without significant alteration. Though Père Necker and daughter may battle à outrance at the whist table, they are absolutely harmonious in questions of politics. For Germaine, and for Benjamin Constant too, Necker is the dishonored Cassandra of the French Revolution. More important still, perhaps, is the cultural triad of Madame de Staël's life: France-England-Germany. This means not only that she is a "European" and cosmopolitan intellectual of the Aufklärung, but that she drinks at the source of Montesquieu's "beau système," which, found in the German forests, has become historically accessible to all Western Europe.

First of all, let us set her mood, which is not without astonishment given the fact that she is the first-seeded blue-stocking of Europe, leading the major intrigues of the Directoire, bearding the terrified Goethe in his den, chatting with Alexander I on the eve of the burning of Moscow. "Chivalry is for the moderns what the heroic ages were for the ancients: all noble memories of the European nations are connected to it." [16] England is "the cavalier armed for the defense of the social order." [17] " [M. Necker] believed in the need for distinctions in society, so as to soften the harshness of power. . . . The aristocracy should, in his conception, be designed to rouse the emulation of all men of merit." [18] "Social distinctions . . . should have no other goal than the utility of all [Madame de Staël is an admiring but not very rigorous Benthamite] . . . men are born free and remain free and equal before the law: but there is a great deal of room for sophisms in such a wide field. . . ." [19]

Madame de Staël's major message may be summarized as *freedom*, yes (especially for the Germaines and Benjamins of this world, except from each other); *equality*, but. . . . It is a very large, but

[14] Dominique Bagge, *Le Conflit des idées politiques en France sous la Restauration* (Paris, 1952), 77.

[15] Benjamin Constant, "Du pouvoir royal" in *Oeuvres politiques* (ed. Louandre, Paris, 1874), 24.

[16] *De l'Allemagne* (5 Vols., Paris, 1958), I, 72–73.   [17] *Ibid.*, I, 8.

[18] *Considérations sur la Révolution française* (Paris, 1862), II, 75. [19] *Ibid.*, I, 217.

still a mixed, *but*. Chivalry, yes; merit, yes: there is no place for poor pardonable stupidity, only for fallible brilliance. Fortunately, French liberalism at its best moments will have more to show than intellectual snobbery.

Madame de Staël is Protestant in background, and so is Constant. This is incalculably important, not simply because it places her genetically in the tradition of modern revolution and "cosmopolitanizes" her rôle—attaching her to the Reformation in Germany, and above all, to the Glorious Revolution of 1688—but because it symbolizes her whole psychological position in the liberal movement. She is intelligent, wealthy, independent, and free—with the candle of the Lord in her soul, when she cares to light it, and money in the bank. Furthermore, her God (and Benjamin's) can become at whim an immanent conscience *à la Rousseau*, a rationalist teleological deity, or a Kantian metaphor that makes liberty immortal; none of the dark, secularized Calvinism of Guizot in her politics, none of the Catholic subordination or dogmatism, either. Instead, a sense that Protestantism, free of consistency and free of priestcraft, taken up or put down at will like a book of poetry, might be a good state religion for France; a sense that Protestantism is ancient and Catholicism modern.

Then there is class. Necker, despite his thousand generosities, is, by dint of birth, an exceedingly rich bourgeois, and his daughter has made a noble "marriage." Consequently, the civil rights of the aristocracy becomes the more tender as Revolutionary France explodes. The *émigrés* in London think Madame de Staël a Jacobin; the Jacobins in Paris, perceiving her adroit underground railway to Coppet which snatches selected aristocratic friends from the hunger of the guillotine, think her a reactionary. No matter: she is true to herself and to a politics that despises the *arbitraire* of death and the pain of exile, that "tomb where the mail continues to arrive."

An unimpeachable member of the aristocracy of merit, denied the aristocracy of birth but consoled through marriage, Germaine has no thought of being neutralized by quaint Republican institutions. It is all right to be a republican, if you can make sure you are a leading one, but you renounce nothing; rather, you adapt. After Terror and banishment, who could fail to discover in the nervous but gay and intrigue-laden Directoire the very atmosphere of liberty? Who could fail to identify in the preposterous Constitution of the Year III the superior virtues—bicameralism, for example [20]—denied in

[20] "Mixed government" was not the only reason why the Directoire appealed to the Liberals. The main sources of their affection were obviously psychological, involving (1) return from exile or concealment; and (2) participation in power and freedom of expression. They were in no way immune to the gush of pseudo-Romanism that burst forth after the austere and violent republicanism of the Terror.

1791 and condemned by the Convention and the Comité de Salut
Public? "Should not property and enlightenment form a natural
aristocracy, exceedingly favorable to the prosperity of the country
and to the very increase of enlightenment?" [21] Here is the *doctrinaire*
and *bourgeoise* Germaine speaking: she has even invented *doctrinaire*
sovereignty long before Royer-Collard turned his mind to philosophical questions: "Is not the single authority that one can establish that
which measures up to the definition of Reason?" [22]

Madame de Staël felt the vicarious gusts of "negative" liberty,
but she had a positive malaise whenever she was in the vicinity of
the *peuple*. Her equality is therefore very abstract, and her aristocracy extremely physical. Let us overtake her in the mood of description: "Twenty thousand men of the lowest class . . . forced their
entry into the King's palace; their physiognomies were stamped with
that moral and physical coarseness which can turn anyone to disgust,
no matter how philanthropic he may be." [23] Again, one sees emerging
from their holes "the crudest classes of society, like vapors rising from
the pestilential swamps." [24] The lower classes, Madame de Staël explains, have "almost no gradations in their feelings or their ideas. . . .
Nothing is more pleasing to men of that class than small talk [*plai-
santerie*]: for, in the excess of their fury against the nobles, they take
pleasure in being treated by them as equals." [25]

These passages should be sufficient to display the De Staëlian
psychology; it remains to see how it worked on politics. Here the
caricature is somewhat softened: first, because the practical question
of governing France in the early XIXth century has little logical rapport with any form of egalitarian sympathy; secondly, because there
is a kind of liberty felt by Madame de Staël and all the Liberals
which, demanding creation of the security for being free, surmounts
the fact of its obvious class connections. Let us see how the notion of
aristocracy contributes to this system of liberty.

First of all, political liberty is resolutely anchored in mixed government. Abstractly at least, the species of government is immaterial:
"The form of government, aristocratic or democratic, monarchical or
republican, is only an organization of powers; and the powers themselves are only a guarantee of liberty. . . . But human wisdom has up
to this time found nothing more conducive to the advantages of the
social order for a great State [than the tripartite separation of pow-
ers]." [26] Montesquieu reveals himself here and also in the observa-

---

[21] "Réflexions sur la paix intérieure," *Oeuvres* (Brussels, 1830), II, 92–93. [22] *Ibid.*
[23] *Considérations*, I, 377.   [24] *Ibid.*, I, 379.   [25] *Ibid.*, I, 391–2.
[26] *Ibid.*, I, 249. See also, 154: "There are in the social as in the natural order
certain principles the neglect of which brings disorder. The three powers are in the
nature of things."

tion that once monarchy is the chosen form it will require a hereditary support: "In France one must abandon royalty or bring back
with it a great part of the political institution of nobility." [27] Circumstance or preference? There is little question that the Germaines
and Benjamins were adroit in adapting themselves to a certain range
of circumstance—republican and monarchical—but we must probably
extract a preference for monarchy and its trappings as well. The
French Republic was a mistake in the first place, as Madame de Staël
points out in her comparison with the American experiment. The
reason is history:

People in France flattered themselves on being able to base themselves on
the principles of government which a new people had been right to adopt;
but, in the midst of Europe and with a privileged class whose pretensions
required appeasement, such a scheme was impractical. . . . The English constitution offered the only example for solving this problem.[28]

So far we have seen that hereditary aristocracy is an obligatory
accompaniment to constitutional monarchy, and that this is the free
type of European government *par excellence,* with England, graced
by "a hundred and twenty years of social perfecting," [29] as the
warrant for its success. "What especially characterizes England is the
mixture of the chivalric spirit with enthusiasm for liberty, the two
most noble feelings of which the human heart is capable." [30] Moreover, "the principal reason for liberty in England is that deliberation
took place in two chambers, and not in three." [31] In England, happily,
the mass is "bien réglée." [32] The English aristocracy is responsible and
progressive and even participates wholeheartedly in those charitable
associations in which Tocqueville, writing of America, will later perceive a substitute for aristocracy itself.[33] English liberty is not just
a passing accident, good in its time, but the cornerstone for all reasonable advance: ". . . after a century of lasting institutions which
have formed the most religious, moral, and enlightened nation of
which Europe can boast, I could not conceive how the prosperity of
the country, that is to say, its liberty, could ever be menaced." [34]

The trick, and for Madame de Staël the whole trick, is to make
this work in France, which, "of all modern monarchies . . . is certainly
the one whose political institutions have been the most arbitrary and
variable." [35] The peerage will be for her the laboratory of *éclat,* char-
acter-building, and example.

Both theoretical and practical considerations enter into her prefer-

[27] "Réflexions," 91. [28] *Considérations,* I, 213. [29] *Ibid.,* II, 283.
[30] *Ibid.,* II, 337. [31] *Ibid.,* I, 14. [32] *De l'Allemagne,* I, 170.
[33] *Considérations,* II, 313–315. [34] *Ibid.,* II, 413. [35] *Ibid.,* I, 105.

ence. In theory, the "hérédité modifiée" can become an agency of liberty, since without it no triple separation of powers is possible. In practice, the peerage can combine the "ancient souvenirs of chivalry" and the modern concerns of merit, and in so doing purge the wastrels and *parvenus* of the aristocracy who belong neither to the great families nor to the nobility of intelligence and achievement. Madame de Staël has an insatiable contempt for everything aristocratic that is not ancient or meritorious. We see this in her description of the Old Regime: "The nobility of the province was still more inflexible than the *grands seigneurs* . . . all these *gentilshommes,* whose titles were known only to themselves, perceived that they might lose distinctions for which no one any longer had any respect." [36] On the other hand, "a privileged body of any sort holds its patent only from history." [37] An institution like the peerage could not possibly injure "the dignity of the first families of France; on the contrary . . . they would be given guaranteed prerogatives and separated more distinctively from the rest of their order." [38] The idea is perfectly consistent with Madame de Staël's notion of constitutional evolution: "Each time that there exists in a country any principle of society, the legislator should draw benefit from it. . . . Most often one institution must be grafted on to another." [39]

Madame de Staël's raptures on her particular conception of the nobility are neither fortuitous nor insignificant, but a continuous *leitmotif:* we have tried to show this by diverse citations from the *Considérations* and other works. "The nobility loses its whole empire over the imagination if it cannot be traced back to the *nuit des temps":* [40] and Germaine de Staël sets no mean store by imagination. This attitude invites a particular contempt for the Bonapartist hereditary creations—a personal as well as historical bias: "What meaning has that *antechamber* of peers, in which are found all the court favorites of Bonaparte ? . . . What a group for founding the aristocracy of a free State, one which should entertain the respect of the monarch as well as of the people!" [41] She takes Benjamin to task for the Cent-Jours: "It was utter foolishness to mask such a man [Napoleon] as a constitutional monarch" [42] "Compared to this, even the Vendean nobles showed a character which makes free men. Give them real and undisputed liberty and they will rally to it." [43]

Finally, the de Staëlian scheme, in all its English grandeur, emerges: fixity and change will meet, tradition and merit will be wedded, the lion and the lamb will lie down together. "You may, I repeat, associate new names with ancient ones, but the color of the past must melt into the present." [44] There are abiding resources and

---

[36] *Ibid.,* I, 157.   [37] *Ibid.,* I, 89.   [38] *Ibid.,* I, 175.   [39] *Ibid.,* I, 288.
[40] *Ibid.,* II, 208. [41] *Ibid.,* II, 265. [42] *Ibid.,* II, 262. [43] *Ibid.,* II, 279. [44] *Ibid.,* II, 265.

new forms of progress toward the light. Aristocracy-meritocracy: this is what Madame de Staël wanted to say. Instinctively she felt herself belonging to both. She wished for the aristocratization of the intellectual bourgeoisie and the refurbishing of old class distinctions in a modern, moderate, and constitutional state.

J.-D. Lanjuinais: Calm Sea, Prosperous Voyage—At Last?

Jean-Denis Lanjuinais is an *ami de la liberté* who has never been to England, never chatted with Goethe, never seen the inside of Coppet: he is a Liberal of the provinces, or rather of a province with a very special flavor—Brittany. Despite all this bourgeois insularity— which relieves us of the duty of rediscussing the psychology of de Staëlian prejudice—he is far from being one of those "men who knew nothing of the world beyond the bounds of an obscure village" [45] who seemed to Burke to be the moving spirits of French legislative bodies; he is an erudite who will translate the Bhagavad-Gītā from Sanskrit in 1826 shortly before his death. But chivalry is not for him "what the heroic ages were for the ancients"; he looks on the French hereditary nobility with a cold and accusing eye. Napoleonic Count of the Empire, Restoration Peer of France, he has one of the qualities Madame de Staël admired—merit—but his ancestors cannot be recovered in the *nuit des temps*.

Born to a comfortable but scarcely *éclatante* bourgeois family of Rennes, Lanjuinais is one of those confident and ardent young men thrown up by the great ferment of the Revolution and the gathering of the Estates. He wins his spurs among the Breton *Tiers* in 1779 by attacking the nobility's *droit des colombiers,* and by the fatal year of 1788 he is pamphleteering against privilege, albeit not quite in a Sieyesian way. The nobles feel his lash:

Imprudent ones, shall we say to you that the nobility with its privileges was, in its origin and nature, nothing but a militia which too often took arms against the citizens; a parasitic body living off the labor of the people while despising it? . . . *In a word, the nobility is not a necessary evil.*[46]

But already he is of the tribe of Montesquieu, and this will not change amid the fortunes of war: "we cherish that mixed form [of government] so desired by the ancient political writers, so applauded by the moderns. . . ." [47]

Lanjuinais goes up to Paris with the Tiers. He will sit as a Moderate in the Constituent, and later be sent by his Breton neighbors

---

[45] Edmund Burke, *Reflections on the Revolution in France* (London, 1955), 43.

[46] "Préservatif contre l'avis à mes compatriotes," cited in *Oeuvres de Jean-Denis Lanjuinais* (4 vols., Paris, 1832), I, 9.

[47] *Ibid.*

to the Convention, where he will bravely vote against the death of the King and will join vociferously with the Girondins (of whom he is not one) to try to stem the fanaticism of the Montagne. Forced to flee from the wrath of the Comité de Salut Public, he will hole up for months in a garret in Rennes and will compel his wife to divorce him temporarily so that she may avoid proscription and possible execution. After Thermidor, he is in all the regimes: *Sénateur à vie* in 1800, Count in 1808, Peer of France in 1814. And by the testimony of his fellow Liberals he is constantly one of the focuses of resistance against all arbitrary despotism.

He is, in fact, the prisoner of his judicious constituents, who rally to him whenever elections are about to take place. They capture him once more to serve in the legislature of the Cent-Jours, and the respect of his colleagues earns him the nomination of President of the Chamber. Napoleon, neo-Liberal in spite of himself, is vexed: Lanjuinais had led the passive resistance in the Imperial Senate. "Êtesvous à moi?" demands the victor of Austerlitz. "Sire," replies Lanjuinais, "je n'ai jamais été à personne, je n'ai appartenu qu'à moi-même." [48] The Emperor's temper is somehow precariously restrained, and Carnot and St.-Jean d'Angely manage to persuade him to accept the wishes of the Assembly. Benjamin Constant, who is not for nothing in these events, describes the Liberal reassurance and undoubtedly his own personal pleasure at the effects of the "Benjamine" in recruiting talent:

M. Lanjuinais's nomination was a proof of respect for morality, discernment, and independence. This respectable and respected citizen had, as senator, shown a constant opposition to the Imperial will, and he had earlier distinguished himself in still more dangerous circumstances by his inalterable courage and inflexible character. This choice was the object of a general approbation. . . .[49]

Within a few months, the Cossacks (horrible to Madame de Staël in much the same way as the *peuple*) are back in Paris and Lanjuinais is back in the Chamber of Peers, where he will find himself in that perpetual minority of seven or eight or fifteen until the end of his days.

But—after such knowledge, what forgiveness? One of the virtues of a moderate constitution and free government is that it allows you to forget what you cannot absolve, but to learn through memory and comparison the ways of action that lie within your power. "The past is no longer ours; but let us be permitted to draw from it the lessons

---

[48] *Ibid.*, I, 66. Constant repeats the anecdote or perhaps gives it its first published currency in *Mémoires sur les Cent-Jours*.

[49] *Mémoires sur les Cent-Jours* (Paris, 1961), 191.

needed against attempts at new injustices." [50] Lanjuinais has lived
with and through all manner of injustices; for him, if the Restoration can be applied with balance and measure, it will represent a vast
breathing space. So he goes to French history in order to breathe and
to establish a stable present, in his survey of the *Constitutions de la
Nation française*. The *mot-clef* is "reasonable liberty" and Lanjuinais
finds the proper guarantees for this quality in the Charte, if it can
be applied in the spirit of Montesquieu:

> We recognize there the measure of liberty reasonably desirable in an old
> civilization, after centuries of despotism and so many intervals of anarchy,
> after thirty years of public disturbance and so many crimes committed in
> the name of liberal doctrines but in the interest of servile doctrines.[51]

Does this, as with Madame de Staël, mean an intermittent praise
of "great families" and the "spirit of chivalry"? Obviously not, given
Lanjuinais's penchant: "The feudal government was only a chaos of
anarchy and despotism." [52] Still, Lanjuinais assigns to hereditary aristocracy "special attributes" [53] and in a much muted way—because
his cosmopolitanism is second-hand—he accepts the Anglophile critique of French institutions. In 1789 "without claiming to imitate
North America, one envied the private and public liberties of the English, and one desired to acquire them as much as an old civilization
could permit." [54] Lanjuinais, in short, is not impressed with the lineage, virtues, and *éclat* of the French hereditary institution—he believes it guilty of countless sins—but he is convinced that history has
made it an overpowering national reality which cannot be ignored, and
must therefore be transformed. The power of history to create habits,
the compulsion of the abstract arguments for mixed government,
the physical fact of the Bourbon Restoration—with the undoubted
observation that a Chamber of Peers might be a barrier against future "chambres introuvables" [55]—his own merited possession of a new
aristocratic title: these are the four criteria to which Lanjuinais repairs for the defense of aristocracy.

Let us see first of all what lessons he draws from his sketch of
constitutional history. First of all, there is little or no "class argument" of Franks and Gauls *à la Guizot:* Lanjuinais will not assimilate
"the chaos of centuries of ignorance and fanaticism" to a single mechanical synthesis. In fact, Lanjuinais's liberty is as ancient as Madame de Staël's and Montesquieu's: it has merely proceeded in a
more interrupted and less optimistic fashion. The earliest Franks

[50] *Oeuvres*, IV, 363.
[51] *Ibid.*, II, 5. [52] *Ibid.*, II, 15. [53] *Ibid.*, II, 17.
[54] *Ibid.*, II, 37. [55] *Ibid.*, II, 101.

were the real fathers of liberty because while ruling the peoples, they were representatives as well, ruling by consent: "The nobility, at the beginning of the kingdom, was only what it ought to be and what no one can prevent it from being—a symbol of the fulfillment of certain functions." [56] In the days of the *première race* "counts and dukes ... were only magistrates elected for a term ... and liable to be deposed just like the King and the *maire du palais*. . . . The last kings of the *seconde race* let slumber in forgetfulness the national assemblies that could have supported them ... thus they lost the crown." [57] When representative monarchy and aristocracy are lost, liberty, too, is lost for Lanjuinais.

Such diverse authorities on liberty as the *abbé* Mably and Germaine de Staël had found a hero in Charlemagne; not so Lanjuinais. With the accession of this "grand roi, cruel vainqueur, convertisseur atroce" the game is over and the "deep shadows" close in.[58] Now comes the ascendancy of the "privileged nobility," which becomes "a nation within the nation," not by right of conquest but precisely because responsibility and election have lapsed. Revolutionary France had the alternative of getting rid of this "oppressive and absurd institution," but what it might also have done was to change it, giving it "nominal qualifications, without privileges and the license for destabilizing action." [59] This should now be the duty of government under the Charte.

In the meantime, there have been various forms of folly. The Constitution of the Year III was an improvement over that of 1791 (despite its radical and hopeless separation of powers) because it restored bicameralism. Napoleon brought back the hereditary institution with a chaotic mixing of old and new creations, which could not but be recognized by the Charte, and at least had the advantage of obscuring the legitimacy of "droits antérieurs," which had been annihilated by six later constitutions.[60] Now the debris of the turbulent past has to be separated and reorganized. The useful transformation of the French aristocracy can be accomplished only by giving it responsibility through a peerage, and by radically separating the notions of rank and heredity (guaranteed by the Charte) from those of nominal privilege and political right (the attributes of the peerage). Real inequalities undoubtedly form ranks of society; but if these ranks are recognized, protected, and created by law, then

---

[56] *Ibid.*, II, 25.   [57] *Ibid.*, II, 27.

[58] For Madame de Staël, let us remember, the question of the feudal age was an open one. It was at least much better for the nobles than royal despotism *à la Richelieu*, and it may have been better for liberty. *Considérations*, I, 9.

[59] Lanjuinais, II, 29.   [60] *Ibid.*, II, 70–81, *passim*.

the law will always be able to regulate them.[61] What will be the legitimizing principle for this inequality? Like Madame de Staël and Constant, Lanjuinais sees it in the nature of society itself and its natural action over time:

Nations that are the most jealous of social equality cannot do without ultimate instances of personal superiority [i.e., political]. . . . These may become hereditary; they tend toward heredity. Finally, without any doubt they constitute that foremost or principal superiority, a nobility which is either attached to the person or transmissible [to his heirs]. This in turn gives existence or protection to all other inequalities; all the others owe it at least the outward respects, the first honors, the first titles, the first ranks in the State, according to the degrees of what is called *hierarchy* or political subordination.[62]

Noble rank is then, according to Lanjuinais, a condition of political merit; proceeding from the monarch down, it is the source and guarantee of order, hierarchy, and mixed government: in paraphrase of Constant, it allows a free society to operate in the sphere which is neither the power of a single man nor of the scaffold. At the same time, by the definition of a peerage, its members represent the nation and not the nobility; the law is above them, ignoring their antecedent rights, and what the law has granted, the law can surely remove.

Benjamin Constant: Dédoublement Aristocratique

"His character," wrote Talleyrand to Bonaparte, "is firm and moderate, his views unhesitatingly Republican and liberal." [63] Sorry as we are to contradict the judgment of a *bel esprit*, contradict we must; and the last adjective alone will suffice, the others being not even controversial. Benjamin Constant, while incontrovertibly liberal, is really no more republican than is the "Republic of letters," and yet he has three forms of doubt about aristocracy which will pursue him, according to circumstances, to his grave. The first is a product of intellectual bias: abstract, metaphysical, and Protestant; it is often also a pose—the pose of a man who delights to celebrate the bucolic feasts of the Directoire among his peasants and play at being a fructidorian Roman. Constant calls this fanciful republicanism "common sense" (as opposed to experience), and we shall let it pass.

The second doubt is derived from Constant's view of French history. After all the notorious indiscretions of the hereditary nobles— history furnishes the catalogue—how is it possible for them to be reborn, like a tired Phoenix, when the Revolution is "won"? It is a wonder that they have the audacity to be there. He relents, however:

---

[61] "Notice sur Jacques Necker," *ibid.*, IV, 437.   [62] *Ibid.*, II, 171.
[63] Quoted by E. W. Schermerhorn, *Benjamin Constant* (London, 1924), 168.

there may be a necessity for their being there. He will force a Chamber of Peers on Napoleon during the Cent-Jours.

Finally, there is doubt in the form of prediction. Constant sees a future, one which our other liberals dying earlier and fatigued by the labors of the past, have not speculated on. In England Madame de Staël has seen prosperity and the perpetuity of free institutions, with commerce entering the aristocracy at a proper rate. Constant, confining his gaze to France, notices industry (of infant proportions) and industrial property growing, a society transforming itself from its earlier roots in feudal and landed holdings—roots very much shaken, besides, by a Revolution that created 2,000,000 new property owners. Moreover, these very changes mean to him increased liberty—at moments they seem to guarantee the impossibility of usurpation (we now know better), the difficulty of *arbitraire* (one can send his property abroad in currency before the slow-footed despot can confiscate it), the disutility of aggressive war, which destroys more than it can ever seize.[64] The march of history has made these things inevitable: "Up to a certain point, the warlike aristocracy counterbalanced the power of the priests just as the despotism of kings later dethroned the military aristocracy and as today industry is upsetting the royal despotism." [65] Constant is proto-Comtean in somewhat the same way as Guizot is proto-Marxian.

Why, under such circumstances, an aristocracy at all, or what kind of an aristocracy? We shall show that, without entirely surmounting his reflexes, Constant will jumble the premises previously expressed and exceed these analyses. First of all, there is Coppet, that "Europe in miniature . . . that Noah's ark of civilization floating on the barbarism of the imperial wars . . . that *phalanstère* of the élite. . . ." [66] Secondly, there is the candid observation of vanished and emerging institutions. Out of this dialectic will come the Restoration Benjamin, the past-all-care Benjamin, the completed Benjamin. Constant did not really believe that men were equal, but he was too intelligent to believe that inequality could be measured and fixed by institutional arrangements. No one who has tried to pierce the history of religions or the pleasures of opium can return to mundane schemes of hierarchy. Madame de Staël's two poles of aristocracy—ancient heredity and merit—are retained in Constant. But the one becomes a mere contrivance of stability "since it is there"—as we saw in Lanjuinais—and the second is sanctioned because intelligence creates

---

[64] See *Cent-Jours*, 65.

[65] *De la religion, considérée dans sa source, ses formes et ses développements* (5 Vols., Paris, 1826–28), V, 175.

[66] Alfred Fabre-Luce, *Benjamin Constant* (Paris, 1938), 161.

and extends liberty—a liberty which, though its components may be separable (religion, press, property, justice, etc.), is basically indivisible and the work of the spirit. The absolute of liberty is guarded by a host of devices which, like property, are themselves less than absolute, "useful social conventions."

Constant's bitterest attacks on the French hereditary nobility are contained in the *Mémoires sur les Cent-Jours,* and his most sympathetic defense of this institution is in the *Principes de politique.* This suggests that he bears the nobles a heavy grudge when he is personally and emotionally involved, but that his wrath subsides when he withdraws to the Olympian calm of political theory. Let us, first of all, follow the diatribe of the *Cent-Jours.* In the extensive note entitled "De la haine contre la noblesse lors du retour de Bonaparte en 1815," Constant is engaged in showing that the unpopularity of the nobility in the country aided powerfully in making Napoleon's return popular.[67] He repairs to the *nuit des temps* to commence his argument. And, quite unlike Madame de Staël and Lanjuinais, he borrows, with generous acknowledgement, M. Guizot's millenial strife of Franks and Gauls. We seem about to hear Voltaire speaking in the following passage: "The least acquaintance with history is enough to convince us that the civilized peoples of the Roman Empire having been enslaved by the barbarian hordes of the North, the calamities of that subjugation and the memories of those calamities established a fundamental difference between the doctrines of ancient and modern political writers on the organization of societies." [68]

Constant's argument now becomes extremely subtle, however; for his purpose is not to prove that the Tiers is the Nation, like Sieyès, or to legitimize middle-class power, like Guizot, but rather to explain why the proper principles of aristocracy, praised by Aristotle, have never functioned in modern Europe. "Among the ancients the nobles were a class of compatriots who had gained wealth or a superior consideration because their ancestors had deserved well of the emerging society," but "among the moderns, inequality of rank had the most revolting origin of all, conquest." An exceedingly vigorous passage on the atrocities of the Middle Ages follows this observation.

Does all this then mean that the entire fabric of illegitimacy must be unwoven so that the nation can come into its kingdom, *à la Sieyès?*

---

[67] *Cent-Jours,* 184–189. Following citations, unless otherwise noted, are from this passage.

[68] *Cf.* Voltaire, "Commentaire sur l'Esprit des lois," *Oeuvres complètes* (Paris, 1880), XXX, 454: "Who were these Franks, whom Montesquieu of Bordeaux calls *our fathers?* Like all other barbarians of the North, they were fierce beasts seeking fodder, shelter, and a few garments against the snow."

Benjamin is more circumspect and draws back from what might seem his only logical conclusion. After all, abstract logic has its limits; has he not written in his *grand ouvrage* on religion: "We detest intolerant power, but we have also some fear of philosophical power"? [69] Time has interceded on behalf of the Northern barbarians, giving them manners, polish, and *éclat.* "Certainly, in recalling these facts, I am far from concluding [like Mably and Sieyès] that it is right to confuse the nobles of the eighteenth century with the conquerors of the fifth, or even with the feudal barons who, for eight hundred years, set thrones shaking and oppressed the peoples." In short, Constant is not intent on proving the iniquity of the nobility; he is rather illustrating why the people hate them. He comments more soberly in the *Principes de politique* that "of all our constitutional institutions, the hereditary peerage is perhaps the only one which opinion rejects with a persistence that nothing up to now has been able to conquer." [70]

Nota bene: it is therefore not the nobility of Louis XV and Louis XVI which is unpardonably guilty, but rather its distant ancestors of the *nuit des temps* so much admired by Germaine de Staël. "The national regeneration of 1789 offered the French nobility a means of expiation for the wrongs of its ancestors." But, of course, with "exceptions which I would like to believe numerous," this class muffed its chance, and would later pay dearly for its imprudence. They muffed it not once, but three times, rallying to the imperial frippery of Bonaparte in 1802 ("how could a man be supposed illegitimate when served by all the families that had served sixty-six kings?" [71]), and finally, having learned and forgotten nothing, comporting themselves with anachronistic cruelty and contempt at the first Restoration and later during the White Terror. The test of their third chance has been the Charte. Though to the Liberals this document "is by no means perfect; . . . it leaves us every faculty for setting up the guarantees necessary for modern peoples," [72] and the nobility, by accepting it "with franchise and without restriction . . . would have effaced wrongs buried in the times of trouble and tumult." [73]

The differing attitudes of Bonaparte and Constant toward the institutionalization of hereditary aristocracy in a peerage are instructive, if only because they illustrate splendidly the diverse motivations that fasten on an object. Constant, as we have seen, holds a low

---

[69] *De la religion,* I, 108.

[70] *Cours de politique constitutionnelle* (2 Vols., ed. Laboulaye, Paris, 1861), I, 308.

[71] *Cent-Jours,* 66.   [72] *Ibid.,* 26.   [73] *Ibid.,* 189.

opinion of the nobility's performance and accuses it of ignoring the nation's interests, but he wishes barriers and balance. "I saw in the hereditary magistracy one more barrier against the authority of a man, and I was seeking everywhere for barriers." [74] Bonaparte, on the other hand, wants no barriers whatever, but he is incurably enamored of all the traditional forms of legitimacy: "he contemplated with not a little joy, in his serving chambers, the brilliant bustle of the courtiers of sixty-six kings." [75] By creating his *pairie* in the Cent-Jours Napoleon hopes to win back, in a certain time, the enthusiasm of that nobility which has now returned to its original Bourbon fealty. He is vexed at their absence, and doubts the success of his project. As Constant reports his troubles: "Where do you expect me to find the kind of aristocracy demanded by a peerage? . . . It was the nobles who gave liberty to England [this is the neo-liberal Napoleon speaking]: the Magna Carta was their work, they grew with the Constitution and became a part of it; but thirty years from now my *champignons de pairs* will be nothing but soldiers or chamberlains." [76] Constant cannot but agree: "Heredity is introduced in the centuries of simplicity or conquest; but it cannot be set up in the midst of civilization. . . . Prestige institutions are never the effect of the will; they are the labor of circumstances." [77] Nevertheless, the two uneasy colleagues in constitutional architecture create their peerage.

With Louis XVIII it is a different story: the sixty-six kings are behind the man and since "the monarch is in some ways an abstract being; one sees in him not an individual, but an entire race of kings, a tradition of several centuries," [78] he deserves and requires all the trappings of his tradition, being "surrounded by *corps intermédiaires* which support and limit him at the same time." [79] Here we meet the theoretical Constant, who, since the days of Jacobinism, has been tracing an argument difficult to reconcile with his outbursts in the *Cent-Jours*. Even in his earlier tract on the Terror we discover him writing: "The chivalric spirit should have been surrounded by barriers that it could not cross, but it should have been left a noble *élan* in the career which nature grants commonly to all. . . ." [80] By the time of the Restoration the noble *élan* seems to have become almost a De Staëlian mania: "I believe that a class elegant in its forms, polished in its manners, rich in example is a precious acquisition for a free

---

[74] *Ibid.*, 157.   [75] *Ibid.*, 187–188.   [76] *Ibid.*, 155.
[77] "De l'usurpation," *Oeuvres politiques*, 51.
[78] *Cours*, II, 186.   [79] *Ibid.*
[80] "De la terreur et de ses effets," *Oeuvres politiques*, 357.

government." [81] Benjamin shows himself to be a very able reconciler when he is not vexed by the memory of the Cent-Jours. Moreover, in a passage he has added to the fourth edition of *De l'Usurpation,* he bestows the blessing of political right:

I admit two kinds of legitimacy: one positive, which derives from a free election, the other tacit, which reposes on heredity; and I add that heredity is legitimate, because the habits which it engenders and the advantages it procures make it the national wish.[82]

We begin here to get the glimmer of another Constantine subtlety. He has not gone over to the Ultras, but is merely indicating the premise: no heredity, no guarantee of property, no liberty. Ranks and titles are a form of property, too, and if they must be included in the bargain, so be it.

After all, there is still the beneficial *éclat,* i.e. if the heretofore irresponsible aristocrats can be taught to put nation above privilege. And the obvious way to teach them to put nation above privilege is to incorporate the best into a peerage. Enter, Anglia. Enter, Montesquieu. "In a hereditary monarchy, the heredity of a class is indispensable. . . . To give additional aid to the monarchy there must be a *corps intermédiaire.*" [83] "No Englishman would believe for an instant that his monarchy was stable if the House of Lords were abolished." [84] But the pre-Revolutionary nobles were not a *corps intermédiaire;* they were "the hazy memory of a system half-destroyed." By means of a peerage, France will have both a "magistracy" and a "dignity"; "monarchy and liberty will be reconciled." [85]

Constant's argument resolves itself into two major themes to which we have already become accustomed: (1) No constitutional system can be stable without a bicameral division of the legislative power; [86] (2) No hereditary monarchy can be stable without organized aristocratic support.[87] We have doubled back on Aristotle and Montesquieu after a good deal of thrashing about, and we have oscillated wildly between Sieyesian invective and De Staëlian admiration.

Still, despite the confidence of the *Principes de politique,* there is a dialectic and there are doubts. The dialectic again leads us toward the realm of Comte, the age of industry and peace: "The absence of civilization gives all individuals a virtually equal color. Civilization, in its progress, develops the differences: but with the excess of civili-

---

[81] "De la doctrine politique qui peut réunir les partis en France," *Cours,* II, 298.   [82] *Op. cit., Cours,* II, 275.

[83] "Principes de politique," *Cours,* I, 35.   [84] *Ibid.,* 36.   [85] *Ibid.,* 310.
[86] *Ibid.,* 311.   [87] *Ibid.,* 35; and *Cent-Jours,* 145.

zation these differences disappear again." [88] "In a century," muses Benjamin, "we will speak of [hereditary differences] the way we now speak of slavery." [89]

The doubt is trenchant when it appears:

I confess that for a long time I doubted the possibility [of a monarchy without a peerage], and that, disposed by character to be content with what is tolerable, I was greatly taken with the example of the British Constitution, which to my way of thinking was supported by the authority of Montesquieu.

Today my opinion, as a general thesis, is greatly shaken. . . . The peerage, when it exists, can get along—as you can see, because we have one; but if it did not exist, I would suggest that it was impossible.[90]

We imagine that the deepest answer to this ring-around must be sought in nothing so simple as an institution itself or its literal corrections and abuses. We refer instead to the nature of "modern liberty": "The danger of modern liberty is that, absorbed in the enjoyment of our private independence and in the pursuit of our particular interests, we might too easily renounce our right of participation in the political power." [91] Hedonism, for Constant, is no solid basis for politics or for liberty. Pleasure is a boon, not an end. The trick is to make the natural orders of society participate in a government of complex equilibrium, satisfying the condition which the ancients perceived as a right and a duty, and at the same time insuring that the social power will be so divided that it can transgress neither against the individual nor against any of its functioning parts. The institutionalized aristocracy is another guarantee of such a commitment.

We look in vain for rigorous consistency in Constant. He lived through his moods—a mood to each book—and through the violent tempers of history. The metaphor for the occasion is the ornate jacket of gold brocade which a Restoration deputy was obliged to wear whenever he mounted the rostrum. Constant had his on continually. Some thought he admired the costume excessively; but whether or not Constant found the gold coat sartorially compelling, he needed it to speak for liberty—and he spoke often and well.

Conclusion

We have seen how the French Liberals attempted to condition

---

[88] *De la religion*, III, 458.   [89] "De l'arbitraire," *Oeuvres politiques*, 91.

[90] *Cent-Jours*, 156.

[91] "De la liberté des anciens comparée avec celle des modernes," *Oeuvres politiques*, 283.

their constitutional and social thought to the preservation of hereditary aristocracy, even on the far side of a cataclysmic event which had been, in great measure, a revolt against privilege. Though there is no single and universal Liberal argument for this procedure, we may extract four major emphases from our examination.

In the first place, the meaning and content of history had changed for French liberalism. The normative abstractness of most of the *philosophes*, often overemphasized but nonetheless real enough, had given way to a more profound feeling for the European and national past and a less obviously dualistic interpretation (ancients vs. barbarians) of European culture. In addition, the Revolution was now a part of this manifold historical experience. Change was an all too familiar and uneasy feeling, but there was no longer much confidence in the possibility of destroying aspects of the past by fiat. Rank and heredity survived this test, at least for the time being, for they helped to guarantee the institution of bourgeois property.

Secondly, the panacea of "mixed government" reigned supreme in constitutional theory. The bloodbath of the previous generation—with all its quaint political experiments—seemed, above all, to show that the single way which had not been tried—the "English system" —could provide the recipe for a free, stable, and prosperous France. The hotly debated question was: did 1814 resemble 1660 or 1688? As events interceded, other significant dates in the constitutional evolution of France and England would be compared. Except in Constant's moments of doubt, which we have recorded, the iron law of Liberal doctrine was: no mixed government, no freedom and security; no hereditary aristocracy, no monarch. As we have seen, the latter axiom was translated into the idea of domesticating the nobility by creation of a peerage in which talent and eminence would rub shoulders.

Thirdly, ancient lineage, both as leaven and example and as a historically formed institution, was held to possess positive merits of its own. It could transmit the monarchical spirit of honor so dear to Montesquieu and could function as a stabilizing *corps intermédiaire* between the pinnacle and the base of society. This action would not automatically take place if the caste were irresponsible, to be sure; but the benefits of aristocracy, if aristocracy was properly exploited, were inherent in its structure. To avoid wanton abuse this class would be placed precisely beneath the law and depend no longer on its mystical connection with "droits antérieurs."

Finally, the Liberals believed in the creative enterprise of the individual liberated from manual toil and confirmed in the independence of his proprietary enjoyment. The hereditary aristocracy was merely the capstone of this governing (and electing) class, no longer separable from the rich *roturiers* by a nexus of feudal privilege but now their senior partners in power and responsibility. A much easier mobility between these classes was envisaged; the old caste would teach the new one "table manners" and the new would infuse the old with its ascendant vitality.

French Liberalism (of all kinds) failed to avoid the much-remarked contradiction between its universalistic principles of liberty —let alone equality—and its obvious class connections, a disparity that would produce the post-1848 conservative trauma of Tocqueville, Thiers, Montalembert, and others. In the Restoration it is clear that French Liberalism set out on the first of its persistent experiments to create a *gouvernement des meilleurs*.[92] Class definitions would shift—often with desultory speed—as democracy and industrialization, literacy and syndicalism advanced. But a pattern of politics had been created that became transmissible and, so to speak, hereditary. The search for a surrogate for bodily aristocracy and new *dépôts* for aristocratic values would frustrate the Liberals throughout the XIXth century.

Harvard University.

---

[92] The "liberal" idea of the *gouvernement des meilleurs* forms the chief and concluding thesis of the remarkable work by Georges Burdeau: *Traité de Science politique, V: L'Etat libéral et les Techniques politiques de la Démocratie gouvernée* (Paris, 1953). Of course, the penchant is as old as Plato's *Republic*, but it is the peculiar liberal contribution to have aspired to fuse limited aristocracy with representative government in the modern state.

XIX

NIETZSCHE AND THE BOURGEOIS SPIRIT

COMMENT BY PAUL TILLICH

None of the three papers on Nietzsche printed above deals directly with Nietzsche as the critic of bourgeois society, though each of them points to his criticism as one element in his whole philosophical attitude. It is indeed impossible to neglect this element in Nietzsche's work; explicitly or implicitly it permeates every part. Even his sense of being "out of season" (*unzeitgemäss*) is primarily a way of expressing his negation of *his own* time. It cannot be interpreted, as Mr. Löwith seems to do, as an abstract timelessness. It makes, of course, a supratemporal claim, like every truth; but it is essentially related to the particular age he is trying to overcome in himself. If he calls this age "decadent," this implies a definite interpretation of history, in which his own appearance—the appearance of "Zarathustra" before the "great midday"—has a definite place. This sense of having a prophetic mandate, of standing at the most crucial moment of history, cannot be left out of the picture.

In expressing the eternal weight of every moment of time in terms of the doctrine of "Eternal Recurrence," Nietzsche is using a classical idea which contradicts his consciousness of the "fullness of time"—just as his ecstatic love of fate contradicts the classical resignation to fate—*cf*. Löwith. This is the reason why his philosophy reveals a dominating dramatic impulse, as Morris brings out. But this dramatic form is no mere aesthetic preference of Nietzsche's; it is not due to the fact that "Nietzsche was nourished on Greek tragedy," as Morris remarks. It is rather his feeling for the dramatic moment in world history in which "man" has come to an end and a being "beyond man" is beginning to appear. The decadence to which Nietzsche opposes his "will to power" is not decadence in general, as Huszar seems to indicate. It is *the* great decadence in which humanity reaches the stage of the "last man," who is a completely rationalized cog in a machine without creative vitality; and in which it reaches at the same time the beginning of the stage "beyond man," the stage of a higher life, embodied in more exalted, more powerful and more creative beings.

It is in the light of this "eschatological consciousness" that we

278

must understand Nietzsche's attack on bourgeois society. Since "life" is the divine-demonic symbol which takes the place for him of the idea of God, whatever is opposed to "life" he challenges with a prophetic wrath. And since the greatest obstacle to "life" is the "objectivating" nature of bourgeois thinking and acting, he wages war against bourgeois society in the name of his ultimate principle, creative life.

There were other attacks on the bourgeois system as it developed after the middle of the nineteenth century. Marx challenged the dehumanization of an economic order in which man is estranged from himself, from society and the world, and is transformed into a commodity, a "thing," a mere object. Kierkegaard challenged the logical necessity of "reason," in Hegel's sense, which destroys man's real existence, his ability to decide and his living in passion and faith. Stirner preached the absolute individual. Dostoievski revealed the demonic forces underneath man's rationality, Jacob Burckhardt prophesied the catastrophe of mass culture. And at the beginning of the twentieth century the creative men in the arts, poetry and philosophy were aware of the approaching earthquake in Western civilization.

We cannot consider Nietzsche apart from this world-historical frame. In his writings there are analogies to some of the ideas of all these men. Like Marx, he describes the development of mankind into a monstrous machine, to serve which has become the only meaning in life. Like Kierkegaard, he defends "becoming" against knowledge and demands a non-detached and passionate attitude towards truth, especially towards historical truth. Like Stirner, he proclaims the value of the strong Ego as over against its dissolution into conventional behavior and moralistic or sentimental self-surrender. Like Dostoievski, he looks into the dangerous forces in the depths of man which control his rational action. Like Burckhardt, he foresees the self-destruction of Europe. And he has influenced most of the critics of bourgeois society and most of the prophets of doom during the beginning of the twentieth century.

Nietzsche shared the fate of many of the great fighters against "objectivation" during the nineteenth century: he fell into a subjectivity the passionate maintenance of which betrayed its own inner insecurity. The paradoxical character of his oracles, the predominance of aggression, his unconquerable hatred for enemies who represent elements of himself, the mannerism of his style: all this reveals the desperate situation of those who were fighting against a foe they were not able to conquer even within themselves. This foe was the world created by the victorious bourgeoisie, the world in which means replaced ends, and everything, man included, had become an object of analysis and control. But it was just analysis and control that Nietzsche applied in his attempt to overcome the world based on them. The tragic implications of this contradiction have become manifest today in the anti-bourgeois revolutions of the twentieth century, one of which, Fascism, has wrongly *and* rightly been linked to Nietzsche's philosophy.

No interpretation of Nietzsche should neglect his grand and tragic war against the spirit of his age, the spirit of bourgeois society. As it does not lessen the proportions of Socrates to emphasize his struggle against the spirit of his age, the spirit of sophistic disintegration, so Nietzsche's stature is not diminished by a strong emphasis on the spirit he was fighting against in his day. The more deeply a man is rooted in the Kairos (the creative moment of time) the better is he able to reach the Logos (universal truth). Nietzsche was great because he struggled against his times out of the deepest experience of his times.

Union Theological Seminary.

XX

JAMES MARSH AND AMERICAN PHILOSOPHY*

By John Dewey

In the years 1829, 1831, and 1832, an event of considerable intellectual importance took place in this University town. For in these years Chauncey Goodrich published in Burlington, Vermont, editions of three of the more important writings of Samuel Taylor Coleridge, namely, *Aids to Reflection, The Friend* and *The Statesman's Manual*. The first of these contains the well-known Introduction by James Marsh, and it is the Centenary of its publication that brings us together to-day.

In associating the name of romantic philosophy with the work of James Marsh, it is important that we should appreciate the sense in which the word "romantic" is employed. Words change their meaning, and to-day such a title may seem to imply a certain disparagement, since realism in some form is the now prevailing mode. In the sense in which the word was earlier used, a somewhat technical one, the opposite of romantic was not realistic, but rather classic. The word was used to denote what was taken to be the modern spirit in distinction from that of antiquity, and more particularly the spirit of the Teutonic and Protestant North in distinction from the Latin and Catholic South.

Fortunately an essay written during Dr. Marsh's last year in Andover Seminary and published in the *North American Review* for July, 1822, enables us to seize, independently of labels, what Marsh himself thought the difference in question to consist of. "The modern mind," he says, "removes the centre of its thought and feelings from the 'world without' to the 'world within'." More in detail he says, in speaking of the Greeks, that "they had no conception of a boundless and invisible world in the bosom of which all that is visible sinks into the littleness of a microcosm."[1]

* Lecture delivered at the University of Vermont, November 26, 1929, in commemoration of the centenary of the publication of James Marsh's "Introduction" to Coleridge's *Aids to Reflection*.

[1] *North American Review.* Vol. XV, p. 107.

In contrast with this attitude he says: "In the mind of a modern all this is changed. His more serious thoughts are withdrawn from the world around him and turned in upon himself. All the phenomena of external nature, with all the materials which history and science have treasured up for the use of the past, are but the mere instruments to shadow forth the fervors of a restless spirit at last conscious of its own powers and expanding with conceptions of the boundless and the infinite." The change is definitely connected with the influence of Christianity in general and of the Protestant and earlier Barbarian North in particular.

I am concerned with the ideas and principles of the philosophical work of Marsh rather than with its historical origin, development, and influence.[2] But it would be unfitting to pass the occasion by without noting the broad and deep scholarship of Marsh as it is made evident even in this the earliest of his published writings. He had mastered Italian, Spanish, and German, as well as Latin, Greek, and Hebrew, at that early date. This was no attainment since he had never been abroad, and since there were few facilities for study at the time. His writings show that he not only knew the languages, but had an extensive and familiar acquaintance with their literatures. I may not go into detail, but it is not too much to say that he was probably the first American scholar to have an intimate first-hand acquaintance with the writings of Immanuel Kant, including not only the *Critiques of Pure* and *Practical Reason,* but his *Anthropology,* and especially his writings on the philosophic basis of natural science. In the latter connection it is worthy of note that Marsh's readings in the scientific literature of his day were wide and influenced his speculations; Oersted with his principle of polarity influenced him chiefly along with Kant. His interpretation of Kant was affected, of course, by his admiration for Coleridge, but also by his reading of Fries.

While his indebtedness to Coleridge was great, it was somewhat less than his distrust of his own powers would intimate. He came to Coleridge with a preparation both in reading and in his thinking, which fitted him to appreciate the latter, but which also absolves him from any charge of being a mere disciple. The

---

[2] A careful and thoroughly trustworthy account of the latter has already been given by Professor Marjorie Nicolson. See the article entitled "James Marsh and the Vermont Transcendentalists," in the *Philosophical Review* for Jan. 1925.

interest that Marsh had in Coleridge sprang primarily from a common interest in religion and a common desire to arouse among believers in Christianity a vital realization of its spiritual truth. There is much in Coleridge's *Aids to Reflection* that is far outside the main currents of present-day thought even in religious circles. Aside from penetrating flashes of insight, a reader to-day is likely to be left indifferent to its substance and repelled by its form. He may easily find it of only antiquarian interest. To employ a juster statement, it is mainly of historical interest. To say this is to say that to grasp its meaning and its influence in its own time we must place it in its own context in the intellectual and moral atmosphere of the early nineteenth century. We must recall that it was a period before Darwin and the evolutionists; before, indeed, modern science had itself left any great impress on the popular mind; a period when the peculiar problems forced upon modern society by the industrial revolution were only beginning faintly to show themselves. It was a time when, outside of a few radicals, there was nominal acceptance of established institutions and doctrines but little concern for their inner meaning. It was, on the whole, a period of intellectual apathy and indifference.

The two essays of John Stuart Mill upon Bentham and Coleridge respectively give a clear picture of the general temper of the day. Among other things Mill says, "The existing institutions in Church and State were to be preserved inviolate, in outward semblance at least, but were required to be, practically, as much of a nullity as possible." More specifically in speaking of the Church he says, "On condition of not making too much noise about religion, or taking it too much in earnest, the church was supported, even by philosophers, as a 'bulwark against fanaticism,' a sedative to the religious spirit, to prevent it from disturbing the harmony of society or the tranquility of states." He sums it up by saying that "on the whole, England had neither the benefits, such as they were, of the new ideas, nor of the old. We had a government which we respected too much to attempt to change it, but not enough to trust it with any power, or look to it for any services that were not compelled. We had a Church which had ceased to fulfill the honest purposes of a Church but which we made a great point of keeping up as the pretence or simulacrum of one. We had a highly spiritual religion (which we were instructed to obey from selfish motives)

and the most mechanical and worldly notions on every other subject.'' As he says, ''An age like this, an age without earnestness,
was the natural era of compromises and half-convictions.''

In this situation, Bentham was the innovator, the critic, and
destroyer of the old. Coleridge was the unusual type of conservative, the thinker who demanded that the *meaning* of the old be
comprehended and acted upon. As Mill says, ''Bentham asked
of every custom and institution 'Is it true?' while Coleridge asked,
'What is its meaning?' '' The latter question, in the existing state
of things, was as disturbing as the other; its import was as radical,
for it was a challenge to the existing state of belief and action.
The more obvious phase of the radicalism of Coleridge in religion
is found in his attack on what he called its bibliolatry. He condemned the doctrine of literal inspiration as a superstition; he
urged the acceptance of the teachings of Scripture on the ground
that they ''find'' one in the deepest and most spiritual part of
one's nature. Faith was a state of the will and the affections, not
a merely intellectual assent to doctrinal and historical propositions. As Mill says, he was more truly liberal than many liberals.

But while he disconnected faith from the Understanding, he
connected it with a higher faculty, the Reason, which is one with
the true Will of man. Coleridge said: ''He who begins by loving
Christianity better than truth will proceed by loving his own sect
or church better than Christianity and end in loving himself better
than all.'' But he held with equal firmness that Christianity is
itself a system of truth which, when rightly appropriated in the
rational will and affection of men, is identical with the truth of
philosophy itself. This assertion of the inherent rationality
of Christian truth was the animating purpose of his *Aids to Reflection,* and it was this which appealed to James Marsh; and it is in
this sense that he may be described as a disciple of Coleridge. It
was in a combination of the teaching of the great English divines
of the seventeenth century, themselves under the spell of Plato,
and the German transcendental philosophy of the late eighteenth
and early nineteenth century, that Coleridge found the especial
philosophical framework by which to support his contention of the
intrinsic philosophical truth of the Christian faith. Since Marsh
himself was already a student of the same sources, all the circumstances conspired to attach his exposition to Coleridge.

If I dwell upon the inherent liberalism of Coleridge's teaching under the circumstances of his own day, as described by Mill, a member of the opposite school, it is because without allusion to that fact we are without the historic key to the work of Marsh also. In our own idea, and under present conditions, the philosophy of Marsh seems conservative. There is comparatively little interest, even in theological circles, in the doctrines to whose clarification, in the light of reason, he devoted himself. One sees his thought in its proper perspective only as one places it against the background of the prevailing interests of his own day. By temperament, Marsh shrank from controversy; he deprecated becoming involved in it. But the most casual reader of the Introduction prefaced to the republication of Coleridge's *Aids to Reflection* will see that its undercurrent is the feeling that what Coleridge says and what he himself says goes contrary to the doctrines that possess the mind of contemporary religious circles, while conjoined with this is the sense that he is under a religious as well as a philosophical obligation to combat the tendency of these beliefs. It was not just the fate or the spread of a particular philosophical system that he was concerned with, but the re-awakening of a truly spiritual religion which had been obscured and depressed under the influence of the prevalent philosophies of John Locke and the Scottish school. It was as an ally of spiritual and personal religion that he turned to the German philosophy, actuated by the conviction that the same evils which Coleridge found in England were found also in his own country.

It is worth while to quote from the Introduction at some length what he has to say upon this subject. "It is our peculiar misfortune in this country that, while the philosophy of Locke and the Scottish writers has been received in full faith as the only rational system and its leading principles especially passed off as unquestionable, the strong attachment to religion and the fondness for speculation, by both of which we are strongly characterized, have led us to combine and associate these principles, such as they are, with our religious interests and opinions, so variously and so intimately, that by most persons they are considered as necessary parts of the same system." He himself held that the philosophical principles thus popularly read into the Christian faith were, in fact, profoundly discordant with the latter. As he says, "A system of philosophy which excludes the very idea of all spiritual power and agency cannot possibly co-exist with a religion essentially spiritual.'' Like Coleridge, he anticipates being regarded as a heretic in religion because he is desirous of searching out a philosophy that is consistent instead of inconsistent with the spiritual truths of Christianity which are to him its essence.

In the attempt, to which I now turn, to expound the positive philosophy of Marsh, one may appropriately return to the essay of 1822, to which allusion has already been made. Christianity presented itself to him not only as the great cause of the intellectual and emotional change from the world of classic to that of modern mind, as expressed in literature, politics, and social life, as well as in religion, but as inherently a revelation of philosophic truth. Revelation from without was required because of the fallen state of man. But the revelation was not external, much less arbitrary in *content*. It was rather a recovery of the essential ultimate truths about nature, man, and ultimate reality. It is for that reason that I said that Christianity was to him a truly philosophic revelation. Were I to attempt to select a single passage that might serve as an illuminating text of what he thought and taught, it would be, I think, the following: A thinking man ''has and can have but one system in which his philosophy becomes religious and his religion philosophical.''

As I have already indicated, the full meaning of this position can hardly be recovered at the present time. It must be considered in relation to the time in which Dr. Marsh lived. It had nothing in common with the views upon philosophy which prevailed in the academic audiences and popular thought of the time. These, as we have also noted, were based upon Locke as modified by the ruling Scotch school, and upon Paley. The orthodox conceived of Christianity as a merely external revelation; the dissenters from orthodoxy relied upon proof from design in nature of the existence of God and upon what Marsh, following Kant and Coleridge, called ''Understanding'' in distinction from ''Reason.'' There is much evidence that Dr. Marsh felt himself between two dangers. One was that he should be thought to reduce Christianity to a mere body of doctrines, a speculative intellectual scheme. The other was that he should be thought faithless to the living power of Christianity in re-making life and thus be classed with unbelieving critics. The situation in which he thus found himself accounts, I think, for the air of apologetic timidity which surrounds the expression of his deepest thoughts. In part it was due, undoubtedly, to his modest distrust of himself, but in larger part, to the situation with which his period confronted him. He was quite right, no one who reads him can doubt that fact, in thinking of himself as a deeply devoted man in his own personality. Indeed, for inner and humble piety and spirituality he had few peers among his contemporaries. But he had, in addition, the distinctively philosophic instinct. He wanted to see the universe and all phases of life as a whole. When he gave rein to his instinct in this direction, he found himself at once conscious that he was coming into conflict with the ideas which dominated not only American society but the churches themselves. He neither mitigated his own Christian sense nor ceased to philosophize. But his activity in the latter field was, it seems to me, restricted. He never developed the independence in thought which matched his philosophic powers. It is probable, as Dr. Nicolson has made clear, that he, as the means of directing Emerson to Coleridge, and indirectly at least, made a profound impress upon the American "transcendental" movement. But he never had the detached position which marked Emerson, for example, and accordingly did not reach an unimpeded development of his own powers.

It is, however, time to turn more directly to his basic thought in which for him the religious truth of Christianity was found to be one with the truth of philosophy as a theory of God, the universe, and man. Formulas are somewhat dangerous. But for the sake of brevity, if for no other reason, a formula or label seems necessary. I shall, accordingly, venture to say that his philosophy is an Aristotelian version of Kant made under the influence of a profound conviction of the inherent *moral* truths of the teachings of Christianity. The formula involves, unfortunately, considerable technical reference to historic systems. The external evidence shows that he was more of a student of Plato and of the great divines of the seventeenth century who are more influenced by Plato, than of Aristotle. But we know also by external testimony that the *Metaphysics* and the *De Anima* of Aristotle were always by him. And it seems fairly evident that his objective interpretation of Kant, his disregard for the phenomenalism and subjective view of nature found in Kant, came to him ultimately, whether directly or through Coleridge, from Aristotle.

To explain what meaning this statement has in connection with Marsh's own metaphysical system, it is necessary to digress into a technical field which I would otherwise gladly avoid. In Kant, as all students know of him, there is a definite separation made between sense, Understanding, and Reason. In consequence, the affections of the mind called sensations are regarded by him as "mental" in character, and as organized by forms of space and time which are themselves ultimately mental in character. The categories of the Understanding, while they provide universality and constancy for these sense impressions, do not, therefore, get beyond knowledge of phenomena. While Reason furnished ideals of unity and complete totality, which go beyond the scope of the Understanding, they are for us unrealizable ideals. When we suppose that Reason gives us knowledge of the real nature of things, we are led into illusions. Knowledge must remain within the bounds of phenomena, that is, of the logical organization of the materials of sense.

Now it is a striking fact that, while Dr. Marsh freely employs the Kantian terminology, and while he uses constantly not only the general distinctions of sense, Understanding, and Reason, but also special conclusions reached by Kant in treating them, he never even refers to the Kantian limitation of knowledge to phenomena— what is usually termed the "subjectivism" of Kant.

For example, while he treats, like Kant, mathematics as a science of space and time as necessary and hence *a priori* forms of perceptual experience, he also has in mind the absolute space and time of Newtonian physics and not just mental forms. They are forms of actual and external things of nature, not merely forms of mind. Thus our geometry and other mathematics is a rational science of the conditions under which all physical things exist, not merely a science of our conditions of experiencing them. In and of themselves as conditions of the possibility of physical things and their changes, they "constitute" in his own words, "the sphere of possibility and of those possible determinations of quantity and form which are the objects of pure mathematical science." The free development of these possibilities, independent of the restric-tions imposed by actual existence, is the work of the productive imagination. But they are also necessary principles of the existence of all physical things and events, since the latter are and occur in space and time. Thus mathematics forms the basis of physical science.

He was probably influenced by Fries in this objective interpretation. But there is the deeper influence which I have called Aristotelian. This influence appears in his treatment of the relations of sense to Understanding and of both to Reason, and also in his entire philosophy of nature, in its relation to mind. Instead of making a separation between sense, Understanding, and Reason, they present themselves in Marsh's account as three successive stages in a progressive realization of the nature of ultimate reality. Each of the two earlier, namely, sense and Understanding, forms the conditions under which the third manifests itself and leads up to it. For each contains in itself principles which point beyond itself and which create the necessity of a fuller and deeper apprehension of the nature of the real.

What I have called the Aristotelianism of his position is seen in the fact that he did not isolate this ascending series of sense, Understanding, and rational will from the natural universe as did Kant, but rather saw in it a progressive realization of the conditions and potentialities found in nature itself. I have not run across in him any allusion to Hegel, although he seems to have known Fichte. But like Hegel, instead of putting the subject in opposition to the object or the world, he regarded the subject, who comes most completely to himself in the rational will, as the culmination, the consummation, of the energies constituting the sensible and physical world. While not a scientist, in any technical sense, Marsh was widely read in the science of his day, and thought he found in it the evidence for the truth of the conception that nature presents to us an ascending scale of energies in which the lower are both the condition and the premonitions of the higher until we arrive at self-conscious mind itself.

His conception of sense is, in the epistemological language of to-day, realistic. He holds that in sense we can distinguish the received material, the seen, heard, and touched qualities from the acts of mind that form seeing, hearing, touching, and that we refer the material of sensed qualities to a ground of reality outside ourselves, just as we refer the acts of sensing to the self as the abiding

ground of their reality.   We perceive qualities of sense as qualities
of an object existing outwardly and independently.   Sense, however, does not give knowledge, even of the physical world, but
only material for knowledge.   The Understanding is necessary
to judge the sensory material and to know *what* is presented in
them.   We have to interpret the material of sense.   The Understanding operates by acts of distinguishing, comparing, and thus
brings out the relations implicit in sensuous material.   Without
these connective and organizing relations, we do not know an object
but merely have a number of qualities before us.   We have the
power to become self-conscious of the relating activities of the
mind.   We note that they proceed by certain necessary laws in as
far as they result in knowledge.   The Understanding is not free to
judge in any arbitrary sense of freedom.   To attain knowledge we
must judge or understand in necessary ways, or else we do not
attain knowledge of objects but only personal fancies.   This law
of understanding or knowing objects proceeds from the mind itself,
and it, when we recognize it and take note of it, forms what is
termed Reason.   In the Understanding (that is, in scientific knowledge of nature) this agency operates spontaneously; but when it
notes its own operation and becomes self-conscious, we recognize
it as rational will, which is the animating principle, one and the
same in character, or universal in all knowing minds; and hence
identical with the divine intellect which is the light that lighteth
every man that cometh into the world.   It is reason because it
operates by necessary principles; it is will when it is viewed as an
agency complete and self-sufficient in itself.

This technical excursion into what Marsh calls rational psychology may help express the sense of what has been called the Aristotelian element in him.   He insists that the powers of the mind or
self are called forth only by objects correlative to them.   The
sensibility remains a mere potentiality until it is called into action
by nature.   We cannot hear or see or touch except as the mind is
affected by things having color, sound, and solidity.   There is no
difference between this and the action and reaction of iron and a
magnet upon each other.   In the same way, the powers of the
Understanding remain mere possibilities until they are called into
action by the actual relations which subsist among objects.   The
orderly, logical structure is both the condition that calls the powers

into action and realizes their potentialities, and the object upon which they expend themselves, just as much as the qualities of things are both the actualizing conditions and the objects upon which the capacities of the mind terminate in exercise or sensibility. Similarly, the objective of self-conscious, rational will is both the condition and the object of the exercise of our Reason.

The essentially Aristotelian nature of this conception of each lower stage forming the conditions of the actualizing of some potentiality of mind and then supplying the material upon which a higher expression of the same mind exercises itself will be obvious, I think, to every philosophic student. It is through the use of this conception that Marsh escapes from the charmed circle of limitation within the self that holds the Kantian philosophy spell-bound. The world in its status as a manifold of qualities, as a logically interconnected whole, and as summed up in universal self-conscious will, has to be there independently of our minds in order that the capacities of our minds may be stimulated into real existence and have material upon which to work.

It was said, however, that this Aristotelian interpretation of Kant is made under the influence of ideas derived from Christian faith. Marsh separates himself from Greek thought, whether that of Plato or Aristotle, in two ways. First, he conceives of mind as identical with the self, the ''I'' or personality, an identification that is like nothing found in ancient thought, and one which he associates with the influence of Christianity. It is another way of saying the same thing to point out that he introduces into the classic conception of reason an element foreign to it in its original statement—namely, the conception of reason as *will*—that is, of a power to institute and seek to realize ends that are universal and necessary, that are supplied by nature but which flow from its own nature as a personal rational self. It is the very nature of these ends that they cannot be realized by themselves or by any merely intellectual process. Their nature demands that they be embodied in the material of sense and of the natural world as an object of knowledge, or that all the material of appetite connected with the senses or of desire directed upon natural objects be subdued and transformed into agencies of expressing the true ultimate nature of the rational will. To put it a little more concretely, Aristotle held that reason could be actualized in contemplative knowledge apart from any effort to change the world of nature and social institutions into its own likeness and embodiment. Following the spirit of Christian teaching, Marsh denied any such possibility. He held that Reason can realize itself and be truly aware or conscious of its own intrinsic nature only as it operates to make over the world, whether physical or social, into an embodiment of its own principles. Marsh constantly condemns what he calls speculation and the speculative tendency, by which he means a separation of knowledge and the intellect from action and the will. By its own nature, reason terminates in action and that action is the transformation of the spiritual potentialities found in the natural world, physical and institutional, into spiritual realities.

The other point of connection of Marsh's philosophy with the Christian faith is more specific, less general. Accepting the idea that man is a fallen creature, he accepted also the idea of Coleridge that original sin is not a mere historic fact, going back to a historic progenitor, but is the act of the will itself by which it takes as the principle and moving spring of its own action something derived not from its own inherent nature but from some source outside itself—the appetites of sense, or the desires that are used by the thought of ends derived from the world about us. I shall not extend my excursion into technicalities to trouble you with his philosophic rendering of the theological doctrines of sin, conscience, and freedom of the will, but no exposition of his basic idea of the equation of philosophy with religion would be complete without reference to the particular way in which he applies his conception of the necessity of a correlative object in order to awaken the potentialities of the self into reality. The correlative object of the conscience and will, through which they, as they exist in man, can be aroused into actuality of operation and being, is no abstract law. As will and conscience are personal, belonging to a self, so their correlative object must also be personal. At this point, the religious character of his philosophy most clearly reveals and expresses itself. This correlative personal object is the manifestation of the divine in Christ. In his own words: "The true end of our being presented by the spiritual law is the realization, practically, in our own being, of that perfect idea which the law itself presupposes, and of which Christ is the glorious manifestation."

And again, "the spiritual principle may be said to have only a
potential reality, or, as it enters into the life of nature, a false and
delusive show of reality, until, awakened from above by its own
spiritual correlatives, it receives the engrafted word, and is empow-
ered to rise above the thralldom of nature."

The discussion will now turn to a consideration of somewhat
more concrete matters (although not, according to the view of
Marsh, more genuinely human interests and concerns)—to what
Marsh has to say upon society in general and education in particular. Unfortunately, what is left to us in the published record is
all too scanty. But there are suggestions adequate to a reconstruction of his fundamental philosophy. Here, too, we may
fittingly begin by recourse to Coleridge, in spite of the fact that
there is less direct evidence of his connection with Coleridge in this
matter than in that of the identification of the Christian religion
with true philosophy. Coleridge, in common with the German
school which he represented, conceived social institutions as essentially educative in nature and function. They were the outward
manifestation of law and reason by means of which the intelligence
and conscience of individuals are awakened and by which they are
nourished till they become capable of independent activity, and
then express themselves in loyalty to social institutions and devotion to improving them until these institutions are still better fitted
to perform their educative task for humanity.

Coleridge with considerable courage applied this conception to
the Church as an institution in distinction from the inward and
spiritual communion of the faithful—an application that took its
point, of course, from the fact that there was an established Church
allied with the political order in England. With rather surprising
daring, he proclaimed that the Church, in this institutional sense,
is not inherently a religious corporation. In his own words, "Religion may be an indispensable ally but is not the essential consti-
tutive end of that national institute which is unfortunately, at least
improperly, styled the church; a name, which in its best sense, is
exclusively appropriate to the Church of Christ." Then with an
obvious etymological reference to the original meaning of clergy
as connected with clerks or writers, he goes on to say "the clerisy
of the nation, or national church in its primary acceptation and
original intention, comprehended the learned of all denominations,

the sages and professors of law and jurisprudence, of medicine and physiology, of music and civil and military architecture, with the mathematical as their common organ; in short, all the arts and sciences, the possession and application of which constitute the civilization of a nation, as well as the theological.'' The latter, he goes on to say, rightfully claimed the precedence but only because ''theology was the root and trunk of the knowledge of civilized man; because it gave unity and the circulating sap of life to all other sciences, by virtue of which alone they could be contemplated as forming the living tree of knowledge.'' It is primarily as educators that those especially called clergy of the established church are to be regarded, and it was even well, according to Coleridge, that they should serve an apprenticeship as village schoolmasters before becoming pastors.

It is evident that, owing to the non-existence of an established church in the United States, this portion of Coleridge's teaching could not directly influence the thought of Marsh. Indeed, he naturally thought that the condition in which the institutional church was but the outward expression or body of the inner and spiritual church represented a higher principle than could be expressed by any politically established church. But indirectly, Marsh's ideas move in a like direction, although with such differences as the difference between the political organization of Great Britain and of our country would naturally suggest.

It is interesting to note that Marsh makes, in a sermon at the dedication of the chapel of the University, a distinction between civilization and culture similar to that drawn by Kant and other German thinkers. Civilization, he says, in effect, is concerned with the adaptation of the acts and services of the individual to the needs and conditions of existing society. It is a discipline of the faculties with reference to the occupations of civil society. Culture is the development of the powers of individuals with reference to the ends that make them truly human; it transcends any existing social order and régime because it elevates them into the possession of the spiritual law of reason, of universal will, and the end of humanity as such. It aims at control by this inner law of rational will instead of by the ordinances and customs of a given society. From the obligations imposed by the interests of higher and common humanity, no state policy can absolve us. The peoples of the East, he says, are, perhaps, more civilized than those of the West, for their institutions and the discipline they provide fit the individual to some definite place and work in the social order. But we, he says, are not destined to be the working instruments for attaining the lower ends imposed by the state of civilization. And he adds these very significant words: "We can hardly, indeed, be said to be subjects of any state, considered in its ordinary sense, as body politic with a fixed constitution and a determinate organization of its several powers. But we are constituent members of a community in which the highest worth and perfection and happiness of the individual free persons composing it constitute the highest aim and the perfection of the community as a whole. With us there is nothing so fixed by the forms of political and civil organization as to obstruct our efforts for promoting the full and free development of all our powers, both individual and social. Indeed, where the principle of self-government is admitted to such an extent as it is in this state, there is, in fact, nothing fixed or permanent, but as it is made so by that which is permanent and abiding in the intelligence and fixed rational principles of action in the self-governed. The self-preserving principle of our government is to be found only in the continuing determination and unchanging aims of its subjects." From this Dr. Marsh draws the inevitable conclusion that the function of an educational institution is a cultivation of the community, which is identical with the full development of all the powers of its individual persons.

It is to be regretted that Dr. Marsh never achieved a complete exposition of his social and political philosophy. While changes in vocabulary might be needed to adapt the principles he here expresses to present conditions, he has stated, it seems to me, a principle which is fundamental to the distinctive American social system, if we have any such system, and one which stands in need of enforcement at the present time. When Dr. Marsh wrote, the idea of nationalism, in its modern sense, had hardly made its appearance in this country. There was little if any worship of the state as a political organization. Individuals were still conscious of their power organized as a free community to make and unmake states—that is, special forms of political organization. There was, indeed, great admiration for the American form of government and much patriotism in loyalty to it. But it was devotion to its under-

lying principle as an expression of a free and self-governing community, not to its form. It was regarded as a symbol and as a
means, not as an end fixed in itself to which the will and conscience
of individuals must be subordinated.

In my judgment, this subordination of the state to the community is the great contribution of American life to the world's
history, and it is clearly expressed in the utterances of Dr. Marsh.
But recent events have tended to obscure it. Forces have been at
work to assimilate the original idea of the state and its organization to older European notions and traditions. The state is now
held up as an end in itself; self-styled patriotic organizations make
it their business to proclaim the identity of the loyalty and patriotism of individuals with devotion to the state as a fixed institution.
The constitution of the state is treated not as a means and instrument to the well-being of the community of free self-governing
individuals, but as something having value and sanctity in and of
itself. We have, unconsciously in large measure but yet pervadingly, come to doubt the validity of our original American ideal.
We tend to submit individuality to the state instead of acting upon
the belief that the state in its constitution, laws, and administration, can be made the means of furthering the ends of a community
of free individuals.

Dr. Marsh wrote in the full if insensible consciousness of the
pioneer period of American life. The true individualism of that
era has been eclipsed because it has been misunderstood. It is
now often treated as if it were an exaltation of individuals free
from social relations and responsibilities. Marsh expresses its
genuine spirit when he refers, as he does constantly, to the *community* of individuals. The essence of our earlier pioneer individualism was not non-social, much less anti-social; it involved
no indifference to the claims of society. Its working ideal was
neighborliness and mutual service. It did not deny the claims of
government and law, but it held them in subordination to the needs
of a changing and developing society of individuals. Community
relationships were to enable an individual to reach a fuller manifestation of his own powers, and this development was in turn to
be a factor in modifying the organized and stated civil and political
order so that more individuals would be capable of genuine participation in the self-government and self-movement of society—so

that, in short, more individuals might come into the possession of that freedom which was their birth-right. Depreciation of the value of our earlier pioneer individualism is but the negative sense of our surrender of the native idea of the subordination of state and government to the social community and our approximation to the older European idea of the state as an end in itself. If I may be allowed a personal word, I would say that I shall never cease to be grateful that I was born at a time and a place where the earlier ideal of liberty and the self-governing community of citizens still sufficiently prevailed, so that I unconsciously imbibed a sense of its meaning. In Vermont, perhaps even more than elsewhere, there was embodied in the spirit of the people the conviction that governments were like the houses we live in, made to contribute to human welfare, and that those who lived in them were as free to change and extend the one as they were the other, when developing needs of the human family called for such alterations and modifications. So deeply bred in Vermonters was this conviction that I still think that one is more loyally patriotic to the ideal of America when one maintains this view than when one conceives of patriotism as rigid attachment to a form of the state alleged to be fixed forever, and recognizes the claims of a common human society as superior to those of any particular political form.

Dr. Marsh's views of education were a reflection of his general social philosophy. It goes without saying that he conceived of education in a deeply religious spirit and that to him religion was, in words reminiscent of a passage already quoted from Coleridge, "the sap of life to the growing tree of knowledge." But we have also in interpreting his words to recall that to him religious truth was one with rational truth about the universe itself and about man's nature in relation to it. In his own words again, religious truth "is not so much a distinct and separate part of what should be taught in a system of instruction, to be learned and stored up in the mind for future use, as a pervading and life-giving principle and power that should act upon the mind in every stage and process of its development, and bring all the powers of the soul, as they are unfolded, under its holy and humanizing influence." The conception of what religion and religious truth are may change; they have undergone change since Marsh taught and wrote. But some organizing, pervading, and life-giving principle to bind together all the spec:alisms and details which so abound is still as greatly needed in education to-day as it was when Marsh spoke.

The ideas of Dr. Marsh upon more specific matters of the organization and conduct of university education reflect his fundamental conceptions. In stating them I depend chiefly upon the record of his successor in the chair of philosophy, Professor Joseph Torrey in the Memoir he prefixed to the collection of Marsh's writings. It was the latter's opinion "that the rules for the admission of students are too limited and inflexible." There is no reason why those unfortunately prevented from taking advantage of the whole of the course should not have the privilege of taking the part that lies within their means. "He was also for allowing more latitude to the native inclinations and tendencies of different minds. It was absurd to expect every young mind to develop in just the same way; and equally absurd to confine each one to the same kind and quantity of study." Again, "he thought the methods of instruction in use too formal and inefficient. There was not enough of actual teaching, and too much importance was attached to textbooks. He wanted to see more constant and familiar intercourse between the mind of teacher and learner." It was more important to invigorate and sharpen the student's powers of independent thought and judgment than to bend them to apprehending the ideas of others. As to college discipline and morals, he also distrusted the system of minute external regulation and conformity. He was also opposed to the then prevailing methods of classification and promotion of students. Merely formal examinations he thought of little value.

These points sound strangely like the criticisms and proposals of educational reformers from his day to this. They were not, however, with him concessions to practical expediency. They were reflections of his fundamental faith in individuality and in the spirit as opposed to the letter and mechanical form. But this emphasis upon the value of individuality was accompanied, in his views on education as elsewhere, with an equal sense that the ultimate end was a community of cultivated individuals. The ultimate purpose of education is "to elevate the condition and character of the great body of the people." Nowhere as much as in the United States were schools "made, as they are here, an important and leading object in the policy of government," and nowhere else was the experiment given a fair trial of "placing all classes and all individuals upon the same level providing for all the same system of free, public instruction."[3]

I have chosen to try to get some idea of the relation of Dr. Marsh's thought to that of his own time rather than to engage in general eulogy of him. But the record discloses a mind at once deeply sensitive and deeply rational. The period was not favorable to far-reaching thought, which always demands a certain audacity lacking both to the period and to Dr. Marsh's temperament. He did not carry his questionings beyond the received order of beliefs in religion. He depended upon others, notably Coleridge and the German idealists, for the language in which to clothe his philosophic speculations. But, none the less, because of his sensitivity one feels that, even when he speaks of things that do not make the appeal now that they did in a time when men were more engrossed in theology, there is nothing second-hand in his thought. There were realities of which he had an intimate personal sense behind his most transcendental speculations. It is characteristic of him that he holds that knowledge of spiritual truth is always more than theoretical and intellectual. It was the product of activity as well as its cause. It had to be lived in order to be known. The low rating which he gave sense as compared with Understanding was not, for example, a merely cognitive matter. The "thralldom of sense" was a moral and personal affair. And so his depreciation of Understanding in comparison with Reason was not technical. In what he called Understanding he saw the root of the skills and the conventions which enable men to make a shrewd adjustment of means to ends, in dealing with nature and with fellowmen. It was the key to what is termed success. But the ends which it prescribed were just those of worldly success, and so Reason was to him the symbol of the ability of man to live on a higher and more inclusive plane which he called that of spirit, and in which he found the distinctive dignity of man. Religion was to him the supreme worth, and yet his conception of what constitutes religion was a virtual condemnation of a large part of that which passed in his time and still passes for religion, as being merely an attempt to include God and the next world in a scheme of personal advance-

[3] These words were spoken, be it noted, before the great public school revival of the eighteen-forties occurred in this country.

ment and success. Underneath the somewhat outmoded form of his philosophy one feels a rare personality, gifted in scholarship, ever eager for more knowledge, who wished to use scholarship and philosophy to awaken his fellowmen to a sense of the possibilities that were theirs by right as men, and to quicken them to realize these possibilities in themselves. His transcendentalism is the outer form congenial in his day to that purpose. The underlying substance is a wistful aspiration for full and ordered living.

Columbia University

PART SIX

PROBLEMATICAL IDEAS IN
THE HISTORY OF POLITICAL THOUGHT

XXI

THE MEANING OF ROMANTICISM FOR THE HISTORIAN OF IDEAS[1]

By Arthur O. Lovejoy

The title of this paper was suggested by the distinguished Committee who planned this Symposium. It presumably conveys a question which the speaker is expected to answer. Questions can hardly be answered unless their terms have an understood meaning, common to those who ask and those who answer, and unless they contain no presuppositions about facts that are contrary to fact. The present question, however, contains two terms having no understood meaning, and at least one supposition contrary to fact. Of these peculiarities of the query propounded, the Committee were, I am sure, fully sensible; and I suspect that their subtle but benevolent design was to formulate the topic in a way which would give the speaker an excuse for calling attention to some still current confusions which pervade the general subject under consideration.

I

The two troublesome terms in the question are "meaning" and "Romanticism." The trouble with them is not that they lack meaning, but that they have too many meanings, so that, when they are used without qualification or explanation, it is impossible to know what the user is talking about. However, of the many senses of "meaning," it is pertinent here to distinguish only two, namely: the sense which the word presumably has when you ask (for example): "What *is* the meaning of 'meaning'?" *viz.*, what is the word the name of, to what object or phenomenon does it point, or of what concept is it the verbal counterpart, in the usage of some person or persons; and second, the group of senses in which the word "meaning" stands for an attribute, not of words, but of things or events, and denotes, not signification, but "significance," or consequence—or major consequences. If one is asked, in this

---

[1] This and the four following papers were contributed to a Symposium on "The Romantic Movement in Europe in the First Half of the Nineteenth Century," at the meeting of the American Historical Association, Section on Intellectual History, held at New York City, December 30, 1940 (see this journal, I, 1940, p. 505). The first paper has been considerably expanded for publication.

second sense, "What is the meaning of Romanticism?" one's answer would express a judgment about what chiefly makes the historical thing called "Romanticism"—if there *is* any such thing —"important," what aspects or what effects of it are most noteworthy or momentous.

It is thus not clear which of two questions this discourse should try to answer—or whether, perhaps, it should try to answer both: *i.e.*, what is the signification of the word "Romanticism," and what, historically considered, is the main significance of the thing, Romanticism? However, it is obvious that the second question cannot be answered until the first is answered, since you cannot communicate to another any observations about a thing unless you and he both understand by the name of it the same thing.

But here the other equivocality of terms in the title presents itself. The first question cannot be answered. No man can say what is "the meaning" of the word "Romanticism"; for meaning, in this sense, is determined by usage, and in its relatively brief life of less than a century and a half this word has acquired so many— and such incongruous and opposed—meanings that no lexicographer has ever yet come near to enumerating them correctly and exhaustively. Next to the word "nature," "romantic," with its derivatives, is possibly the most equivocal in the language—a fact which it is of some importance for historians to remember. That it is sufficiently remembered by most writers on literary, philosophical, political or social history cannot, I fear, be said—though the historians of modern literature are perhaps the greatest sinners in this way, one of their favorite employments being to introduce new explicit or implicit senses of Romanticism, with a fine indifference to the others already in use. The amazing diversity of its meanings I have already attempted to exhibit—though incompletely —in a paper read before another learned body, composed of philologists and literary historians.[2] I shall, for the sake of brevity, assume that it furnishes sufficient proof, if any were needed, that "Romanticism" has no generally understood meaning and has therefore come to be useless as a verbal symbol. And thus, finally, the question propounded contains an assumption contrary to fact, namely, that there is such a thing as *the* meaning of "Romanticism" for "*the* historian of ideas."

These semasiological preliminaries may seem an unduly pedantic

[2] "On the Discrimination of Romanticisms," read before Modern Language Association of America, 1923; published in *PMLA*, XXXIX, pp. 229–253.

and logic-chopping approach to what is presumably meant, after all, to be a discussion of a historical topic. But few things, I think, are more needful for historians of ideas—and every good historian is in some degree a historian of ideas—than to get rid of the logical confusions associated with the use of this linguistically extraordinary word "Romanticism," and, in fact, to cease asking, and trying to answer, the first question suggested by the title of this paper. For an answer to it, whether expressed or implied, will either (a) contain the factually false assumption which I have indicated—*viz.,* that the word has one understood and accepted meaning—or else (b) it will be a personal definition of the word, conveying no information except about the definer's private taste in terminology, and not open to discussion, or comparison with any objective matters of fact—since personal preferences in the definition of terms are not discussable, provided the definitions are not self-contradictory. Yet those who propound definitions—new or old—of "Romanticism," appear usually to suppose that they are *not* merely uttering a verbal proposition—a statement of the signification which they choose to attach to a term—but are putting forth a proposition of historical fact, capable of discussion and verification. This singular confusion in most instances can be seen to rest upon a vague, tacit assumption that there is a kind of determinate entity existing prior to the definition, an object or an essence, or Platonic Idea—which *must* be the thing that the word "Romantic" or "Romanticism" denotes, but which, when it is discovered, must then be assumed to be exemplified or embodied in all the writers or writings which have been conventionally called, or which the particular historian or critic is accustomed to call, "Romantic." In determining what this Romantic essence is, the inquirer is usually guided by his own associations of ideas with the word, the connotations which it chiefly has for him,—or sometimes, in the case of those for whom "Romantic" is an adjective of disparagement, guided only by a determination to apply that damning epithet to all the ideas or tastes which they most dislike. The result of this sort of procedure is not only the vast terminological confusion to which I have already referred, but a vast amount of bad history—the reading into texts or doctrines which have come to be commonly classified as "Romantic," of all the characteristics or theses which one has, by a largely *a priori,* non-historical method, determined to be the pure quiddity of "the Romantic," *das Wesen des Romantischen*. These are, I am aware, dogmatic-sounding assertions; but probative examples could be cited by the dozen, if there were time for them.

Nothing, then, but confusion and error can result from the quest of some supposititious intrinsic nature of a hypostatized essence called "Romanticism." But there is a quite different sort of inquiry into which our initial question may be converted; and such an inquiry would make for the elimination of confusion, and is indispensable for the understanding of the history of the past century and a half, and, consequently, for the understanding of the contemporary intellectual, moral and political situation; and this inquiry is primarily the business of the historian of ideas, and requires the application of a specific method of analysis proper to that study. Its starting-point is a massive historical fact which no one is likely to deny—namely, that in the last quarter of the eighteenth century, especially in the 1780s and 1790s, there were discovered, invented or revived, chiefly in Germany, a large number of ideas which had been relatively, though not always absolutely, unfamiliar or uninfluential through most of the seventeenth and eighteenth centuries; and that the total impact of what we may call, for short, the new ideas of the 1780s and 1790s (including revivals of old ideas under "new"), as they developed, ramified, and were diffused during the following decades, profoundly altered the habitual preconceptions, valuations, and ruling catchwords of an increasingly large part of the educated classes in Europe, so that there came into vogue in the course of the nineteenth century and in our own a whole series of intellectual fashions—from styles in poetry and styles in metaphysics to styles in government—which had no parallels in the preceding period. The result was—to resort to the hackneyed but apt metaphor—not one, but a whole set of "climates of opinion," in which species of plants either unknown to the earlier eighteenth century or only germinant then, came to flourish mightily. The "newness" of these ideas of (*e.g.*) the 1790s was, for the most part, not an absolute newness; it lies in the contrast with the dominant ideas of the immediately antecedent age, and with what may be called the "old ideas" of the 1790s, exemplified, on the political side, in the French Revolution. For, roughly, in that decade two revolutions were taking place— one, external and political, in France, which was the culmination of the *Aufklärung*, the other, primarily in the realm of abstract ideas, mainly in Germany, which was only somewhat later to manifest its political consequences—some of them, indeed, only in our own unhappy day.

To call these new ideas of the 1780s and 1790s "Romanticism" is confusion-breeding and productive of historical error above all because it suggests that there was only one such idea, or, if many, that they were all implicates of one fundamental "Romantic" idea, or, at the least, that they were harmonious *inter se* and formed a sort of systematic unity. None of these things are true. The new ideas of the period—even when held, as they often were, by the same individual minds—were in large part heterogeneous, logically independent, and sometimes essentially antithetic to one another in their implications, though their full implications were not always at once discerned; and some writers traditionally labelled "Romantic" were influenced by some of them, others by others, and yet others, I suspect, by none. But though there is no such thing as Romanticism, there emphatically *was* something which—for lack of any other brief name—may still be called a Romantic period; and one may perhaps speak of—not a, but several, Romantic movements: the period in which this array of new or newly energized ideas emerged into prominence, and the movements which consist in the propagation of one or many of them, in the drawing out of their initially latent consequences, logical or pseudo-logical, in their alliances with one another or with various older ideas and fashions of thought, and in their interaction with certain more or less permanent affective elements of human nature. For my own part, at any rate, I am—in a spirit of compromise—willing to speak of such a period and of such movements—meaning, approximately, the half-century 1780–1830, but especially its second decade, and the movements in which any one or more of these ideas conspicuously manifested themselves. In what follows I shall be chiefly concerned with some of the ideas of those German writers who, in the 1790s, first introduced the *term* "Romantic" as the designation of a new tendency or fashion of thought.

Now the question: What were the new, or newly *active* and peculiarly influential, ideas of the 1790s and what were their vicissitudes and developments in the subsequent decades? is a factual and therefore a properly historical question. But it is a question in the history of ideas; and it therefore, as I have said, requires the application of a method of investigation appropriate to that study. And the nature of this method, as applied, not to the life-history of a particular idea but to the integral study of a period, still appears to need some explanation. Given the prerequisite knowledge of the relevant texts, the first task of the historiographer of ideas is a task of logical analysis—the discrimination *in* the texts, and the segregating *out of* the texts, of each of what I shall call the basic or germinal ideas, the identification of each of them so that it can be recognized wherever it appears, in differing contexts, under different labels or phrasings, and in diverse provinces of thought. And in this part of the task the historian—unhappily—must usually begin by carefully scrutinizing the most recurrent and crucial terms in his texts—the most prevalent formulas or phrases or sacred words—in order to determine what and how many distinct ideas appear to be expressed by, or associated with, each of these terms in the minds of the various users of it. For once a word or phrase or theorem has gained vogue and sanctity, it is likely to be used by different writers in quite different senses—usually without their being clearly aware that they are doing so.

For example: it is, I suppose, commonly recognized that *one* of the relatively new phenomena of the Romantic period was a new or, at all events, a much wider and intensified, vogue of the highly abstract and equivocal term "infinite." It is notorious that such phrases as *Streben ins Unendliche* or *Sehnsucht nach dem Unendlichen* or *Annäherung zu einer unendlichen Grösse,* were peculiarly dear to the German *Frühromantiker* as expressions of their ideal of life or of art. But, as I have elsewhere pointed out, the term "infinite," as used by one or another of these writers, had at least five distinct, thought not in all cases mutually exclusive, senses or applications.[3] All of these senses obviously had something in common, and that something was, historically, highly important. The common element was the negative element. The "infinite," whatever positive meaning might be connected with the word, meant at least the not-limited or not-completed, the *Unbegrenzt* or *Unvollendet*—in *some* sense of limit or completion. And the sanctity of

    [3] "Schiller and the Genesis of Romanticism," *Mod. Lang. Notes,* 1920, pp. 138 ff. *Cf.* also H. Rehder: *Die Philosophie der unendlichen Landschaft: ein Beitrag zur Geschichte der romantischen Weltanschauung,* 1932; E. L. Schellenberg, *Das Buch der deutschen Romantik, die Sehnsucht nach dem Unendlichen,* 1924; F. Strich, *Deutsche Klassik und Romantik; oder Vollendung und Unendlichkeit,* 1928.

the word in most of the new writers of the period was evidence of a tendency to a new presupposition about what is excellent or valuable—and also about the nature of things, the constitution of the universe or the course of history. It was a presupposition contrary to a feature of what may be fairly called the main—not the only—earlier tradition of European thought, at least in value-judgments of all kinds, and not in these alone. There were important opposing strains in the older tradition, but the most prevalent and orthodox tendency had been to think in terms of finites, and to regard limitation as an essential element of excellence, at least for mortals. In logic and science, the first thing needful was to have precisely *defined* concepts and terms; in a work of art, the first essential was that it should have one limited theme and a clear-cut and readily recognizable "form," so that, as Schiller declared in the essay that gave the decisive initial impetus to the early Romantic movement in Germany,[4] the essence of classical art is that is a *Kunst der Begrenztheit;* in literary style, the supreme merit was the clarity that comes from using words which immediately convey clear and distinct ideas, express exact and therefore limited meanings; and in human character and conduct, the mark of excellence was to observe metes and bounds and to be moderate in all one's desires, ambitions and pretensions. The historic process, too, in the Christian tradition—in spite of opposing Aristotelian and other influences—was conceived as a finite thing, having a beginning, a middle and an end—neither an interminable undulation, nor an endless recurrence of similar cycles, nor even a perpetual movement towards an infinitely distant and therefore unattainable goal. Now the German Romantics of the 1790s were in conscious and zealous—though not in consistent or unwavering—revolt against all these assumptions, but first of all in the theory of art. They conceived and proclaimed themselves to be the prophets of a new, a "modern," art—and "modern" is what *they* primarily meant by "Romantic"[5]—which should be a *Kunst des*

[4] *Ueber naive und sentimentalische Dichtung;* see my "Schiller and the Genesis of Romanticism" in *Mod. Lang. Notes, loc. cit.*

[5] *Cf.* my "The Meaning of 'Romantic' in Early German Romanticism" in *Mod. Lang. Notes,* XXXII, 1917. For an example, *cf.* A. W. Schlegel's Berlin *Vorlesungen über schöne Litteratur und Kunst,* 1803–4 (ed. Minor, 1884, Pt. I, III, p. 7): "eine romantische, d. h. nicht nach den Mustern des Alterthums gebildete Poesie." So the title of the Third Series, *Ueber die romantische Poesie,* is explained as meaning "eine Geschichte und Charakteristik der Poesie der Haupnationen des neueren Europa, oder der romantischen."

Unendlichen. The new valuation, the revolt against "the finite," speedily passed over into other provinces; and since one of the most pregnant differences of taste or habit in categories is that between a habitual preference for the limited and well-defined and a habitual preference for "the infinite," this one among the ideas of the 1790s has had many and far-reaching consequences.

But in spite of this common element in the new vogue of the word "infinite," when any more positive and concrete significations were attached to it by German writers of the 1790s, it could serve as the catchword for several quite distinct and, in part, mutually antagonistic tendencies, since there are numerous varieties of "the infinite." These, again, I may not take the time to enumerate; I merely recall the general fact in order to illustrate the indispensability of a careful semasiological analysis in the first phase of the intellectual historian's study of a period.

When this phase is completed—when he has discriminated and listed as exhaustively as he can the separate "ruling ideas" which distinguish the period, or the particular group of writers in it with whom he is concerned, his next task is to examine the relations between these ideas. And the relations he will need to look for are of three kinds: logical, psychological, and historical—and especially, under the latter, genetic—relations.

The first two of these inquiries I have distinguished from the strictly historical because they are procedures of analysis and construction which need in some measure to be carried out in the historian's own mind before he goes on to confront their results with the historical evidence to be found in his sources. It corresponds to the phase of constructing tentative hypotheses in the work of the natural scientist. By logical relations I mean relations of implication or opposition between categories, or tacit presuppositions, or express beliefs or doctrines. When he has ascertained the currency and influence of a given idea in his period, the historian does well to ask himself, what does this idea logically presuppose, what does it imply, and with what other ideas is it implicitly incompatible—whether or not these logical relations were recognized by those who embraced the idea. For if it should turn out that some of its implications were not recognized, this may become a highly important, though negative, historical fact. Negative facts are of much more significance for the intellectual historian than is usually appreciated. The things that a writer, given his premises, might be expected to say, but doesn't say—the consequences which legitimately and fairly evidently follow from his theses, but which he never sees, or persistently refuses to draw—these may be even more noteworthy than the things he does say or the consequences he does deduce. For they may throw light upon peculiarities of his mind, especially upon his biases and the non-rational elements in his thinking—may disclose to the historian specific points at which intellectual processes have been checked, or diverted, or perverted, by emotive factors. Negative facts of this kind are thus often indicia of positive but unexplicit or subconscious facts. So, again, the determination of not-immediately-obvious *in*compatibilities between ideas may lead to the recognition of the historically instructive fact that one or another writer, or a whole age, has held together, in closed compartments of the mind, contradictory preconceptions or beliefs. Such a fact—like the failure to see necessary positive implications of accepted premises—calls for psychological explanation, if possible; the historian must at least seek for a hypothesis to account for it.

By the psychological relations of ideas, I mean, so to say, elective affinities between them not properly logical in character—the tendency of one, through some process of association by similarity, or often through the ambiguity of the terms used to express it, to suggest or evoke others. These transitions often pass, with the writers in whom they appear, for logical ones. But especially important for the historian, under this head, is the consideration of the natural *affective* concomitants of various ideas—the kinds of feeling—even, if you like, of "bodily set"—which, when entertained, they tend to arouse, the moods or attitudes to which they are congenial, what I have elsewhere called the "types of metaphysical pathos" which go with various types even of highly abstract notions or doctrines, and are perhaps the real secret of their appeal, at least to the lay public. Philosophy, historically considered, like Nanki Poo in the opera, can sing, and has sung, songs adapted to every—or almost every—changing mood or passion. Into the highly controversial question whether changes of dominant mood beget the philosophies, or changes in philosophy the moods—or sometimes one and sometimes the other—I do not propose here to enter; I merely suggest that the historiographer of ideas must be alert to note the connection between specific ideas and philosophies and specific moods. "Connection" here includes repugnancies. A not uncommon historical phenomenon is a repugnancy between a dominant doctrine in, for example, aesthetics, and the actual tastes of those who feel obliged to subscribe to that doctrine. It has been pointed out by acute students of seventeenth- and eighteenth-century English criticism that most critics of the period seem to have really liked and admired Shakespeare, while the critical principles many of them professed required them to damn him— at least with faint, or much-qualified, praise. This is even more apparent, I think, in those German critics of the early 1790s who were still classicists of the straitest sect, but were, in a few years, to promulgate the new program of *die romantische Poesie*. One factor—though only one—in causing them to reverse their position was, I suspect, that their strong, but repressed, taste for Shakespeare predisposed them to accept a new philosophy of art—and in particular, of poetry—which would justify their taste.

When the intellectual historian of a period has thus considered the logical and the hypothetical psychological relations of the major unit-ideas which he has found prevalent in the period, he must then, of course, return to the historical data, to observe how far the logical relations between these ideas were in fact manifested as operative factors in the thought-tendencies of the time, and what psychological relations among them can be actually seen at work in the minds of their spokesmen. In this latter inquiry he will often, if lucky, be able to discern a sort of genetic relationship between one logically distinct idea and another—to note the nature of the transitions in thought by which one gave rise to a quite different one, and into what combinations or idea-complexes it entered.

For example: the *original* "Romanticists"—the German introducers of the term, the Schlegels and their group—were preoccupied at the outset chiefly with two peculiar problems: (a) What are the essential and distinguishing characteristics of classical, *i.e.*, Greek, art and thought and culture, on the one hand, and of non-classical, *i.e.*, modern art, etc., on the other? (b) How are these differences to be explained historically? They began their reflection on these problems while still assuming the superiority of the "classical;" their lucubrations on the subject are an episode in the history of the quarrel over the Ancients and Moderns. Now their answer to the second question was that the fundamental differences between classical and "modern" ways of thinking must be due to one or both of the two great historic events which brought the ancieht culture to an end: the introduction of Christianity and the invasions of the Nordic or Germanic peoples. This suggested to them, in part, the answer to their other question. If you want to know, in terms of basic ideas—of preconceptions, valuations, or emotional susceptibilities—what distinguishes the classical from the modern or "Romantic," you have but to determine wherein the Christian view of life or of the universe fundamentally differs from the Greek, or the Germanic or Nordic from the Latin or Mediterranean. At first they (certainly Friedrich Schlegel) conceived the former, at least, to be a difference for the worse. But in their attempt— much influenced by Schiller's essay to which I have referred—to formulate the "essence" of the "modern" or Christian *Lebensanschauung,* they came (through processes which, once more, it would take too long to analyze here) to find this in certain propensities or assumptions such as the craving (to which I have already referred) for infinite values or infinite objects for thought or imagination to contemplate, or for the will to aim at, a love of mystery, otherworldliness, an awareness of the duality of man's constitution, a preoccupation with the inner life, and a sense of man's inner corruption—all of these being contrasted with the classical sense for "form" and limits, the supposed Greek love of clarity, absorption in the beauty of this world, "objectivity" (*i.e.,* looking out and not in), untroubled unity of personality, and "serenity." And some, at least, of the former propensities or assumptions these writers found congenial to their own imaginations or temperaments; and they thereupon abruptly turned from what they conceived (with a good deal of historical error) to be the classical mode of art and thought to its opposite, which they had already named "Romantic."

But this conversion was clearly much facilitated by the influence of another idea which has its own pre-history, but was especially potent in the Romantic decades: the idea that a man—and especially an artist—ought to be of his own time, to express in his life or art the characteristics, the ideas, the spirit of his age.[5a] He will neither be true to himself nor *en rapport* with his contemporaries if he does not do so. If, for example, he is a dramatist, he must

---

[5a] This became an especially influential idea among the French Romantic writers and artists of the 1820s. On this see George Boas, "*Il faut être de son temps,*" in *Jour. of Aesthetics,* I, 1, 1941, pp. 52–65.

exhibit in his characters the emotions and motives which he understands—those by which men of his time are moved. A modern
man, then, should *be* "modern." But since "modern" or "Romantic" meant mainly, for the early German Romanticists, "Christian," and since for them the spirit of Christianity was best exemplified in the Middle Ages, what at first looked like a sort of
revolutionary modernism proved to be identical (in part) with a
kind of medievalism.

Now in noting these phenomena which I have roughly sketched,
the historian is at once (a) discriminating certain (by no means
all) of the more characteristic ideas of the Romantic period, (b)
observing the processes by which some of them generated others,
and (c) recognizing the complex groupings which they formed in
individual—in fact, in numerous individual—minds of the time.
When he has done this, the ideas fall into a pattern, of which the
diverse modes of relation, logical or psychological, between them
are, as it were, the framework. And—though this is perhaps a
counsel of perfection—one has not, I think, fully understood the
Romantic period as a historic phenomenon—has not grasped what
was then going on—until he has apprehended this pattern. It
could be at least suggestively portrayed graphically, though the
diagram would need to be an extremely large and intricate one.

But when the historian has thus traced these genetic processes,
the passing-over from one idea to another, and noted one particular
combination of ideas which resulted, he has still to observe that
each of the units of *that* complex presently broke loose from its
original context and went on its own separate way, generating, in
different minds, yet other ideas or entering into other combinations. Thus, out of one group of assumptions made or theorems
evolved by the Schlegels, Novalis, and their circle, of which I have
tried to suggest roughly the components and their genesis, a whole
series of distinct notions and thought-movements emerged. Was
it to be assumed, for example, that "modern" or "Romantic" art,
as a result of the preoccupation of Christianity with the inner life,
is, or should be, peculiarly introspective? Then modern "poetry"
has before it as its special province the whole field of subjective
states and their infinite nuances, and finds its best expression in
the psychological novel or play, especially in those exhibiting subtle
moral conflicts in the soul of the hero—already exemplified, or supposed to be exemplified, in Shakespeare's *Hamlet*. This, it will

be remembered, is one of the themes of Chateaubriand's *Génie du Christianisme*.[6] With this, the novel, as the form best adapted to this purpose, tended to assume a new dignity and pre-eminence among the literary *genres*. But it was no far cry from this idea to that of the superiority of the *realistic*—but the psychologically realistic—novel in general; so that a French literary historian has not unintelligibly written of "the realism of the Romantics." *Madame Bovary* is certainly neither medieval, nor mysterious, nor vague, nor otherworldly, nor particularly characterized by *Unbegrenztheit;* it has often been described as an attack upon the "Romantic" temper; but it has nevertheless a filiation with one of the elements in the idea-complex of the *Frühromantiker* of the 1790s and the French Romantics of the following decade, as that element developed in isolation from the others. But, on the other hand, Mr. Lascelles Abercrombie assures us that "there is an element directly opposed to romanticism; it is realism." Thus a truly romantic taste in "Views," or landscapes, finds the "pleasant thing in them" to be "a certain blur or dimness, which prevents the eye from being lost in a throng of things positively known, and at the same time stirs one to guess at the infinite possibility the blur contains of things which might be known." "The best thing our minds can do for us is

> In keeping us in hope strange things to see
> That never were, nor are, nor e'er shall be."[7]

Now in insisting that this is the *truly* "romantic" thing, Mr. Abercrombie was simply expressing his own taste in the use of that adjective; but it happens to be true that this note, as well as the other I have just mentioned, was one of the elements in the original idea-complex of the German Romanticists of the 1790s; so that from it a literary tendency opposite to realism could also develop, or at least could gain reënforcement: the cultivation of a mysterious vagueness, the poetry that hints at what cannot be expressed, at least in words, the art that seeks always to convey a sense of something vast and ineffable in even "the meanest flower that blows." This too is "Romantic" in the sense of one, but only one, of Friedrich Schlegel's definitions: "romantisch . . . in jenem weitern

[6] Pt. I, Livre ii, chap. 1; iii, chap. 1, 8, 9.
[7] *Romanticism* (1926), p. 44.

Sinn des Wortes wo es die Tendenz nach einem tiefen unendlichen Sinn bezeichnet.'"[8]

In a similar way, then, could be pointed out the later separate fortunes, vicissitudes and alliances of each one of the ideas that constituted the particular combination, in the minds of the original avowed Romanticists, of which I have attempted to indicate summarily the process of formation. But let it not be supposed that this combination contained *all* the new or peculiarly potent ideas of the 1790s. It includes only a group of them which were, at that time, especially associated with the *word* "Romantic." There were others, equally important, which sprang from other sources and developed in other ways—though often absorbed by the same minds and in that sense combined with the former. In the total pattern, these, too, with their relations to the others, would have to be incorporated. But that is too large an enterprise to be attempted here.

II

I suppose, however, that most of the learned company I am addressing are primarily interested in political and social history; but most of the slight illustrations hitherto given of the application of the method of the historian of ideas to the study of the Romantic period have not been obviously pertinent to political or social history. They have had to do with seemingly non-political notions, belonging initially to the fields of literary criticism, aesthetics, or quasi-aesthetic valuations, or religion, or metaphysics. The reason for this lies in a fact which the political historian needs to bear in mind—namely, that most of the new ideas of the 1780s and 1790s *were* originally aesthetic or religious or metaphysical ideas. But they are not on that account less pertinent to political history. For they were the sort of ideas that, when accepted and developed, could modify men's general ways of thinking profoundly, and because profoundly, widely—in many diverse fields, including the political. And if one were to consider the "meaning," in the sense of the historic significance, of—not "Romanticism," but certain ideas of the Romantic period—from the point of view of 1940, their political consequences may well be regarded as the most significant. For a particular group of these ideas, continuously at work on the minds of the educated and reading public for fifteen decades, have produced in our own time a sort of culminating joint-effect, which is

[8] *Gespräch über die Poesie,* 1800.

at least an essential and conspicuous part of the monstrous scene presented by Germany and by Europe today. That the revolutionary—or counter-revolutionary—political events of the past twenty years would not have occurred but for these earlier alterations in fashions of thought, it would be hazardous to maintain. For most of these events are merely new instances of familiar types of historical phenomena which seem to repeat themselves in ages or among peoples whose ruling ideologies are extremely dissimilar. The rise of dictatorships, for example, is an old story. It is, doubtless, possible only under certain conditions; but no uniform underlying general ideas seem to be among those conditions. A political phenomenon which, even in our own time, appears almost simultaneously in, e.g., Germany, Italy, Russia and Spain—countries whose recent intellectual history has certainly been very different —can hardly be explicable as due to the prior prevalence among their peoples of identical fashions of thought. Equally old is the lust of conquest and the emergence of military conquerors on the grand scale—though we had fondly and foolishly supposed the day for such things to be over. I am, therefore, far from suggesting that the rise of the dictatorships and the return of an era of wars of territorial aggrandizement in Europe have their sufficient condition in the changes in ideas which marked the Romantic period; and I recognize that there is room for question whether those changes were even among the necessary conditions for the present recrudescence of those ancient evils. Nevertheless, it is certain— and notorious—that all these contemporary revolutions have had distinctive ideologies—i.e., idea-complexes—associated with them, and that their leaders—some of whom are past masters of practical political psychology—seem to regard the inculcation of these ideologies as indispensable to the success of their revolutionary enterprises and the permanence of the "new orders" they wish to establish. The ideologies may be, in great part they indubitably are, only "rationalizations" of the ambitions, or delusions of grandeur, of the leaders or of the passions of their followers; but even so, the rationalizations are found necessary, before those ambitions are converted into deeds or those latent passions into mass-action. A Hitler or a Mussolini is not more sedulous in the strengthening of his armaments than in the propagating of his ideas—the ideas which, on the one hand, serve his purpose, but on the other, can appeal to the minds of his followers because those minds have already been "conditioned" for their reception.

Now, out of the many "new ideas of the 1780s and 1790s," there were three which—though at the outset they were not political at all in their reference—were destined to be transferred to the domain of political thought and sentiment; to which the German—and in less degree the general European—mind was increasingly conditioned by a series of influential nineteenth-century writers; and the *fusion or combination* of which, I suggest, has been a factor in the production of the state of mind upon which the totalitarian ideologies depend for their appeal.   These three are by no means the only ones of which the same might be said; but they are, I incline to think, the most fundamental and most important, though the estimate is certainly debatable.   They consist in a sort of apotheosis of conceptions associated with three words; the German words are for the present purpose the most appropriate: *das Ganze, Streben,* and *Eigentümlichkeit.*   If terms ending in *-ism* must be had to designate these ideas, they may be called holism or organicism, voluntarism or "dynamism," and diversitarianism.

1. The first—which is now familiar enough—was a relatively new idea about the relation of the individual to the whole—the idea of organism, in its logical or metaphysical sense.   The political liberalism of the seventeenth and eighteenth centuries had, it need hardly be recalled, usually conceived the individual as primary. This is the essence of the doctrine of natural rights; it is not really less characteristic of the presuppositions of political utilitarianism. The reality with which politics was concerned was the human person, conceived as a possessor of intrinsic rights, or as a claimant for the means of happiness.   He had, admittedly, relations to other individuals, and—at least in the natural rights theory—moral obligations towards them.   But the relations and obligations were *between* individuals as such; and though the interests or instincts of the individuals required them to combine in organized aggregates, such as the State, these were secondary, derivative, and merely instrumental to the assurance and adjustment of individual rights or the satisfaction of individual needs and desires.   The whole was just the aggregate of its parts, and apart from them was nothing; and the dominant conception of scientific method, like the dominant political theory, proceeded, in its investigation of any complex thing, by an "analysis" or "resolution" of it into its ultimate component parts.   To understand *it,* you had but to take it to pieces, to know the parts and *their* characteristics and the laws

of their action, and how many of them there were in the given complex—and your problem was solved. But a strain of German thought in the late eighteenth century—which had had earlier foreshadowings in Shaftesbury, Stahl, and others—tended increasingly towards a reversal of this whole way of thinking—towards giving primacy and a mystical sanctity to what was called "the Idea of the Whole," as defined by Kant in the *Critique of Judgment:* "An Idea [of something] which must determine *a priori* all that is contained *in* it"—of a "product of nature" in which, "just as every part of it exists *through* all the others, so every part is also thought as existing *for* all the others and for the sake of the Whole (*um . . . des Ganzen willen*), that is, as a tool or organ (*Werkzeug, Organ*)."[9] Kant was talking about a natural organism—a tree; but, as is well known, the conception was speedily carried over into the provinces of metaphysics, of morals and, especially, of politics. The "Idea of the Whole" came increasingly to mean, in its practical application, the idea of the political State.   The details of this process are exceedingly various and complex, and cannot be analyzed here; happily, Professor Anderson and Professor Briefs are to deal with some important parts of the story in their papers. But the general result of the repetition of this conception, by many greater and lesser teachers, in diverse forms and with or without qualifications, was the conditioning of the mind of individuals to think of themselves (to a degree perhaps unprecedented in history) as *mere* members of *das Ganze,* as "tools or organs" of the national State—as existing *um des Ganzen willen*—and as finding the interest and value of their existence in the realization of the ends of the State, which are by no means merely the summation of the private ends even of all of its members.   Without a long prior conditioning, then, to this idea, among others, the totalitarian ideology would not, I suggest, have the potency that it has, either in Germany or Italy.

The distinguished president of the American Association for the Advancement of Science, Professor Cannon, in his recent presidential address, has argued that the political analogue of the biological organism is democracy, and that "the human body is the best democracy." I venture to disagree, but there is no time to state the distinctions which would justify this disagreement. But in any case the historical effects of a conception, especially of one

[9] *Kr. d. Urteilskraft,* Pt. II, 65; A288.

of the great metaphors which play so large a part in the history of ideas, are not necessarily, or, perhaps, normally identical with its logical implications; and it will, I think, be generally agreed by historians that the vogue of the organismic conception in the nineteenth century has *not* made for what is commonly understood by democracy.

2. But the practical tendency of this idea is profoundly modified by its fusion with another idea of the 1790s. This is the assumption of the primacy, in reality and in value, of process, striving, cumulative becoming, over any static consummation—the dislike of finality, *das Abgeschlossene,* and in particular, the peculiar sensibility to the pathos of struggle, which is, by necessary implication, a struggle *against* something or somebody, some *Anstoss* or antagonist. *Streben,* as everyone knows, was one of the most sacred words of the German Romantics—and it was necessarily, for them, a *Streben ins Unendliche,* a striving without a terminus; and in spite of the various other senses and applications which this formula could and did receive, its vogue tended in the main towards that apotheosis of "the Will" which, astonishingly combined in Schopenhauer with its polar opposite, a Vedantist and Buddhistic quietism and otherworldliness, found its natural culmination in Nietzsche's gospel of the *Wille zur Macht,* that "Dionysian philosophy" of which "the decisive feature," as he writes in *Ecce Homo,* is "the yea-saying to contradiction and war, the postulation of Becoming, together with the radical rejection even of the concept *Being*"—the "tragic" temper which seeks "to be far beyond terror and pity and to be the eternal lust of Becoming itself—that lust which also involves the joy of destruction.'"[10] The notion of *Streben* was originally, and even in Nietzsche largely remained, an ideal for the individual. But it too, naturally enough, has been converted into a political idea; and Nietzsche, as Professor Brinton has shown,[11] has become the chief official philosopher of Nazism—after Hitler. But as a political idea, this second notion has been fused with the first. The individual, as essentially an organ of *das Ganze,* the State, does his striving through the

[10] *The Complete Works of Friedrich Nietzsche,* tr. by A. M. Ludovici: *Ecce Homo,* p. 72. Part of the citation is quoted by Nietzsche himself from *The Twilight of the Idols* (*Götzendämmerung*).

[11] Crane Brinton, "The National Socialists' Use of Nietzsche," JOUR. OF THE HIST. OF IDEAS, I, No. 2.

State, which is the embodiment of the Will to Power. If it is to be effective in this capacity, it must be completely integrated; it can permit no struggles within itself, between its parts—for example, no class-struggle and no party-conflicts. The parts must be strictly regimented, *gleichgeschaltet*, for the service of the whole. But the nation or State itself takes on the rôle of the insatiable Romantic hero—in which its members can, indeed, vicariously share. It must ever strive for expansion, external power, and yet more power, not as a regrettably necessary means to some final rationally satisfying goal, but because continuous self-assertion, transcending of boundaries, triumph over opposition, is its vocation. As the personification of the present German State, Adolf Hitler is Carlyle's "infinite bootblack" endowed with all the power of a great people and a vast military machine. It is true that, somewhere in *Mein Kampf*, Hitler shows, in one passage, some embarrassment at the thought of the finitude of this planet. When the "superior man," *der höchsstehende Mensch*, through struggle has once made himself master of the world, there will be no more opportunity for struggle, but only a tedious reign of universal peace. But Hitler puts the awkward thought from his mind; the evil day is at least a long way off; *also, erst Kampf, und dann kann man sehen was zu machen ist.* Hitler is, in short, a kind of vulgar, political and sanguinary Faust, *der immer strebend sich bemüht* upon the international scene—a Faust, I need hardly add, before his redemption.

3. One of the most revolutionary of the ideas of the 1790s was an assertion of the value of diversity in human opinions, characters, tastes, arts and cultures. This had, it is true, a long prehistory, which cannot be told here;[12] but in the original German Romanticists of that decade it reached a climax and became one of the chief articles of their creed. It was revolutionary because it reversed a presupposition that had been dominant for some two centuries: the presupposition which may be called uniformitarianism. By this term I do not mean the assumption that individuals and peoples are *in fact* identical in their characters and beliefs and ways of living. It was evident—to the reformer of the Enlightenment all too painfully evident—that they are not. Uniformitarianism is the assumption that what is most important, most valuable,

12 I have dealt with it more fully and tried to show its sources in *The Great Chain of Being;* see especially Lecture X.

normal, in men consists in what is the same in all men, and that
their actual diversities in opinion and cultures and forms of government are evidences of departures from the norm of human life.
And this was a natural and seemed an obvious inference from a
very common assumption concerning the nature of truth. To any
given question that can be asked or any practical problem with
which men are confronted, it seemed evident that there can be only
one true or correct answer. There is one right generic way of per-
forming any kind of task—of writing a play or an epic, painting a
landscape, building a house, organizing and governing a society—
and (this was a postulate usually tacitly or explicitly associated
with the uniformitarian preconception) any man having normal
human faculties is capable of discovering the one true view or the
one correct rule of practice, for himself, by the unaided—provided
it be also the uncorrupted—light of nature. For there is, in that
admittedly very mixed compound called human nature, a faculty,
the *gemeine Menschenverstand,* which is the organ for apprehending or revealing the one true answer to any question to which an
answer is needful for man, the universal and invariant objective
truth. What is rational is uniform; and what is not uniform is
eo ipso not rational; and diversity is therefore the easily recognizable mark of error. In a sense, every man has a latent potential
knowledge of such truth, by virtue of his possession of *le bon sens
ou raison* which, as Descartes declared, is *la chose du monde la
mieux partagée* and is *naturellement égale en tous les hommes*—
and therefore has nothing to do with time or place or race. But in
most of mankind it has been buried under a vast mass of accumulated error—that is to say, of differences in beliefs, valuations,
laws, practices. These errors were the product of a long, increasing series of unhappy accidents—*i.e.,* of lapses from rationality on
the part of the multitude, misled by a few men actuated by the love
of power—priests and kings. The vehicles of the transmission of
these errors—what were called *les préjugés*—from generation to
generation, were tradition, custom, (whose tyranny was so bitterly
denounced by Montaigne and Charron and many lesser writers),
and above all, the early education of children. The task of the
lover of humanity, the reformer, the educator, therefore, was less
to discover and show to men new truths, than to purge their minds
of the historic accretion of non-rational prejudices, and thus to
allow the pure, clear light of nature within them to shine forth of

itself. For, among all the extremely numerous senses of the sacred word "nature," in its normative use, from the sixteenth to the late eighteenth century, the most common and potent was that in which it summed up this whole uniformitarian complex of ideas.

But to the Romantics of the 1790s (following Herder) it appeared that the diversity of men and ages and peoples, in their ways of thinking and feeling and expressing themselves in arts and institutions, is "natural" and necessary, and also supremely desirable and right. And from this pregnant premise they drew two opposite consequences, of which the second was to prevail over the first. The assumption made initially for tolerance and catholicity. All the historic manifestations of human nature are good, and the cultivated man will train himself to appreciate and enjoy them all. But the other inference was that it is the first duty of an individual or a people to cherish and intensify the differentness, idiosyncrasy, *Eigentümlichkeit,* with which nature has endowed him or it. This, like the ideal of *Streben,* was, at the outset, applied largely to the individual, especially to the artist; but it also tended to be applied, and in the end to be chiefly applied, to the nation or race. So applied, it eventually destroyed, in many minds, the conception of a universal standard of human conduct and the sense of a common human destiny. It gave respectability to what the eighteenth century had meant by *les préjugés.* It seemed to lend a new philosophic sanction to that unreflective or animal nationalism which had long been a potent factor in European politics, but which, in the *Aufklärung,* had appeared to be on the wane among enlightened men. It tended to substitute for the piety towards humanity as such an exclusive piety towards one's own folk and its peculiarities; the very word "humanity," beloved by the earlier liberals, began to be *démodé,* and it became, as is well known, almost a commonplace in the Romantic period to say that there are no "men" but only Frenchmen, Germans, Englishmen, *et al.* Finally, when combined with that "permanent affective element of human nature," the collective, mutually re-enforcing *amour-propre* of the group, it was easily transformed into a conviction of the superiority of what is distinctive of one's own people —its "blood," its *Volksgeist,* traditions, *mores* and institutions— and of its right to dominate all lesser breeds.

Of these three among the ideas of the 1790s, any one, by itself, might have worked out to historic issues quite different from those that actually resulted—and, in fact, when not combined with the others, did so. For example, if the first had not been combined with the third, the "whole" to which the individual is to subordinate himself and whose ends he is to seek might have been construed as humanity—which is, in fact, the only real social totality —and a tendency towards this interpretation may be seen in Novalis's *Die Christenheit oder Europa;* and the second and third, when taken as ideals for the individual, have always been at variance with the first. But when, and in so far as, these three ideas are (however incongruously) combined, one may discern, I think, an important part (though, assuredly, far from all) of the pattern of ideas behind—or associated with—the fateful political events of our own time: the idea of a national State whose members are but instruments to its own vaster ends; in which, therefore, no internal oppositions or disagreements in individual opinion can be permitted; which, however, is itself dedicated to a perpetual struggle for power and self-enlargement, with no fixed goal or terminus, and is animated by an intense and obsessing sense of the differentness of its own folk, of their duty of *keeping* different and uncorrupted by any alien elements, and by a conviction of the immeasurable value of their supposedly unique characteristics and culture. A host of other factors and events between the 1790s and the present, of which nothing has been said here, have, of course, contributed to this outcome; I have merely attempted to suggest, in a deplorably but unavoidably sketchy fashion, that there is a certain specific historical connection between the intellectual revolution of the Romantic period and the tragic spectacle of Europe in 1940.

Johns Hopkins University

XXII

THE MEANINGS OF "INDIVIDUALISM"

BY STEVEN LUKES

We shall begin with the fact that the same word, or the same concept in most cases, means very different things when used by differently situated persons.[1]

"The term 'individualism'," wrote Max Weber, "embraces the utmost heterogeneity of meanings," adding that "a thorough, historically-oriented conceptual analysis would at the present time be of the highest value to scholarship."[2] His words remain true. "Individualism" is still used in a great many ways, in many different contexts and with an exceptional lack of precision. Moreover, it has played a major role in the history of ideas, and of ideologies, in modern Europe and America. The present study seeks to contribute to the analysis Weber desired. But clearly, what is still needed is to carry the analytical task further: to isolate the various distinct unit-ideas (and intellectual traditions) which the word has conflated—unit-ideas whose logical and conceptual relations to one another are by no means clear.[3]

Like "socialism" and "communism," "individualism" is a nineteenth-century expression. In seeking to identify its various distinct traditions of use, I shall concentrate on its nineteenth-century history, for this is what chiefly determined its twentieth-century meanings. My main purpose is to indicate both the variety and the directions of the main paths traced during the term's rich semantic history. The interest of such an account is, however, neither merely semantic nor merely historical. The meanings of words generally incapsulate ideas, even theories. Accordingly, where semantic divergences systematically tend to follow social and cultural (in this case national) lines, to explain those divergences becomes a challenging problem in the sociology of knowledge.

(i) *France.* The first uses of the term, in its French form "*individualisme*," grew out of the general European reaction to the French Revolution and to its alleged source, the thought of the Enlightenment.[4] Conservative thought in the early nineteenth century was virtually unanimous in condemning the appeal to the reason,

[1]K. Mannheim, *Ideology and Utopia* (London, 1960), 245. In what follows I am particularly indebted to the studies by Koebner, Swart, and Arieli, cited *infra.*

[2]M. Weber, *The Protestant Ethic and the Spirit of Capitalism,* (1904-5), tr. T. Parsons (London, 1930), 222 (amended translation: S. L.).

[3]Cf. my article on "Individualism" in *Dictionary of the History of Ideas* (New York, 1972)

[4]H. Peyre, "The Influence of Eighteenth Century Ideas on the French Revolution," *JHI*, X (1949), 63–87; W. F. Church (ed.), *The Influence of the Enlightenment on the French Revolution* (Boston, 1964).

interests, and rights of the individual; as Burke had said: "Individuals pass like shadows; but the commonwealth is fixed and stable."[5] The Revolution was proof that ideas exalting the individual imperilled the stability of the commonwealth, dissolving it into "an unsocial, uncivil, unconnected chaos of elementary principles."[6] Conservative thinkers, above all in France and Germany, shared Burke's scorn for the individual's "private stock of reason" and his fear lest "the commonwealth itself would, in a few generations, crumble away, be disconnected into the dust and powder of individuality, and at length dispersed to all the winds of heaven," as well as his certainty that "Society requires" that "the inclinations of men should frequently be thwarted, their will controlled, and their passions brought into subjection."[7]

These sentiments were found at their most extreme among the theocratic Catholic reactionaries in France. According to Joseph de Maistre, the social order had been "shattered to its foundations because there was too much liberty in Europe and not enough Religion"; everywhere authority was weakening and there was a frightening growth of "individual opinion [*l'esprit particulier*]."[8] The individual's reason was "of its nature the mortal enemy of all association": its exercise spelt spiritual and civil anarchy. Infallibility was an essential condition of the maintenance of society, and indeed government was "a true religion," with "its dogmas, its mysteries, its priests; to submit it to individual discussion is to destroy it."[9] In the earliest known use of the word, de Maistre spoke in 1820 of "this deep and frightening division of minds, this infinite fragmentation of all doctrines, political protestantism carried to the most absolute individualism."[10]

The theocrats agreed in giving to "society" the same exclusive emphasis that they accused the eighteenth-century *philosophes* of giving to "the individual." Society for de Maistre was God-given and natural, and he wished the individual's mind to lose itself in that of the nation "as a river which flows into the ocean still exists in the mass of the water, but without name and distinct reality"[11]; while for

[5]"Speech on the Economic Reform" (1780), *Works* (London, 1906), II, 357.

[6]*Reflections on the Revolution in France* (1790) (London, 1910), 94.

[7]*Ibid.*, 84, 93, 57. Cf. D. Bagge, *Les Idées Politiques en France sous la Restauration* (Paris, 1952); K. Mannheim, "Conservative Thought," *Essays in Sociology and Social Psychology* (London, 1953).

[8]J. de Maistre, *Du Pape* (1821), bk. III, ch. II, *Oeuvres Complètes* (Lyon, 1884-7), II, 342, 346.

[9]J. de Maistre, *Etude sur la Souveraineté* (1884), bk. I, ch. X, *Oeuvres Complètes*, I, 375-6.   [10]"Extrait d'une Conversation," *Oeuvres Complètes*, XIV, 286.

[11]*Etude sur la Souvenaineté* (1884) bk. I. ch. X, *Oeuvres Complètes*, I, 326.

de Bonald "man only exists for society and society only educates him for itself."[12] The ideas of the *philosophes* were, they thought, not merely false; they were wicked and dangerous. According to Lamennais, they proclaimed the individual as sovereign over himself in the most absolute sense:

His reason—that is his law, his truth, his justice. To seek to impose on him an obligation he has not previously imposed on himself by his own thought and will is to violate the most sacred of his rights .... Hence, no legislation, no power is possible, and the same doctrine which produces anarchy in men's minds further produces an irremediable political anarchy, and overturns the very bases of human society.

Were such principles to prevail, "what could one foresee but troubles, disorders, calamities without end, and universal dissolution?" Man, Lamennais argued, "lives only in society" and "institutions, laws, governments draw all their strength from a certain concourse of thoughts and wills." "What," he asked, "is power without obedience? What is law without duty?" and he answered:

Individualism which destroys the very idea of obedience and of duty, thereby destroying both power and law; and what then remains but a terrifying confusion of interests, passions, and diverse opinions?[13]

It was the disciple of Claude Henri de Saint-Simon,[14] who were the first to use "*individualisme*" systematically, in the mid-1820's.[15] Saint-Simonism shared the ideas of the counter-revolutionary reactionaries—their critique of the Enlightenment's glorification of the individual, their horror of social atomization and anarchy, as well as their desire for an organic, stable, hierarchically organized, harmonious social order. But it applied these ideas in a historically progressive direction: that social order was not to be the ecclesiastical and feudal order of the past, but the industrial order of the future. Indeed, the proselytizing Saint-Simonians systematized their master's ideas into an activist and extremely influential secular religion, an ideological force serving as a kind of Protestant ethic for the expanding capitalism of the Catholic countries in nineteenth-century Europe.

History for the Saint-Simonians was a cycle of "critical" and "organic" periods. The former were "filled with disorder; they destroy former social relations, and everywhere tend towards egoism"; the latter were unified, organized, and stable (the previous instances in

---

[12]L. de Bonald, *Théorie du Pouvoir* (1796), Preface, *Oeuvres* (Paris, 1854), I, 103.

[13]F. de Lamennais, *Des Progrès de la Révolution et de la Guerre contre l'Eglise* (1829), ch. I, *Oeuvres Complètes* (Paris, 1836-7), IX, 17-18.

[14]Cf. my chapter on Saint-Simon in T. Raison (ed.), *Founding Fathers of Social Science* (London, 1969).   [15]Cf. *Le Producteur*, Vols. I-IV, *passim*.

Europe being the ancient polytheistic preclassical society and the Christian Middle Ages). The modern critical period, originating with the Reformation was, the Saint-Simonians believed, the penultimate stage of human progress, heralding a future organic era of "universal association" in which "the organization of the future will be final because only then will society be formed directly for progress." They used *"individualisme"* to refer to the pernicious and "negative" ideas underlying the evils of the modern critical epoch, whose "disorder, atheism, individualism, and egoism" they contrasted with the prospect of "order, religion, association, and devotion." The "philosophers of the eighteenth century"—men such as Helvetius, with his doctrine of "enlightened self-interest," Locke, Reid, Condillac, Kant, and the "atheist d'Holbach, the deist Voltaire, and Rousseau"—all these "defenders of individualism" refused to "go back to a source higher than individual conscience." They "considered the individual as the center" and "preached egoism," providing an ideological justification for the prevailing anarchy, especially in the economic and political spheres. The "doctrine of individualism" with its two "sad deities . . . two creatures of reason—conscience and public opinion" led to "one political result: opposition to any attempt at organization from a center of direction for the moral interests of mankind, to hatred of power."[16]

Partly perhaps because of the extraordinarily pervasive influence of Saint-Simonian ideas, *"individualisme"* came to be very widely used in the nineteenth century. In France, it usually carried, and indeed still carries, a pejorative connotation, a strong suggestion that to concentrate on the individual is to harm the superior interests of society. The latest edition of the Dictionary of the *Académie Française*[17] defines it simply as "subordination of the general interest to the individual's interest," and one recent writer, noting its naturally pejorative sense, has remarked on its "tinge of *'ubris,'* of *'démesuré'* " which "does not exist in English,"[18] while another observes that in France "until the present day the term individualism has retained much of its former, unfavorable connotations."[19] It is true that there was a group of French revolutionary republican *Carbonari* in the 1820's who proudly called themselves the "Société d'Individualistes," and that various individual thinkers adopted the label, among them Proudhon—though

---

[16]*The Doctrine of Saint-Simon: An Exposition, First Year 1828-9* (1830) tr. G. Iggers (Boston, 1958), 28, 70, 247, 178-80, 182.   [17]Paris, 1932-5.

[18]L. Moulin, "On the Evolution of the Meaning of the Word 'Individualism'," *International Social Science Bulletin*, VII (1955), 185.

[19]K. W. Swart, " 'Individualism' in the Mid-Nineteenth Century (1826-60)," *JHI*, XXIII (1962), 84.

even Proudhon saw society as "a *sui generis* being" and argued that "outside the group there are only abstractions and phantoms."[20] From the mid-nineteenth century, liberal Protestants and eventually a few *laissez-faire* liberals started to call themselves individualists and one wrote a comprehensive history of "economic and social individualism," incorporating a variety of French thinkers[21]—yet the tone was always one of defensive paradox. Few have welcomed the epithet, and many, from Balzac onwards,[22] stressed the opposition between *"individualisme,"* implying anarchy and social atomization, and *"individualité,"* implying personal independence and self-realization. For the Swiss theologian Alexandre Vinet, these were "two sworn enemies; the first an obstacle and negation of any society; the latter a principle to which society owes all its savor, life and reality." The "progress of individualism" meant "the relaxation of social unity because of the increasingly pronounced predominance of egoism," while the "gradual extinction of individuality" meant "the increasingly strong inclination for minds ... to surrender themselves to what is known as public opinion or the spirit of the age."[23] In general, *"individualisme"* in French thought points to the sources of social dissolution, though there have been wide divergences concerning the nature of those sources and of the social order they are held to threaten, as well as in the historical frameworks within which they are conceptualized.

For some, individualism resides in dangerous ideas, for others it is social or economic anarchy, a lack of the requisite institutions and norms, for yet others it is the prevalence of self-interested attitudes among individuals. For men of the right, from de Maistre to Charles Maurras, it is all that undermines a traditional, hierarchical social order. Thus Louis Veuillot, the militant Catholic propagandist, wrote in 1843 that "France has need of religion" which would bring "harmony, union, patriotism, confidence, morality ...":

The evil which plagues France is not unknown; everyone agrees in giving it the same name: *individualism.*

It is not difficult to see that a country where individualism reigns is no longer in the normal conditions of society, since society is the union of minds and interests, and individualism is division carried to the infinite degree.

[20]P. J. Proudhon, *Lettres sur la Philosophie du Progrès* (1853), Letter I, pts V and IV, *Oeuvres Complètes,* new ed. (Paris, 1868–76), XX, 39–40, 36.

[21]A. Schatz, *L'Individualisme Economique et Sociale* (Paris, 1907). *Cf.* H.-L. Follin, "Quelle est la Véritable Définition de L'Individualisme," *Journal des Economistes* (April 15, 1899).

[22]Swart, *art. cit.,* 84.

[23]Quoted *ibid.,* 84–5. *Cf.* Arieli, *Individualism and Nationalism in American Ideology* (Cambridge, Mass., 1964), ch. X.

All for each, each for all, that is society; each for himself, and thus each against all, that is individualism.[24]

Similarly, during the Dreyfus Affair, Ferdinand Brunetière, the strongly *anti-Dreyfusard* literary historian, defended the army and the social order, which he saw as threatened by "individualism" and "anarchy," and poured scorn on those intellectuals who had presumed to doubt the justice of Dreyfus's trial. Individualism, he wrote, was

the great sickness of the present time.... Each of us has confidence only in himself, sets himself up as the sovereign judge of everything ... when intellectualism and individualism reach this degree of self-infatuation, one must expect them to be or become nothing other than *anarchy*....[25]

Among socialists, individualism has typically been contrasted with an ideal, cooperative social order, variously described as "association," "harmony," "socialism," and "communism"; the term here refers to the economic doctrine of *laissez-faire* and to the anarchy, social atomization, and exploitation produced by industrial capitalism. Pierre Leroux, aiming at a new humanitarian and libertarian socialism, used it to mean the principle, proclaimed by political economy, of "everyone for himself, and ... all for riches, nothing for the poor," which atomized society and made men into "rapacious wolves"[26]; "society," he maintained, "is entering a new era in which the general tendency of the laws will no longer have individualism as its end, but association."[27] For Constantin Pecqueur, "the remedy lies in association precisely because the abuse springs from individualism"[28] and the utopian Etienne Cabet wrote that

Two great systems have divided and polarized Humanity ever since the beginning of the world: that of Individualism (or egoism, or personal interest), and that of Communism (or association, or the general interest, or the public interest).[29]

Likewise, the conspiratorial revolutionary Auguste Blanqui asserted that "Communism is the protector of the individual, individualism his extermination."[30]

Other socialists used the term in more complex ways. Louis Blanc saw individualism as a major cultural principle, encompassing Protes-

[24]L. Veuillot, "Lettre à M. Villemain" (August, 1843), *Mélanges Religieux, Historiques, Politiques et Littéraires* (1842–56) (Paris, 1856–60), 1ère série, I, 132–3.

[25]F. Brunetière, "Après le Procès," *Revue des Deux Mondes*, LXVII (15 March 1898), 445. *Cf.* my article: "Durkheim's 'Individualism and the Intellectuals'," *Political Studies*, XVII (1969), 14–19.   [26](1832 and 1833), quoted in Arieli, *op. cit.*, 233.

[27](1841), quoted in J. Dubois, *Le Vocabulaire Politique et Sociale en France de 1869 à 1872* (Paris, 1962), 220.

[28](1840) quoted *ibid.*, 322.   [29](1845) quoted *ibid.*   [30](1869) quoted *ibid.*, 267.

tantism, the Bourgeoisie, and the Enlightenment, bringing a historically necessary, though false and incomplete, freedom. Its progressive
aspect was a new self-assertion, a new independence of traditional
structures and rejection of Authority in the religious, economic, and
intellectual spheres; but it needed to be transcended and completed,
pointing towards a future age of socialist Fraternity. In Blanc's own
words:

Three great principles divide the world and history: Authority, Individualism, and Fraternity.

The principle of individualism is that which, taking man out of society,
makes him sole judge of what surrounds him and of himself, gives him a
heightened sense of his rights without showing him his duties, abandons
him to his own powers, and, for the whole of government, proclaims *laisser-
faire*.

Individualism, inaugurated by Luther, has developed with an irresis-
tible force, and, dissociated from the religious factor ... it governs
the present; it is the spiritual principle of things.

... individualism is important in having achieved a vast progress. To
provide breathing-space and scope to human thought repressed for so long,
to intoxicate it with pride and audacity; to submit to the judgment of every
mind the totality of traditions, centuries, their achievements, their beliefs; to place man in an isolation full of anxieties, full of perils, but sometimes also full of majesty, and to enable him to resolve personally, in the
midst of an immense struggle, in the uproar of a universal debate, the problem of his happiness and his destiny ...—this is by no means an achievement without grandeur, and it is the achievement of individualism. One
must therefore speak of it with respect and as a necessary transition.[31]

Again, the disciples of Charles Fourier denied any basic opposition between individualism and socialism,[32] while at the end of the century,
Jean Jaurès argued that "socialism is the logical completion of individualism,"[33] a formula echoed by Emile Durkheim, who saw a kind
of centralized guild socialism as a means of "completing, extending,
and organizing individualism."[34] For all these socialist thinkers,
individualism signified the autonomy, freedom, and sacredness of the
individual—values which had hitherto taken a negative, oppressive,
and anarchic form but could henceforth only be preserved within a
cooperative and rationally-organized social order.

[31]From his *Histoire de la Révolution Française* (1846), quoted in R. Koebner, "Zur
Begriffbildung der Kulturgeschichte: II: Zur Geschichte des Begriffs 'Individualismus'
(Jacob Burckhardt, Wilhelm von Humboldt und die französische Soziologie)," *Histor-
ische Zeitschrift*, CXLIX (1934), 269.   [32]Swart, *art. cit.*, 85.
[33]J. Jaurès, "Socialisme et Liberté," *Revue de Paris*, XXIII (Dec. 1898), 499.
[34]E. Durkheim, "Individualism and the Intellectuals" (1898), tr. S. and J. Lukes,
Political Studies, XVII (1969), 29. *Cf.* Lukes, "Durkheim's 'Individualism and the
Intellectuals'," *loc. cit.*

French liberals also spoke of individualism, but they characteristically saw it as a threat to a pluralist social order, with minimum
state intervention and maximum political liberty. Benjamin Constant,
perhaps the most eloquent exponent of classical liberalism, was clearly
groping for the word when he observed that "when all are isolated by
egoism, there is nothing but dust, and at the advent of a storm, nothing but mire."[35] It was, however, that aristocratic observer of early
nineteenth-century America, Alexis de Tocqueville, who developed
its most distinctive and influential liberal meaning in France. For
Tocqueville, individualism was the natural product of democracy
("Individualism is of democratic origin and threatens to develop
insofar as conditions are equalized"), involving the apathetic withdrawal of individuals from public life into a private sphere and their
isolation from one another, with a consequent weakening of social
bonds. Such a development, Tocqueville thought, offered dangerous
scope for the unchecked growth of the political power of the state.

More specifically, "individualism"—a "recent expression to which
a new idea has given birth"—was "a deliberate and peaceful sentiment which disposes each citizen to isolate himself from the mass of
his fellows and to draw apart with his family and friends," abandoning "the wider society to itself." At first, it "saps only the virtues of
public life; but, in the long run, it attacks and destroys all others and
is eventually absorbed into pure egoism." In contrast to aristocratic
society, in which men were "linked closely to something beyond them
and are often disposed to forget themselves" and which "formed of
all the citizens a long chain reaching from the peasant to the king,"
democracy "breaks the chain and sets each link apart," and "the
bond of human affections extends and relaxes." With increasing social mobility, the continuity of the generations is destroyed; as classes
become fused, "their members become indifferent and as if strangers
to one another"; and as individuals become increasingly self-sufficient,
"they become accustomed to considering themselves always in isolation, they freely imagine that their destiny is entirely in their own
hands." Democracy, Tocqueville concluded, "not only makes each
man forget his forefathers, but it conceals from him his descendants
and separates him from his contemporaries; it ceaselessly throws
him back on himself alone and threatens finally to confine him entirely
in the solitude of his own heart."[36]

Individualism for Tocqueville thus sprang from the lack of intermediary groups to provide a framework for the individual and protec-

[35]Quoted in H. Marion, "Individualisme," *La Grande Encyclopédie* (Paris, n.d.),
Vol. XX.

[36]A. de Tocqueville, *De la Démocratie en Amérique* (1835) bk. II, pt. II, ch. II,
Oeuvres Complètes, ed. J. P. Mayer (Paris, 1951-), I, II, 104–6.

tion against the State. (As for the Americans, they only avoided its destructive consequences because of their free institutions and active citizenship: they conquered individualism with liberty.) It was, moreover, a peculiarly modern evil: "Our fathers," Tocqueville wrote, "did not have the word 'individualism,' which we have coined for our own use, because in their time there was indeed no individual who did not belong to a group and who could be considered as absolutely alone."[37]

No less diverse than these conceptions of the sources and the dangers of individualism have been the historical frameworks within which French thinkers have placed it. It is variously traced to the Reformation, the Renaissance, the Enlightenment, the Revolution, to the decline of the aristocracy or the Church or traditional religion, to the Industrial Revolution, to the growth of capitalism or democracy, but, as we have seen, there is wide agreement in seeing it as an evil and a threat to social cohesion. Perhaps the role of *"individualisme"* in French thought is partly due to the very success of "individualist" legislation at the time of the Revolution,[38] the elimination of intermediary groups and bodies in the society, and the ensuing political and administrative centralization of the country. The basis for this had been laid, as Tocqueville observed, in the municipal and fiscal policies of the French Kings in the seventeenth and eighteenth centuries, which had systematically prevented the growth of spontaneous, organized activities and informal groupings.[39] One can even reasonably postulate that the lack of such activities and groupings is a basic and distinctive French cultural trait.[40]

However that may be, the mainstream of French thought, above all in the nineteenth century, has expressed by *"individualisme"* what Durkheim identified by the twin concepts of "anomie" and "egoism"[41] —the social, moral, and political isolation of individuals, their dissociation from social purposes and social regulation, the breakdown of social solidarity. General de Gaulle was using it in its paradigm French sense when, in his New Year's broadcast to the nation on 31 December 1968, recalling the *Evènements* of May, he observed:

At the same time, it is necessary that we surmount the moral malaise which—above all among us by reason of our individualism—is inherent in modern mechanical and materialist civilization. Otherwise, the fanatics of destruction, the doctrinaires of negation, the specialists in demagogy, will once more have a good opportunity to exploit bitterness in order to provok: agita-

[37]*L'Ancien Régime et la Révolution* (1856), bk. II, ch. IX, *ibid.*, II, 1, p. 158.

[38]R. R. Palmer, "Man and Citizen: Applications of Individualism in the French Revolution," *Essays in Political Theory* (Ithaca, N.Y., 1948).

[39]*L'Ancien Régime et la Révolution*, bk. II, chs. 3, 6, 9, 12.

[40]M. Crozier, *The Bureaucratic Phenomenon* (London, 1964), esp. ch. 8.

[41]*Suicide* (1897), trans. J. A. Spaulding and G. Simpson (Glencoe, Ill., 1951).

tion, while their sterility, which they have the derisory insolence to call revolution, can lead to nothing else than the dissolution of everything into nothingness, or else to the loss of everything under the grinding oppression of totalitarianism.[42]

Despite wide divergences in views about the causes of social dissolution and the nature of an acceptable or desirable social order, the underlying perspective conveyed by the term is unmistakable.

(ii) *Germany.* This characteristically French meaning was certainly subject to cultural diffusion beyond the borders of France. It was, for instance, adopted by Friedrich List, precursor of the German Historical School of economics and advocate of economic nationalism, who used it in the sense developed by the Saint-Simonians and the socialists. List's major work, *The National System of Political Economy*,[43] written in Paris, stressed the organic nature of society and the economy, and the historical and national framework of economic activity; and it attacked the classical economists for abstracting economic life from its social context. Thus List accused classical economics, which supported free trade and *laissez-faire,* of "*Kosmopolitismus,*" "*Materialismus,*" "*Partikularismus,*" and, above all, of "*Individualismus*"—sacrificing the welfare of the national community to the individual acquisition of wealth.

There is, however, quite distinct from this French use of the term, another use whose characteristic reference is German. This is the Romantic idea of "individuality" (*Individualität*), the notion of individual uniqueness, originality, self-realization—what the Romantics called "*Eigentümlichkeit*"—in contrast to the rational, universal, and uniform standards of the Enlightenment, which they saw as "quantitative," "abstract," and therefore sterile. The Romantics themselves did not use the term "*Individualismus,*" but it came to be used in this sense from the 1840's when a German liberal, Karl Brüggemann, contrasted with its negative French meaning, as found in List, that of a desirable and characteristically German "infinite" and "whole-souled" individualism, signifying "the infinite self-confidence of the individual aiming to be personally free in morals and in truth."[44]

Thereafter, the term soon became, in this, chiefly German, use, virtually synonymous with the idea of individuality, which had originated in the writings of Wilhelm von Humboldt, Novalis, Friedrich Schlegel, and Friedrich Schleiermacher. Thus Georg Simmel wrote of the "new individualism" which he opposed to "eighteenth-century individualism" with its "notion of atomized and basically undif-

---

[42]*Le Monde,* 2 Jan. 1969.   [43](1841) tr. (London, 1928).
[44]K. H. Brüggemann, *Dr. Lists nationales System der politischen Ökonomie* (Berlin, 1842) quoted in Koebner, *art. cit.,* 282.

ferentiated individuals"; the new, German, individualism was "the individualism of difference, with the deepening of individuality to the point of the individual's incomparability, to which he is 'called' both in his nature and in his achievement." The individual became "this specific, irreplaceable, given individual" and was "*called* or destined to realize his own incomparable image." The "new individualism," Simmel wrote, "might be called qualitative, in contrast with the quantitative individualism of the eighteenth century. Or it might be labeled the individualism of uniqueness *(Einzigkeit)* as against that of singleness *(Einzelheit)*. At any rate, Romanticism was perhaps the broadest channel through which it reached the consciousness of the nineteenth century. Goethe had created its artistic, and Schleiermacher its metaphysical basis: Romanticism supplied its sentimental experiential foundation."[45]

The German idea of individuality has had a remarkable history. Having begun as a cult of individual genius and originality, especially as applied to the artist, stressing the conflict between individual and society and the supreme value of subjectivity, solitude, and introspection, it developed along various lines. In one direction, it led to an uninhibited quest for eccentricity and to the purest egoism and social nihilism. This development found perhaps its most extreme expression in the thought of Max Stirner, whose "individualism" amounted to an amoral and anti-intellectualistic vision of freely cooperating and self-assertive egoists. For Stirner,   ·

I, the egoist, have not at heart the welfare of this "human society." I sacrifice nothing to it. I only utilize it: but to be able to utilize it completely I must transform it rather into my property and my creature—i.e., I must annihilate it and form in its place the Union of Egoists.[46]

The main development, however, of the idea of individuality was in the direction of a characteristically German *Weltanschauung,* or cosmology, a total view of the (natural and social) world, fundamentally in conflict with the essentially humanist and rationalist thought typical of the rest of Western civilization. In a justly famous essay, Ernst Troeltsch contrasted the two systems of thought, the "west-European" and the German: on the one side, "an eternal, rational, and

---

[45]G. Simmel, "Individual and Society in Eighteenth- and Nineteenth-Century Views of Life: an Example of Philosophical Sociology" (1917) tr. in *The Sociology of Georg Simmel*, tr. and ed. K. H. Wolff (Glencoe, Ill., 1950), 78-83. *Cf.* L. Furst, *Romanticism in Perspective* (London, 1969), pt. I: "Individualism."

[46]M. Stirner, *The Ego and its Own: The Case of the Individual against Authority* (1844) tr. S. T. Byington (London and New York, 1907), quoted in G. Woodcock, *Anarchism* (London, 1963), 93. Cf. V. Basch, *L'Individualisme Anarchiste: Max Stirner* (Paris, 1904).

divinely ordained system of Order, embracing both morality and law";
on the other, "individual, living, and perpetually new incarnations of
an historically creative Mind." Thus,

> Those who believe in an eternal and divine Law of Nature, the Equality of
> man, and a sense of Unity pervading mankind, and who find the essence of
> Humanity in these things, cannot but regard the German doctrine as a curious
> mixture of mysticism and brutality. Those who take an opposite view—who
> see in history an ever-moving stream, which throws up unique individual-
> ities as it moves, and is always shaping individual structures on the basis of a
> law which is always new—are bound to consider the west-European world of
> ideas as a world of cold rationalism and equalitarian atomism, a world of
> superficiality and Pharisaism.[47]

Friedrich Meinecke summed up the revolution in thought which
he saw Romanticism as bringing to Western civilization in the following way:

> Out of this deepening individualism of uniqueness, there henceforth arose
> everywhere in Germany, in various different forms, a new and more living
> image of the State, and also a new picture of the world. The whole world now
> appeared to be filled with individuality, each individuality, whether personal
> or supra-personal, governed by its own characteristic principle of life, and
> both Nature and History constituting what Friedrich Schlegel called an "abyss
> of individuality".... Individuality everywhere, the identity of mind and na-
> ture, and through this identity an invisible but strong bond unifying the other-
> wise boundless diversity and abundance of individual phenomena—these were
> the new and powerful ideas which now burst forth in Germany in so many
> different ways.[48]

In particular, the personal "individualism" of the early Romantics
very soon became transformed into an organic and nationalistic theory
of community, each unique and self-sufficient, according to which, as
one recent scholar has said, the individual was "fated to merge with
and become rooted in nature and the Volk" and would thus be "able to
find his self-expression and his individuality."[49] Moreover, individuality was ascribed no longer merely to persons, but to supra-personal
forces, especially the nation or the state. Meinecke paints a vivid
picture of this transformation:

> This new sense for what was individual resembled a fire which was capable of
> consuming, not all at once, but gradually, every sphere of life. At first, it seized

[47]E. Troeltsch, "The Ideas of Natural Law and Humanity in World Politics"
(1922), O. Gierke, *Natural Law and the Theory of Society, 1500-1800,* tr. E. Barker
(Boston, 1957), 204.

[48]F. Meinecke, *Die Idee der Staatsräson* (1924), *Werke* (Munich, 1957–62), I, 425.

[49]G. L. Mosse, *The Crisis of German Ideology* (London, 1966), 15. *Cf.* Mannheim's
attempt to explain the conservative direction taken by Romanticism in Mannheim,
"Conservative Thought," *loc. cit.*

only the flimsiest and most inflammable materials—the subjective life of the individual, the world of art and poetry; but then it went on to consume heavier substances, above all the state.[50]

The same progression from the individuality of the person to that of the nation or state occurred in countless German thinkers of the early nineteenth century—notably, in Fichte, Schelling, Schleiermacher, and even, in a sense, Hegel. The state and society were no longer regarded as rational constructions, the result of contractual arrangements between individuals in the manner of the Enlightenment; they were "super-personal creative forces, which build from time to time out of the material of particular individuals, a spiritual Whole, and on the basis of that Whole proceed from time to time to create the particular political and social institutions which embody and incarnate its significance."[51] As Simmel wrote, the "total organism" of society "shifts, so to speak into a location high above [individuals]" and, accordingly, "this individualism, which restricts freedom to a purely inward sense of the term, easily acquires an antiliberal tendency"; it is "the complete antithesis of eighteenth-century individualism which . . . could not even conceive the idea of a collective as an organism that unifies heterogeneous elements."[52]

While the characteristically French sense of "individualism" is negative, signifying individual isolation and social dissolution, the characteristically German sense is thus positive, signifying individual self-fulfillment and (except among the earliest Romantics) the organic unity of individual and society. The distinction was drawn with particular force by Thomas Mann, in a passage written at the close of the First World War, which argues that German life reconciles the individual and society, freedom and obligation:

It remains the uniqueness of German individualism that it is entirely compatible with ethical socialism, which is called "state socialism" but which is quite distinct from the philosophy of the rights of man and Marxism. For it is only the individualism of the Enlightenment, the liberal individualism of the West, which is incompatible with the social principle.

The German variety, Mann thought, "includes the freedom of the individual." To "reject the individualistic Enlightenment does not amount to a demand for the submergence of the individual in society and the state": the German theory of organic community protected freedom, whereas ideas deriving from the Enlightenment (among which Mann included Marxism) led to Jacobinism, state absolutism, political tyranny. "Organism" was a word that is "true to life," for "an organism is more than the sum of its parts, and that more is its spirit,

---

[50]*Op. cit.*426.   [51]Troeltsch, *loc. cit.*, 210–11.   [52]*Loc. cit.*, 82.

its life."[53] Here one can see that individualism does not, as with the French, endanger social solidarity; it is its supreme realization.

(iii) *Burckhardt.* A striking and influential synthesis of French and German meanings of "individualism" is to be found (appropriately enough) in the work of the Swiss historian, Jacob Burckhardt. A central theme of Burckhardt's *The Civilization of the Renaissance in Italy*[54] was the growth of "individualism." Summing up the "principal features in the Italian character of that time," Burckhardt maintained that its "fundamental vice ... was at the same time a condition of its greatness, namely, excessive individualism."[55] The second part of the work is entitled "The Development of the Individual" and, in general, Burckhardt treated the Italians of the Renaissance as a people "who have emerged from the half-conscious life of the race and become themselves individuals."[56]

Schematically, one can say that Burckhardt's use of "individualism" combines the notion of the aggressive self-assertion of individuals freed from an externally given framework of authority (as found in Louis Blanc) and that of the individual's withdrawal from society into a private existence (as in Tocqueville) with the early Romantic idea, most clearly expressed by Humboldt, of the full and harmonious development of the individual personality, seen as representing humanity and pointing towards its highest cultural development. The Italian of the Renaissance was for Burckhardt "the firstborn among the sons of modern Europe"[57] in virtue of the autonomy of his morality, his cultivation of privacy, and the individuality of his character.

"The individual," Burckhardt wrote,

first inwardly casts off the authority of a State which, as a fact, is in most cases tyrannical and illegitimate, and what he thinks and does is now, rightly or wrongly, called treason. The sight of victorious egotism in others drives him to defend his own right by his own arm.... In face of all objective facts, of laws and restraints of whatever kind, he retains the feeling of his own sovereignty, and in each single instance forms his decision independently, according as honor or interest, passion or calculation, revenge or renunciation, gain the upper hand in his own mind.[58]

As to privacy, Burckhardt wrote of "the different tendencies and manifestations of private life ... thriving in the fullest vigour and variety" and cited "Agnolo Pandolfini (d. 1446), whose work on domestic economy is the first complete programme of a developed private life." "The private man," he argued, "indifferent to politics, and busied partly with serious pursuits, partly with the interests of a *dilettante,*

---

[53]T. Mann, *Betrachtungen eines Unpolitischen* (Berlin, 1918), 267.
[54](1860) tr. S.G.C. Middlemore (London, 1955). *Cf.* Koebner, *art. cit.*
[55]*Ibid.*, 279.   [56]*Ibid.*, 200.   [57]*Ibid.*, 80.   [58]*Ibid.*, 279.

seems to have been first fully formed in these despotisms of the fourteenth century."[59] Finally, he identified the "impulse to the highest individual development" and saw Italy at the close of the thirteenth century as beginning to "swarm with individuality; the ban upon human personality was dissolved; and a thousand figures meet us each in his own special shape and dress." Dante, "through the wealth of individuality which he set forth," was "the most national herald of his time"; much of Burckhardt's book treats of "this unfolding of the treasures of human nature in literature and art." An acute and practised eye could trace

the increase in the number of complete men during the fifteenth century. Whether they had before them as a conscious object the harmonious development of their spiritual and material existence, is hard to say, but several of them attained it, so far as is consistent with the imperfection of all that is earthly.[60]

It is worth adding that for Burckhardt this growth of individualism was, as for so many philosophers of history, no accident but a "historical necessity." Transmitted by Italian culture, and infusing the other nations of Europe, it

has constituted since then the higher atmosphere which they breathe. In itself it is neither good nor bad, but necessary; within it has grown up a modern standard of good and evil—a sense of moral responsibility—which is essentially different from that which was familiar to the Middle Ages.[61]

(iv) *America.* It was in the United States that "individualism" primarily came to celebrate capitalism and liberal democracy. It became a symbolic catchword of immense ideological significance, expressing all that has at various times been implied in the philosophy of natural rights, the belief in free enterprise, and the American Dream. It expressed, in fact, the operative ideals of nineteenth- and early twentieth-century America (and indeed continues to play a major ideological role), advancing a set of universal claims seen as incompatible with the parallel claims of the socialism and communism of the Old World. It referred, not to the sources of social dissolution or the painful transition to a future harmonious social order, nor to the cultivation of uniqueness or the organic community, but rather to the actual or imminent realization of the final stage of human progress in a spontaneously cohesive society of equal individual rights, limited government, *laissez-faire,* natural justice and equal opportunity, and individual freedom, moral development, and dignity. Naturally it carried widely varying connotations in differing contexts and at different times.

---

[59]*Ibid.,* 82–3.   [60]*Ibid.,* 81–4.   [61]*Ibid.,* 279.

It was imported, in the negative French sense, *via* the writings of
various Europeans, among them the socialists, as well as Tocqueville,
List, and the Saint-Simonian Michel Chevalier, whose *Lettres sur
l'Amérique du Nord* (1836) contrasted the anarchic individualism of
the Yankees with the more socially inclined and organizable French.
Already in 1839, an article in the *United States Magazine and Democratic Review* identified it positively with national values and ideals
seen in evolutionary and universal terms. The course of civilization

> is the progress of man from a state of savage individualism to that of an in-
> dividualism more elevated, moral and refined.... The last order of civiliza-
> tion, which is democratic, received its first permanent existence in this coun-
> try.... The peculiar duty of this country has been to exemplify and embody
> a civilization in which the rights, freedom, and mental and moral growth of
> individual men should be made the highest end of all social restrictions and
> laws.[62]

This abrupt change in the evaluative significance of the term is strikingly illustrated in one of the earliest American discussions of Tocqueville's *Democracy in America* by a Transcendentalist writer in the
Boston Quarterly Review. The writer, inaccurately but significantly,
expounded Tocqueville's concept of individualism as expressing "that
strong confidence in self, or reliance upon one's own exertion and resources" and as "the strife of all our citizens for wealth and distinction
of *their own*, and their contempt of reflected honors." "Individualism," he continued, "has its immutable laws ... which ... when allowed to operate without let or hindrance ... must in the end assimilate
the species, and evolve all the glorious phenomena of original and
eternal *order*;—that order which exists in man himself, and alone
vivifies and sustains him."[63]

"Individualism" had, by the end of the Civil War, acquired an important place in the vocabulary of American ideology. Indeed, even
those who criticized American society, from New England Transcendentalists to the Single Taxers and the Populists, often did so in the
name of individualism. The term acquired differing layers of meaning
under the successive influences of New England Puritanism, the Jeffer-
sonian tradition, and natural rights philosophy; Unitarianism, Transcendentalism, and evangelicalism; the need of the North to develop
an ideological defence against the challenge of the South; the immensely popular evolutionary and *laissez-faire* ideas of Herbert
Spencer and the growth of Social Darwinism; and the permanent and

---

[62]"The Course of Civilization," *United States Magazine and Democratic Review,*
6 (1839), 208ff, 211, quoted in Arieli, *op. cit.*, 191–2.

[63]"Catholicism," *Boston Quarterly Review* (1841), 320ff, quoted in Arieli, *op. cit.*,
199.

continuing impetus of alternative, European-born ideologies. The course of this development has been admirably traced in Yehoshua Arieli's book, *Individualism and Nationalism in American Ideology*,[64] which rightly treats the American version of "individualism" as a symbol of national identification. As Arieli concludes,

Individualism supplied the nation with a rationalization of its characteristic attitudes, behaviour patterns and aspirations. It endowed the past, the present and the future with the perspective of unity and progress. It explained the peculiar social and political organization of the nation—unity in spite of heterogeneity—and it pointed towards an ideal of social organization in harmony with American experience. Above all, individualism expressed the universalism and idealism most characteristic of the national consciousness. This concept evolved in contradistinction to socialism, the universal and messianic character of which it shared.[65]

It can, indeed, be argued that the lack of a real socialist tradition in America is in part a function of the very pervasiveness of the ideology of individualism.

Certainly, a perusal of the various American uses of the term reveals a quite distinctive range of connotations. For Emerson, contemplating the failure of Brook Farm, individualism, which he endowed with an exalted moral and religious significance, had "never been tried"[66]; it was the route to perfection—a spontaneous social order of self-determined, self-reliant and fully developed individuals. "The union," he wrote, "is only perfect when all the uniters are isolated. . . . Each man, if he attempts to join himself to others, is on all sides cramped and diminished. . . . The Union must be ideal in actual individualism."[67] Society was tending towards a morally superior voluntary social order, a "free and just commonwealth" in which "property rushes from the idle and imbecile to the industrious, brave and persevering."[68] For the historian John William Draper, writing immediately after the Civil War, in celebration of the social system of the North, its

population was in a state of unceasing activity; there was a corporeal and mental restlessness. Magnificent cities in all directions were arising; the country was intersected with canals, railroads . . . companies for banking, manufacturing, commercial purposes, were often concentrating many millions of capital. There were all kinds of associations . . . churches, hospitals, schools abounded. The foreign commerce at length rivaled that of the most powerful nations of Europe. This wonderful spectacle of social de-

---

[64]See note 23 above.   [65]*Op. cit.*, 345–6.
[66]R. W. Emerson, *Journals* (1846), (Cambridge, Mass., 1909–14), VII, 322–3.
[67]R. W. Emerson, "New England Reformers" (1844), *Complete Writings* (New York, 1929), I, 317–8.   [68]"Wealth" (1860), *ibid.*, 551.

velopment was the result of INDIVIDUALISM; operating in an unbounded theatre of action. Everyone was seeking to do all that he could for himself.[69]

And for Walt Whitman, likewise celebrating the democratic system of the North, it incarnated the progressive force of modern history— "the singleness of man, individualism,"[70] reconciling liberty and social justice.

In the hands of the Social Darwinists, such as William Graham Sumner, "individualism" acquired a harsher and altogether less idealistic significance. Sumner, who maintained that "liberty, inequality, survival of the fittest . . . carries society forward and favors all its best members,"[71] offered a purportedly scientific rationale for a ruthlessly competitive society where the individual "has all his chances left open that he make out of himself all there is in him. This is individualism and atomism."[72] In this context, the influence of Herbert Spencer's doctrines as a justification for unrestrained rivalry in business and unscrupulous dealings in politics was immense; he was widely seen as "the shining light of evolution and individualism."[73] These ideas entered into an evolving ideology of private enterprise and *laissez-faire*, postulating absolute equality of opportunity and the equivalence of public welfare and private accumulation. The word was used in this sense by Andrew Carnegie, and by Henry Clews, author of *The Wall Street Point of View* (1900), who spoke of "that system of Individualism which guards, protects and encourages competition," whose spirit was "the American Spirit—the love of freedom,—of free industry,— free and unfettered opportunity. . . ."[74] It was also used favorably by Theodore Roosevelt, Woodrow Wilson, and William J. Bryan. Despite counter trends to the "Gospel of Wealth" and the "Gospel of Success," the term continued to have wide currency until a temporary eclipse during the Depression and the New Deal. It was in 1928 that Herbert Hoover gave his famous campaign speech on the "American system of rugged individualism"; yet the term regained its resonance, as can be seen by the sales of the writings of the contemporary novelist-philosopher, Ayn Rand, in defence of "reason, individualism, and capitalism."

In short, with regard to the American sense of "individualism," James Bryce was right when he observed that, throughout their history, "individualism, the love of enterprise, and pride in personal

[69] J. W. Draper, *History of the American Civil War*, 3 vols. (New York, 1868–70), I, 207–8.

[70] W. Whitman, *Democratic Vistas* (1871), *Complete Prose Works* (Philadelphia, 1891), II, 67.

[71] Quoted in R. Hofstadter, *Social Darwinism in American Thought* (New York, 1959), 51, *q. v. passim., esp.* ch. 3.

[72] W. G. Sumner, *Earth Hunger and Other Essays* (New Haven, 1913), 127–8.

[73] J. R. Commons quoted in Hofstadter, *op. cit.*, 34.

[74] H. Clews, *Individualism versus Socialism* (New York) 1907, 1–3.

freedom, have been deemed by Americans not only their choicest, but their peculiar and exclusive possession."[75]

(v) *England*. In England, the term has played a smaller role, as an epithet for nonconformity in religion, for the sterling qualities of self-reliant Englishmen, especially among the nineteenth-century middle-classes, and for features common to the various shades of English liberalism. French and German influences can, of course, also be found. Its first use was in Henry Reeve's translation of Tocqueville's *De la Démocratic en Amérique* in 1840. The word was also used pejoratively in the French sense by a great number of thinkers, but especially socialists, to refer to the evils of capitalist competition. Thus, Robert Owen, in specifying his cooperative socialist ideals, argued that to "effect these changes there must be . . . a new organisation of society, on the principle of *attractive union*, instead of *repulsive individualism* . . . ,"[76] while John Stuart Mill (who was much influenced by the Saint-Simonians) asserted that "the moral objection to competition, as arming one human being against another, making the good of each depend upon evil to others, making all who have anything to gain or lose, live in the midst of enemies, by no means deserves the disdain with which it is treated by some of the adversaries of socialism. . . . Socialism, as long as it attacks the existing individualism, is easily triumphant; its weakness hitherto is in what it proposes to substitute."[77] Mill, expounding, not unsympathetically, the ideas of "the present Socialists," wrote that, in their eyes,

the very foundation of human life as at present constituted, the very principle on which the production and repartition of all material products is now carried on, is essentially vicious and anti-social. It is the principle of individualism, competition, each one for himself and against all the rest. It is grounded on opposition of interests, not harmony of interests, and under it every one is required to find his place by a struggle, by pushing others back or being pushed back by them. Socialists consider this system of private war (as it may be termed) between every one and every one, especially fatal in an economical point of view and in a moral.[78]

And the socially-conscious Bishop of Durham, Brooke Foss Westcott argued in 1890 that "individualism regards humanity as made up of disconnected or warring atoms: socialism regards it as an organic whole, a vital unity formed by the combination of contributing members mutually interdependent."[79]

[75]J. Bryce, *The American Commonwealth* (London and New York, 1888), II, 404. For a contemporary statement defending nonconformity and privacy against "groupism," v. D. Riesman, *Individualism Reconsidered* (Glencoe, Ill., 1954).

[76]R. Owen, *Moral World* (1845), quoted in Arieli, *op. cit.*, 406.

[77]J. S. Mill, *Newman's Political Economy* (1851) in *Collected Works* (Toronto, London, 1963--), V, 444.   [78]J. S. Mill, *Chapters on Socialism* (1879), *ibid.*, 715.

[79]*The Guardian* (8 Oct. 1890), quoted in O.E.D.

As to the German sense, this can be seen in the writings of the Unitarian minister William McCall, claimed as a precursor in expounding "the doctrine of Individuality" (along with Humboldt, the German Romantics, Goethe, and Josiah Warren) by John Stuart Mill.[80] McCall, who was influenced by German Romanticism, wrote declamatory books and pamphlets, such as *Elements of Individualism* (1847) and *Outlines of Individualism* (1853), in which he preached the gospel of a new way of life dominated by the "Principle of Individualism," which he hoped England would be the first country to adopt.

Among indigenous uses, the term's reference to nonconformity is evident in the condemnation by Gladstone, who for a time advocated a single state religion, of "our individualism in religion"[81] and in Matthew Arnold's contrast between the Catholics' ecclesiastical conception of the Eucharist and its origin "as Jesus founded it" where "it is the consecration of absolute individualism."[82] The term's reference to the English character can be seen in Samuel Smiles, that ardent moralist on behalf of the Manchester School of political economy. "The spirit of self-help," he wrote, "as exhibited in the energetic action of individuals, has in all times been a marked feature of the English character"; even "the humblest person, who sets before his fellows an example of industry, sobriety, and upright honesty of purpose in life, has a present as well as a future influence upon the well-being of his country." It was this "energetic individualism which produces the most powerful effects upon the life and action of others, and really constitutes the best practical education."[83]

It was as a central term in the vocabulary of English liberalism that "individualism" came to be mainly used in the latter half of the nineteenth century, in contrast with "socialism," "communism," and, especially, "collectivism." Thus the *Pall Mall Gazette* in 1888 spoke of holding "the scales between individualists and Socialists"[84] and the *Times* in 1896 of "the individualists" holding "their own against the encroachments of the State."[85] Though scarcely used by the political economists and the Benthamites, and though, as we have seen, Mill used it in a different and negative sense, "individualism" came to be embraced by the whole spectrum of English liberals, from those advocating the most extreme *laissez-faire* to those supporting quite extensive state intervention.

Among the former was Herbert Spencer, concerned to assist the

[80]Mill's *Autobiography* (1873) (New York, 1960), 179.
[81]W. E. Gladstone, *Church Principles Considered in their Results* (London, 1840), 98, quoted in O.E.D.
[82]M. Arnold, *Literature and Dogma* (1873), (London, 1876), 312, quoted in O.E.D.
[83]S. Smiles, *Self Help* (1859), (London, 1958), 38, 39.
[84]10 Sept. 1888, quoted in O.E.D.   [85]30 Jan. 1896, quoted in O.E.D.

general course of social evolution by arresting the imminent "drift towards a form of society in which private activities of every kind, guided by individual wills, are to be replaced by public activities guided by governmental will," that "lapse of self-ownership into ownership by the community, which is partially implied by collectivism and completely by communism."[86] Even more extreme than Spencer was Auberon Herbert, author of *The Voluntaryist Creed* (1906) and editor in the 1890's of *The Free Life*, where he described his creed as "thorough-going individualism," advocating among other things voluntary taxation and education, and "the open market and free trade in everything." At the other end of the scale were liberals, such as T. H. Green and L. T. Hobhouse, who favored positive political action for the promotion of a liberal society. For Green, individualism was "the free competitive action of the individual in relation to the production and distribution of wealth," as opposed to "the collective action of society operating through society or the executive"; he believed individualism in this sense to be "a fundamental principle of human nature and an essential factor of the well-being of society."[87] Hobhouse put the matter very clearly: "to maintain individual freedom and equality we have to extend the sphere of social control," and thus "individualism, when it grapples with the facts, is driven no small distance along Socialist lines."[88]

Perhaps the most influential use was that typified by Dicey, who equated individualism with Benthamism and utilitarian Liberalism. For Dicey,

Utilitarian individualism, which for many years under the name of liberalism, determined the trend of English legislation, was nothing but Benthamism modified by the experience, the prudence, or the timidity of practical politicians.

The "individualistic reformers," he wrote, "opposed anything which shook the obligations of contracts, or, what is at bottom the same thing, limited the contractual freedom of individuals" and, in general, they "tacitly assumed that each man if left to himself would in the long run be sure to act for his own true interest, and that the general welfare was sufficiently secured if each man were left free to pursue his happiness in his own way, either alone or in combination with his fellows."[89]

[86]H. Spencer, *Principles of Sociology* (London, 1876-96), III, 594. For Spencer's first account of his ideas as the philosophy of individualism v. the introduction to the American edition of his *Social Statics* (New York, 1865), x.

[87]Quoted in M. Richter, *The Politics of Conscience: T. H. Green and his Age* (London, 1964), 343.

[88]L. T. Hobhouse, *Liberalism* (1911), (New York, 1964), 54.

[89]A. V. Dicey, *Law and Public Opinion in England* (1905) (London, 1962), 125, 151, 156.

"Individualism" has, in this sense, been widely used to mean the absence or minimum of state intervention in the economic and other spheres, and has usually been associated, both by its adherents and its opponents, with classical, or negative liberalism.

Balliol College, Oxford.

XXIII

THE ECONOMIC PENETRATION OF POLITICAL THEORY:
SOME HYPOTHESES

By C. B. Macpherson

I propose to look at the record, over the centuries, of the varying relation between political theory, on the one hand, and on the other, ideas or assumptions that we may properly call economic. Can we explain why economic ideas at some times seem to enter into political theories only slightly if at all, and at other times are there in such strength that they may be said to penetrate the political theory? This is the economic penetration referred to in my title. If there is also in the title an implication that the penetrating quality of a political theory, its ability to get to the root of the political problems it is concerned with, depends somewhat on its economic grasp, I shall not disavow that position. But the economic penetration I am directly concerned with is the penetration of political theory by economic ideas.

I do not say "by economic theory." That would narrow the enquiry too far. For the relation between formal economic theory and political theory is only a small part of the relation I want to look at. It is true that some of the outstanding political theorists have also written treatises or tracts or papers in economic theory—Bodin and Locke, for instance, in monetary theory; Hume and Burke on various problems of economic policy; Bentham on public finance especially; and of course both James and John Stuart Mill produced complete *Elements* or *Principles* of political economy. But it is not always clear whether, or how much, their political thinking was shaped by their formal economic theorizing. With Bentham at least, it seems to be the other way around. In any case, I am after something broader than the relation between formal economic theory and political theory. The economic penetration I want to look at is the entry into political theories, on the ground floor or perhaps one should say in the basement, of ideas or assumptions which may properly be called economic.

I take "economic ideas" to be ideas or assumptions about the necessary or possible relations between people in their capacity as producers of the material means of life. This is not, of course, recognizable as a description of the content of modern economics. In so describing "economic ideas," I am deliberately going back to the classical political economy tradition. There is good reason for doing that, rather than seeking a starting point in modern economics. For, since the late nine-

* Slightly revised version of paper presented at the 1974 meeting of the Conference for the Study of Political Thought, at York University, Toronto, April 19, 1974.

teenth century, economics has largely turned its attention away from that concern which had made earlier economic thought so congruous with political thought, namely, its concern with the relations of dependence and control in which people are placed by virtue of a given system of production. Modern economics has turned instead to treating people as undifferentiated demanders of utilities. Autonomous consumer demand has been taken as the motor of the whole economic system. People are economically related to each other as demanders and exchangers of things which have market values. The central concern has become the market values of the things. Economic relations between people have in effect been reduced to relations between things: the underlying economic relations of dependence and control between people have dropped out of sight.

Twentieth-century economics has thus rendered itself incapable of illuminating political theory. Economic ideas which are confined to relations between things, or to relations between disembodied persons who appear only as the holders of demand schedules, cannot enter into political theory at any fundamental level, since political theory is about relations of dependence and control between people.

We may notice here, incidentally, one unfortunate side-effect of this change in the focus of economic theory. In giving economics a new precision, it made economics an object of admiration and imitation on the part of mid-twentieth century political scientists (who saw that they were far behind in precision). This induced political scientists to carry over into their thinking, by a superficial analogy, the impersonal market model of the marginal-utility equilibrium economists. Hence we have had in recent decades many attempts to explain the democratic political process as a political analogue of the competitive market economy. These explanations do not go very deep.[1] They read back into the political process an economic relation which had already had the real relations of dependence and control taken out of it: they read back a consumers' sovereignty model of the economy without recognizing that the purchasing powers of various consumers are determined by their place in the relations of production.

The twentieth-century political scientists' application of economists' equilibrium models to the modern democratic process might seem to be an outstanding example of the penetration of political theory by economic ideas. But in my view, penetration is just what it is not. The equilibrium market model cannot penetrate political theory because it has abstracted from the power relations with which political theory is concerned. In what follows, therefore, I shall not treat this borrowing

[1] Cf. "Market Concepts in Political Theory," in my *Democratic Theory: Essays in Retrieval* (Oxford, 1973), and Ch. IV of my *Life and Times of Liberal Democracy* (Oxford and New York, 1977).

of an economic model by political scientists as a case of economic penetration of political theory.

To return, then, to the question what are to be counted as economic ideas for the purposes of this enquiry. Most broadly, for the reasons just given, I take them to be ideas about the necessary or possible relations between people as producers. And those relations may include, and at least from Aristotle on usually have been taken to include, relations between *classes*, distinguished by their function in the productive system or, more sloppily, by their share of the whole social product.

Moreover, since these relations between individuals and between classes require, and become congealed in, some institutions of *property*, we may take economic ideas to include ideas about the relation of property to other political rights and obligations. I say *other* political rights and obligations, because property is a right which has to be maintained politically. Property, as Bentham said, "is entirely the work of law."[2]

Finally, since observed relations between people as producers are apt to be read back, at a conceptual level, into assumptions about the necessary social relations between people as such, and even into assumptions about the very nature of man, we may include, under the head of economic penetration of political theory, any influence of this sort which we can see in the political theorists' models of society and of man.

How, then, are we to measure the extent of the economic penetration of political theory? As a first approximation we might say that the criterion is the extent to which actual or supposedly necessary or possible economic relations are seen as setting the *problem* of the best possible political order, or setting the problem of justice. As a closer approximation we might take the extent to which economic relations are thought to set not merely the problems, but the inescapable *requirements*, of the political system. Or, if you like, the extent to which it is thought that (to adapt Marx's much quoted statement), the anatomy of political society is to be sought in political economy.[3] And we may treat, as signals of such penetration, the amount of attention, or the centrality of the attention, given to property, or to class.

Another dimension that might be considered is the extent to which the economic assumptions are conscious and explicit, or more accurately, the extent to which there is a conscious and explicit assumption that economic relations set the political problem and set the inescapable requirements of a system of political obligation. But the consciousness and explicitness of this assumption cannot be used as a single measure

[2] *Principles of the Civil Code*, ed. C. K. Ogden (New York, 1931), Part 1, Chap. 8, paragr. 1.

[3] *Contribution to the Critique of Political Economy* (Chicago, 1904; Moscow, 1970), Preface.

of the economic penetration of political theories. For the economic assumptions may get into the political theory only indirectly (but none-theless powerfully) at the level of a generalized model of man or of society which then determines the political theory. Since these models are generally presented as models of man or society as such, their authors cannot be expected to be conscious that they reflect any particu-lar set of economic relations.

In looking for explanations of the varying penetration of political theory by economic assumptions, we may look first for mere correla-tions between the changing penetration and some other factors, and then enquire if the correlations suggest causal relations.

Looking at the whole sweep of Western political theory—ancient, medieval and modern—one correlation suggests itself, and I shall make this my first hypothesis. I shall state it first in an oversimple form, which is irresistibly suggested by a famous formulation (about something else, namely, the division of labor) by the father of political economy. I shall accordingly offer as my first hypothesis: (1) *That the economic penetration of political theory varies with the extent of the market.* More accurately this should be, varies with the extent to which market relations have permeated the society, or, the extent to which the rela-tions between people as producers are market relations.

This hypothesis is suggested by looking simply as the broad con-trasts between ancient, medieval, and modern theory. The political theorists in all three eras paid some attention to property and class, and to economic relations more generally, but the extent of their inter-est in them was rather different, and they let them enter their political theories in different ways.

Plato and Aristotle lived in a somewhat market-oriented society, a society more market-oriented than the medieval, though nothing like as much so as the modern. Their society was still near enough to a household or simple peasant and artisan exchange economy, that stan-dards appropriate to those could be thought natural. And the rest of the productive labor was mainly slave labor, not labor exchanged in a market between laborers and buyers of labor. So the market had not permeated society, although Aristotle's strictures on unnatural money-making show that he was dealing with a fairly commercialized society. Yet Plato and Aristotle neither created man in the image of market man nor allowed that economic relations between men set the main problems or the inescapable requirements of the polity. They saw the state as not at all *for* the economy, but as having a much higher purpose. The household and the village were for the material require-ments of life, the *polis* was for the good life. They did not, that is to say, allow economic assumptions to penetrate their political thinking very far. They not only put other values higher than material ones—almost all political theorists have done that—but they tried to design a polity which would provide the good life by counteracting or limiting the play of economic motives which they thought deplorable, sometimes unnatural, and at any rate always less than fully human.

Medieval society was on the whole less market-oriented; and medieval theory, at least before the rediscovery of Aristotle, showed even less economic penetration. Until then, there was not much more economic content than the Augustinian explanation of private property as punishment for, and partial remedy for the effects of, original sin.

As we move into the modern period, in which society becomes more and more permeated with market relations, with labor itself soon becoming a market commodity, the penetration of economic assumptions into political theory becomes increasingly evident. From relatively small beginnings in Machiavelli, who saw at least a necessary correspondence between a political system and the class structure, and made the class structure depend not just on amounts of property but on the kind of property (feudal vs. mercantile), there is an increasingly full assumption that economic relations set the dominant requirements of the political system. Hobbes deduced his whole system of political obligation from a model of bourgeois man, and a model of society as a market in men's powers. Locke, seeing a man's labor as an alienable and generally alienated commodity, and consequently seeing society as naturally class-divided, was able from those assumptions to justify a class state from his initial postulate of equal natural rights. For Hume, the origin of justice, and the whole need for the state, lay in man's numberless material wants and the consequent need not only for joint labor but also for exchange and contracts. Burke and Bentham made capital accumulation through market operations the *sine qua non* of civilization, and made security for capital accumulation an essential, if not the essential, function of the state.

So one could go on. The overall pattern is fairly clear: the penetration of political theory by economic assumptions has varied roughly with the extent to which market relations have permeated society. As far as it goes, then, the pattern supports my first hypothesis.

But granting that there is historically such a correlation, is there any reason for it? Is there any causal relation? One such relation suggests itself at once. Market society requires a kind of individual freedom not found in non-market societies. It requires that men be owners of something, free to sell what they own, exempt from most of the constrictions that prevail in non-market societies. Market society encourages, even enforces, rational maximizing behavior by all individuals. In doing so, it makes man restless. So the emergence and development of market relations raises new problems for political stability, and for any other political goals; and it is only a matter of time until perceptive political theorists see the source of the new problems, and see that they require an economic perspective.

This suggests a second subsidiary hypothesis, which must however be treated with some caution and probably should be discarded. *Hypothesis 2* is: *That the economic penetration of political theory varies with the extent of recent or current change in actual economic relations.* The actual change could of course only be correlated with the theorists' awareness of the change, which is obviously the operative factor, if we assume a standard acuteness or standard time-lag in the theorists' perception. This is a risky assumption, but it might be allowed over a very long run.

The main support for the second hypothesis lies in the contrast between the medieval period and either the ancient or the modern. There was not, comparatively speaking, much economic change in medieval society; and the comparative lack of change does correspond to the comparative lack of economic penetration of political theory in the medieval era.

But when one looks within either the ancient or the modern period, the hypothesis seems rather shaky. For in many cases it is not clear whether the theorist saw the actual economic relations which he did admit into his political thinking, as something new, something recently changed, or currently changing.

Aristotle certainly saw and deplored an accumulative mercantile society. But did he see it as a recent change? One might conclude, by inference from the position he took about unnatural money-making and about limited property, that he did not, or at least that he did not see it as an irreversible change. For what he did was to apply standards appropriate to a household or simple exchange economy to what was, by his own account of it, an advanced exchange economy driven by desire to accumulate without limit.

And in the modern period, the towering figure of Hobbes presents similar doubts. Hobbes saw (and regretted) that market man and market society were here to stay, but he fell short of recognizing clearly that this was a recent change. Now he saw it, now he didn't. His analysis of the causes of the Civil War, in *Behemoth,* does recognize it. But in *Leviathan,* and his other two theoretical treatises, there is no such recognition: in them he presents his models of man and society, which we can see are bourgeois models, as models of man and society as such. Not until the eighteenth century, in Millar and Ferguson, Hume and Adam Smith, with their three or four stages, do we find a clear recognition that society *has* changed by virtue of changes in the productive relations; and not until Rousseau do we find both a recognition that man and society have so changed, and a belief that man may change, or be changed, again.

In view of these outstanding doubtful cases, I think we should discard the second hypothesis. We are back then with nothing but the extent of the market. But this does not take us far with the changes observable within the period of the modern market society, particularly the changes within the liberal tradition from, say, Locke to the present.

There I see one fairly clear pattern of economic penetration of political theory, but it is not at all clear, at first sight, to what other factors this corresponds. The pattern is one of increasing economic penetration of liberal political theory from Locke through to Bentham and James Mill, and decreasing economic penetration from John Stuart Mill to the present. In the first period it is increasingly fully and explicitly assumed that economic relations are what set the problem and the requirements of political obligation and rights, set the problem of justice and the purpose of the state. To see this one need only compare Locke's fudge with the clarity of Hume and Bentham about the centrality of economic relations. Parallel with this, there is the increasing explanatory depth of political economy, from Petty and Boisguille-bert, through the Physiocrats and Adam Smith, to Ricardo.

One is tempted to the simple hypothesis that, with the increase of the scale of the full market economy, political economy got an increasingly better grasp of the essentials of the economy, and that, correspondingly, political theorists were more influenced by political economy. Certainly the personal links became closer—Hume and Adam Smith, Adam Smith and Burke, Economistes and Encyclopédistes, James Mill and Ricardo.

Now the improvement in political economy was due to its increasing recognition of a class of industrial and agricultural (rather than mercantile) capitalists, whose share of the whole annual produce of the nation, i.e., profit, was seen to be not wages of superintendance, nor akin to rent or interest, nor merely from taking advantage of momentary terms of trade. Instead, it was seen to be the excess of the value added by the current labor which that capital employed over the wage paid. This amounts to a recognition that profit was due to the extractive or exploitive power of capital. One is therefore tempted to the further hypothesis that the economic penetration of liberal theory varies directly with the recognition, by the political and economic theorists, of the necessarily exploitive or extractive nature of market relations in a fully capitalist society.

Let us see if this is a feasible working hypothesis. An immediate objection that may be made to it is that the political economists, although they increasingly saw profit as a deduction from the value added by labor, did not see this as exploitive. It is true they did not. That is, in their formal economic theories of wages and profits there is no notion of exploitation. The reason for this is plain. *Given* the pattern of ownership which they assumed, everyone got a fair reward for what he put in. They assumed the necessary and permanent division of all modern and progressive societies into three classes: those whose income derived from (a) ownership of land, (b) ownership of capital, and (c) ownership only of their own capacity to labor. They assumed this without asking how these classes were formed. But they were well enough aware that that pattern of ownership itself was broadly exploitive. They saw that in any society in which there was a class without any material productive property (and this included the capitalist market society), that class was *used* by the others. Adam Smith made this point, and drew a political conclusion, in a well-known passage: "Whenever there is great property, there is great inequality. For one very rich man, there must be at least five hundred poor, and the affluence of the rich supposes the indigence of the many. The affluence of the rich excites the indignation of the poor, who are often both driven by want, and prompted by envy, to invade his possessions. It is only under the shelter of the civil magistrate that the owner of that valuable property, which is acquired by the labour of many years, or perhaps of many successive generations, can sleep a single night in security. . . . The acquisition of valuable and extensive property, therefore, necessarily requires the establishment of civil government. Where there is no property, or at least none that exceeds the value of two or three days' labour, civil government is not so necessary."[4] And again: "Civil government, so far as it is instituted for the security of property is in reality instituted for the defence of the rich against the poor, or of those who have some property against those who have none at all."[5]

The classical liberal political theorists, whether or not they also wrote economics, were similarly outspoken, and increasingly so from Locke to Bentham. And this went along with an increasing tendency to see the job of the state as set by economic relations: in other words it went along with an increasing economic peneration of political theory. So I shall put as *Hypothesis 3: That the economic penetration of political theory varies with the theorists' recognition of the necessarily exploitive or extractive nature of market relations in a society divided into owners and non-owners of productive material property.* A glance at some highlight of liberal theory from Locke to Bentham offers some support for this.

Locke, in making the protection of property the chief end for which men enter civil society and set up government, blurred the relation by including in "property" life, liberty, and estate. But he was explicit that it was *unequal* material property that was to be protected, and he took for granted a society in which some had nothing but their labor to sell. He combined this with a rudimentary labor theory of value, but he did not draw the conclusion that the laboring class was exploited.

Hume, more clearly than Locke, saw government as needed only when great and unequal property had been accumulated, and went

---

[4] *Wealth of Nations,* Bk. V, Ch. 1, part ii (Modern Library ed., 670).
[5] *Ibid.,* 674.

beyond Locke in relating this to the emergence of the market: government is needed when the market comes to include men totally unknown to us. Hume goes on from a utilitarian justification of individual property in land and goods to an explicit recognition that *market* relations are the fundamental relations of society. The right of private property, the right to exchange property, and the obligation of contracts are asserted to be the three fundamental natural laws because they are all necessary for a market society. He assumed that there would always be a class of laboring poor, but he was still some way from seeing this as exploitive. That is, he did not single this out as *the* exploitive relation, though he thought almost all social relations were determined by the avidity of conflicting individual material desires.

Diderot likewise made property the *raison d'être* of the state, but went further in seeing the exploitive nature of property. Not only did he see that wage-labor is employed only because it produces a profit for the employer: he also saw that it condemned many to an inhuman existence.

Les mines du Hartz recèlent dans leurs immenses profondeurs des milliers d'hommes qui connaissent à peine la lumière du soleil et qui atteignent rarement l'âge de trente ans. C'est là qu'on voit des femmes qui ont eu douze maris.
Si vous fermez ces vastes tombeaux, vous ruinez l'État et vous condamnez tous les sujets de la Saxe ou à mourir de faim ou à s'expatrier.
Combien d'ateliers dans la France même, moins nombreux, mais presque aussi funestes![6]

Diderot saw no alternative to the exploitive wage-relation, but hoped for some regulation of it. And he was a more consistent utilitarian than Bentham was to be, for he held that a smaller net product equally distributed is better than a larger net product so unequally distributed as to divide people into rich and poor classes.[7] Diderot saw no way out of the contradiction between the wage relation and human values, but at least he saw the contradiction.

Burke, who insisted that there was a natural functional order of subordination between laborers and capitalists, and wrote that "the laws of commerce . . . are the laws of nature, and consequently the laws of God,"[8] made capital accumulation the *sine qua non* of civilization. He recognized, in words very like Diderot's, the exploitation inseparable from it, but he would permit no interference with it. Referring to "the innumerable servile, degrading, unseemly, unmanly, and often most

---

[6] *Réfutation d'Helvétius, Oeuvres Complètes de Diderot, éd. Assezat* (Paris, 1875), II, 430-31.

[7] *Encyclopédie,* art. Homme (politique).

[8] *Thoughts and Details on Scarcity, Works* (Oxford World's Classics, 1907), VI, 22.

unwholesome and pestiferous occupations, to which by the social economy so many wretches are inevitably doomed," he insisted that it would be "pernicious to disturb the natural course of things, and to impede, in any degree, the great wheel of circulation which is turned by the strangely-directed labour of these unhappy people."[9]

Bentham similarly did not mince matters. "In the highest state of social prosperity," he wrote, "the great mass of citizens will have no resource except their daily industry; and consequently will be always near indigence. . . ."[10] It was the fate of those without property to be so used. This was the inevitable outcome of the fact that "human beings are the most powerful instruments of production, and therefore everyone becomes anxious to employ the services of his fellows in multiplying his own comforts. Hence the intense and universal thirst for power; the equally prevalent hatred of subjection."[11] And Bentham was clear that security of property must have priority over the claims of equality: "When security and equality are in conflict, it will not do to hesitate a moment. Equality must yield."[12] This was in spite of the fact that Bentham had shown that, by the principle of diminishing utility, aggregate utilities would be maximized by complete equality of property. But equality was incompatible with capital accumulation and hence with maximization of wealth.

If I might venture a slight digression, I should say that Bentham had done the same thing as the neo-classical economists were to do at the end of the nineteenth century. As Joan Robinson has pointed out about Marshall et al.: "The method by which the egalitarian element in the [marginal utility] doctrine was sterilized was mainly by slipping from utility to physical output as the object to be maximized. A small total of physical goods, equally distributed, admittedly may yield more utility than a much larger total unequally distributed, but if we keep our eye on the total of goods it is easy to forget about utility."[13] This is just what Bentham had done. Security of property, he argued, must be put ahead of equality because security is necessary to maximize physical output, not utility: he did not notice that he had slipped from one to the other.

With James Mill we touch the high point of recognition of the exploitive nature of market society, though he fetched it from a principle of human nature which he held to be universal. "The desire . . . of that power which is necessary to render the persons and properties of human beings subservient to our pleasures, is a grand governing law of human nature. . . . The grand instrument for attaining what a man

---

[9] *Reflections on the Revolution in France* (Pelican Classics ed. 1968, 271).
[10] *Principles of the Civil Code,* Part I, Chap. 14, Sect. 1.
[11] *Economic Writings* (ed. Stark), 1954, III, 430.
[12] *Principles of the Civil Code,* Part I, Chap. 11, para. 3.
[13] *Economic Philosophy* (London, 1962), 55.

likes is the actions of other men."[14] So everyone seeks exploitive power over others. This view is not carried into his formal economic analysis of wages and profits. But there is in his *Elements of Political Economy* a suggestive passage about slave labor and wage labor. "The only difference" between the manufacturer who operates with slaves and the manufacturer who operates with free laborers, "is, in the mode of purchasing. The owner of the slave purchases, at once, the whole of the labour which the man can ever perform: he, who pays wages, purchases only so much of a man's labour as he can perform in a day, or any other stipulated time. Being equally, however, the owner of the labour, so purchased, as the owner of the slave is of that of the slave, the produce, which is the result of this labour, combined with his capital, is all equally his own."[15] Mill's readers would assume that the slave relation was wholly exploitive. For Mill to say, then, that the only difference between it and the wage relation is in the mode of purchasing, is to leave a pretty plain implication that the wage relation is equally exploitive.

It may be noted that, in this catalogue of classical liberal theorists, those who held most strongly that society was necessarily contentious and hence exploitive—namely, Hume, Bentham, and James Mill— asserted this of society as such, not just of capitalist society. But they were able to assert it to be inherent in any society only because they had put into the very nature of man the motivations of bourgeois man. Hume deduced the necessary opposition of passions and consequent opposition of actions from a postulate of insatiable material desire: "This avidity alone, of acquiring goods and possessions for ourselves and our nearest friends, is insatiable, perpetual, universal. . . ."[16] James Mill's "grand governing law of human nature" takes this a step further, as does Bentham's self-evident proposition, already quoted, that because human beings are the most powerful instruments of production, everyone tries to use everyone else. And Bentham brought this to a finer point by making the pleasure of acquisition stronger than the pleasure of possession. "It is the pleasure of acquisition, not the satisfaction of póssessing, which gives the greatest delights."[17] Possession is of course needed to consolidate acquisition, and is helpful as a means to further acquisition.

Thus all three theorists read back into human nature their observation of bourgeois man—man as infinite appropriator. Having done this,

[14] *Government*, Sect. IV, ed. Barker (Cambridge, 1937), 17.

[15] *Elements*, Chap. 1, Sect. 2 (in Winch, ed., *Selected Economic Writings* (1966), 219).

[16] *Treatise*, Bk. III, Part 2, Sect. 2, in F. Watkins, ed., *Hume, Theory of Politics* (1961), 41.

[17] *Principles of the Civil Code*, Part I, Chap. 6; in *Theory of Legislation*, ed. C. K. Ogden, 105.

and having made this the reason why government was necessary, they saw no need for further explanation nor any need to make excuses for the social relations it produced.

I find, then, in the classical liberal tradition from Locke to Bentham and James Mill, an increasing recognition of the exploitative nature of a society based on the capital/wage-labor relation, and a corresponding increase in the extent to which the job of the state was thought to be set by economic relations.

With John Stuart Mill and T. H. Green (and their twentieth-century liberal followers) there is a remarkable change. There is in them no recognition, indeed there is a denial, of the exploitative nature of capital; and there is correspondingly a decline in the extent to which the job of the state was thought to be set by economic relations.

It may seem strange to take John Stuart Mill as the watershed, as the beginning of a declining economic penetration of political theory. For in no other theorist is there such a massive relation between political theory and political economy: no one wrote more about both, or linked them so deliberately. But the link is not direct: both are linked to social philosophy. And it was a social philosophy which departed from the utilitarian tradition precisely in its denial that all human values could or should be furthered by or reduced to the market: that was the upshot of Mill's introduction of qualitative differences in pleasures. Mill was concerned to rescue human values from their then subordination to the market. The job of the state was not to facilitate an endless increase in the production of wealth but to fashion a society with higher ends. He was thus, we might say, opposed in principle to the economic penetration of political theory.

At the same time he failed to see that the wage/capital relation was by its nature extractive or exploitive. He saw indeed the exploitation in nineteenth-century society, and denounced it in the strongest terms. Nothing was more unjust than the prevailing relation between work and reward, by which the produce of labor is apportioned "almost in an inverse ratio to the labour—the largest portions to those who have never worked at all, the next largest to those whose work is almost nominal, and so in a decreasing scale, the remuneration dwindling as the work grows harder and more disagreeable, until the most fatiguing and exhausting bodily labour cannot count with certainty on being able to earn even the necessaries of life. . . ."[18] But he insisted, as did T. H. Green, that this was not inherent in the capital/labor relation, but was due to something else—the original (feudal) forcible seizure of the land, and the failure of subsequent governments to counteract its effects.

---

[18] *Principles of Political Economy* (Toronto and London, 1965), Bk. II, Chap. 1, Sect. 3. (*Collected Works*, II, 207).

He even argued that "industry" has for many centuries been modifying the work of force (*ibid.*).

Thus, where the earlier liberals had seen that capitalist profit was a deduction from labor's production, but had seen no need to reconcile this with a principle of equity because the system led to increased wealth all around, Mill rejected wealth as the criterion, insisted on a principle of equity, preferred a stationary economy to the rat-race of his contemporary society, but did not see that the prevailing inequity, and the trampling and elbowing, were inherent in the capitalist relation.

It is not just that he did not put exploitation into his economic theory of the determinants of wages and profits. No more, as we have noticed, did Adam Smith or James Mill. But in their cases it was because they made the wealth of the nation the grand criterion, and assumed the inevitability of existing classes, so did not see any need to justify or excuse the prevailing distribution. John Stuart Mill did see that that distribution was not automatically justified. He was the first of the liberals to see this, and to say it. He saw that there was a gap between his idea of maximized utility and the actual utilities that were produced by the class-divided society of his time. He saw that there was something to be explained. But he could not explain it except by denying that the exploitive relation was inherent in the capitalist relation.

Some would argue that Mill's well-known disjunction between the laws of production and the pattern of distribution[19] was his answer to, or his way of avoiding, the difficulty that a competitive market economy in which every bargain was entirely fair would result in a distribution which was utterly inequitable. If this disjunction was intended as such, it was a very poor logical resolution of the difficulty. For the disjunction he made was not between the social relations of production and the social distribution of the product, but merely between the physical laws (e.g. of the fertility of the soil, and hence diminishing returns on increasing applications of labor to the same land) which limit production in any system, whatever are the social relations of production, and any particular system of social distribution. His disjunction was perfectly valid, but it did not meet the difficulty. He simply did not see that capitalist production entailed capitalist distribution, or that the distribution was a co-requisite of the production. Instead, he attributed the inequity of the existing distribution to an historical factor extraneous to the system of production.

Accordingly, he did not see that men's economic relations set the requirements of the political system. In moving away from utility, by redefining it qualitatively, he moved his political theory away from political economy. And T. H. Green, starting from a different base,

---

[19] *Principles*, Bk. II, Chap. 1, Sect. 1 (*Works*, II, 199-200).

came full circle back to the Greek ideal of the good life as something apart from and even opposed to material maximization.

This retreat from economic assumptions was not, I think, simply coincidental with the failure to see the necessarily exploitive nature of capitalist productive relations. Both were perhaps due to a third factor: the increasingly evident incompatibility, in the nineteenth century, between the dehumanizing actual economic relations and any morally acceptable vision of a human society. All political theorists, not least those in the liberal tradition, have some vision of human needs and human excellence, and hence a vision of a humanly desirable society. Incompatibility between the exploitive nature of capitalist market relations and a humanistic ethic had not been a serious problem for the seventeenth- and eighteenth-century political theorists. They could, and did, square the massive inequality of the accumulative society based on free contract and wage-labor with a humanistic vision, by pointing out that the market society raised and could continue to raise the general level of material well-being. Since they saw this as a *necessary* condition of moral and cultural improvement, they did not look too closely at the question whether it was also a *sufficient* condition for that improvement.

But by the middle of the nineteenth century this would no longer suffice. The quality of life for the mass of the people in that unequal society had become so blatantly wretched that it could no longer be excused by the ability of the system to go on increasing the national wealth. Sensitive liberals such as Mill found the condition of the working class morally insupportable. Mill's way out, as we have seen, was to attribute the evil to something other than the capitalist relation.

But now we must notice another factor which contributed to the liberal change of position. Not only did sensitive liberals find the conditions of the working-class insupportable. So did some emerging working-class movements which were making their weight felt politically. There was thus an objective factor, a factor beyond the subjective humanistic perception of sensitive liberals, and it was the objective change that sparked the subjective one. Mill, writing in 1845 of the effects of the Chartist movement, which he described as "the revolt of nearly all the active talent, and a great part of the physical force, of the working classes, against their whole relation to society" said that "among the more fortunate classes . . . some by the physical and moral circumstances which they saw around them, were made to feel that the conditions of the labouring classes *ought* to be attended to, others were made to see that it *would* be attended to, whether they wished to be blind to it or not." He concluded: "It was no longer disputable that something must be done to render the multitude more content with the existing state of things."[20]

[20] *The Claims of Labour,* in *Dissertations and Discussions,* II, 188-90; and in *Collected Works* (1967), IV, 369-70.

This suggests that my third hypothesis can be taken one step further. Hypothesis 3 was that the penetration of political theory by economic ideas varies with the theorists' recognition of the necessarily exploitive or extractive nature of market relations in a society divided into owners and non-owners of productive material property. What may be thought a weakness of that hypothesis is that it merely relates one mental operation with another: the theorist's admission of economic assumptions with his *perception* of a certain inherent relation in society.

But now, if my point about Mill is right, we may substitute an external factor for that perception. Instead of a theorist's perception of the inherent exploitiveness of the capitalist relation, we may look to the *exploited class's* perception of its exploitation, and its consequent political action. Thus, for liberal theory, we would have the following proposition: the economic penetration of political theory varies *inversely* with the political strength of an exploited class. And, of course, for socialist theory, which speaks in the name of the exploited class, the economic penetration of the political theory would be expected to vary *directly* with the political strength of an exploited class.

We may frame this as *Hypothesis 4: That the economic penetration of political theory varies with the political strength of an exploited class; directly in socialist theory, inversely in liberal theory.* This hypothesis is borne out pretty well in both traditions.

In the socialist tradition, Marx may fairly be regarded as the high point of economic penetration of political theory, and his was the period of maximum political strength of class-conscious working-class action in the Western nations. Revisionist and Fabian theory, and subsequent democratic socialist theory, have corresponded with (and no doubt contributed to) declining class-conscious political action.

In the liberal tradition the inverse correspondence is fairly clear for the seventeenth to nineteenth centuries, in the line I have already sketched: the economic penetration increasing from Locke to Bentham, a period when the threat from below was at least quiescent if not decreasing—(it is true that Burke and Malthus saw a threat in the repercussions of the French Revolution, but Bentham and Ricardo and James Mill did not); then, from John Stuart Mill on through the rest of the nineteenth century, the economic penetration decreasing as the threat from below increased.

What about subsequent liberal tradition? I see, in the twentieth century, a continuation of that line. From Ernest Barker and A. D. Lindsay and John Dewey to, say, Maurice Cranston and John Rawls,[21] the economic penetration of liberal politicial theory has decreased. And its decrease is correlated with an increase in the apprehended threat

---

[21] Cf. my "Rawls's Models of Man and Society," *Philosophy of the Social Sciences* (Dec. 1973), 341-47.

to bourgeois liberal societies, not so much a threat by any *indigenous* class-conscious exploited class (for these have not amounted to much in the economically advanced Western nations in this century) but by the global threat of the socialist and Third World societies. It would be astonishing if liberal theorists in countries which, either directly, or indirectly as client states or nostalgic states, rely on global exploitation, did not respond, even if only subconsciously, to that threat. I see them as having done so, and hence as bearing out Hypothesis 4.

It may be objected that I have contradicted myself in referring the twentieth-century change in the Western *socialist* tradition to a *decline* in the political strength of the exploited, and the change in the *liberal* tradition to an *increase* in the threat from those presently or formerly transnationally exploited; it may be thought that the distinction I have made between indigenous and transnational threats is too artificial to hold my case together. But we may see a further unifying factor here, namely, the increasingly uncertain viability of capitalist society. The perception of this by liberal theorists makes them retreat from economic penetration to idealism. The same perception by socialist theorists in the affluent countries easily leads them to think that capitalism cannot keep going without submitting to steadily erosive reforms, and so leads them to press for concessions rather than confrontation, and to bend their theory towards reformism, with some lack of economic penetration.

I doubt if this explanation can be pressed very far, at least without a good deal of refinement and qualification. And since it concerns only the twentieth century (and only some developments within that time-span) it cannot serve as a general hypothesis. But it does suggest one further general hypothesis which is applicable to the whole rise and fall of the economic penetration of political theory from the seventeenth century on. If we look back over that stretch, which comprises the emergence and maturation and faltering of capitalism, we may entertain the idea, as *Hypothesis 5, That the economic penetration of political theory varies with the theorists' confidence in the ability of an emerging or established economic order to maximize human well-being and to achieve or maintain political dominance.* This may be said to hold both for the rise and decline of the economic penetration of liberal theory from the seventeenth century till now, and for its decline in Western socialist theory from Marx till now. It also appears to hold for the continuance and revival of Marxism in the non-Western world in this century.

The same weakness might be seen in this hypothesis as was seen in Hypothesis 3, namely, that it merely relates one mental operation to another—the theorists' use of economic assumptions with their confidence in some actual or possible economic relations. It would no doubt be tidier if we could reduce the latter to some external factor such as the actual performance of an economic system. We can do so in part, but not entirely.

An improving performance is indeed apt to bring increasing confidence in an existing system. And a faltering performance is apt to bring decreasing confidence in an existing system by its beneficiaries. But the faltering performance of an existing system also brings an *increasing* confidence, by its *non*-beneficiaries, in the possibilities of what they see as an emerging alternative system. This I take to have been as true of Adam Smith as of Marx.

To put the point most generally, confidence in an established or emergent economic system is not reducible to any external factor, because the possibility of an emergent one depends partly on people's perception of such new possibility. I do not see any determinate relation between actual performance and such perception. There are time-lags. There are variations induced by the operation of the system itself. There are different perceptions, by different sections of the community, of the relative value of aggregate affluence and general quality of life. Opinion in one nation may be compelled by changes outside to make a different valuation of the limits of the prevailing system and the possibility of alternatives.

All these things may be seen as happening in our own day. Even some economists have begun to count the cost of economic growth. An optimistic view is that quality of life will get the upper hand, and that we will move away from a society permeated by market behavior and material maximization. If my first hypothesis still governed then, the economic penetration of political theory would decline. But we should not expect a constant ratio to be maintained during such a move. At the theoretical end-point we might indeed expect it: with zero market there would presumably be zero economic penetration of political theory, if only because there would be zero political economy. Indeed, if, as I suppose, the full transcendence of market behavior requires an end of scarcity, might there not in that case be zero political theory? That is the logical conclusion that would follow from the postulates of classical liberal theory, which tied political obligation, rights and justice to scarcity; as Hume put it: "it is only from the selfishness and confined generosity of men, along with the scanty provision nature has made for his wants, that justice derives its origin . . . it is evident that the . . . extensive generosity of man, and the perfect abundance of everything, would destroy the very idea of justice . . . because they render it useless."[22]

However that may be—and it is surely not just one's professional bias as a political theorist that makes one resist the notion of the end

[22] *Treatise of Human Nature*, Bk. III, Part 2, Sect. 2 (in F. Watkins, ed.), 45-46.

of political theory—any move from a market-dominated society to a non-market-dominated society will clearly need the services both of political theory and political economy. And it will need a political theory that recognizes the determining role of necessary and possible relations between people as producers. If need always brought forth what is needed, we would be sure of a continued presence, indeed a revival from the present low point in Western political theory, of economic penetration. But if demand creates supply, we should still have to ask, whose demand? and the answer might not be very encouraging. Or if supply creates demand, we are no better off, for economic thought of the fundamental sort needed by political theory is now in rather short supply. The conclusion which seems inescapable is that we ourselves as political theorists will have to augment the supply, and take the lead in restoring to political theory the economic insight it once enjoyed.

University of Toronto.

XXIV

POLITICAL PHILOSOPHY AND HISTORY[1]

By Leo Strauss

Political philosophy is not a historical discipline. The philosophic questions of the nature of political things and of the best, or just, political order are fundamentally different from historical questions, which always concern individuals: individual groups, individual human beings, individual achievements, individual "civilizations," the one individual "process" of human civilization from its beginning to the present, and so on. In particular, political philosophy is fundamentally different from the history of political philosophy itself. The question of the nature of political things and the answer to it cannot possibly be mistaken for the question of how this or that philosopher or all philosophers have approached, discussed or answered the philosophic question mentioned. This does not mean that political philosophy is absolutely independent of history. Without the experience of the variety of political institutions and convictions in different countries and at different times, the questions of the nature of political things and of the best, or the just, political order could never have been raised. And after they have been raised, only historical knowledge can prevent one from mistaking the specific features of the political life of one's time and one's country for the nature of political things. Similar considerations apply to the history of political thought and the history of political philosophy. But however important historical knowledge may be for political philosophy, it is only preliminary and auxiliary to political philosophy; it does not form an integral part of it.

This view of the relation of political philosophy to history was unquestionably predominant at least up to the end of the eighteenth century. In our time it is frequently rejected in favor of "historicism," *i.e.*, of the assertion that the fundamental distinction between philosophic and historical questions cannot in the last analysis be maintained. Historicism may therefore be said to question the possibility of political philosophy. At any rate it challenges a premise that was common to the whole tradition of politi-

[1] A Hebrew translation of this paper appeared in *Eyoon—Hebrew Journal of Philosophy*, I (1946), 129 ff.

cal philosophy and apparently never doubted by it. It thus seems to go deeper to the roots, or to be more philosophic, than the political philosophy of the past. In any case, it casts a doubt on the very questions of the nature of political things and of the best, or the just, political order. Thus it creates an entirely new situation for political philosophy. The question that it raises is to-day the most urgent question for political philosophy.

It may well be doubted whether the fusion of philosophy and history, as advocated by historicism, has ever been achieved, or even whether it can be achieved. Nevertheless that fusion appears to be, as it were, the natural goal toward which the victorious trends of nineteenth- and early twentieth-century thought converge. At any rate, historicism is not just one philosophic school among many, but a most powerful agent that affects more or less all present-day thought. As far as we can speak at all of the spirit of a time, we can assert with confidence that the spirit of our time is historicism.

Never before has man devoted such an intensive and such a comprehensive interest to his whole past, and to all aspects of his past, as he does to-day. The number of historical disciplines, the range of each, and the interdependence of them all are increasing almost constantly. Nor are these historical studies carried on by thousands of ever more specialized students considered merely instrumental, and without value in themselves: we take it for granted that historical knowledge forms an integral part of the highest kind of learning. To see this fact in the proper perspective, we need only look back to the past. When Plato sketched in his *Republic* a plan of studies he mentioned arithmetic, geometry, astronomy, and so on: he did not even allude to history. We cannot recall too often the saying of Aristotle (who was responsible for much of the most outstanding historical research done in classical antiquity) that poetry is more philosophic than history. This attitude was characteristic of all the classical philosophers and of all the philosophers of the Middle Ages. History was praised most highly not by the philosophers but by the rhetoricians. The history of philosophy in particular was not considered a philosophic discipline: it was left to antiquarians rather than to philosophers.

A fundamental change began to make itself felt only in the

sixteenth century. The opposition then offered to all earlier philosophy, and especially to all earlier political philosophy, was marked from the outset by a novel emphasis on history. That early turn toward history was literally absorbed by the "unhistorical" teachings of the Age of Reason. The "rationalism" of the seventeenth and eighteenth centuries was fundamentally much more "historical" than the "rationalism" of pre-modern times. From the seventeenth century onward, the rapprochement of philosophy and history increased almost from generation to generation at an ever accelerated pace. Toward the end of the seventeenth century it became customary to speak of "the spirit of a time." In the middle of the eighteenth century the term "philosophy of history" was coined. In the nineteenth century, the history of philosophy came to be generally considered a philosophical discipline. The teaching of the outstanding philosopher of the nineteenth century, Hegel, was meant to be a "synthesis" of philosophy and history. The "historical school" of the nineteenth century brought about the substitution of historical jurisprudence, historical political science, historical economic science for a jurisprudence, a political science, an economic science that were evidently "unhistorical" or at least a-historical.

The specific historicism of the first half of the nineteenth century was violently attacked because it seemed to lose itself in the contemplation of the past. Its victorious opponents did not, however, replace it by a non-historical philosophy, but by a more "advanced," and in some cases a more "sophisticated" form of historicism. The typical historicism of the twentieth century demands that each generation reinterpret the past on the basis of its own experience and with a view to its own future. It is no longer contemplative, but activistic; and it attaches to that study of the past which is guided by the anticipated future, or which starts from and returns to the analysis of the present, a crucial philosophic significance: it expects from it the ultimate guidance for political life. The result is visible in practically every curriculum and textbook of our time. One has the impression that the question of the nature of political things has been superseded by the question of the characteristic "trends" of the social life of the present and of their historical origins, and that the question of the best, or the just, political order has been superseded by the question of the probable or desirable future. The questions of the modern state, of modern government, of the ideals of Western civilisation, and so forth, occupy a place that was formerly occupied by the questions of *the* state and of *the* right way of life. Philosophic questions have been transformed into historical questions— or more precisely into historical questions of a "futuristic" character.

This orientation characteristic of our time can be rendered legitimate only by historicism. Historicism appears in the most varied guises and on the most different levels. Tenets and arguments that are the boast of one type of historicism, provoke the smile of the adherents of others. The most common form of historicism expresses itself in the demand that the questions of the nature of political things, of *the* state, of the nature of man, and so forth, be replaced by the questions of the modern state, of modern government, of the present political situation, of modern man, of our society, our culture, our civilization, and so forth. Since it is hard to see, however, how one can speak adequately of the modern state, of our civilization, of modern man, etc., without knowing first what a state is, what a civilization is, what man's nature is, the more thoughtful forms of historicism admit that the universal questions of traditional philosophy cannot be abandoned. Yet they assert that any answer to these questions, any attempt at clarifying or discussing them, and indeed any precise formulation of them, is bound to be "historically conditioned," *i.e.*, to remain dependent on the specific situation in which they are suggested. No answer to, no treatment or precise formulation of, the universal questions can claim to be of universal validity, of validity for all times. Other historicists go to the end of the road by declaring that while the universal questions of traditional philosophy cannot be abandoned without abandoning philosophy itself, philosophy itself and its universal questions themselves are "historically conditioned," *i.e.*, essentially related to a specific "historic" type, *e.g.*, to Western man or to the Greeks and their intellectual heirs.

To indicate the range of historicism, we may refer to two assumptions characteristic of historicism and to-day generally accepted. "History" designated originally a particular kind of knowledge or inquiry. Historicism assumes that the object of historical knowledge, which it calls "History," is a "field," a "world"

of its own fundamentally different from, although of course related to, that other "field," "Nature." This assumption distinguishes historicism most clearly from the pre-historicist view, for
which "History" as an object of knowledge did not exist, and
which therefore did not even dream of a "philosophy of history"
as an analysis of, or a speculation about, a specific "dimension of
reality." The gravity of the assumption in question appears only
after one has started wondering what the Bible or Plato, *e.g.*, would
have called that X which we are in the habit of calling "History."
Equally characteristic of historicism is the assumption that restora-
tions of earlier teachings are impossible, or that every intended
restoration necessarily leads to an essential modification of the
restored teaching. This assumption can most easily be understood
as a necessary consequence of the view that every teaching is essentially related to an unrepeatable "historical" situation.

An adequate discussion of historicism would be identical with
a critical analysis of modern philosophy in general. We cannot
dare try more than indicate some considerations which should prevent one from taking historicism for granted.

To begin with, we must dispose of a popular misunderstanding
which is apt to blur the issue. It goes back to the attacks of early
historicism on the political philosophy which had paved the way
for the French Revolution. The representatives of the "historical
school" assumed that certain influential philosophers of the eighteenth century had conceived of the right political order, or of the
rational political order, as an order which should or could be
established at any time and in any place, without any regard to
the particular conditions of time and place. Over against this
opinion they asserted that the only legitimate approach to political
matters is the "historical" approach, *i.e.*, the understanding of the
institutions of a given country as a product of its past. Legitimate
political action must be based on such historical understanding, as
distinguished from, and opposed to, the "abstract principles" of
1789 or any other "abstract principles." Whatever the deficiencies of eighteenth-century political philosophy may be, they certainly do not justify the suggestion that the non-historical philosophic approach must be replaced by a historical approach. Most
political philosophers of the past, in spite or rather because of the
non-historical character of their thought, distinguished as a matter

of course between the philosophic question of the best political order, and the practical question as to whether that order could or should be established in a given country at a given time. They naturally knew that all political action, as distinguished from political philosophy, is concerned with individual situations, and must therefore be based on a clear grasp of the situation concerned, and therefore normally on an understanding of the causes or antecedents of that situation. They took it for granted that political action guided by the belief that what is most desirable in itself must be put into practice in all circumstances, regardless of the circumstances, befits harmless doves, ignorant of the wisdom of the serpent, but not sensible and good men. In short, the truism that all political action is concerned with, and therefore presupposes appropriate knowledge of, individual situations, individual commonwealths, individual institutions, and so on, is wholly irrelevant to the question raised by historicism.

For a large number, that question is decided by the fact that historicism comes later in time than the non-historical political philosophy: "history" itself seems to have decided in favor of historicism. If, however, we do not worship "success" as such, we cannot maintain that the victorious cause is necessarily the cause of truth. For even if we grant that truth will prevail in the end, we cannot be certain that the end has already come. Those who prefer historicism to non-historical political philosophy because of the temporal relation of the two, interpret then that relation in a specific manner: they believe that the position which historically comes later can be presumed, other things being equal, to be more mature than the positions preceding it. Historicism, they would say, is based on an experience which required many centuries to mature—on the experience of many centuries which teaches us that non-historical political philosophy is a failure or a delusion. The political philosophers of the past attempted to answer the question of the best political order once and for all. But the result of all their efforts has been that there are almost as many answers, as many political philosophies as there have been political philosophers. The mere spectacle of "the anarchy of systems," of "the disgraceful variety" of philosophies seems to refute the claim of each philosophy. The history of political philosophy, it is asserted, refutes non-historical political philosophy as such, since the many irreconcilable political philosophies refute each other.

Actually, however, that history does not teach us that the political philosophies of the past refute each other. It teaches us merely that they contradict each other. It confronts us then with the philosophic question as to which of two given contradictory theses concerning political fundamentals is true. In studying the history of political philosophy, we observe, *e.g.*, that some political philosophers distinguish between State and Society, whereas others explicitly or implicitly reject that distinction. This observation compels us to raise the philosophic question whether and how far the distinction is adequate. Even if history could teach us that the political philosophy of the past has failed, it would not teach us more than that non-historical political philosophy has hitherto failed. But what else would this mean except that we do not truly know the nature of political things and the best, or just, political order? This is so far from being a new insight due to historicism that it is implied in the very name "philosophy." If the "anarchy of systems" exhibited by the history of philosophy proves anything, it proves our ignorance concerning the most important subjects (of which ignorance we can be aware without historicism), and therewith it proves the necessity of philosophy. It may be added that the "anarchy" of the historical political philosophies of our time, or of present-day interpretations of the past, is not conspicuously smaller than that of the non-historical political philosophies of the past.

Yet it is not the mere variety of political philosophies which allegedly shows the futility of non-historical political philosophy. Most historicists consider decisive the fact, which can be established by historical studies, that a close relation exists between each political philosophy and the historical situation in which it emerged. The variety of political philosophies, they hold, is above all a function of the variety of historical situations. The history of political philosophy does not teach merely that the political philosophy of Plato, *e.g.*, is irreconcilable with the political philosophy, say, of Locke. It also teaches that Plato's political philosophy is essentially related to the Greek city of the fourth century B.C., just as Locke's political philosophy is essentially related to the English revolution of 1688. It thus shows that no political philosophy can reasonably claim to be valid beyond the historical situation to which it is essentially related.

Yet, not to repeat what has been indicated in the paragraph before the last, the historical evidence invoked in favor of historicism has a much more limited bearing than seems to be assumed. In the first place, historicists do not make sufficient allowance for the deliberate adaptation, on the part of the political philosophers of the past, of their views to the prejudices of their contemporaries. Superficial readers are apt to think that a political philosopher was under the spell of the historical situation in which he thought, when he was merely adapting the expression of his thought to that situation in order to be listened to at all. Many political philosophers of the past presented their teachings, not in scientific treatises proper, but in what we may call treatise-pamphlets. They did not limit themselves to expounding what they considered *the* political truth. They combined with that exposition an exposition of what they considered desirable or feasible in the circumstances, or intelligible on the basis of the generally received opinions; they communicated their views in a manner which was not purely "philosophical," but at the same time "civil."[2] Accordingly, by proving that their political teaching as a whole is "historically conditioned," we do not at all prove that their political philosophy proper is "historically conditioned."

Above all, it is gratuitously assumed that the relation between doctrines and their "times" is wholly unambiguous. The obvious possibility is overlooked that the situation to which one particular doctrine is related, is particularly favorable to the discovery of *the* truth, whereas all other situations may be more or less unfavorable. More generally expressed, in understanding the genesis of a doctrine we are not necessarily driven to the conclusion that the doctrine in question cannot simply be true. By proving, *e.g.*, that certain propositions of modern natural law "go back" to positive Roman law, we have not yet proven that the propositions in question are not *de jure naturali* but merely *de jure positivo*. For it is perfectly possible that the Roman jurists mistook certain principles of natural law for those of positive law, or that they merely "divined," and did not truly know, important elements of natural

---

[2] Compare Locke, *Of Civil Government*, I, Sect. 109, and II, Sect. 52, with his *Essay Concerning Human Understanding*, III, ch. 9, Sects. 3 and 22.

law. We cannot then stop at ascertaining the relations between a doctrine and its historical origins. We have to interpret these relations; and such interpretation presupposes the philosophic study of the doctrine in itself with a view to its truth or falsehood. At any rate, the fact (if it is a fact) that each doctrine is "related" to a particular historical setting does not prove at all that no doctrine can simply be true.

The old fashioned, not familiar with the ravages wrought by historicism, may ridicule us for drawing a conclusion which amounts to the truism that we cannot reasonably reject a serious doctrine before we have examined it adequately. In the circumstances we are compelled to state explicitly that prior to careful investigation we cannot exclude the possibility that a political philosophy which emerged many centuries ago is *the* true political philosophy, as true to-day as it was when it was first expounded. In other words, a political philosophy does not become obsolete merely because the historical situation, and in particular the political situation to which it was related has ceased to exist. For every political situation contains elements which are essential to all political situations: how else could one intelligibly call all these different political situations "political situations"?

Let us consider very briefly, and in a most preliminary fashion, the most important example. Classical political philosophy is not refuted, as some seem to believe, by the mere fact that the city, apparently the central subject of classical political philosophy, has been superseded by the modern state. Most classical philosophers considered the city the most perfect form of political organization, not because they were ignorant of any other form, nor because they followed blindly the lead given by their ancestors or contemporaries, but because they realized, at least as clearly as we realize it today, that the city is essentially superior to the other forms of political association known to classical antiquity, the tribe and the Eastern monarchy. The tribe, we may say tentatively, is characterized by freedom (public spirit) and lack of civilization (high development of the arts and sciences), and the Eastern monarchy is characterized by civilization and lack of freedom. Classical political philosophers consciously and reasonably preferred the city to other forms of political association, in the light of the standards of freedom and civilization. And this preference was not a peculiarity bound up with their particular historical situation. Up to and including the eighteenth century, some of the most outstanding political philosophers quite justifiably preferred the city to the modern state which had emerged since the sixteenth century, precisely because they measured the modern state of their time by the standards of freedom and civilization. Only in the nineteenth century did classical political philosophy in a sense become obsolete. The reason was that the state of the nineteenth century, as distinguished from the Macedonian and Roman empires, the feudal monarchy, and the absolute monarchy of the modern period, could plausibly claim to be at least as much in accordance with the standards of freedom and civilization as the Greek city had been. Even then classical political philosophy did not become completely obsolete, since it was classical political philosophy which had expounded in a "classic" manner the standards of freedom and civilization. This is not to deny that the emergence of modern democracy in particular has elicited, if it has not been the outcome of, such a reinterpretation of both "freedom" and "civilization" as could not have been foreseen by classical political philosophy. Yet that reinterpretation is of fundamental significance, not because modern democracy has superseded earlier forms of political association, or because it has been victorious—it has not always been victorious, and not everywhere—but because there are definite reasons for considering that reinterpretation intrinsically superior to the original version. Naturally, there are some who doubt the standards mentioned. But that doubt is as little restricted to specific historical situations as the standards themselves. There were classical political philosophers who decided in favor of the Eastern monarchy.

Before we can make an intelligent use of the historically ascertained relations between philosophic teachings and their "times," we must have subjected the doctrines concerned to a philosophic critique concerned exclusively with their truth or falsehood. A philosophic critique in its turn presupposes an adequate understanding of the doctrine subjected to the critique. An adequate interpretation is such an interpretation as understands the thought of a philosopher exactly as he understood it himself. All historical evidence adduced in support of historicism presupposes as a matter of course that adequate understanding of the philosophy of the past is possible on the basis of historicism. This presupposition is open to grave doubts. To see this we must consider historicism in the light of the standards of historical exactness which, according to common belief, historicism was the first to perceive, to elaborate, or at least to divine.

Historicism discovered these standards while fighting the doctrine which preceded it and paved the way for it. That doctrine was the belief in progress: the conviction of the superiority, say, of the late eighteenth century to all earlier ages, and the expectation of still further progress in the future. The belief in progress stands midway between the non-historical view of the philosophic tradition and historicism. It agrees with the philosophic tradition in so far as both admit that there are universally valid standards which do not require, or which are not susceptible of, historical proof. It deviates from the philosophic tradition in so far as it is essentially a view concerning "the historical process"; it asserts that there is such a thing as "the historical process" and that that process is, generally speaking, a "progress": a progress of thought and institutions toward an order which fully agrees with certain presupposed universal standards of human excellence.

In consequence, the belief in progress, as distinguished from the views of the philosophic tradition, can be legitimately criticized on purely historical grounds. This was done by early historicism, which showed in a number of cases—the most famous example is the interpretation of the Middle Ages—that the "progressivist" view of the past was based on an utterly insufficient understanding of the past. It is evident that our understanding of the past will tend to be the more adequate, the more we are interested in the past. But we cannot be passionately interested, seriously interested in the past if we know beforehand that the present is in the most important respect superior to the past. Historians who started from this assumption felt no necessity to understand the past in itself; they understood it only as a preparation for the present. In studying a doctrine of the past, they did not ask primarily, what was the conscious and deliberate intention of its originator? They preferred to ask, what is the contribution of the doctrine to our beliefs? What is the meaning, unknown to the originator, of the doctrine from the point of view of the present? What is its meaning in the light of later discoveries or inventions?

They took it for granted then that it is possible and even necessary to understand the thinkers of the past better than those thinkers understood themselves.

Against this approach, the "historical consciousness" rightly protested in the interest of historical truth, of historical exactness. The task of the historian of thought is to understand the thinkers of the past exactly as they understood themselves, or to revitalize their thought according to their own interpretation. If we abandon this goal, we abandon the only practicable criterion of "objectivity" in the history of thought. For, as is well-known, the same historical phenomenon appears in different lights in different historical situations; new experience seems to shed new light on old texts. Observations of this kind seem to suggest that the claim of any one interpretation to be *the* true interpretation is untenable. Yet the observations in question do not justify this suggestion. For the seemingly infinite variety of ways in which a given teaching can be understood does not do away with the fact that the originator of the doctrine understood it in one way only, provided he was not confused. The indefinitely large variety of equally legitimate interpretations of a doctrine of the past is due to conscious or unconscious attempts to understand its author better than he understood himself. But there is only one way of understanding him as he understood himself.

Now, historicism is constitutionally unable to live up to the very standards of historical exactness which it might be said to have discovered. For historicism is the belief that the historicist approach is superior to the non-historical approach, but practically the whole thought of the past was radically "unhistorical." Historicism is therefore compelled, by its principle, to attempt to understand the philosophy of the past better than it understood itself. The philosophy of the past understood itself in a non-historical manner, but historicism must understand it "historically." The philosophers of the past claimed to have found *the* truth, and not merely the truth for their times. The historicist, on the other hand, believes that they were mistaken in making that claim, and he cannot help making that belief the basis of his interpretation. Historicism then merely repeats, if sometimes in a more subtle form, the sin for which it upbraided so severely the "progressivist" historiography. For, to repeat, our understanding of the thought of the past is liable to be the more adequate, the less the historian is convinced of the superiority of his own point of view, or the more he is prepared to admit the possibility that he may have to learn something, not merely about the thinkers of the past, but from them. To understand a serious teaching, we must be seriously interested in it, we must take it seriously, *i.e.*, we must be willing to consider the possibility that it is simply true. The historicist as such denies that possibility as regards any philosophy of the past. Historicism naturally attaches a much greater importance to the history of philosophy than any earlier philosophy has done. But unlike most earlier philosophies, it endangers by its principle, if contrary to its original intention, any adequate understanding of the philosophies of the past.

It would be a mistake to think that historicism could be the outcome of an unbiased study of the history of philosophy, and in particular of the history of political philosophy. The historian may have ascertained that all political philosophies are related to specific historical settings, or that only such men as live in a specific historical situation have a natural aptitude for accepting a given political philosophy. He cannot thus rule out the possibility that the historical setting of one particular political philosophy is the ideal condition for the discovery of *the* political truth. Historicism cannot then be established by historical evidence. Its basis is a philosophic analysis of thought, knowledge, truth, philosophy, political things, political ideals, and so on, a philosophic analysis allegedly leading to the result that thought, knowledge, truth, philosophy, political things, political ideals, and so on, are essentially and radically "historical." The philosophic analysis in question presents itself as the authentic interpretation of the experience of many centuries with political philosophy. The political philosophers of the past attempted to answer the question of the best political order once and for all. Each of them held explicitly or implicitly that all others had failed. It is only after a long period of trial and error that political philosophers started questioning the possibility of answering the fundamental questions once and for all. The ultimate result of that reflection is historicism.

Let us consider how far that result would affect political philosophy. Historicism cannot reasonably claim that the fundamental questions of political philosophy must be replaced by questions of a historical character. The question of the best political order, *e.g.*, cannot be replaced by a discussion "of the operative ideals which maintain a particular type of state," modern democracy, *e.g.*; for "any thorough discussion" of those ideals "is bound to give some consideration to the absolute worth of such ideals."[3] Nor can the question of the best political order be replaced by the question of the future order. For even if we could know with certainty that the future order is to be, say, a communist world society, we should not know more than that the communist world society is the only alternative to the destruction of modern civilization, and we should still have to wonder which alternative is preferable. Under no circumstances can we avoid the question as to whether the probable future order is desirable, indifferent or abominable. In fact, our answer to that question may influence the prospects of the probable future order becoming actually the order of the future. What we consider desirable in the circumstances depends ultimately on universal principles of preference, on principles whose political implications, if duly elaborated, would present our answer to the question of the best political order.

What historicism could reasonably say, if the philosophic analysis on which it is based is correct, is that all answers to the universal philosophic questions are necessarily "historically conditioned," or that no answer to the universal questions will in fact be universally valid. Now, every answer to a universal question necessarily intends to be universally valid. The historicist thesis amounts then to this, that there is an inevitable contradiction between the intention of philosophy and its fate, between the non-historical intention of the philosophic answers and their fate always to remain "historically conditioned." The contradiction is inevitable because, on the one hand, evident reasons compel us to raise the universal questions and to attempt to arrive at adequate answers, *i.e.*, universal answers; and, on the other hand, all human thought is enthralled by opinions and convictions which differ from historical situation to historical situation. The historical limitation of a given answer necessarily escapes him who gives the answer. The historical conditions which prevent any answer from being universally valid have the character of invisible walls. For

[3] A. D. Lindsay *The Modern Democratic State* (Oxford, 1943), I, 45.

if a man knew that his answer would be determined, not by his free insight into the truth, but by his historical situation, he could no longer identify himself with or wholeheartedly believe in, his answer. We should then know with certainty that no answer which suggests itself to us can be simply true, but we could not know the precise reason why this is the case. The precise reason would be the problematic validity of the deepest prejudice, necessarily hidden from us, of our time. If this view is correct, political philosophy would still have to raise the fundamental and universal questions which no thinking man can help raising once he has become aware of them, and to try to answer them. But the philosopher would have to accompany his philosophic effort by a coherent reflection on his historical situation in order to emancipate himself as far as possible from the prejudices of his age. That historical reflection would be in the service of the philosophic effort proper, but would by no means be identical with it.

On the basis of historicism, philosophic efforts would then be enlightened from the outset as to the fact that the answers to which they may lead will necessarily be "historically conditioned." They would be accompanied by coherent reflections on the historical situation in which they were undertaken. We might think that such philosophic efforts could justly claim to have risen to a higher level of reflection, or to be more philosophic, than the "naive" non-historical philosophy of the past. We might think for a moment that historical political philosophy is less apt to degenerate into dogmatism than was its predecessor. But a moment's reflection suffices to dispel that delusion. Whereas for the genuine philosopher of the past all the answers of which he could possibly think were, prior to his examination of them, open possibilities, the historicist philosopher excludes, prior to his examining them, all the answers suggested in former ages. He is no less dogmatic, he is much more dogmatic, than the average philosopher of the past. In particular, the coherent reflection of the philosopher on his historical situation is not necessarily a sign that, other things being equal, his philosophic reflection is on a higher level than that of philosophers who were not greatly concerned with their historical situation. For it is quite possible that the modern philosopher is in much greater need of reflection on his situation because, having abandoned the resolve to look at things *sub specie aeternitatis,* he is much more exposed to, and enthralled by, the convictions and "trends" dominating his age. Reflection on one's historical situation may very well be no more than a remedy for a deficiency which has been caused by historicism, or rather by the deeper motives which express themselves in historicism, and which did not hamper the philosophic efforts of former ages.

It seems as if historicism were animated by the certainty that the future will bring about the realization of possibilities of which no one has ever dreamt, or can ever dream, whereas non-historical political philosophy lived not in such an open horizon, but in a horizon closed by the possibilities known at the time. Yet the possibilities of the future are not unlimited as long as the differences between men and angels and between men and brutes have not been abolished, or as long as there are political things. The possibilities of the future are not wholly unknown, since their limits are known. It is true that no one can possibly foresee what sensible or mad possibilities, whose realization is within the limits of human nature, will be discovered in the future. But it is also true that it is hard to say anything at present about possibilities which are at present not even imagined. Therefore, we cannot help following the precedent set by the attitude of earlier political philosophy toward the possibilities which have been discovered, or even realized since. We must leave it to the political philosophers of the future to discuss the possibilities which will be known only in the future. Even the absolute certainty that the future will witness such fundamental and at the same time sensible changes of outlook as can not even be imagined now, could not possibly influence the questions and the procedure of political philosophy.

It would likewise be wrong to say that whereas non-historical political philosophy believed in the possibility of answering fundamental questions once and for all, historicism implies the insight that final answers to fundamental questions are impossible. Every philosophic position implies such answers to fundamental questions as claim to be final, to be true once and for all. Those who believe in " the primary significance of the unique and morally ultimate character of the concrete situation," and therefore reject the quest for "general answers supposed to have a universal meaning that covers and dominates all particulars," do not hesitate to offer what claim to be final and universal answers to the questions as to what "a moral situation" is and as to what "*the* distinctively moral traits," or "*the* virtues" are.[4] Those who believe in progress toward a goal which itself is essentially progressive, and therefore reject the question of the best political order as "too static," are convinced that their insight into the actuality of such a progress "has come to stay." Similarly, historicism merely replaced one kind of finality by another kind of finality, by the final conviction that all human answers are essentially and radically "historical." Only under one condition could historicism claim to have done away with all pretense to finality, if it presented the historicist thesis not as simply true, but as true for the time being only. In fact, if the historicist thesis is correct, we cannot escape the consequence that that thesis itself is "historical" or valid, because meaningful, for a specific historical situation only. Historicism is not a cab which one can stop at his convenience: historicism must be applied to itself. It will thus reveal itself as relative to modern man; and this will imply that it will be replaced, in due time, by a position which is no longer historicist. Some historicists would consider such a development a manifest decline. But in so doing they would ascribe to the historical situation favorable to historicism an absoluteness which, as a matter of principle, they refuse to ascribe to any historical situation.

Precisely the historicist approach would compel us then to raise the question of the essential relation of historicism to modern man, or, more exactly, the question as to what specific need, characteristic of modern man, as distinguished from pre-modern man, underlies his passionate turn to history. To elucidate this question, as far as possible in the present context, we shall consider the argument in favor of the fusion of philosophic and historical studies which appears to be most convincing.

Political philosophy is the attempt to replace our opinions about political fundamentals by knowledge about them. Its first task consists therefore in making fully explicit our political ideas, so that they can be subjected to critical analysis. "Our ideas" are only partly our ideas. Most of our ideas are abbreviations or residues of the thought of other people, of our teachers (in the broadest sense of the term) and of our teachers' teachers; they are abbreviations and residues of the thought of the past. These

[4] John Dewey, *Reconstruction in Philosophy* (New York, 1920), 189 and 163 f.

thoughts were once explicit and in the center of consideration and discussion. It may even be presumed that they were once perfectly lucid. By being transmitted to later generations they have possibly been transformed, and there is no certainty that the transformation was effected consciously and with full clarity. At any rate, what were once certainly explicit ideas passionately discussed, although not necessarily lucid ideas have now degenerated into mere implications and tacit presuppositions. Therefore, if we want to clarify the political ideas we have inherited, we must actualize their implications, which were explicit in the past, and this can be done only by means of the history of political ideas. This means that the clarification of our political ideas insensibly changes into and becomes indistinguishable from the history of political ideas. To this extent the philosophic effort and the historical effort have become completely fused.

Now, the more we are impressed by the necessity of engaging in historical studies in order to clarify our political ideas, the more we must be struck by the observation that the political philosophers of former ages did not feel such a necessity at all. A glance at Aristotle's *Politics, e.g.,* suffices to convince us that Aristotle succeeded perfectly in clarifying the political ideas obtaining in his age, although he never bothered about the history of those ideas. The most natural, and the most cautious, explanation of this paradoxical fact would be, that perhaps our political ideas have a character fundamentally different from that of the political ideas of former ages. Our political ideas have the particular character that they cannot be clarified fully except by means of historical studies, whereas the political ideas of the past could be clarified perfectly without any recourse to their history.

To express this suggestion somewhat differently, we shall make a somewhat free use of the convenient terminology of Hume. According to Hume, our ideas are derived from "impressions"— from what we may call first-hand experience. To clarify our ideas and to distinguish between their genuine and their spurious elements (or between those elements which are in accordance with first-hand experience and those which are not), we must trace each of our ideas to the impressions from which it is derived. Now it is doubtful whether all ideas are related to impressions in fundamentally the same way. The idea of the city, *e.g.,* can be said to be derived from the impressions of cities in fundamentally the same way as the idea of the dog is derived from the impressions of dogs. The idea of the state, on the other hand, is not derived simply from the impression of states. It emerged partly owing to the transformation, or reinterpretation, of more elementary ideas, of the idea of the city in particular. Ideas which are derived directly from impressions can be clarified without any recourse to history; but ideas which have emerged owing to a specific transformation of more elementary ideas cannot be clarified but by means of the history of ideas.

We have illustrated the difference between our political ideas and earlier political ideas by the examples of the ideas of the state and of the city. The choice of these examples was not accidental; for the difference with which we are concerned is the specific difference between the character of modern philosophy on the one hand, and that of pre-modern philosophy on the other. This fundamental difference was described by Hegel in the following terms: "The manner of study in ancient times is distinct from that of modern times, in that the former consisted in the veritable training and perfecting of the natural consciousness. Trying its powers at each part of its life severally, and philosophizing about everything it came across, the natural consciousness transformed itself into a universality of abstract understanding which was active in every matter and in every respect. In modern times, however, the individual finds the abstract form ready made."[5] Classical philosophy originally acquired the fundamental concepts of political philosophy by starting from political phenomena as they present themselves to "the natural consciousness," which is a pre-philosophic consciousness. These concepts can therefore be understood, and their validity can be checked, by direct reference to phenomena as they are accessible to "the natural consciousness." The fundamental concepts which were the final result of the philosophic efforts of classical antiquity, and which remained the basis of the philosophic efforts of the Middle Ages, were the starting-point of the philosophic efforts of the modern period. They were partly taken for granted and partly modified by the

[5] *The Phenomenology of the Mind,* tr. J. B. Baillie, 2nd edition (London, New York, 1931), 94. I have changed Baillie's translation a little in order to bring out somewhat more clearly the intention of Hegel's remark.—For a more precise analysis, see Jacob Klein, "Die griechische Logistik und die Entstehung der modernen Algebra," *Quellen und Studien zur Geschichte der Mathematik, Astronomie und Physik,* vol. 3, Heft 1 (Berlin, 1934), 64–66, and Heft 2 (Berlin, 1936), 122 ff.

founders of modern political philosophy. In a still more modified form they underlie the political philosophy or political science of our time. In so far as modern political philosophy emerges, not simply from "the natural consciousness," but by way of a modification of, and even in opposition to, an earlier political philosophy, a tradition of political philosophy, its fundamental concepts cannot be fully understood until we have understood the earlier political philosophy from which, and in opposition to which, they were acquired, and the specific modification by virtue of which they were acquired.

It is not the mere "dependence" of modern philosophy on classical philosophy, but the specific character of that "dependence," which accounts for the fact that the former needs to be supplemented by an intrinsically philosophic history of philosophy. For medieval philosophy too was "dependent" on classical philosophy, and yet it was not in need of the history of philosophy as an integral part of its philosophic efforts. When a medieval philosopher studied Aristotle's *Politics, e.g.*, he did not engage in a historical study. The *Politics* was for him an authoritative text. Aristotle was *the* philosopher, and hence the teaching of the *Politics* was, in principle, *the* true philosophic teaching. However he might deviate from Aristotle in details, or as regards the application of the true teaching to circumstances which Arisotle could not have foreseen, the basis of the medieval philosopher's thought remained the Aristotelian teaching. That basis was always present to him, it was contemporaneous with him. His philosophic study was identical with the adequate understanding of the Aristotelian teaching. It was for this reason that he did not need historical studies in order to understand the basis of his own thought. It is precisely that contemporaneous philosophic thought with its basis which no longer exists in modern philosophy, and whose absence explains the eventual transformation of modern philosophy into an intrinsically historical philosophy. Modern thought is in all its forms, directly or indirectly, determined by the idea of progress. This idea implies that the most elementary questions can be settled once and for all so that future generations can dispense with their further discussion, but can erect on the foundations once laid an ever-growing structure. In this way, the foundations are covered up. The only proof necessary to guarantee their solidity seems to be that the structure stands and grows. Since philosophy demands, however, not merely solidity so understood, but lucidity and truth, a special kind of inquiry becomes necessary whose purpose it is to keep alive the recollection, and the problem, of the foundations hidden by progress. This philosophic enquiry is the history of philosophy or of science.

We must distinguish between inherited knowledge and independently acquired knowledge. By inherited knowledge we understand the philosophic or scientific knowledge a man takes over from former generations, or, more generally expressed, from others; by independently acquired knowledge we understand the philosophic or scientific knowledge a mature scholar acquires in his unbiased intercourse, as fully enlightened as possible as to its horizon and its presuppositions, with his subject matter. On the basis of the belief in progress, this difference tends to lose its crucial significance. When speaking of a "body of knowledge" or of "the results of research,"e.g., we tacitly assign the same cognitive status to inherited knowledge and to independently acquired knowledge. To counteract this tendency a special effort is required to transform inherited knowledge into genuine knowledge by re-vitalizing its original discovery, and to discriminate between the genuine and the spurious elements of what claims to be inherited knowledge. This truly philosophic function is fulfilled by the history of philosophy or of science.

If, as we must, we apply historicism to itself, we must explain historicism in terms of the specific character of modern thought, or, more precisely, of modern philosophy. In doing so, we observe that modern political philosophy or science, as distinguished from pre-modern political philosophy or science, is in need of the history of political philosophy or science as an integral part of its own efforts, since, as modern political philosophy or science itself admits or even emphasizes, it consists to a considerable extent of inherited knowledge whose basis is no longer contemporaneous or immediately accessible. The recognition of this necessity cannot be mistaken for historicism. For historicism asserts that the fusion of philosophic and historical questions marks in itself a progress beyond "naïve" non-historical philosophy, whereas we limit ourselves to asserting that that fusion is, within the limits indicated, inevitable on the basis of modern philosophy, as distinguished from pre-modern philosophy or "the philosophy of the future."

New School for Social Research